# The Sound of Empire: Soundscapes, Aesthetics and Performance between *Ancien régime* and Restoration

# Specvlvm Mvsicae

Edendum Curavit
Roberto Illiano

Volume LI

Publications of the Centro Studi Opera Omnia Luigi Boccherini
Pubblicazioni del Centro Studi Opera Omnia Luigi Boccherini
Publications du Centro Studi Opera Omnia Luigi Boccherini
Veröffentlichungen des Centro Studi Opera Omnia Luigi Boccherini
Publicaciones del Centro Studi Opera Omnia Luigi Boccherini
Lucca

# The Sound or Empire

## Soundscapes, Aesthetics and Performance between *Ancien régime* and Restoration

Edited by

Federico Gon and Emmanuel Reibel

✤

BREPOLS
TURNHOUT
MMXXIII

*The present volume has been made possibile by the friendly support of the*

Palazzetto Bru Zane – Centre de musique romantique française

© BREPOLS 2023

All rights reserved. No part of this publication may be reproduced,
stored in a retrieval system, or transmitted, in any form or by any means,
electronic, mechanical, photocopying, recording, or otherwise, without
the prior permission of the publisher.

D/2023/0095/259

ISBN 978-2-503-60849-5

Printed in Italy

# Contents

Federico Gon – Emmanuel Reibel
    Preface                                                                                                         ix

## Politics and National Identity

Galliano Ciliberti
    Francesco Morlacchi, Napoleone I
    e il sound imperiale tra Italia e Germania             3

Magdalena Oliferko-Storck
    Napoleonic Warsaw: The Emperor's Sojourns
    and the French Culture in the Soundscape
    of the Capital of Poland before Chopin                  41

Eric Boaro
    «Non essendovi più capelle in veruna chiesa...».
    Finanziamento e impiego musicale nella Modena giacobina
    e la stagione al Teatro Rangone tra il 1798 e il 1799     77

Federico Gon
    'Feast, Flour, and Gallows': Haydn's *Creation*
    in Naples (1821) and the Politics of Restoration           95

Matthieu Cailliez
    Étude des transferts musicaux franco-allemands
    à l'époque napoléonienne à travers le prisme de
    l'*Allgemeine musikalische Zeitung*                            109

## Opera, Theatre and Performance

Maria Bribili
    The Sound of Empire: Politicised Dramaturgy
    in French Opera from the French Revolution
    to Napoleon      151

Martin Barré
    Dans l'ombre de Paris. Circulation et diffusion
    de la musique de scène sous l'Empire :
    l'exemple du théâtre de Versailles      167

Annelies Andries
    Caroline Branchu: A Model of
    Nineteenth-Century Womanhood?      195

Claudia Chibici-Revneanu
    Moving towards Exclusion:
    A Case Study of the 'Female Viennese School'      221

## Music Publishing and Teaching

Henri Vanhulst
    Les relations entre Jean-Jérôme Imbault
    et ses compositeurs d'après des lettres de
    Jean-Louis Duport et Ferdinando Paër      245

David Rowland
    Music Publishing and Markets c.1750-1830      259

## Soundscapes and Aesthetics

Emmanuel Reibel
    The Empire's Mechanical Musics:
    From Soundscape to Reception      275

Inês Thomas Almeida
    Imaginary Soundscapes:
    The Sounds of Portuguese Music as Captured by
    German Travellers at the End of the *Ancien Régime*      295

Alban Ramaut
    Le Napoléon d'Hector Berlioz, proposition de lecture      313

Abstracts and Biographies      333

Index of Names      343

# Preface

THE SECOND HALF of the eighteenth century and the first half of the nineteenth century was a time of great historical and social upheavals — a melting pot of events the repercussions of which are still felt. The first industrial revolution, the American Revolution, the French Revolution, the Napoleonic wars, the first Empire: such were the events that gradually undermined the *status quo* of the *ancien régime*.

«The old world ended and a new era began» said Goethe, as a beaten and retreating soldier, witnessing the crushing French victory at Valmy (20 September 1792) against the army of the First Coalition; the author of *Faust* could not have been more prophetic: shortly thereafter, the rapid rise of the star of Napoleon represented the keystone of this period, given Napoleon's role as an innovator in the military, political, civil, artistic and cultural life of his time.

However, the harbingers of modernity had been making their way into Europe since the mid-eighteenth century, especially in England and France. Thanks to the exploitation of steam and mechanics for production purposes, factories had grown in number and productivity, giving rise to the first Industrial Revolution, a phenomenon that indelibly changed society on the continent, attracting thousands of peasants from the countryside and contributing to the uncontrolled demographic and urban growth of the big capitals, with devastating social implications: the endemic poverty and the extreme physical precariousness into which the workers were forced by exhausting shifts and unworthy working conditions were the material from which were crafted immortal masterpieces of social denunciation such as *David Copperfield* (1850) and *Hard Times* (1854) by Charles Dickens or *Les Misérables* (1862) by Victor Hugo.

The purely musical *Zeitgeist* of the time could not remain isolated from all of this: the roar of battlefields and the deafening noise of industrial machinery forever changed soundscapes, aesthetics and performance practice: there was, for example, the music of revolutionary marches and ceremonies that crept into the great symphonic repertoire through Cherubini, Méhul and Beethoven, shaping both the peculiarities of writing and orchestration; or again there was the idea of obsessive repetition inherent in the mechanical production by machinery and looms that is glimpsed in the obsessive iterative and hammering formulas of certain rhythmic and formal figurations of Rossini. The great Pesarese himself bears witness to how the succession of upheavals that Europe witnessed between the 1750s and 1830s had marked a profound *caesura* in musical aesthetics; always suspicious about the progress of his times, he succinctly described its salient features, stating that it was an era devoted just to 'steam, robbery and barricades'.

Such radical and sudden changes of both a social and artistic nature were not to be understood, in their real scope, even by the greatest protagonists who were the actual architects of those changes; this was not least the case for Napoleon himself, who «in music had remained an Italian of the eighteenth century, full of *nostalgia* for the amiable cantilenes of Paisiello and Piccinni: the noisy orchestration of Cherubini and the dramatic energy of Spontini's declamation annoyed the emperor, who wanted to distract himself in the theatre and escape from the care of the state. He did not realise that it was he himself who destroyed the world in which the delightful *ariettas* of eighteenth-century bel canto could thrive», as the great musicologist Massimo Mila said with his usual analytical wit.

The studies contained in this volume are grafted onto this dichotomy, one which still makes the overall classification of the rapid and shocking socio-cultural changes of the time difficult, even when organised into vast and exhaustive thematic areas such as 'Politics and National Identity', 'Opera, Theatre and Performance', 'Music Publishing and Teaching', and 'Soundscapes and Aesthetics'.

So we begin with the essay by Galliano Ciliberti, which opens the first part of the volume, on the soundscape relating to the Dresden Congress of May 1812 organised by Napoleon before the disastrous Russian campaign, which was attended by the host, Frederick Augustus I King of Saxony, the Emperor of Austria and the King of Prussia. From 1810 the *Kapellmeister* was Francesco Morlacchi, who took an active part in the event having overseen the musical elements within the royal chapel, as well as at court and at the theatre. The most important result of this event was the composition of two cantatas, the Cantata in praise of Napoleon *Quella che qui s'aggira* and the Cantata performed in the presence of Napoleon I and the royal participants in the Congress *No non menton gli dei*, together with the offertory *Domine salvum fac imperatorem nostrum Napoleonem*, all works which contribute to underline the Imperial sound world around the Congress of Dresden.

The Polish musical environment and its relationship with French culture due to Napoleon's creation of the Duchy of Warsaw (1807) is investigated by Magdalena Oliferko-Storck, with an essay focussed on the sphere of performance practice and composition present in the Polish capital in the years preceding the beginning of the artistic parable of the one who would later become its antonomastic symbol, namely Fryderyk Chopin, who grew up in a musical environment strongly influenced by French culture. It was a bond that was to lead to thousands of Polish families emigrating to France.

# Preface

Eric Boaro focusses on the repercussions created by the secularisation of the state, a situation brought about by the effect the new French revolutionary administration had on the musical chapels of Modena in the two-year period 1798-1799 (immediately after the creation of the Cisalpine Republic). Following the removal of their two main patrons through the suppression of the religious orders and the delegitimisation of the aristocracy, city musicians suddenly fell into a state of profound poverty, evidenced by the pleas addressed to the pro-French government that dramatically testify to the repercussions of the changed social and political order on the musical profession during the first Napoleonic age in Italy. They constitute precious testimonies about the daily life of professional musicians at the end of the eighteenth century.

The possibility that the Symphony No. 100 by Haydn (renamed 'Military' due to the presence of percussion instruments of direct wartime derivation) is not a simple, naive and general oleographic exaltation of the military world — as has often been thought — but an attempt to illustrate the field events of 1793 is the central point of the investigation of the essay by Federico Gon included in this collection: through the use of quotations, formal patterns and its particular orchestration, Haydn may instead have left us a vivid description of the European war and political situation of the time, anticipating the relationship between history and aesthetics that governs, for example, Beethoven's *Eroica*.

Matthieu Cailliez investigates the musical transfer between France and Germany (enemies and belligerent contestants on the fields of half of Europe) as captured through the reviews and chronicles that appeared in the contemporary *Allgemeine musikalische Zeitung*. Published from 1798 onwards, this periodical is an invaluable source of information for understanding the musical relations between these two countries in a period extending to the definitive Napoleonic fall of 1815, as seen through the privileged observation point of some great German composers such as Johann Friedrich Reichardt, Louis Spohr, August von Kotzebue and Ignaz Franz Castelli, who crossed Europe and resided extensively in Paris during this period.

The second part of the volume, oriented towards problems relating to the operatic world, opens with an essay by Maria Birbili concerning some general peculiarities of French opera between the dawn of the Revolution and the consequent Napoleonic hegemony. She considers titles such as *Péronne sauvée*, *La prise de la Bastille*, *La prise de Toulon*, *Toulon soumis*, *Le siège de Lille*, *Le siège de Thionville*, *La prise du pont de Lodi*, along with the 'siege-opera' genre that depicts various authentic sieges, battles, and political events from the Revolutionary wars against the European coalition, often transposed into Greek or Roman antiquity, including such works as *Léonidas ou Le siège des Thermopyles*, *Miltiade à Marathon*, *Toute la Grèce, ou Ce que peut la liberté Marathon*, *Fabius*, and *Horatius Coclès*. Through depicting the political ideas of democracy in 'siege-opera', specific new models in dramaturgy, staging, and music were created.

Martin Barré analyses the circulation of a particular type of repertoire, that of incidental music, at the Court Theatre of Versailles at the beginning of the 19th century, examining the dramatic repertoire and the musical practices of the hall from a rich collection of orchestral material (not yet inventoried) that was used in the city theatre and housed in the municipal library of Versailles. This unpublished collection of 589 manuscripts (*vaudevilles*, melodramas and ballets) illuminates the musical practices of a provincial town very close to Paris, and demonstrate how it developed an artistic identity of its own. The Versailles case also helps to examine the diffusion and circulation of incidental music between the capital and its suburbs, as well as their reception.

Linked by interest in the female figure are the two essays that conclude this section; the first, by Annelies Andries, analyses how, after the Code Napoleon (1804) that limited female roles to the domestic sphere, womanhood was imagined in elite circles during the Napoleonic era at the Opéra and in the salon. This chapter analyses the public persona of Caroline Branchu, a star singer at the Paris Opéra during the first quarter of the nineteenth century, focussing first on Gaspare Spontini's *La Vestale* (1807) and Charles-Simon Catel's *Les Bayadères* (1810). While these operas offered examples of women's active participation in public life, this essay shows how the female roles and the way they were musically shaped also portrayed them as 'other': they are imagined as defenders of tradition (rather than champions of progress), as 'unknowable' for practising sexual abstinence, and at times as oriental or exotic.

The second essay, by Claudia Chibici-Revneanu, deals with the phenomenon of the 'Viennese School' but from the point of view of the female musicians who worked there, and especially Marianna Martinez, Maria Theresia von Paradis and Josepha Barbara Auernhammer. Marianna Martinez, for instance, like her contemporary Mozart, was granted the prestigious membership of the Accademia dei Filarmonici. Indeed, there was an intense interconnection between members of the 'male' and 'female' Viennese school. Haydn was Martinez's teacher; Auernhammer and Martinez often performed with Mozart and the latter even incorporated some of Martinez's compositions into his work. However, whereas Haydn, Mozart and Beethoven went on to be celebrated as semi-divine musical heroes, Martinez, Auernhammer and Paradis were all but forgotten, except for some attempts at dismissing them and their work, disregarding the recognition they had received during their lifetimes. This is not only a matter of gender injustice — it also resulted in the cultural loss and ignorance of many significant lives and works. The question remains whether the genius myth arose in part as a socio-cultural mechanism actively intended to exclude women.

Henri Vanhulst opens the third part of the volume with a study of some letters from composers Jean-Louis Duport and Ferdinando Paer. The relations between Jean-Jérôme Imbault

# Preface

and the composers are little known due to the absence of sources. These letters demonstrate some peculiarities of Imbault's business and publishing strategies, shedding light on new aspects of early 19th-century music publishing.

The changing conditions of trade between 1750 and 1830 are the subject of David Rowland's essay: it was a period of growing internationalism, when music publishers took steps to cooperate with each other across borders in so far as they were able at a time when copyright provision was inadequate. The major upheavals that occurred with the French Revolution and the Napoleonic wars had a major impact on the ways in which these businesses were able to trade with each other. Britain was especially, although not uniquely, affected. However, in spite of prolonged attempts by the French to weaken British trade with Europe and the upheavals caused by war, the internationalisation of the music business continued even through uncertain times during which the free movement of goods and intellectual property were hampered. Part of the continuing success of Britain's music businesses lay in the development of trade with its current and former colonies, demonstrating how the dissemination of music was affected. The chapter considers how some of the major figures of the period, including Beethoven, Clementi and Pleyel, fared as composers and as leaders of the music industry.

The last part of the volume is opened by Emmanuel Reibel, whose contribution deals with mechanical instruments during the Napoleonic Era. Mechanical music was omnipresent, sometimes as one simple element of a soundscape, sometimes as a spectacular object on display. Special attention is paid to Maelzel's instruments: in reconstructing the Parisian trajectory of the first Panharmonicon and the trumpet-player automaton, this chapter shows that these instruments contributed to the circulation of repertoire and that they also served a transcultural dynamic, at a moment when the Austrian and French Empires faced each other on the battlefield. It also shows that listeners and critics became so familiar with mechanical music that it came to structure their perception and judgments of taste: the ideal of non-mechanicity would soon become widely held.

There follows the contribution of Inês Thomas Almeida on the nature of the Portuguese soundscape at the end of the *ancien régime* as read through the privileged lens of the testimonies of some travellers from Germany, who tended to seek the manifestation of a national character, mirroring the Pre-Romantic sensibility of their own homeland, and reacted negatively when they failed to find in Portugal the same elements they had in their own country. Portuguese musical practice, embedded with Iberian, Italian and Counter-Reformist influences (such as the overlapping of the profane and sacred spheres and the preference for Italian operatic models), was viewed with perplexity, leading to rejection and a vivid critique by the German travellers, who searched for the imagined elements of what they thought to be the true Portuguese nation. These elements would be found, so they believed, in the common people, expressing a primordial naturalness that had not yet been corrupted, in a manner of perception that stresses the delicate balance between the observed and the imagined.

The volume concludes with an essay by Alban Ramaut on the Napoleonic influences in the life, and above all in the music, of Hector Berlioz. Of the specifically Napoleonic musical projects planned by Berlioz, few works reached maturity, with the exception of the *Cinq Mai* Cantata (which he called *Napoléon* on 9 November 1840). The idea, inspired by the journey to Lodi on his return from Rome, of composing a third symphony celebrating the return of the army from Italy in 1831-1835 did not materialise, not even in the arranged form of the *Fête musicale funèbre* (1835). When Napoleon's ashes were returned to France in late 1840, Berlioz also refused to compose a march, for lack of time to meditate on such a solemnity. Fragments of this imagined and sketched music nevertheless migrated into other of his most notable works, the *Grande messe des morts*, the *Symphonie funèbre et triomphale*, and the *Te Deum*, the latter, ironically, performed under Napoleon III.

From the review of the studies that make up this volume, it emerges even more clearly how the Napoleonic era coincided not only with an upheaval of the centuries-old European political structures, but also with a change in the relationship between art and the masses, and between aesthetics and pragmatics, as has happened so often on those occasions in which history has connected an entire era with a man as a symbol of his time. Stendhal, albeit with his usual inclination to hyperbole, hit the mark when he wrote, in *The Charterhouse of Parma* (1839): «On 15 May 1796, General Bonaparte entered Milan at the head of that young army which had lately crossed the bridge of Lodi and announced to the world that after so many centuries Caesar and Alexander had a successor». This was a man capable of exerting decisive influence on both the political front and on the purely aesthetic one, proving the truth that «each age has a characteristic relation to the past. This relation depends on the extent to which it takes tradition more or less tacitly for granted, and on the ways it receives the legacy of still earlier ages. Whether composers take their bearings from general rules of composition, generic conventions, or individual works is just as much subject to the vicissitudes of time as the system of aesthetic categories which guides them as they assimilate earlier traditions». This was a reflection by Carl Dahlhaus on the product of these upheavals: the nineteenth-century music (DAHLHAUS, Carl. *Nineteenth-Century Music*, English translation by J. Bradford Robinson, Berkeley-Los Angeles, University of California Press, 1989, p. 26).

The transition between the eighteenth and nineteenth centuries therefore represented an epochal change from every point of view, a change well illustrated with lightning genius by a verse that Alessandro Manzoni, in his famous ode *Il 5 maggio* (1821) dedicated to that

# Preface

turbulent period: «Two centuries, armed one against the other»; it was the roar of a clash that would lead to the Napoleonic Empire and the Restoration, forever and irreversibly changing the profound relationship between music and society.

***

The present volume includes fourteen of the twenty-one contributions presented during the international conference held online in November 2021. Many thanks are due to the Centro Studi Opera Omnia Luigi Boccherini and the Palazzetto Bru Zane - Centre de musique romantique française for organising this conference. We would like to thank sincerely all the authors for kindly accepting our invitation to participate. Many thanks are also due to David Force, for his assistance with some revisions of the English texts. We also warmly thank the editorial staff of the Centro Studi Opera Omnia Luigi Boccherini — Roberto Illiano, Fulvia Morabito, and Massimiliano Sala — for his invaluable help in the editorial preparation of the volume and for the enthusiasm with which he accompanied us in undertaking this fascinating project.

*Federico Gon & Emmanuel Reibel*
Summer 2023

# Politics and National Identity

# Francesco Morlacchi, Napoleone I e il sound imperiale tra Italia e Germania

*Galliano Ciliberti*
(Conservatorio 'Nino Rota' di Monopoli)

La posizione di Francesco Morlacchi (Perugia, 1784 - Innsbruck, 1841) nel panorama musicale europeo del suo tempo è davvero peculiare[1]. Se confrontiamo infatti i suoi dati anagrafici con altri musicisti nati nello Stato Pontificio possiamo constatare che il musicista era di sei anni più vecchio di Nicola Vaccai (Tolentino, 1790 - Pesaro, 1848) e di ben otto rispetto al pesarese Gioachino Rossini (Pesaro, 1792 - Passy, 1868). Se però Rossini esordì nel 1810 a Venezia con *La cambiale di matrimonio*, il più anziano Morlacchi aveva invece debuttato sulle scene teatrali solo tre anni prima a Firenze con la breve farsetta in un atto intitolata *Il poeta disperato*[2]. Vaccai dovrà aspettare addirittura il 1815 per il suo esordio teatrale avvenuto a Napoli con l'opera *I Solitari di Scozia* (quindi dopo aver terminato tardivamente gli studi con il vecchio Paisiello). Sia Morlacchi che Vaccai comporranno opere dopo il 'fatidico' 1829, cioè oltre la data dell'ultima opera rossiniana, il *Guillaume Tell*, e l'inizio in Europa della nuova 'era romantica'.

In soli 3 anni (cioè dal 1807 al 1810) il compositore perugino scrisse ben 10 opere. Da quando assunse il prestigioso incarico di *Hofkapellmeister* presso la corte di Sassonia a Dresda (ruolo che svolse ininterrottamente per 31 anni dal 1810 sino alla morte avvenuta nel 1841)[3], creò 16 melodrammi[4] — di cui uno non rappresentato, un altro incompleto e un altro ancora rifacimento di se stesso[5] —, dedicando il maggior tratto delle proprie forze alla composizione

---

[1]. Rossi Scotti 1860; Ricci Des Ferres-Cancani 1958; Sabatini 1977; Brumana – Ciliberti 1986; Brumana – Ciliberti – Guidobaldi 1987; Brumana 2013a; Brumana 2017; Brumana 2021b.
[2]. Brumana – Ciliberti – Guidobaldi 1987, n. 16, pp. 48, 116-118; Brumana 2017, pp. 19-48.
[3]. Steindorf 2018.
[4]. Surian 1986.
[5]. Tavola 1.

di cantate celebrative, canzoni da camera per canto e pianoforte[6], musica sacra[7], e accentuando negli ultimi anni della carriera l'attività di direttore d'orchestra.

TAVOLA 1: ELENCO CRONOLOGICO DELLE OPERE DI FRANCESCO MORLACCHI

| c *Il poeta disperato* | primavera 1807, Firenze, Pergola |
|---|---|
| c *Il ritratto o sia La forza dell'astrazione* | estate 1807, Verona, Filarmonico |
| ss *Corradino* | carnevale (25 febbraio) 1808, Parma, Imperiale |
| s *Enone e Paride* | autunno (ottobre) 1808, Livorno, Avvalorati |
| s *Oreste* | carnevale (26 dicembre) 1808, Parma, Imperiale |
| c *La principessa per ripiego* | primavera (15 aprile) 1809, Roma, Valle |
| c *Il Simoncino* | primavera (giugno) 1809, Roma, Valle |
| c *Il tutore deluso ossia Rinaldo d'Asti* | estate 1809, Parma, Filo-Musico-Drammatico |
| *c *Le avventure d'una giornata* | autunno (26 settembre) 1809, Milano, Scala |
| *s *Le danaidi* | carnevale (11 febbraio) 1810, Roma, Argentina |
| *ss *Raoul di Créquy* | primavera (aprile) 1811, Dresda, Reale |
| c *La capricciosa pentita* | carnevale (10 gennaio) 1816, Dresda, Reale |
| c *Il barbiere di Siviglia* | primavera (27 aprile) 1816, Dresda, Reale |
| c *La semplicetta di Pirna* | estate (9 settembre) 1817, Pillnitz, Teatrino; 1817, Dresda, Reale |
| *s *Boadicea* | carnevale (31 gennaio) 1818, Napoli, S. Carlo |
| *c *Gianni di Parigi* | primavera (29 maggio) 1818, Milano, Scala |
| *c *Donna Aurora o sia Il romanzo all'improvviso* | autunno (2 ottobre) 1821, Milano, Scala |
| *s *Tebaldo e Isolina* | carnevale (4 febbraio) 1822, Venezia, Fenice |
| c *La gioventù di Enrico V* | estate (18 settembre) 1823, Castello di Pillnitz; (4 ottobre) Dresda, Reale |
| *s *Ilda d'Avenel* | carnevale (27 gennaio) 1824, Venezia, Fenice |
| *s *I saraceni in Sicilia ovvero Eufemio di Messina* | carnevale (23 febbraio) 1828, Venezia, Fenice |
| *s *Colombo* | primavera (21 giugno) 1828, Genova, Carlo Felice |
| c *Il disperato per eccesso di buon cuore* | non rappresentata |
| *s *Il rinnegato* | (10 marzo) 1832, Dresda, Reale |
| s *Francesca da Rimini* | 1839, incompiuta, non rappresentata |

\* = con impiego di banda nell'organico orchestrale; c = comica; s = seria; ss = semiseria.

A Dresda Morlacchi dovette immediatamente confrontarsi anche con una tradizione mitteleuropea estremamente rilevante e qualificata: non solo erano conosciute le migliori opere italiane (da Domenico Cimarosa, Giovanni Paisiello sino a Gaspare Spontini, Luigi Cherubini, Rossini, Vincenzo Bellini e Gaetano Donizetti), ma anche quelle tedesche (Wolfgang Amadeus

---

[6]. DALMONTE 1986.
[7]. KANTNER 1986; JAHRMÄRKER 1998.

Ill. 1: Carl Christian Vogel von Vogelstein, *Ritratto del compositore e direttore d'orchestra Francesco Morlacchi*, 1823, D-Dl.

Mozart, Ludwig van Beethoven, Carl Maria von Weber) e soprattutto francesi di tradizione rivoluzionaria e napoleonica (André-Ernest-Modeste Grétry, François-Adrien Boieldieu, Étienne-Nicolas Méhul, Louis-Joseph-Ferdinand Hérold)[8].

Riconosciuto per la sua egregia attività di *Hofkapellmeister*, Morlacchi fu apprezzato particolarmente anche quale eccellente, raffinato e applaudito interprete di Johann Sebastian Bach (la cui musica conosceva molto bene), Georg Friedrich Händel, Franz Joseph Haydn, Mozart, Beethoven, Giacomo Meyerbeer e Rossini[9].

## L'apprendimento del sound napoleonico: la formazione musicale di Morlacchi a Bologna

> Giovani Armonisti italiani, accogliete ora con docile animo le mie parole: tenetevi saldi alla sola imitazione de' Classici antichi che da filosofi studiarono la bella natura e di que' pochi che oggi ne seguono le tracce gloriose: non vi seduca la pericolosa novità, né la bizzaria dell'omai nauseante sistema della musica *napoleonica* la quale trasporta sul teatro i fragorosi stromenti di guerra[10].

Così scriveva nel novembre del 1834 il professore di lettere greche presso l'Università di Perugia Antonio Mezzanotte, recensendo *Il canto XXXIII della Divina Commedia di Dante Alighieri, declamato con musica* per basso e pianoforte dell'amico Francesco Morlacchi edito da Giovanni Ricordi nel 1832. L'atteggiamento antiromantico e classicista di Mezzanotte (fortemente legato a Vincenzo Monti) però non rispecchiava esattamente la posizione estetica di Morlacchi, che conobbe personalmente Napoleone I e che non solo risultò sempre legato culturalmente agli ambienti bonapartisti[11] ma ne fu fortemente influenzato sia nel modo di comporre (attraverso l'impiego di diverse 'bande sul palco', nonché di organici per soli fiati) che in quello di direttore d'orchestra (la disposizione degli esecutori secondo la tradizione francese), da un vero e proprio sound napoleonico[12].

Pur non essendo mai stato in Francia, i rapporti tra il nuovo mondo ideologico francese e la musica di Morlacchi furono molto stretti così come i legami con le successive idee politiche di Napoleone che segnarono la vita del musicista sin dall'età di quattordici anni. Morlacchi, infatti, sin da adolescente era stato in contatto con le utopie rivoluzionarie (il suo maestro Luigi Caruso aveva innalzato nel 1798 «l'albero di libertà nella piazza detta dei Corsi di Perugia»)[13].

---

[8]. Fambach 1985.
[9]. Ciliberti 2021.
[10]. Mezzanotte 1834, p. 244.
[11]. Guarraccino – Perni 2014, pp. 36-37.
[12]. Fleischmann 1965, pp. 256-259.
[13]. Agretti 1798.

# Francesco Morlacchi, Napoleone I e il sound imperiale tra Italia e Germania

Nelle proprie *Memorie biografiche* Morlacchi affermò che all'età di 20 anni «prese le nozioni necessarie di tutti gli istrumenti» e «che per qualche tempo esercitò, specialmente il Clarinetto»[14]. La notizia venne suffragata diversi anni più tardi in un 'Verzeichniss sämmtlicher Compositionen des Kapellmeisters Ritter Morlacchi bis 1822' apparso il 12 marzo 1823 nel periodico *Allgemeine musikalische Zeitung* di Lipsia:

> Im zwanzigsten Jahre machte er in Bologna unter Pater Mattei einen regelmässigen Kursus in allen Musikgattungen, besonders der Kirchenmusik, und fing dabey an, die Klarinette, die Flöte, den Fagott, das Waldhorn und das Violoncell zu spielen, um die Kenntnisse aller dieser Instrumente zu erlangen[15].

Frutto di queste pratiche strumentali bolognesi fu la composizione di un versetto del *Gloria*, che si avvale espressamente di un organico di voci e strumenti a fiato: *Originale. Quoniam tu solus a due bassi con banda di Fran[cesc]o Morlacchi A[ccademico] F[ilarmonico] L'agosto 1806* recita il titolo del manoscritto autografo oggi custodito presso l'Archivio musicale della cattedrale di San Lorenzo di Perugia[16]. La partitura possiede una precisa postilla del conte Giovanni Battista Rossi-Scotti, già possessore dell'autografo, nella quale si afferma che il componimento è opera «giovanile del M[aestro] Morlacchi il quale appunto nel 1806 fu in Bologna dichiarato nel Liceo Musicale Maestro Compositore»[17]. L'organico è costituito per la parte strumentale da 4 clarinetti, 2 corni, 2 trombe, fagotto e continuo mentre per la parte vocale da 2 bassi[18].

E fu proprio durante i suoi studi bolognesi con padre Stanislao Mattei tra il 1804 e il 1805 che il giovane Morlacchi entrò in contatto con i cenacoli filofrancesi e filonapoleonici. Nel maggio del 1805, in occasione dell'incoronazione di Napoleone a Re d'Italia Morlacchi compose due cantate per l'Accademia musicale dei Concordi di Bologna: *Quando fia che ai nostri danni*[19] e *Che più si tarda*[20]. L'Accademia musicale bolognese, che suscitò anche l'interesse e la partecipazione del giovane Rossini, era stata fondata da Tommaso Marchesi (1773-1852), accademico filarmonico, maestro di cembalo e allievo come Morlacchi di Stanislao Mattei. Soprannominati i «filarmonici tedeschizzanti» per esser soliti promuovere esecuzioni di componimenti lontani dalla tradizione italiana del bel canto — come l'allestimento dell'oratorio *La creazione* (*Die Schöpfung* Hob. XXI:2) di Haydn il 6 aprile 1808 — il sodalizio risultò costituito perlopiù da professori e dilettanti di musica[21].

---

[14]. Morlacchi 1841, pp. 148-149.
[15]. *Allgemeine musikalische Zeitung* [d'ora in avanti: *AmZ*], XXV/11 (12 marzo 1823), coll. 174-176: 174.
[16]. Brumana – Ciliberti – Guidobaldi 1987, n. 106, p. 58.
[17]. Brumana 1993, n. 302, pp. 58-59.
[18]. Edizione in Morlacchi 1806.
[19]. Brumana – Ciliberti – Guidobaldi 1987, [n. 122], p. 34. Libretto in I-Bc.
[20]. *Ibidem*, [n. 132], p. 34.
[21]. Bosdari 1914, pp. 6-7, 24-26.

Delle due cantate napoleoniche bolognesi la musica è andata dispersa. Resta il libretto della prima *Quando fia che ai nostri danni* per voce (Pallade) e coro su testo di Odoardo Zurla. Napoleone è descritto come «Quel semideo che primo» nelle «contrade» d'Italia «sparse» la «libertade», e grazie al quale poté risorgere «dal lungo squallor». Per questa ragione Bonaparte vien visto non solo come «Grand'Eroe divin Spirto che il Cielo | Scelse a render la pace» ma soprattutto «Padre» «Amico» e «Rè» del «popol d'Italia».

Ma è sotto il governo napoleonico di Parma tra il 1808 e il 1810 che avvenne l'affermazione definitiva del giovane maestro perugino. Morlacchi arrivò in città il 9 gennaio del 1808 e fu definito nell'elenco dei *Forestieri entrati e sortiti*: «Francois, musicien de Bologna»[22]. Proprio a Parma per il Teatro Imperiale scrisse due opere importanti per la sua carriera: *Corradino* (25 febbraio 1808)[23] e *Oreste* (26 dicembre 1808)[24]. Inoltre il 15 agosto del 1808 in occasione dell'onomastico di Napoleone fu eseguito un *Inno* di Morlacchi[25]. Ma la sua presenza in città lo vide attivo anche nei cenacoli culturali e soprattutto nella casa del primo *Maire* di Parma, il conte Stefano Sanvitale per il quale Morlacchi compose nel marzo del 1809 un «gran Concertone Istrumentale»[26] e dove fu rappresentato nell'estate dello stesso anno il suo *Rinaldo d'Asti*[27].

## Morlacchi a Dresda: l'incontro con Napoleone

La nomina di *Hofkapellmeister* nonché direttore dell'Opera italiana a Dresda, dapprima nel 1810 come assistente di Joseph Schuster e dal 1811 come titolare a vita, collocò il compositore perugino in una dimensione internazionale. Nomina che Morlacchi dovette all'intermediazione di Vincenzo Rastrelli, che aveva studiato a Bologna con padre Mattei e che era dal 1793 maestro di canto e di musica a Dresda presso il conte Camillo Marcolini, primo ministro del gabinetto reale. Fu, infatti, proprio Marcolini ad avere grande parte nella chiamata del musicista perugino alla corte di Sassonia[28].

Quando Morlacchi giunse a Dresda il 10 luglio del 1810 regnava Federico Augusto I che aveva assunto il titolo di Re di Sassonia dopo Jena (1806) e aveva pagato a Napoleone un milione e mezzo di talleri prelevato dall'Erario dello Stato per conservare il Regno. Il maestro perugino era dunque arrivato nella capitale Sassone nel momento di massima espansione della

---

22. Ferrara 1986, p. 179.
23. Brumana – Ciliberti – Guidobaldi 1987, n. 6, pp. 47, 89-92.
24. *Ibidem*, n. 15, pp. 48, pp. 114-116.
25. Ferrara 1986, p. 180 (nota 14).
26. Morlacchi 1841, p. 150.
27. Brumana – Ciliberti – Guidobaldi 1987, n. 19, pp. 47, 125-126.
28. Brumana 2021a, p. 18.

potenza francese, con l'Austria battuta a Wagram e dopo che Napoleone aveva ripudiato la prima moglie Giuseppina e sposato Maria Luisa figlia dell'Imperatore sconfitto.

Federico Augusto aveva dato un assetto costituzionale alla monarchia, il suo vivere in semplicità con la famiglia e l'interesse della corte, alle lettere, alle arti e alle scienze, abbandonando rigide etichette del passato, lo avvicinavano ideologicamente e politicamente all'Imperatore dei Francesi[29].

Tra il 1811 e il 1812 (anno del Congresso di Dresda) Morlacchi è impegnato in tutta una serie di iniziative che vedono la glorificazione di Napoleone e dell'Impero.

Nella prima opera scritta per il Teatro reale di Dresda, il *Raoul di Créquy* allestita nell'aprile del 1811[30], Morlacchi profuse tutte le energie nell'intento di adeguarsi al gusto 'neofrancese' (il duca di Créquy che salva la propria sposa Adele e il figlioletto Riccardo dall'usurpatore omicida Gastone)[31]. Discostandosi dalle consuetudini italiane, abolì i recitativi secchi e introdusse, secondo lo stile di Mayr, danze e cori in un insieme drammaturgicamente unitario e coerente. Le turbinose scene di tempesta, l'impiego 'francese' della banda turca sul palco (alla fine del I atto *Coro e danza* con timpani e tamburo e al termine del II atto, la *Congiura*, con flauto, ottavino, tromba e timpani) nonché l'uso in orchestra di «martelli e picconi» (anticipando l'utilizzo di «suoni concreti» come nella scena III del *Das Rheingold* wagneriano), per rendere l'immagine dei minatori che faticano nelle viscere della terra, trasportano l'opera in un clima volutamente 'imperiale', anche se la presenza di alcuni elementi comici risulta retrospettiva.

Nella sala del barone Jean-François de Bourgoing, ministro plenipotenziario del re Federico Augusto I di Sassonia e raffinato letterato, venne eseguita nel maggio del 1811 la sua Cantata *Anche sì frettoloso* per la nascita del re di Roma Napoleone II[32].

Dal 16 al 28 maggio 1812 Napoleone organizzò un incontro diplomatico di alto livello, il Congresso di Dresda, per definire quella che sarà la disastrosa conclusione della 'campagna di Russia', incontro al quale presero parte l'imperatore d'Austria, i sovrani di Prussia e di Sassonia con la maggior parte dei membri della Confederazione Renana e nel corso del quale promisero formale fedeltà al Bonaparte[33]. Francesco Morlacchi ne fu testimone oculare oltreché protagonista indiscusso per la parte musicale avendo provveduto a dirigere la *Hofkapelle* nelle varie manifestazioni che si svolsero a corte, a teatro e nella Katholische Hofkirche.

La cronaca di queste settimane, che a parere del musicista perugino fecero «epoca nell'Istoria del Mondo, perché una riunione di Sovrani simile difficilmente si è data e si darà»,

---

[29]. Ricci Des Ferres-Cancani 1958, pp. 37-38.
[30]. Brumana – Ciliberti – Guidobaldi 1987, n. 18, pp. 47, 122-124.
[31]. Ciliberti 2013a.
[32]. Brumana – Ciliberti – Guidobaldi 1987, n. 32, p. 50.
[33]. Ricci Des Ferres-Cancani 1958, p. 38.

viene sinteticamente riferita dal maestro in una lettera al padre Alessandro datata «Dresda, 8 giugno 1812»[34] (Ill. 2). Morlacchi informa innanzi tutto degli arrivi dei vari personaggi. La sera del 16 maggio vigilia di Pentecoste giunse primo fra tutti Napoleone «con la sua Sposa e una quantità di Duchi e principi» per un totale di «64 gran carrozze di seguito». Il 17 maggio domenica di Pentecoste arrivarono il Gran Duca di Toscana Ferdinando «con seguito», Caterina Sofia Dorotea di Württemberg, regina di Westfalia e sposa di Girolamo Bonaparte fratello di Napoleone, a «mezzodì» il re di Prussia Federico Guglielmo III, con «20 carrozze di seguito», e la notte il principe ereditario di Prussia. Il lunedì 18 maggio alle 11 giunse l'imperatore Francesco I con la sua sposa e «con un seguito di 40 vetture».

«Tutti i duchi e i principi regnanti della Sassonia erano già» a Dresda «per ricevere questi sovrani» accolti ogni volta, testimonia ancora Morlacchi, «con sparo di cannoni» e «suono di campane» alloggiando tutti «magnificamente al Palazzo Reale»

La sola corte di Napoleone era costituita da «600 persone, immaginate il resto», scriveva con enfasi il musicista al padre. Secondo la testimonianza di Morlacchi, tre furono i pranzi ufficiali offerti dal re di Sassonia con servizio «tutto in oro» che «non l'ha nessun Monarca», durante i quali «noi, ed io in specie, abbiamo goduto, perché sempre presenti a tutto quello che si faceva alla Corte, giacché sempre musica istrumentale a tavola, e dopo vocale in tempo del giuoco». «Illuminazione, feste, teatro, concerti, insomma», narra Morlacchi al padre, «vedete in tanto poco tempo quante cose si fanno».

Napoleone si era portato da Parigi il suo «compositeur et directeur de la musique particulière», Ferdinando Paer che era stato predecessore di Morlacchi a Dresda (1802-1806) prima che Bonaparte lo assumesse definitivamente (1807) dopo la battaglia di Jena sottraendolo alla corte assieme ai bottini di guerra.

L'*Allgemeine musikalische Zeitung* riferisce che furono rappresentate due opere di Paer[35]: nel piccolo teatro dell'opera vennero date alcune scene del *Sargino*; nel teatro di corte il compositore aveva portato «einige neue Opern» tra le quali l'*Agnese* che aveva già visto alcune rappresentazioni a Dresda nel precedente inverno e che «Sie enthält vieles recht Gute». Paer, stando al giornale di Lipsia, avrebbe strategicamente ingrandito la portata del suo intervento e della sua presenza a Dresda avendo avuto l'onore di intrattenere «einige der hohen Herrschaften mit Gesang und Spiel, und meist scherzhaft», afferma con non poca ironia l'anonimo corrispondente del periodico.

Il re di Sassonia Federico Augusto I dal canto suo oppose a Paer, che era stato precedentemente maestro di cappella ai tempi del suo elettorato ma che ora era al servizio di colui che aveva messo in ginocchio la Sassonia, il nuovo direttore della *Hofkapelle*, il giovane Francesco Morlacchi.

---

[34]. I-PEmazza e pubblicata in *ibidem*, pp. 39-40.
[35]. *AmZ*, XIV/28 (8 July 1812), col. 468.

ILL. 2: Lettera di Francesco Morlacchi al padre Alessandro, Dresda, 8 giugno 1812, I-PEmazza.

GALLIANO CILIBERTI

Il musicista perugino documentò nell'autobiografia che

> Nel maggio 1812 compose a Dresda *due* Cantate per solennizzare la presenza di S. M. I. Napoleone con l'Imperatrice, S. M. Imperiale Francesco I con l'Imperatrice, il Re di Prussia, il Re di Olanda, il Re di *Vestfalia* con la Regina, il Re di Napoli con la Regina, e tutti gli Arciduchi e Duchi dell'Alemagna, che fu eseguita nel Gran teatro alla Loro presenza[36].

Le due cantate furono eseguite non «la sera del 18», secondo quanto recita la già citata lettera del compositore al padre[37], ma quella del 20 maggio del 1812, come testimonia il frontespizio dell'autografo della prima cantata[38]. Ambedue i brani furono composti «per ordine di S.M. il Re di Sassonia» tra il 4 e il 12 maggio 1812 intonando i versi poetici di Ferdinando Orlandi. Le due cantate sono strettamente collegate: nella prima si inneggia alla venuta di Napoleone, mentre nella seconda è il personaggio Sassonia a ringraziarlo della sua presenza.

La prima cantata *No non menton gli Dei*[39] è articolata in tre grandi sezioni chiamate «scene» nelle quali è previsto anche l'impiego di un apparato scenografico composto essenzialmente da un tempio collocato in mezzo al palcoscenico. I personaggi sono due: Albi (tenore), il cui appellativo fa riferimento all'abbreviazione del nome latino di Albino e nello stesso tempo alla città occitana di Albi, la Gran Sacerdotessa (soprano) nonché il coro di Sacerdoti e Sacerdotesse. L'ambientazione neoclassica è tipicamente napoleonica, dove imitare l'antico nel suo spirito, nei suoi principi e nelle sue massime, diventa la finalità prioritaria degli artisti dell'epoca.

Nella scena I Albi narra come l'oracolo abbia predetto che il giorno che seguirà «del nascente sole | ai primi rai, | maggior sole apparir | tu qui ne vedrai». Colui che risplenderà più del sole sarà, ovviamente, Bonaparte. Nel sonno Albi vede scendere dal cielo Giove e la dea Afrodite («la vaga dea di Gnido») ma è svegliato dal canto degli «inni festivi» che «i sacri ministri» fanno nel «tempio risuonar». Il «Coro dentro il tempio chiuso dai ridò», predice che questo *ignoto numini* sarà più splendente del sole: «Di lui men grande | ed è men chiaro il sole». Albi ormai è cosciente che «quest'aurora» è foriera di un «giorno felice».

La scena II è ambientata nel tempio e vede protagonista il coro di Sacerdoti e di Sacerdotesse. La narrazione è marcatamente ideologica e si entra subito in *medias res*: a «Napoleon» onore del trono e «amore e felicità» del suo «possente imperio» si inchina e «porta gli omaggi suoi | la Sassone città». Il decantato eroe «novelle leggi crea» e il «Mondo» è pieno dei suoi vanti.

---

[36]. MORLACCHI 1841, p. 151.
[37]. RICCI DES FERRES-CANCANI 1958, p. 40.
[38]. I-Rn, Mss. musicali 75, f. 1r.
[39]. BRUMANA – CILIBERTI – GUIDOBALDI 1987, n. 69, p. 54.

Nella scena III e ultima la Gran Sacerdotessa dissipa gli ultimi dubbi di Albi: «Napoleon lume del Sol maggiore» porta amicizia a Dresda. In fine tutti esaltano Napoleone e la sua grandezza.

I lunghi declamati che celebrano allegoricamente Napoleone sono inframezzati da poche arie a questi strettamente collegate ma nessuna con il consueto 'da capo', questo probabilmente per creare una coesa continuità musicale nonché una omogeneità drammaturgica. Sia l'aria di Albi 'Vidi dal ciel discendere', collocata nella scena I, che l'aria della Gran Sacerdotessa 'Quando dirà che un giorno', nella scena III, possiedono uno stile marcatamente melodico. Le fioriture di bravura si trovano nella sola parte della Sacerdotessa, quella collocata nel concertato finale, tramite melismi che si intrecciano con la severa omoritmia del coro prima del breve Maestoso conclusivo che ha la funzione di una coda.

La seconda cantata *Quella che qui s'aggira*[40] è molto più semplice della precedente. Protagonista è Sassonia (soprano) e il coro di Ninfe e Pastori che interviene dopo l'inizio e possiede una funzione concertante alla fine del componimento. Si tratta di un saluto deferente per la presenza di Napoleone; Sassonia infatti canta usando nei suoi confronti parole divinatorie: «splendor felicità del Gallo impero, | gloria del secol nostro | che dalla Senna» qui a Dresda «come già un dì riporti amico il piede». L'unico *coup de théâtre* è l'apertura del tempio «dove vedesi, al di sopra | d'un arco, circondato da grandissima luce il nome | di Napoleone». Anche in questo caso, come nella precedente cantata, l'imperatore è visto come sole e come luce, concetto molto simile alla tradizione filosofica della lotta tra luci e tenebre presente nella *Zauberflöte* K. 620 di Mozart e nel *Fidelio* Op. 72b di Beethoven.

Morlacchi nella lettera al padre testimonia anche di

> [...] un gran concerto nel gran Teatro ridotto a sala composto da 126 individui tra cantanti e suonatori, dove intervennero parimenti tutti i Sovrani e dove si eseguì molta musica mia, e tutto andò a meraviglia. Tutti vestiti sempre in gran gala, cioè in spada. Io avevo ricevuto in regalo pochi giorni prima una bellissima spada tutta d'acciaio del valore di 20 zecchini, ma all'ultima moda[41].

È ancora l'*Allgemeine musikalische Zeitung*[42] a specificare che il concerto avvenne il 24 marzo dove fu eseguita «ausser einer unbedeutenden Ouvertüre», alcuni *ensemble* de *Le danaidi*[43] e del *Corradino* del *Kapellmeister* Morlacchi, un duetto degli *Orazi e Curiazi* di Domenico Cimarosa e simili, e la marcia trionfale e il coro della *Vestale* di Gaspare Spontini. Il tutto durò circa un'ora e, indipendentemente dalle dimensioni della sala, la

---

[40]. *Ibidem*, n. 79, p. 55.
[41]. Ricci Des Ferres-Cancani 1958, p. 40.
[42]. *AmZ*, XIV/28 (8 luglio 1812), col. 468.
[43]. Brumana – Ciliberti – Guidobaldi 1987, n. 7, pp. 47, 92-95.

musica fu «recht gut», e la *Hofkapelle* e tanto più il suo direttore Morlacchi vennero molto ben apprezzati.

E risulta di nuovo il compositore perugino a narrare nella sua lettera al padre che «i coristi della cantata e del gran concerto» furono «la cappella medesima», aggiungendo: «Immaginate Sassaroli corista!», ovvero Germano Sassaroli celebre basso solista italiano attivo a Dresda che *obtorto collo* dovette cantare con il coro. E ancora: il basso Gioacchino Benincasa che «ha cantato al Gran Concerto e 2 volte in camera, ed ha ricevuto un regalo di 10 Napoleoni d'oro»[44].

Vi furono anche diverse funzioni liturgiche alle quali presero parte le teste coronate presenti al Congresso di Dresda in particolare la domenica 22 maggio dove, sempre secondo la lettera di Morlacchi al padre, «ho dovuto ripetere tre volte la mia Messa. Ho dovuto comporre in un'ora il *Domine salvum fac Imperatorem* ecc.»[45]. La messa a cui fa riferimento il compositore è la sua *Messa I* composta nel 1810, appena arrivato a Dresda, che lo portò immediatamente all'attenzione del pubblico e della critica[46]. Preceduta da una Sinfonia *ad Missam*[47], le prime quattro parti dell'*ordinarium* si articolano solennemente con una ricca orchestrazione, mentre a contrastare questo carattere grandioso è l'*Agnus Dei* «senza i strumenti, cosa non usitata che produsse un grand'effetto», come testimonia il maestro nell'autobiografia[48]. Per l'occasione del Congresso di Dresda e rispettando la tradizione liturgica francese, Morlacchi dovette comporre in aggiunta il *Domine salvum fac* per coro e orchestra che era cantato alla fine della messa dopo il *post communio*[49].

Napoleone per ringraziare la cappella donò 1000 zecchini d'oro da ripartirsi tra tutti i suoi componenti. Scrive ancora Morlacchi al padre:

> Io poi sono stato distinto da tutti, ed ho ricevuto un grande anello in turchina contornato da grossi brillanti, come per una memoria dell'Imperatore Napoleone, unitamente a grazioso complimento. In detto anello che è il più bello di tutti quelli regalati e ai Militari e ai Ministri, si trovano 16 brillanti in giro di non mediocre grandezza, e poi un doppio giro di brillanti più piccoli legati a giorno. Il mio anello è valutato 1000 scudi[50].

I fasti napoleonici, com'è noto, durarono poco. Mutata la situazione politica, costretti i regnanti ad abbandonare Dresda in balìa dell'occupazione russa, Morlacchi dovette comporre

---

44. RICCI DES FERRES-CANCANI 1958, p. 40.
45. *Ibidem*.
46. BRUMANA – CILIBERTI – GUIDOBALDI 1987, n. 92, p. 57.
47. *Ibidem*, n. 215, p. 67.
48. RICCI DES FERRES-CANCANI 1958, p. 150.
49. BRUMANA – CILIBERTI – GUIDOBALDI 1987, n. 144, p. 62.
50. RICCI DES FERRES-CANCANI 1958, p. 40.

una cantata (*Della felice Neva*) per festeggiare «il giorno natalizio» dello zar Alessandro che andò in scena il 24 dicembre 1813[51]. «N.B.» specifica il maestro nella sua autobiografia: «Questa cantata fu composta in 48 ore, e forzatamente con la graziosa minaccia fatta dal Baron [Alexander von] Rosen, allora Ministro della Polizia Russa a Dresda, o di fare la cantata, o di *andare in Siberia!!*»[52]. Al ritorno di Federico Augusto I di Sassonia Morlacchi compose la cantata *Fortuna che giri* eseguita il 17 aprile 1814, dove si inneggia alla conquista di Parigi da parte delle truppe della sesta coalizione dopo il tramonto dell'astro napoleonico[53].

## Il sound napoleonico nella produzione di Morlacchi

### *Fiati e banda*

L'impiego di quei «fragorosi stromenti di guerra» napoleonici tanto criticati dall'amico Mezzanotte non avvenne nelle musiche celebrative composte da Morlacchi espressamente per la corte (come le cantate del Congresso di Dresda che rispecchiavano le 'classiche' consuetudini stilistiche dei brani encomiastico-celebrativi tipici della tradizione musicale della capitale sassone) o per la cappella reale, quanto nelle composizioni paraliturgiche e nei melodrammi scritti proprio durante la sua direzione della *Hofkapelle*. Negli oratori che egli compose per la Chiesa cattolica della capitale sassone fece tesoro dell'esperienza bolognese. Ne *La passione di Gesù Cristo* del 1812 su testo di Metastasio[54], Morlacchi iniziò la *Parte seconda* con una *Introduzione* dove nell'organico appose solo strumenti a fiato: flauto, oboe, corno I e II, tromba I, II e III, fagotto e continuo. La recensione apparsa il 15 aprile 1812 nell'*Allgemeine musikalische Zeitung* sottolineò il carattere 'sperimentale' del componimento affermando quanto Morlacchi avesse fatto sfoggio di una nuova strumentazione:

> Er hatte alles Glänzende der neuen Instrumentation auf geboten, um interessant zu seyn: Posaunen, die wir in dieser Kirche noch nie gehört hatten, und die sich sehr gut ausnehmen, vier Violoncells, gedämpfte Trompeten etc.[55]

Ma in questo brano più che utilizzare quel 'fortissimo' fragore imperiale di rivoluzionaria memoria[56], il compositore sembrò praticare ancora i modelli haydniani conosciuti a Bologna

---

[51]. Brumana – Ciliberti – Guidobaldi 1987, n. 44, p. 51.
[52]. Ricci Des Ferres-Cancani 1958, p. 151.
[53]. Brumana – Ciliberti – Guidobaldi 1987, n. 56, p. 52.
[54]. Brumana 1985; Brumana – Ciliberti – Guidobaldi 1987, n. 107, p. 58.
[55]. *AmZ*, XIV/16 (15 aprile 1812), col. 265.
[56]. Biget 1989, pp. 78-84.

sempre in ambienti filonapoleonici, ispirandosi in particolare all'idea della strumentazione per soli fiati dell'*Introduzione* della parte II della versione corale e orchestrale dell'oratorio *Die sieben letzten Worte unseres Erlösers am Kreuze* Hob. XX/2, appunto, di Haydn.

Ed ancora: il sabato santo del 1821 nella Chiesa cattolica di Dresda venne eseguito un altro oratorio di Morlacchi ancora su testo di Metastasio: *La morte d'Abele*[57]. Nella corrispondenza del successivo 16 maggio l'*Allgemeine musikalische Zeitung* espresse non solo un giudizio favorevole sul componimento ma si soffermò in particolare sull'impiego dei fiati nell'orchestrazione:

> Umso lieblicher trat dann wieder eine Arie von Abel: "L'ape e la serpe spesso etc." in H Dur ein welche hauptsächlich von Blasinstrumenten begleitet ward, und eine schöne Wirkung hervorbrachte. Adams Auftreten ist mit Posaunen und Hörnern begleitet, und seine Recitative werden fortdauernd von diesen gehalten, wodurch der Charakter eine ansprechende Kraft erhält[58].

Il soggetto della morte di Abele era anch'esso di provenienza napoleonica (la *tragédie lyrique La mort d'Abel* di Rodolphe Kreutzer su un libretto di François-Benoît Hoffman era stata allestita all'Opéra per la prima volta il 23 marzo 1810 in pieno Primo Impero)[59], così come le trame di alcuni melodrammi di Morlacchi quali: *Enone e Paride* del 1808[60] (l'*Œnone* opera postuma in due atti di Christian Kalkbrenner fu data all'Opéra il 26 maggio del 1812)[61]; *Le danaidi* del 1810[62] (una ripresa de *Les Danaïdes* di Antonio Salieri era stata progettata dallo stesso Napoleone I all'Opéra per l'autunno del 1810, programma che però non fu realizzato)[63]; il *Gianni di Parigi* del 1818[64] (*Jean de Paris* di Boieldieu era stata data il 4 aprile del 1812 all'Opéra-Comique).

Per quanto concerne i generi[65], cinque melodrammi seri composti da Morlacchi rimandavano proprio a quegli argomenti classici tanto preferiti da Napoleone[66]: *Boadicea*[67], *Le danaidi*, *Enone e Paride*, *Oreste*. Sette opere avevano, invece, soggetti storici, temi analogamente prediletti dall'Imperatore soprattutto per l'esaltazione dell'eroismo[68]: *Corradino*, *Raoul di*

---

[57]. Brumana 1986; Brumana – Ciliberti – Guidobaldi 1987, n. 108, p. 59.
[58]. *AmZ*, XXIII/20 (16 maggio 1821), col. 345.
[59]. Chaillou 2004, pp. 174-175, 433.
[60]. Brumana – Ciliberti – Guidobaldi 1987, n. 10, pp. 48, 101; Brumana 2013b.
[61]. Chaillou 2004, p. 434.
[62]. Brumana – Ciliberti – Guidobaldi 1987, n. 7, pp. 47, 93-95.
[63]. Chaillou 2004, p. 175.
[64]. Brumana – Ciliberti – Guidobaldi 1987, n. 12, pp. 48, 103-107.
[65]. Tavola 1.
[66]. Chaillou 2004, pp. 251-259; Noiray 2004.
[67]. Brumana – Ciliberti – Guidobaldi 1987, n. 3, pp. 47, 79-82.
[68]. Chaillou 2004, pp. 279-282; Noiray 2004.

*Créquy*, *Tebaldo e Isolina*[69], *Ilda d'Avenel*[70], *I saraceni in Sicilia*[71], *Colombo*[72], *Il rinnegato*[73], tra i quali spiccavano per le loro ambientazioni esotiche e ispano-moresche tipiche dell'opera napoleonica[74], *I saraceni in Sicilia* e il *Colombo* ambedue del 1828 (il *Fernando Cortez* di Spontini aveva già debuttato il 28 novembre 1809 all'Opéra, mentre *Les Abéncerages* di Cherubini il 6 aprile 1813 sempre all'Opéra)[75].

Parallelamente all'affermarsi di contenuti specifici nei libretti e di soggetti ricorrenti prescritti dal gusto napoleonico, si andò a imporre nell'opera proprio il sound di quella fragorosa *musique militaire* della *Garde nationale républicaine* della Rivoluzione francese, trasformatasi poi in *Garde consulaire* e infine in *Garde impériale*, con il suo *ensemble* sempre più ricco di strumenti a fiato e a percussione nonché sempre di più plasmato quale complesso sonoro identitario delle truppe napoleoniche, frutto di volontà unite per rafforzare lo spirito di corpo, la sua coesione e il suo orgoglio. Tale *corpus* costituì il modello (con i dovuti aggiustamenti rispondenti sia di gusto teatrale che a tradizioni melodrammatiche autoctone) della cosiddetta «banda sul palco» impiegata in alcune scene descrittive e di movimento di masse nell'opera coeva[76].

Anche Morlacchi ne rimase affascinato. La solida conoscenza tecnica dei fiati, padronanza acquisita durante la formazione giovanile del compositore e legata al gusto filo-francese, portò il musicista perugino a estendere l'uso di questa tecnica anche nella propria produzione operistica. Su 25 melodrammi composti dal 1807 al 1839 Morlacchi inserì l'elemento bandistico in 12 opere[77]. Di queste 2 furono semiserie (*Corradino*, *Raoul di Créquy*), 3 comiche (*Le avventure d'una giornata*[78], *Gianni di Parigi*, *Donna Aurora*[79]) e le rimanenti 7 serie (*Le danaidi*, *Boadicea*, *Tebaldo e Isolina*, *Ilda d'Avenel*, *I saraceni in Sicilia*, *Il Colombo*, *Il rinnegato*). Interessante constatare come, a eccezione de il *Corradino*, i primi melodrammi — cioè quelli scritti tra il 1807 e il 1809 — non contemplino nell'organico strumentale l'uso della banda, così come le opere comiche scritte per Dresda (*La capricciosa pentita*[80], *Il barbiere di Siviglia*[81],

---

69. Brumana – Ciliberti – Guidobaldi 1987, n. 25, pp. 49, 139-144.
70. *Ibidem*, n. 14, pp. 48, 110-113.
71. *Ibidem*, n. 22, pp. 49, 132-135.
72. *Ibidem*, n. 5, pp. 47, 86-89.
73. *Ibidem*, n. 20, pp. 49, 126-129.
74. Chaillou 2004, pp. 261-264.
75. Noiray 2004.
76. Longyear 1978; Maehder 1987; Beghelli 2003, pp. 242-249; Cardoni 2009, pp. 161-207.
77. Tavola 1.
78. Brumana – Ciliberti – Guidobaldi 1987, n. 1, pp. 47, 73-76.
79. *Ibidem*, n. 9, pp. 47, 97-101.
80. *Ibidem*, n. 4, pp. 47, 83-85.
81. *Ibidem*, n. 2, p. 47, 76-79.

*La semplicetta di Pirna*[82], *La gioventù di Enrico v*[83], *Il disperato per eccesso di buon cuore*[84]). Al contrario i melodrammi comici composti espressamente per la Scala di Milano[85] possiedono tutti nell'organico strumentale la banda (*Le avventure d'una giornata, Gianni di Parigi, Donna Aurora*) così come l'insieme della produzione seria compresa tra il 1810 e il 1832.

Senza distinguere tra banda, banda militare, banda castigliana e banda turca (quest'ultima associata normalmente ad un nutrito gruppo di fiati), Morlacchi impiegò tali peculiari mezzi timbrici in 65 brani: 5 nelle Sinfonie d'apertura, 31 nel I atto, 28 nel II e 1 solo nel III. Particolare attenzione è affidata ai finali (12) — specificamente a quelli del I atto (8 sui 4 del II) —, alle introduzioni (8), ai cori (6) a volte uniti ad altre forme (7), alle marce (5) anche di vario genere (3), alle scene (4), alle scene e duetto (3), alle arie con coro (2), alle scena e cavatina (2), nonché alle cavatine (2)[86].

I melodrammi in cui Morlacchi utilizzò in modo marcato l'elemento bandistico furono: *Tebaldo e Isolina* con 13 brani; *I Saraceni in Sicilia* e *Colombo* con 9; *Boadicea* e *Ilda d'Avenel* con 8; *Il rinnegato* con 5; *Le danaidi, Raoul di Créquy* e *Donna Aurora* con 4; *Gianni di Parigi* con 3; il *Corradino* e *Le avventure d'una giornata* con 1[87].

Ognuna di queste opere possedeva poi all'interno delle forme chiuse rappresentative o referenziali per l'inserimento della banda nell'orchestrazione[88]: per le introduzioni *I saraceni in Sicilia*; per i finali *Le danaidi, Donna Aurora* e *Tebaldo e Isolina*; per le marce *Boadicea*; per le danze il *Raoul di Créquy*; per i cori *Colombo* (che presentava anche un *Coro doppio indiano e spagniolo*) così come per le arie con coro[89].

Morlacchi impiegò gli strumenti della banda non solo come effetto strumentale d'assieme ma anche in particolari situazioni drammaturgiche che richiedevano l'uso di significative sottolineature timbriche. Nel *Raoul di Créquy* abbiamo l'inserimento della banda turca alla fine del I atto (*Coro e danza*), nel n. 5 del II atto (*Coro dei minatori e danze* con «martelli e picconi»), alla fine del II atto (*Congiura* con flauto, ottavino, tromba e timpani). Nel II atto del *Gianni di Parigi* la banda turca partecipa con l'orchestra alla *Canzone e ballata con danza campestre*. Dopo la Sinfonia, in *Ilda d'Avenel* è collocata una *Melodia nazionale scozzese* che precede l'*Introduzione* (nell'organico oltre agli archi sono previsti anche flauti, oboi, clarinetti, corni, trombe, tromboni, fagotti, timpani e banda turca) e un successivo *Coro nazionale* (con in più arpa e tamburi). Interessante anche il *Colombo* con l'impiego massiccio della banda turca sia

---

[82]. *Ibidem*, n. 23, pp. 49, 135-137.
[83]. *Ibidem*, n. 13, pp. 48, 107-109.
[84]. *Ibidem*, n. 8, pp. 47, 95-97.
[85]. TAVOLA 1.
[86]. APPENDICE 1.
[87]. APPENDICE 2.
[88]. APPENDICE 1.
[89]. APPENDICE 2.

nel I atto (*Coro di cacciatori e cacciatrici*; *Coro di Castigliani*; *Coro doppio indiano e spagniolo* dove si unisce anche una banda castigliana) che nel II (*Coro lugubre* con i sistri; *Marcia castigliana* dove è prevista altresì la banda sul teatro). Infine ne *Il rinnegato* il II atto è aperto da un *Coro di Saraceni* in cui è possibile rilevare l'impiego della banda turca assieme all'ottavino, clarinetto, corno, tromba e tamburo sulla scena[90].

Spesso questi gruppi strumentali non avevano una collocazione dentro l'orchestra ma venivano posti sia sulla scena o dietro le quinte. La dicitura «sul palco» è scritta: nel *Tebaldo e Isolina* alla cavatina di Tebaldo «Di tanti prodi al vincitore» (con timpani, banda turca e banda); ne *I saraceni in Sicilia* al finale del I atto (con clarinetto, corno, tromba e trombone). L'indicazione «sul palcoscenico» accompagna invece i seguenti brani: nella *Boadicea* la *Marcia trionfale* (con flautini); nell'*Ilda d'Avenel* il *Coro nazionale* (con ottavino, clarinetto, corno, fagotto, banda turca, tamburi), l'aria di Aroldo 'Già nel lucro in pianto assai' (con ottavino, clarinetto, corno, tromba, fagotto, banda turca e tamburi) e il finale del I atto (con tamburi e trombe); ne *I saraceni in Sicilia* la scena e cavatina d'Eufemio 'Né Alamir tornò' (unico caso in cui sono indicati gli strumenti della banda turca: ottavino, clarinetto, corno, tromba, trombone). La didascalia «sulla scena» appare invece nel *Coro dei saraceni* che apre il II atto de *Il rinnegato* (con ottavino, clarinetto, corno, tromba, trombone, tamburo), mentre la dicitura «sul teatro» è apposta: nel *Tebaldo e Isolina* alla *Sinfonia* (con banda turca e banda militare) e all'*Introduzione* del I atto (con timpani, triangolo, banda turca e musica a parte); nell'*Ilda d'Avenel* alla cavatina di Riccardo 'Io primier ti rendo omaggio' (con ottavino, clarinetto, tromba, trombone, fagotto, timpani, banda turca, tamburi); ne *I sarceni in Sicilia* all'*Introduzione* del I atto (con 6 trombe) e al coro 'Vittoria! Si uccidano i vinti infedeli' del II atto (con ottavino, clarinetto, corno, tromba, fagotto, trombone, tamburo, banda turca); ne il *Colombo* alla *Marcia castigliana* (con ottavino, clarinetto, corno, tromba, fagotto, trombone, tamburi, gran cassa); ne *Il rinnegato* al finale del I atto (con clarinetto, corno, tromba, tromboni)[91].

Nell'*Introduzione* del I atto de *I saraceni in Sicilia* possiamo inoltre trovare l'indicazione «sul teatro di dentro» (con ottavino, clarinetto, corno, tromba, fagotto, trombone) analogamente all'*Introduzione* del I atto de *Il rinnegato* (ma senza fagotto).

Quattro risultano i brani espressamente scritti da Morlacchi per soli fiati e collocati nei suoi melodrammi: la *Marcia lugubre* del III atto del *Raoul di Créquy* (con trombone, corno, tromba e trombone basso): la *Marcia trionfale sul palcoscenico* del II atto della *Boadicea* (con flautini, oboe, clarinetto, corno, tromba, fagotto, trombone, banda turca, violoncello e contrabbasso); il terzettino di Isolina, Tebaldo ed Ermanno (con flauto, oboe, clarinetto, corno, fagotto, violoncello e contrabbasso) nel I atto di *Tebaldo e Isolina* e una scena posta

---

[90]. Appendice 2.
[91]. Appendice 2.

dopo l'aria n. 9 di Boemondo nel II atto della stessa opera (con 2 trombe moderne, 4 trombe, 4 corni, 2 tamburi)[92].

L'importanza dell'uso della banda nella produzione operistica di Morlacchi venne sottolineata anche da alcuni significativi passi dell'*Allgemeine musikalische Zeitung*. In una corrispondenza da Dresda del 18 marzo 1812, l'anonimo recensore scrisse a proposito di una replica de *Le danaidi* all'Opera italiana:

> Im 2[ten] Act wird in einem unterirdischen Mysterientempel, im ägyptisch-colossalen Geschmack, die ganze hintere Mauer in Zeit von 20 bis 30 Secunden eingeschlagen; eine Armee Aegypter, mit türkischer Musik und dem blanken halben Mond mit Glöckchen des Garderegiments, erfüllet den Tempel; man trägt Hypermestra davon: wo diese aber hergekommen, da Aegypten doch keinen Krieg mit Danao führte, weiss ich nicht zu sagen, und andere Leute wissen es auch nicht[93].

A proposito di un allestimento viennese de *Il Gianni di Parigi* al Theater an der Wien (settembre-ottobre 1820), un articolo del medesimo periodico lipsiense datato 6 dicembre 1820 si soffermò particolarmente sulla *Canzone e ballata con danza campestre* 'Mira o bella il Trovatore' (II atto), osservando quanto al:

> No. 11. Der Troubadour, ein ausgezeichnet gehaltvolles Tonstück, voll Originalität und überreich an harmonischen Schönheiten. Die erste Strophe intoniert der Page [Oliviero] in Fis moll, und endigt in A dur, die folgenden des Johann, und der Prinzessin beginnen in A moll und schließen in C dur. Wunderlieblich ist die zarte: Harfeubegleitung, und die Zephirs hauche der Blasinstrumente; sinnreich die Benützung eines ächt provençalischen Thema's, und meisterhaft desselben Ausarbeitung im a tre[94].

Un ampio resoconto di Giannagostino Perotti relativo alla prima veneziana di *Tebaldo e Isolina* (e tradotto in tedesco nel numero del 14 agosto 1822 dell'*Allgemeine musikalische Zeitung*) affermava come:

> Der Chor, welcher der Sortita der Isolina vorausgeht, ist sehr lieblich, die Octavflöten thun dabey schöne Wirkung. Das mit Blaseinstrumenten begleitete Terzett bringt die angenehmste Ueberraschung hervor ; Kunst und glückliche Erfindungsgabe wetteifern darin [...]. Hr. R. Morlacchi hat in dieser Oper häufig und mit Geschicklichkeit die Blaseinstrumente angewandt, um den Ausdruck der verschiedenen aus den Situationen hervorgehenden Empfindungen zu erhöhen und

---

[92]. APPENDICE 2.
[93]. *AmZ*, XIV/12 (18 marzo 1812), coll. 188-191: 190.
[94]. *AmZ*, XXII/49 (6 dicembre 1820), coll. 825-828: 828.

stärkere Fortes anzubringen, wo eine stärkere Kraft nöthig war, ohne jedoch diese
Mittel zu missbrauchen, wie diess jetzt sonst so häufig geschieht[95].

Il 4 e l'11 luglio 1832 l'*Allgemeine musikalische Zeitung* — attraverso il corrispondente Gottfried Wilhelm Fink — dedicò due ponderosi articoli di analisi alla prima rappresentazione de *Il rinnegato*. L'erudita disamina fece riferimento in diversi passi all'uso dei fiati e della banda:

> Nach wenigen Einleitungs-Tacten (4/4, D dur, Maestoso) der Blasinstrumente heben die Violinen *p*. tremulirend zu Triolenbewegungen des Basses und zu hineingeworfenen Accordklängen der Bläser ein All. 2/4 an; mit dem eilften Tacte setzen die Trompeten der türkischen Banda auf dem Theater in *a* ein und mit dem zwölften singt der Männerchor: "Ascoltate! Risuona più forte lo squillar delle trombe frementi" [...][96].
>
> Nachdem im kurzen drey stimmigen Chore die Versammelten zu ihrem Golt um Rettung fleheten, verkünden die Trompeten der Banda mit ihren übrigen Instrumenten die Ankunft des Gesandten [...]. Alles fasst sich leicht, Orchester und Banda sind zweckmässig verwendet und die Harmonie ist reicher, als man sie in italienischen Opern, besonders jetzt, zu sehen oder zu hören gewohnt ist [...][97]. Das Volk steigt die Stufen herab unter Glockengeläut (Triangel und Banda) während einer religiösen Musik und die Mädchen bringen Palmen und Kränze: "Vieni fra gl'inni, e i cantici, vieni, donzella eletta"[98]. 2ter Act. [...]. Auf dem Theater lässt sich die Banda im einfachen, kriegerisch rhythmischen Accorde zwischen dem Orchester vernehmen und das All. marziale 2/4 ist gleichfalls italisch wirksam [...][99]. [Nella scena di Selene 'Oh qual silenzio intorno'] Da erklingt, die Orgel nachahmend, vom Theater her Larghetto religioso, 4/4, G dur, choralmässig von Flöten, Oboen, Clarinetten, Fagotten und Posaunen vorgetragen[100].

Questi giudizi espressi dal periodico lipsiense sono estremamente significativi poiché riconsideravano radicalmente alcune critiche taglienti e decisamente parziali su Francesco Morlacchi compositore[101] espressione degli ambienti filo-weberiani. Preme sottolineare, inoltre, quanto a partire dal *Tebaldo e Isolina* vengano sempre più esaltati i caratteri stilistici tedesco-italiani impiegati nella produzione operistica del musicista perugino. Valga per tutti questo ulteriore quanto esemplare giudizio dell'*Allgemeine musikalische Zeitung*: «Als Künstler

---

95. *AmZ*, xxiv/33 (4 agosto 1822), coll. 545-547: 545-546.
96. *AmZ*, xxxiv/27 (4 luglio 1832), coll. 437-446: 438.
97. *Ibidem*, col. 439.
98. *Ibidem*, col. 441.
99. *Ibidem*, coll. 441-442.
100. *AmZ*, xxxiv/28 (11 luglio 1932), coll. 457-462: 458.
101. Mori 1989.

rühmen wir zuvörderst den Verf. in seiner Instrumentation [...], die dem Teutschen eigener ist, als jedem Andern»[102]. E tale elogio passava anche attraverso l'uso raffinato e proprio che Morlacchi faceva nelle sue opere dei fiati e della banda.

### Il coro come popolo

Morlacchi aveva raffinati gusti letterari dovuti ad una solida preparazione umanistica; fu questa la ragione per cui si avvalse sempre di librettisti di qualità come: Jacopo Ferretti (*La principessa per ripiego*); Giovanni Battista Bordesi (*Boadicea*); Antonio Sografi (*Corradino*); Stefano Scatizzi (*Le danaidi*); Luigi Bottioni (*Oreste*); Niccolò Perotti (*Raoul di Créquy*); Bartolomeo Merelli (*Il disperato per eccesso di buon cuore*); Luigi Romanelli con tre opere comiche (*Il ritratto, Le avventura d'una giornata, La capricciosa pentita*); Gaetano Rossi con due opere serie (*Tebaldo e Isolina, Ilda d'Avenel*); Felice Romani con ben sette opere, tre comiche (*Gianni di Parigi, Donna Aurora, La gioventù di Enrico V*) e quattro serie tutte collocate nella tarda produzione (*I saraceni in Sicilia, Colombo, Il rinnegato*, l'incompleta *Francesca da Rimini*).

All'inizio della sua carriera il giovane Morlacchi predilesse soprattutto i soggetti classici, allora molto alla moda e pienamente inseriti nel filone post-rivoluzionario e napoleonico. In tutte queste opere vi fu, naturalmente, l'impiego del coro ma l'unico melodramma del periodo giovanile in cui comparve esplicitamente il «popolo» in qualità di personaggio agente della vicenda[103], risultò *Le danaidi*[104]. Esso interagisce nella vicissitudine della trama dell'opera soprattutto nell'atto II. La prima scena si svolge nell'«atrio delle carceri». Il popolo è in tumulto contro Danao re d'Argo che ha imprigionato la figlia Ipermestra perché innamorata di Linceo figlio d'Egitto. Danao, sfidando apertamente il volere degli dei che esigevano il matrimonio tra Ipermestra e Linceo, vede ora ribellarsi il popolo con odio contro di sé. L'arrivo del popolo è annunziato da sinistri squilli di fanfara a cui seguono i ritmi puntati in omoritmia del coro (T I e II – B I e II) che ben esprimono l'aspra invettiva del popolo contro Danao («Re tiranno, re crudo, re folle») decretandone l'imminente rovina («a cader, a morir sei vicino») e preconizzando, con le sonorità a piena orchestra rinforzata dalla banda turca, «un re giusto» che sul suo «soglio» si siederà. L'*ignoto numini* sarà Linceo che alla fine dell'opera potrà palesarsi finalmente vittorioso sul palcoscenico proprio grazie al popolo dopo aver fatto crollare la facciata del tempio tra il fragore orchestrale e della banda.

Nell'ambito della primissima produzione per il Teatro reale di Dresda si colloca un tentativo 'sperimentale' di Morlacchi al fine di creare un melodramma anticipatore, per certi versi, di ciò che sarà — circa vent'anni dopo — il *grand opéra* francese: si tratta del *Raoul di Créquy*

---

[102]. *AmZ*, XXXIV/28 (11 luglio 1932), col. 460.
[103]. Ciliberti 1995.
[104]. Brumana 2013c.

rappresentato nel 1811[105]. Peculiare è, infatti, l'articolazione dell'opera in tre atti, l'impiego sostanzioso di cori di danze (poste alla fine del I e del III ed entro il II atto), nonché l'unione di caratteri buffi con personaggi seri. Il sottotitolo apposto al libretto e al componimento è di «dramma semiserio» costituendo una interessante prova di fondere assieme elementi stilistici italiani, francesi e tedeschi. Di italiano vi sono da un lato la figura saggia di Gerardo, padre di Raoul, e dall'altra (quasi a mediare l'opera comica italiana con i generi dell'*opéra-comique* e del *Singspiel*) la comicità di Uguccione, servo di Raoul che addirittura citerà testualmente e musicalmente nel II atto la *Canzone* (*sic* nella partitura) 'Nel cor più non mi sento' dalla *Molinara* di Paisiello. Di tedesco si possono riscontrare sia il rapporto con la natura — come la grande Tempesta nel I atto in cui il compositore sembra esprimere non solo il turbamento dello stato d'animo di Adele (la protagonista) sconvolta dalla prospettiva di matrimonio con l'usurpatore Gastone (cugino di Raoul) ma congiuntamente anche il terrore delle potenti forze del tutto — sia le numerose indicazioni scenografiche apposte nel libretto da Perotti. Di francese vi è, poi, il soggetto — tratto dal *Raoul di Créquy* di Jacques-Marie Boutet de Monvel su musica di Nicolas-Marie Dalayrac, rappresentato per la prima volta a Parigi nel 1789 alla Comédie Italienne — nonché l'impiego dei cori, di una grande orchestra e l'uso di abbondanti francesismi nel testo del libretto.

Le scelte musicali del compositore costituiscono per alcuni aspetti, linee coerenti con la struttura 'nuova' dell'opera e la modernità esplicitamente filonapoleonica della trama: per ogni atto esistono introduzioni strumentali; l'orchestrazione è consistente nonché ben adatta a sottolineare le vicende del dramma (come la presenza di una grande marcia funebre nell'atto I); si assiste, poi, all'abolizione del tradizionale recitativo a favore di un declamato più abbondantemente melodico; vi è infine, l'utilizzo di un linguaggio aperto all'uso di dissonanze.

Con tali premesse il concetto di 'popolo' acquista in quest'opera un senso identitario e politico. Nel *Raoul di Créquy* (atto II, scena 3) di Morlacchi la massa è costituita dai minatori i quali — per usare alcuni dei francesismi tratti dal testo del libretto — «travagliano» nella «gran cava» di una montagna. Al fine di rappresentare con maggior vigore musicale la loro immagine mentre faticano nelle viscere della terra, il musicista perugino prescrive nell'orchestra «martelli e picconi» obbligati che, assieme alla banda turca, scandiscono con un arpeggio ascendente l'accordo di Re maggiore. I minatori vengono oppressi dalla tirannide di Gastone e nonostante cantino «Siam qui condannati | la pena a portare | de' nostri delitti», il senso di ribellione trova la sua catarsi nei versi successivi: «non giova il pensarci | dobbiam lavorare | [...] Evviva! cantiamo | Si scacci il rancor». Quasi ad alleviare la tensione timbrica espressa dalla fatica 'martellante' e continua dei minatori, segue una melodica preghiera di Raoul imprigionato tra questi e condannato ai lavori forzati dove non si invoca né giustizia né vendetta, ma solo pietà. I minatori si trasformeranno ben presto in congiurati a fianco di Raoul

---

[105]. Ciliberti 2013a.

nella «marcia funebre» dell' atto III, in cui il feretro, ove il duca di Créquy finge la morte, viene scortato dall'amata Adele e, appunto, dal «coro dei congiurati». Il dolore espresso dal trombone tenore solista scandisce, accompagnato da un gruppo di ottoni, la melodia funebre con un *tactus* 'alla francese' e con un *sound* 'imperiale'. Raoul, che esce improvvisamente dalla tomba e sconfigge l'impostore aiutato da semplici minatori, ha senza dubbio il fascino di un eroe romantico, sorta di Masaniello (pensando alla *Muette de Portici* di Auber) o di Tell *ante litteram*. Nonostante il finale si concluda con il perdono dell'usurpatore, il *Raoul di Créquy* di Morlacchi costituisce in realtà una eccezione nella produzione operistica italiana del tempo. Il popolo dei minatori, infatti, sembra partecipare all'appassionante vicenda dei personaggi e le loro ambizioni di riscatto dalla sofferenza fanno già parte di un mondo diverso, quello napoleonico.

Dell'ultima opera di Morlacchi rappresentata a Dresda nel 1832, *Il rinnegato* (rifacimento de *I saraceni in Sicilia* del 1828)[106] — melodramma in cui compare «il popolo» come soggetto interagente nell'atto I della vicenda —, esiste la già ricordata ampia e puntuale analisi di Fink pubblicata nell'*Allgemeine musikalische Zeitung*. A proposito della scena IV, l'attento recensore afferma quanto:

> Im All. 4/4, G dur, hört man ferne Volksstimmen: "Zum Tempel!". Rauschend drücken die Instrumente das Wogen und Treiben der Menge aus. Man sieht einen freyen Platz in Catania; im Hintergrunde das Hospiz, wohin Selene flüchtete. Das Volk stürmt hieher. Innerhalb des Klosters vernimmt man fernes Chorgeschrey: "Sie gehe! Das Vaterland fordert es! Sie sey uns eine neue Judith!"[107].

Anche qui, dunque, un grande spostamento di masse sul palcoscenico, l'impiego di diversi piani fonici (sia a scena aperta che dietro le quinte) e la suddivisione del dramma in quattro grandi parti. Il popolo de *Il rinnegato* è rappresentato dai catanesi, fedeli sudditi dell'esarca di Sicilia Teodoto che inorridiscono all'idea che la di lui figlia Selene sia innamorata e, quindi sacrificata, a Eufemio condottiero dei Saraceni. Vi è una sottomissione non solo religiosa ma anche patriottica nei confronti dell'ambizioso esarca. Tutti sembrano consapevoli dell'identico destino che lega Catania a Teodoto: sorte funesta che sarà mitigata grazie all'appagamento dei sentimenti amorosi che costituiscono il fulcro centrale della vicenda. L'opera è concepita spettacolarmente, ma ciò doveva apparire un carattere esclusivo della tradizione teatrale della capitale sassone, se anche Wagner troverà con il suo *Rienzi* proprio a Dresda, sette mesi dopo la morte di Morlacchi, il primo significativo successo (20 ottobre 1842). Capolavoro che gli varrà anche quel posto lasciato ormai vuoto dal compositore perugino.

---

[106]. CILIBERTI 2013B.
[107]. *AmZ*, XXXIV/27 (4 luglio 1832), coll. 437-446: 400.

# Francesco Morlacchi, Napoleone I e il sound imperiale tra Italia e Germania

## Dirigere Bach con un sound francese

Subito dopo la morte di Weber (Londra, 5 giugno 1826), Morlacchi divenne la personalità dominante della vita musicale di Dresda. Il suo prestigio raggiunse il culmine proprio nel 1826 quando fu coronato il suo desiderio di costituire un fondo pensione per le vedove e gli orfani dei membri della cappella reale tramite lo svolgimento di concerti di beneficenza, che si svolsero a partire dal 1827 il giorno della Domenica delle Palme[108], contribuendo così al miglioramento della situazione sociale dei musicisti e delle loro famiglie[109].

Tavola 2: Concerti per il fondo pensione delle vedove e degli orfani della cappella reale di Dresda

| *Data del concerto* | *Componimenti diretti da Francesco Morlacchi* |
|---|---|
| 29.XII.1826, concerto inaugurale | Franz Joseph Haydn, *Die Schöpfung* Hob. XXI:2 [in italiano] |
| 8.IV.1827, Domenica delle Palme | Friedrich Schneider, *Das Weltgericht* |
| 12.IV.1829, Domenica delle Palme | Ludwig van Beethoven, *Kyrie* e *Gloria* dalla *Missa solemnis* in Re maggiore Op. 123<br>Giovanni Battista Pergolesi, *Stabat mater* P. 77<br>Ludwig van Beethoven, Sinfonia n. 3 in Mi♭ maggiore Op. 55 'Eroica'<br>Georg Friedrich Händel, *Halleluja* da *Der Messias* HWV 56 |
| 4.IV.1830, Domenica delle Palme | Ludwig van Beethoven, *Christus am Ölberge* Op. 85 [in italiano traduzione ritmica di Franz Sales Kandler]<br>Wolfgang Amadeus Mozart, Sinfonia n. 41 in Do maggiore K. 551 'Jupiter' |
| 27.III.1831, Domenica delle Palme | Wolfgang Amadeus Mozart, *Requiem* K. 626<br>Franz Joseph Haydn, *Die Jahreszeiten* [solo: *Frühling* e *Sommer*] Hob. XXI:3 [in italiano] |
| 15.IV.1832, Domenica delle Palme | Luigi Cherubini, *Messe solennelle en re* BV 295<br>Francesco Morlacchi, *Il Rinnegato*, «Canto religioso» [n. 14, Scena e Romanza di Selene: «Oh! Qual silenzio intorno / Dì sereni, dì ridenti'] |
| 31.III.1833, Domenica delle Palme | Johann Sebastian Bach, *Matthäus-Passion* BWV 244 |
| 23.III.1834, Domenica delle Palme | Georg Friedrich Händel, *Der Messias* HWV 56 |
| 12.IV.1835, Domenica delle Palme | Georg Friedrich Händel, *Jephta* HWV 70 |
| 27.III.1836, Domenica delle Palme | Carl Heinrich Graun, *Der Tod Jesu* |
| 19.III.1837, Domenica delle Palme | Georg Friedrich Händel, *Der Messias* HWV 56 |
| 8.IV.1838, Domenica delle Palme | Ludwig van Beethoven, Sinfonia n. 4 in Si♭ maggiore Op. 60 |
| 24.III.1839, Domenica delle Palme | Georg Friedrich Händel, *Samson* HWV 57<br>Ludwig van Beethoven, Sinfonia n. 7 in La maggiore Op. 92 |
| 12.IV.1840, Domenica delle Palme | Johann Sebastian Bach, *Matthäus-Passion* BWV 244 |

---

108. Tavola 2.
109. Börner-Sandrini 1876, p. 231: «Für die königliche Capelle hat er hingebungsvoll gewirkt, indem er den Pensionsfonds für die Wittwen und Waisen der königlichen Capellmitglieder begründete». Steindorf 2018, p. 665.

Così scriveva Morlacchi nelle *Memorie autobiografiche*:

> Nel Dec. *1826* fondò l'istituzione del Concerto della Domenica delle Palme, per formare il fondo di penzione per le Veddove dei membri della Cappella Reale, vincendo con gran pena tutte le difficoltà che si opponevano. Prese tutte le misure perché la istituzione fosse immutabile[110].

Nell'ambito di questa meritoria iniziativa Morlacchi diresse il 31 marzo del 1833 al Großes Opernhaus am Zwinger di Dresda un'Accademia musicale e strumentale della Königliche musikalische Kapelle, quale fondo di sostegno per le vedove e gli orfani dei membri della cappella reale, con in programma la *Matthäus-Passion* BWV 244 di Johann Sebastian Bach[111]. Si trattò di una esecuzione pubblica e Morlacchi inoltre non utilizzò come base per il suo allestimento di Dresda la versione di Mendelssohn[112] ma la partitura a stampa pubblicata a Berlino nel 1830 dall'editore Schlesinger:

> Grosse | Passionmusik | nach dem Evangelium Matthaei | von | Johann Sebastian Bach | Partitur | Seiner Königlichen Hoheit | dem Kronprinzen von Preussen | in tiefster Ehrfurcht vom Verleger | zugeeignet | [...] | Berlin, 1830 | In der Schlesinger'schen Buch — und Musikalienhandlung[113].

L'edizione di Schlesinger è la prima fonte completa del capolavoro bachiano, essa infatti contiene la medesima sequenza e gli stessi brani dell'edizione moderna a cura di Alfred Dürr[114]. Per la prima volta questa musica venne interpretata usando una fonte autorevole e ufficiale rifiutando l'ancora controversa tradizione manoscritta.

In una lettera del compositore al Gonfaloniere di Perugia cav. Lodovico Baldeschi[115], Morlacchi fornisce una pianta dettagliata costituente «un piccolo sbozzo del come era formata l'Orchestra, composta di più di *300* individui»[116]. Ma il dato più interessante riguarda la disposizione degli esecutori. Il coro vocale è collocato entro un emiciclo dal quale sporgono due alette trapezoidali laterali dove sono posti una parte dei soprani e dei contralti: a sinistra quelli del I coro a destra quelli del II. I cantori sia a destra che a sinistra sono posti davanti al direttore generale (Morlacchi) collocato in un podio rialzato di 1 braccio (Ill. 3-4). A

---

[110]. Morlacchi 1841, p. 155.
[111]. Ciliberti 2021.
[112]. Come invece sostiene Steindorf 2018, p. 667.
[113]. Dal catalogo online della D-Dl risultano conservati tre esemplari: 5.Mus.2.2083; Mus.2405.D.11; Mus.2405.D.7.
[114]. Bach 1972.
[115]. I-PEmazza [Dresda, 1833].
[116]. Brumana – Ciliberti – Guidobaldi 1987, p. 18.

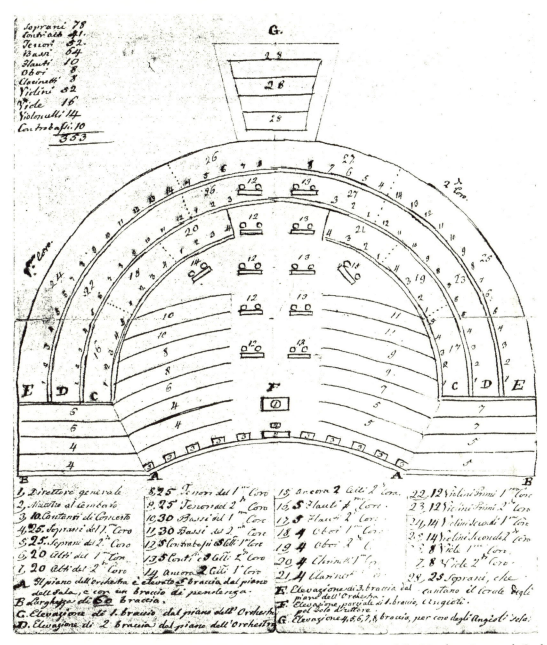

Ill. 3: Francesco Morlacchi, Pianta per la disposizione degli esecutori della *Matthäus-Passion* di Bach, I-PEmazza.

separare le due compagini un corridoio centrale di violoncelli e contrabbassi (anch'essi ripartiti equamente nei rispettivi cori) posto difronte al direttore generale. Subito dietro di lui si trova il maestro al cembalo (Carl Gottlieb Reißiger) in due postazioni verticali probabilmente corrispondenti a due strumenti di sonorità diverse: uno per il continuo durante i pezzi con

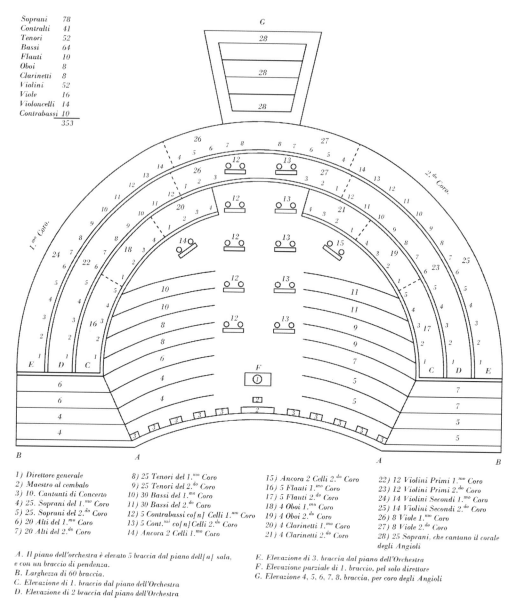

Ill. 4: Realizzazione planimetrica della pianta di Francesco Morlacchi per la disposizione degli esecutori della *Matthäus-Passion* di Bach.

le voci e l'orchestra e l'altro proprio davanti al pubblico per i recitativi secchi. Quest'ultima postazione è perfettamente centrale e distribuisce i solisti paritariamente: 5 collocati alla sua sinistra e 5 alla sua destra ma tutti davanti al pubblico. L'emiciclo rialzato sopra il coro prevede tre gradoni semicircolari suddivisi in due sezioni: quella di sinistra ospita il I coro mentre quella di destra il II. Nel primo gradone sono collocati (partendo dal pubblico verso l'interno) flauti, oboi e clarinetti; nel secondo i violini I e nel terzo, più alto, i violini II. Dietro il terzo gradone

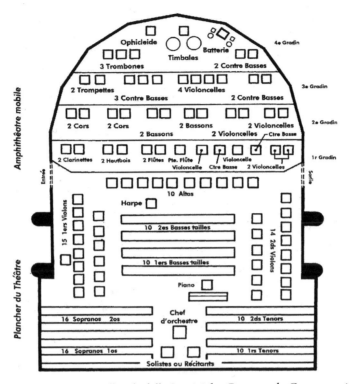

Ill. 5: Disposizione degli esecutori nella sala della Société des Concerts du Conservatoire di Parigi.

dell'emiciclo, al centro, è collocata un'altra struttura trapezoidale a gradoni per i soprani che cantano il corale del n. 1.

Morlacchi sembrò adottare la stessa disposizione dell'orchestra «secondo gli usi di Parigi»[117] che aveva compiuto Gaspare Spontini il 30 aprile 1828 all'Opernhaus in occasione del *Bußtag* (il Giorno di penitenza), dirigendo oltre a musiche di Beethoven anche il *Credo* della Messa in Si minore BWV 232 di Bach[118].

Il disappunto di Adolf Bernhard Marx (e della stessa Singakademie) per l'orchestra collocata da Spontini su palchi a terrazze come a Parigi, con i fiati dietro gli archi e la loro relativa perdita di suono soprattutto nei passi solistici)[119] fu probabilmente recepito da Morlacchi distribuendo tutti i fiati sul primo gradone in modo da renderli più udibili e più vicini al pubblico di quanto lo avesse fatto Spontini a Berlino. Se si confronta la pianta di Morlacchi (Ill. 3-4) con quella della sala della Société des Concerts du Conservatoire di Parigi (Ill. 5) si può evincere come della disposizione parigina rimanessero: il terrazzamento a gradoni degli esecutori, il posizionamento del coro attorno al direttore, i solisti sistemati proprio davanti al

---

117. Sità 2016, p. 153.
118. *Berliner Allgemeine musikalische Zeitung*, v/18 (30 aprile 1828), p. 146.
119. Sità 2016, p. 153.

pubblico, l'utilizzazione di parti di 14/15 violini, le viole vicino ai violini, la collocazione in diversi punti dei violoncelli e dei contrabbassi[120].

Maturità ed esperienza portarono il maestro a riproporre una nuova esecuzione della *Matthäus-Passion* nel concerto della Domenica delle Palme del 1840[121].

Fu per Francesco Morlacchi l'ultimo concerto. Le sue condizioni di salute andarono man mano peggiorando. La morte lo colse a Innsbruck il 28 ottobre del 1841 a soli 57 anni mentre stava tornando a Perugia per un congedo.

## Appendice

### 1.
### Forme chiuse dei melodrammi di Morlacchi con fiati, percussioni e banda

Aria. I atto: *Ilda d'Avenel*.

Aria con coro. I atto: *Colombo*; II atto: *Colombo* [2].

Canzone, e ballata, con danza campestre [e recitativo]. II atto: *Gianni di Parigi*.

Cavatina. I atto: *Tebaldo e Isolina* [con coro], *Ilda d'Avenel*.

Coro. I atto: *Ilda d'Avenel* [«Coro nazionale»], *Colombo*; II atto: *Gianni di Parigi*, *Donna Aurora*, *Colombo* [«Coro lugubre»], *Il rinnegato*.

Coro, cavatina e duetto. I atto: *Ilda d'Avenel*.

Coro doppio. I atto: *Colombo*.

Coro e danza. I atto: *Raoul di Créquy*.

Coro e danze. II atto: *Raoul di Créquy*.

Coro e marcia. I atto: *Boadicea*.

Duetto e coro. II atto: *Boadicea*.

Finale. I atto: *Le danaidi*, *Boadicea*, *Donna Aurora*, *Tebaldo e Isolina* [con scena precedente], *Ilda d'Avenel*, *I saraceni in Sicilia*, *Colombo*, *Il rinnegato*; II atto: *Le danaidi*, *Raoul di Créquy*, *Donna Aurora*, *Tebaldo e Isolina*.

Introduzione. I atto: *Tebaldo e Isolina*, *Ilda d'Avenel*, *I saraceni in Sicilia*, *Colombo*, *Il rinnegato*; II atto: *Le danaidi*, *Donna Aurora*, *I saraceni in Sicilia* [«Coro Introduzione»].

Marcia. I atto: *Boadicea*; II atto: *Colombo* [«Marcia castigliana»].

Marcia lugubre e coro. III atto: *Raoul di Créquy*.

Marcia trionfale sul palcoscenico. II atto: *Boadicea*.

Melodia nazionale scozzese. I atto: *Ilda d'Avenel*.

Quartetto. II atto: *Corradino*.

Romanza. II atto: *Tebaldo e Isolina*.

Scena. I atto: *I saraceni in Sicilia*; II atto: *Boadicea*, *Tebaldo e Isolina*, *I saraceni in Sicilia*.

Scena, coro ed aria: II atto: *Tebaldo e Isolina*.

Scena e cavatina: I atto: *I saraceni in Sicilia*, *Il rinnegato*.

---

[120]. Elwart 1864, pp. 114-115; Di Grazia 1998, p. 196 (Plate 3); Hervé 2010.

[121]. Tavola 2.

# Francesco Morlacchi, Napoleone I e il sound imperiale tra Italia e Germania

SCENA E MARCIA. I atto: *Boadicea*.
SCENA E DUETTO. I atto: *I saraceni in Sicilia*; II atto: *Tebaldo e Isolina*, *I saraceni in Sicilia*.
SCENA E TERZETTO E FINALE. II atto: *Il rinnegato*.
SINFONIA. *Le avventure d'una giornata, Gianni di Parigi, Tebaldo e Isolina, Ilda d'Avenel, I saraceni in Sicilia*.
TERZETTINO. I atto: *Tebaldo e Isolina*.
TERZETTO E CORO. II atto: *Le danaidi*.

## 2.
## Banda e strumenti sul palco nei melodrammi di Morlacchi

*Corradino* [1]
– II Atto: [n. 3]. Quartetto. Vl, vla, ott, cl, cor, tr, fag, Eufrosina (S), Melisa (S), Corradino (T), Sussidio (B), coro (T, B), b [timp, gran cassa, banda turca a parte]. Coro: «Su cantiamo la vittoria».

*Le avventure d'una giornata* [1]
– Sinfonia. Vl, vla, fl, ob, cl, tr, cor, fag, timp, banda, vlc, b.

*Le danaidi* [4]
– I Atto: n. 9. Finale. Vl, vla, fl, cl, cor, trb, fag, Ipermestra (S), Linceo (A), Danao (T), coro (T, B), vlc, b [timp, banda turca a parte]. Ipermestra: «Da questi solitari aditi ignoti».
– II Atto: n. 1. Introduzione. Vl, vla, fl, cl, cor, fag, timp, Alceo (T), coro (T, B), b [banda turca a parte]. Coro: «Re tiranno, re crudo, re folle».
– II Atto: n. 3. Terzetto e coro. Vl, vla, fl, ob, cl, cor, fag, Ipermestra (S), Linceo (A), Alceo (T), coro (T, B), b [tr, timp, banda turca a parte. Coro: «Ah figlia sconsigliata di te non senti orror».
– II Atto: n. 6. Finale. Vl, vla, fl, ob, cl, cor, tr, fag, timp, tutti gli strumenti turchi, Ipermestra (S), Linceo (A), Danao (T), coro (T, B), b. Ipermestra: «Ah come in un momento».

*Raoul di Créquy* [4]
– I Atto: Coro e danza. Vl, vla, fl, ob, cl, cor, tr, fag, timp, banda turca, coro (S, A, T, B), vlc, b. Coro: «O dea di grazia, madre d'amor».
– II Atto: Coro e danze. Vl, vla, ott, fl, ob, cl, cor, tr, fag, timp, banda turca, martelli e picconi, coro (S, A, T, B), cb. Coro di minatori: «All'opra compagni, su via travagliamo».
– II Atto: Congiura: Finale. Vl, vla, fl, ob, cl, cor, tr, fag, Raoul (T), Uguccione (B), Gerardo (B), coro (S, A, T, B), b [fl, ott, cor, tr, timp, banda turca a parte]. Uguccione: «Per esempio se Raoul».
– III Atto: Marcia lugubre e coro di congiurati. Trb, cor, tr, Adele (S), coro (S, A, T, B), trb basso; Adele: «Quel mi rianima come delirante».

*Boadicea* [8]
– I Atto: [n. 2]. – [Scena e marcia] Vl, vla, fl, ob, d, cor, tr, fag, timp, Agaulo (T), coro (S, T, B), vlc, cb [trb, banda turca a parte]. Agaulo: «Ma quai veggo apparir britanne insegne».
– I Atto: [n. 4]. – [Marcia.] Vl, vla, fl, ob, cl, cor, tr, fag, vlc, cb [tr, banda turca a parte].
– I Atto: [n. 6]. Coro e marcia – [Marcia.] Vl, vla, fl, ob, cl, cor, tr, trb, fag, timp, banda turca, vlc, cb.– [Coro] Vl, vla, fl, ob, cl, cor, tr, fag, trb, Boadicea (S), Mario (T), Agaulo (T), Svetonio (B), timp, banda turca, coro (S, T, B), vlc, cb. Coro: «Deh serbate o Dei di Roma».

- I Atto: [n. 10]. Finale. Vl, vla, fl, ob, cl, cor, fag, Boadicea (s), Elcida (s), Mario (t), Agaulo (t), Publio (b), Svetonio (b), coro (s, t, b), vlc, cb [cor, tr, trb, timp, banda turca a parte]. Mario: «Se all'amor mio non cedi».
- II Atto: n. 2. Duetto [e coro]. Vl, vla, fl, ob, cl, cor, tr, fag, trb, timp, Publio (b), Svetonio (b), coro (t, b), vlc, cb [banda turca a parte]. Coro: «Deh serena signore il tuo ciglio».
- II Atto: n. 4. Scena. Vl, vla, fl, ob, cl, cor, tr, trb, fag, timp, banda turca, Agaulo (t), Mario (t), vlc, cb. Agaulo: «Sia compiuto da' ministri il sacro rito».
- II Atto: n. 7. [Scena] Vl, vla, fl, cl, cor, tr, fag, trb, timp, Elcida (s), coro (s), vlc, cb [banda turca a parte]. Elcida: «Ferve la pugna intanto».
- II Atto: [n. 9]. Marcia trionfale sul palcoscenico. Flautini, ob, cl, cor, tr, fag, trb, banda turca, Boadicea (s), coro (t, b), vlc, cb; Boadicea: «Ma chi si avanza o Numi».

*Gianni di Parigi* [3]
- Sinfonia, nel Gianni di Parigi. Vl, vla, fl, ob, cl, cor, tr, fag, trb, timp, vlc, cb [banda turca a parte].
- II Atto: n. 9, Coro. Vl, vla, flautini, ob, cl, cor, tr, fag, trb, coro (s i e ii, t i e ii, b), vlc, cb [timp, banda turca a parte]. Coro: «La Dea della festa si canti e si onori».
- II Atto: n. 10. Canzone, e ballata, con danza campestre [e recitativo]. Vl, vla, fl, ob, cl, cor, tr, fag, timp, Principessa (s), Oliviero (s), Gianni (t), arpa, vlc, cb [trb, banda turca a parte]. Oliviero: «Mira, o bella il Trovatore». – Recitativo dopo la canzone. Vl, vla, Principessa (s), Siniscalco (b), Gianni (t), vlc, cb. Principessa: «Bravo, signor Borghese». – Vl, vla, fl, ob, cl, cor, tr, fag, Principessa (s), Lorezza (s), Oliviero (s), Gianni (t), Pedrigo (b), Siniscalco (b), coro (s, t, b), vlc, cb [tr, trb, timp, banda turca a parte]. Gianni: «Sì questo è l'amabile oggetto bramato».

*Donna Aurora* [4]
- I Atto: n. 6. Finale Primo. – Vl, vla, fl, ob, cl, fag, Donna Aurora (s), Lisetta (s), Giulia (s), Adolfo (t), Frontino (b), Don Marziale (b), coro (s, t, b), vlc, cb [cor, tr, trb, timp, banda a parte]. Coro: «È già salva non temete».
- II Atto: n. 7. Introduzione. Vl, vla, fl, ott, ob, cl, cor, tr, trb, fag, timp, Lisetta (s), Don Marziale (b), coro (t, b), vlc, cb [banda turca a parte]. Coro: «Noi soldati».
- II Atto: n. 12. Coro. Vl, vla, fl, ob, cl, cor, trb, fag, coro (t, b), vlc, cb [timp e banda turca a parte]. Coro: «Venerandi seggioloni».
- II Atto: n. 14. Finale 2.do. Vl, vla, fl, ob, cl, fag, Donna Aurora (s), Lisetta (s), Giulia (s), Adolfo (t), Frontino (b), Don Marziale (b), coro (s, t, b), vlc, cb [cor, tr, trb, timp, banda turca a parte]. Donna Aurora: «Tutto il rigor d'un giudice».

*Tebaldo e Isolina* [13]
- Sinfonia. Vl, fl, ott, ob, cl, cor, tr, fag, trb, timp, banda turca, banda militare sul teatro, vlc, cb.
- I Atto: n. 1. Introduzione [...]. Vl, vla, fl, ob, cl, cor, tr, fag, trb, Clemenza (s), Geroldo (t), Ermanno (b), coro (t, b), vlc, cb [timp, banda turca, musica sul teatro a parte]. Coro: «Dai tuoi figli, dagli amici».
- I Atto: n. 3. Cavatina di Tebaldo. Vl, vla, fl, ob, cl, cor, tr, fag, trb, Tebaldo (s), coro (t, b), vlc, cb [timp, banda turca, banda sul palco a parte]. Coro: «Di tanti prodi al vincitore».
- I Atto: n. 2. Coro e Cavatina d'Isolina. Vl, vla, fl, ott, cl, cor, tr, fag, Isolina (s), coro (t, b), vlc, cb [timp, triangolo, banda turca a parte]. Coro: «Bella stella mattutina».
- I Atto: Dopo la Cavatina d'Isolina. Isolina (s), Ermanno (b), Clemenza (s), Geroldo (t), bc, tr sul teatro. Isolina: «Cavalieri, una figlia».

- I Atto: n. 3. Cavatina di Tebaldo. Vl, vla, fl, ob, cl, cor, tr, fag, trb, Tebaldo (s), coro (t, b), vlc, cb [timp, banda turca, banda sul palco a parte]. Coro: «Di tanti prodi al vincitore».
- I Atto: n. 4. Terzettino. Fl, ob, cl, cor, fag, Isolina (s), Tebaldo (s), Ermanno (b), vlc, cb. Tebaldo: «In quel soggiorno».
- I Atto: n. 7. Scena e Finale Primo. Vl, vla, fl, ott, ob, cl, cor, fag, Isolina (s), Clemenza (s), Tebaldo (s), Boemondo (t), Geroldo (t), Ermanno (b), vlc, cb [tr, trb, timp, banda turca a parte ]. Tebaldo: «Er'io... che orror!... La morte».
- II Atto: n. 10. [*recte*: n. 9]. Scena, Coro ed Aria di Boemondo. Vl, vla, fl, ob, cl, cor, tr, trb, fag, Boemondo (t), coro (t, b), vlc, cb, [timp, banda turca a parte]. Boemondo: «Oh! Sposa oh figlia!».
- II Atto: [scena] Dopo l'aria di Boemondo. 2 tr moderne, 4 tr, 4 cor, 2 tamburi, Isolina (s), Ermanno (b), Tebaldo (s), bc. Isolina: «Io più non reggo».
- II Atto: n. 10. Scena e duetto. Vl, vla, fl, ob, cl, cor, tr, fag, Isolina (s), Tebaldo (s), vlc, cb [trb, timp, banda turca a parte]. Isolina: «Che dici? Ah, no».
- II Atto: [n. 12]. Romanza. Vl, vla, fl, Tebaldo (s), arpa sul palco, cb. Tebaldo: «Morir ciel qual contento».
- II Atto: [n. 15]. Finale 2°. Vl, vla, fl, ob, cl, cor, tr, fag, Isolina (s), Clemenza (s), Tebaldo (s), Boemondo (t), Ermanno (b), coro (t, b), vlc, cb [trb, timp, banda turca a parte]. Isolina: «Ferma!».

*Ilda d'Avenel* [8]
- Sinfonia dell'Opera Ilda [...]. Vl, vla, fl, ob, cl, cor, tr, fag, trb, timp, banda turca, vlc, cb.
- I Atto: [n. 1]. Melodia nazionale scozzese che precede l'introduzione. Vl, vla, fl, ob, cl, cor, tr, trb, fag, timp, banda turca, vlc, cb.
- I Atto: [n. 2]. Introduzione. [...]. – Vl, vla, fl, ob, cl, cor, tr, trb, fag, timp, banda turca, Fergusto (t), Aroldo (b), coro (t, b), vlc, cb. Fergusto: «La speranza avrò concessa».
- I Atto: n. 4. Coro, Cavatina, e Duetto. Vl, vla, fl, ott, ob, cl, cor, fag, banda turca, triangolo, Rovena (ms), coro (s, t, b), vlc, cb. Coro: «Della beltà e d'amor eccoti il serto».
- I Atto: n 6. Coro nazionale. Vl, vla, fl, ott, ob, cl, cor, tr, trb, fag, timp, banda turca, arpa, coro (s, t, b), vlc, cb [ott, cl, cor, fag, banda turca, tamburi sul palcoscenico]. Coro: «Acclamate, celebrate».
- I Atto: [n. 7]. Cavatina Riccardo. [...]. Vl, vla, fl, ob, cl, cor, tr, trb, fag, timp, banda turca, Riccardo (s), coro (t, b), vlc, cb [ott, cl, tr, trb, fag, timp, banda turca, tamburi sul teatro]. Riccardo: «Io primier ti rendo omaggio».
- I Atto: n. 9. Aria. Vl, vla, fl, ob, cl, cor, tr, trb, fag, timp, banda turca, Aroldo (b), vlc, cb [ott, cl, cor, tr, trb, fag, banda turca, tamburi sul palcoscenico]. Aroldo: «Già nel lutto in pianto assai».
- I Atto: n. 11. Finale primo. Vl, vla, fl, ob, cl, cor, tr, trb, fag, timp, banda turca Ilda (s), Rovena (ms), Riccardo (s), Valtero (s), Fergusto (t), Aroldo (b), Gilberto (t), coro (t, b), vlc, cb [tamburi, tr sul palcoscenico]. Coro: «Qual d'allarme segnale repente».

*I Saraceni in Sicilia* [9]
- Sinfonia dell'opera I Saraceni in Sicilia. Vl, vla, fl, ob, cl, cor, tr, fag, trb, timp, banda turca, vlc, cb.
- I Atto: n. 1. Introduzione. – Vl, vla, fl, ob, cl, cor, tr, fag, trb, timp, 6 trombe sul teatro, coro (t, b), vlc, cb [banda turca a parte]. Coro: «Ascoltate... rimbomba più forte lo squillar delle trombe». – Vl, vla, fl, ob, cl, cor, tr, fag, trb; sul teatro di dentro: ott, cl, cor, tr, fag, trb; Lucerio (t), Niceto (b), coro (t, b), b. Niceto e coro: «Ascoltate... egli è giunto».
- I Atto: n. 2. Scena che precede la cavatina di Teodoto. Vl, vla, fl, ob, cl, cor, tr, fag, trb, timp, banda turca, coro (t, b), vlc, cb. Coro: «Si vada, il chiede, il vuol la patria afflitta».

- I Atto: n. 4. Dopo la Cavatina di Teodoto, scena e duetto [coro]. [...] – Coro. Vl, vla, fl, ob, cl, cor, tr, fag, trb, timp, banda turca, triangolo, campana, Selene (S), Teodoto (T), coro (T, B), b; Coro: «Vieni, vieni fra gl'inni e i cantici».
- I Atto: n. 5. Scena e cavatina d'Eufemio. Vl, vla, fl, ob, cl, cor, tr, fag, trb, banda turca, Eufemio (S), coro (T, B), b; banda turca sul palcoscenico: ott, cl, cor, tr, trb. Eufemio: «Né Alamir tornò».
- I Atto: n. 8. Finale primo. – Vl, vla, fl, ob, cl, cor, tr, fag, trb, Teodoto (T), Niceto (B), Lucerio (T), b [timp, banda turca a parte]. Teodoto: «Perché vacillo? E qual gelo nel cor mi scende». – Vl, vla, fl, ott, ob, cl, cor, fag, trb, banda sul palco (cl, cor, tr, trb), coro (T, B), Teodoto (T), Niceto (B), Selene (S), Eufemio (S), Lucerio (T), Alamir (S), vlc, cb. Teodoto: «Ma qual solenne pompa».
- II Atto: n. 9. Coro Introduzione dell'Atto II. Vl, vla, fl, ob, cl, cor, tr, trb, banda sul teatro (ott, cl, cor, tr, fag, trb, tamburo, banda turca), coro (T, B), b. Coro: «Vittoria! Si uccidano i vinti infedeli».
- II Atto: n. 10. Scena e duetto Eufemio e Teodoto. – Vl, vla, fl, ob, cl, cor, tr, fag, trb, timp, Eufemio (S), Teodoto (T), b. Teodoto: «Tutto è perduto... il dì finale è giunto». – Vl, vla, fl, ob, cl, cor, tr, fag, trb, Eufemio (S), Teodoto (T), vlc, cb [timp e banda turca a parte]. Teodoto: «Trema, trema asciutto cuor».
- II Atto: n. 16. Scena [...]. - Vl, vla, fl, ob, cl, cor, tr, fag, trb, timp, banda turca, Selene (S), Eufemio (S), vlc, cb. Selene: «Misera ne! Qual tetro batter di squille».

*Colombo* [9]
- I Atto: [n. 1]. Introduzione. Vl, vla, fl, ob, cl, cor, tr, trb, fag, timp, banda turca, Zamoro (T), Jarico (B), coro (T I e II, B), vlc, cb;. Coro: «Oh qual narrasti orribile».
- I Atto: n. 2. Coro di cacciatori e cacciatrici. Vl, vla, fl, ob, cl, cor, fag, trb, banda turca, coro (S, T, B), vlc, cb. Coro: «Bella è l'argentea stella».
- I Atto: n. 5. Coro di Castigliani. [...] – Aria con coro. Vl, vla, fl, ob, cl, cor, tr, trb, fag, timp, banda turca, Colombo (B), coro (T I e II, B), b. Coro: «E puoi sperarlo tu?».
- I Atto: n. 6. Coro doppio indiano e spagniolo. Vl, vla, fl, ob, cl, cor, tr, trb, fag, timp, banda castigliana, banda turca, coro (S, A, T, B), b. Coro: «Per voi grappoli, e poma odorose».
- I Atto: n. 9. Finale I. Vl, vla, fl, ob, cl, cor, tr, trb, fag, timp, banda turca, Zamoro (T), Jarico (B), coro (S, A, T, B), b. Jarico: «Regna silenzio intorno».
- II Atto: n. 3. Scena e aria [aria con coro]. [...] – Aria con coro. Vl, vla, fl, ob, cl, cor, tr, trb, fag, timp, banda turca, Fernando (S), coro (T I e II, B), b. Fernando: «Non pensar ch'io compri mai».
- II Atto: n. 4. Scena ed aria Zamoro. [...]. – Aria. Vl, vla, fl, ob, cl, cor, tr, trb, fag, timp, banda turca, Zamoro (T), Zilia (S), coro (T I e II, B), b. Zamoro: «Non tentata segreta isoletta».
- II Atto: n. 5. Coro lugubre. Vl, vla, fl, ob, cl, cor, trb, fag, timp, sistri, banda turca, Jarico (B), coro (S, T, B), vlc, cb. Jarico: «Pria che i notturni spirti».
- II Atto: n. 9. Marcia castigliana. Vl, vla, fl, ob, cl, cor, tr, trb, fag, timp, banda turca, banda sul teatro (ott, cl, cor, tr, fag, trb, tamburi, gran cassa), Diego (T), vlc, cb. Diego: «Fiesco ritorna e navigli e nocchieri a te conduce».

*Il rinnegato* [5]
- I Atto: n. 1. Introduzione dell'Opera Il Rinegato | Morlacchi. Vl, vla, fl, ob, cl, cor, tr, fag, trb, timp, banda turca, sul teatro di dentro (ott, cl, cor, tr, trb), coro (T, B), vlc, cb. Coro: «Ascoltate rimbomba più forte».
- I Atto: n. 4. Scena e Cavatina d'Eufemio. Vl, vla, fl, ob, cl, cor, tr, trb, fag, timp, banda turca, Eufemio (S), coro (T, B), vlc, cb. Eufemio: «Ne' Alamir tornò» | Eufemio: «Ah! Selene io tal non era».
- I Atto: [n. 7]. Finale I. Vl, vla, fl, ott, ob, cl, cor, tr, trb, fag, timp, sul teatro (cl, cor, tr, trb), Teodoto (B), coro (S, T, B), vlc, cb. Teodoto: «Perché vacillo? E qual gelo nel cor mi scende?».

– II Atto: n. 8. Coro di Saraceni. Vl, vla, ott, ob, cl, cor, tr, trb, fag, banda turca, sulla scena (ott, cl, cor, tr, trb, tamburo), coro (T, B), vlc, cb; Coro: «Vittoria, si uccidano i vinti infedeli».
– II Atto: n. 15. Scena, terzetto e Finale. Vl, vla, fl, ob, cl, cor, tr, trb, fag, timp, banda turca, campane, Selene (s), vlc, cb. Selene: «Misera me! Qual tetro batter di squilla».

## Bibliografia

### Agretti 1798
Agretti, Giovanni Battista. *Canzone del cittadino Agretti da cantarsi il giorno del solenne innalzamento del nuovo albero di libertà nella piazza detta dei Corsi di Perugia messa in musica dal cittadino Luigi Caruso celebre maestro di cappella*, Perugia, Carlo Baduel e figli stampatori nazionali, 1798.

### Bach 1972
Bach, Johann Sebastian. *Matthäus-Passion BWV 244*, a cura di Alfred Dürr, Kassel, Bärenreiter, 1972 (Neue Ausgabe Sämtlicher Werke. Serie II: Messen, Passionen, oratorische Werke, 5).

### Beghelli 2003
Beghelli, Marco. *La retorica del rituale nel melodramma ottocentesco*, Parma, Istituto di studi verdiani, 2003 (Premio Rotary Club, 6).

### Biget 1989
Biget, Michelle. *Musique et Révolution Française: La longue durée*, Besançon-Parigi, Université de Besançon-Les Belles Lettres, 1989 (Annales Litteraires de l'Université de Besançon, 397).

### Börner-Sandrini 1876
Börner-Sandrini, Marie. *Erinnerungen einer alten Dresderin*, Dresda, Verlag der K. S. Hofbuchhandlung von Hermann Burdach-Warnatz & Lehmann, 1876.

### Bosdari 1914
Bosdari, Filippo. *La Vita Musicale a Bologna nel periodo napoleonico*, Bologna, Cooperativa Tipografica Azzoguidi, 1914.

### Brumana 1985
Brumana, Biancamaria. *Una «Passione» contrastata. Note e commenti dei contemporanei sulla «Passione» di Morlacchi*, Perugia, Sagra Musicale Umbra, 1985.

### Brumana 1986
Ead. 'L'oratorio La morte di Abele di Francesco Morlacchi e la sua tradizione', in: Brumana – Ciliberti 1986, pp. 247-295.

### Brumana 1993
Ead. *L'archivio musicale della cattedrale di San Lorenzo a Perugia. Catalogo*, Perugia, Regione dell'Umbria-Volumnia Editrice, 1993 (Cataloghi dell'Umbria. Biblioteche e strumenti, 11).

BRUMANA 2013A
«Caro suono lusinghier...» Tutti i libretti di Francesco Morlacchi, vol. I: *Studi*; vol. II: *Testi*, a cura di Biancamaria Brumana, Perugia, Morlacchi Editrice, 2013 (Quaderni di *Esercizi Musica e Spettacolo*, 19).

BRUMANA 2013B
BRUMANA, Biancamaria. '*Enone e Paride* [dramma serio, 2 atti]', in: BRUMANA 2013A, vol. I, pp. 48-55.

BRUMANA 2013C
EAD. '*Le danaidi* [dramma serio, 2 atti]', in: BRUMANA 2013A, vol. I, pp. 92-103.

BRUMANA 2017
EAD. *Morlacchiana. Nuovi autografi di Francesco Morlacchi*, Perugia, Morlacchi Editore University Press, 2017 (Quaderni di *Esercizi Musica e Spettacolo*, 21).

BRUMANA 2021A
EAD. '*L'Ugolino* di Pelagio Pelagi e Francesco Morlacchi, con una nota su altri interessi d'arte del compositore', in: BRUMANA 2021B, pp. 15-29.

BRUMANA 2021B
*Morlacchiana II. Il Dante in musica di Francesco Morlacchi*, a cura di Biancamaria Brumana, Perugia, Morlacchi Editore University Press, 2021 (Quaderni di *Esercizi Musica e Spettacolo*, 25).

BRUMANA – CILIBERTI 1986
"Francesco Morlacchi e la musica del suo tempo (1784-1841)". Atti del convegno internazionale di studi (Perugia 26-28 ottobre 1984), a cura di Biancamaria Brumana e Galliano Ciliberti, Firenze, Olschki, 1986 (Quaderni della RivistaItaliana di Musicologia, 11)

BRUMANA – CILIBERTI – GUIDOBALDI 1987
BRUMANA, Biancamaria – CILIBERTI, Galliano – GUIDOBALDI, Nicoletta. *Catalogo delle composizioni musicali di Francesco Morlacchi (1784-1841)*, Firenze, Olschki, 1987 (Historia Musicæ Cultores. Biblioteca, 47).

CARDONI 2009
CARDONI, Fabien. *La Garde républicaine: D'une République à l'autre (1848-1871)*, Rennes, Presses universitaires de Rennes, 2009.

CHAILLOU 2004
CHAILLOU, David. *Napoléon et l'Opéra. La politique sur la scène 1810-1815*, Parigi, Librairie Arthème Fayard, 2004.

CILIBERTI 1995
CILIBERTI, Galliano. 'Il popolo come topos drammaturgico nelle opere di Francesco Morlacchi', in: «*Weine, weine, du armes Volk*». *Das verführte und betrogene Volk auf der Bühne. Gesammelte Vorträge des*

# Francesco Morlacchi, Napoleone I e il sound imperiale tra Italia e Germania

*Salzburger Symposions 1994. 1*, a cura di Peter Csobádi, Gernot Gruber, Jürgen Kühnel, Ulrich Müller, Oswald Panagl e Franz Viktor Spechtler, Anif-Salisburgo, Verlag Ursula Müller-Speiser, 1995 (Wort und Musik. Salzburger Akademische Beiträge, 28), pp. 289-299.

### Ciliberti 2013a
Ciliberti, Galliano. '*I saraceni in Sicilia ovvero Eufemio di Messina* [melodramma serio, 2 atti]', in: Brumana 2013a, vol. i, pp. 192-198.

### Ciliberti 2013b
Id. '*Raoul di Créquy* [dramma semiserio, 3 atti]', in: Brumana 2013a, vol. i, pp. 106-111.

### Ciliberti 2021
Id. 'Francesco Morlacchi direttore d'orchestra e la *Matthäus-Passion* BWV 244 di Johann Sebastian Bach', in: «Helicon Resonans». Studi in onore di Alberto Basso per il suo 90º compleanno. *1*, a cura di Cristina Santarelli, Lucca, LIM, 2021 (Studi e Saggi, 45), pp. 63-123.

### Dalmonte 1986
Dalmonte, Rossana. 'Le canzoni di Francesco Morlacchi', in: Brumana – Ciliberti 1986, pp. 209-237.

### Di Grazia 1998
Di Grazia, Donna M. 'Rejected Traditions: Ensemble Placement in Ninteenth-Century Paris', in: *19th-Century Music*, xxii/2 (1998), pp. 190-209.

### Elwart 1864
Elwart, Antoine. *Histoire de la Société des concerts du Conservatoire impérial de musique, avec dessins, musique, plans, portraits, notices biographiques, etc.*, Parigi, Librarie Castel, ²1864.

### Fambach 1985
Fambach, Oscar. *Das repertorium des Königlichen Theaters und der Italienischen Oper zu Dresden 1814-1832*, Bonn, Bouvier Verlag Herbert Grundmann, 1985 (Mitteilungen zur Theatergeschichte der Goethezeit, 8).

### Ferrara 1986
Ferrara, Adriana. 'Francesco Morlacchi a Parma (1808-1809)', in: Brumana – Ciliberti 1986, pp. 177-184.

### Fleischmann 1965
Fleischmann, Théo. *Napoléon et la musique*, Bruxelles-Parigi, Brepols, 1965.

### Guarraccino – Perni 2014
Guarraccino, Monica – Perni, Giulia. *Napoleone e la musica. Un itinerario musicale*, Livorno, Sillabe, 2014.

HERVÉ 2010
HERVÉ, Emmanuel. 'La disposition des musiciens de l'orchestre de l'Opéra de Paris d'après Alexandre Choron et Adrien de Lafage', in: *Musique, images, instruments. Revue française d'organologie et d'iconographie musicale*, n. 18 (2010), pp. 80-90.

JAHRMÄRKER 1998
JAHRMÄRKER, Manuela. 'Die Kirchenmusik der Italiener Ferdinando Paer und Francesco Morlacchi für Katholische Hofkirche: Tradition und Restauration', in: *Die Dresdner Kirchenmusik im 19. und 20. Jahrhundert*, a cura di Mathias Hermann, Laaber, Laaber-Verlag, 1998, pp. 61-80 (Musik in Dresden. Schriftenreihe der Hochschule für Musik 'Carl Maria von Weber', 3).

KANTNER 1986
KANTNER, Leopold. 'La musica sacra di Morlacchi in rapporto allo stile del suo tempo', in: BRUMANA – CILIBERTI 1986, pp. 239-245.

LONGYEAR 1978
LONGYEAR, Rey Morgan. 'The «Banda sul palco»: Wind Bands in Nineteenth-century Opera', in: *Journal of Band Research*, XV (1978), pp. 25-40.

MAEHDER 1987
MAEHDER, Jürgen. '«Banda sul palco» – Variable Besetzungen in der Bühnenmusik der italienischen Oper des 19. Jahrhunderts als relikte alter Besetzungstraditionen?', in: *«Alte Musik als ästhetische Gegenwart: Bach, Händel, Schütz». Internationaler Kongreß der Gesellschaft für Musikforschung (Stuttgart 15-20 September 1985). 2*, a cura di Dietrich Berke e Dorothee Hanemann, Kassel, Bärenreiter, 1987, pp. 293-310.

MEZZANOTTE 1834
MEZZANOTTE, Antonio. 'Parte del Canto XXXIII. dell'Inferno di Dante Alighieri, posta in Musicale Declamazione con accompagnamento di Piano-Forte Dal Cav. Francesco Morlacchi Perugino, e dedicata a S. A. R. il Principe Giovanni Duca di Sassonia – Milano e Firenze, presso Gio. Ricordi – Prezzo Fr. 4. 50.', in: *Oniologia scientifico letteraria di Perugia*, pubblicata sotto la direzione di Ferdinando Speroni, XVII/3 (novembre 1834), pp. 227-244.

MORI 1989
MORI, Cristina. 'L'attività operistica di Francesco Morlacchi e l'*Allgemeine musikalische Zeitung*', in: *Itinerari musicali italo-tedeschi*, a cura di Johannes Streicher e Armando Menicacci, Roma, Herder, 1989, pp. 47-63.

MORLACCHI 1806
MORLACCHI, Francesco. '*Quoniam tu solus* (1806), per 2 bassi, 2 clarinetti di concerto, 2 clarinetti di ripieno, 2 corni, 2 trombe, fagotto e basso continuo', revisione di Mario Venturi, in: *Il repertorio sommerso. Musica storica per la banda d'oggi. Atti del convegno (Palermo 13-15 dicembre 1991)*, a cura di Gaetano Pennino, Palermo, Regione Siciliana, Assessorato ai Beni culturali e ambientali e alla Pubblica istruzione, 2000, pp. 197-224.

MORLACCHI 1841
ID. *Memorie biografiche di Francesco Morlacchi e sue composizioni*, autografo in I-PEc, Ms 3059/18, in: RICCI DES FERRES-CANCANI 1958), pp. 148-157.

NOIRAY 2004
NOIRAY, Michel. 'Le nouveau visage de la musique française', in: *L'Empire de Muses. Napoléon, les Arts et les Lettres*, a cura di Jean-Claude Bonnet, Parigi, Belin, 2004, pp. 199-227.

RICCI DES FERRES-CANCANI 1958
RICCI DES FERRES-CANCANI, Gabriella. *Francesco Morlacchi. Un maestro italiano alla corte di Sassonia (1784-1841)*, Firenze, Olschki, 1958 (Historia Musicæ Cultores. Biblioteca, 11).

ROSSI-SCOTTI 1860
ROSSI-SCOTTI, Giovanni Battista. *Della vita e delle opere del Cav. Francesco Morlacchi di Perugia*, Perugia, Tipografia Bartelli, 1860.

SABATINI 1977
SABATINI, Renato. *Francesco Morlacchi (1784-1841)*, Perugia, Guerra, 1977.

SITÀ 2016
SITÀ, Maria Grazia. 'Una fatale congiuntura (storiografica): la ripresa della *Matthäus-Passion* di Bach-Mendelssohn nel 1829', in: «*Il giovane Mendelssohn*». *Atti del convegno internazionale di studi (Perugia, Conservatorio 'F. Morlacchi', 4-5 dicembre 2009)*, a cura di Bianca Maria Antolini, Costantino Mastroprimiano e Francesco Scarpellini Pancrazi, Lucca, LIM, 2016, pp. 143-188.

STEINDORF 2018
STEINDORF, Eberhard. *Die Konzerttätigkeit der Königlichen musikalischen Kapelle zu Dresden (1817-1858). Institution geschichtliche Studie und Dokumentation*, Baden-Baden, Tectum Verlag, 2018 (Dresdner Schriften für Musik Hochschule für Musik 'Carl Maria von Weber', 11).

SURIAN 1986
SURIAN, Elvidio. 'Morlacchi compositore operistico. Sua carriera e circolazione delle sue opere in Italia', in: BRUMANA – CILIBERTI 1986, pp. 77- 86.

# Napoleonic Warsaw
## The Emperor's Sojourns and the French Culture in the Soundscape of the Capital of Poland before Chopin

*Magdalena Oliferko-Storck*
(Universität Bern, CH)

The common history of Poland and France, based on mutual influences and the intermingling of cultures, only really began in the Napoleonic era. The two-year episode of the elected French king Henri de Valois 1573-1575 did not bring about the assimilation of French culture on Polish soil, or vice versa, and two centuries later, the representatives of the *ancien régime* supported the partitioning of Poland and the disappearance of the country from the map of Europe. A significant reversal of this situation was brought about by the policy of Napoleon Bonaparte whose armies — bearing the slogans of freedom, equality and brotherhood — achieved the short-term liberation of Poland at the beginning of the 19th century. Although Poland and France were not neighbouring countries, in the early years of the 19th-century France could not exist without the Polish nation, just as the Polish nation could not exist without France. This important aspect influenced the role that Napoleon was to entrust to Poland in the era of his glory, which then paved the way for the further common history of both nations.

The Napoleonic period, from the conquest of Warsaw at the end of 1806 and the establishment of the Duchy of Warsaw in 1807 up to the Congress of Vienna in 1815, is an extraordinary case of a short episode in partitioned Poland, the scope of which was much wider than the long-lasting influence of the three Polish invaders: Prussia, Austria and Russia. This is related to the fact that France was not an invader nor an oppressor rejected by the Polish nation but, on the contrary, a liberator who promised to restore its recently lost freedom. The future long-term ties between Poland and France were based on that paradigm, which placed French culture on a pedestal in partitioned Poland after the defeat of the November Uprising, during the so-called Great Polish Emigration to France that occurred after 1831. I refer not

Ill. 1: Bernardo Bellotto, *View of Warsaw from Praga*, oil on canvas, 1770, Royal Castle in Warsaw.

only to military emigration, but also the emigration of the cultural and artistic élite of the Polish nation, which constituted nearly 6,000 people[1]. The Polish élite, including Frédéric Chopin, then settled in Paris and they established there a centre of Polish culture that also permeated French culture. Its activity in the field of music has been the subject of my other studies[2].

## Warsaw after 1795: From Prussian Rule to Napoleon

Warsaw at the beginning of the 19th century, right after the last partition of Poland, was the former capital of the Polish-Lithuanian Commonwealth, which still remembered the days of its splendour as the cultural centre of Central Europe during the reign of the last king of Poland, Stanisław August, a man passionate about art and architecture. After 1795, it was briefly under Prussian rule. Soon, in 1807, liberated by Napoleon along with the lands from the second and third Prussian partition, it became the capital of a substitute of the former Polish-Lithuanian Commonwealth, the Duchy of Warsaw. It was a small state with

---

[1]. Bielecki 1986, p. 21.
[2]. See, i.a., Oliferko-Storck forthcoming; Oliferko 2014.

Ill. 2: Marcello Bacciarelli, *Granting of the Constitution of the Duchy of Warsaw by Napoleon*, oil on canvas, 1811, National Museum in Warsaw, inv. No. MP 2950.

its own constitution, government and army, actually dependent on the French Empire and subordinated to the French emperor, and ruled by the King of Saxony, Frederick Augustus I. In 1809, after the Peace of Vienna, part of the lands under the Austrian Partition, including Kraków, were attached to it. After Napoleon's fall in 1814 and the decisions of the Congress of Vienna, the Duchy of Warsaw ceased to exist and Warsaw became the capital of the Kingdom of Poland. Its rulers for over a hundred years were to be the tsars of Russia, suppressing the cultural efforts of the capital.

Let us, however, return to the period shortly before the liberation of Warsaw by Napoleon. After the liquidation of the royal court in 1795 and its departure from the former capital, the number of its inhabitants fell by almost half, rebuilding itself only at the beginning of the 19th century. While before the last Partition Warsaw had approximately 110,000 inhabitants, the Prussian census in 1806 showed only 68,000 people[3]. Under the rule of the Prussian invaders, however, Warsaw remained the cultural and scientific centre of the country. At the end of the Prussian period, due to the positive economic situation, it had become crowded with carnival entertainment, as well as private and public balls. The largest of them took place in 1804 at the National Theatre, housing 2,500 people[4]. The influence of the Habsburgs ruling Warsaw from 1795 was visible in the repertoire (the dominance of the Viennese and Mannheim schools) and in the field of cultural institutionalisation, which was continued with greater or lesser success in the following years.

## Warsaw in the Napoleonic Era: The Influence of the Political Situation on Art

The period of the liberation of Warsaw by Napoleon was a time of turmoil and unrest. The culture and art were strongly influenced by political and social events. French troops entered Warsaw on 28 November 1806[5], when the Prussians, having been defeated at the battles of Jena and Auerstedt, fled in panic without a fight. The Grand Duke of Berg, Marshal Joachim Murat, commanding the French cavalry at the time, reported to Napoleon about the great 'enthusiasm' that exploded in Warsaw, «[…] I am unable to describe it, because I have never seen such strongly expressed national feelings before. I entered Warsaw with repeated cheers "Long live Emperor Napoleon, our Liberator"»[6]. Adoration of the French as heroes

---

3. Szymkiewicz 1959, pp. 130-136.
4. Kosim 1980, p. 148.
5. Perrot 1846, p. 268.
6. «[…] il m'est impossible de vous [Napoleon] le dépeindre; je n'ai jamais vu de ma vie un esprit national si fortement prononcé; je suis entré dans Varsovie aux cris mille fois répétés de 'Vive l'Empereur Napoléon, notre libérateur'». See Joachim Murat's letter to Napoleon Bonaparte of 28 November 1806, in Lettres 1910, p. 483.

prevailed in the city. The director of the National Theatre, Wojciech Bogusławski, referring to the years 1806 and 1807, recalled: «Who in such a fortunate change of the fate of the Mother Land would not predict a better life for everything that lived on it?»[7]. Established in July 1807, the Duchy of Warsaw at that time was naively perceived as a state given by Napoleon, «a new Poland»[8]. With all the euphoria and adoration for France, the Polish nation, however, was aware of the transitional nature of this political construct, hoping that under the emperor's leadership the Polish state would regain its sovereignty and its former borders[9], and «Napoleon would return Poland to us»[10]. Faith and optimism were manifested in the generally prevailing merriment at that time. Until the departure of the Great Army in 1812, society in Warsaw did not lack entertainment, balls and other events[11]. As Prot Lelewel recalled, «the light came along with the French, merriment, singing, dancing, and honour»[12]. Writers, including Julian Ursyn Niemcewicz, fled to Warsaw[13]. The efforts of the Duchy of Warsaw focused primarily on military issues, not on culture. As Wojciech Bogusławski deplored, «the theatrical circumstances did not get any better, neither with the influx of several dozen thousand [sic] French soldiers to the capital [Warsaw], nor with the arrival of the famous Victor [Napoleon] himself [...]»[14]. The newly created small Polish state had to support French and Polish troops, taking part in Napoleon's numerous campaigns, which significantly weakened its economic condition. The community was plagued by taxes and military levies. At that time Warsaw was a great military camp, and in the years of intensified fighting in 1807, 1809 and 1812/1813 it became a huge military hospital with tens of thousands of wounded soldiers[15]. In December 1806, as many as 60,000 French troops arrived in the city. Julian Ursyn Niemcewicz recalled that «Warsaw, designated as the headquarters, was filled to the brim. Only generals were counted as 96 [sic]. What about other staff, field officers and civilian officials?»[16]. At that time, the Duchy of Warsaw was plagued by crop failures and floods[17]. The limitation on cultural activity was also influenced by frequent changes of authorities. In April 1809, after the outbreak of the next Austro-French war, Austrian troops under the command of Archduke Ferdinand d'Este invaded the Duchy of

---

[7]. BOGUSŁAWSKI 1820, p. 195.
[8]. LELEWEL 1966, p. 112.
[9]. For more on the perception of the Duchy of Warsaw created by Napoleon by contemporary Poles, see ROLNIK 2007.
[10]. WYBICKI 1927, p. 259.
[11]. BŁĘDOWSKA Z DZIAŁYŃSKICH 1960, p. 123; TARCZEWSKA Z TAŃSKICH 1967, pp. 83-89 and 93; LELEWEL 1966, p. 118.
[12]. LELEWEL 1966, p. 142.
[13]. KOŹMIAN 1972, vol. III, p. 404.
[14]. BOGUSŁAWSKI 1820, p. 190.
[15]. SZWANKOWSKI 1954, p. 12.
[16]. Quoted after BYSTROŃ 1949, p. 149.
[17]. SZWANKOWSKI 1954, p. 13.

Warsaw, taking advantage of the fact that there were almost no military forces stationed there, as they had been sent by Napoleon to the war in Spain. The Austrians occupied Warsaw for several months, leaving it in July 1809, after which the Polish army captured the territory of Galicia, and the Austrians lost the battle with the French at Wagram. The unexpected arrival of the Austrian army in April 1809 removed half of the population from Warsaw. Theatre performances were interrupted for six weeks, resuming only in June 1809[18]. Warsaw's culture experienced similar difficulties in 1812, during Napoleon's Moscow campaign, when nearly 100,000 Polish soldiers left the Duchy of Warsaw, and in winter Warsaw was invaded by the Russians. At that time Warsaw was a city occupied by different armies. Bogusławski reported that «[...] the National Theatre [...] was miraculously saved many times almost from complete extermination»[19]. Despite this, until the outbreak of the November Uprising in 1830, the artistic life of the capital was continued. The most successful year for culture during Napoleon's reign was the 1807/1808 season. It was a period in which the public grew to include a large group of officials, officers and wealthy nobility coming to the capital[20].

## Musical Culture in Warsaw at the Beginning of the 19th Century: Cultural Institutions, National Theatre, Public Spaces, Repertoire, Education, Music Publishing

The Napoleonic period in the history of Warsaw (1806-1814) is part of the so-called 'Polish Classicism', and therefore a classicism with nationalistic tendencies. It manifested itself primarily through quotations from folklore, by the means of which attempts were made to recall the image of the lost motherland. At that time, the National Theatre continued to exist, and its opera performances from 1779 were successfully staged in the newly built edifice on Krasiński Square[21]. Despite the unstable political situation, it regularly staged public opera performances, conveying national and cosmopolitan ideas. During the partitions, the National Theatre was the only musical institution that managed to operate continuously and dynamically, despite the subsequent repressions, and was the most important entertainment in the Duchy of Warsaw. In 1800, Józef Elsner, a later mentor of Chopin, and a rector at the Main School of Music, became the musical director of the Theatre. It was he who was to greet Napoleon musically during his splendid visit to Warsaw in January 1807. And in 1810, Karol Kurpiński joined

---

[18]. Bogusławski 1820, pp. 203-204.
[19]. *Ibidem*, p. 238.
[20]. Szwankowski 1954, pp. 13-14.
[21]. For more on the activities of the National Theatre in Warsaw, see, i.a., Wierzbicka 1955; Szwankowski 1970; Miziołek 2015.

him, in later years becoming the sole conductor of the opera. The repertoire of the Theatre flattered the tastes of the audience, applying the *varietas* principle. The premieres and benefit performances, attracting a large audience, were the most popular[22]. Italian and Polish operas from before the partitions were repeated, but also premieres of works played on the stages of Europe at that time: Italian and French operas, ballets, and comedy operas. Polish music, created by Elsner and, after 1810, also by Kurpiński, was very popular. However, it occupied less space in concert programmes than foreign music[23]. The audience showed cosmopolitan aspirations. In 1807, seven years after the Paris premiere, the opera by François-Adrien Boieldieu *Le Calife de Baghdad* was staged in Warsaw, followed by his works *Jean de Paris* or *Le nouveau Seigneur de village*, for a year or two after their French premieres[24]. Soon after the fall of Napoleon, in the years of Chopin's youth, the National Theatre was already staging all the latest works, including those by G. Rossini, F.-A. Boieldieu and G. Spontini, or canons of literature, including works by W. A. Mozart. Rossini's repertoire completely dominated the Polish opera scene of the 1820s, in the period of Chopin's youth[25]. According to the testimony of Kurpiński, who visited the most important theatres in Europe in 1823, Warsaw was not inferior at all to the largest centres of the time.

In Warsaw at the beginning of the 19th century, the so-called 'public space' was emerging. The concerts moved from royal and magnate courts to public theatres, churches, and concert halls. These included, first of all, both halls of the National Theatre, but from 1822 also the Theatre's subordinate amphitheatre in the Royal Baths Park 'Łazienki', where summer concerts were held, eagerly visited by the inhabitants of Warsaw. The public space of instrumental concerts also included the Social Music Club in Mniszech Palace at Senatorska Street, founded in 1805 or the Social Club for Merchants opened in 1820 in Młodziejowski Palace at Miodowa Street. In Warsaw, there were many musical games, balls, and occasional concerts. The role of patronage gradually dwindled and financial support was supplied by the bourgeoisie, allowing art to develop independently of the royal authority. The opera was also becoming public, available not only to the royal community, but to everyone, financed by the sale of tickets[26]. The concert repertoire depended on the tastes of music buyers. Light music was practised, cyclical works were avoided, and the formula of benefit concerts reigned, the so-called 'medley'. This was also evident in the printed repertoire. Large instrumental forms were performed primarily as *entr'actes* between dramatic plays, and sometimes after theatrical performances as the second part of the event. Some information about the music that was performed at that time is provided

---

[22]. LELEWEL 1966, p. 115.
[23]. See PUKIŃSKA-SZEPIETOWSKA 1973, p. 63.
[24]. *Ibidem*, pp. 35-104.
[25]. For more about Chopin's interest in opera spectacles, see, i.a., REMBOWSKA 1995.
[26]. See BOGUSŁAWSKI 1820.

by the Warsaw press, which, however, did not always record all the concerts, giving evidence only of a certain part of the musical life of the capital of the Duchy of Warsaw[27]. This picture is complemented by the memories of contemporary Warsaw composers, especially Józef Elsner[28] and the director of the National Theatre, Wojciech Bogusławski[29].

Music societies played an important role in the Napoleonic era in Warsaw. At the end of the Prussian rule, following the Enlightenment ideas instilled by the last Polish king, Stanisław August, the *Harmoniegesellschaft* was established in 1801, followed by the Music Society founded by E. T. A. Hoffmann, also called the Social Music Club, in 1805. The latter, based in the Mniszech Palace on Senatorska Street from 1806 (today the Belgian embassy), enrolled 120 members, also Poles, including Józef Elsner. The Society conducted regular enterprise activities, not only teaching, but in particular organising symphonic and chamber concerts open to the public once a week[30]. They performed, *inter alia*, L. van Beethoven's symphonies, works by Ch. W. Gluck and L. Cherubini[31]. «[...] in a short time the Social Music Club became a centre bringing together all kinds of local artistry, and had a very positive influence on the musical development of the contemporary Warsaw society»[32]. The institutions of musical life in partitioned Warsaw, however, were rather ephemeral. Hoffman's Society was dissolved shortly after the defeat of Prussia by Napoleon and the entry of French troops into Warsaw, when French officials also arrived, displacing the Prussian ones. The Society concert hall, however, continued to function until the Duchy of Warsaw was established in July 1807, attracting numerous Polish and French audiences, including Ferdinando Paër[33]. After the dissolution of the Hoffmann Music Society, there was no one in Warsaw who could conduct such a work, despite the fact that the Mniszech Palace on Senatorska Street was perfectly arranged for this purpose, and the Warsaw audience managed to become attached to the cultural offering of this institution[34]. It was not until 1812 that efforts to establish the Society of Friends of Religious and National Music began, which started its activity only after Napoleon's fall, in 1815. Two years later, in 1817, 150 of its members founded the Amateur Music Society, creating a permanent orchestra and organising weekly concerts with symphonies by W. A. Mozart, L. van Beethoven and É. Méhul. The seat of the association was initially in Miodowa Street, and then it was moved to the Salvator house on Freta Street in the New Town. However, it also operated

---

[27]. Information on the musical life of the Duchy of Warsaw under the auspices of Napoleon can be found in *Gazeta Korrespondenta Warszawskiego i Zagranicznego*, *Kurjer Warszawski*, *Gazeta Polska* and *Gazeta Warszawska*.
[28]. [ELSNER] 1809; ELSNER 1957.
[29]. BOGUSŁAWSKI 1820.
[30]. See, i.a., STATUTEN 1805.
[31]. KOSIM 1973.
[32]. POLIŃSKI 1896A.
[33]. POLIŃSKI 1896B, p. 225.
[34]. *Ibidem*, pp. 225-226.

for only a few years, and until the November Uprising in 1830 and the departure of the Polish Great Emigration to France, no other permanent music society was established in Warsaw[35]. Public concerts were held by the Warsaw Charitable Society, founded in 1815, among others. The artistic *tournées* of outstanding soloists visiting Warsaw on their way to St. Petersburg, such as Angelica Catalani (1819), Johann Nepomuk Hummel (1828), Nicolò Paganini (1829) and others gained momentum only after the Congress of Vienna, when a period of peace began in the capital of the newly created Kingdom of Poland. In 1822, the press reported that «in Warsaw, the love for music becomes more and more fashionable»[36].

At the beginning of the 19th century, education, writing and music publishing developed in Warsaw. In 1810, the Drama School was established at the opera, from which the Elsner Music Conservatory in Warsaw emerged several years later. At the same time, other Conservatories were established in Europe, in Prague (1811), Brussels (1813), and later in Vienna (1817). The Conservatory in Paris was in this sense a pioneering project, established as early as 1795. The production of musical instruments was developing in Warsaw. The capitalist publishing industry existed there only from the period of the partitions, having been previously limited by royal patronage, and was now developing at an extraordinary pace due to the demand of the bourgeoisie for musical novelties in salons[37]. The publishing market was supported by the music institutions, mainly the National Theatre, and later also the Conservatory. From the beginning of the 19th century, and especially later in the 1820s and 1830s, Warsaw was well-stocked with music prints. Printing houses acted as libraries, and therefore the European repertoire circulated not just in concert halls. In addition to the editions of works by native composers, the newest works of European music literature were brought to Warsaw[38]. Numerous music printing houses appeared there, such as those of Jan Engel (1772), of Józef Elsner and Izydor Józef Cybulski (1802), of Antoni Płachecki (1802), of Franciszek Klukowski (1805, 1816), and later also of Jan Brzezina (1822), who until 1830 published nearly 570 music prints[39]. There were sheet music supplements to newspapers, sheet music periodicals, such as the *Selection of Beautiful Musical Works and Polish Songs* published by Elsner (1803-1805), and later also *Terpsichore, or the Collection of the Newest and the Most Liked Various Dances for Piano-Forte in Warsaw Societies* (1821). It should be added at this point that the repertoire published in Warsaw was limited mainly to salon music, although at that time excellent larger-scale forms were also composed there. They remained in handwritten circulation, and some of them were printed abroad, as there was no demand from the bourgeoisie for them. Therefore, the real

---

[35]. *Ibidem*.
[36]. *Kurjer Warszawski*, no. 295 (10 December 1822), no pagination.
[37]. ELSNER 1957, p. 78.
[38]. For more on this topic, see GOLDBERG 2008, p. 104.
[39]. For more on music printing in partitioned Poland to the November Uprising, see, i.a., TOMASZEWSKI 1992; PROKOPOWICZ 1971.

Ill. 3: Józef Elsner, *The Selection of Beautiful Musical Works and Polish Songs for 1805*, Warsaw, 1805.

repertoire of the capital should not be equated with the repertoire of scores printed in Warsaw in the early years of the 19th century[40].

All the facts mentioned here allow us to create a certain stereotypical image of Warsaw as a cultural city of Central Europe at the beginning of the 19th century. Despite the ravages of war, music developed there on a level that did not differ much from other European centres. There was an opera theatre which performed, although with some delay, the most important works of the world literature as well as native works. Following the example of other European cities, music societies were formed, even if they were short-lived. The foundations of the Music Conservatory were created, and the newest music prints were imported and published. But what influence did Napoleon himself have on Polish culture? What effect did his extended stay in Warsaw in January 1807 and the French sovereignty over the Polish state (thereafter called the Duchy of Warsaw) have, which organisation survived in this form until 1815, influencing the entire period of Polish partition until the country regained its independence in 1918?

---

[40]. Gołębiowski 1831, p. 264.

# Napoleonic Warsaw

## French Culture in Warsaw at the Beginning of the 19th Century before and after Napoleon's Reign

The presence of French culture in Warsaw in the first decades of the 19th century was reflected in many fields. «[...] the French language [...] seemed [then in Warsaw] so common that [even] and the valets understood everything [...]»[41]. This was due to the military cooperation of both nations, which had been ongoing for some time. In 1797, Gen. Jan Henryk Dąbrowski, naively counting on the support for the Polish cause, founded the Polish Legions alongside the French army, fighting for Napoleon in Italy and on the Rhine. It comprised a total of about 35,000 soldiers, of whom about 20,000 died[42]. Some Legions were sent by Napoleon in 1801 to suppress the uprising of Afro-American slaves in Spaniola (today's Haiti), which lasted until 1804. Some of them settled on the island, effecting the first significant incorporation of Polish culture into the Caribbean[43], before the spectacular 'expedition' of Chopin's closest friend and pupil, Julian Fontana, to Cuba in 1844[44]. After Napoleon's victories at Jena in 1806, the possibility for the Polish Legions' return to their mother country finally came to pass. The French emperor then ordered the formation of the Polish Army, the nucleus of the future army of the Duchy of Warsaw, the first one since the last Polish partition. It is symbolic that *Dąbrowski's Mazurka* [Poland Is Not Yet Lost] (1797), dating from this very period, referring to the creation of the Polish Legions in Italy under Napoleon and the emperor's supremacy («Bonaparte set an example for us of how we should prevail»), has been the official national anthem of Poland since 1927. The French nation showed its appreciation to the Polish Legions for their support in the Napoleonic war campaigns, for which they later repaid by offering hospitality for the Great Polish Emigration after the fall of the November Uprising (1831). And the Polish nation similarly expressed special gratitude to Napoleon, who opened the gates to regaining its independence, although no one realised how short-lived this profit would be. At that time, an extraordinary Francophilia was born that engulfed the blinded Warsaw. The atmosphere of ardent adoration of Napoleon as the resurrector of lost Poland and the great hopes placed in his strategic genius can be understood from the press reports, memories, works of fine art and music. Polish Napoleonians were counted in their thousands.

Let us return to the musical issues. In 1829, Karol Kurpiński stated: «We Poles [are] surrounded by a flood of [opera] works by these three nations [French, Italian and German] [...]»[45]. In fact, French repertoire was as widespread in Warsaw as that of Italy, which dominated

---

[41]. Magier 1963, p. 122.
[42]. For more about the Polish Legions in Italy, see Bielecki – Tyszka 1984.
[43]. In fact, there is still a genre of *mazurka mélancolique* to be found in Haiti, mistakenly identified with Chopin's mazurka, and whose roots go back to the period of the Polish Legions.
[44]. For more on this topic, see Oliferko 2013; Tieles 1988.
[45]. Kurpiński 1830.

the opera there alongside native works. During the Warsaw stage of the Napoleonic era (1806-1814), apart from works by Polish composers, Józef Elsner, Jan Stefani and the Italians, French works were performed very often: François-Adrien Boieldieu had 55 performances in Warsaw until 1820, Étienne-Nicolas Méhul — 70 performances, Nicolas Dalayrac — 109 performances, Ferdinando Paër (being an imperial favourite and court composer with Italian roots) — nearly 50 performances[46]. Francophilia reigned in the National Theatre. The performances, however, were translated into Polish for the audience.

## Napoleon in Warsaw

Although Napoleon only stayed in Warsaw for a short time, his influence on the life of the city was significant, during the entire period of French rule. The extraordinary enthusiasm, which translated into Warsaw's musical repertoire, manifested itself just after the arrival of French troops in the city on 28 November 1806[47], while awaiting the emperor's arrival. A few days later, on 2 December 1806, the celebrations of the second anniversary of Napoleon's coronation began in Warsaw. In the morning, in St. John's Archcathedral, a solemn mass was held, accompanied by a performance from the orchestra and singers of the National Theatre of the *Te Deum*. The Royal Castle hosted a ball visited by French generals and officers, and the National Theatre restaged the one-act opera *Mieszkańcy wyspy Kamkatal* [Residents of the Kamkatal Island] by Józef Elsner and Ludwik Dmuszewski[48], which had been played in Warsaw since 1804[49]. The opera, in which melodramatic action is set in a utopian land, was then given a new subtitle *Wylądowanie Francuzów* [The Landing of the French], referring to the rescue of the title characters by French soldiers. *The Warsaw Newspaper* reported:

> [On 2 December 1806] the National Theatre [in Warsaw], open free of charge, was filled with soldiers and local residents. Polish and French actors applied to play this assembly with a representation of two operas, in both languages, with songs used for that day. Finally, the ballet ended with the display of an inscription, the letters of which, held separately by the dancers in a selected shape, consisted of *Vive l'Empereur des Français*. This inscription was repeated many times to cheers from the audience. During the performance and later, after the show, the Redoute Rooms were open for the ball, where food and drink were given free of charge, the French and Poles charged their glasses for the health of the Emperor [Napoleon]

---

[46]. Dmuszewski 1820.
[47]. Perrot 1846, p. 268.
[48]. *Gazeta Warszawska*, no. 97 (5 October 1806), p. 1515.
[49]. Dmuszewski 1820.

and The Honourable Duke of Berg [Joachim Murat]. The dances lasted until late at night[50].

Ill. 4: Józef Peszka, *Allegorical scene with Napoleon*, National Musem in Warsaw, oil on canvas, after 1810, sign. MP 2119. The painting refers to Virgil's *Aeneid*: Napoleon is depicted as Aeneas leaving Dido (Poland), symbolised by a fainting woman in a *corona muralis* and a heraldic shield with a white eagle at her feet, held in the arms of Napoleon's great love, Maria Walewska.

---

[50]. *Gazeta Warszawska*, no. 97 (5 October 1806), p. 1515.

Even greater emotions were awakened a few days later, on 9 December 1806, by the appearance of General Jan Henryk Dąbrowski, the leader of the Polish Legions, in the audience at the Theatre, a man to whom Poland owed its intercession to Napoleon. During the performance of *Krakowiacy i Górale* [Cracovians and Highlanders] by Jan Stefani — the first Polish national opera — he was carried in the hands of the crowd amid the applause of the large audience, who shouted «Long live the emperor! Long live the French»[51]. Another gala performance, ordered by the government, was held at the National Theatre on 19 December 1806, the day after Napoleon's first arrival in Warsaw[52]. Another event was the performance of the song *Homage to His Majesty Napoleon* (*What a Providence Over Us*) by Elsner in the Masonic Lodge 'Temple of Wisdom' in December 1806. It was later published by him in the collection *Music to Masonic Songs* (1811)[53]. This song was sometimes mistaken with a Cantata in honour of Napoleon, created in December 1806 and premiered in January 1807 as the culmination of the opera *Andromeda*.

Napoleon visited Warsaw three times. He first came to the city after conquering Vienna, achieving victories at Austerlitz and Jena, and capturing Berlin. He arrived in Warsaw on 18 December 1806 and departed after five days, on 23 December 1806. His troops had been there for less than a month. Napoleon returned to Warsaw on 2 January 1807 and stayed almost a whole month until 29 January 1807. He returned to Warsaw again on 10 December 1812[54]. The reason for his longer than necessary sojourn in Warsaw in 1807 was not just a political one, but was related to his obsessive love for Maria Walewska (1786-1817), whom he met there. Walewska, after Napoleon's many promotions and insistences, became his official mistress, and was called by historians 'Napoleon's Polish wife'. She later visited him in Finckenstein in East Prussia, at the Schönbrunn Palace in Vienna, and then settled in Paris. She was the mother of his biological son, born in 1811 — the first confirmed descendant of the emperor who had previously suspected his infertility. Walewska was to play a significant role. She took on the mission of influencing Napoleon to bring about the restoration of Poland[55]. As history has shown, it did not happen. Walewska learned French and German, music and dancing[56]. Chopin's father, Nicolas Chopin, was her siblings' tutor for six years. Her love for music certainly to some extent transferred to Napoleon's interest in Polish music. Walewska and Napoleon met at a carnival ball in honour of the emperor at the Tepper Palace at Miodowa Street. *The Newspaper of the Warsaw and Foreign Correspondent* reported that:

---

[51]. *Gazeta Warszawska*, no. 99 (12 December 1806), pp. 1569-1570.
[52]. WIERZBICKA 1955, pp. 85 and 87.
[53]. ELSNER, Józef. *Muzyka do pieśni wolnomularskich*, Warsaw, s.n., 1811.
[54]. PERROT 1846, pp. 269-271 and 561.
[55]. See, i.a., BRANDYS 1995.
[56]. *Ibidem*, p. 24.

# Napoleonic Warsaw

On Saturday [17 January 1807], the Brightest Emperor [Napoleon Bonaparte] was at the ball at Prince of Benevento [Charles-Maurice de Talleyrand-Périgord], during which he *danced the contredance* [my emphasis] with the Right Honourable Mrs Walewska and played happily during his stay[57].

ILL. 5: François-Pascal-Simon Gérard, *Maria Walewska*, oil on canvas, after 1810, National Musem in Warsaw, inv. No. 210233.

---

[57]. *Gazeta Korrespondenta Warszawskiego i Zagranicznego*, no. 6 (20 January 1807), Appendix, p. 77.

*The Warsaw Newspaper* added that in the evening «The Emperor [Napoleon] [...] was in the audience there for a long time after midnight, danced a quadrille, which, apart from the Monarch was composed by the Great Prince of Berg [Joachim Murat], Prince Borghese [Camillo Filippo Ludovico Borghese, the second husband of Napoleon's sister], Duke of Neuchâtel and four Polish ladies»[58]. Napoleon appreciated the art of dance of the Varsovians. In one of his letters to Walewska, he wrote to her that the Poles from her *milieu* knew better about dancing the polonaise than about politics[59].

The famous Warsaw carnival ball for Napoleon on 17 January 1807, was not, however, the first official musical greeting of the emperor in Warsaw. It was preceded by private concerts, organised for Napoleon from 13 January 1807 at the Royal Castle, where he stayed. They were arranged by Józef Elsner and Wojciech Bogusławski at the request of the emperor's court composer, Ferdinand Paër, who came with him to Warsaw. There were deliberately no operas in the Theatre on these days[60]. Each concert for Napoleon consisted mostly of a short allegro symphony followed by three vocal numbers. These concerts had an intimate character: «Emperor Napoleon used to leave the adjoining apartments to the concert hall, dressed modestly, without a ribbon, only with the silver cross of the Legion of Honour on his chest, in white shoes and stockings; he took the programme from Paër's hands and sat in his armchair, placed some distance away from the piano»[61]. First-class musicians performed in Napoleon's concerts at the Royal Castle: among them were the wife of Paër, the soprano Francesca Riccardi, the Italian tenor residing in Warsaw, Luigi de Santis, and the famous tenor Brizzi, as well as members of the orchestra and choir of the National Theatre, including Józef Elsner as the first violinist[62]. The Érard piano was transported to the hall, which Elsner accepted on commission in 1806 after his visit to Paris and unsuccessfully tried to sell to Resursa until 1830[63]. These concerts were reported in detail in the press:

> [During Napoleon's visit to Warsaw] there was music at the court [at the Royal Castle] on certain days in the evening, conducted by the famous composer Mr. Paër. On 13 [January 1807] there was a great concert, attended by several dozen Polish Ladies. It was sung by Mrs. Paër, Mr. Brizzi, the famous Italian virtuoso, and Mr. de Santis, who remained here from the past Italian operas. Mr. Elsner, director

---

[58]. *Gazeta Warszawska*, no. 6 (20 January 1807), p. 89.
[59]. BRANDYS 1995, p. 111.
[60]. POLIŃSKI 1896a, [ELSNER] 1809, p. 233.
[61]. ELSNER 1957, p. 121.
[62]. [ELSNER] 1809, p. 233; ELSNER 1957, pp. 120-122; POLIŃSKI 1896a.
[63]. ELSNER 1957, pp. 123-129; POLIŃSKI 1896a; VOGEL 1995, p. 82.

of the orchestra of the Polish Theatre, was also called to perform with some people selected from the orchestra[64].

The concerts and balls held in honour of France did not stop after Napoleon left Warsaw. Shortly after his departure, on 10 February 1807, at the seat of the Musical Society in the Mniszech Palace, a large, impressive ball was organised to celebrate «the victories of the French army over their enemies»[65]. The civil and military elite of the French present in Warsaw were invited. After the dancing, starting with a Polish dance, a refined dinner followed.

Let us return, however, to the events related to the emperor's stay in Warsaw. Its musical highlights were glamorous performances of the opera *Andromeda* by Józef Elsner, composed to celebrate Napoleon's arrival. It was created in December 1806[66] and performed at the National Theatre for the first time on 14 January 1807[67]. Napoleon, however, did not honour the Theatre with his presence until 18 January 1807[68], perhaps being unaware of the premiere[69]. Elsner used the history of the mythical Andromeda as an allegory of Poland. Osiński linked his libretto with mythology very loosely, mainly using the names of the characters from the ancient prototype. The princess of Syria (in mythology Ethiopia), remains in captivity, defeated by the king of the Thracians. Famous for her extraordinary beauty, in an act of revenge, she is chained to a rock and left to be devoured by the sea monster, Ketos. At the last moment, Perseus manages to save her, returning from an expedition against Medusa with mortal eyesight. Symbolising Napoleon Bonaparte, who repulsed Poland's enemies, Perseus is presented in the opera «like the God of war», the one whom «the Nation considers as a saviour»[70].

As a quasi-epilogue or «quasi-second act»[71] and a climax of the performance of the opera *Andromeda*, a Cantata in honour of Napoleon by Osiński and a composition by Elsner was performed. The musical arrangement has not survived to this day but included a recitative, aria, duet and a choir. Only the text of the Cantata has survived:

---

[64]. *Gazeta Warszawska*, no. 5 (16 January 1807), Appendix, p. 73.
[65]. *Gazeta Korrespondenta Warszawskiego i Zagranicznego*, no. 13 (15 February 1807), p. 163.
[66]. ELSNER 1957, p. 45.
[67]. OSIŃSKI 1807, manuscript, f. 1.
[68]. Several years later Józef Elsner recalled in *Warsaw Diary* not quite strictly that «the greatest of the heroes [Napoleon Bonaparte] [...] honoured the Polish Theatre [Teatr Narodowy] (on 14 January 1807) [...]». [ELSNER] 1809, p. 233. In fact, the emperor did not appear in the Theatre until 18 January 1807, after the premiere of the opera, as evidenced by press reports directly from that period (fn. 83).
[69]. See fn. 80-81.
[70]. OSIŃSKI 1807, manuscript, f. 15.
[71]. ELSNER 1957, p. 45.

Ill. 6: Paolo Veronese, *Perseus rescuing Andromeda*, 1576-1578, oil on canvas, Musée des Beaux-Arts Rennes.

| [Recitativo:] | [Recitativo:] |
|---|---|
| Fate has brought Poland to life | Tak Polska z losów kolei |
| From the ruins to be able go on. | Z gruzów swoich ożywiona |
| And she saw that her hope is alive | Ujrzała cel swych nadziei |
| In the great NAPOLEON! | Wielkiego NAPOLEONA! |
| | |
| With his breath the graves trembled, | Jego tchnieniem owiane wstrzęsły się mogiły |
| Astonished knight rises from his crypt | Nowym życiem zdumiony rycerz z grobu wstaie |
| And with the use of the old kings' sabre, | I szablą Chrobrych, którey spoczynek niemiły |
| He tries to recapture the lands that were seized. | Wydarte sobie wskazuie kraie. |
| | |
| [One Voice:] | [Jeden głos:] |
| This change is due to the great man, | Mąż wielki zrządził tę zmianę |
| The earth is amazed with a day glorious. | Zdumiewa się ziemia cała |
| He had barely left the Seine, | Ledwie opuścił Sekwanę |
| The Vistula already saw him victorious. | Iuż Go zwycięzcą Wisła uyrzała. |
| | |
| [Two Voices:] | [Dwa głosy:] |
| He takes big steps when he strolls, | On krokami olbrzymiemi |
| And the world is dazed with his bravery. | Dziwi świat odgłosem męstwa |
| And soon on the Earth Pole | I wnet na biegunie ziemi |
| He will plant the banner of victory. | Zatknie chorągiew zwycięstwa. |
| | |
| [Choir:] | [Chór:] |
| Fate has brought Poland to life, etc. | Już Polska z losów kolei, itd.[72] |

The climax and the sensation of this memorable theatrical performance visited by Napoleon, accompanying the performance of the Cantata, was the banner hung at the National Theatre at the end of the performance. Made by the former royal decorator, Jan Bogumił Plersch, who had remained in the service of the National Opera since 1803[73], it depicted the apotheosis of Napoleon. «[...]. All of this beautiful and interesting spectacle took place without an interval in one act for the sake of uninterrupted attention and maintaining the general relationship». As it was reported, «the show ended with a Cantata to the music of the said composer [Józef Elsner]. At the beginning, the new decoration was unveiled to the sound of trumpets and kettle drums, as a banner»[74]. In the banner by Plersch, Napoleon was depicted as the rising sun, in a laurel wreath, with a winged personification of fame with a trumpet in its hand above him.

---

[72]. Osiński 1807, manuscript, f. 19v. The text of the Cantata in honour of Napoleon was also published in the *Gazeta Warszawska* together with excerpts from some scenes of the opera *Andromeda* (no. 5 [16 January 1807], Appendix, p. 80). Translated by Tadeusz Oliferko.

[73]. Obidzińska 1956, p. 156.

[74]. *Gazeta Warszawska*, no. 5 (16 January 1807), Appendix, p. 78.

At the bottom, in the centre, there was an altar with a burning fire. On its left side, a kneeling personification of Poland, at whose feet there were shattered Polish and Lithuanian coats of arms, pointing to Napoleon and saying the words «SPES IN TE» («Hope in you»). On the right, a winged figure was visible, having one hand pointing towards the emperor, and the other releasing a Polish Sarmatian dressed in armour from a Polish grave, on which plate there was an inscription «RESURGAM» («I will rise again»)[75]. The role of Polonia was played by Józefa Ledóchowska, the first actress of the National Theatre, while the Sarmatian was acted by the director of the Theatre, Wojciech Bogusławski. The banner made by Plersch, the 'sacrificial altar', was a symbolic allegorical image expressing hopes for regaining independence associated with the person of Napoleon. In order to perpetuate this unusual 'living image', an occasional engraving by Jan Ligber was released for the Warsaw community, made according to a drawing by Kazimierz Wojniakowski taken from the original of Plersch's work[76]. It contained a refrain and a strophe from the Cantata in honour of Napoleon, sung in January 1807 at the National Theatre[77], and a sentence in French referring to the content of the banner. This «large sheet of copperplate on a beautiful vellum paper, taken from the painting» by Plersch was available in monochrome and in colours, as announced in the Warsaw press[78]. Moreover, a copy of two pages of the programme of the premiere of the show from 14 January 1807 has been preserved[79].

The emperor graced the National Theatre with his presence four days after the premiere of *Andromeda*. On its premiere, 14 January 1807, he participated in important meetings at the Royal Castle, during which the Governing Commission of the provisional Polish state was established and its statutes were drawn up[80]. Elsner recalled: «As it was reported to Emperor Napoleon I that the opera *Andromeda* and Cantata were written on his arrival, he ordered them to be repeated for a second time on the first Sunday after New Year 1807 [in fact, the third, on 18 January]»[81]. Napoleon arrived at the Theatre in the company of numerous French generals, ministers and princes, whose list was published by *Gazeta Warszawska*. Prince Aleksander Antoni Sapieha, who in January 1807 organised Napoleon's stay in Warsaw, took care of him and translated live into French. The press reported the sensational and long-awaited appearance of Napoleon at the National Theatre:

---

[75]. An in-depth analysis of the symbolism of the *Apotheosis of Napoleon* by Jan Bogumił Plersch was presented two days later in the Warsaw press. See *Gazeta Warszawska*, no. 5 (16 January 1807), Appendix, p. 78.

[76]. *Apotheosis of Napoleon* based on a banner by Jan Bogumił Plersch. Aquatint by Jan Ligber according to a drawing by Kazimierz Wojniakowski, Cabinet of Prints of the National Museum in Warsaw, inv. No. Gr. Pol. 18674.

[77]. See fn. 72.

[78]. *Gazeta Korrepondenta Warszawskiego i Zagranicznego*, no. 13 (15 February 1807), Appendix, p. 174.

[79]. Wierzbicka-Michalska 1993.

[80]. *Gazeta Warszawska*, no. 6 (20 January 1807), pp. 81-84.

[81]. Elsner 1954, p. 114.

Ill. 7: *Apotheosis of Napoleon* based on a banner by Jan Bogumił Plersch. Aquatint by Jan Ligber according to a drawing by Kazimierz Wojniakowski, National Museum in Warsaw, inv. No. Gr. Pol. 18674.

> As soon as the Monarch [Napoleon] entered the loge, the trumpets and the kettle drums rang, but the sound of them disappeared in the cries of the assembly filling the hall, which, in the most vivid heart-stirring way and fired by enthusiasm, could not quickly refrain from repeating the words expressing his sincere wish: *Vive l'Empereur*! [...]. The emperor, having a French translation [in prose] of the play [*Andromeda* by Elsner and Osiński] for himself, looked through it during the performance. After a short ballet, the altered decoration, displaying a bust of NAPOLEON the Great, again aroused applause and similar to the first cheers. During the Cantata, Prince [Aleksander Antoni] Sapieha translated the words to His Majesty. All the time when he enjoyed himself at the Theatre until the end of the Cantata at the Theatre, the Monarch clearly showed cheerfulness and contentment. His departure was accompanied by the same cries, with which he was coming in. [...] it was a voice bursting from the hearts of children to their Father. If an apt, animated brush had been able to grasp all the expressions of the soul on the faces of this numerous assembly, how tender and interesting a picture it would have displayed[82]!

Napoleon's visit to the National Theatre on 18 January 1807 caused great euphoria throughout Warsaw. Elsner recalled that «[...] this high grace of the first monarch will always be remembered in the annals of the Polish Theatre»[83]. In his honour, the Theatre was hastily renovated and decorated with great splendour[84]. Already during the premiere of the opera on 14 January 1807, «the [Theatre] hall [...] filled to the crowd [...] with an audience of both French and Polish, sounded with applause and joyful cries of *Vivat*»[85]. Napoleon was undoubtedly pleased with the performance. The director of the National Theatre, Wojciech Bogusławski, recalled:

> [Napoleon], showing himself at the National Theatre just once, on 18 January [1807], was greeted there by the heroic opera *Andromeda*, written in verse, appropriate to the moment in time, by Ludwik Osiński, with beautiful music by Józef Elsner, adorned with a cantata and a ballet. That true connoisseur of talent, with which, in the home of all excellence, he had been surrounded since childhood, found objects worthy of his praise also on the Polish stage. He liked the voice of the leading singer, [Zofia] Dmuszewska, the transparencies suited to the circumstances [the Apotheosis of Napoleon], painted by the excellent artist [Jan Bogumił] Plesz [Plersch], and even the idea of the opera presented to him, which was served him translated into his language and printed out[86].

---

[82]. *Gazeta Warszawska*, no. 6 (20 January 1807), Appendix, p. 89.
[83]. [ELSNER] 1809, p. 233.
[84]. WIERZBICKA 1955, pp. 88-89 and 101.
[85]. *Gazeta Korrespondenta Warszawskiego i Zagranicznego*, no. 5 (16 January 1807), Appendix, p. 78.
[86]. BOGUSŁAWSKI 1820, pp. 190-191.

# Napoleonic Warsaw

Napoleon's satisfaction was also emphasised by Józef Elsner, who was disappointed that he had missed the emperor's generous gesture of gratitude. In his *Register* he recalled:

> [...] the emperor [Napoleon] appeared with a retinue at the [National] Theatre, and although he and those who came with him (with a small exception) did not understand Polish, he stayed, however, until the very end of the Cantata. [...] The next morning, after the performance, the emperor deigned to send to the Theatre through his aide-de-camp 600 Napoleons in gold[87], of which neither I, as a music composer, nor Mr. Osiński, the author of poems, received anything at all, at least one piece as a souvenir; more I can say that we were gladly expecting the result of the generous imperial generosity [*sic*], but we did not even know that it had taken place[88].

Indeed, during Napoleon's stay, Elsner suffered a financial deficit throughout. Apart from the loss of the emperor's generous fee for creating an opera in his honour, he did not receive the promised payment for the concerts at the Royal Castle co-organised by Ferdinando Paër[89], for which he had invested money from his own pocket. Paër left the court with Napoleon on his way to Puławy, without paying either Elsner or the ad hoc orchestra that Elsner created. The Napoleonic retinue also did not pay for the Érard piano, which was on the Elsner commission, and transferred to the Royal Castle[90].

Let us return, however, to the reception of *Andromeda*. Kajetan Koźmian was a lawyer, poet and literary critic, known for his reluctant attitude towards the art of the word. He later became a Referendary in the Council of State of the Duchy of Warsaw. Although not a direct witness to the events of January 1807, he regarded Ludwik Osiński as a literary competitor, and mentioned the haste with which the latter was forced to create the libretto of the opera dedicated to the French emperor:

> When the Battle of Jena smashed the might of Prussia and Napoleon stood in Warsaw and demanded to go to the Theatre, [Wojciech] Bogusławski and people in general with one voice obliged [Ludwik] Osiński to write a play that would portray the nation's feelings towards the saviour of Poland. The deadline was extremely short, around twenty-four hours, but Osiński wrote a one-act play entitled *Andromeda Chained to the Rock*. Perseus, having decapitated Medusa, frees Andromeda from her chains; the parallel with Napoleon is quite plain. That play,

---

[87]. The sum of 600 gold napoleons (3,000 francs) mentioned by Elsner was acknowledged by the director and intendant of the National Theatre, Wojciech Bogusławski on 24 January 1807. See Centre Historique des Archives Nationales, Paris, manuscript, sign. O²/36. Quoted after Kuligowska-Korzeniewska 2009, pp. 114-115.

[88]. Elsner 1957, pp. 114-117.

[89]. See fn. 62-64.

[90]. Elsner 1957, pp. 120-122.

ILL. 8a: Libretto of the *Andromeda* by Osiński, Warsaw 1808, title page.

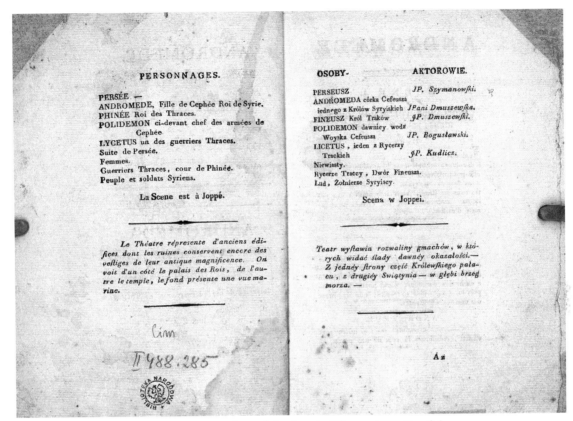

Ill. 8b: Libretto of the *Andromeda* by Osiński, Warsaw 1808, list of characters.

plaiting prose with lyrical verse, was poor. The excuse was the haste; it also had to be translated into French, so that Napoleon might have it before him. The enthusiasm of the audience and the playing of the actors compensated on the stage for what the play lacked in artistry; Osiński himself was not happy, but Napoleon left the Theatre contented, having sat through it to the end[91].

In defence of Osiński, the words of Prot Lelewel should be quoted here, who mentioned that Kajetan Koźmian was, after all, a man «respected in public and private life» and «an excellent classic poet», however, in his *Memoirs* he «throws mud on the merits, abuses honourable people without being guided by the truth»[92]. The Libretto of *Andromeda* by Osiński, presented to the emperor in French translation on 18 January 1807, was published in two languages in Warsaw a year later[93].

---

[91]. Koźmian 1972, vol. III, p. 403. On the literary value of Osiński's libretto, see also Uljasz 2017.
[92]. Lelewel 1966, p. 112.
[93]. [Osiński] 1808.

Let us look at the musical arrangement of the opera, which unfortunately has not survived today (except for the overture printed by Breitkopf & Härtel). Some information about the work is provided by the libretto, reminiscences and reports in the press, as well as E. T. A. Hoffmann's review of the Overture to the opera, printed in 1814 in Leipzig. Elsner's opera in one act *Andromeda* was the first entirely composed opera by a Polish composer[94], devoid of spoken elements. It included arias, duets, trios, recitatives and a chorus and dances[95]. At the same time, it was the only opera series in the *œuvre* by Elsner. In the review published by *Gazeta Warszawska*, its musical qualities were praised:

> The music [of *Andromeda*] by Mr. Elsner, the director of the orchestra of the Polish Theatre and opera, responding to the poet's [Osiński's] beautiful poems, with accurate and expressive tones, helps to delight the mind, lifts the soul with the idea of what is present, and will capture the heart with the charm of good harmony[96].

In terms of style, E. T. A. Hoffmann looked in *Andromeda* for the influence of Cherubini and the lack of the 'imperial' character characteristic of the opera series, present in the operas of Gluck or Puccini[97]. The music by Elsner, however, was only a background for the symbolic content of the textual layer[98]. Hoffmann stated: «Poles are fond of all kinds of allegories and always prefer everything that has at least the slightest reference to [their] homeland»[99].

The opera *Andromeda* by Elsner and Osiński was staged a dozen more times in Warsaw[100], such as on the occasion of the patriotic celebrations on 3 May 1807 (together with the Cantata)[101] and on 26 March 1809[102], as well as in Gdańsk on 22 August 1811[103]. On these occasions, a spectacular banner by Plersch was also presented, in which small details were changed. During the celebration of the anniversary of the Constitution of 3 May in 1807, the banner appeared while the Cantata was being performed, to which Osiński added an additional stanza[104]. On 13 October 1808, it was exhibited at the National Theatre in Warsaw after the first act of a comedy by Alojzy Fryderyk Brühl. And on 14 August 1809, it appeared on the stage in Kraków,

---

[94]. CHECHLIŃSKA 2013, p. 136.
[95]. *Gazeta Warszawska*, no. 5 (16 January 1807), Appendix, p. 78.
[96]. *Ibidem*, p. 78.
[97]. [HOFFMANN] 1814.
[98]. See JACHIMECKI 1929, p. 13.
[99]. «Man liebt in Polen dergleichen Allegorien, und vorzüglich wurde von jeher alles, was nur im mindesten auf [ihren] Vaterland Bezug hat [...]». See [HOFFMANN] 1814, p. 42.
[100]. ELSNER 1857, p. 128.
[101]. *Gazeta Warszawska*, no. 38 (12 May 1807), Appendix, p. 610.
[102]. WIERZBICKA 1955, p. 110.
[103]. ELSNER 1957, pp. 128-129; SZWANKOWSKI 1954, p. 12.
[104]. BRUMER 1929, p. 105.

presented at the end of the opera by Henri Berton, accompanied by Ludwik Dmuszewski's song expressing gratitude for Napoleon[105]. A new, equally impressive apotheosis was prepared by Plersch on the occasion of Napoleon's birthday on 15 August 1811[106].

The music programme in honour of Napoleon in Warsaw also included religious music. On 15 August 1807, when the emperor stayed for several weeks in Paris, during a service at the Church of the Holy Cross Church, the motet *Salvum fac emperatorem* Op. 6 by Józef Elsner for 4 voices and orchestra[107] composed on the occasion of Bonaparte's birthday was performed. Elsner's wife, Karolina Elsner née Drozdowska, took part in its execution, winning the praise of the audience[108]. The emperor's birthday celebrations were repeated in the following years. I am going to mention here the celebration of 1812, which was the peak of patriotic sentiment and faith in the restoration of sovereign Poland due to Napoleon's Moscow campaign. On the very day of the event, the Cantata by Józef Elsner was performed again to words by Ludwik Osiński, composed in honour of Napoleon in 1807[109], and poems written for this occasion by Julian Ursyn Niemcewicz were sung as well. It was reported in the press that[110]:

> On the preceding day [14 August 1812], at sunset, a 5-time cannon shot announced the upcoming celebration; on the same evening, at the National Theatre, to which all seats were free of charge for the public [...], a great opera was performed under the title *Zauberflöte* [by W. A. Mozart]; after the completion of the play, a banner with a bust of the emperor [Napoleon] turned out; the audience, which filled all the places in great numbers, shouted three times with elation: *Long live!* to the sound of trumpets and kettle drums in which it had shown the due respect and love it had for her Resurrector [Napoleon]. Artists of the National Theatre, with the music composed by His Lordship Elsner, the director of the Polish opera, sang a Cantata in front of the banner in honour of the Hero of Europe [...], accompanied by constant applause of joy. This performance was honoured by the presence of the Honourable General Governor, Count du Taillis [Adrien Jean-Baptiste du Bosc], as well as some members of the French Embassy[111].

The next day, on Napoleon's birthday, in the Church of St. Cross, there were numerous celebrations, including a solemn mass for the emperor, during which the Te Deum and the

---

[105]. KULIGOWSKA-KORZENIEWSKA 2009, pp. 105 and 116.

[106]. *Gazeta Korrespondenta Warszawskiego i Zagranicznego*, no. 67 (20 August 1811), p. 1044.

[107]. ELSNER 1957, p. 33.

[108]. [ELSNER] 1820, pp. 233-234; ELSNER 1957, p. 33.

[109]. See fn. 72.

[110]. The texts of the poems by J. U. Niemcewicz, sung at the National Theatre during Napoleon's birth- and nameday celebrations on 15 August, 1812, were printed in the Warsaw press. See *Gazeta Korrespondenta Warszawskiego i Zagranicznego*, no. 66 (18 August 1812), Appendix, p. 1053.

[111]. *Gazeta Korrespondenta Warszawskiego i Zagranicznego*, no. 66 (18 August 1812), Appendix, p. 1051.

motet *Salvum fac emperatorem* were performed[112]. This was probably a motet Op. 6 by Józef Elsner, composed for the emperor in 1807[113]. The Government Palace was decorated with impressive illuminations with Napoleon's apotheosis, and in the evening, in the palace garden, «Music[ians] placed in two amphitheatres played various symphonies». As reported in the press, «[...] excellent music was heard, and many cheers of the gathered people could be heard late at night»[114]. Napoleon was presented as «the saviour of the homeland», «the resurrector of Poland»[115].

Napoleon's glory was also reflected in the works of other Polish composers. As early as 1799, the politician and amateur musician Prince Michał Kleofas Ogiński (1765-1833), who met Napoleon personally[116], dedicated to him his one-act opera *Zélis et Valcour ou Bonaparte au Caïre*[117]. It praised the General's successes in Egypt, where he waged a military campaign in 1798-1801, wanting to cut off England from its colonies in India. Napoleon's army finally capitulated in 1801, but in Ogiński's opera, however, he was presented as the winner and liberator of Egypt, which was a reference to the situation of Poland. The opera was the crowning of the mission that Ogiński undertook as a Polish diplomat in 1796, addressing Napoleon as the commander-in-chief of the Italian army with a request for Poland's support[118]. The libretto was written in French by the composer himself. Musically, the work represents the genre of *opéra-comique*, where the spoken parts are intertwined with instrumental passages, arias, duets, ensembles and choruses. Unfortunately, Ogiński's opera has never been staged in modern times.

A work directly related to Napoleon's presence in Polish culture at the peak and at the same time the end of his glory was the programmatic symphony by Karol Kurpiński *Bitwa pod Możajskiem* [The Battle of Mozhaysk]. Its later title, *Wielka symfonia bitwę wyobrażająca* [The Great Symphony of Battle], was changed due to censorship. The work refers to one of the most famous battles in the history of Napoleon's army fought between 5-7 of September 1812 at Borodino near Mozhaysk. The French emperor was then accompanied by nearly 100,000 Poles who naively believed that their state would be rebuilt after the triumphant victory. The loss of the Russians opened the way to Moscow for Napoleon. This aroused a climax of patriotic feeling in Poles, whose hopes of regaining a sovereign state had never been stronger. As it turned out later, after the first victories, Napoleon's army, surprised by

---

[112]. *Ibidem*, p. 1052.
[113]. See fn. 108.
[114]. *Gazeta Korrespondenta Warszawskiego i Zagranicznego*, no. 66 (18 August 1812), Appendix, pp. 1052-1053.
[115]. *Ibidem*, p. 1053.
[116]. See fn. 118.
[117]. OGIŃSKI, Michał Kleofas. *Zélis et Valcour ou Bonaparte au Caïre*, manuscript, Biblioteka Jagiellońska in Kraków.
[118]. JACHIMECKI 1929, pp. 5-6.

the frost, suffered a complete defeat. These events marked the beginning of the collapse of the great emperor's domain, ending with the final defeat at Leipzig in 1813. In his work, not knowing what the future would bring, Kurpiński referred to Napoleon's last glorious victory. It was the last Polish work devoted to Napoleon Bonaparte, whose rule would soon come to an end whereafter Poland's hope of regaining independence would be ruined. The Symphony by Kurpiński was performed for the first time at the National Theatre two months after the historic events of the Battle of Borodino and few days after Napoleon's last visit in Warsaw, on 18 December 1812. It was played as an *entr'acte* between the new plays (a one-act comedy *Chase* translated from French and the comedy-opera *Forest near Sandomierz*)[119]. The next performance of the work took place on 17 August 1817, already in Congress Poland, also interspersed by comedy stage works[120]. The work by Kurpiński distances itself from the traditional form of a multi-movement symphony with a sonata form. Here the composer programmatically imitates great fight scenes, cannon shots and other sounds of nature. The symphony has a free ABA structure with an introduction, internally divided into fragments with a change of tempo, in a form similar to a fantasy. Its individual parts are entitled: 'Night', 'Dividing', 'Sunrise', 'Reading the Daily Command', 'Grand March', 'Battle', 'Grand March da capo'. As Zofia Chechlińska notes, in his other instrumental works, Kurpiński also avoided using sonata form[121]. The score contains 'stage directions' describing the meaning of the musically expressed images (e.g. «The French are attacking, the enemy is afraid», «The Poles then resist», «shouting victory»), hymns of praise ('Long live the Emperor [Bonaparte]'), imitation of the sounds of nature, artillery shots, battle scenes. The musical means used to convey the extra-musical programme refer to naive, easy-to-read associations: the use of cymbals symbolised the clash of sabres, the beating of the timpani recreated sounds of artillery, and dotted rhythms represented the gallop of horses. Kurpiński's work was a success. The *Gazeta Korrespondenta Warszawskiego...* praised the virtues of the composition, stating with some exaltation: «About this music ['Battle of Mozhaysk' by Kurpiński], depicting a great battle, we will say, without offence to the opinion of the experts, that it bears the stamp of genius that Mr. Kurpiński shows in his works [...]»[122].

With his Symphony 'The Battle of Mozhaysk', Kurpiński is a part of the programmatic music trend that illustrates historical events. Programmatic symphonies with historical content were already known in the 18th century, and the most recognisable example related to the Napoleonic period is the *Grande sinfonie caractéristique pour la paix avec la République*

---

[119]. KURPIŃSKI 1812, manuscript, f. 1; *Gazeta Korrespondenta Warszawskiego i Zagranicznego*, no. 100 (15 December 1812), pp. 1611-1612 and no. 104 (29 December 1812), Appendix, pp. 1674-1675.

[120]. *Gazeta Korrespondenta Warszawskiego i Zagranicznego*, no. 65 (16 August 1817), Appendix, p. 1447.

[121]. CHECHLIŃSKA 2013, p. 120.

[122]. *Gazeta Korrespondenta Warszawskiego i Zagranicznego*, no. 104 (29 December 1812), Appendix, p. 1675.

Ill. 9: Karol Kurpiński, *Battle of Mozhaysk*, Ms., Biblioteka Jagiellońska, sign. No. P.I.73 Partyt., front page.

*Françoise*, Op. 31 (1797) by Pavel Vranický, a respected Austrian composer of Czech origin, director of the Theatre am Kärntnertor and Burgtheater in Vienna.

\*\*\*

In 1815, the Napoleonic era came to an end. After several years of continuous wars in Europe, a period of peace finally came to Warsaw in the new reality established during the Congress of Vienna. The former Duchy of Warsaw lost part of its lands and from then on it remained under Russian rule as the Kingdom of Poland. During this period, Warsaw fell victim to prohibitions and repressions in the sphere of culture and science, for example the closure of the Warsaw Conservatory and the Warsaw University. After the November Uprising, as a result of the so-called Great Polish Emigration, many were forced to flee to France to avoid the death penalty; Warsaw lost its intellectual and artistic élite, which from that moment exerted their influence from a distance. Paris became 'la petite Pologne', where Polish books and sheet music were published, numerous cultural and scientific institutions were established, and the artistic life was organised[123]. There, Chopin was able to preserve his Polish identity and instill

---

[123]. See fn. 2.

it from afar in his countrymen. He became the symbol of a fusion of Polish and French culture in the post-restoration era. The intense activity of the Polish elite in Paris contributed to an interpenetration of the cultures of the two nations unprecedented in history. The seeds sown by Napoleon bore their crops. In fact, the eight-year period of Polish-French statehood influenced Polish culture more than did the 120-year period of partition.

## Bibliography

Bielecki 1986
Bielecki, Robert. *Zarys rozproszenia Wielkiej Emigracji we Francji 1831-1837. Materiały z archiwów francuskich*, Warsaw, PWN, 1986.

Bielecki – Tyszka 1984
Bielecki, Robert – Tyszka, Andrzej Tadeusz. *Dał nam Przykład Bonaparte. Wspomnienia i relacje żołnierzy polskich 1796-1815. 1*, Kraków, Wydawnictwo Literackie, 1984.

Błędowska z Działyńskich 1960
Błędowska z Działyńskich, Henrieta. *Pamiątka przeszłości. Wspomnienia z lat 1794-1832*, edited by Ksenia Kostenicz and Zofia Makowiecka, Warsaw, PIW, 1960.

Bogusławski 1820
Bogusławski, Wojciech. *Dzieie Teatru Narodowego na trzy części podzielone oraz wiadomość o życiu sławnych artystów*, Warsaw, Glücksberg, 1820.

Brandys 1995
Brandys, Marian. *Kłopoty z Panią Walewską*, Kraków, Studio 90, ²1995.

Brumer 1929
Brumer, Wiktor. 'Raz jeszcze o «Andromedzie»', in: *Muzyka*, vi/2 (1929), pp. 104-105.

Bystroń 1949
Bystroń, Jan Stanisław. *Warszawa*, Warsaw, Wydawnictwo Ludwika Fiszera, 1949.

Chechlińska 2013
Chechlińska, Zofia. *Romanticism. 1795-1850. 5: The History of Music in Poland*, Warsaw, Sutkowski Edition, 2013.

Dmuszewski 1820
Dmuszewski, Ludwik Adam. 'Spis wszystkich oper granych w polskim języku na teatrach warszawskich od założenia polskiej sceny do miesiąca października 1820 roku', in: *Tygodnik Muzyczny*, no. 26 (25 October 1820), no pagination.

[Elsner] 1809
[Elsner, Józef]. 'O wirtuozach, którzy w tych czasach popisywali się z talentami swemi w Warszawie', in: *Pamiętnik Warszawski*, II/5 (1 September 1809), pp. 227-234.

Elsner 1957
Id. *Sumariusz moich utworów muzycznych*, edited by Alina Nowak-Romanowicz, Kraków, PWM, 1957.

Goldberg 2008
Goldberg, Halina. *Music in Chopin's Warsaw*, Oxford-New York, Oxford University Press, 2008.

Gołębiowski 1831
Gołębiowski, Łukasz. *Gry i zabawy różnych stanów w kraju całym, lub niektórych tylko prowincyach*, Warsaw, Glücksberg, 1831.

[Hoffmann] 1814
[Hoffmann, Ernst Theodor Amadeus]. 'Ouverture à grand Orchestre de l'Opéra Andromeda par Jos[eph] Elsner à Leipsic, chez Breitkopf & Härtel', in: *Allgemeine musikalische Zeitung*, XVI/3 (19 January 1814), pp. 42-46.

Jachimecki 1929
Jachimecki, Zdzisław. *Dwie opery polskie o Napoleonie 1799-1807*, Muzyka, VI/1 (1929), pp. 5-13.

Kosim 1973
Kosim, Jan. 'Ernst Theodor Amadeus Hoffmann i Towarzystwo Muzyczne w Warszawie', in: *Szkice o kulturze muzycznej XIX wieku. Studia i materiały. 2*, edited by Zofia Chechlińska, Warsaw, PWN, 1973, pp. 105-180.

Kosim 1980
Id. *Pod pruskim zaborem. Warszawa w latach 1796-1806*, Warsaw, PIW, 1980.

Koźmian 1972
Koźmian, Kajetan. *Pamiętniki*, edited by Marian Kaczmarek and Kazimierz Pecold, 3 vols., Wrocław, Zakład Narodowy im. Ossolińskich, 1972.

Kuligowska-Korzeniewska 2009
Kuligowska-Korzeniewska, Anna. 'Apoteoza Napoleona', in: *Antreprener. Księga ofiarowana profesorowi Janowi Michalikowi w jego 70. rocznicę urodzin*, edited by Jacek Popiel, Kraków, Wydawnictwo UJ, 2009, pp. 105-118.

Kurpiński 1812
Kurpiński, Karol. *Bitwa pod Możajskiem grana przez Wielką Orkiestrę na Teatrze Wielkim Narodowym d[nia] 18, grudnia r[oku] 1812 ułożona przez Karola Kurpińskiego*, manuscript, Biblioteka Jagiellońska, sign. No. P.I.73 Partyt.

Kurpiński 1830
Id. 'Rzut oka na operę polską', in: *Roczniki Towarzystwa Przyjaciół Nauk*, XXI (1830), p. 183.

## Napoleonic Warsaw

Lelewel 1966
Lelewel, Prot. *Pamiętniki i diariusz domu naszego*, edited by Irena Lelewel-Friemannowa, Wrocław, Zakład Narodowy im. Ossolińskich, 1966.

Lettres 1910
*Lettres et documents pour servir à l'histoire de Joachim Murat, 1767-1815 publiés par s.a. le prince Murat. 4: Campagne d'Autriche (1805) Gouvernement de Paris Duchés de Clèves et de Berg Grand-duché de Berg Campagne de Prusse (1806)*, Paris, Plon-Nourrit & Cie, 1910.

Magier 1963
Magier, Antoni. *Estetyka miasta stołecznego Warszawy*, [c.1833], edited by Hanna Szwankowska, Wrocław, Zakład Narodowy im. Ossolińskich, 1963.

Miziołek 2015
Miziołek, Jerzy. *The Grand Theatre in Warsaw: The 250$^{th}$ Anniversary of Public Theatre in Poland 1765-2015*, translated by John Comber, Warsaw, Teatr Wielki-Opera Narodowa, 2015.

Obidzińska 1956
Obidzińska, Janina. 'Jan Bogumił Plersch (1732-1817). Zarys działalności', in: *Biuletyn historii sztuki*, XVIII/1 (1956), pp. 150-160.

Oliferko 2013
Oliferko, Magdalena. 'Chopin and Liszt in Fontana's Cuban Episode', in: *«Grandeur et finesse»: Chopin, Liszt and the Parisian Musical Scene*, edited by Luca Lévi Sala, Turnhout, Brepols, 2013 (Speculum Musicae, 20), pp. 311-326.

Oliferko 2014
Ead. 'Fryderyk Chopin i Towarzystwo Politechniczne Polskie w Paryżu – nieznana korespondencja oraz aspekty emigracyjnej aktywności Chopina', in: *Muzyka*, LIX/2 (2014), pp. 37-60.

Oliferko-Storck forthcoming
Ead. 'Chopin w środowisku Klubu Polskiego oraz innych polskich organizacji w Paryżu', forthcoming.

Osiński 1807
Osiński, Ludwik. *Andromeda. Drama liryczne w jednym akcie z muzyką Józefa Elsnera zaprezentowane pierwszy raz w Teatrze Narodowym w Warszawie dnia 14 stycznia 1807* [libretto of the opera *Andromeda*], manuscript, Biblioteka Narodowa w Warszawie, sign. Rps 6152 I.

[Osiński] 1808
[Id]. *Andromede: drame lyrique en un acte represénté pour la prèmiere fois sur le Théâtre national à Varsovie le 14. janvier 1807 / Andromeda: drama liryczne w 1 akcie z muzyką Józefa Elsnera reprezentowane pierwszy raz na Teatrze Narodowym w Warszawie dnia 14 stycznia 1807*, Warsaw, s.n., 1808.

PERROT 1846
PERROT, Aristine Michel. *Itinéraire général de Napoléon, chronologie du consulat et de l'empire*, Paris, Martinon 1846.

POLIŃSKI 1896A
POLIŃSKI, Aleksander. 'Warszawskie Towarzystwo Muzyczne', in: *Tygodnik Illustrowany*, XXVII/11 (14 March 1896), p. 208.

POLIŃSKI 1896B
ID. 'Warszawskie Towarzystwo Muzyczne', in: *Tygodnik Illustrowany*, XXVII/12 (21 March 1896). pp. 225-228.

PROKOPOWICZ 1971
PROKOPOWICZ, Maria. 'Z działalności warszawskich księgarzy i wydawców muzycznych w latach 1800-1831', in: *Szkice o kulturze muzycznej XIX w. 1*, edited by Zofia Chechlińska, Warsaw, PWN, 1971, pp. 33-50.

PUKIŃSKA-SZEPIETOWSKA 1973
PUKIŃSKA-SZEPIETOWSKA, Hanna. 'Życie koncertowe w Warszawie (lata 1800-1830)', in: *Szkice o kulturze muzycznej XIX wieku. 2*, edited by Zofia Chechlińska, Warsaw, PWN, 1973, pp. 35-104.

REMBOWSKA 1995
REMBOWSKA, Aleksandra. 'Nic nie robię, tylko łażę na teatr', in: *Ruch Muzyczny*, XXXIX/21 (1995), pp. 16-17, XXXIX/22, pp. 12-15, XXXIX/23, pp. 33-35 and XXXIX/25, pp. 32-34.

ROLNIK 2007
ROLNIK, Dariusz. 'Księstwo Warszawskie w świadomości Polaków – świadectwo pamiętników', in: *Roczniki humanistyczne*, LV/2 (2007), pp. 83-105.

STATUTEN 1805
'Statuten der musikalischen Gesallschaft zu Warschau', in: *Allgemeine musikalische Zeitung*, VIII/2 (9 October 1805), pp. 18-28 and VIII/3 (16 October 1805), pp. 43-48.

SZWANKOWSKI 1954
SZWANKOWSKI, Eugeniusz. *Teatr Wojciecha Bogusławskiego w latach 1799-1814*, Wrocław, Zakład im. Ossolińskich, 1954.

SZWANKOWSKI 1970
ID. 'Teatr warszawski 1799-1863', in: *Warszawa XIX wieku: 1795-1918. 1*, edited by Ryszard Kołodziejczyk, Jan Kosim and Janina Leskiewiczowa, Warsaw, PWN, 1970 (Varsaviana. Studia Warszawskie, 6).

SZYMKIEWICZ 1959
SZYMKIEWICZ, Samuel. *Warszawa na przełomie XVIII i XIX w. w świetle pomiarów i spisów*, edited by Barbara Grochulska and Eugeniusz Szwankowski, Warsaw, PWN, 1959.

TARCZEWSKA Z TAŃSKICH 1967
TARCZEWSKA Z TAŃSKICH, Aleksandra. *Historia mego życia. Wspomnienia Warszawianki*, edited by Izabela Kaniowska-Lewańska, Wrocław, Ossolineum, 1967.

TIELES 1988
TIELES, Cecilio. 'Julián Fontana. El introductor de Chopin en Cuba', in: *Revista de musicología*, IX/1 (1988), pp. 123-150.

TOMASZEWSKI 1992
TOMASZEWSKI, Wojciech. *Warszawskie edytorstwo muzyczne w latach 1772-1865*, Warsaw, Biblioteka Narodowa, 1992.

ULJASZ 2017
ULJASZ, Adrian. 'Libretto Ludwika Osińskiego do opery Józefa Elsnera Andromeda z 1807 r. w zbiorach rękopiśmiennych Biblioteki Naukowej PAU i PAN w Krakowie', in: *Rocznik Biblioteki Naukowej PAU i PAN w Krakowie*, LXII (2017), pp. 79-103.

VOGEL 1995
VOGEL, Beniamin. *Fortepian polski. Budownictwo fortepianów na ziemiach polskich od poł. XVIII w. do II wojny światowej*, Warsaw, Sutkowski Edition, 1995 (Historia muzyki polskiej, 10).

WIERZBICKA 1955
WIERZBICKA, Karyna. *Źródła do historii teatru warszawskiego od roku 1762 do roku 1883, part II (1795-1833)*, Wrocław, Zakład im. Ossolińskich, 1955.

WIERZBICKA-MICHALSKA 1993
WIERZBICKA-MICHALSKA, Karyna. 'Teatry w Warszawie w latach 1806-1814', in: *Dzieje teatru polskiego. 2: Teatr polski od schyłku XVIII wieku do roku 1863*, edited by Tadeusz Sivert, Warsaw, PWN, 1993, pp. 199-275.

WYBICKI 1927
WYBICKI, Józef. *Życie moje oraz wspomnienie o Andrzeju i Konstancji Zamoyskich*, edited by Adam Mieczysław Skałkowski, Kraków, Krakowska Spółka Wydawnicza, 1927.

# «Non essendovi più capelle in veruna chiesa…».
# Finanziamento e impiego musicale nella Modena giacobina e la stagione al Teatro Rangone tra il 1798 e il 1799

*Eric Boaro*
(Independent Researcher, Milan)

Durante l'*ancien régime*, il mercato del lavoro, per quanto riguarda le occupazioni di tipo musicale in Italia, era sostenuto essenzialmente da due attori: l'aristocrazia e il clero locali. La prima creava opportunità di impiego sostenendo finanziariamente i teatri d'opera e assumendo musicisti nei propri palazzi. Il secondo, per assicurarsi la presenza della musica durante le più disparate funzioni religiose, era solito assumere alle proprie dipendenze strumentisti e cantanti con contratti a breve e lungo termine. Con l'avvento degli stati napoleonici nel Nord Italia e del laicismo giacobino, entrambi gli attori persero progressivamente potere e ricchezza. Cessarono dunque di foraggiare realtà teatrali e musicali locali e di assumere a proprio servizio professionisti della musica. Tale congiuntura storica e culturale fu dunque un momento critico per intere famiglie di musicisti, private improvvisamente della loro principale fonte di sostentamento.

È proprio questo il quadro che emerge dalle carte d'archivio illustrate nel presente contributo. Relative ad alcune vicende avvenute a Modena tra il 1798 e il 1799, e conservate presso l'Archivio di Stato di Milano[1], esse mostrano chiaramente che il mercato del lavoro musicale locale di quel biennio fu influenzato in modo negativo — se non addirittura drammatico — dal nuovo ordine anti-aristocratico e anticlericale. Oltre alla cessazione delle attività teatrali cittadine, che lasciò molti musicisti senza alcuna fonte di reddito, numerose istituzioni religiose interruppero le loro attività, licenziando gli artisti delle loro cappelle. Intere famiglie modenesi di musicisti, ridotte in miseria, rivolsero dunque alcune petizioni al nuovo governo napoleonico per ottenere un aiuto finanziario. Queste petizioni, giunte fino a noi, testimoniano in modo

---

[1]. D'ora in poi, ASMi.

crudo le ripercussioni del mutato assetto sociale e politico sulla professione musicale nella prima età napoleonica a Modena, e costituiscono una preziosa testimonianza della vita quotidiana del musicista professionista nello stesso periodo.

Le stesse carte fanno anche emergere con molta chiarezza la strategia che il neonato stato napoleonico adottò per venire incontro ai musicisti modenesi: approvò, quantunque dopo una lunga negoziazione, una nuova fonte di finanziamento per l'organizzazione di una stagione operistica al Teatro Rangone tra il 1798 e il 1799. I documenti qui esaminati, dunque, aprono uno spiraglio inedito sulle modalità di gestione proprie degli stati napoleonici in Italia in materia di impiego musicale.

## Il contesto locale: Modena dopo la Campagna d'Italia (1796)

Al termine della Campagna d'Italia del 1796, Napoleone istituì la Repubblica Cispadana. La neonata repubblica sorella della Francia comprendeva ampi possedimenti territoriali nelle zone di Bologna, Ferrara, Modena, Reggio, Massa e Carrara. Nel 1797, Napoleone unì la Repubblica Cispadana agli altri territori che aveva precedentemente occupato in Lombardia, per creare la Repubblica Cisalpina. Tutte queste città e regioni, che per secoli erano state governate da organismi statali tipici dell'*ancien régime*, si trovarono in una dimensione completamente nuova nel giro di pochi mesi.

Modena, prima della Campagna d'Italia, era la capitale del Ducato di Modena e Reggio, retto dall'antica famiglia aristocratica degli Este. Il 7 maggio 1796, all'avvicinarsi delle truppe francesi, il duca Ercole III riparò a Venezia, portando con sé il proprio patrimonio. Prima di abbandonare il soglio, il duca diede ordine a dei suoi rappresentanti lasciati in città di negoziare la neutralità con i napoleonici. Questi ultimi, tuttavia, imposero al Ducato un armistizio in quanto, negli anni precedenti, Ercole III aveva condannato alcuni repubblicani e aveva permesso il transito di truppe austriache nei propri domini. L'armistizio diede luogo a pesanti imposizioni di carattere economico da parte francese.

Angustiati dal malcontento diffusosi in città a causa di tali imposizioni, i legati rimasti a Modena chiesero aiuto al Duca in Laguna. Emisero un proclama rassicurante in cui si prometteva che questi avrebbe utilizzato le proprie finanze per soddisfare le richieste dei francesi, ma Ercole lo smentì immediatamente. La situazione si sbloccò solo all'inizio di ottobre, quando Bonaparte, dopo aver sconfitto la controffensiva austriaca nel Veneto, dichiarò rotto l'armistizio di giugno e decretò la decadenza del Duca.

Il 7 ottobre 1796, 2000 soldati francesi presero possesso di Modena. L'8 ottobre, il Ducato di Modena e di Reggio fu consegnato alla Francia napoleonica. A capo dell'ex ducato estense fu posto un comitato esecutivo di nomina francese, i cui membri giurarono fedeltà a Parigi; i notabili che Ercole aveva lasciato a Modena dopo la sua fuga furono invece espulsi.

La statua equestre del duca venne abbattuta; il 12 ottobre venne emanato un proclama che bandiva titoli nobiliari, stemmi, livree, e diritti feudali. Il 13 ottobre Bonaparte arrivò a Modena accolto con grandi onori e festeggiamenti[2]. A poco meno di due anni più tardi risalgono le prime testimonianze sulle conseguenze di questo cambio di regime in ambito musicale.

Per una più agevole comprensione del carteggio oggetto del presente articolo, è d'uopo accennare ai quattro principali livelli istituzionali coinvolti nella vicenda. Al livello inferiore si trovava la «Municipalità di Modena», una sorta di governo comunale locale. La Municipalità di Modena era a sua volta dipendente dalla «Amministrazione centrale del Dipartimento del Panaro»[3], un corpo governativo di ordine regionale — il Dipartimento del Panaro aveva come capoluogo Modena — che fungeva da anello di congiunzione tra le sue Municipalità e il governo centrale. Governo centrale che, per lo meno in questo carteggio, è principalmente rappresentato dal Ministro dell'Interno[4], nelle persone di Antonio Tadini prima e di Diego Guicciardi poi. A sua volta, il Ministro dell'Interno doveva rispondere all'autorità suprema della Repubblica: il Direttorio Esecutivo. Il seguente schema può aiutare a comprendere le diverse figure istituzionali coinvolte nella vicenda:

| Livello centrale | Direttorio Esecutivo | | |
| --- | --- | --- | --- |
| | Ministro dell'Interno | | |
| Livello locale | Amministrazione centrale del Dipartimento del Panaro | | |
| | Altre Municipalità | Municipalità di Modena | Altre Municipalità |

La maggior parte delle lettere che verranno illustrate sono state scambiate tra l'Amministrazione centrale del Dipartimento del Panaro e il Ministro dell'Interno, e cioè, tra gli attori che costituivano l'anello di congiunzione tra istanze locali e governo centrale.

## Maggio-giugno 1798: i musicisti modenesi sul lastrico e una prima proposta di soluzione

La prima fonte di rilievo emersa dai faldoni milanesi è infatti una lettera proveniente dall'Amministrazione centrale del Dipartimento del Panaro e indirizzata al Ministro dell'Interno.

---

[2]. Le informazioni in queste due paragrafi sono state tratte da ROMBALDI 2001. Per informazioni su Modena in questo periodo, vedasi la bibliografia ivi indicata.

[3]. Nelle fonti, la dicitura «Amministrazione centrale del Dipartimento del Panaro» appare anche in altre fogge, dal significato analogo. L'articolo uniforma preferendo questa forma.

[4]. Nelle fonti, la dicitura «Ministro dell'Interno» appare anche come «Ministro degli Affari Interni». L'articolo uniforma preferendo la prima forma.

Datata 30 maggio 1798[5], il suo mittente è Valentino Contri[6], vicepresidente del Dipartimento del Panaro. Nella missiva, Contri rende note al Ministro dell'Interno le sue preoccupazioni per il destino dei musicisti modenesi. Con l'avvento della Repubblica Cisalpina, infatti, i musicisti locali avevano visto svanire le loro principali opportunità di lavoro: prestare servizio a corte, nelle diverse chiese cittadine, e insegnare. Incoraggia quindi il Ministro dell'Interno a consentire l'apertura di un teatro in città, per dare un parziale sollievo alle famiglie di musicisti. Con questi toni preoccupati il funzionario scriveva al Ministro dell'Interno:

> Permetteteci però, Cittadino Ministro, che su tale proposito noi vi invitiamo a volere riflettere alla situazione di questo nostro capoluogo, che, come rileverete dal promemoria dell'Ispettore municipale ai teatri, è la più critica per quelle non poche famiglie, che ritraevano il sostentamento dalla loro professione di suonatori, e che tutto hanno perduto, non facendosi ora più funzioni di culto, non avendo più le funzioni ducali, e per fine avendo perduti moltissimi scolari. Se a questi non si dà pane col teatro, essi sono ridotti all'ultima miseria, non essendo certo possibile, che si possano ora che sono avvanzati in età aplicare ad altri mestieri[7].

Il notabile modenese prosegue sulla stessa linea d'onda cercando di convincere il Ministro dell'Interno a permettere l'apertura di un teatro in città facendo leva anche sulle potenzialità propagandistiche di un'attività spettacolare repubblicanamente intesa:

> Una città di 25 mila abitanti, e nella quale si ritrovano spessissimo molte truppe certo dovrebbe anco politicamente avere un teatro, ove potessero li cittadini fraternizzare, e che facilitasse il modo di impedire delle riunioni in luoghi assai pericolosi. Altre comuni hanno provvisoriamente ottenuti mezzi, onde avere qualche spettacolo, che occupi lodevolmente il popolo nelle ore di riposo.
> Alcuni bravi cittadini hanno, Cittadino Ministro, cominciato già a loro spese una società per rappresentare delle tragedie, e commedie repubblicane, e virtuose; ma questa società privata non potrà anche condotta a termine avere l'effetto di dar pane alla povera professione musicale e non può occupare, ed istruire il pubblico che una sol volta per decade, e poi, Cittadino Ministro, una società, che non ha fondi, ed è basata su la generosità di pochi individui non può essere riguardata che come precaria. Affidati al vostro civismo, e zelo noi ci lusinghiamo che vorrete procurare qualche risorsa a tante povere persone, tanto più, che facendo questo voi certo promovete in questa comune lo spirito pubblico[8].

---

[5]. Per comodità, le date indicate in calendario rivoluzionario sono state convertite in calendario gregoriano, almeno nel corpo del testo.

[6]. Sulla figura di Valentino Contri, vedasi ROVATTI – BRIZZI 1997, pp. 13-14.

[7]. ASMi, Atti di Governo, Spettacoli Pubblici Parte Antica, cartella 21, lettera firmata «Valentino Contri | D. Cortese | N.[?] Bernardoni vicesegretario», e datata 11 Pratile Anno 6 [30 maggio 1798].

[8]. *Ibidem.*

## «Non essendovi più capelle in veruna chiesa…»

Contri scrisse questa lettera al Ministro dell'Interno in risposta a una missiva da parte dello stesso datata 15 maggio, di cui però non è rimasta traccia negli incartamenti milanesi. Le prime righe della lettera del 30 maggio, tuttavia, suggeriscono che il Ministro dell'Interno avesse chiesto a Contri un resoconto sullo stato degli edifici teatrali nella sua regione:

> Per riscontrare colla dovuta precisione la vostra del 26 Fiorile scorso [15 maggio] n° 284, v'inoltriamo copia dei riscontri, che abbiamo ricevuti dalle municipalità nel di cui comune esistono teatri[9].

E infatti, alla stessa lettera sono allegati altri documenti in copia: i resoconti che ogni singola Municipalità del Dipartimento del Panaro aveva inviato all'Amministrazione centrale dello stesso territorio. La municipalità di Sassuolo informa Contri che:

> […] in questa comune esiste un teatro di proprietà di questa municipalità, ma non è istrutto di alcun fondo, che ne costruisca la dote. I palchi poi sono nella massima parte di regime di private famiglie[10].

Analogamente sintetica è la risposta delle autorità di Carpi:

> Un solo teatro esiste in questo nostro comune, ed è di proprietà della Nazione tranne i palchi, o le loggie, che sono dei particolari. Poche tele di un assai tenue valore ne costruiscono la dote[11].

I notabili di Mirandola sono meno lapidari, e informano Contri che:

> […] in questa città esiste un solo teatro già costrutto in una parte del fabbricato detto "il castello" spettante alla Nazione. Questo teatro è di particolar ragione del cittadino Ottavio Greco, al quale fu ceduto dall'ex Ducal Camera per titolo piuttosto lucrativo, che oneroso il locale, ov'è eretto il teatro suddetto, oltre la cessione d'altri fondi, e fabbricati staccati dal teatro medesimo […]. Vi perveniamo poi che l'intiero fabbricato, come inserviente all'abitazione, delli ex principi Pichi della Mirandola fu dall'Impero ceduto con tutti gli altri diritti dell'ex Ducato mirandolese, e con tutti li beni allodiali della famiglia Pico a titolo di feudo nell'anno 1711 a Rinaldo I già Duca di Modena[12].

---

[9]. *Ibidem*.

[10]. ASMi, Atti di Governo, Spettacoli Pubblici Parte Antica, cartella 21, lettera firmata «P. Teggia presidente | C. Carnivali | Rognoni segretario», e datata 3 Pratile Anno 6 [22 maggio 1798] (copia).

[11]. ASMi, Atti di Governo, Spettacoli Pubblici Parte Antica, cartella 21, lettera firmata «G. Federico Mazzoni presidente | Antonio Paltrinieri | Pittori segretario», e datata 4 Pratile Anno 6 [23 maggio 1798] (copia).

[12]. ASMi, Atti di Governo, Spettacoli Pubblici Parte Antica, cartella 21, lettera firmata «Giuseppe Gobbi presidente», e datata 2 Pratile Anno 6 [21 maggio 1798] (copia).

Di gran lunga più interessante è la risposta della Municipalità di Modena. Firmata «Tamburini presidente», invita esplicitamente Contri a

> [...] fare presente al medesimo [Ministro dell'Interno] le critiche circostanze di tante famiglie, che ritraevano il sostentamento dal teatro, e che ora per mancanza di sussidi trovansi nelle più grandi angustie[13].

L'esigenza di provvedere al sostentamento dei musicisti modenesi è dunque emersa a causa di un'iniziativa della Municipalità di Modena, non dell'Amministrazione centrale del Dipartimento del Panaro. La carta del Tamburini, a sua volta, presenta come allegato un lungo resoconto sullo stato dei teatri a Modena durante la prima età napoleonica — il già citato «promemoria dell'Ispettore municipale dei teatri» — elaborato da un sovrintendente locale degli spettacoli, un certo Bellencini. Vista l'estrema lucidità con cui ricostruisce almeno parte delle cause della rovina di molti musicisti modenesi, e la rilevanza per la storia del teatro d'opera a Modena, è qui proposta una trascrizione integrale:

> Notizie intorno ai teatri esistenti nella comune di Modena.
>
> Tre sono li teatri ch'esistono nella città di Modena, e nessun altro ve ne ha fuori di città entro i limiti distrettuali di questa Comune. Fra questi, due sono di privata ragione, l'altro di spettanza, e proprietà nazionale.
>
> Di privata spettanza evvi un picciolo teatro denominato di San Rocco, di cui sono proprietari, come soci in solido li cittadini Fantini, Orlandini, Scozia; teatro che rimane quasi sempre chiuso.
>
> Di privata spettanza evvi un teatro grande, detto il Teatro Rangone di cui ne ha la proprietà il cittadino Ghirardo Rangone di Modena, ed in questo teatro soltanto si danno costantemente li pubblici spettacoli.
>
> Vi è finalmente un terzo picciolo teatro, che rimane sempre chiuso denominato oggigiorno Teatro nazionale, ch'era in addietro di spettanza dell'ex Duca come facente parte del già palazzo di corte, ed al quale si ha accesso dagl'appartamenti del palazzo stesso, oltre l'ingresso, che smonta sulla pubblica via.
>
> Niun fondo avvi originariamente assegnato a questo, siccome a nessun altro dei teatri di questa Comune. Nei passati tempi e fino alla partenza dell'ex Duca eravi un annuo assegno a favore dei teatri del suo Stato per la somma di lire quindicimila di Milano. Questa si lasciava a un intraprenditore il quale aveva l'obbligo di dare un'opera in musica in Modena nel Carnevale, un'altra in Reggio per la Fiera, col patto di trasportarla successivamente a Modena, ed altra finalmente in autunno a Sassuolo; questa somma si traeva parte dalla Cassa ex Ducale, e parte da quella di Finanza.
>
> Il nuovo ordine di cose ha fatto cessare questo assegnamento. Da ciò ne deriva la impossibilità di trovare intraprenditori, che vogliano avventurarsi ad una

---

13. ASMi, Atti di Governo, Spettacoli Pubblici Parte Antica, cartella 21, lettera firmata «Tamburini presidente | S. [?] Bellencini | Tardini vicesegretario», e datata 10 Pratile Anno 6 [29 maggio 1798] (copia).

> quasi sicura perdita. Quindi raro è che possa aversi un'opera in musica in questa città. Infinito però è il danno che risentono quaranta, e più povere famiglie di suonatori, ed artigiani dalla cessazione di questi spettacoli, dal che traevano esse il loro sostentamento buona parte dall'anno. Assediano queste, ed opprimono colle continue rimostranze a tale oggetto le autorità costituite, che sono bensì penetranti della loro situazione, e convincenti dalla necessità di ripararvi, ma impotenti a farlo quantunque siano giunti i loro reclami.
> In vista di ciò non può il soprintendente agli spettacoli, che instare con tutto l'ardore avanti la Municipalità affinché essa interponga efficacemente i suoi uffizi presso le autorità superiori, onde sia fissato un congruo assegnamento ai teatri di questa Comune a sollievo di tanti indigenti che rimangono inoperosi, mancando gli spettacoli teatrali, e principalmente all'oggetto di promuovere, ed animare lo spirito pubblico, che senza tali mezzi non può, che paralizzarsi, e languire[14].

Il resoconto del Bellencini ricostruisce con estrema chiarezza le cause dell'indigenza di molti musicisti in città, e le collega, senza mezzi termini, al «nuovo ordine» napoleonico, che ha abolito di fatto le quindici mila lire milanesi destinate alle attività spettacolari durante l'epoca ducale.

Non ci sono carte, nel fondo considerato da questo contributo, che includano la risposta del Ministro dell'Interno a Contri. Sembra infatti che i funzionari dell'Amministrazione centrale del Dipartimento del Panaro non avessero ricevuto alcuna risposta. L'8 giugno la stessa istituzione scrisse ancora al Ministro dell'Interno sollecitando risposta. Lo informava anche che la Municipalità di Modena aveva ideato un progetto a suo giudizio conveniente per produrre un'opera buffa in città, e che questo progetto aveva già trovato l'approvazione a livello locale:

> La municipalità di questa comune, alla quale sono stati portati diversi progetti per un'opera buffa, ha la medesima scelto il più vantaggioso, ed atto nello stesso tempo a dare un conveniente divertimento per la corrente stagione. Questo progetto è formato in modo, che non pone in azzardo la cassa municipale di perdere che una piccola somma di £ 1500 milanesi tutt'al più, e tale perdita è anche incerta, e remota [...]. Su tale incertezza però, benché lontana, e nonostante che la rimessa potesse essere di così leggiera entità, non abbiamo voluto approvare il progetto della municipalità senza riportarne prima la vostra approvazione. Siccome ravvisiamo questa misura atta non solo a sollevare de' poveri cittadini che ritraggono il loro sostentamento dal solo teatro [...], così noi appoggiamo la dimanda della municipalità medesima invitandovi a volerci sollecitamente abilitare ad approvare l'indicato progetto[15].

---

[14]. ASMi, Atti di Governo, Spettacoli Pubblici Parte Antica, cartella 21, «Notizie intorno ai teatri esistenti nella comune di Modena», allegato alla lettera del 10 Pratile Anno 6 [29 maggio 1798], e firmato «Bellencini V[ice] presidente agli spettacoli».

[15]. ASMi, Atti di Governo, Spettacoli Pubblici Parte Antica, cartella 21, lettera firmata «Soragni presidente | D. Cortese | Bernardoni vicesegretario», e datata 20 Pratile Anno 6 [8 giugno 1798].

# Eric Boaro

Questo progetto, tuttavia, cadde nel vuoto. Dalla risposta del 14 giugno, si intuisce che il Ministro dell'Interno, almeno per ora, fosse disinteressato al sostentamento dei musicisti modenesi:

> A sfogo della vostra [del] 20 corrente con cui mi esponete il progetto già scelto dalla municipalità per un'opera buffa da farsi in cotesto teatro, rispondo che il governo non prende parte per in simili imprese[16].

## Agosto 1798: le petizioni dei musicisti modenesi

I toni di una lettera inviata dall'Amministrazione centrale del Dipartimento del Panaro al Ministro dell'Interno l'11 agosto seguente sembrano suggerire ulteriormente che quest'ultimo avesse poco interesse negli affari musicali della città emiliana[17]. L'importanza di questa missiva risiede non tanto nel suo contenuto, che ripete sostanzialmente quanto riferito nelle lettere precedenti, ma nel fatto che allega in copia alcune petizioni di musicisti, probabilmente al fine di muovere a compassione il Ministro dell'Interno. Tali petizioni erano state precedentemente raccolte in città dalla Municipalità di Modena il 10 agosto, e, benché riguardino solo i professori Lorenzo Solignani, Ignazio Picchioretti e Vincenzo Navi, testimoniano, a detta dei municipalisti che le fecero produrre, la situazione di moltissimi altri loro colleghi in città:

> La situazione in cui si trovano questi [tre] infelici è comune a tutti gli altri professori di musica. Privi d'ogni mezzo di esercitare la loro professione, ed incapaci ad appigliarsi a qualche altra per avere impiegato la maggior parte della loro vita ad apprendere, ed esercitare la professione, a cui si sono addetti, non hanno più ove rivolgersi per sussistere, e in conseguenza trovansi ridotti all'estremo della miseria, senza alcuna loro colpa, o demerito[18].

Le petizioni allegate risultano di enorme interesse in quanto lasciano trasparire — quasi come istantanee — la condizione precaria dei musicisti modenesi nel 1798. Anche qui, mi permetto di riportare le petizioni per intero.

La prima petizione allegata alla lettera del 10 agosto descrive la situazione del violinista Vincenzo Navi, in serie difficoltà economiche a causa, principalmente, del nuovo laicismo giacobino:

---

[16]. ASMi, Atti di Governo, Spettacoli Pubblici Parte Antica, cartella 21, lettera firmata «Tadini», e datata 26 Pratile Anno 6 [14 giugno 1798] (copia).

[17]. ASMi, Atti di Governo, Spettacoli Pubblici Parte Antica, cartella 21, lettera firmata «Bacciolanini [?] presidente | P. [?] Campi | Parise segretario», e datata 24 Termidoro Anno 6 [11 agosto 1798].

[18]. ASMi, Atti di Governo, Spettacoli Pubblici Parte Antica, cartella 21, lettera firmata «G. Ferraresi presidente | P. [?] Balugani | Nalluri [?] segretario», e datata 23 Termidoro Anno 6 [10 agosto 1798] (copia); allegato alla lettera del 24 Termidoro Anno 6 [11 agosto 1798].

## «Non essendovi più capelle in veruna chiesa…»

> Trovandosi deluso dalla sua professione il cittadino petente, e non avendo maniera alcuna di poter seguire la carriera per la detta professione già abbolita, non essendovi più capelle in veruna chiesa che da molti anni copriva in qualità di violino già sua professione quella della chiesa del Novo, ed avendo anche perdute molte funzioni, non sapendo più la maniera di guadagnarsi un poco di pane, per darlo a' suoi poveri figli, essendo ridotto quasi all'estrema necessità, non avendo più che a vendere pochi otensigli di casa. Il medesimo si fa coraggio, e ricorre per tanto alli cittadini municipali acciò volgano il suo cuore republicano verso l'infelice petizionario, e sua famiglia, e gli diano braccio con soccorrerlo di un qualche impiego, impiego però atto all'abilità del detto, acciò possa rimediare alle sue vigenti circostanze, e bisogni di che avrà il petente una eterna gratitudine, e memoria dei loro animi repubblicani, e si chiamerà felice, e fortunato godendo la beata libertà, ed eguaglianza[19].

La seconda petizione è di Ignazio Picchioretti, professore di violoncello. All'altezza del 1789, Picchioretti era primo violoncello nella cappella ducale di Modena[20]. Nove anni prima ricopriva un incarico simile: professore di violoncello dell'Accademia Filarmonica[21]. Nella petizione ritorna, grosso modo, sugli stessi punti indicati da Navi. Non può più suonare né in chiesa, né per la corte ducale:

> Ignazio Picchioretti professore di violoncello, vi espone che egli è già caduto nell'estremo dell'indigenza con la moglie, cinque figli per essere cessate tutte le funzioni di chiesa, aboliti i prodotti delle capelle, e per fino precluso il modo di qualche guadagno fuori di queste per tanto tempo che è chiuso il teatro. Egli è persuaso che sia ben giusto, che nella Repubblica non debbansi abbandonare delle famiglie allo squallore della miseria, né debbansi queste condannare senza veruna colpa alla più crudele delle morti, quale quella della fame. Con questo sicuro principio, che parte immediatamente [*illeggibile*], tutta diretta a favorire la classe indigente, e molto più quella, che non per propria colpa, ma per avverso destino resta priva di sussistenza egli ricorre a voi, o cittadini, affinché esercitiate quella umanità, che esigge la di lui circostanza col migliore, e più sollecito modo possibile provvedendolo d'immediata sussistenza, giacché egli è privo del modo di procacciarsi in altra maniera del vivere, non sapendo esercitare altra professione, se non se l'indicativi, e non avendo più altro con che sussistere, che le £ 70 mensuali della Nazione[22].

---

[19]. ASMi, Atti di Governo, Spettacoli Pubblici Parte Antica, cartella 21, lettera firmata «Vincenzo Navi Suonatore di professione», e datata 17 Termidoro Anno 6 [4 agosto 1798] (copia); allegato alla lettera del 23 Termidoro Anno 6 [10 agosto 1798].

[20]. *Calendario di corte* 1789, p. 26. La grafia del suo cognome, nei documenti, non chiara, e sembra talvolta rimandare ad una seconda lezione: «Ignazio Picchiarotti».

[21]. *Calendario di corte* 1780, p. 69.

[22]. ASMi, Atti di Governo, Spettacoli Pubblici Parte Antica, cartella 21, lettera firmata «Ignazio Picchioretti», non datata (copia); allegato alla lettera del 23 Termidoro Anno 6 [10 agosto 1798].

La terza e ultima petizione è di Lorenzo Solignani. A partire dagli anni Settanta, egli fu primo leggio dei secondi violini dell'orchestra del teatro ducale[23]; nel 1789 è infatti registrato come professore di violino dell'Accademia Filarmonica[24]. Era anche impiegato come solista dalla corte[25]. Il Gandini narra che Solignani fosse ben voluto in società a causa delle sue taglienti trovate di spirito[26]. Ma, all'altezza del 1798, Solignani aveva ben altro da pensare:

> Trovandosi il cittadino petente escluso da qualunque guadagno della sua professione, ed essendo carco di una numerosa famiglia, quale è composta d'otto persone merita bene, o rispettabili cittadini, la vostra pietà, ed aiuto; massime in oggi, in cui regna la Beata Fratellanza. La beneficenza deve segnalarsi in dar braccio ai bisognosi perseguitati dalla sfortuna, e quei che si trovano ridotti da sì calamitose vicende, solo per la colpa del dover suo. Questo nuovo ordine di cose, [*illeggibile*] ha rapito il pane al suddetto petizionario e sua famiglia suonatore di professione da lui sul principio di sua fanciullezza onestamente applicassi faticando incessantemente e ritraendo il mantenimento per sé e suoi figli. Il petente, [*illeggibile*], è costretto a chiedere il vostro sostegno, ed appoggio, onde gli somministrate un'opportunità di [*illeggibile*] e guadagno. Ottene bensì dalla benefica nazione un'annua pensione di zecchini 24 per gratificazione dei servigi prestati, ma non è in verun modo sufficiente, per riparare agli estremi bisogni della famiglia. Si rivolge però a noi, o cittadini municipalisti, onde mossi a compassione [*illeggibile*] vi segnate di accordargli un onesto impiego tanto al padre, come al figlio pure suonatore di professione il più presto possibile, giacché è urgente la necessità, [*illeggibile*] coerentemente alla loro abilità, domandandovi pane un cittadino, ed aiutando così una povera e desolata famiglia[27].

Le tre petizioni sono preziose testimonianze di un delicatissimo momento storico e culturale per la storia della musica a Modena. Probabilmente, furono presentate per muovere il

---

[23]. GANDINI 1873, vol. I, p. 129.

[24]. *CALENDARIO DI CORTE* 1780, p. 68.

[25]. TORELLI 1966, p. 126.

[26]. GANDINI 1873, vol. I, pp. 129-130: «Il Solignani era ben accolto in società, per essere assai faceto. Molti sono i tratti di spirito che di lui si narrano, fra quali ciò che disse ad un signore suo scolaro di violino, il quale, avendo poca attitudine a tal arte, gli chiese osservando un pezzo di musica che tempo fosse quello che si trovava in chiave? Egli rispose "è tempo perduto". Un'altra volta in una prova d'opera al teatro, e mentre una poco abile cantatrice si compiaceva di far replicare la sua aria (per udire un motivo non ancora da lei ben accennato dall'orchestra) lasciandosi ad arte assalire da un attacco di tosse, si rivolgeva ai suonatori dicendo loro che essendo raffreddata li pregava di nuovo a ripetere. Il Solignani reso impaziente le rispose: "ella dunque ci ritiene per tante pastiglie stomatiche, se dobbiamo farle cessare la costipazione a forza di prove?"».

[27]. ASMi, Atti di Governo, Spettacoli Pubblici Parte Antica, cartella 21, lettera firmata «Lorenzo Solignani», datata 16 Termidoro Anno 6 [3 agosto 1798] (copia); allegato alla lettera del 23 Termidoro Anno 6 [10 agosto 1798].

Ministro dell'Interno a maggior compassione: un secondo progetto ideato dalla Municipalità di Modena, differentemente dal primo, venne infatti accolto dal Ministro dell'Interno e dal Direttorio Esecutivo, come si vedrà.

## Agosto-settembre 1798: un nuovo progetto per la sopravvivenza dei musicisti modenesi

Questa seconda soluzione avrebbe previsto la riattivazione di una sala teatrale in città. In una lunga lettera spedita dall'Amministrazione centrale del Dipartimento del Panaro al Ministro dell'Interno il 14 agosto, l'Amministrazione centrale ribadisce la necessità di riaprire una sala cittadina. Oltre al sollievo economico per le famiglie di musicisti e operai che traevano sostentamento dalle attività spettacolari in epoca pre-napoleonica, i due funzionari del Panaro Cortese e Vaccari fanno presente, forse artatamente, che l'assenza di una stagione teatrale in città avrebbe potuto generare malcontento popolare. I due notabili fanno anche notare che le truppe francesi stanziatesi in città chiedevano a gran voce l'apertura del teatro cittadino: è dunque «da temersi che trascurando [queste richieste] il buon ordine, e la tranquillità possano essere compromesse». I due rappresentanti vedono inoltre nell'apertura di una sala in città l'opportunità di avere «un luogo di riunione in cui i partiti purtroppo tuttora divisi l'uno all'altro si accosterebbero e giungerebbero fors'anche ad estinguersi»[28]. Non è dato sapere se i due intendenti fossero sinceri nel manifestare queste preoccupazioni. Il fatto che, nell'ampio carteggio, quest'ultimo tipo di assilli — ordine pubblico, malcontento del popolo, eventuale ruolo conciliatore del teatro — emerga principalmente nelle lettere indirizzate al Ministro dell'Interno, fa pensare che Cortese e Vaccari lo usassero proprio come strumento persuasivo.

Sembra che la tattica messa in atto da Cortese e Vaccari fosse azzeccata. Con una lettera del 24 agosto seguente, infatti, il Ministro dell'Interno Diego Guicciardi invita i due a presentare un progetto per un'opera in musica, cercando però di «aver riguardo alla massima economia possibile, perché giovando in certo modo a' particolari, non ne risenta alcun pregiudizio lo Stato»[29]. Una ventina di giorni dopo, l'Amministrazione centrale del Dipartimento del Panaro propone la soluzione ideata dalla Municipalità di Modena al Ministro dell'Interno:

> La municipalità però ci fa il seguente progetto, che noi non possiamo, che collaudare, ed appoggiare presso di voi col maggiore valore. La stessa municipalità in grazia di una migliore amministrazione delle rendite del Civico Collegio, ed in grazia

---

[28]. Le ultime due citazioni in ASMi, Atti di Governo, Spettacoli Pubblici Parte Antica, cartella 21, lettera firmata «Diotebo Cortese | L. Vaccari», datata 27 Termidoro Anno 6 [14 agosto 1798].

[29]. ASMi, Atti di Governo, Spettacoli Pubblici Parte Antica, cartella 21, lettera firmata «Guicciardi | Sassi», datata 7 Fruttidoro Anno 6 [24 agosto 1798].

di aver essa abolite le recite pubbliche, che dai convittori si facevano in Carnevale, avanzerà annualmente in detto Civico Collegio la somma di lire dieci mila circa milanesi. Qualora pertanto si abilitasse la municipalità a valersi di queste lire dieci mila pel teatro, tenuissima somma mancherebbe all'intento, ed a cui potrebbe pure abilitarsi la municipalità a supplire con parte delle sue rendite comunali. Questo è, Cittadino Ministro, l'espediente a nostro avviso opportuno per provvedere al mantenimento del teatro, cioè per avere due, o tre corsi di recite, che bene distribuiti bastano per tutto l'anno[30].

I notabili modenesi si riferiscono, con tutta probabilità, al Teatro del Collegio dei Nobili di Modena. Fondato nel 1626, esso si curava dell'educazione dei nobili rampolli locali. A completare la loro educazione erano anche le arti drammatiche: per questo, in seno a tale Collegio, venivano praticate anche attività spettacolari. Dal 1732 il Collegio venne dotato anche di un teatro. Caleidoscopici erano gli spettacoli proposti dai convittori. Erano

[...] spettacoli articolati nel succedersi di azioni recitate, di balli, di cori, di cantate e di intermezzi d'arme. I canovacci drammatici, quasi sempre opera dei Collegiali, erano frequentemente di soggetto mitologico e allegorico con intrecci e opposizioni allusive a personaggi e fatti dinastici[31].

Evidentemente, il nuovo ordine giacobino dovette causare una battuta di arresto per quanto riguarda le attività drammatiche del Collegio. Già il Gandini aveva osservato che

[...] gli sconvolgimenti politici che agitarono l'Italia dalla metà di quest'anno [1796] in avanti portarono naturalmente una lacuna in questo Teatro[32].

I documenti milanesi chiarificano la ragione di questa «lacuna»: fu il Collegio stesso a sospendere le sue recite. Il denaro che veniva di solito investito per tali spettacoli, dunque, poteva essere riutilizzato per la riapertura di una sala in Modena.

Forte del parere positivo del Commissario generale del potere esecutivo del Dipartimento del Panaro[33], l'Amministrazione centrale del Dipartimento del Panaro può dunque sottoporre al Ministro dell'Interno il piano elaborato dalla Municipalità di Modena. A sua volta, il Ministro dell'Interno avrebbe dovuto ottenere l'approvazione del Direttorio Esecutivo. Nell'incartamento

---

[30]. ASMi, Atti di Governo, Spettacoli Pubblici Parte Antica, cartella 21, lettera firmata «A. [?] Soragni pel presidente | P. [?] Campi | Parise segretario», datata 28 Fruttidoro Anno 6 [14 settembre 1798].

[31]. BENASSATI 1991 p. 238. Dallo stesso articolo sono tratte le altre informazioni sul Collegio. Vedasi inoltre GANDINI 1873, vol. II, pp. 166-224.

[32]. GANDINI 1873, vol. II, p. 224

[33]. ASMi, Atti di Governo, Spettacoli Pubblici Parte Antica, cartella 21, lettera firmata «Luigi Vaccari | Panelli pel segretario», non datata (copia).

mancano documenti relativi all'approvazione, da parte del Ministro dell'Interno, del piano elaborato dall'Amministrazione centrale del Dipartimento del Panaro; ma sono sopravvissuti — quantunque in copia — i documenti che lo stesso Ministro dell'Interno presentò al Direttorio Esecutivo, da cui emerge una valutazione positiva da entrambe le parti. In questo modo, infatti, il Ministro dell'Interno scrive all'amministrazione del Panaro:

> Con mio rapporto di questa mattina ho presentato al Direttorio Esecutivo il progetto di cotesta municipalità riguardante il teatro di cui voi mi parlate colla vostra lettera segnata n. 48 29 Fruttidoro scaduto. Egli avuto riguardo all'esportegli circostanze ha voluto annuire ed agevolare per quanto lo permette il momento l'apertura del teatro medesimo, ed ha concluso, che sia permesso alla municipalità di Modena di prevalersi a quest'oggetto, e per una volta sola, della somma di 10 mila lire sulla cassa di cotesto Collegio Civico[34].

Dopo lunghe contrattazioni, la Municipalità di Modena era dunque riuscita a risparmiare ai musicisti cittadini il lastrico. Nei mesi seguenti vennero infatti organizzate tre opere al Teatro Rangone. Nella prima metà dell'agosto 1799 venne data l'opera seria *Zulema*[35]; mentre i due drammi giocosi *La vera somiglianza* ossiano *I due gobbi*[36] e *Il re Teodoro in Venezia*[37] vennero proposti nel Carnevale[38]. *Zulema* e *La vera somiglianza* erano due melodrammi di Marcos António da Fonseca Simão (1762-1830; anche conosciuto in Italia come «Marco Portogallo»)[39], mentre *Il re Teodoro in Venezia* era una riproposta dell'omonima opera di Giovanni Paisiello. Il libretto di *Zulema* include il nome di Lorenzo Solignani come «primo violino de' secondi»[40]. Finalmente, una boccata d'aria per i musicisti modenesi.

Oltre alla riapertura del Rangone, la Municipalità di Modena cercò di garantire ai suoi musicisti degli stipendi mensili. Il Gandini ci informa infatti che

> [...] 14 marzo [1799]: dietro reclami fatti dai professori di musica già addetti al servizio della Corte la Municipalità prese la determinazione di favorire detta classe

---

[34]. ASMi, Atti di Governo, Spettacoli Pubblici Parte Antica, cartella 21, lettera firmata «Guicciardi | Sassi», 5 Vendemmiaio Anno 7 (spedita il) [26 settembre 1798]. A questa lettera è allegata una sua minuta e il rapporto che il Ministro presentò al Direttorio, che sostanzialmente ripete quanto riferito dalla municipalità precedentemente.

[35]. GANDINI 1873, vol. I, p. 189: «1799. 31 luglio. Si aprì il teatro colla rappresentazione dell'opera in musica *Zulema* che terminò poco dopo la metà del successivo agosto». Copia consultata: Cremona, Biblioteca Statale, CIV.A.LL.5.12.6. Vedasi inoltre SARTORI 1990, libretto n. 25433.

[36]. Copia consultata: Modena, Biblioteca Estense Universitaria, M.T.Ferr.Mor.31.02.

[37]. Copia consultata: Fratta Polesine, Biblioteca privata «Giorgio Fanan». Vedasi inoltre SARTORI 1990, libretto n. 19653a.

[38]. TARDINI 1902, p. 1407.

[39]. Su Simão vedasi CRANMER 2001.

[40]. *Zulema, dramma per musica da rappresentarsi in Modena nel Teatro Rangone l'estate dell'anno 1799*, Modena, Soliani, [1799], p. 3.

di persone coll'assegnar loro uno stipendio mensile regolato come indicherò più sotto, e ciò affine di sostenere un'arte indispensabile e compagna del progresso, della civiltà, e necessaria al decoro d'ogni pubblico spettacolo. Detti stipendii venivano pagati in una parte dalla Nazione, e nell'altra dal Municipio, come si vedrà dal seguente elenco:

[...]

2. Solignani Lorenzo, primo de' secondi [violini], a carico della nazione [mensili lire modenesi] 60, a carico della municipalità [mensili lire modenesi] 30.

[...]

8. Nava Vincenzo [suonatore di violino], a carico della municipalità [mensili lire modenesi] 45.

[...]

11. Picchioretti Ignazio, suonatore di violoncello, a carico della nazione [mensili lire modenesi] 70[41].

Non si deve tuttavia pensare che tali rendite fossero adatte per la sopravvivenza dei loro beneficiari: già nel 1798 Picchioretti e Solignani obiettavano che le rendite a loro erogate dalla Nazione erano insufficienti. La citazione dal Gandini riporta qui per brevità solo i musicisti di cui sono sopravvissute le petizioni — Nava, Picchioretti, Solignani — ma ne includerebbe, in totale, ventotto. Poco meno di trenta erano, dunque, le famiglie che erano state messe in pericolo dal nuovo ordine, e che la municipalità modenese seppe tutelare — quantomeno parzialmente — riaprendo il Rangone.

## Conclusioni

Le carte d'archivio relative alle vicende accadute a Modena tra il 1798 e il 1799 si fermano qui. Hanno illustrato come il mercato del lavoro musicale della città risentì del cambio di regime. Col nuovo ordine napoleonico, le attività teatrali cittadine, così come quelle musicali in ambito ecclesiastico, cessarono, lasciando molti musicisti senza alcuna fonte di reddito. Alcuni tra questi, le cui famiglie erano ormai sul lastrico, presentarono dunque diverse petizioni ai notabili della Municipalità di Modena. Essi le accolsero, e cercarono di convincere le autorità governative a loro superiori ad aprire un teatro in città, di modo da scongiurare il peggio. Dopo lunghe contrattazioni, il Direttorio Esecutivo e il Ministro dell'Interno accolsero il progetto di finanziare una stagione al Teatro Rangone con dei fondi originariamente stanziati per le attività spettacolari del Collegio Civico, che nel frattempo erano però cessate.

Le petizioni dei musicisti testimoniano in modo drammatico le conseguenze del mutato assetto sociopolitico della Modena del tempo sulla vita quotidiana dei musicisti durante la

---

[41]. Gandini 1873, vol. II, pp. 61-63.

prima età napoleonica in Italia. Le lunghe contrattazioni descritte dal carteggio tra i vari livelli di governo — locale e centrale — palesano invece la strategia che la Repubblica Cisalpina adottò per venire incontro ai musicisti modenesi ridotti in miseria. In una fase iniziale, il Ministro dell'Interno sembrava restio a concedere anche solo 1500 lire. Dopo che l'Amministrazione centrale del Dipartimento del Panaro gli presentò le petizioni dei musicisti, e che fece leva sui possibili rischi derivanti dalla mancanza di un teatro in città, cambiò idea, approvando il progetto finanziario proposto dall'amministrazione emiliana e presentandolo al Direttorio Esecutivo.

In senso più generale, questo articolo mostra come il subitaneo cambio di governo — da *ancien régime* a napoleonico — influenzò negativamente il mercato del lavoro musicale in Italia, a causa della perdita di potere e ricchezza di due attori fondamentali nella storia della musica dell'Italia pre rivoluzionaria: il clero e l'aristocrazia.

### Bibliografia

Benassati 1991
Benassati, Giuseppina. 'Il teatro del Collegio dei Nobili', in: *Il Collegio e la Chiesa di San Carlo a Modena*, a cura di Daniele Benati, Lucia Peruzzi e Vincenzo Vandelli, Modena, Banca Popolare dell'Emilia, 1991, pp. 236-247.

*Calendario di corte* 1780
*Calendario di corte per l'anno 1780*, Modena, Bartolomeo Soliani, 1780.

*Calendario di corte* 1879
*Calendario di corte per l'anno 1789*, Modena, Bartolomeo Soliani, 1789.

Cranmer 2001
Cranmer, David. 'Portugal [Portogallo], Marcos António', in: *Oxford Music Online*, 2001 <https://www.oxfordmusiconline.com>, visitato ad agosto 2023.

Gandini 1873
Gandini, Alessandro. *Cronistoria dei teatri di Modena dal 1539 al 1871*, Modena, Tipografia sociale, 1873.

Rombaldi 2001
Rombaldi, Odoardo. 'Dalla Repubblica Cispadana alla Repubblica Cisalpina: Giovanni Paradisi e Iacopo Lamberti', in: *Lo stato di Modena. Una capitale, una dinastia, una civiltà nella storia d'Europa. 1*, a cura di Angelo Spaggiari e Giuseppe Trenti, Roma, Direzione generale per gli archivi, 2001, pp. 69-81.

Rovatti – Brizzi 1997
Rovatti, Antonio – Brizzi, Gian Paolo. *Dall'aquila imperiale al ritorno dei francesi, 1799-1801*, Modena, Fondazione Cassa di risparmio di Modena, 1997.

Sartori 199

Sartori, Claudio. *I libretti italiani a stampa dalle origini al 1800*, Cuneo, Bertola & Locatelli, 1990-1994.

Tardini 1902

Tardini, Vincenzo. *I teatri di Modena*, Modena, Vincenzi, 1902.

Torelli 1966

Torelli, Armando. *Cronachette teatrali, mondane, sportive di Modena capitale (1750-1859)*, Modena, Cooperativa tipografi, 1966.

## Appendice

### Fonti archivistiche in ordine cronologico

| N. doc. | Calendario rivoluzionario | Calendario gregoriano | Mittente | Destinatario | Contenuto |
|---|---|---|---|---|---|
| 1 | 2 Pratile Anno 6 | 21 maggio 1798 | «Mirandola»: «Giuseppe Gobbi presidente» | «All'Amministrazione centrale del Dipartimento del Panaro» | Resoconto dei teatri esistenti nella comune di Mirandola, copia allegata al doc. 6 |
| 2 | 3 Pratile Anno 6 | 22 maggio 1798 | «Sassuolo»: «P. Teggia presidente», «C. Carnivali» | «All'Amministrazione centrale del Panaro» | Resoconto dei teatri esistenti nella comune di Sassuolo, copia allegata al doc. 6 |
| 3 | 4 Pratile Anno 6 | 23 maggio 1798 | «La Municipalità di Carpi»: «G. Federico Mazzoni presidente», «Antonio Paltrinieri» | «All'Amministrazione centrale del Panaro» | Resoconto dei teatri esistenti nella comune di Carpi, copia allegata al doc. 6 |
| 4 | 10 Pratile Anno 6 | 29 maggio 1798 | «La Municipalità di Modena»: «Tamburini presidente», «Bellencini» | «All'Amministrazione centrale» | Resoconto dei teatri esistenti nella città di Modena, copia allegata al doc. 6 |
| 5 | [10 Pratile Anno 6] | [29 maggio 1798] | [La Municipalità di Modena]: «Bellencini vicepresidente agli spettacoli» | [All'Amministrazione centrale del Dipartimento del Panaro] | «Notizie intorno ai teatri esistenti nella comune di Modena», allegato alla lettera precedente, copia allegata al doc. 4, a sua volta allegato al doc. 6 |

| | | | | | |
|---|---|---|---|---|---|
| 6 | 11 Pratile Anno 6 | 30 maggio 1798 | «L'Amministrazione centrale del Dipartimento del Panaro»: «Valentino Contri vicepresidente», «D. Cortese» | «Al Ministro dell'Interno» | Fa presente al Ministro dell'Interno la situazione dei musicisti di Modena ed esorta ad aprire una sala in città |
| 7 | 20 Pratile Anno 6 | 8 giugno 1798 | «L'Amministrazione centrale del Dipartimento del Panaro»: «Soragni presidente», «D. Cortese» | «Al Ministro dell'Interno» | Presenta al Ministro il progetto per un'opera buffa in città |
| 8 | 26 Pratile Anno 6 | 14 giugno 1798 | [Ministro dell'Interno]: «Tadini» | «All'Amministrazione centrale del Panaro» | Rifiuta il progetto dell'opera buffa, copia allegata al doc. 7 |
| 9 | 16 Termidoro Anno 6 | 3 agosto 1798* | «Il cittadino Lorenzo Solignani vi espone quanto segue»: «Lorenzo Solignani» | «Alli cittadini componenti la Municipalità di Modena» | Petizione di Lorenzo Solignani, copia allegata al doc. 12, a sua volta allegato al doc. 13 |
| 10 | 17 Termidoro Anno 6 | 4 agosto 1798* | «Il cittadino Vincenzo Navi espone quanto segue»: «Vincenzo Navi suonatore di professione» | «Alli cittadini componenti la Municipalità di Modena» | Petizione di Vincenzo Navi, copia allegata al doc. 12, a sua volta allegato al doc. 13 |
| 11 | [16/17 Termidoro Anno 6] | [3/4 agosto 1798] | «Ignazio Picchioretti» | «Cittadini municipali» | Petizione di Ignazio Picchioretti, copia allegata al doc. 12, a sua volta allegato al doc. 13 |
| 12 | 23 Termidoro Anno 6 | 10 agosto 1798 | «La Municipalità di Modena»: «Ferraresi presidente», «Balugani» | «All'Amministrazione centrale» | Resoconto dello stato dei musicisti di Modena, copia allegata al doc. 13 |
| 13 | 24 Termidoro Anno 6 | 11 agosto 1798 | «L'Amministrazione centrale del Dipartimento del Panaro»: «Bacciolanini presidente», «P. Campi» | «Al Ministro degli Affari Interni» | Ribadisce al governo la necessità per Modena di avere un teatro funzionante |

| | | | | | |
|---|---|---|---|---|---|
| 14 | 27 Termidoro Anno 6 | 14 agosto 1798 | «Milano; Delegati dell'Amministrazione centrale del Panaro»: «Diotebo Cortese», «L. Vaccari» | «Al Ministro dell'Interno» | Ribadiscono al Ministro dell'Interno la necessità della apertura di un teatro in Modena, copia allegata al doc. 16 |
| 15 | 7 Fruttidoro Anno 6 | 24 agosto 1798 | [Ministro dell'Interno]: «Guicciardi», «Sassi» | [All'Amministrazione centrale del Dipartimento del Panaro] | Invitano a proporre un nuovo progetto, copia allegata al doc. 16 |
| 16 | 28 Fruttidoro Anno 6 | 14 settembre 1798 | «L'Amministrazione centrale del Dipartimento del Panaro»: «Soragni pel presidente», «P. Campi» | «Al Ministro degli Affari Interni» | Presenta il nuovo progetto riguardante il riutilizzo dei fondi precedentemente destinati al Civico Collegio |
| 17 | [Prima del 5 Vendemmiaio Anno 7] | [Prima del 14 settembre 1798] | «Il Commissario del potere esecutivo nel Dipartimento del Panaro»: «Vaccari» | [Al Ministro dell'Interno] | Ribadisce la necessità dell'apertura di un teatro in Modena |
| 18 | 5 Vendemmiaio Anno 7 (spedita il) | 26 settembre 1798 (spedita il) | [Ministro dell'Interno]: «Guicciardi», «Sassi» | «All'Amministrazione centrale del Panaro» | Informa che il Direttorio ha approvato il progetto (copia) |
| 19 | [5 Vendemmiaio Anno 7] | [26 settembre 1798] | [Ministro dell'Interno] | [Al Direttorio Esecutivo] | Presentazione del progetto al Direttorio Esecutivo, copia allegata al doc. 18. |

\*. Erroneamente, il documento converte questa data in «16 agosto 1798».

# 'FEAST, FLOUR AND GALLOWS':
# HAYDN'S *CREATION* IN NAPLES (1821)
# AND THE POLITICS OF THE RESTORATION

*Federico Gon*
(CONSERVATORIO DI TRIESTE)

1.

DURING LENT OF 1821 (specifically the evenings of 10 and 12 April) Joseph Haydn's *The Creation* was performed in Italian, under the title *La creazione del mondo*[1], at the Teatro S. Carlo in Naples under the direction of Gioachino Rossini, with a cast of great quality: there were, among others, absolute legends of *bel canto* such as Andrea Nozzari, Giovanni Battista Rubini, Filippo Galli, Michele Benedetti and Adelaide Comelli[2].

Naples was, however, one of the Italian cities in which Haydn's music enjoyed the greatest credit and diffusion[3]. Thus this Neapolitan staging of *The Creation* assumed a

---

[1]. «LA CREAZIONE DEL MONDO | ORATORIO | ESEGUITO IN NAPOLI | NEL REAL TEATRO S. CARLO | Nella Quaresima del 1821 | NAPOLI | Dalla Tipografia Flautina | 1821».

[2]. On the same libretto: «PARTI PRIMARIE | Signora Comelli Rubini | Signori Nozzari | Benedetti | Galli | Rubini | Ambrosi | Ciccimarra. | PARTI CONCERTANTI | Signore De Bernardis | Terracciani | Signori Gargiulo | Sabatini | Chizzola | Orlandini | Spiriti | Con numero 30 Coristi d'ambo i sessi».

[3]. In a letter dated 14 March 1786, the secretary of the Austrian ambassador to the Neapolitan court, Norbert Hadrava, recounts a curious episode in this regard. During the interludes of the French comedies that were given at the Court Theatre, «court violinists were ordered to play. His Majesty the King could no longer bear the rubbish that these people were playing, and ordered the first violin to play Haydn's symphonies, which are available in large copies in the King's music collection, and to play them one after the other from time to time in the interludes. Now at least there was good music, albeit poorly played. [The king then] ordered that at the end of the French comedy the entire orchestra was taken to the guard post; that the guard officer left everyone on the picket post until further notice. This lesson had good effects: the next time they played a new symphony by Haydn quite well, so that all the listeners were heartily rejoiced». GIALDRONI

certain importance because it fitted into a particular and very delicate political-social context: the year before (June-July 1820) Naples had been the scene of a clear attempt at revolution (led by Guglielmo Pepe, whom we will discuss shortly) that culminated in the granting of the Constitution (7 July), an act of liberation badly received by the great European rulers, and in particular Austria[4].

Let us first try to retrace those events.

2.

In Sicily the growing discontent with the Neapolitan authorities (together with the recent constitutional changes), caused the outbreak — on 15 June 1820 — of a popular riot, while Francesco di Borbone, son of Ferdinand and General Lieutenant of Sicily, on 27 June was forced to leave Palermo and come back to Naples.

Even in the shadow of Vesuvius this growing request for renewal led, on the night between 1 and 2 July 1820, to the conspiracy — near Nola — of a group of soldiers of chivalry, led by second lieutenants Michele Morelli and Giuseppe Silvati, in the hope that it would have the same success that the Spanish constitutional riot of January 1820 had previously achieved. The *coup d'état* in the Kingdom of the Two Sicilies was carried out with the help of the so-called *Carboneria*[5] and senior officers of the Royal Army, including General Guglielmo Pepe, who hired the command of the revolutionary forces.

King Ferdinand, having ascertained the impossibility of stopping the riot (which rapidly spread to many provinces), on 7 July 1820 granted the Constitution on the model of the Spanish one of 1812 and appointed his son Francesco as his viceroy. On 1 October, work began on the new Neapolitan parliament elected at the end of August, in which prevailed the bourgeois ideals spread during the decade of French domination (1806-1815). Among the acts of the parliament there were the reorganisation of the provincial and municipal administrations and the introduction of laws on the freedom of the press and of worship: «Here everything is quiet;

---

1996, p. 96. The passionate king — let's remember that Ferdinando was married to Maria Carolina of Austria since 1768 — in 1786 was also the client and the dedicatee of the five concerts for Lire organizzate and had done everything to bring Haydn to his court. The composer, after the death of 'his' prince (Nikolaus Esterházy) in 1790, and before choosing London as a destination, was in discussion with King Ferdinand to go to Naples, because he thought that as a musician, in Italy, he could become a famous composer of operas. Then, as we know, he made other choices.

[4]. For references to the historical facts cited, see LEPRE 1967.

[5]. *Carboneria* was a secret political society with liberal republican aims, particularly engaged in the struggle for Italian unification during the 19th century.

## 'Feast, Flour and Gallows': Haydn's *Creation* in Naples (1821)

our good Sovereign has signed the constitution, and I assure you that the Neapolitans have done an inevitable action», Rossini wrote to his mother on 11 July 1820[6].

In the meantime, on 16 July there was the establishment in Palermo of a provisional but clearly independent government, which requested the revolutionary government of Naples to restore the Kingdom of Sicily, albeit under Bourbon leadership, and its own parliament. The Neapolitan government initially sent General Florestano Pepe to Sicily on 30 August, who, with the Termini Imerese agreement of 22 September, granted the Sicilians the possibility of electing their own assembly of deputies, an agreement which, however, was not ratified by the newly-elected parliament of Naples.

The bourgeoisie of Sicily saw in this act the betrayal of their aspirations for independence, which forced the Neapolitan government to send General Pietro Colletta on 14 October, with the order to forcefully impose on the Sicilians the unitary will of the central government. The lack of coordination of the forces of the various Sicilian cities led to the weakening of the provisional government (Messina and Catania opposed Palermo's claim to want to capital city), which soon fell under the blows of Bourbon repression. Thus, on 22 November, Sicily returned under the control of the constitutional government of Naples.

However, the innovations introduced in the Two Sicilies Kingdom with the riots of 1820 were not appreciated by the governments of the great European powers, especially by Metternich's Austria, which, after the Troppau congress of 27 October 1820, summoned King Ferdinand to the next Congress of Laibach (nowadays Liubljana) to clarify his attitude regarding the constitution he had granted. Metternich, worried about the consequences that the Neapolitan riot could have aroused in other Italian states, organised an Austrian armed intervention (of about 50,000 soldiers) which, with the favour of Ferdinand, had the aim of suppressing the Neapolitan constitutional government, despite the conflicting opinions of other European powers. The Neapolitan government, which hoped in vain for a defence of the Constitution by King Ferdinand in Ljubljana, decided for armed resistance against Austrian aggression.

In March 1821 the Kingdom of the Two Sicilies was attacked and then militarily occupied by the Austrian troops, which defeated the Neapolitan constitutional army (despite the latter being compounded by 40,000 people) led by Guglielmo Pepe and Michele Carrascosa in the battle of Rieti-Antrodoco (7-10 March 1821), often referred to as the 'First battle of the Italian Risorgimento'[7].

---

[6]. Letter from Rossini to his mother, 11 July 1820 in *GRLD* 2004, p. 146. All translations are by the author.

[7]. The Risorgimento is the period stretching from the early nineteenth century to 1861 and the proclamation of the Kingdom of Italy, which saw considerable upheaval and change. Political and personal freedom took on new importance as the events of the French Revolution unfolded. The Risorgimento paved the way for the unification of Italy in 1871.

General Angelo D'Ambrosio led the extreme resistance of the constitutional troops in the fortress on the Volturno river and was then forced to sign the end of hostilities on 20 March. To weaken the fighting spirit of the other troops of the Neapolitan army, a proclamation was issued by King Ferdinand who, following the Austrians troops, ordered the dissolution of the army and invited the revolutionaries to lay down their weapons and not fight «those who came to restore order in the Kingdom»[8].

The revolutionary uprisings ended definitively on 24 March, the day on which the Austrian troops entered Naples escorting King Ferdinand without encountering further resistance and, as a first act of force, closed the newborn parliament, without due respect to the so-called 'policy of no revenge' required since 1815 by the Holy Alliance.

The 'good', so to speak, obviously had to come: in a couple of months, King Ferdinand revoked the Constitution and gave to the powerful Prince of Canosa — the feared minister of police — the task of capturing all those suspected of conspiracy[9].

The repression was harsh and inexorable: following the investigations, Canosa publicly posted a long, persuasive and paternalistic manifest in the newspaper *Il giornale delle Due Sicilie* on 15 April, from which we present some short excerpts:

> The demagogues, the leaders of the proscribed sects, hiding under the name now of Jacobins, now of liberals, now of Carbonari [...] have plunged you into misfortunes. God had given us a legitimate King, son and emulating the virtues of Charles III, a King descendant of Henry IV, a King nephew and son of Saint Louis. The iniquitous took it from you twice, in 1799 and in 1806. But after having tried everything to humiliate him in 1820, behind so many perjuries and so many ingratitudes, did they then make you as happy as they promised[10]?

Canosa continues:

---

[8]. Edict proclaimed on 6 March, see LEPRE 1967, p. 54.

[9]. Among these, curiously, also appears the young Vincenzo Bellini, then a student at the Royal College of Music at the convent of San Sebastiano in Naples — who, demonstrating the same clear temper of future musical and non-musical occasions — denied his belonging to the riots and, therefore, obtained the amnesty.

[10]. «I demagoghi, i capi delle sette proscritte, nascosi sotto il nome ora di giacobini, ora di liberali, ora di carbonari [...] vi hanno immersi nelle sventure. Iddio ci aveva dato un Re legittimo, figlio ed emulo delle virtù di Carlo III, un Re discendente da Enrico IV, un Re nipote e figlio di S. Luigi. Gli iniqui ve lo tolsero due volte, nel 1799 e nel 1806. Ma dopo aver tutto tentato per umiliarlo nel 1820, dietro tanti spergiuri e tante ingratitudini, vi hanno poi renduti così felici come promisero?». *Il giornale delle Due Sicilie*, 15 April 1821, p. 23. Canosa was right: indeed, King Ferdinand was obviously related to the Bourbons of France and, therefore also to the Capetians, who ruled by 'divine right'. In the Bourbons' coat of arms, the red stripe indicates that the Bourbons are a cadet branch of the Capetian house, and, in the coat of arms of Bourbon of two Sicilies it is shown by the central red frame around the lilies.

## 'Feast, Flour and Gallows': Haydn's *Creation* in Naples (1821)

> Since I will go spying on them [the Carbonari] right into the most secret hiding places, I hope that for your part you will contribute to public safety [...] quite sure that since I will be inexorable against repeat offenders, and enemies of public order, so I will be the friend and confidant of all those who show themselves as friends of the order[11].

The legislative effect of these warnings was soon to come. On both 9 and 12 April the Marquis of Circello, Prime Minister of the king, promulgated two edicts, signed in place of the sovereign, with which (to say with the words of Gabriele Rossetti, poet, patriot and *carbonaro*)[12] «that unfaithful king finally gave free rein to his ill-repressed hatred against all liberals by striking to death, with martial law, every *carbonaro*»[13].

The edict of 9 April (which appeared on the *Il Giornale delle Due Sicilie*) is a text clearly dictated by contingencies, which aims to make a 'clean sweep' of the insurgents, giving legal tender to the not-too-veiled threats uttered by Canosa and using every means, such as searches, conspiracy of silence, death penalty, prison and impunity for whistleblowers:

> Art. 1 – A court-martial will be created with the faculty of a war council
>
> Art. 2 – This court will strictly execute the articles [...] against the takers of prohibited weapons, condemning to the death penalty as a murderer whomever is caught with them, and having the sentence carried out without delay
>
> Art. 3 – The director of the Police [Canosa...] is authorised to order home visits as soon as prudence dictates [...]
>
> Art. 4 – The same Court is charged against any secret union, and against the society of the so-called Carbonari [...]
>
> Art. 5 – Since the purpose of the Carbonari society is the upheaval and destruction of governments, anyone who belongs to it will be punished with the death penalty as an offender of high treason [...]
>
> Art. 6 – All those who, even if not Carbonari, find themselves in the flagrant union of unions intended to upset public order will be subject to the same death penalty
>
> Art. 7 – The same Court-Martial will proceed with an extraordinary sentence of imprisonment from three to ten years against those who, knowing the place both in the city or countryside, in which the aforementioned frenzied join together, do not go immediately to denounce them
>
> Art. 8 – A person belonging to the aforementioned gangs, if repentant and provides the names of members and the aims of the conspirators to the Police, will

---

11. «Dal momento che io andrò spiandoli [i carbonari] fin dentro i più secreti nascondigli, mi auguro che dal canto vostro concorrerete alla tranquillità pubblica [...] ben sicuri che siccome io sarò inesorabile contro i recidivi, e nemici dell'ordine pubblico, così sarò amico e il confidente di tutti coloro che si mostrano amici dell'ordine». *Ibidem*.

12. *Carbonaro* means affiliated to the so-called *Carboneria*, see note 5.

13. BENELLI 1898, p. 134.

enjoy impunity. His name will remain hidden among the archives of the Police, and be not recorded in any paper[14].

This last sentence perhaps casts a dark shadow over how Bellini was released by the authorities… The document continues with two further articles, the first of which declares that «all free companies and all so-called National Guard corps [...] established after 5 July 1820 up to the day of the installation of the provisional government, are abolished».

The second edict instead, that of 12 April, appears to be more a text that aims to consolidate the power of censorship and control, since it establishes «Four scrutiny councils» in charge of examining the conduct, respectively, of ecclesiastics, of teachers, writers and academics, of employees in the judicial branch and finally of employees in public administration.

All this resulted, in practice, in 13 life sentences and 30 death sentences, all carried out within a year: among the condemned there were also the aforementioned Morelli and Silvati, who were executed by hanging.

But, how does all this liberticidal horror relate both to Rossini and Haydn's *Creation*?

## 3.

If we look at the previously mentioned edict of 9 April, we can see that, right after the text that gave way to this very harsh repression, appears the following announcement, under the heading 'Teatri':

> Tomorrow, on the 10<sup>th</sup> day of the current month, will take place in the theatre of San Carlo *La creazione del mondo* by the immortal Haydain [*sic*] Which will be

---

[14]. «Art. 1 – Sarà creata una Corte marziale con facoltà di consiglio di guerra subitaneo. / Art. 2 – Questa corte eseguirà rigorosamente gli articoli [...] contro gli asportatori d'armi vietate, condannando alla pena capitale come assassino chiunque sarà sorpreso con le medesime, e facendo senza indugio eseguire la condanna. / Art. 3 – Il direttore delle Polizia è abilitato ad ordinare visite domiciliari, secondocché la prudenza gli detterà [...]. / Art. 4 – È la stessa Corte incaricata [...] contro di qualunque unione segreta, e specialmente contro la società de' cosi detti Carbonari [...] / Art. 5 – Essendo scopo della società Carbonaria lo sconvolgimento e la distruzione de' governi, sarà punito di morte qual reo di alto tradimento chiunque [...] vi si ascrivesse [...]. / Art. 6 – Alla stessa pena di morte saranno soggetti tutti quelli, i quali, ancorché non Carbonari, si ritrovassero nella flagranza di unioni intese allo sconvolgimento dell'ordine pubblico. / Art. 7 – Procederà l'istessa Corte Marziale con estraordinaria pena di prigionia da tre a dieci anni contro quei che sapendo il luogo di città o di campagna in cui si uniscono gli anzidetti forsennati, non vadano subito a denunziarli. / Art. 8 – Qualunque persona appartenente alle suddette combriccole, se pentita scovre alla Polizia i membri e le mire de' complottati, godrà l'impunità. Il suo nome resterà occulto tra gli arcani della Polizia, e non registrato in veruna carta». *Il giornale delle Due Sicilie*, 9 April 1821, p. 57.

## 'Feast, Flour and Gallows': Haydn's *Creation* in Naples (1821)

performed by the main singers: Mrs. Comelli and Mr. Nozzari, Rubini, Ciccimarra, Galli, Ambrogi and Benedetti. There will be four concertante parts, forty choristers and one hundred orchestra professors. The company will not omit any care to have this masterpiece of German music performed with the utmost decency.

*La Creazione del mondo* was then played two days later: two performances, on the 10 and 12 April, scheduled exactly on the days in which King Ferdinand, Canosa and Circello legally and juridically began the harsh repression of the insurrectional uprisings (let us remember that the aforementioned two edicts were signed almost on the same days, 9 and 12 April).

There is more than one well-founded suspicion that the contemporaneity of these facts may not be accidental; but, in any case, let us proceed in order.

Rossini — who had spent a carefree Roman carnival performing the brand new *Matilde di Shabran* on 24 February 1821 — had returned to Naples on 23 March, following the Austrian troops[15], and was therefore called to conduct *La creazione del mondo* just a few days later, if it is true that rehearsals took place on the day of the first performance, as Ferdinand Hérold tells us in a letter to his mother dated 10 April[16].

Two details of the manuscript originally used by Rossini[17] are surprising[18]. The first is the absolute fidelity to the Haydnian original: very little has been retouched in the musical part (just in some points where the vocal lines needed to be fitted to the Italian language's accentuation and metrics) and, considering the singers he had available, it is almost miraculous that there are no *abbellimenti* or additions that could enhance their vocal skills (although this does not exclude the fact that they may have been added during rehearsals, without being recorded on paper). The only real mystery concerns the number of the soloists: as we have seen, on the title page of the libretto there are seven described as «primary parts» and also seven «concertante parts», but Haydn's score includes only three (soprano, tenor and bass) for a maximum of five different roles (Uriel, Raphael, Gabriel, Adam and Eve). Perhaps we could attribute the enlargement to seven by making a distinction between arias and recitatives and a division (of the seven other singers) of those employed in the *concertati* but not in the arias.

The second detail is the choice of the libretto. The most popular Italian translation of *The Creation* was without doubt the one by the well-known Giuseppe Carpani (1801), a personal friend of Haydn[19]; however, the text of this Neapolitan performance is another, of a much

---

[15]. Letter from Rossini to his mother, 23 march 1821, in *GRLD* 2000, p. 290.

[16]. *GRLD* 1992, p. 491.

[17]. «La Creazione del Mondo | Oratorio | Musica | del Maestro | Haydn». I-NaC, Minutolo 21.3.14.

[18]. I had the opportunity to prepare the revision of the score of this 'Neapolitan' *Creation* on the occasion of the performance which took place at the Belcanto Festival 'Rossini in Wildbad', Summer 2021.

[19]. Giuseppe Carpani (1752-1825), poet, writer, journalist and musician, wrote *Le Haydine, ossia lettere sulla vita e le opere di Giuseppe Haydn* (1812), one of the first reliable biographies about Haydn (together with

lower literary level, which matches with that used by the manuscript of the piano reduction produced by Tipografia Flautina[20], which bears the words «Translated into Italian by Mr. Ignazio Pleyel», the well known composer, and Haydn's pupil, who had edited its publication in Paris in 1801 (in a bilingual version: in French, translated by the librettist Philippe Desriaux, and in Italian by Pleyel himself).

The translation used in Naples was considered in itself so poor that in the libretto we find a so-called *excusatio non petita* (an apology) as follows, which also demonstrates the hurry with which the entire operation was set up:

> The administration of the royal theatres, in presenting this Oratory to the public, flatters itself that, by virtue of the music, the imperfect translation of the poem will be pitied, having thus received it from abroad. The desire to let lovers of fine arts enjoy one of the masterpieces of the famous Haydn, did not allow, due to lack of time, to have a better version performed.

So, why was the less convincing translation of the Austro-French musician chosen and not the one, poetically much more convincing and popular, of the Italian writer? The reasons, in fact, could be many: Pleyel's libretto — albeit with some minimal variations — had already been used for the performance of 1808 at the Accademia de' Concordi in Bologna[21] at the time when Rossini was a student at the local Liceo Musicale, and it is probable that this version is the one that he then knew and admired most, as he had occasion to affirm in his old age during the famous (and, luckily, recorded) conversations with both Ferdinand Hiller and Edmond Michotte[22].

Secondly, Pleyel had been a well-known name for decades at the Neapolitan court (in 1785, for the San Carlo, he had composed *Ifigenia in Aulide*) and was in close relations with the King himself. Moreover, during the Reign of Terror of the French Revolution, he was repeatedly targeted by the notorious Committee of Public Safety and labelled as a «royalist

---

the ones by Dies and Griesinger, both 1810).

[20]. «Creazione del Mondo | Oratorio | per Cembalo, o Pianoforte | Del Sig.r Giuseppe Haydn | Tradotta in lingua Italiana | Dal Sig.r Ignazio Pleyel». I-NaC, 33.6.36.

[21]. Copies of this libretto can be found in I-Bc and I-Nc.

[22]. «Above all, I knew *The Creation* by heart, even in the smallest recitatives; I had played it and accompanied it often enough [...] In Bologna, in my youth, I had assembled a string quartet in which I played viola as best as I could. At first, the first violin had only a few pieces of Haydn, but I was always behind him, to make him more and more, and so slowly I learned a considerable number of them. At that time I was studying Haydn with a particular predilection. You should have been there when I directed The Creation at the Lyceum of Bologna: I did not really leave anything to the performers, because I knew every note by heart. I also directed The Seasons when, after leaving the Lyceum, they appointed me as director of philharmonic concerts». HILLER 1868, p. 21.

collaborator»[23]: a reputation that, given the situation, was certainly not an obstacle to the setting of *The Creation* in Naples in 1821.

However, beyond these purely biographical reasons, the choice of the libretto certainly followed that of the score; therefore, the first question to ask is: why *The Creation* itself?

Of course, this wonderful *oratorio*, drawing the argument both from Genesis and from Milton's *Paradise Lost*, is in itself a text whose dramaturgical structure, we may argue, places every interlocutor — archangel or human being — in a subordinate position facing the divine majesty, who is praised and to which the whole world prostrates itself at every possible moment. In short, it was a praiseworthy text *par excellence*, and very well known to the Italian audiences: it had already been performed in seven Italian cities including Naples, Rome, Venice, Milan, Bergamo, Bologna and Siena between 1804 and 1820[24].

Therefore, it seems likely that there was a particular symbolic aim to reprise this *oratorio*, which may be seen as a clear desire to underline musically the Restoration of the *status quo* — expressly desired by the Habsburg occupiers at the Ljubljana congress — through a work that could represent not only a peak of Viennese music, but could establish a clear link with both the people and the Neapolitan nobility and bourgeoisie (among whose ranks there were numerous conspirators), and between the creative power of divine majesty and the regained political stability due to the power of King Ferdinand, a sovereign related to saints and — let us not forget — invested by God himself (as Canosa stated in the aforementioned manifest). Canosa also knew Rossini personally, if it is true that the first private performance of the pastoral *cantata La riconoscenza* took place in his house in the same year, 1821[25].

Yet the initial question regarding the libretto remains unchanged, however: why the 'bad' Pleyel version instead of the more widespread and euphonic Carpani?

The reason could lie in some of the variants, that is to say, elements that were more appreciated and better in line with the praiseworthy and patronal intent of the occasion.

We may try to match the German original libretto of Haydn's *Die Schöpfung* (made by baron Gottfried van Swieten)[26] with these two Italian translations.

Part I, scene IV
Terzetto with chorus 'Die Himmel erzählen die Ehre Gottes', in the original section addressed to the soloist, there appears this text:

---

[23]. To save his life, in 1794 he soon composed some Revolutionary works, especially for Strasbourg, like *La Prise de Toulon, Hymne de Pleyel chanté au Temple de la Raison, Hymne à l'Être Suprême* and *La Révolution du 10 août*, see HONEGGER 1987, p. 115.

[24]. RICCIARDI 2003, pp. 10-24.

[25]. And then replicated at Teatro San Carlo on 27 December 1821.

[26]. Van Swieten also made a translation, since the original libretto (anonymous) that Haydn brought with him from London was in English, see TEMPERLEY 1994, p. 16.

Dem kommenden Tage sagt es der Tag,
Die Nacht, die verschwand, der folgenden Nacht
[...]
In alle Welt ergeht das Wort,
Jedem Ohre klingend, Keiner Zunge fremd

This means: «Each day announces a new day; last night introduces the night that follows [...] The Word spreads throughout the world, resounds in every ear and is not foreign to any language».

Carpani's translation is much closer to the original («Le annunzia al seguente / il giorno che muore / la notte cadente / all'altra così [...] non v'è nel mondo / luogo remoto / non v'è profondo / recesso ignoto / che lui non lodi / che lui non canti»). Pleyel, on the other hand, translates the last part with an arbitrary «Humble homage to the King of heaven, of the mighty and wise God let's <u>worship the power</u>».

*Part III, Scene I*
Recitativo of Uriel. The original version is:

Aus Rosenwolken bricht,
Geweckt durch süßen Klang,
Der Morgen jung und schön.

This means: «Among pink clouds, awakened by sweet sounds, the morning appears young and beautiful». Carpani translates it similarly: «Among the pink clouds in the sky the beautiful dawn rises / awakens from a sweet sound», while Pleyel freshly invents a new line which could be related to the well-known Bourbon lilies, a symbol also well known in Bourbon Naples: «Above the clouds appears the dawn, with hair adorned with lilies and roses».

*Part III, Scene III*
Recitativo of Adam. The original version is:

Nun ist die erste Pflicht erfüllt,
Dem Schöpfer haben wir gedankt.
Nun folge mir, Gefährtin meines Lebens!

This means: «Now the first duty is done; we gave thanks to the Creator. Now follow me, companion of my life!» (he is obviously speaking to Eve). Carpani, as usual, translates it in a very similar way: «Of our duties to the first / we gave vent, oh my consort / to the supreme factor we gave thanks. / Now follow me, my sweet life / Dear companion». While Pleyel, arbitrarily, translates it as «It is the first of duties, done. In the meantime / towards our King, follow / my footsteps, lovable companion».

# 'Feast, Flour and Gallows': Haydn's *Creation* in Naples (1821)

Also in the same scene III, Eve says to Adam:

O du, für den ich ward,
Mein Schirm, mein Schild, mein All!
Dein Will' ist mir Gesetz

This means: «O you for whom I was born! / My asylum, my shield, my everything! / Your will is my law». Carpani translates it as: «O You, for whom I was born / my good, my life, my support and everything / Your will is my law»; but instead Pleyel has: «O you, who will be my soul ever / everything, the King, yes, with you / I will always be».

After this comparison it is clear how Pleyel's text (either by chance or following a specific will of the clumsy translator) has clear references to God identified as a King, readily useful for *propaganda* and praiseworthy aims, but absent both in the original German and in the widely known version of Carpani. We should not forget that King Ferdinand was, obviously, present at the performance, sitting in his Royal loge.

It is therefore not surprising that, for a highly celebratory occasion such as the return to the city under the absolute power, Rossini chose one of the most important monuments of his contemporary musical repertoire, admired and studied by him since his apprenticeship years[27]. The fact that a particular textual edition was chosen but barely a note of the score was changed represents a tribute not only to that Habsburg Vienna that had brought back (with guns...) law and order to Naples, but also an opportunity to pay homage to one of his favourite German masters (perhaps at the suggestion of the Haydn fan King Ferdinand, or of Canosa).

We also know that Rossini was later commissioned to compose other music related to the Restoration, such as the cantatas *La Santa alleanza* and *Il vero omaggio*, both written for Metternich's Congress of Verona in 1822, and also *Zelmira*, which was written in the same year both for Naples and Vienna, with a precise intent to strengthen the artistic, cultural and politic ties between these two cities[28].

So, the choice of this text, in the global theocentric conception and in some encomiastic details, therefore appears in line with the spirit of those days of great celebrations at the Teatro San Carlo, with the greatest composer and some of the most famous singers of Europe engaged in a magniloquent self-affirmation of the power of the *ancien régime*, which occurred at the same time as the beginning of the great reactionary repressions (events later advertised by *Il giornale delle Due Sicilie* as if they were related and a consequence of the other). This accords with the sadly famous *motto* addressed to King Ferdinand (but probably invented by Alexandre

---

[27]. For an overview of the influences of the Wiener Klassik on Rossini see Gon 2014.
[28]. See Lamacchia 2006.

Dumas *père*)[29], a monarch known for wanting to govern his subjects through a game of balances between paternalistic instincts and violent sentences, known as 'feasts, flour and gallows'. It could not be more different and far removed from the ecumenic, goodhearted and positive spirit that is encapsulated in the universalistic masterpiece that is Haydn's *Creation*.

### Bibliography

Benelli 1898
Benelli, Zulia. *Gabriele Rossetti: notizie biografiche e bibliografiche raccolte e ordinate da Zulia Benelli*, Florence, Fratelli Bocca, 1898.

Dumas 1862
Dumas, Alexander. *I Borboni di Napoli: questa istoria, pubblicata pe' soli lettori dell'Indipendente, è stata scritta su documenti nuovi, inediti e sconosciuti, scoperti dall'autore negli archivi segreti della polizia*, Naples, L'indipendente, 1862.

Gialdroni 1996
Gialdroni, Giuliana. 'La musica a Napoli alla fine del XVIII secolo nelle lettere di Norbert Hadrava', in: *Fonti musicali italiane*, I (1996), pp. 75-143.

Gon 2014
Gon, Federico. *«Scolaro sembra dell'Haydn». Il problema dell'influenza di Haydn su Rossini*, Pesaro, Fondazione Rossini, 2014 (Tesi rossiniane, 2).

*GRLD* 1992
*Gioachino Rossini, lettere e documenti. 1: 29 febbreio 1792-17 marzo 1822*, edited by Bruno Cagli and Sergio Ragni, Pesaro, Fondazione Rossini, 1992.

*GRLD* 2000
*Gioachino Rossini, lettere e documenti. 3: 17 ottobre 1826-31 dicembre 1830*, edited by Bruno Cagli and Sergio Ragni, Pesaro, Fondazione Rossini, 2000.

*GRLD* 2004
*Gioachino Rossini, lettere e documenti. 3a: Lettere ai genitori: 18 febbraio 1812-22 giugno 1830*, edited by Bruno Cagli and Sergio Ragni, Pesaro, Fondazione Rossini, 2004.

Hiller 1868
Hiller, Ferdinand. 'Plaudereien mit Rossini', in: *Aus dem Tonleben unserer Zeit*, Leipzig, Hermann Mendelssohn, 1868, pp. 1-84.

---

[29]. Dumas 1862, p. 176.

HONEGGER 1987
HONEGGER, Geneviève. 'Pleyel à Strasbourg Durant La Terreur', in: *Revue de Musicologie*, LXXIII/1 (1987), pp. 113-119.

LAMACCHIA 2006
LAMACCHIA, Saverio. *Zelmira*, Pesaro, Fondazione Rossini, 2006 (I libretti di Rossini, 13).

LEPRE 1967
LEPRE, Aurelio. *La rivoluzione napoletana del 1820-1821*, Rome, Editori Riuniti, 1967 (Biblioteca di storia, 6).

RICCIARDI 2003
RICCIARDI, Simonetta. 'Gli oratori di Haydn in Italia nell'800', in: *Il Saggiatore musicale*, X/1 (2003), pp. 23-61.

TEMPERLEY 1994
TEMPERLEY, Nicholas. *Haydn: The Creation*, Cambridge, Cambridge University Press, 1994 (Cambridge Music Handbook).

# ÉTUDE DES TRANSFERTS MUSICAUX FRANCO-ALLEMANDS À L'ÉPOQUE NAPOLÉONIENNE À TRAVERS LE PRISME DE L'*ALLGEMEINE MUSIKALISCHE ZEITUNG*

*Matthieu Cailliez*
(Université Jean Monnet - Saint-Étienne)

Le 3 octobre 1798 commence à Leipzig la publication hebdomadaire de l'*Allgemeine musikalische Zeitung*, le principal périodique musical allemand de la première moitié du XIXe siècle créé par la maison d'édition Breitkopf und Härtel. Un an plus tard, le coup d'État du 9 novembre 1799 et l'instauration du Consulat marquent symboliquement la fin de la Révolution française, la prise de pouvoir de Napoléon Bonaparte et le début de l'ère napoléonienne en Europe. Un dépouillement de l'*Allgemeine musikalische Zeitung* entre 1798 et 1815, voire légèrement au-delà, permet d'observer et d'analyser l'évolution des transferts musicaux franco-allemands sous le Consulat et l'Empire. Ce dépouillement est enrichi par l'analyse des écrits de compositeurs et de dramaturges allemands, tels que Johann Friedrich Reichardt, Louis Spohr, August von Kotzebue et Ignaz Franz Castelli, qui voyagent à travers toute l'Europe et séjournent longuement à Paris durant cette période. C'est donc le point de vue allemand qui est privilégié dans cette étude.

Tandis que les œuvres théâtrales et lyriques françaises connaissent une très large diffusion dans le monde germanique sous la forme de traductions et d'adaptations, le succès de la musique allemande en France se limite alors en grande partie à la musique instrumentale et aux compositions de Haydn et de Mozart. Le goût prononcé de Napoléon pour l'opéra italien est un frein très puissant à la diffusion en France de l'art lyrique allemand.

Dans cet article, le terme Allemagne est employé dans le sens du monde germanique dans son ensemble, autrement dit des pays de langue allemande, Autriche incluse. L'étude des transferts musicaux franco-allemands a été en particulier étendue à plusieurs villes qui appartiennent aujourd'hui à la Pologne, à l'Ukraine, aux pays baltes ou à la Russie, mais qui étaient placées au XIXe siècle sous le contrôle direct ou sous l'influence culturelle de la Prusse ou de l'Autriche: Breslau, Danzig, Königsberg, Lemberg, Riga, Stettin et Warschau (orthographe allemande).

La première partie de cette étude est consacrée à l'importante diffusion, via l'édition musicale, des œuvres françaises et des méthodes du Conservatoire de Paris. Les deux parties suivantes évoquent respectivement l'exécution et la représentation d'œuvres françaises dans le monde germanique et d'œuvres allemandes en France, avant une quatrième et dernière partie centrée sur les rapports entre musique et politique.

## Diffusion des œuvres françaises et des méthodes du Conservatoire de Paris via l'édition musicale

Originaire d'Autriche où il fut l'élève de Joseph Haydn, le compositeur Ignace-Joseph Pleyel (1757-1831) s'installe à Strasbourg en 1784, puis à Paris en 1795. Au mois de juillet 1796, il ouvre une maison d'édition musicale qui devient rapidement l'une des principales de la capitale française avec plus de 4.000 titres publiés entre 1796 et 1834. Pleyel contribue à la diffusion des œuvres de Haydn, Beethoven et Hummel en France, outre la publication de nombreuses œuvres de compositeurs français et italiens[1]. Il joue ainsi un rôle clé dans les transferts musicaux franco-allemands via l'édition musicale. Dès sa première année de publication en 1798-1799, l'*Allgemeine musikalische Zeitung* fait régulièrement paraître les recensions de nouvelles partitions en provenance de la maison d'édition parisienne Pleyel, dont des pièces de Pleyel lui-même, mais aussi de Luigi Boccherini, Muzio Clementi, Martin Pierre d'Almivare, Giacomo Gotifredo Ferrari, Joseph Haydn, François-Joseph Hérold, Franz Anton Hoffmeister, Johann Christian Hennig, Joseph Martin Kraus, F. H. Salingre, Armand Trial et Giovanni Battista Viotti[2]. Pour ne citer que les œuvres musicales de Pleyel qui sont alors recensées par le journal allemand, celles-ci comprennent de grandes sonates pour le clavecin ou pianoforte, avec accompagnement d'un violon et violoncelle (Opus 55), deux concertos pour flûte ou hautbois et pour violoncelle (Opus 1 et 4), trois duos pour deux violoncelles (Opus 5), six duos pour deux violons et une « Simphonie périodique » pour instruments à cordes frottées et à vent. Quoique la réputation du compositeur soit fermement établie, le ton des articles qui sont consacrés à ses œuvres varie des louanges à la critique féroce[3]. Dans son édition du 20 mars 1799, l'*Allgemeine musikalische Zeitung* propose la recension de diverses

---

[1]. Devriès-Lesure 2003.
[2]. *AMZ* 1799[C]; *AMZ* 1799[F-G]; *AMZ* 1799[K]; *AMZ* 1799[O-P]; *AMZ* 1799[S]; *AMZ* 1800[N]; *AMZ* 1800[Q]; *AMZ* 1800[S-T]; *AMZ* 1800[V]; *AMZ* 1800[Z]; *AMZ* 1800[B1]; *AMZ* 1801[A]; *AMZ* 1801[E]; *AMZ* 1801[K]; *AMZ* 1801[N]; *AMZ* 1801[R].
[3]. *AMZ* 1799[C]; *AMZ* 1799[F-G].

pièces françaises éditées par Pleyel. Le genre de la romance[4] et l'emploi de la harpe[5] retiennent en particulier son attention. Les *Trois Romances avec Accompagnement de Harpe ou Fortépiano* d'Armand Trial, fils du célèbre acteur-chanteur Antoine Trial et compositeur de quelques opéras-comiques, suscitent de curieuses observations quatre ans seulement après la création du Conservatoire de Paris: «Für uns Deutsche kann der Titel des Komponisten merkwürdig seyn. Er unterzeichnet sich *Professeur d'Accompagnement et de Fortépiano, Elève du Conservatoire de Musique*. Uebrigens möchte es mit der Harfe bey so vielen dissonirenden Akkorden schlecht vorwärts gehen. Die Melodien sind ganz artig»[6]. La création par Mendelssohn en 1843 à Leipzig du premier conservatoire supérieur de musique allemand devait en effet être postérieure d'un demi-siècle à celle du Conservatoire de Paris, ce qui explique l'absence de familiarité du public allemand avec une telle institution en 1799[7]. La parution de vingt-quatre nouvelles romances de Giacomo Gotifredo Ferrari offre l'occasion au périodique allemand de manifester une certaine forme de condescendance vis-à-vis du genre français, même si le compositeur italien semble plutôt épargné:

> Liebhabern des französischen Gesanges können diese beyden Sammlungen mit allem Recht empfohlen werden. Die Romanzen haben sehr hübsche, meist italienische Melodien und da eine bequeme Begleitung untergelegt ist, die ohne Ueberladung dennoch füllt, so können sie am Fortepiano wirklich eine recht angenehme Unterhaltung gewähren, um so mehr, da die Scansion besser und die Harmonie mannigfaltiger ist, als sie in französischen gewöhnlichen Chansons zu seyn pflegt[8].

À propos de la grande scène intitulée *Le Départ* du même compositeur, le critique musical remarque l'inhabituelle virtuosité de l'accompagnement écrit pour harpe, semblable à celle d'un accompagnement pour pianoforte, ce qui témoigne selon lui d'une facture instrumentale et d'une école de harpe nettement plus développées en France qu'en Allemagne[9]. Le *Recueil de six Airs et Romances, avec Accompagnement de Fortepiano* de Martin Pierre d'Almivare permet au critique de souligner une fois de plus la difficile réception outre-Rhin de ce genre vocal jugé spécifiquement français: «Mehr Nationalfranzösisch und holperich; also für Deutsche unbrauchbar, wenigstens viel zu theuer»[10]. Enfin, le critique n'est pas tendre avec l'intégrité de la maison d'édition parisienne. La publication de *Six nouvelles Sonatines pour le Clavecin ou Pianoforte* sous le nom de Muzio Clementi est jugée à la fois mensongère et honteuse: «Man

---

4. Voir *AMZ* 1802[T]; *AMZ* 1804[H]; *AMZ* 1806[A]; *AMZ* 1807[D]; *AMZ* 1811[G].
5. Voir *AMZ* 1807[A-C]; *AMZ* 1807[I].
6. *AMZ* 1799[K]. Voir *AMZ* 1803[H].
7. Voir *AMZ* 1810[F].
8. *AMZ* 1799[K].
9. Voir *IBAMZ* 1806[I].
10. *AMZ* 1799[K].

muss eilen, das deutsche Publikum vor diesem schändigen Betruge zu warnen. Nicht eine Note darin kann Clementi geschrieben haben; es ist die elendeste Leyer- und Bierhausmusik. Solche Versündigung gegen einen noch lebenden Künstler, ist Rec. noch nicht vorgekommen »[11]. Volontaires ou non, les erreurs d'attribution ne semblent pas être un problème ponctuel. En décembre 1799, Franz Anton Hoffmeister fait paraître une annonce dans laquelle il dément être l'auteur de trois grands duos pour flûtes publiés sous son nom par la maison d'édition parisienne. À la décharge de Pleyel, cette erreur est également commise par d'autres éditeurs établis à Offenbach, Berlin, Amsterdam, Braunschweig et Vienne[12].

Loin de se limiter à la maison d'édition Pleyel, l'intérêt du périodique de Leipzig pour les dernières publications parisiennes est soutenu, même si les compositeurs mis en valeur ne sont pas forcément français. Le 3 avril 1799, ce sont les dernières nouveautés de la maison d'édition Le Duc qui sont au centre de l'attention et l'objet de recensions, avec des pièces de Mozart, Giuseppe Maria Cambini, Armand Vanderhagen et Frédéric Blasius[13].

Le 13 mars 1799, le périodique annonce avec bienveillance la parution mensuelle à Hambourg du *Musikalisches Journal* contenant des extraits arrangés pour piano des derniers opéras allemands et français donnés dans la ville hanséatique :

> Es herrscht in diesem Journal nicht allein eine grössere Mannigfaltigkeit als in den bekannten Rellstabschen Sammlungen dieser Art, indem die beliebtesten Stücke aus französischen Opern, die in Hamburg gegeben werden, darin stehen; sondern Druck und Papier sind weit geschmackvoller, und zum Anblick und Gebrauch angenehmer, auch ist ein weit besseres Arrangement der Auszüge darin. Von gleichem Werth kann natürlich nicht alles seyn; aber der allgemeine Geschmack ist das auch nicht. Und da man nun so vielerley Operngesänge einmal bedarf, so ist diesem Journal, das jährlich in 12 Heften erscheint, aller gute Fortgang zu wünschen[14].

Fait remarquable, de nombreuses représentations d'opéras-comiques sont données en français entre 1790 et 1805 à Hambourg, une ville devenue depuis 1793 un centre de l'émigration française, avant que les événements politiques ne modifient la neutralité du public allemand. Selon le musicologue Herbert Schneider, l'impression à Hambourg de livrets d'opéras français en langue originale est attestée pour vingt-sept nouveaux ouvrages en 1795, puis pour cinq à dix-sept nouveaux ouvrages par an jusqu'en 1805[15].

Une courte partition est parfois ajoutée en supplément d'un numéro de l'*Allgemeine musikalische Zeitung*. Il s'agit d'une pratique très courante au sein des périodiques musicaux

---

[11]. *Ibidem*.
[12]. IBAMZ 1799ᴱ.
[13]. *AMZ* 1799ᴸ.
[14]. *AMZ* 1799ᴴ.
[15]. Schneider 1997.

européens du XIXe siècle dont la plupart sont la propriété d'une maison d'édition musicale. Dans le périodique de Leipzig, il n'est pas rare que la partition proposée en supplément soit extraite d'une œuvre française. Entre le 12 novembre 1800 et le 28 octobre 1801 sont ainsi publiés trois romances extraites des opéras-comiques *L'Opéra-comique* (1798) de Domenico Della Maria[16], *Les Deux Journées* (1800) de Luigi Cherubini[17] et *Annette et Lubin* (1800) de Johann Paul Aegidius Martini[18], un air et un chœur extraits des *Mystères d'Isis* (1801), adaptation par Étienne Morel de Chédeville pour le livret et Ludwig Wenzel Lachnith pour la musique du Singspiel *Die Zauberflöte* (1791) de Mozart[19], et un rondo de Pierre-Jean Garat[20]. Dans son édition du 15 juillet 1801, le périodique justifie son choix éditorial de publier un extrait des *Deux Journées*, une décision prémonitoire quand on connaît l'incroyable succès de cet ouvrage de Cherubini dans le monde germanique au XIXe siècle[21]:

> Wir haben seit der Erscheinung der Cherubini'schen Oper: *Les deux journées*, aus Ueberzeugung von ihrem hohen Werth, mehreremal Gelegenheit genommen, auf sie aufmerksam zu machen; aber zu unsrer Befremdung wissen wir sie noch auf nicht Einem deutschen Theater, indess hundert sehr alberne, Sinn und Geschmack verderbende Produkte mit Eifer immerfort verbreitet werden. Vielleicht achtet man auf jenes Meisterstück mehr wenn wir einen kleinen Satz daraus im Klavierauszuge geben. Nur bitten wir dabey sich zu erinnern, dass er einzeln stehend wenig von dem würken *kann* und *darf*, was er im Zusammenhange würkt, eben weil das Ganze, in Text und Musik, Eins ist.
>
> d. Redakt[22].

Propriétaire du périodique musical, la maison d'édition Breitkopf und Härtel publie dès l'année suivante une réduction piano-chant de cet opéra-comique traduit en allemand sous le titre *Der Wasserträger*. Parue le 11 août 1802, une recension de cette partition encense une nouvelle fois l'ouvrage de Cherubini, qualifié d'excellent et considéré comme l'un des meilleurs du genre de l'*opera semiseria*[23].

La diffusion des œuvres françaises dans le monde germanique via l'édition musicale est largement documentée par les annexes, intitulées *Intelligenz-Blatt zur Allgemeine musikalische Zeitung*, qui sont régulièrement placées à la fin des numéros du périodique musical avec une

---

16. *AMZ* 1800$^{C1}$. Voir *AMZ* 1800$^{P}$.
17. *AMZ* 1801$^{V}$.
18. *AMZ* 1801$^{Z}$.
19. *AMZ* 1801$^{D1}$.
20. *AMZ* 1801$^{D}$.
21. Cailliez 2021.
22. *AMZ* 1801$^{U}$. Voir *AMZ* 1802$^{E1\text{-}F1}$.
23. *AMZ* 1802$^{B1}$.

pagination qui leur est propre[24]. Comme beaucoup d'autres, l'annexe publiée en mai 1799 donne une liste d'œuvres publiées par différents éditeurs qui sont disponibles à la vente chez Breitkopf und Härtel à Leipzig. De nouvelles partitions de Frédéric Blasius, Joseph-François-Narcisse Carbonel, Richard Dautrive, François Devienne, Ignace Joseph Pleyel, Étienne Ozi et Jean-Jacques Rousseau y figurent, ainsi que les œuvres de compositeurs étrangers installés à Paris, tels que les Italiens Giovanni Battista Viotti et Giuseppe Maria Cambini, ou le Flamand Armand Vanderhagen[25]. Huit annexes similaires parues en décembre 1805 et janvier 1806 mentionnent plusieurs centaines d'œuvres publiées par différents éditeurs et mises en vente à Leipzig. La grande quantité d'œuvres françaises ou d'origine française présentes dans ce corpus est manifeste. On y trouve notamment des pièces d'Olivier Aubert, Henri-Montan Berton, Frédéric Blasius, François-Adrien Boieldieu, Luigi Cherubini, Nicolas Dalayrac, J. J. Depuis, François Devienne, Charles Doisy, Victor Dourlen, Jérôme Duval, Frédéric Duvernoy, André-Frédéric Eler, A. H. Forestier, Georg Friedrich Fuchs, Pierre-Jean Garat, Joseph-François Garnier, Luigi Gianella, André-Ernest-Modeste Grétry, Nicolas Isouard, Rodolphe Kreutzer, Antoine Lacroix, Jean-Xavier Lefèvre, Joseph Le Gros, Jean-François Lesueur, Louis-Luc Loiseau de Persuis, Martin, Étienne-Nicolas Méhul, J. Michel, Ignace Joseph Pleyel, Félix Rault, Anton Reicha, Pierre Rode[26], Jean-Joseph Rodolphe, Nicolas Roze, F. de Salin, Gaspare Spontini, Bernard Viguerie et Giovanni Battista Viotti[27]. La variété des genres représentés est également impressionnante: ouvertures et airs d'opéras ou d'opéras-comiques, musique de ballet, romances, pièces pour piano, études pour le violon ou le cor, concertos et pièces concertantes, musique de chambre, musique militaire, méthodes pour différents instruments, etc. De cette manière, le public allemand dispose alors d'un accès privilégié à la production musicale française dans toute sa diversité, sans être limité à quelques œuvres ou compositeurs emblématiques.

La diffusion outre-Rhin via l'édition musicale des méthodes du Conservatoire de Paris ou d'autres ouvrages pédagogiques d'origine française est aussi largement documentée par les annexes de l'*Allgemeine musikalische Zeitung*. L'une des annexes publiées en janvier 1806 fait par exemple la promotion du *Jeu d'Apollon ou nouvelle méthode pour apprendre, en jouant, les principes de la musique* de Joseph Le Gros, des *Éléments de musique, en forme de dialogue, servant d'introduction au solfège d'Italie* de Charles Doisy, de la *Neue theoretische und praktische Flötenschule* de François Devienne, de la *Méthode de clarinette* de Jean-Xavier Lefèvre, de la *Méthode pour le cor suivie de duos et de trios pour cet instrument* de Frédéric Duvernoy et de la *Méthode pour le hautbois* de Joseph-François Garnier. Les trois dernières méthodes sont

---

[24]. *IBAMZ* 1799[A-D]; *IBAMZ* 1800[A-K]; *IBAMZ* 1801[A-K]; *IBAMZ* 1802[A-I]; *IBAMZ* 1805[A-E]; *IBAMZ* 1806[A-J].
[25]. *IBAMZ* 1799[A].
[26]. Voir *AMZ* 1801[F].
[27]. *IBAMZ* 1805[A-E]; *IBAMZ* 1806[A-D].

proposées à la vente en langue originale et en traduction allemande[28]. L'annexe de juin 1806 fait également la réclame de trois méthodes instrumentales, celle pour cor de Duvernoy, celle pour flûte du Conservatoire en langue originale et en traduction allemande, ainsi que la méthode de basson du Conservatoire d'Étienne Ozi traduite en allemand[29]. Outre la méthode de flûte du Conservatoire éditée par Antoine Hugot et Fritz Wunderlich et traduite en allemand, l'une des annexes publiées en février 1806 propose également en traduction quatre recueils d'exercices de chant du Conservatoire, les deux premiers pour voix de soprano, le troisième pour ténor et le quatrième pour baryton et basse[30]. Certaines méthodes font l'objet d'une recension particulière. Une illustration parmi d'autres est l'article de quatre pages consacré le 14 avril 1802 à la *Méthode de clarinette* de Michel Woldemar[31]. Plus imposants encore sont les trois articles de seize pages au total dédiés en juillet et août 1807 à la méthode de piano du Conservatoire, une méthode rédigée par Jean-Louis Adam, traduite en allemand et publiée directement par Breitkopf und Härtel[32]. Au-delà de ces quelques exemples, c'est ainsi une très grande partie de la littérature pédagogique du Conservatoire de Paris qui est proposée à la vente par la maison d'édition de Leipzig.

Certains livres français sur la musique, d'ordre plus esthétique ou historique, sont aussi traduits dans la langue de Goethe. C'est le cas notamment des *Mémoires, ou Essais sur la musique* (1797) de Grétry. En septembre 1799, Karl Spazier annonce en effet la future publication par Breitkopf und Härtel de larges extraits de cet ouvrage traduits par ses soins en allemand et s'honore de bénéficier des conseils du compositeur Johann Friedrich Reichardt, lequel a longuement séjourné à Paris, pour mener à bien ce projet éditorial. Spazier insiste sur le fait que Méhul, Dalayrac, Cherubini, Lesueur et Gossec ont signé en France une pétition, afin que la publication de l'ouvrage de leur confrère soit faite au nom de la nation française. Il estime aussi que l'ouvrage de Grétry est écrit de manière plus lisible et divertissante que la plupart des écrits allemands sur la musique[33]. Intitulée *Gretry's Versuche über die Musik*, la traduction de Spazier paraît en 1800[34]. La grande importance accordée à cette traduction est soulignée par une recension exceptionnellement longue, ne comptant pas moins de quatorze pages au total, placée le 3 février 1802 en première page de l'*Allgemeine musikalische Zeitung*[35]. Dans son texte intitulé *Seltsame Leiden eines Theater-Direktors* (1819), dialogue fictif entre deux directeurs de théâtre, E. T. A. Hoffmann intègre une longue citation de l'ouvrage de Grétry à

---

[28]. *IBAMZ* 1806[C].
[29]. *IBAMZ* 1806[H].
[30]. *IBAMZ* 1806[E]. Voir *AMZ* 1805[C].
[31]. *AMZ* 1802[K].
[32]. *AMZ* 1807[F]. Voir *AMZ* 1809[J].
[33]. *IBAMZ* 1799[B].
[34]. Spazier 1800.
[35]. *AMZ* 1802[B]. Voir *AMZ* 1799[A]; *AMZ* 1806[J]; *AMZ* 1807[E]; *AMZ* 1813[H-I].

propos de la taille jugée souvent trop grande des nouveaux théâtres, inadaptés à l'art vocal et à l'oreille de l'auditeur moyen[36]. Ce passage est repris presque mot pour mot d'un article publié le 27 octobre 1813 dans l'*Allgemeine musikalische Zeitung*[37]. Le 17 mai 1817, Carl Maria von Weber fait paraître dans l'*Abend-Zeitung* de Dresde une notice de présentation de l'opéra-comique *Raoul Barbe-bleue* (1789) de Grétry. Le chef d'orchestre et compositeur allemand estime la production musicale de son confrère français, mais critique l'ignorance et la naïveté de son activité en tant que musicographe:

> Auch als politischer Schriftsteller hat sich Grétry 1801 ("De la Vérité", 3 Vol.) gezeigt. Seine musikalischen Abhandlungen aber beweisen die gänzlichste Unwissenheit in der musikalischen Literatur und wie sehr er alles aus eigenem Gefühle geworden und gefunden, indem er Dinge, die in Deutschland fast jeder Chorknabe seit Jahrzehnten kennt, für ganz neu gemachte Entdeckungen ansieht. Doch das gehört in das große Register der französischen Gelehrsamkeit[38].

Autre exemple d'intérêt pour la littérature française liée à la musique, Goethe traduit lui-même *Le Neveu de Rameau* de Diderot, une entreprise appréciée par le périodique de Leipzig qui qualifie l'œuvre de «géniale» dans son édition du 18 décembre 1805[39]. Cette traduction est d'autant plus remarquable que l'œuvre du célèbre philosophe et encyclopédiste est alors inédite en France et que le texte original ne devait être retrouvé qu'à la fin du XIXe siècle. Par ailleurs, une série de quatre articles totalisant trente-deux pages de recension est consacrée en 1808 au *Cours complet d'harmonie et de composition, d'après une théorie neuve et générale de la musique* (1806) de Jérôme-Joseph de Momigny[40]. D'autres ouvrages ou écrits de Jean-Jacques Rousseau, Jacques-Antoine de Révéroni Saint-Cyr, Joachim Le Breton, François Fayolle et Alexandre Choron sont également recensés[41].

En résumé, la production musicale française diffusée via l'édition à Leipzig reflète la grande variété des compositeurs actifs à Paris sous le Consulat et l'Empire, à travers de nombreuses romances et pièces pour instruments à vent, guitare[42] ou harpe, de multiples pièces de musique de chambre[43], symphonies concertantes et arrangements d'opéras, ainsi que la traduction en allemand d'un vaste corpus de méthodes instrumentales françaises et d'essais sur la musique. Confrontée à ce répertoire pléthorique, l'*Allgemeine musikalische*

---

36. Hoffmann 2017, pp. 482-484, 1068.
37. *AMZ* 1813[I].
38. Weber 1975, p. 205.
39. *AMZ* 1805[L].
40. *AMZ* 1808[D]; *AMZ* 1808[E].
41. Voir aussi *AMZ* 1800[A1]; *AMZ* 1804[E]; *AMZ* 1811[B]; *AMZ* 1812[C]; *AMZ* 1813[A].
42. *AMZ* 1801[X].
43. Voir *AMZ* 1802[H1]; *AMZ* 1809[E]; *AMZ* 1812[B]; *AMZ* 1813[G]; *AMZ* 1813[K]; *AMZ* 1814[B]; *AMZ* 1815[E].

*Zeitung* peut se montrer parfois très critique, voire pleine de préjugés vis-à-vis de l'école française, telle qu'elle s'illustre dans certains genres musicaux plus connus outre-Rhin que celui de la romance. Publiée dans l'édition du 12 février 1806, une longue recension de la sonate pour pianoforte Opus 64 de Daniel Steibelt et d'un air arrangé en rondo pour le pianoforte par le même compositeur, rapporte le grand succès des œuvres pianistiques de Steibelt en France et en Angleterre, contrairement à leur moindre diffusion en Allemagne. L'article développe des considérations sur l'école pianistique française qui serait focalisée sur la vitesse d'exécution et la virtuosité au détriment du style et de la clarté polyphonique, à l'opposé de l'école pianistique allemande. La musique allemande serait plus profonde, la musique française plus superficielle. Le public allemand serait mieux éduqué musicalement que le public français. Enfin, la recherche d'équilibre entre les différents mouvements d'une même œuvre serait plus poussée en Allemagne qu'en France[44]. Parue le 23 juillet 1806, la recension de trois sonates pour le pianoforte d'Armand de Villeblanche est une nouvelle occasion pour le périodique de critiquer vertement l'école française de piano:

> Rec. hat Gelegenheit, seit langer Zeit so ziemlich alle französische Novitäten, wenigstens alle von nur einiger Bedeutung, kennen zu lernen, und er lässt diese Gelegenheit nicht unbenutzt. Da, muss er gestehen, hat es für ihn wirklich etwas Niederschlagendes gehabt, zu bemerken, wie es, seit etwa zehn bis zwölf Jahren, allen jungen französischen Komponisten (— ihm wenigstens ist auch nicht Eine beträchtliche Ausnahme vorgekommen —) ganz und gar an dem fehlt, was in der Tonkunst wirklich poetisch ist; zu bemerken, wie es jetzt unter diesen jungen Männern auch nicht einen einzigen eigentlich dichtenden Musiker giebt, und sie nun mit göttlicher Frechheit nicht nur von sich werfen, alles was Rechtens ist, und an dessen Statt eine wilde oder frivole Willkühr setzen, sondern auch alles, was unter den Namen solider Ausführung begriffen wird — nicht verstehen, oder nicht vermögen, oder verachten; mit Einem Worte, dass die jungen Franzosen mit den Noten umgehen, als wären's nur — Königreiche[45].

Dans le même esprit, le 18 juin 1806 paraît la recension de douze pièces pour orgue de Michael Gotthard Fischer, un compositeur allemand actif à Erfurt. Cet article présente une critique de l'influence française, jugée néfaste, dans le domaine de la musique pour orgue en Allemagne[46].

---

44. *AMZ* 1806[F]. Voir *AMZ* 1811[H]. Voir aussi *AMZ* 1800[E1]; *AMZ* 1800[R].
45. *AMZ* 1806[P]. Voir *AMZ* 1798[A]; *AMZ* 1801[H1]; *AMZ* 1802[G-H]; *AMZ* 1802[I1]; *AMZ* 1807[G-H]; *AMZ* 1808[B]; *AMZ* 1809[F].
46. *AMZ* 1806[M].

MATTHIEU CAILLIEZ

Exécution et représentation d'œuvres
françaises dans le monde germanique

Entre 1798 et 1848, la page de titre de chaque volume annuel de l'*Allgemeine musikalische Zeitung* est, à de rares exceptions près, toujours illustrée par le portrait d'un compositeur. Quinze des dix-sept premiers volumes publiés jusqu'en 1815 honorent ainsi la mémoire d'un compositeur, les deux autres célébrant le physicien Ernst Florens Friedrich Chladni[47] et le musicographe Johann Nikolaus Forkel. Douze des quinze compositeurs mis en valeur durant cette période sont allemands et l'École de Berlin, avec cinq membres, est particulièrement bien représentée. Johann Sebastian Bach occupe la page de titre du premier volume, suivi par Johann Abraham Peter Schulze, Carl Philipp Emanuel Bach, Georg Friedrich Händel, Christoph Willibald Gluck, Johann Adam Hiller, Joseph Haydn, Wolfgang Amadeus Mozart, Johann Philipp Kirnberger, Carl Friedrich Christian Fasch, Johann Adolph Hasse et Johann Friedrich Reichardt. Seuls trois compositeurs étrangers bénéficient du même traitement, Jean-Philippe Rameau en 1809-1810, Luigi Cherubini[48] en 1813 et Giovanni Pierluigi da Palestrina en 1815, c'est-à-dire un compositeur français, un compositeur italien naturalisé français et un compositeur italien. Le choix par le périodique de deux compositeurs français essentiellement connus pour leur répertoire lyrique est signe de la grande diffusion de l'opéra français dans le monde germanique.

Parmi les milliers de comptes rendus sur l'actualité musicale d'une ville européenne publiés dans l'*Allgemeine musikalische Zeitung* jusqu'en 1815, plusieurs centaines évoquent la représentation d'opéras-comiques ou d'opéras français dans le monde germanique et à sa périphérie[49]. Mentionnée précédemment, l'excellente diffusion de l'opéra français à Hambourg entre 1790 et 1805, aussi bien en langue originale qu'en traduction, apparaît clairement à la lecture de comptes rendus publiés en 1799. Dans les éditions du 19 juin[50] et du 31 juillet, le correspondant du périodique regrette vivement le départ pour Saint-Pétersbourg d'Alexis Paris, le bien nommé directeur du Théâtre français. Celui-ci a fait connaître au public de la ville hanséatique un large répertoire et sa perte est jugée irremplaçable:

> Mit der französischen Oper sieht es hier freylich nicht ganz so schlecht, doch aber auch nicht viel besser aus, als mit der deutschen. Als Mad. Chevalier, Mad. le Roi, Madem. Duquénoy die ältere, die Herren Dusauzin und Raimond etc. noch hier waren, und vor allen andern, als Paris, dessen ich auch schon bereits

---

47. Voir *AMZ* 1809^A; *AMZ* 1810^C.
48. Voir *AMZ* 1811^A; *AMZ* 1811^I; *AMZ* 1814^H.
49. Voir *AMZ* 1800^H; *AMZ* 1800^I; *AMZ* 1800^W; *AMZ* 1801^O; *AMZ* 1802^A; *AMZ* 1802^I; *AMZ* 1802^L; *AMZ* 1804^F; *AMZ* 1806^D; *AMZ* 1806^{Q-R}.
50. *AMZ* 1799^Q.

in meinem vorigen Briefe erwähnte, noch Direktor dieser Oper war – ja freylich!
damals kannte ich fast kein grösseres Vergnügen, als mir die Vorstellungen mehrerer
sowohl älterer als neuer, grosser und kleiner Opern, unter denen ich nur *Œdipe à
colonne, Didon, Euphrosine ou le tyran corrigé, Camille ou les souterrains, Panurge,
la fausse Magie, le Prisonier* etc. anführen will, gewährten. Wurde eine neue Oper
einstudiert, so freuete ich mich auf die erste Vorstellung, wie sich nur immer ein
Kind auf ein Weihnachtsgeschenk freuen kann[51].

Le 24 juillet, le correspondant se plaint de l'état du théâtre allemand et estime que les interprètes allemands seraient incapables d'égaler leurs confrères français à Hambourg dans le répertoire de l'opéra-comique :

In welchem Zustande unsere Opern sich gegenwärtig befinden, soll ich
Ihnen schreiben? Ach in dem allerschlimmsten traurigsten Zustande, worin sie nur
seyn können, besonders die deutsche, worüber ich denn auch zuerst mein Klagelied
anstimmen werde! […]
Wer überhaupt dergleichen Opern, wie diese und ähnliche, als z. E. *le petit
Matelot, Rose et Colas, Blaise et Babet, le Prisonnier, l'Opéra comique* etc. von, auch
nur mittelmässigen, geschweige denn guten französischen Operisten, die durch so
manche und den Deutschen fast unnachahmliche Nüancen ihr Spiel und ihren
Gesang zu erheben und interessant zu machen wissen, gesehen hat, kann unmöglich
einer solchen deutschen Darstellung davon, Geschmack abgewinnen[52].

Plutôt que de multiplier les exemples, un tour d'horizon géographique de l'année 1806 donne un aperçu assez fidèle de l'ensemble de la période. Les éditions des 19 février, 12 mars et 2 avril relatent les représentations à l'Opéra de Vienne ou au Theater an der Wien, de trois ouvrages français, *Les Mariages samnites* (1776) de Grétry, *L'Intrigue aux fenêtres* (1805) d'Isouard et *Faniska* (1806) de Cherubini, ce dernier étant une création[53]. Les 23 et 30 avril sont évoquées les représentations de *Michel-Ange* (1802) d'Isouard et d'*Emma ou La Prisonnière* (1799) de Cherubini à Leipzig[54], puis des *Deux Journées* (1800) de Cherubini, d'*Une Folie* (1802) de Méhul, de *Raoul Barbe-Bleue* (1789) de Grétry et d'*Aline, reine de Golconde* (1804) de Boieldieu à Danzig[55]. Le 2 juillet, ce sont la mise en scène de *L'Intrigue aux fenêtres* (1805) d'Isouard et la mise en répétition de *Lodoïska* (1791) de Cherubini à Stuttgart qui retiennent l'attention[56]. Le projet avorté de tournée d'une troupe française à Berlin est rapporté dans

---

51. *AMZ* 1799[U].
52. *AMZ* 1799[T]. Voir *AMZ* 1799[V]; Reichardt 2002, p. 118.
53. *AMZ* 1806[G-I].
54. *AMZ* 1806[K].
55. *AMZ* 1806[L].
56. *AMZ* 1806[O].

l'édition du 10 septembre, alors que deux opéras-comiques de Boieldieu, *Ma Tante Aurore* (1803) et *La Jeune Femme colère* (1805), avaient été annoncés au programme[57]. Ces quelques exemples non exhaustifs pour l'année 1806 sont néanmoins représentatifs. Dans le même esprit, un rapide coup d'œil sur le mois de février 1814 permet de relever les représentations d'ouvrages lyriques de Dalayrac (3), Isouard, Solié, Devienne et Gluck à Stockholm[58], de Cherubini et Méhul à Königsberg[59], de Cherubini et Spontini à Vienne[60], et d'Isouard et Cherubini à Lemberg[61].

Le goût prononcé du public allemand pour l'art lyrique français transparaît également à la lecture des nombreuses recensions consacrées par le périodique de Leipzig aux partitions d'opéras ou d'opéras-comiques — et à leurs multiples produits dérivés — de Berton[62], Boieldieu[63], Bruni[64], Catel[65], Cherubini[66], Dalayrac[67], Gaveaux[68], Gluck[69], Grétry[70], Isouard[71], Jadin[72], Kreutzer[73], Méhul[74], Solié[75], etc.

En dehors d'une couverture très large, mais nécessairement partielle, des milliers de représentations d'opéras-comiques et d'opéras français données outre-Rhin sous le Consulat et l'Empire, l'intérêt du lectorat de l'*Allgemeine musikalische Zeitung* pour la musique française est également entretenu à travers la rubrique 'Anekdote' qui est régulièrement placée en fin de journal. Plusieurs dizaines de ces anecdotes se rapportent à un instrumentiste, chanteur

---

57. *AMZ* 1806[T].
58. *AMZ* 1814[E].
59. *AMZ* 1814[F].
60. *AMZ* 1814[I].
61. *AMZ* 1802[E1-F1]; *AMZ* 1803[R]; *AMZ* 1814[J].
62. *AMZ* 1804[A]; *AMZ* 1802[N]. Voir REICHARDT 2002, pp. 100, 347-348.
63. *AMZ* 1813[J]; *AMZ* 1814[S]. Voir WEBER 1975, pp. 200-203; REICHARDT 2002, pp. 226, 305-307; KOTZEBUE 1804, p. 183.
64. *AMZ* 1802[N].
65. *AMZ* 1814[T]. Voir WEBER 1908, pp. 300-301.
66. *AMZ* 1801[U-V]; *AMZ* 1802[B1]; *AMZ* 1802[J]; *AMZ* 1806[S]; *AMZ* 1813[C]. Voir WEBER 1975, pp. 126-128, 206-209; REICHARDT 2002, pp. 68-69; SPOHR 1861, pp. 114-116; KOTZEBUE 1804, p. 177.
67. *AMZ* 1802[J]; *AMZ* 1802[N]. Voir WEBER 1908, pp. 113-115; REICHARDT 2002, p. 226.
68. *AMZ* 1799[D]. Voir WEBER 1908, pp. 268-269; REICHARDT 2002, p. 130.
69. *AMZ* 1808[E]; *AMZ* 1812[L]. Voir *AMZ* 1799[I]. Voir aussi *AMZ* 1800[A]; *AMZ* 1804[Q].
70. *AMZ* 1805[B]; *AMZ* 1806[N]; *AMZ* 1814[L]. Voir WEBER 1975, pp. 203-205; REICHARDT 2002, pp. 222-223; SPOHR 1861, pp. 115-116; KOTZEBUE 1804, p. 179; CASTELLI 1861, p. 88.
71. *AMZ* 1812[E]. Voir WEBER 1908, pp. 102-104, 266-268, 289-291; REICHARDT 2002, p. 200.
72. *AMZ* 1802[J]; *AMZ* 1802[N]. Voir REICHARDT 2002, p. 146.
73. *AMZ* 1803[J]. Voir SPOHR 1861, pp. 118-119.
74. *AMZ* 1802[J]; *AMZ* 1803[R]; *AMZ* 1812[K]. Voir WEBER 1975, pp. 197-200; REICHARDT 2002, pp. 69, 77-79, 130, 340-341, 423, 428-429; SPOHR 1861, p. 140; KOTZEBUE 1804, p. 175; HOFFMANN 2007, pp. 453-460.
75. *AMZ* 1802[J]. Voir *AMZ* 1812[I].

ou compositeur de nationalité française ou actif en France, parfois en contact avec un ancien roi de France ou l'empereur Napoléon I[er], ou bien ont trait à un quelconque fait divers lié à la musique française[76]. Parmi les musiciens concernés figurent les compositeurs Cimarosa[77], Gluck[78], Lully[79], Paisiello[80], Piccinni[81] et Rousseau[82], la cantatrice Mademoiselle de Maupin[83], le chanteur Charles-Louis-Dominique Chassé de Chinais[84] et le violoncelliste Duport[85]. À notre connaissance, l'article le plus improbable publié dans le très sérieux périodique allemand est constitué de deux lettres traduites du français, parues en février 1802 et consacrées à l'influence supposée de la musique sur la sexualité des éléphants, à la suite d'un concert orchestral spécialement organisé au jardin des Plantes à Paris en mai 1798 pour un couple de pachydermes. Le lecteur apprend que le gardien des deux animaux les a surpris de nuit en plein ébat, alors qu'ils étaient toujours restés chastes auparavant. Cet événement inédit étant survenu peu de temps après le concert, l'auteur de l'article spécule sur un éventuel lien de causalité. Il souhaite tester l'effet de la musique sur les deux éléphants placés en semi-liberté dans un parc et observer si de nouveaux ébats seraient occasionnés par l'audition musicale. Les musiciens et le gardien seraient placés hors de vue des animaux[86].

## Exécution et représentation d'œuvres allemandes en France

Entre 1798 et 1815, l'*Allgemeine musikalische Zeitung* possède un excellent réseau de correspondants répartis non seulement dans les principales villes allemandes, mais aussi dans la plupart des centres musicaux européens. Ce réseau lui permet de publier chaque année une centaine de comptes rendus consacrés à l'actualité musicale d'une ville en particulier, qu'elle appartienne ou non au monde germanique. Dans ce vaste corpus, Paris est de loin la ville étrangère qui bénéficie du plus grande nombre d'articles. Cette différence apparaît de manière flagrante à la lecture des tables des matières annuelles du périodique, lorsque l'on compare les villes présentées de manière alphabétique à la rubrique 'Nachrichten' entre 1798 et 1805, puis

---

76. *AMZ* 1798[B]; *AMZ* 1799[A]; *AMZ* 1799[M]; *AMZ* 1799[R]; *AMZ* 1799[W-X]; *AMZ* 1799[Z]; *AMZ* 1800[E]; *AMZ* 1801[M]; *AMZ* 1802[C1]; *AMZ* 1805[J]; *AMZ* 1814[F]; *AMZ* 1814[G]. Voir *AMZ* 1812[G-H].
77. *AMZ* 1798[C]; *AMZ* 1800[D].
78. *AMZ* 1800[G]; *AMZ* 1802[V].
79. *AMZ* 1800[I]; *AMZ* 1802[X].
80. *AMZ* 1798[C]; *AMZ* 1800[D]. Voir *AMZ* 1806[C]. Voir aussi 1806[E].
81. *AMZ* 1798[C]; *AMZ* 1800[G]. Voir *AMZ* 1801[S].
82. *AMZ* 1800[X]. Voir *AMZ* 1799[Y].
83. *AMZ* 1800[U].
84. *AMZ* 1814[A].
85. *AMZ* 1803[P].
86. *AMZ* 1799[E].

'Correspondenz' entre 1805 et 1815. Publié en 1801-1802, le quatrième volume ne contient ainsi pas moins de seize comptes rendus consacrés à Paris[87], contre deux seulement à Prague et un à Copenhague, Londres, Moscou, Saint-Pétersbourg et Varsovie. Dans ce volume, la capitale française compte même plus d'articles que les principales villes germaniques, telles que Dresde (11), Hambourg (8), Vienne (8), Leipzig (6) ou Stuttgart (5), alors que Brême, Cologne, Francfort-sur-le-Main, Hanovre, Munich ou Nuremberg ne sont pas mentionnées. Seule Berlin, avec vingt comptes rendus, dépasse la capitale française. De même, Paris compte dix-sept comptes rendus dans le cinquième volume[88], treize dans le sixième volume[89], huit dans le septième volume[90], etc[91]. Sur la seule foi des tables des matières annuelles, on obtient le tableau suivant:

Tableau 1
Nombre de comptes rendus par volume et par ville à la rubrique 'Nachrichten'
dans les tables des matières annuelles de l'*Allgemeine musikalische Zeitung* entre 1798 et 1815

| Vol. | Année | Berlin | Vienne | Leipzig | Paris | Dresde | Hambourg | Milan | Londres | Copenhague | Moscou |
|---|---|---|---|---|---|---|---|---|---|---|---|
| 1 | 1798-99 | 2 | – | 2 | 2 | – | 10 | – | – | 1 | – |
| 2 | 1799-00 | 5 | 1 | 3 | 6 | – | – | 1 | 1 | – | – |
| 3 | 1800-01 | 11 | 19 | – | 12 | 9 | 2 | 2 | 2 | – | 3 |
| 4 | 1801-02 | 20 | 8 | 6 | 16 | 11 | 8 | – | 1 | 1 | 1 |
| 5 | 1802-03 | 16 | 15 | 9 | 17 | 10 | 1 | 1 | 3 | 1 | 1 |
| 6 | 1803-04 | 13 | 17 | 7 | 13 | 4 | – | – | 1 | – | – |
| 7 | 1804-05 | 20 | 18 | 11 | 8 | 1 | – | – | 2 | – | – |
| 8 | 1805-06 | 20 | 12 | 8 | 4 | 6 | – | – | – | – | – |
| 9 | 1806-07 | 18 | 12 | 16 | 1 | 3 | – | – | 1 | – | – |
| 10 | 1807-08 | 21 | 12 | 14 | 3 | 1 | 1 | – | – | – | – |
| 11 | 1808-09 | 15 | 15 | 16 | 6 | 1 | – | – | – | – | – |
| 12 | 1809-10 | 26 | 17 | 12 | 7 | 4 | 1 | 3 | – | – | – |
| 13 | 1811 | 17 | 12 | 10 | 5 | – | 2 | 2 | – | – | – |
| 14 | 1812 | 13 | 13 | 10 | 4 | 9 | 1 | 3 | – | 1 | – |
| 15 | 1813 | 11 | 14 | 5 | 3 | 2 | – | 5 | – | 1 | – |
| 16 | 1814 | 11 | 13 | 8 | – | 6 | – | 5 | – | – | – |
| 17 | 1815 | 13 | 13 | 7 | – | 3 | – | 1 | 2 | 1 | – |
| TOT. |  | 252 | 211 | 144 | 107 | 70 | 26 | 23 | 13 | 6 | 5 |

---

87. *AMZ* 1801[B1-C1]; *AMZ* 1801[E1]; *AMZ* 1801[G1]; *AMZ* 1802[C-D]; *AMZ* 1802[M]; *AMZ* 1802[O-R]; *AMZ* 1802[U]; *AMZ* 1802[W]; *AMZ* 1802[Y-Z]; *AMZ* 1802[D1]; *AMZ* 1802[G1].
88. *AMZ* 1802[J1-N1]; *AMZ* 1803[A-G]; *AMZ* 1803[I]; *AMZ* 1803[K-O].
89. *AMZ* 1803[Q]; *AMZ* 1803[S-U]; *AMZ* 1804[B-C]; *AMZ* 1804[G]; *AMZ* 1804[I-M].
90. *AMZ* 1804[N-P]; *AMZ* 1805[A]; *AMZ* 1805[D-G].
91. Voir *AMZ* 1800[B-C]; *AMZ* 1800[F]; *AMZ* 1800[J-K]; *AMZ* 1800[M]; *AMZ* 1800[O]; *AMZ* 1800[Y]; *AMZ* 1800[F1-G1]; *AMZ* 1801[B-C]; *AMZ* 1801[G-J]; *AMZ* 1801[L]; *AMZ* 1801[P-Q]; *AMZ* 1801[T]; *AMZ* 1801[Y]; *AMZ* 1801[F1]; *AMZ* 1808[A]; *AMZ* 1808[G]; *AMZ* 1809[A-B]; *AMZ* 1809[D]; *AMZ* 1809[G-I]; *AMZ* 1809[K-L]; *AMZ* 1810[A-B]; *AMZ* 1810[D-E]; *AMZ* 1811[C-F]; *AMZ* 1812[A]; *AMZ* 1812[F]; *AMZ* 1812[J]; *AMZ* 1813[B]; *AMZ* 1813[E-F].

## ÉTUDE DES TRANSFERTS MUSICAUX FRANCO-ALLEMANDS À L'ÉPOQUE NAPOLÉONIENNE

L'idée première de ce tableau est de comparer Paris avec neuf autres villes, à savoir cinq des principales villes du monde germanique, trois capitales européennes et Milan qui devient au XIXe siècle le premier centre musical italien. Il s'agit nécessairement d'un choix arbitraire, car une centaine de villes seraient à considérer sur l'ensemble de la période étudiée. Avec 107 articles, Paris est certes distancée par les deux plus grands centres musicaux du monde germanique, Berlin (252) et Vienne (211), mais soutient la comparaison avec Leipzig (144) et Dresde (70), devance largement Hambourg (26) et laisse à très grande distance Milan (23), Londres (13), Copenhague (6) et Moscou (5). C'est sous le Consulat que l'intérêt pour la capitale française semble être le plus développé, avant de décliner progressivement sous l'Empire. Les années 1814 et 1815 sont les seules où Paris ne compte aucun compte rendu, c'est-à-dire au moment de l'effondrement de l'Empire et d'une période très perturbée en France sur le plan politique. Seules deux autres villes françaises apparaissent à la rubrique 'Nachrichten' entre 1798 et 1815: Versailles avec un article en 1801 et Strasbourg avec dix articles au total en 1814 et 1815. Tous ces nombres sont à prendre avec précaution, car ils ne tiennent pas compte de la longueur relative des articles, ni de l'absence de plusieurs centaines d'articles dédiés à la vie musicale parisienne, à travers les domaines de l'édition, de la facture instrumentale[92], de questions d'ordre esthétique, d'anecdotes, etc., qui ne figurent pas à la rubrique 'Nachrichten'. De plus, certains articles qui appartiennent de toute évidence à cette rubrique ont été omis dans les tables des matières, ce qui relativise la valeur absolue des nombres présentés ci-dessus.

À l'instar des récits de voyage de Kotzebue, Reichardt, Spohr et Castelli[93], la centaine de comptes rendus consacrés à Paris jusqu'en 1813 dans le périodique musical de Leipzig examinent de manière préférentielle l'activité des trois théâtres lyriques de la capitale: l'Opéra de Paris, l'Opéra-Comique et le Théâtre-Italien. D'autres sujets récurrents concernent l'activité des théâtres secondaires, l'organisation de concerts, l'actualité des interprètes et des compositeurs, le Conservatoire de Paris, l'Académie des Beaux-Arts, etc. Dans ce vaste corpus, un certain nombre d'articles évoquent l'exécution ou la représentation d'œuvres allemandes en France et seront analysés ici.

Sans surprise, l'ouvrage allemand représenté à Paris qui requiert la plus grande attention outre-Rhin est *Die Zauberflöte* de Schikaneder et Mozart, adapté sous le nom de *Mystères d'Isis* par Morel de Chédeville et Lachnith[94]. C'est sous cette forme que le *Singspiel* mozartien est connu du public de l'Opéra de Paris entre 1801 et 1827. La première représentation des *Mystères d'Isis* est donnée sur cette scène le 20 août 1801. Un artiste allemand anonyme installé dans la capitale française fait paraître le 28 octobre son analyse de l'ouvrage, tandis qu'un extrait de la

---

[92]. Voir *AMZ* 1799[N]; *AMZ* 1801[X]; *IBAMZ* 1806[I].

[93]. Kotzebue 1804; Kotzebue 1805; Reichardt 1804; Spohr 1860; Spohr 1861, pp. 113-143; Castelli 1861.

[94]. Valle 2014.

partition est ajouté en supplément au même numéro de l'*Allgemeine musikalische Zeitung*[95]. Avant une étude détaillée de l'opéra, l'artiste commence son article par un jugement général d'une grande sévérité:

> Seyn Sie vorsichtig, und urtheilen Sie nicht ganz sicher aus dem, was Sie von den Aeusserungen der hiesigen Musikkenner und des hiesigen Publikums über diese Vorstellung zu lesen bekommen möchten, über den Stand der hiesigen musikal. Kultur und des Geschmacks an musik. Kunstprodukten bey beyden: es ist eigentlich nicht wahr, dass man Mozarts Zauberflöte gegeben habe; es war eine Oper aus dieser, aus D. Juan, der Clemenza di Tito, und Figaro von Mozart, nebst eigenen Zusätzen des Hrn. Lachnith zusammengemacht. Alle die M. Oper schon genauer kannten, sind darüber erbittert, und lassen Bonmots auf Herrn Lachn. regnen. Die "Opéra" nennen sie seine "Opération"; die "les mystères d'Isis", "les misères d'ici" u. dgl. Es ist unmöglich, alle die Veränderungen, Zusätze, Abkürzungen, Versetzungen der Stücke aus der Zauberfl., mit welchen Hr. L. nicht etwa nur den Text, sondern die Musik zusammengearbeitet hat, anzuführen. Doch Einiges zur Probe muss ich Ihnen geben[96].

À la fin du compte rendu, Lachnith est raillé pour sa vanité face au succès de «son opéra», lequel lui assure de très confortables revenus, et pour sa menace d'adapter un second opéra de Mozart destiné au divertissement du public parisien. Témoignage précieux sur la vie musicale française sous le Consulat, les lettres de Johann Friedrich Reichardt écrites à Paris en 1802 et 1803 sont publiées à Hambourg en 1804 et font aussitôt l'objet d'une longue recension parue dans l'édition du 15 février de l'*Allgemeine musikalische Zeitung*[97]. Dans une lettre datée du 24 décembre 1802, Reichardt estime que *Les Mystères d'Isis* sont une «caricature de l'original» et une «abomination»[98]. Par la suite, Louis Spohr[99], Ferdinand Hérold[100] et Hector Berlioz ne se montreront pas moins critiques avec l'adaptateur, ce dernier qualifiant Lachnith de «crétin» et de «profanateur» dans ses *Mémoires*[101]. Pour revenir à la période étudiée, le périodique de Leipzig fait paraître le 17 février 1802 une recension de la *Fantaisie avec neuf Variations sur un air des Mystères d'Isis* pour le pianoforte de Steibelt[102]. Le 10 août 1803, c'est un très court article qui vient une nouvelle fois dénoncer l'adaptation de Lachnith sous la forme d'un trait d'esprit: «*Pariser Zauberflöte*. / Nehmt unsern Dank; ihr halft sankt Mozart aus den Nöthen! / Der

---

[95]. *AMZ* 1801[D1].
[96]. *AMZ* 1801[C1]. Voir *AMZ* 1805[H1], *AMZ* 1812[D].
[97]. *AMZ* 1804[D].
[98]. Reichardt 2002, pp. 225-228. Voir *ibidem*, pp. 101-102; *AMZ* 1814[K].
[99]. Spohr 1861, pp. 117-118.
[100]. Dratwicki 2009. p. 338.
[101]. Berlioz 1991, pp. 105-107, 111.
[102]. *AMZ* 1802[E].

Zauber ist nun weg, habt ihr doch noch die Flöten!»[103]. Suite aux représentations des *Mystères d'Isis*, l'intérêt du public français pour Mozart gagne le terrain de la littérature. La traduction en français d'anecdotes sur ce compositeur, précédemment publiées dans l'*Allgemeine musikalische Zeitung* par son rédacteur Johann Friedrich Rochlitz, est ainsi l'objet d'une recension dans l'édition du 4 août 1802. Installé à Paris depuis 1795, le traducteur d'origine allemande Carl Friedrich Cramer est loué pour la qualité de son travail, mais est critiqué pour ne pas avoir cité ses sources et pour avoir remplacé le prénom Amadeus par Gottlieb[104]. Une courte notice nécrologique de Cramer est publiée le 9 mars 1808[105].

Seules cinq tournées de troupes lyriques allemandes sont organisées à Paris dans la première moitié du XIXᵉ siècle, au Théâtre de la Cité en 1801[106], au Théâtre-Italien en 1829, 1830 en 1831, puis au Théâtre Ventadour en 1842, outre un projet avorté de saison allemande au Théâtre Nautique en 1834[107]. La première d'entre elles est donc l'unique saison allemande mise en place dans la capitale française avant 1815. À l'automne 1801, soit quelques mois après la création des *Mystères d'Isis*, le Théâtre de la Cité est opportunément rebaptisé «Théâtre Mozart» et accueille les représentations de six *Singspiele* contemporains en langue originale: *Die Entführung aus dem Serail* (1782) de Mozart le 16 novembre 1801, *Das rote Käppchen* (1788) de Karl Ditters von Dittersdorf le 21 novembre, *Das neue Sonntagskind* (1793) de Wenzel Müller le 25 novembre, *Der Spiegel von Arkadien* (1794) de Franz Xaver Süssmayer le 29 novembre, *Der Tyroler Wastel* (1796) de Jakob Heibel le 30 novembre et *Das Sonnenfest der Braminen* (1790) de Wenzel Müller le 3 décembre. La saison compte douze représentations au total: trois pour le premier ouvrage, deux pour les quatre suivants et une pour le dernier. La troupe allemande qui interprète ce répertoire réunit une quinzaine de chanteurs et chanteuses placés sous la direction administrative de Haselmayer et la direction musicale du chef d'orchestre Blasius. Les premiers rôles sont confiés au ténor Walter, à la basse Ellmenreich et aux chanteuses Lüders et Lange. Cette dernière, de son nom de jeune fille Aloysia Weber, est la belle-sœur de Mozart, un lien de parenté apparemment ignoré du public parisien[108]. L'organisation de la saison allemande au Théâtre de la Cité et le recrutement des chanteurs sont annoncés par l'*Allgemeine musikalische Zeitung* dans son édition du 11 novembre 1801: «Paris, Ende Okt. Die Gesellschaft, die die Errichtung einer deutschen Oper entworfen hat, und den Enthusiasmus, der für deutsche Opernmusik sich hier zu zeigen anfängt, zu benutzen gedenkt, gehet rasch zu Werke in der Ausführung ihres Plans»[109]. Le déroulement de la saison est rapporté de manière détaillée dans

---

103. *AMZ* 1803ᴸ.
104. *AMZ* 1802^{A1}.
105. *AMZ* 1808ᶜ.
106. Mongrédien 1986.
107. Cailliez 2014.
108. Mongrédien 1986.
109. *AMZ* 1801^{E1}.

l'édition du 10 février 1802. Le correspondant du périodique est choqué par le faible niveau de la troupe, par le voisinage du *Singspiel* de Mozart avec ceux de Dittersdorf, Müller, Süssmayer et Haibel, qu'il juge triviaux en comparaison, ainsi que par le comportement malhonnête du directeur Haselmayer, lequel fuit ses responsabilités :

> [...] man gab nun mit dem übrigen Kram zwey Vorstellungen – wovon? von dem neuen Sonntagskind, zwey, von dem Spiegel aus Arkadien, und zwey vom – Tyroler Wastel – vom Tyroler hier! Vom Wastel und Praterwirth hier! Die Entweihung des Namens Mozart durch solches Zeug war dem Publikum ein Greuel; und trotz den Zeitungen, die immer so galant waren, mehr Gutes als Böses von diesem Theater zu sagen, kam niemand mehr, welches denn den Direktor bewog, sich Nachts aus dem Staube zu machen, und alle seine Leute, nebst dem ganzen Orchester, unbezahlt, in der grössten Verlegenheit zu lassen[110].

Sous l'ère napoléonienne, certains compositeurs allemands tentent leur chance au Théâtre de l'Opéra-Comique avec des fortunes diverses. Reichardt souhaite sans succès y faire représenter en 1803 son *Singspiel* intitulé *Die Geisterinsel* (1798)[111]. Ancien rival pianistique de Beethoven à Vienne, Joseph Wölfl compte deux opéras-comiques représentés sur cette scène, *L'Amour romanesque* le 3 mars 1804[112] et *Fernando ou les Maures* le 11 février 1805[113]. Daniel Steibelt[114], Bernhard Heinrich Romberg et Joseph Weigl y font représenter chacun un ouvrage, respectivement *Roméo et Juliette* le 19 octobre 1801, *Dom Mendoze ou le Tuteur portugais* le 15 février 1802 et *La Vallée suisse* le 31 octobre 1812[115]. La version originale allemande de ce dernier ouvrage, *Die Schweizerfamilie* (1809), connaît au même moment une large diffusion dans le monde germanique[116].

Alors que le périodique de Leipzig ne publie aucun compte rendu sur l'actualité musicale de Strasbourg entre 1798 et 1813, la situation change radicalement à partir de 1814. Entre 1814 et 1847, la vie théâtrale strasbourgeoise, aussi bien française qu'allemande, suscite en effet des rapports annuels systématiques et circonstanciés, sauf en 1828[117]. Dix comptes rendus sur l'actualité musicale de Strasbourg, cinq par an, sont ainsi publiés en 1814 et 1815[118]. Deux saisons allemandes sont étudiées avec attention, celle d'une troupe originaire d'Augsbourg et

---

[110]. *AMZ* 1802[C].
[111]. *AMZ* 1803[D].
[112]. *AMZ* 1804[I]. Voir *AMZ* 1801[G1].
[113]. *AMZ* 1805[E].
[114]. Voir *AMZ* 1802[C].
[115]. Wild – Charlton 2005.
[116]. Weber 1975, pp. 191-192.
[117]. Cailliez 2014.
[118]. *AMZ* 1814[O]; *AMZ* 1814[R]; *AMZ* 1814[V.W]; *AMZ* 1814[Y]; *AMZ* 1815[C-D]; *AMZ* 1815[F-H].

dirigée par Müller durant l'été 1813, puis celle d'une troupe en provenance de Mayence et dirigée par le Baron von Lichtenstein, laquelle donne vingt représentations dans la capitale alsacienne entre le 22 juin et le 24 septembre 1814. Le répertoire des troupes allemandes de passage à Strasbourg dans la première moitié du XIXᵉ siècle est typique du répertoire habituel des théâtres lyriques allemands de cette époque, avec un mélange d'opéras allemands en langue originale et d'opéras français et italiens en traduction.

Tandis que le théâtre lyrique allemand reste peu familier du public français sous le Consulat et l'Empire, la musique instrumentale germanique connaît une large diffusion à Paris depuis la deuxième moitié du XVIIIᵉ siècle et les œuvres de Joseph Haydn en particulier y jouissent d'une solide réputation, comme cela a été vu dans la première partie de cet article. Cette diffusion se poursuivra tout au long du XIXᵉ siècle, en particulier dans le domaine de la musique de chambre[119]. Le 16 septembre 1801, le périodique de Leipzig publie *in extenso* et en langue originale une «Copie de la lettre adressée à J. Haydn par les artistes françois, en lui faisant agréer l'hommage de la Médaille-d'or, qu'ils lui ont décernée». Réunis à l'Opéra de Paris pour une exécution de l'oratorio *La Création*, les artistes français, «pénétrés d'une juste admiration» pour le génie de Haydn, multiplient les louanges: «Il ne se passe pas une année qu'une nouvelle production de ce Compositeur sublime ne vienne enchanter les artistes, éclairer leurs travaux, ajouter aux progrès de l'art, étendre encore les routes immenses de l'harmonie, et prouver qu'elles n'ont pas de bornes en suivant les traces lumineuses dont Haydn embellit le présent et sait enrichir l'avenir»[120]. Le 20 février 1811, c'est la *Notice historique sur la vie et les ouvrages de Joseph Haydn* (1810) de Joachim Le Breton, destinée à célébrer la mémoire du prestigieux membre associé de l'Institut de France, qui donne lieu à une recension[121].

## Musique et politique

L'actualité politique et les guerres napoléoniennes exercent une influence indéniable sur une partie de la production musicale publiée, diffusée ou recensée par l'*Allgemeine musikalische Zeitung* entre 1798 et 1815, qu'il s'agisse d'œuvres de circonstance, de pièces aux titres explicites, de dédicaces à l'Empereur français ou à des membres de sa famille, ou bien encore des commentaires de certains rédacteurs[122]. Le compte rendu de l'actualité musicale parisienne publié dans l'édition du 20 novembre 1805 évoque l'atmosphère nationaliste liée aux dernières conquêtes napoléoniennes. Le correspondant du périodique insiste en particulier

---

[119]. Fauquet 1986.
[120]. *AMZ* 1801^A1.
[121]. *AMZ* 1811^B. Voir *AMZ* 1802^D; Reichardt 2002, pp. 271-272.
[122]. Voir *AMZ* 1799^B.

sur la perméabilité des genres entre musique dramatique et musique militaire, manifeste dans la plupart des théâtres de la capitale française:

> Die üppigen Ballette auf dem grossen kaiserlichen, und die bald wilden, bald militairischen, Pomp-Spektakel – und Maschinenstücke auf kleinern, aber viel besuchten Theatern, werden immer mehr Hauptsache; und nur einige der immer fes[t]stehenden, ältern Opern, besonders der Gluckschen, (z. B. je[t]zt die Armide,) behandelt man immer noch mit gewissem Anstand, vielleicht dürft' ich sagen, respektuöser, patriotischer Scheu — ungefähr wie die Hauptwerke Corneille's und Racine's[123].

Le correspondant poursuit sa chronique avec l'analyse des dernières créations au Théâtre de l'Opéra-Comique, à savoir *Gulistan ou le Hulla de Samarcande* de Dalayrac, *Le Grand-Père ou les Deux Âges* de Jadin et *Chacun son tour* de Solié, trois œuvres représentées pour la première fois aux mois de septembre et d'octobre 1805. Il donne ensuite quelques nouvelles des autres théâtres parisiens, avant de conclure son article sur un ton ironique et désabusé: «in fast allen Theatern tönen zwischen den Akten Jubelgesänge auf die Siege der grossen Armee nach Volksmelodieen: sagen Sie, um Himmels willen, was wollen die Kunstfreunde mehr — die eleganten, die feinen?»[124]. Le compte rendu de l'actualité musicale parisienne publié dans l'édition du 15 janvier 1806 est également riche d'éléments à cet égard: «Es hat etwas Schauerliches für den Freund der Werke des Friedens, zu sehn, wie das ungeheure Glück unsrer Waffen hier aufgenommen und genossen wird. Man achtet die Gaben der Musen nicht mehr — wenigstens ists Ton, Geringschätzung derselben zu Tage zu legen; und vielleicht bedarf es nur noch weniger Jahre, und es ist Ton, sie zu verachten»[125]. Le correspondant continue son article en rapportant les nombreuses créations qui s'enchaînent au Théâtre du Vaudeville. Alors qu'il s'apprête à détailler le contenu d'une pièce patriotique française intitulée *La Prise de Vienne*, la suite de son compte rendu est volontairement coupée par le rédacteur du périodique allemand, lequel justifie immédiatement le motif de son intervention:

> Auf dieser Bühne schiessen die Neuigkeiten auf, wie Schwämme; es wäre aber vergebens, sie Ihnen zu nennen, weil sie auch so schnell wie Schwämme wieder verschwinden und immer nur zunächst ein lokales Interesse haben — ich müsste Ihnen denn das Stück, was eben je[t]zt vielfältig beklatscht wird: La prise de Vienne, anführen, das zu grosser Erbauung des deutschen Publikums verpflanzt werden könnte und worin —

---

[123]. *AMZ* 1805ᴷ.
[124]. *Ibidem.*
[125]. *AMZ* 1806ᴮ.

> (Der Herr Verfasser muthe uns nicht zu, dass wir diese Stelle, so witzig sie ist, in einem Journal zunächst für dieselbe Nation abdrucken lassen, die man möglichst unglücklich gemacht hat. Es ist nicht im Charakter der Deutschen, über dieselben Ereignisse zu scherzen, deren Druck man unverschuldet und eben je[t]zt noch so tief fühlt — wenn es auch im Charakter des Franzosen ist, und er darin das beste Erleichterungsmittel findet.            D. Redakt[126].)

L'entrée triomphale de Napoléon I[er] à Vienne le 14 novembre 1805, à la tête de sa Grande Armée et fort de sa victoire décisive lors de la bataille d'Ulm, est en effet peu susceptible de réjouir le lectorat allemand. La suite de l'article précise les concerts et représentations donnés à l'Opéra de Paris, au Théâtre-Italien, à l'Opéra-Comique et au Théâtre de la Porte-Saint-Martin avant le 26 décembre 1805. La fin elliptique du compte rendu, sous-entendant la vaste diffusion de pièces patriotiques dans la capitale, provoque une nouvelle intervention amère du rédacteur de l'*Allgemeine musikalische Zeitung*:

> Oder, können Sie etwa die musikalischen Neuigkeiten brauchen, die man je[t]zt hier überall trödeln trägt, überall absingt, und wovon ich hier nur beylege, was ich eben ohne Mühe zusammenraffen kann? Es versteht sich, dass sich viel mehr zusammen bringen liessen! –
>
> (Es sind Kriegs-, Sieges-, Jubellieder, meistens auf Melodieen bekannter Operncouplets und dgl., und nur – neunzehn an der Zahl, wovon aber auch nicht Eins einigen, nur mässigen poetischen Werth hat. Die meisten sind den „braven Soldaten" in den Mund gelegt, und wenn man bedenkt, dass eine gewisse Art der Bildung wirklich selbst unter den Gemeinen der ältern französischen Regimenter herrscht, so muss man gestehn, dass allerdings „die braven Kameraden" so gedichtet haben könnten. Wir verschonen unsre Leser damit. Sie werden nun lieber Friedenslieder singen – die nämlich, denen die Lust zu singen überhaupt noch geblieben ist.            D. Redakt)[127].

Alors que le monde germanique a soif de liberté, le refus du périodique de mettre en valeur le répertoire nationaliste du peuple conquérant est parfaitement compréhensible. De nombreuses pièces aux titres explicites sont cependant évoquées par ailleurs dans le même journal. Certaines sont en faveur de Napoléon, de ses victoires militaires, de son sacre et de sa famille. Le 20 mars 1799 paraît ainsi une recension de la *Marche du Général Buonaparte, variée et dédiée à Madame Loehr née Bause*, d'August Eberhard Müller[128]. Deux pièces de Daniel Steibelt sont recensées les 3 mars et 15 juin 1802, à savoir la *Grande Sonate pour le Pianoforte composée*

---

[126]. *Ibidem*.
[127]. *Ibidem*. Voir *AMZ* 1800[D1]; *AMZ* 1809[C].
[128]. *AMZ* 1799[J].

*et dédiée à Madame Bonaparte*[129] et *La grande Marche de Bonaparte en Italie, composée pour le Fortépiano avec accompagnement de Tambourin*[130]. La deuxième recension commence par un jugement lapidaire sur la piètre valeur musicale de ce répertoire apologétique: «Man verstehe das grande auf dem Titel recht; es soll, ausserdem, dass es das Werkchen besser verkaufen helfen soll, diesen Marsch von dem allgemein bekannten und so oft variirten sogenannten Bonaparte-Marsch unterscheiden: übrigens ist gar nichts Grosses daran und darin»[131]. Les annexes de l'*Allgemeine musikalische Zeitung* indiquent quelques pièces similaires publiées par différents éditeurs et disponibles à la vente chez Breitkopf und Härtel. En juillet 1802 est ainsi mentionnée la *Victoire de l'armée d'Italie ou Bataille de Montenolle* pour le pianoforte ou orgue de Jacques-Marie Beauvarlet-Charpentier[132]. Suite à la bataille du 2 décembre 1805, le même auteur compose une œuvre similaire qui, à notre connaissance, n'a pas été mise en vente à Leipzig: *Bataille d'Austerlitz / Surnommée la Journée / Des Trois Empereurs / pièce militaire et historique / Pour le Forte-Piano / Avec Accompagnement de Violon / Précédée des Réjouissances du Camp Français / pour l'Anniversaire du Couronnement de S. M. / l'Empereur Napoléon / dédiée / à la Grande Armée*. Trois pièces louant le sacre de l'empereur et son nouveau statut apparaissent pourtant dans les annexes du périodique en décembre 1805 et janvier 1806: la *Marche à l'entrée de l'Empereur Napoléon au Dôme des Invalides* de Méhul et la *Marche au Couronnement de l'Empereur Napoléon* de Lesueur, toutes deux arrangées pour le pianoforte[133], ainsi que la partition et les parties séparées du *Vivat in aeternum*, le motet du sacre de Napoléon I[er] composé par Nicolas Roze[134].

Dans l'autre sens et plus tardivement, l'*Allgemeine musikalische Zeitung* met aussi en valeur dans ses colonnes le répertoire patriotique allemand, se joignant à l'élan nationaliste impulsé par les *Befreiungskriege* entre 1813 et 1815. Une recension parue le 2 février 1814 encourage la publication des *Sechs deutsche Kriegslieder* pour une ou plusieurs voix, avec chœur et accompagnement de piano *ad libitum*, mis en musique par Albert Methfessel:

> Es ist ganz recht, dass zu einer Zeit, wo jeder sein Opfer auf den Altar des Vaterlands legt, auch der Künstler nicht zurückbleibe; und kann er nicht für dasselbe fechten, fehlen ihm auch Mittel, die Fechtenden zu unterstützen, diese wenigstens ermuntern und erfreuen will – allerdings, ohne dafür selbst noch nebenbey einigen Vortheil zu suchen. Das hat denn Hr. M. gethan, indem er diese Lieder zum Besten kranker und verwundeter Krieger herausgab; und da sich mit ihm eine liberale Handlung zum Debit ohne alle Entschädigung verband: (hoffentlich werden ihr mehrere folgen:) so konnte der Preis, des anständigen Aeussern ungeachtet, so sehr

---

[129]. *AMZ* 1802[F]. Voir *AMZ* 1813[D].
[130]. *AMZ* 1802[S].
[131]. Ibidem.
[132]. *IBAMZ* 1802[H].
[133]. *IBAMZ* 1805[E].
[134]. *IBAMZ* 1806[B].

> gering angesetzt, und doch wird, bey beträchtlichem Absatz, ein Namhaftes für
> jenen wohltätigen Zweck erreicht werden[135].

L'article de six pages propose ensuite une analyse des six chants de guerre avec quelques exemples sur partition. L'exemple musical le plus long correspond au troisième chant, intitulé *Schlachtgesang*, dont les paroles exaltent l'éveil de la nation allemande, la soif de liberté et le combat pour la patrie. Ces paroles sont soutenues par le rythme martial d'un soliste renforcé par un chœur à trois voix chantant en *ré* majeur sur la nuance *fortissimo*. La recension se conclut par une très nette prise de position en faveur des guerres de libération, soulignée par le point d'exclamation final: «Möge übrigens dies Werkchen, zu dem wir den Dichtern und dem Componisten Glück wünschen, recht viel beytragen, jenen Sinn unter den deutschen Kriegern zu befestigen, mit dem man nicht blos siegt, sondern auch zu siegen, und dann des Friedens zu geniessen, wahrhaft würdig ist!»[136]. La partition du Lied *Des Deutschen Vaterland* de Carl Theodor Moritz est ajoutée en supplément à l'édition du 1ᵉʳ juin 1814. Les huit couplets de ce chant strophique soutiennent l'idée selon laquelle la patrie allemande ne correspondrait pas à une ou plusieurs régions déterminées, telles que la Bavière, la Poméranie, la Westphalie, la Prusse, la Rhénanie, le Tyrol ou la Styrie, mais à «toute l'Allemagne», c'est-à-dire à l'ensemble du monde germanique, Suisse et Autriche incluses[137]. Basée sur l'accord parfait ascendant de *fa* majeur, la mélodie est à interpréter selon les indications «kraftvoll und feurig». Le même numéro du périodique de Leipzig propose la recension d'un autre chant patriotique, *Zuruf an die deutschen Brüdern am Rhein*, sur un texte d'Oswald mis en musique par Seidel, édité par Schlesinger à Berlin. Il s'agit d'un chant de circonstance composé après la bataille de Leipzig, dite «bataille des nations», qui a opposé du 16 au 19 octobre 1813 la Grande Armée à une large coalition réunissant des troupes venues de Prusse, d'Autriche, de Suède et de Russie[138]. Une recension de la petite cantate *Der Engel auf dem Schlachtfeld* de Johann Philipp Samuel Schmidt, pour voix soliste et chœur, paraît dans l'édition du 10 août 1814[139]. Le 24 août, c'est au tour du *Patriotischer Rundgesang für fröhliche Zirkel*, extrait de la pièce de théâtre *Das Dorf an der Gränze* mise en musique par Bernhard Anselm Weber, de faire l'objet d'un article analytique[140]. Deux autres recensions de chants patriotiques suivent à la fin de l'année 1814, consacrées respectivement au *Lobgesang auf die Retter Deutschlands, die allerhöchsten verbündeten Monarchen* de Heinrich Anton Hoffmann le 26 octobre[141], et aux *Kriegslieder* de

---

[135]. *AMZ* 1814ᴰ.
[136]. *Ibidem*.
[137]. *AMZ* 1814ᴺ.
[138]. *AMZ* 1814ᴹ.
[139]. *AMZ* 1814ᴾ.
[140]. *AMZ* 1814ᵠ.
[141]. *AMZ* 1814ᵁ.

Johann Otto Heinrich Schaum le 7 décembre[142]. L'intérêt pour ce répertoire reste soutenu en 1815 avec de nouvelles publications[143]. Des compositeurs de premier plan, tels que Ludwig van Beethoven, Louis Spohr et Carl Maria von Weber, ne dédaignent pas non plus la composition de pièces patriotiques de circonstance, le premier avec sa pièce orchestrale *Wellingtons Sieg oder die Schlacht bei Vittoria* qui triomphe à Vienne en 1813[144], le second avec sa cantate *Das befreite Deutschland* composée en 1814[145] et le troisième avec sa cantate *Kampf und Sieg* en 1815 pour fêter la victoire de Waterloo. Weber écrit en janvier 1816 un long article explicatif sur sa cantate, enrichi de nombreux exemples musicaux[146]. L'article ne sera cependant pas publié de son vivant. De son côté, Ernst Theodor Amadeus Hoffmann profite de sa recension négative du *Nouveau Seigneur de village* de Boieldieu, parue le 5 octobre 1814 dans l'*Allgemeine musikalische Zeitung*, pour condamner la très large diffusion des opéras-comiques français en Allemagne, une diffusion qu'il associe de manière transparente en fin d'article à l'invasion du monde germanique par les troupes napoléoniennes[147].

En conclusion, le dépouillement comparatif des dix-sept premiers volumes annuels de l'*Allgemeine musikalische Zeitung* offre une multitude d'informations complémentaires sur l'ampleur et l'intensité des transferts musicaux franco-allemands en action sous le Consulat et l'Empire. Le rôle central de l'édition musicale est favorisé par l'implantation de nombreux professionnels allemands de ce secteur dans la capitale française. La circulation des partitions dans les deux sens entre Paris et Leipzig est ainsi grandement facilitée. Que ce soit en langue originale ou en traduction, le public allemand dispose chez Breitkopf und Härtel d'un accès privilégié à un répertoire pléthorique d'œuvres françaises, de méthodes instrumentales du Conservatoire de Paris et d'essais sur la musique, et peut même se procurer les dernières nouveautés de la facture parisienne, telles que des harpes à pédales ou des archets[148]. Tandis que l'actualité musicale parisienne est suivie avec la plus grande attention, l'incroyable diffusion de l'art lyrique français dans le monde germanique est attestée par des centaines de comptes rendus et par de nombreuses recensions de partitions d'opéras ou de produits dérivés. Le lectorat est également informé de manière détaillée des représentations d'œuvres allemandes données à Paris. Alors que la rédaction du périodique exprime peu souvent une position politique dans les années 1800 et semble adopter une forme de neutralité vis-à-vis du régime napoléonien, la donne change au début des années 1810 avec la mise en valeur éditoriale des chants patriotiques allemands sur fond de *Befreiungskriege* ou guerres de libération.

---

[142]. *AMZ* 1814$^{\text{X}}$.
[143]. *AMZ* 1815$^{\text{A-B}}$.
[144]. *AMZ* 1814$^{\text{C}}$.
[145]. Spohr 1860, pp. 195-197.
[146]. Weber 1908, pp. 199-218.
[147]. *AMZ* 1814$^{\text{S}}$; Hoffmann 2007, pp. 355-359. Voir Spohr 1861, p. 123; Weber 1975, pp. 188, 215.
[148]. *IBAMZ* 1806$^{\text{I}}$.

# ÉTUDE DES TRANSFERTS MUSICAUX FRANCO-ALLEMANDS À L'ÉPOQUE NAPOLÉONIENNE

## Bibliographie

*AMZ* 1798

A. 'Kurze Anzeigen / Sonate pour le Pianoforte, par Grasset. Œuv. 3. Bey Ebend. [Offenbach bey André] (1 Fl.)', in: *Allgemeine musikalische Zeitung*, I/10 (5 décembre 1798), p. 158.

B. 'Anekdote', I/11 (12 décembre 1798), p. 176.

C. 'Anekdote', I/13 (26 décembre 1798), pp. 207-208.

*AMZ* 1799

A. 'Anekdoten [Duni, Grétry]', in: *Allgemeine musikalische Zeitung*, I/14 (2 janvier 1799), p. 224.

B. CHRISTMANN. 'Einige Ideen über den Geist der französischen Nationallieder, vom Pfarrer Christmann', I/15-17 (9, 16 et 23 janvier 1799), pp. 228-236, 246-250, 261-269.

C. 'Recensionen / *Suite des grandes Sonates pour le Clavecin ou Pianoforte, avec Accompagnement d'un Violon et Violoncelle, composées et dédiées à Mad. Martilière, par I. Pleyel*. Œuv. 55. liv. 7. 8. 9. Hummel. (chacune 1 Fl. 16 Xr.)', I/18 (30 janvier 1799), pp. 282-283.

D. 'Kurze Anzeigen / *Ouvertüre und Favoritgesänge aus der Oper: Der kleine Matrose, zum Singen am Fortepiano eingerichtet, in Musik gesetzt von Gaveaux*. Berlin bey Rellstab (1 Rthlr. 4 Gr.)', I/18 (30 janvier 1799), p. 288.

E. 'Von der Gewalt der Musik über die Thiere, und von dem Conzerte, das zu Paris den beyden Elephanten gegeben worden ist (aus dem Franz.)', I/19-20 (6 et 13 février 1799), pp. 298-304, 312-320.

F. 'Recension / Neueste Pariser Musikalien, sämtlich aus dem Verlage des Herrn Pley[e]l', I/21 (20 février 1799), pp. 328-329.

G. 'Recension / Neueste Pariser Musikalien, sämtlich aus dem Verlage des Herrn Pleyl. (Fortsetzung.)', I/22 (27 février 1799), pp. 342-346.

H. 'Kurze Anzeigen / *Musikalisches Journal, aus den neuesten deutschen und französischen Opern ausgezogen und fürs Klavier oder Fortepiano eingerichtet, von F. H. Lütgert*. Ein Jahrgang und sieben Hefte. Hamburg in der Meynschen Musikhandlung. (Auch unter dem Titel *Journal de musique etc*. – Preis des Jahrgangs 5 Rthlr.)', I/24 (13 mars 1799), pp. 382-383.

I. 'Abhandlungen / Ueber Glucks Alceste', I/25 (20 mars 1799), p. 388.

J. 'Recensionen / *Marche du Général Buonaparte, variée et dédiée à Madame Loehr née Bause, par A. E. Müller*. Œuvre 15. à Leipsic au Magasin de Musique de Breitkopf et Härtel', I/25 (20 mars 1799), pp. 395-396.

K. 'Kurze Anzeigen. / Neueste Pariser Musikalien, sämtlich aus dem Pleyelischen Verlage', I/25 (20 mars 1799), pp. 398-400.

L. 'Neueste Pariser Musikalien aus Le Duc's Verlag. (Auch bey Breitkopf und Härtel in Leipzig zu finden.)', I/27 (3 avril 1799), pp. 430-431.

M. 'Anekdote', I/29 (17 avril 1799), p. 464.

N. D. REDAKT. 'Korrespondenz. Neuerfundene französische Saiten', I/33 (15 mai 1799), pp. 522-523.

O. 'Recensionen [Pleyel]', I/36 (5 juin 1799), pp. 570-573.

P. 'Recensionen [Pleyel]', I/37 (12 juin 1799), pp. 585-587.

Q. 'Briefe über Tonkunst und Tonkünstler. Dritter Brief. (Fortsetzung aus dem 8. Stück dieser Zeitung.) Hamburg, Ende des Mays 1799', I/38 (19 juin 1799), pp. 602-607.

R. 'Anekdote', I/40 (3 juillet 1799), p. 640.

S. 'Recensionen [Pleyel]', I/42 (17 juillet 1799), pp. 679-683.

T. 'Briefe über Tonkunst und Tonkünstler. Vierter Brief. (Fortsetzung aus dem 39. Stück.) Hamburg, Ende Juny 1799', I/43 (24 juillet 1799), pp. 711-715.

<sup>U.</sup> 'Briefe über Tonkunst und Tonkünstler. Vierter Brief. (Fortsetzung aus dem vorigen Stück.) Hamburg, Ende Juny 1799', I/44 (31 juillet 1799), pp. 727-732.

<sup>V.</sup> 'Korrespondenz / Aus einem Briefe aus Hamburg. Im August 1799', I/48 (28 août 1799), p. 816.

<sup>W.</sup> 'Anekdote', II/2 (9 octobre 1799), p. 32.

<sup>X.</sup> 'Anekdote', II/5 (30 octobre 1799), p. 103.

<sup>Y.</sup> 'Zustand der Musik unter Italienern, Teutschen, Franzosen und Engländern', II/6 (6 novembre 1799), pp. 112-113.

<sup>Z.</sup> 'Anekdote', II/6 (6 novembre 1799), p. 128.

*AMZ* 1800

<sup>A.</sup> 'Ueber die italienisch-französische Musik', in: *Allgemeine musikalische Zeitung*, II/14 (1<sup>er</sup> janvier 1800), pp. 241-243.

<sup>B.</sup> 'Kurze Nachrichten [Paris]', II/17 (22 janvier 1800), p. 298.

<sup>C.</sup> 'Kurze Nachrichten [Paris]', II/19 (5 février 1800), pp. 330-331.

<sup>D.</sup> 'Anekdote', II/19 (5 février 1800), p. 336.

<sup>E.</sup> 'Anekdote', II/20 (12 février 1800), p. 360.

<sup>F.</sup> 'Nachricht / Konservatorium der Musik zu Paris', II/24 (12 mars 1800), pp. 426-429.

<sup>G.</sup> 'Anekdote', II/25 (19 mars 1800), pp. 446-448.

<sup>H.</sup> 'Nachricht / Berlin, Anfangs März', II/29 (16 avril 1800), pp. 508-512.

<sup>I.</sup> 'Anekdoten [Lully]', II/30 (23 avril 1800), p. 536.

<sup>J.</sup> 'Kurze Nachrichten [Paris]', II/32 (7 mai 1800), pp. 564-565.

<sup>K.</sup> 'Nachricht / Gegenwärtiger Zustand der Musik in Paris. A. d. Französischen / No. 1. Frimaire an 8', II/33-34 (14 et 21 mai 1800), pp. 588-591, 605-607.

<sup>L.</sup> 'Nachrichten / Ueber die Oper Medea, von Cherubini, und deren Aufführung in Berlin', II/39-40 (25 juin et 2 juillet 1800), pp. 683-688, 700-704.

<sup>M.</sup> 'Kurze Nachrichten [Paris]', II/39 (25 juin 1800), p. 688.

<sup>N.</sup> 'Recensionen [Pleyel]', II/40 (2 juillet 1800), pp. 696-697.

<sup>O.</sup> 'Nachrichten / Gegenwärtiger Zustand der Musik in Paris. A. d. Französischen / Zweyter Brief, vom Anfang des Juny dieses Jahres', II/41-43 (9, 16 et 23 juillet 1800), pp. 711-714, 732-736, 745-751.

<sup>P.</sup> 'Nachrichten / Einige Worte über den kürzlich verstorbenen Komponisten Domenico Della Maria, nach einem Aufsatz von Alexander Düval im 4ten St. des Journ. Frankreich und einigen Privat-Nachrichten', II/41 (9 juillet 1800), pp. 714-716.

<sup>Q.</sup> 'Recension / *Sonate à quatre mains pour le Forte-Piano, composée par I. F. Tapray*. Œuvre 29. à Paris chez Pleyel. (Pr. 1 Thlr. 4 Gr.)', II/43 (23 juillet 1800), pp. 743-744.

<sup>R.</sup> 'Kurze Anzeige / *Douze Walzes pour deux Flûtes, par D. Steibelt*. à Paris chez J. Pleyel. (Pr. 1 Thlr. 8 Gr.)', II/43 (23 juillet 1800), p. 752.

<sup>S.</sup> 'Kurze Anzeige / *Trois Sonates pour le Fortepiano, avec Accompagnement d'un Violon, composées par F. Amon*. Œuvre 11, à Paris chez F. Pleyel. (Pr. 2 Thlr. 12 Gr.)', II/44 (30 juillet 1800), p. 768.

<sup>T.</sup> 'Recensionen [Pleyel]', II/45 (6 août 1800), pp. 780-783.

<sup>U.</sup> 'Anekdote', II/46 (13 août 1800), pp. 798-800.

<sup>V.</sup> 'Kurze Anzeigen / *Trois Duos concertan[t]s pour deux Flûtes, composées par A. Peichler*. Œuvre I. (Pr. 1 Thlr. 18 Gr.) et II. (Pr. 2 Thlr. 12 Gr.) à Paris chez J. Pleyel', II/49 (3 septembre 1800), p. 848.

<sup>W.</sup> 'Nachricht / Darstellung des Musikzustandes im Meklenburgischen überhaupt, und in Schwerin in'sbesondere', II/50 (10 septembre 1800), pp. 858-859.

X. 'Anekdoten', II/52 (24 septembre 1800), pp. 895-896.

Y. 'Nachricht / Gegenwärtiger Zustand der Musik in Paris. A. d. Französischen / Paris, Ende des Augusts', III/2 (8 octobre 1800), pp. 36-40.

Z. 'Kurze Nachrichten [Pleyel]', III/2 (8 octobre 1800), p. 40.

A1. 'Notizen über die Erfindung der Oper aus Rousseaus Manuscript', III/3 (15 octobre 1800), pp. 54-55.

B1. 'Kurze Anzeige / Rondeau, avec Accompagnement de Fortepiano Paroles de ***, Musique d'Augustin Caron. (Prix 2 Fl.) À Paris, chez Pleyel', III/4 (22 octobre 1800), p. 72.

C1. 'Beylage zur allgemeinen musikalischen Zeitung No. 1 / Romanze aus der Oper: L'Opéra comique von Domenico Della Maria', III/7 (12 novembre 1800), partition en supplément intercalée entre les pages 120 et 121.

D1. 'Recensionen / Collection de tous les Airs patriotiques arrangés pour le Fortépiano. Livrais. I. Imprimés à Paris. (Pr. 1 Thlr. 8 Gr.)', III/10 (3 décembre 1800), pp. 163-165.

E1. 'Recensionen / Douze Walzes pour le Pianoforte avec Accompagnement de Tambourin et Triangle par D. Steibelt. Op. 36. à Paris chez J. Pleyel et Leipsic chez Breitkopf et Härtel. (7 Liv. 10 S.)', III/11 (10 décembre 1800), pp. 178-179.

F1. 'Kurze Nachrichten [Paris]', III/11 (10 décembre 1800), pp. 182-183.

G1. 'Korrespondenz / Briefe über Musik und Musiker in Paris. A. d. Französischen / (Fortsetzung a. d. 3ten St. d. 3ten Jahrg.) / Vierter Brief. Paris, Ende des Octobers', III/13 (24 décembre 1800), pp. 211-218.

*AMZ* 1801

A. 'Recensionen [Pleyel, Della Maria]', in: *Allgemeine musikalische Zeitung*, III/15 (7 janvier 1801), pp. 249-251.

B. 'Korrespondenz / Paris, den 28ten Decemb. 1800 / (Von einem deutschen Kunstkenner daselbst.)', III/16 (14 janvier 1801), pp. 269-270.

C. 'Nachricht / Zustand der Musik in Versailles', III/16 (14 janvier 1801), pp. 270-272.

D. 'Beylage zur allgemeinen musikalischen Zeitung No. 2 / Rondo von Garat', III/17 (21 janvier 1801), partition en supplément intercalée entre les pages 296 et 297.

E. 'Recension [Pleyel]', III/20 (11 février 1801), pp. 346-347.

F. 'Kurze Anzeigen / Sixième Concerto pour le Violon, composé par P. Rode. À Offenbach, chez J. André. (Pr. 2¾ Fl.)', III/20 (11 février 1801), p. 352.

G. 'Kurze Nachrichten [Paris]', III/22 (25 février 1801), pp. 387-388.

H. 'Korrespondenz / Briefe über Musik und Musiker in Paris. A. d. Französischen / Fünfter Brief', III/24 (11 mars 1801), pp. 411-419.

I. 'Nachricht / Bruchstücke aus der Rede des franz. Ministers bey der Austheilung der Preise an die Zöglinge des Conservatoriums / (Als Beylage zu dem Briefe aus Paris im vorigen Stücke.)', III/25 (18 mars 1801), pp. 432-435.

J. 'Kurze Nachrichten [Paris]', III/27 (1er avril 1801), p. 468.

K. 'Recensionen / Six Airs variées pour le Violon avec accompagn. d'un Violon par St. George, 1 Œuvre Posthume. À Paris, chez Pleyel. (Pr. 6 Francs.)', III/29 (15 avril 1801), p. 492.

L. 'Korrespondenz / Briefe über Musik und Musiker in Paris. A. d. Französischen / Sechster Brief / Paris, Ende März, 1801', III/30 (22 avril 1801), pp. 509-515.

M. 'Anekdote', III/30 (22 avril 1801), p. 516.

N. 'Recensionen / Trois Pot-Pourri. En Quatuors concertants, pour Flûte, Clarinette, Cor et Basson, par E. R. Gebauer. À Paris, chez Pleyel. (Prix 8 Francs. 10 Sous.)', III/31 (29 avril 1801), pp. 525-526.

O. 'Korrespondenz / Briefe über Tonkunst und Tonkünstler / Siebenter Brief / (Fortsetzung a. d. 23sten St. d. 2ten Jahrg.) / Hamburg, den 22 April 1801', III/32 (6 mai 1801), pp. 545-546.

P. 'Kurze Nachrichten / Paris', III/32 (6 mai 1801), p. 547.

<sup>Q</sup> 'Korrespondenz / Briefe über Musik und Musiker in Paris. A. d. Französischen / Siebenter Brief / (Fortsetzung a. d. 30ten St. d. 3ten Jahrg.) / Paris, 15ten April, 1801', III/33 (13 mai 1801), pp. 556-560.

<sup>R</sup> 'Kurze Anzeige / Duo pour Deux Violons par la Croix. Op. 12. À Paris, chez Pleyel. (Pr. 3 Francs.)', III/34 (20 mai 1801), p. 580.

<sup>S</sup> 'Biographische Nachrichten / Ueber Piccini's Leben und Werke / A. d. Französischen', III/40 (1<sup>er</sup> juillet 1801), pp. 661-668.

<sup>T</sup> 'Kurze Nachrichten / Paris', III/41 (8 juillet 1801), p. 692.

<sup>U</sup> D. REDAKT. 'Ueber die musik. Beylage No. VIII [Cherubini]', III/42 (15 juillet 1801), p. 707.

<sup>V</sup> 'Beylage zur allgemeinen musikalischen Zeitung No. 8 / Romanze aus der Oper: Les deux journées, von Cherubini', III/42 (15 juillet 1801), pp. xxvii-xxviii [partition en supplément intercalée entre les pages 708 et 709].

<sup>W</sup> 'Nachrichten / Dresden d. 8ten Aug.', III/47 (19 août 1801), pp. 784-785.

<sup>X</sup> 'Einige Worte über die neue französische Lyra. (Lyre-Guitarre.)', III/47 (19 août 1801), pp. 786-788.

<sup>Y</sup> 'Fortsetzung der Nachrichten über die neuesten musikalischen Angelegenheiten in Paris. / Anfang des Augusts', III/50-51 (9 et 16 septembre 1801), pp. 821-831, 837-842.

<sup>Z</sup> 'Beylage zur allgemeinen musikalischen Zeitung No. 9. a) / Romanze aus der Oper: Annette et Lubin von Martini', III/50 (9 septembre 1801), p. xxix [partition en supplément intercalée entre les pages 836 et 837].

<sup>A1</sup> 'Copie de la lettre adressée à J. Haydn par les artistes françois, en lui faisant agréer l'hommage de la Médaille-d'or, qu'ils lui ont décernée', III/51 (16 septembre 1801), pp. 842-843.

<sup>B1</sup> 'Kurze Nachrichten / Paris', IV/3 (14 octobre 1801), p. 47.

<sup>C1</sup> 'Korrespondenz / Nachrichten eines deutschen Künstlers in Paris über die Aufführung der Zauberflöte daselbst', IV/5 (28 octobre 1801), pp. 69-74.

<sup>D1</sup> 'Beylage zur allgemeinen musikalischen Zeitung No. 1 / Arie und Chor aus Mystères d'Isis', IV/5 (28 octobre 1801), pp. i-iii [partition en supplément intercalée entre les pages 80 et 81].

<sup>E1</sup> 'Kurze Nachrichten / Paris, Ende Okt.', IV/7 (11 novembre 1801), pp. 111-112.

<sup>F1</sup> APEL, August. 'Abhandlung / Musik und Deklamation / (Bey Gelegenheit der Preisausgabe des französischen Nationalinstituts.)', IV/9-14 (25 novembre, 2, 9, 16, 23 et 30 décembre 1801), pp. 129-139, 145-151, 161-170, 177-188, 193-204, 209-226.

<sup>G1</sup> 'Kurze Nachrichten / Paris, den 4ten November', IV/10 (2 décembre 1801), pp. 156-157.

<sup>H1</sup> 'Recension / *Trois Sonates pour le Fortepiano, dédiées à son ami Rode par A. Boieldieu*. Œuvr. I. à Paris, chez Imbault etc. (Pr. 10 Livr.)', IV/14 (30 décembre 1801), pp. 226-227.

*AMZ* 1802

<sup>A</sup> 'Nachricht / Uebersicht dessen, was in Leipzig während des le[t]zten Vierteljahrs für Musik öffentlich gethan worden', in: *Allgemeine musikalische Zeitung*, IV/16 (13 janvier 1802), pp. 256-257.

<sup>B</sup> 'Recension / *Gretry's Versuche über die Musik. Im Auszuge und mit kritischen und historischen Zusätzen herausgegeben von D. K. Spazier*. Leipzig, bey Breitkopf und Härtel. 1800. XVI. und 446 S. 8. (Pr. 1 Thlr. 12 Gr.)', IV/19 (3 février 1802), pp. 297-310.

<sup>C</sup> 'Nachrichten / Fortsetzung der Brief eines deutschen Künstlers in Paris / den 7. Nivose, An 10', IV/20 (10 février 1802), pp. 320-324.

<sup>D</sup> 'Nachrichten / Paris / d. 16. Nivose', IV/21 (17 février 1802), pp. 337-339.

<sup>E</sup> 'Kurze Anzeigen / *Fantaisie avec neuf Variations sur un air des Mystères d'Isis, pour le Pianoforte composée par D. Steibelt*. à Paris. (6 Liv)', IV/21 (17 février 1802), pp. 351-352.

<sup>F</sup> '*Grande Sonate pour le Pianoforte composée et dédiée à Madame Bonaparte par D. Steibelt*. Bey Breitkopf et Härtel, à Leipsic. (Pr. 1 Thlr.)', IV/23 (3 mars 1802), pp. 383-384.

# ÉTUDE DES TRANSFERTS MUSICAUX FRANCO-ALLEMANDS À L'ÉPOQUE NAPOLÉONIENNE

G. 'Recension / *Genres de Musique des différen[t]s peuples arrangés pour le Piano par L. Félix Despréaux (5me Partie du Cours d'Éducation de Musique et Piano du même Auteur.)* À Paris. (6 Liv.)', IV/26 (24 mars 1802), pp. 426-427.

H. 'Recension / *Trois Sonates pour Fortépiano comp. et dédiées à son ami Rodolphe Kreutzer par C. Dumonthau. Œuvr. I.* à Paris. (Pr. 9 Liv.)', IV/27 (31 mars 1802), pp. 437-438.

I. 'Nachrichten / Ueber die französische Oper zu Braunschweig', IV/27 (31 mars 1802), pp. 439-441.

J. 'Recensionen [Cherubini, Méhul, Jadin, Tarchi, Dalayrac, Solié]', IV/28 (7 avril 1802), pp. 457-461.

K. 'Recension / *Méthode de Clarinette. Contenant tous les Principes de cet Instrument, les nouveaux coups de langue, les Cadences, les Gammes, l'Étude des Intervalles, des Préludes et des airs modernes, par Woldemar.* à Paris. etc. (Preis 2 Thlr. 6 Gr.)', IV/29 (14 avril 1802), pp. 475-478.

L. 'Nachrichten / Berlin, d. 29sten März 1802', IV/29 (14 avril 1802), pp. 478-480.

M. 'Nachrichten / Paris, d. 18ten April', IV/31 (28 avril 1802), pp. 508-510.

N. 'Recensionen / Zweyte Lieferung neuer französischer Opern und Operetten [Dalayrac, Jadin, Trial, Bruni, Auvray, Berton]', IV/32 (5 mai 1802), pp. 523-528.

O. 'Nachrichten / Paris, den 28sten Apr.', IV/33 (12 mai 1802), pp. 539-543.

P. 'Nachrichten / Paris, d. 10ten May', IV/35 (26 mai 1802), pp. 572-575.

Q. 'Nachrichten [Paris]', IV/36 (2 juin 1802), p. 591.

R. 'Nachrichten / Paris, d. 16ten May', IV/37 (9 juin 1802), pp. 604-605.

S. 'Recensionen / *La grande Marche de Bonaparte en Italie, composée pour le Fortépiano avec accomp. de Tambourin par D. Steibelt.* à Paris. (Pr. 21 Gr.)', IV/38 (15 juin 1802), pp. 621-622.

T. 'Recensionen [recueils de romances]', IV/39 (23 juin 1802), p. 640.

U. 'Nachrichten / Paris, den 10ten Juni', IV/42 (14 juillet 1802), pp. 681-686.

V. 'Anekdote [Gluck in Paris]', IV/42 (14 juillet 1802), p. 688.

W. 'Nachrichten / Paris, den 1sten Juli', IV/43 (21 juillet 1802), pp. 689-695.

X. 'Anekdote [Lully]', IV/43 (21 juillet 1802), p. 704.

Y. 'Nachrichten [Paris]', IV/44 (28 juillet 1802), pp. 718-720.

Z. 'Nachrichten / Paris, d. 14. Juli', IV/45 (4 août 1802), pp. 733-735.

A1. 'Kurze Anzeige / *Anecdotes sur W. G. (A., Mozart schrieb sich nie Gottlieb, sondern Amadeus) Mozart. Traduites de l'Allemand par Ch. Fr. Cramer.* À Paris, chez l'éditeur, rue des Bons-Enfans. etc.', IV/45 (4 août 1802), p. 736.

B1. 'Recension / *Der Wasserträger (Les deux journées), ein Singspiel in drey Akten, in Musik gese[t]zt von Cherubini. Im Klavierauszuge von G. B. Bierey.* Leipzig, bey Breitkopf und Härtel. (Pr. 3 Thaler.)', IV/46 (11 août 1802), pp. 750-752.

C1. 'Anekdote [mauvais chanteur à Paris]', IV/47 (18 août 1802), p. 768.

D1. 'Nachrichten / Paris, den 8ten Aug.', IV/48 (23 août 1802), pp. 779-781.

E1. 'Ueber die musikal. Beylage No. VIII', IV/49 (1er septembre 1802), p. 800.

F1. 'Beylage zur allgemeinen musikalischen Zeitung No. VIII / Romanze aus der Oper: Une Folie, von Méhul', IV/49 (1er septembre 1802), pp. xix-xxvi [partition en supplément intercalée entre les pages 800 et 801].

G1. 'Nachrichten / Paris, d. 20sten Aug.', IV/50 (8 septembre 1802), pp. 815-816.

H1. 'Recensionen / *Deux grands Trios pour Pianoforte avec Violon et Violoncelle obligés par le Chevalier de la Lance.* Augsburg, bey Gombart', IV/52 (22 septembre 1802), pp. 851-852.

I1. '*IX[e] Potpourri, arrangé pour le Fortepiano par Hermann.* à Paris, chez Imbault. (Preis 18 Gr.)', IV/52 (22 septembre 1802), p. 856.

J1. 'Nachrichten / Paris, den 22ten Sept.', V/2 (6 octobre 1802), pp. 32-37.

[K1]. 'Nachrichten / Paris, den 14ten Oktober', v/7 (10 novembre 1802), pp. 112-115.

[L1]. 'Nachrichten [Paris]', v/8 (17 novembre 1802), pp. 140-143.

[M1]. 'Nachrichten [Paris]', v/9 (24 novembre 1802), p. 159.

[N1]. 'Nachrichten / Paris, d. 22sten Nov.', v/11 (8 décembre 1802), pp. 190-191.

*AMZ* 1803

[A]. 'Nachrichten / Paris, den 16ten Dec.', in: *Allgemeine musikalische Zeitung*, v/15 (5 janvier 1803), pp. 258-260.

[B]. 'Nachrichten [Conservatoire de Paris]', v/15 (5 janvier 1803), pp. 263-264.

[C]. 'Nachrichten [Conservatoire de Paris]', v/21 (16 février 1803), pp. 345-353.

[D]. 'Nachrichten / Paris, den 10sten Januar', v/21 (16 février 1803), p. 358.

[E]. 'Nachrichten [*Journal de Paris*]', v/22 (23 février 1803), p. 373.

[F]. 'Nachrichten / Paris, den 12ten Febr.', v/24 (9 mars 1803), pp. 402-406.

[G]. 'Nachrichten / Paris, den 3ten März', v/26 (23 mars 1803), pp. 439-443.

[H]. 'Recensionen / *Trois Quatuors pour deux Violons, Alto et Basse, dédiés à Mr. Lesueur, Inspecteur de l'Enseignement au Conservatoire de Musique, composés par J. Martinn. Œuvre 5ᵉ et 2me liv. de Quatuors*. à Bonn, chez Nicolas Simrock. (Pr. 9 Fr.)', v/31 (27 avril 1803), pp. 526-528.

[I]. 'Nachrichten [Paris]', v/37 (8 juin 1803), pp. 621-622.

[J]. 'Recensionen / *Introduction et Marche de l'Opéra Lodoiska composée de Kreutzer, arrangés pour Pianoforte par le B. N. et K. T.* À Vienne au Bureau d'arts et d'industrie. (Prix 30 Xr.)', v/42 (13 juillet 1803), p. 698.

[K]. 'Nachrichten / Paris, d. 6ten July', v/45 (3 août 1803), pp. 741-746.

[L]. 'Pariser Zauberflöte', v/46 (10 août 1803), p. 768.

[M]. 'Nachrichten / Paris, d. 24sten Jul.', v/48 (24 août 1803), pp. 791-794.

[N]. 'Nachrichten / Paris, den 20sten Aug.', v/49 (31 août 1803), pp. 816-818.

[O]. 'Nachrichten / Paris, d. 3ten Septbr.', v/52 (21 septembre 1803), pp. 863-865.

[P]. 'Anekdote [Duport]', v/52 (21 septembre 1803), pp. 866-867.

[Q]. 'Nachrichten / Paris, d. 14ten Septbr.', vi/1 (5 octobre 1803), pp. 15-16.

[R]. 'Recensionen / *Der Schatzgräber (Le Trésor supposé) ein Singspiel in Einem Akt, mit Musik von Méhul. Im Klavierauszuge von A. E. Müller*. Leipzig, bey Breitkopf und Härtel. (Preis 1 Thlr. 12 Gr.)', vi/2 (12 octobre 1803), pp. 25-27.

[S]. 'Nachrichten / Paris, d. 20sten Septbr. [Nécrologies de Devienne et Hugot, professeurs de flûte au Conservatoire]', vi/2 (12 octobre 1803), pp. 28-31.

[T]. 'Nachrichten / Paris, d. 18ten Octbr.', vi/6 (9 novembre 1803), pp. 93-96.

[U]. 'Nachrichten / Paris, d. 18ten Octbr.', vi/7 (16 novembre 1803), pp. 109-110.

*AMZ* 1804

[A]. 'Recensionen / *Le grand Deuil, Opéra en un Acte, Musique de H. Berton. Die tiefe Trauer, Operette in einem Aufzuge. Klavierauszug*. Bey Breitkopf und Härtel in Leipzig. (Preis 2 Thlr. 12 Gr.)', in: *Allgemeine musikalische Zeitung*, vi/15 (11 janvier 1804), pp. 245-247.

[B]. 'Nachrichten / Paris, den letzten Dec. 1803', vi/18 (1ᵉʳ février 1804), pp. 290-292.

[C]. 'Nachrichten / Paris', vi/19 (8 février 1804), pp. 312-315.

[D]. '*Johann Friedrich Reichardts vertraute Briefe aus Paris geschrieben in den Jahren 1802 und 1803. Zwey Theile. Hamburg, bey B. G. Hoffmann. 1804*', vi/20 (15 février 1804), pp. 317-331.

^E^. Michaelis, E. F. 'Gedanken eines Franzosen über die Analogie zwischen Gesichts- un Gehörsvorstellungen, zwischen Malerey und Musik', VI/21 (22 février 1804), pp. 333-338.

^F^. 'Vorschlag zur eben so leichten, als zuverlässigen Emporbringung der deutschen Oper, in Absicht auf neue Kompositionen unsrer grössten Meister', VI/23 (7 mars 1804), pp. 365-377.

^G^. 'Nachrichten / Paris, d. 18. Febr.', VI/23 (7 mars 1804), pp. 377-384.

^H^. 'Recensionen / *Six Romances françaises avec accompagnement de Pianoforte, composées par F. de Dalberg. Œuvre 21. À Bonn, chez Simrock. (Pr. 1 Fl. 10 Xr.)*', VI/23 (7 mars 1804), p. 387.

^I^. 'Nachrichten / Paris, den 24sten März', VI/29 (18 avril 1804), pp. 473-480.

^J^. 'Nachrichten / Paris, den 16ten May', VI/35 (30 mai 1804), pp. 583-586.

^K^. 'Nachrichten / Paris, den 18ten Juny', VI/40 (4 juillet 1804), pp. 674-676.

^L^. 'Nachrichten / Paris, den 30sten July', VI/47 (22 août 1804), pp. 785-787.

^M^. 'Nachrichten / Paris, den 30sten Aug.', VI/50 (12 septembre 1804), pp. 834-837.

^N^. 'Nachrichten / Paris, d. 3ten Octbr.', VII/3 (17 octobre 1804), pp. 44-47.

^O^. 'Nachrichten / Paris, den 20sten Oct.', VII/6 (7 novembre 1804), pp. 85-86.

^P^. 'Nachrichten / Paris, d. 7ten Nov.', VII/9 (28 novembre 1804), pp. 139-143.

^Q^. C. in Paris, 'Ueber den Charakter, den die italienische und deutsche Musik haben, und die französische haben sollte', VII/10 (5 décembre 1804), pp. 149-155.

*AMZ* 1805

^A^. 'Nachrichten / Paris, d. 1sten Jan.', in: *Allgemeine musikalische Zeitung*, VII/16 (16 janvier 1805), pp. 245-252.

^B^. 'Kurze Anzeige / *Ausgewählte Stücke aus dem Singspiel: Raul der Blaubart, von Grétry und Fischer, für das Pianoforte*. Wien, b. Thade Weigl', VII/18 (30 janvier 1805), pp. 291-292.

^C^. 'Recension / *Singschule des Konservatoriums d. Musik in Paris. Mit franz. u. deutsch. Texte, in 3 Abtheilungen.* [...] Leipzig, bey Breitkopf und Härtel. Pr. 6 Thlr.', VII/19-20 (6 et 13 février 1805), pp. 293-303, 309-315.

^D^. 'Nachrichten / Paris, d. 20sten Jan.', VII/19 (6 février 1805), pp. 303-306.

^E^. 'Nachrichten / Paris, d. 4ten März', VII/26 (27 mars 1805), pp. 417-424.

^F^. 'Nachrichten / Paris, den 25sten April', VII/33 (15 mai 1805), pp. 525-532.

^G^. 'Nachrichten / Paris, den 3ten August', VII/47 (21 août 1805), pp. 750-756.

^H^. 'Nachrichten [Paris]', VIII/1 (2 octobre 1805), pp. 10-11.

^I^. 'Nachrichten / Paris, den 3ten Oktober', VIII/3 (16 octobre 1805), pp. 33-43.

^J^. 'Anekdote', VIII/5 (30 octobre 1805), p. 80.

^K^. 'Nachrichten / Paris, d. 7ten November', VIII/8 (20 novembre 1805), pp. 115-119.

^L^. 'Fragmente von Diderot', VIII/12 (18 décembre 1805), pp. 177-183.

*AMZ* 1806

^A^. 'Ueber den zweckmässigen Gebrauch der Mittel der Tonkunst', in: *Allgemeine musikalische Zeitung*, VIII/16 (15 janvier 1806), pp. 248-249.

^B^. 'Nachrichten / Paris, den 26sten December', VIII/16 (15 janvier 1806), pp. 249-253.

^C^. 'Nachrichten [Paisiello]', VIII/19 (5 février 1806), pp. 299-300.

^D^. 'Nachrichten / Berlin, den 25sten Januar', VIII/19 (5 février 1806), pp. 300-301.

^E^. 'Nachrichten [Crescentini]', VIII/19 (5 février 1806), pp. 301-302.

^F^. 'Recension [Steibelt]', VIII/20 (12 février 1806), pp. 305-312.

[G.] 'Nachrichten / Wien, den 9ten Februar', VIII/21 (19 février 1806), pp. 328-329.

[H.] 'Nachrichten / Wien, den 26sten Februar', VIII/24 (12 mars 1806), p. 376.

[I.] 'Nachrichten / Wien, den 20sten März', VIII/27 (2 avril 1806), p. 426.

[J.] APEL, Johann August, 'Musik und Poesie [Grétry]', VIII/29 (16 avril 1806), pp. 449-452.

[K.] 'Nachrichten. Musik in Leipzig. (Neujahr bis Ostern)', VIII/30 (23 avril 1806), p. 471.

[L.] 'Nachrichten / Danzig, den 28sten März', VIII/31 (30 avril 1806), p. 490.

[M.] 'Recension / *Zwölf Orgelstücke verschiedener Art, v. M. G. Fischer, Organist und Musikdirektor in Erfurt. Op. 9. Erster Heft. Bei Breitkopf und Härtel in Leipzig* (Pr. 18 Gr.)', VIII/38 (18 juin 1806), pp. 598-605.

[N.] 'Kurze Anzeigen / *Variations faciles sur la Marche de l'Opéra Raul Barbe-Bleue, comp. par N. Gyrowetz. À Vienne, au Bureau des Arts et d'Industrie* (Pr. 45 Xr.)', VIII/39 (25 juin 1806), p. 624.

[O.] 'Nachrichten / Stuttgart, den 24sten May', VIII/40 (2 juillet 1806), pp. 637-638.

[P.] 'Recension / *Trois Sonates pour le Pianoforte, composée par Armand de Villeblanche et dédiées à son Père. Œuvre 1. à Paris, chez Maillard.* (Pr. 9 Livr.)', VIII/43 (23 juillet 1806), pp. 683-686.

[Q.] 'Nachrichten / Wien, den 12ten July 1806', VIII/44 (30 juillet 1806), pp. 700.

[R.] 'Nachrichten / Wien, d. 2ten Aug.', VIII/46 (13 août 1806), pp. 728-729.

[S.] 'Kurze Anzeigen / *Ouverture d'Anacréon par Cherubini. Chez Breitkopf et Härtel à Leipsic.* (Pr. 8 Gr.)', VIII/49 (3 septembre 1806), p. 784.

[T.] 'Nachrichten / Berlin, d. 26. Aug.', VIII/50 (10 septembre 1806), pp. 796-797.

*AMZ 1807*

[A.] 'Recension / *Trois Sonates pour la Harpe – par M. P. Dalmivare. Œuvre 1. à Paris, chez Gaveaux.* (Pr. 7 Liv. 10 S.)', in: *Allgemeine musikalische Zeitung*, IX/16 (14 janvier 1807), pp. 253-254.

[B.] 'Kurze Anzeigen / *Airs variés pour la Harpe par Venier fils – Œuvr. 14. à Paris. À la Nouveauté. (!) Chez Gaveaux.* (Pr. 7 Liv. 10 S.)', IX/17 (21 janvier 1807), pp. 271-272.

[C.] 'Kurze Anzeigen / *Six Airs variés pour la Harpe tirés des Opéras — par Venier fils. Œuvr. 6. à Paris, chez Gaveaux.* (Pr. 7 Liv. 10 S.)', IX/18 (28 janvier 1807), p. 287.

[D.] 'Recension / *Six Romances pour le Pianoforte av. accomp. de Violon, paroles du Comte Alexandre de T–y, musique de Vi[n]cent Righini — Œuvr. 1.* (Preis 16 Gr.)', IX/19 (4 février 1807), pp. 302-304.

[E.] SIEVERS, G. L. P. 'Charakteristik der italienischen und französischen Musik', IX/32 (5 mai 1807), pp. 503-512.

[F.] 'Recension / *Pianoforte des Conservatorium der Musik in Paris, herausgegeben von L. Adam, Mitglied des Conservatorium. Beym Unterricht in diesem Institute eingeführt*, Leipzig, bey Breitkopf u. Härtel', IX/43, 45, 46 (22 juillet, 5 et 12 août 1807), pp. 689-692, 719-724, 729-734.

[G.] 'Recension / 1) *Trois Sonates pour le Clavecin ou Pianoforte par Méhul. Op. 1. (Liv. 1.)* (Pr. 6 Livr.) und / 2) *Trois Sonates p. l. Clav. ou Pianoforte, av. acc. de Violon ad libit. (nur zwey mit Violin) par Méhul. Op. 1. Liv. 2. à Paris, au magasin de musique, dirigé par Cherubini, Méhul etc.* (Pr. 6 Livr.)', X/1 (30 septembre 1807), pp. 11-15.

[H.] 'Recension / *Sonate pour le Piano av. acc. de Violon, extraite du IVme Duo de Piano et Harpe d'An. Bojeldieu. Op. 7. à Paris, au magasin de Musique, dirigé par Cherubini, Méhul etc.* (Pr. 6 Livr.)', X/1 (30 septembre 1807), p. 16.

[I.] 'Kurze Anzeige / *Deux Sonates pour Harpe ou Piano (avec Violon) comp. et déd. à son Elève Madem. A. de – par A. Boieldieu. à Paris, au magasin de musiq. dirigé par Chérubini, Méhul etc.* (Pr. 7 Livr. 10 Cent.)', X/6 (4 novembre 1807), p. 96.

# ÉTUDE DES TRANSFERTS MUSICAUX FRANCO-ALLEMANDS À L'ÉPOQUE NAPOLÉONIENNE

*AMZ* 1808

A. 'Kurze Notizen, aus Briefen / In Paris', in: *Allgemeine musikalische Zeitung*, x/20 (10 février 1808), pp. 318-319.

B. 'Recension / *Trente six Fugues pour le Pianoforte, composées d'après un nouveau système par Antoine Reicha*. Vienne, au Magasin de l'Imprim. chym. Querfolio, 127 S. Nebst 2 Bogen Text, über das neue Fugensystem. (Pr. 9 Fl.)', x/23 (2 mars 1808), pp. 353-361.

C. 'Kurze Notizen [nécrologie de Carl Friedrich Cramer]', x/24 (9 mars 1808), p. 383.

D. 'Nachrichten / In Paris [Momigny]', x/37 (9 juin 1808), p. 590.

E. 'Recensionen / *Iphigénie en Aulide etc. Iphigenia in Aulis, lyrische Tragödie in drey Aufzügen, in Musik gesetzt von dem Ritter Gluck, frey übersetzt und in einen Auszug zum Singen beym Pianoforte gebracht von J. D. Sander*. Erster Akt. Berlin, in Sanders Buchhandlung. (Pr. 3. Thlr. 8 Gr.)', x/49 (31 août 1808), pp. 776-778.

F. 'Recensionen / *Cours complet d'Harmonie et de Composition d'après une théorie neuve et générale de la musique* [...] *par Jérôme-Joseph De Momigny*. A Paris, chez l'auteur [...]', xi/1-2, 4-5 (5, 12 et 26 octobre, 2 novembre 1808), pp. 3-10, 19-27, 49-54, 65-73.

G. 'Bericht über die Arbeiten der Sektion der Musik in der Klasse der schönen Künste des Instituts zu Paris vom 1sten Okt. 1807 bis zum 1sten Okt. 1808', xi/9 (30 novembre 1808), pp. 136-143.

*AMZ* 1809

A. 'Nachrichten / Paris, d. 1sten März [Chladni]', in: *Allgemeine musikalische Zeitung*, xi/27 (5 avril 1809), pp. 430-432.

B. 'Nachrichten / Paris, d. 28sten März', xi/29 (19 avril 1809), pp. 460-461.

C. '*Vertrauen auf Gott*. Eine Friedenskantate mit Chören von Herklots; für das Conservatoire der Blas-Instrumente in Berlin komponirt von Bernhard Anselm Weber, Königl. Preuss. Kapellmeister', xi/33 (17 mai 1809), pp. 525-527.

D. 'Nachrichten / Paris. Ende des Mays', xi/38 (21 juin 1809), pp. 600-607.

E. 'Kurze Anzeige / *Trois Duos pour 2 Violons, dédiés à son ami Montbeillard, par P. Baillot*. Op. 8. Liv. 1. Offenbach, chez J. André. (Pr. 2 Fl.)', xi/41 (12 juillet 1809), pp. 655-656.

F. 'Recension / *Trois Sonates et trois Fugues pour le Pianoforte, dans le Style de Haydn, Mozart et Clementi, déd. à Mdm. de Montherot et comp. par Charles Dumonchau*. Œuvr. 50. à Paris, chez Dahan. (Pr. 9 Francs.)', xi/45 (9 août 1809), pp. 713-719.

G. 'Nachrichten / Paris, d. 6ten Aug.', xi/47 (23 août 1809), pp. 748-751.

H. 'Nachrichten / Paris', xi/48 (30 août 1809), pp. 763-766.

I. 'Nachrichten / Paris, den 6 October', xii/4 (25 octobre 1809), pp. 54-61.

J. 'Recension / *Grande Méthode pour le Forte-Piano en trois parties par Démar*. Paris, chez Pollet. Partie I. II. (Pr. 30 Livr.)', xii/5 (1$^{er}$ novembre 1809), pp. 75-80.

K. 'Nachrichten / Paris, im Octbr.', xii/7 (15 novembre 1809), pp. 97-104.

L. 'Kurze Notizen aus Briefen / In Paris [*Requiem* de Cherubini]', xii/7 (15 novembre 1809), p. 111.

*AMZ* 1810

A. 'Nachrichten / Paris, den 18ten Dec.', in: *Allgemeine musikalische Zeitung*, xii/14 (3 janvier 1810), pp. 212-218.

B. 'Nachrichten / Paris, d. 15ten Febr.', xii/21 (21 février 1810), pp. 325-333.

^C^. 'Etwas über die Schicksale und Beschäftigungen des Hrn. D. Chladni während seines Aufenthalts in Paris. Aus einem Briefe von ihm, von Strasburg d. 11ten März', XII/27 (4 avril 1810), pp. 419-422.

^D^. 'Miscellen / Orchester des grossen Concerts und der grossen Oper in Paris', XII/46 (15 août 1810), pp. 729-731.

^E^. ORION. 'Nachrichten / Paris, den 10ten Nov.', XII/62 (5 décembre 1810), pp. 985-992.

^F^. D. K. 'Ueber die Errichtung musikalischer Conservatorien in Deutschland', XII/64 (19 décembre 1810), pp. 1021-1029.

*AMZ* 1811

^A^. 'Kurze Anzeigen / *Messe à 3 voix et Chœurs, arrangée p. l. Pianoforte, comp. par L. Cherubini.* à Leipsic, chez Fred. Hofmeister. (Pr. 4 Thlr.)', in: *Allgemeine musikalische Zeitung*, XIII/5 (30 janvier 1811), pp. 91-92.

^B^. 'Recension / *Notice historique sur la vie et les ouvrages de Joseph Haydn, Membre Associé de l'Institut de France et d'un grand nombre d'Académies, lue dans la séance publique du 6. Octobre 1810, par Joachim Le Breton, Secrétaire perpétuel de la Classe [...]. Chez Baudouin, Imprimeur de l'Institut de France*', XIII/8 (20 février 1811), pp. 148-151.

^C^. 'Nachrichten / Paris, den 18ten April', XIII/20 (15 mai 1811), pp. 346-348.

^D^. 'Nachrichten / Paris, d. 8ten July', XIII/31 (31 juillet 1811), pp. 526

^E^. 'Nachrichten / Paris. Anfang October', XIII/43 (23 octobre 1811), pp. 713-721.

^F^. 'Nachrichten / Paris', XIII/44 (30 octobre 1811), pp. 729-739.

^G^. 'Recensionen / *Six Romances françaises av. acc. de Guitarre, paroles et musique de Poly Delaurier.* à Offenbach, chez André. (Preis 1 Fl.)', XIII/45 (6 novembre 1811), pp. 757-758.

^H^. 'Notizen / Vermischte Bemerkungen aus dem Schreiben eines Deutschen in Paris', XIII/45 (6 novembre 1811), pp. 761-762.

^I^. 'Recension / *Messe à 3 voix et chœurs par L. Cherubini.* Partition. à Paris, chez Cherubini, Méhul et Compagnie', XIII/47 (20 novembre 1811), pp. 781-789.

*AMZ* 1812

^A^. 'Nachrichten / Paris, d. 21sten Dec. 1811', in: *Allgemeine musikalische Zeitung*, XIV/3 (15 janvier 1812), pp. 41-45.

^B^. 'Kurze Anzeige / *Trois Nocturnes — p. le Pianof. et Flûte (ou Violon) par Jadin.* Œuvr. 10. à Leipzig, chez Kühnel. (Pr. 1 Thlr.)', XIV/7 (12 février 1812), p. 116.

^C^. 'Recensionen / *Dictionnaire historique des Musiciens [...] par Al. Choron et F. Fayolle.* [...] Paris. 1. Band. XCII. 435 S. 1810. 2. Band. 470 S. 1811', XIV/14 (1^er^ avril 1812), pp. 217-221.

^D^. 'Nachrichten / Paris, den 21sten März', XIV/16 (15 avril 1812), pp. 258-262.

^E^. 'Recensionen / *Cendrillon, Prinzessin Aschenbrödel, Oper in drey Acten, franz. u. deutsch, v. Nicolo.* Klavierauszug. Leipzig, bey Breitkopf und Härtel. (Pr. 3 Thlr.)', XIV/22 (27 mai 1812), pp. 367-368.

^F^. 'Nachrichten / Paris, Ende Mays', XIV/25 (17 juin 1812), pp. 413-416.

^G^. 'Miscellen [Giroust]', XIV/27 (1^er^ juillet 1812), pp. 447-448.

^H^. 'Fontenelle', XIV/30 (22 juillet 1812), p. 502.

^I^. 'Nachrichten [nécrologie de Solié]', XIV/37 (9 septembre 1812), p. 613.

^J^. 'Nachrichten / Paris, den 3ten Octbr.', XIV/45 (4 novembre 1812), pp. 734-736.

^K^. 'Recensionen / *Ouverture à grand Orchestre, du jeune Henri Chasse par F. Méhul.* Chez Breitkopf et Härtel à Leipsic. (Preis 1 Rthlr. 8 Gr.)', XIV/46 (11 novembre 1812), pp. 743-747.

ᴸ. 'Recensionen / *Iphigenia in Tauris, tragische Oper in vier Acten vom Ritter Gluck, aus dem Franz. des Gaillard frey übers. v. Sander. Vollständiger Klavierauszug, mit deutsch. und franz. Texte, von Ludw. Hellwig.* Berlin, bey Schlesinger. (Pr. 4 Thlr.)', xɪᴠ/51 (16 décembre 1812), pp. 834-835.

*AMZ 1813*
ᴬ. Oʀɪᴏɴ '*Allgemeine historische Uebersichten der Musik*. N. d. Französ. des Hrn. Choron, mit einigen Anmerkungen', in: *Allgemeine musikalische Zeitung*, xᴠ/5-6 (3 et 10 février 1813), pp. 73-79, 89-97.
ᴮ. 'Nachrichten / Paris, den 15ten Jan.', xᴠ/5 (3 février 1813), pp. 82-83.
ᶜ. 'Kurze Anzeigen / *Ouverture de l'Opéra Anacréon, arrangée pour 2 Pianofortes à 8 mains, comp. par Cherubini*. à Leipzig, chez Kühnel. (Preis 1 Rthlr. 4 Gr.)', xᴠ/5 (3 février 1813), p. 86.
ᴰ. 'Kurze Anzeigen / *Favorit-Walzer der Kaiserin von Frankreich – für 2 Violinen, 2 Clarinetten, 2 Fagotte, 2 Hörner, Piccoloflöte, Posaune, Trompete und Bass*. Leipzig, bey Kühnel. (Preis 1 Thlr.)', xᴠ/16 (21 avril 1813), p. 276.
ᴱ. 'Nachrichten [Paris]', xᴠ/18 (5 mai 1813), pp. 302-303.
ᶠ. 'Nachrichten / Paris, den 10ten Jun.', xᴠ/26 (30 juin 1813), pp. 437-439.
ᴳ. 'Kurze Anzeigen / *Six Airs variés ou Etudes pour le Violon, av. accomp. d'un second Viol. par P. Baillot.* Œuvr. 12. Leips. et Berlin, au Bureau des arts. (Pr. 20 Gr.)', xᴠ/41 (13 octobre 1813), pp. 679-680.
ᴴ. 'Miscellen [Grétry]', xᴠ/42 (30 octobre 1813), pp. 688-695.
ᴵ. 'Miscellen [Grétry]', xᴠ/43 (27 octobre 1813), pp. 705-708.
ᴶ. 'Recensionen / 1. *Johann von Paris, grosse komische Oper in zwey Aufzügen, in Musik gesetzt von A. Boieldieu. Vollständiger Klavier-Auszug.* Leipzig und Berlin, im Kunst- u. Industrie-Comptoir. (Pr. 2 Thlr. 16 Gr.) / 2. *Johann von Paris etc. Vollständiger Klavier-Auszug.* Leipzig, bey Kühnel. (Pr. 4 Thlr.)', xᴠ/43 (27 octobre 1813), pp. 708-709.
ᴷ. 'Kurze Anzeigen / *Trois Duos concertants pour 2 Flûtes, compos. – par T. Berbiguier*. 2 Livre[s] de Duos. Œuvr. 15. à Leipsic et Berlin, au bureau des arts. (Preis 1 Rthlr. 20 Gr.)', xᴠ/51 (22 décembre 1813), pp. 838-839.

*AMZ 1814*
ᴬ. 'Anekdoten', in: *Allgemeine musikalische Zeitung*, xᴠɪ/1 (5 janvier 1814), p. 20.
ᴮ. 'Kurze Anzeigen / *Nouveau mélange d'airs choisis des Opéras français et italiens, arr. pour 2 Flûtes par Berbiguier*. N° 4. Leipz., chez Breitk. et Härtel. (Pr. 16 Gr.)', xᴠɪ/3 (19 janvier 1814), p. 52.
ᶜ. 'Nachrichten / Wien, d. 7ten Jan.', xᴠɪ/24 (26 janvier 1814), pp. 70-72.
ᴰ. 'Recension / *Sechs deutsche Kriegslieder für eine und mehrere Stimmen, mit Chören, und willkürlicher Begleitung des Pianof., in Musik gesetzt – von Alb. Methfessel*. 35stes W. Rudolstadt, in Commiss. d. Hof- Buch u. Kunsthandl. (Preis 8 Gr.)', xᴠɪ/5 (2 février 1814), pp. 83-88.
ᴱ. 'Nachrichten / Stockholm. Monat November', xᴠɪ/5 (2 février 1814), p. 88.
ᶠ. 'Nachrichten. Königsberg', xᴠɪ/6 (9 février 1814), pp. 103-107.
ᴳ. 'Anekdote', xᴠɪ/6 (9 février 1814), p. 108.
ᴴ. 'Miscellen [Cherubini]', xᴠɪ/7 (16 février 1814), pp. 122-123.
ᴵ. 'Nachrichten / Wien, d. 1ten Febr.', xᴠɪ/8 (23 février 1814), pp. 131-132.
ᴶ. 'Nachrichten / Lemberg in Gallizien, den 29sten Januar', xᴠɪ/8 (23 février 1814), pp. 133-135.
ᴷ. 'Brief über das musikalische Publicum, an dasselbe. Erster Brief', xᴠɪ/9 (2 mars 1814), pp. 141-148.
ᴸ. 'Kurze Anzeige / *Richard Löwenherz, Oper in drey Aufzügen, in Musik gesetzt von Andr. Emil Grétry – Vollständiger Klavierauszug von Friedrich Ludwig Seidel, königl. preuss. Musikdirector*. Berlin, in der Schlesingerschen Musikhandlung. (Pr. 3 Thlr. 8 Gr.)', xᴠɪ/16 (20 avril 1814), pp. 275-276.

^M^ 'Kurze Anzeige / *Zuruf an die deutschen Brüder am Rhein – von Oswald, in Musik ges. von Seidel* – Berlin, bey Schlesinger. (Pr. 4 Gr.)', XVI/22 (1ᵉʳ juin 1814), p. 380.

^N^ 'Beylage zur allgemeinen musikalischen Zeitung N. 3 / Lied *Des Deutschen Vaterland*, comp. von K. T. Moritz', XVI/22 (1ᵉʳ juin 1814), partition en supplément intercalée entre les pages 380 et 381.

^O^ 'Nachrichten / Strasburg', XVI/32 (10 août 1814), pp. 530-534.

^P^ 'Kurze Anzeige / *Der Engel auf dem Schlachtfeld, von F. W. Gubitz, in Musik gesetzt mit Begl. des Pianof. von J. P. Schmidt.* Berlin, bey Schlesinger. (Pr. 14 Gr.)', XVI/32 (10 août 1814), p. 540.

^Q^ 'Kurze Anzeigen / *Patriotischer Rundgesang für fröhliche Zirkel, aus d. Schauspiel: Das Dorf an der Gränze, mit Begleitung des Pianof. oder der Guitarre. Musik von Bernh. Ans. Weber.* Berlin, bey Schlesinger. (Pr. 6 Gr.)', XVI/34 (24 août 1814), p. 576.

^R^ 'Nachrichten / Strasburg, im September', XVI/40 (5 octobre 1814), pp. 668-669.

^S^ 'Recension / *Der neue Gutsherr, (le nouveau Seigneur de Village,) Singspiel, im Klavierauszug, mit französischem und deutschem Texte. Musik von Adrien Boieldieu.* Bonn, bey N. Simrock. (Preis 9 Franks.)', XVI/40 (5 octobre 1814), pp. 669-673.

^T^ 'Kurze Anzeigen / *Ouverture pour le Pianoforte de l'Opéra les Aubergistes de qualité, par Catel.* à Leipzig, chez Breitkopf et Härtel. (Pr. 8 Gr.)', XVI/42 (19 octobre 1814), p. 712.

^U^ 'Kurze Anzeige / *Lobgesang auf die Retter Deutschlands, die allerhöchsten verbündeten Monarchen, in Mus. ges. von H. A. Hoffmann*, Concertmeister in Frankfurt am Mayn. Bonn, bey Simrock', XVI/43 (26 octobre 1814), p. 728.

^V^ 'Nachrichten / Strasburg, d. 10ten Nov.', XVI/48 (30 novembre 1814), pp. 804-807.

^W^ 'Nachrichten / Strasburg. (Fortsetzung aus der 48sten No.)', XVI/49 (7 décembre 1814), pp. 820-826.

^X^ 'Kurze Anzeigen / *Kriegslieder in Musik gesetzt, und zum Besten verwundeter Krieger herausgegeben, von J. O. H. Schaum.* Breslau, bey Grass und Barth', XVI/49 (7 décembre 1814), pp. 831-832.

^Y^ 'Nachrichten / Strasburg. (Beschluss aus der 49sten No.)', XVI/50 (14 décembre 1814), pp. 838-842.

*AMZ* 1815

^A^ 'Beylage zur allgemeinen musikalischen Zeitung No. 2 / Nachtlied der Krieger', in: *Allgemeine musikalische Zeitung*, XVII/12 (22 mars 1815), partition en supplément intercalée entre les pages 212 et 213.

^B^ Fröhlich. 'Recension / *Opfergesang am Altar des Vaterlandes, von K. G. Kapf und F. W. Berner.* Breslau, bey Förster und Hoffmann. Partitur. Op. 10. (Preis 16 Gr.)', XVII/14 (5 avril 1815), pp. 229-232.

^C^ 'Strasburg', XVII/14 (5 avril 1815), pp. 233-236.

^D^ 'Strasburg', XVII/15 (12 avril 1815), pp. 252-255.

^E^ Fröhlich. 'Recension / *Grande Sonate pour Piano et Violon obligé avec accomp. de Violoncelle ad libit. par L. Jadin.* [...] Leipsic et Berlin, au Bureau des arts et d'industrie', XVII/18 (3 mai 1815), pp. 297-300.

^F^ 'Strasburg', XVII/18 (3 mai 1815), pp. 305-309.

^G^ 'Strasburg', XVII/42 (18 octobre 1815), pp. 704-707.

^H^ 'Strasburg', XVII/43 (25 octobre 1815), pp. 725-728.

Berlioz 1991

Berlioz, Hector. *Mémoires*, édition présentée et annotée par Pierre Citron, Paris, Flammarion, 1991.

Cailliez 2014

Cailliez, Matthieu. *La Diffusion du comique en Europe à travers les productions d'«opere buffe», d'opéras-comiques et de «komische Opern» (France - Allemagne - Italie, 1800-1850)*, thèse de doctorat, Universités de Paris-

Sorbonne, Bonn et Florence, 2014, pp. 287-318, publication en ligne: <https://bonndoc.ulb.uni-bonn.de/xmlui/handle/20.500.11811/6808>, visité en octobre 2023.

CAILLIEZ 2021
ID. 'Étude comparée de l'influence musicale et institutionnelle de Cherubini en France et dans le monde germanique entre 1787 et 1842', in: *Luigi Cherubini: A Multifaceted Composer at the Turn of the 19th Century*, Massimiliano Sala éd., Turnhout, Brepols Publishers, 2021 (Studies on Italian Music History, 14), pp. 391-395.

CASTELLI 1861
CASTELLI, Ignaz Franz. *Memoiren meines Lebens. 2: Vom Jahre 1814 bis zum Jahre 1830*, Vienne, Kober & Markgraf, 1861.

DEVRIÈS-LESURE 2003
DEVRIÈS-LESURE, Anik. 'Pleyel, Ignace-Joseph', in: *Dictionnaire de la musique en France au XIXe siècle*, Joël-Marie Fauquet dir., Paris, Fayard, 2003, p. 981.

DRATWICKI 2009
*Hérold en Italie*, ouvrages coordonné par Alexandre Dratwicki, Lyon, Symétrie, 2009 (Perpetuum mobile).

FAUQUET 1986
FAUQUET, Joël-Marie. *Les Sociétés de musique de chambre à Paris de la Restauration à 1870*, Paris, Aux Amateurs de livres, 1986.

HOFFMANN 2007
HOFFMANN, Ernst Theodor Aamadeus. *Die Elixiere des Teufels – Werke 1814-1816*, Hartmut Steinecke éd. avec la collaboration de Gerhard Allroggen, Francfort, Deutscher Klassiker Verlag, ²2007 (Deutscher Klassiker Verlag im Taschenbuch, 17).

HOFFMANN 2017
ID. *Nachtstücke – Klein Zaches – Prinzessin Brambilla – Werke 1816-1820*, Hartmut Steinecke éd. avec la collaboration of Gerhard Allroggen, Francfort, Deutscher Klassiker Verlag, ²2017 (Deutscher Klassiker Verlag im Taschenbuch, 36).

*IBAMZ* 1799
A. 'Neue Musikalien, von verschiedenen Verlegern, welche bey Breitkopf und Härtel zu haben sind', in: *Intelligenz-Blatt zur Allgemeinen Musikalischen Zeitung*, I/12 (mai 1799), pp. 63-64.
B. SPAZIER, Karl. 'Ankündigung eines deutschen Auszugs aus Gretry's Essais sur la Musique', I/18 (septembre 1799), pp. 89-91.
C. 'Neue Musikalien, von verschiedenen Verlegern, welche bey Breitkopf und Härtel zu haben sind', II/1 (octobre 1799), pp. 2-4.
D. 'Neue Musikalien, von verschiedenen Verlegern, welche bey Breitkopf und Härtel zu haben sind', II/4 (novembre 1799), pp. 13-16.
E. HOFFMEISTER, Franz Anton. 'Anzeige', II/5 (décembre 1799), pp. 19-20.

*IBAMZ* 1800

A. 'Neue Musikalien, von verschiedenen Verlegern, welche bey Breitkopf und Härtel zu haben sind', in: *Intelligenz-Blatt zur Allgemeinen Musikalischen Zeitung*, II/12 (avril 1800), pp. 53-54.

B. 'Neue Musikalien, von verschiedenen Verlegern, welche bey Breitkopf und Härtel zu haben sind', II/15 (juillet 1800), pp. 64-66.

C. 'Neue Musikalien, welche bey Joh. Aug. Böhme in Hamburg zu haben sind', II/20 (septembre 1800), pp. 68-69.

D. 'Neue Musikalien, von verschiedenen Verlegern, welche bey Breitkopf und Härtel zu haben sind', II/18 (août 1800), pp. 75-78.

E. 'Musikalien-Anzeige / In der Falterischen Musikhandlung in München haben nachstehende Werke die Presse verlassen', II/19 (septembre 1800), pp. 79-82.

F. 'Neue Musikalien, von verschiedenen Verlegern, welche bey Breitkopf und Härtel zu haben sind', II/20 (septembre 1800), pp. 83-86.

G. 'Neue Musikalien, von verschiedenen Verlegern, welche bey Breitkopf und Härtel zu haben sind', III/3 (novembre 1800), pp. 11-12.

H. 'Neue Musikalien, von verschiedenen Verlegern, welche bey Breitkopf und Härtel zu haben sind', III/4 (décembre 1800), pp. 16.

*IBAMZ* 1801

A. 'Neue Musikalien, von verschiedenen Verlegern, welche bey Breitkopf und Härtel zu haben sind', in: *Intelligenz-Blatt zur Allgemeinen Musikalischen Zeitung*, III/6 (février 1801), pp. 23-24.

B. 'Neue Musikalien, von verschiedenen Verlegern, welche bey Breitkopf und Härtel zu haben sind', III/7 (avril 1801), pp. 25-26.

C. 'Ankündigung [Pleyel, Dussek]', III/7 (avril 1801), p. 28.

D. 'Neue Musikalien, von verschiedenen Verlegern, welche bey Breitkopf und Härtel zu haben sind', III/10 (juillet 1801), pp. 37-40.

E. 'Neue Musikalien in Verlag von Breitkopf und Härtel', III/11 (juillet 1801), pp. 42-43.

F. 'Neue Musikalien, von verschiedenen Verlegern, welche bey Breitkopf und Härtel zu haben sind', III/12 (juillet 1801), pp. 47-48.

G. 'Neue Musikalien, von verschiedenen Verlegern, welche bey Breitkopf und Härtel zu haben sind', III/13 (septembre 1801), pp. 51-52.

H. 'Neue Musikalien, von verschiedenen Verlegern, welche bey Breitkopf und Härtel zu haben sind', III/14 (septembre 1801), pp. 55-56.

I. 'Neue Musikalien, von verschiedenen Verlegern, welche bey Breitkopf und Härtel zu haben sind', IV/2 (novembre 1801), pp. 7-8.

J. 'Neue Musikalien, von verschiedenen Verlegern, welche bey Breitkopf und Härtel zu haben sind', IV/3 (novembre 1801), pp. 11-12.

K. 'Neue Musikalien, von verschiedenen Verlegern, welche bey Breitkopf und Härtel zu haben sind', IV/5 (décembre 1801), pp. 19-20.

*IBAMZ* 1802

A. 'Neue Musikalien, von verschiedenen Verlegern, welche bey Breitkopf und Härtel zu haben sind', IV/8 (mars 1802), pp. 29-32.

B. 'Neue Musikalien, von verschiedenen Verlegern, welche bey Breitkopf und Härtel zu haben sind', IV/9 (mars 1802), p. 36.
   C. 'Neue Musikalien, von verschiedenen Verlegern, welche bey Breitkopf und Härtel zu haben sind', IV/10 (mars 1802), pp. 38-40.
   D. 'Neue Musikalien, von verschiedenen Verlegern, welche bey Breitkopf und Härtel zu haben sind', IV/13 (mai 1802), pp. 50-52.
   E. 'Neue Musikalien, von verschiedenen Verlegern, welche bey Breitkopf und Härtel zu haben sind', IV/14 (mai 1802), pp. 55-56.
   F. 'Neue Musikalien, von verschiedenen Verlegern, welche bey Breitkopf und Härtel zu haben sind', IV/15 (juin 1802), p. 60.
   G. 'Neue Musikalien, von verschiedenen Verlegern, welche bey Breitkopf und Härtel zu haben sind', IV/16 (juin 1802), pp. 63-64.
   H. 'Neue Musikalien, von verschiedenen Verlegern, welche bey Breitkopf und Härtel zu haben sind', IV/17 (juillet 1802), p. 68.
   I. 'Neue Musikalien, von verschiedenen Verlegern, welche bey Breitkopf und Härtel zu haben sind', IV/18 (juillet 1802), pp. 71-72.

   *IBAMZ* 1805
   A. 'Neue Musikalien im Verlage von Breitkopf u. Härtel in Leipzig', in: *Intelligenz-Blatt zur Allgemeine musikalische Zeitung*, VIII/1 (décembre 1805), pp. 1-2.
   B. 'Neue Musikalien von verschiedenen Verlagern, welche bey Breitkopf und Härtel zu haben sind', VIII/1 (décembre 1805), pp. 2-4.
   C. 'Neue Musikalien von verschiedenen Verlegern, welche bey Breitkopf und Härtel zu haben sind', VIII/2 (décembre 1805), pp. 5-8.
   D. 'Neue Musikalien von verschiedenen Verlegern, welche bey Breitkopf und Härtel zu haben sind', VIII/3 (décembre 1805), pp. 11-12.
   E. 'Neue Musikalien von verschiedenen Verlegern, welche bey Breitkopf und Härtel zu haben sind', VIII/4 (décembre 1805), pp. 13-16.

   *IBAMZ* 1806
   A. 'Neue Musikalien von verschiedenen Verlegern, welche bey Breitkopf und Härtel zu haben sind', in: *Intelligenz-Blatt zur Allgemeine musikalische Zeitung*, VIII/5 (janvier 1806), pp. 17-20.
   B. 'Neue Musikalien von verschiedenen Verlegern, welche bey Breitkopf und Härtel zu haben sind', VIII/6 (janvier 1806), pp. 21-24.
   C. 'Neue Musikalien von verschiedenen Verlegern, welche bey Breitkopf und Härtel zu haben sind', VIII/7 (janvier 1806), pp. 25-28.
   D. 'Neue Musikalien von verschiedenen Verlegern, welche bey Breitkopf und Härtel zu haben sind', VIII/8 (janvier 1806), pp. 29-32.
   E. 'Neue Musikalien im Verlage von Breitkopf u. Härtel in Leipzig', VIII/9 (février 1806), pp. 33-35.
   F. 'Neue Musikalien von verschiedenen Verlegern, welche bey Breitkopf und Härtel zu haben sind', VIII/9 (février 1806), pp. 35-36.
   G. 'Neue Musikalien von verschiedenen Verlegern, welche bey Breitkopf und Härtel zu haben sind', VIII/10 (avril 1806), pp. 37-40.

H. 'Neue Musikalien von verschiedenen Verlegern, welche im Verlag der Breitkopf u. Härtelschen Musikhandlung erschienen sind', VIII/11 (juin 1806), pp. 41-44.

I. Breitkopf u. Härtel. 'Anzeige', VIII/12 (août 1806), p. 45.

J. 'Neue Musikalien von verschiedenen Verlegern, welche bey Breitkopf u. Härtel zu haben sind', VIII/12 (août 1806), pp. 47-48.

Kotzebue 1804
Kotzebue, August von. *Erinnerungen aus Paris im Jahre 1804*, Carlsruhe, s.n., 1804.

Kotzebue 1805
Id. *Souvenirs de Paris en 1804. Traduits de l'allemand, sur la deuxième Édition*, 2 vol., Paris, Barba, 1805.

Mongrédien 1986
Mongrédien, Jean. *La Musique en France des Lumières au Romantisme (1789-1830)*, Paris, Flammarion, 1986.

Reichardt 1804
Reichardt, Johann Friedrich. *Vertraute Briefe aus Paris geschrieben in den Jahren 1802 und 1803*, 2 vol., Hambourg, B. G. Hoffmann, 1804.

Reichardt 2002
Id. *Un hiver à Paris sous le Consulat: 1802-1803*, traduction française d'Arthur Laquiante [1895], Thierry Lentz éd., Paris, Tallandier, 2002 (Bibliothèque napoléonienne).

Schneider 1997
Schneider, Herbert. 'Die deutschen Übersetzungen französischer Opern zwischen 1780 und 1820. Verlauf und Probleme eines Transfer-Zyklus', in: *Kulturtransfer im Epochenumbruch. Frankreich-Deutschland 1770-1815*, Hans-Jürgen Lüsebrink et Rolf Reichardt éd., Leipzig, Leipziger Universitätsverlag, 1997 (Deutsch-Französische Kulturbibliothek, 9), pp. 593-676.

Spazier 1800
Spazier, Karl. *Gretry's Versuche über die Musik*, Leipzig, Breitkopf & Härtel, 1800.

Spohr 1860
Spohr, Louis. *Selbstbiographie. 1*, Cassel-Göttingen, Georg H. Wigand, 1860.

Spohr 1861
Id. *Selbstbiographie. 2*, Cassel-Göttingen, Georg H. Wigand, 1861.

# Opera, Theatre and Performance

# The Sound of Empire:
# Politicised Dramaturgy in French Opera
# from the French Revolution to Napoleon

*Maria Birbili*
(Universität des Saarlandes)

The late 18th century and the first half of the 19th century in France were a time of frequent upheavals, everchanging unstable regimes, and a series of events the repercussions of which, in their great significance, shaped the course of history of Europe and the Americas and are still very relevant in the 21st century. After the French Revolution, Napoleon Bonaparte became a controversial key figure not just due to his role in European (and American) politics from the last phase of the French Revolution until after the restoration of monarchy in France, but also in terms of the impact of his legacy on Napoleon III, president of the 2nd French Republic and later self-proclaimed second Emperor of France, from the late 1840s until the 1870s. Napoleon Bonaparte, however, was primarily an innovator of the military and one of the greatest army commanders of all times, while his strategy for war and expedition campaigns are still studied in military schools all over the world today.

Napoleon's influence on the arts and culture of 19th-century France (and Italy) are very closely related to the depiction of the use of military forces, expeditions, and war strategy also on the opera stage. As Napoleon himself said: «En général, la meilleure façon de me louer est de faire des choses qui inspirent des sentiments heroïques à la Nation, à la jeunesse et à l'armée»[1].

In this article I will discuss the profound changes in the aesthetics, the politicised dramaturgy, and the music brought upon French opera during the French Revolution and the Napoleonic wars. Phenomena will be explored such as the diminishing of the protagonist vs. the chorus as a dramatis persona, the collective revolutionary oath-taking by the unisono male

---

[1]. Letter from Napoleon to Jean-Baptiste de Nompère de Champagny (Duc de Cadore), minister of foreign affairs, quoted in Joly 1985, p. 240.

chorus, and the realistically staged depiction of a siege, battle, and military expedition on stage, all introduced by the French Revolution but still dominant and evolving during the Napoleonic era. As discussed in my first book[2], two specific new opera sub-genres, the 'siege-opera' and the 'expedition-opera', were introduced at the Paris Opéra respectively during the French Revolution and during the Napoleonic era. These two new operatic subgenres not only reflect the organised propaganda of the Revolutionary regime and of Napoleon's regime (both as a consul and as an emperor), but constitute a direct acculturisation process, with the representation of a number of contemporary historic events on the opera stage, often just months after their occurrence. With works such as Nicolas Dezède's *Péronne sauvée* (1783), *La prise de la Bastille* (anonymous, 1790), Antoine Rochefort's *La prise de Toulon* (anonymous, 1794), *Toulon soumis* (anonymous, 1789), Armand-Emmanuel Trial's *Le siège de Lille* (1794), Louis Jadin's *Le siège de Thionville* (1793), Étienne-Nicolas Méhul's *La prise du pont de Lodi* (1797), the 'siege-opera' genre depicts various historically authentic sieges, battles, and political events from the Revolutionary wars against the European coalition, often transposed into Greek or Roman antiquity, with works such as *Léonidas ou Le siège des Thermopyles* (unknown, 1791), Jean-Baptiste Lemoyne's *Miltiade à Marathon* (1793) and *Toute la Grèce, ou Ce que peut la liberté Marathon* (1794), Nicolas le Froid de Méraux' *Fabius* (1794), and Étienne-Nicolas Méhul's *Horatius Coclès* (1794). In the course of depicting the political ideas of democracy in 'siege-opera', specific new models in dramaturgy, staging, and music were created. For instance, the official protagonists listed in the libretti of the Revolutionary 'siege-opera' were neglected in their solo appearances vs. a *coryphée* from the chorus («un soldat», «un député») who remained nameless in the libretto and yet appeared in an important scene where the *coryphée* from the chorus completely dominated the dramaturgy and impressed with his revolutionary ethos. This musico-dramatic concept of neutralising the protagonists vs. anonymous figures from the chorus was related to the fact that the French Revolutionaries felt threatened by the idea of separate individuality, as it is known that unstable democracy has often favoured the collective over the individual. Another staple of the French Revolutionary 'siege-operas' was the homophonic male chorus of the Revolutionary oath-taking over the text 'Que + subjonctif', as in: 'Jurons tous!'. The oath-taking chorus frequently also reached a dissonant passage in which a «traitor» was mentioned, clearly related to King Louis XVI[3]. A similar oath-taking chorus with a dissonant passage where a «traitor» is mentioned was even used by federalist librettist Étienne de Jouy in Act II of Rossini's *Guillaume Tell* (Paris, 1829)[4].

These strong Revolutionary impressions also lingered throughout the Napoleonic era, during which many of these 'siege-operas' (such as Lemoyne's *Miltiade à Marathon* and Méhul's

---

[2]. BIRBILI 2014, pp. 39-93.
[3]. See BARTLET 1992B.
[4]. BIRBILI 2014, pp. 55-72 and pp. 171-213, as well as BIRBILI 2013.

*Horatius Coclès*) were performed from 1794 onward. The evolution of the genre from the Revolution into the Napoleonic era can be identified in Méhul's *Le pont de Lodi* and *Adrien*, and Spontini's/Étienne de Jouy's *Fernand Cortez*, which no longer depict the ideals of democracy and the contemporaneous historically authentic Revolutionary wars, but in which period an obsession with strategic expeditions reached the opera stage. These 'expedition operas' were ordered so as to celebrate Napoleon's glory during the Napoleonic expeditions in Egypt and in Spain, and the libretti mainly depict an expedition on the opera stage. *Fernand Cortez*, an opera which Napoleon disliked (he left the premiere before the end of the performance), is the most fascinating of these works, remaining politically ambiguous in its sophisticated dramaturgy and its conflicted approach to colonialism, while, in its complex historicism, it paves the road to the later genre of *grand opéra*.

The continuity of the politicised sub-genres from the French Revolution to Napoleon's era can be identified in Étienne-Nicolas Méhul's *Adrien*. This opera meant to be performed during the French Revolution, on 6 March 1792 at the Paris Opéra[5], but was suspected of being too 'imperial', also due to the fact that it was based on a libretto by Metastasio and was considered to be too close to Vienna and its emperor Leopold II, with the libretto of *Adrien* celebrating an emperor's *clemenza*. The following discussion in the newspaper *Annales Patriotiques* goes so far as to refer to Marie-Antoinette:

> Il faut espérer que les spectateurs ne lui [Marie-Antoinette] donneront pas lieu de croire que les Parisiens soient de sitôt prêts à s'atteler au char de l'empereur son frère[6].

The belated first production of a starkly modified version[7] of Méhul's *Adrien* took place on 4 June 1799 at the Paris Opéra for only four nights, as the libretto apparently was still considered too 'imperial'. *Adrien* depicts an emperor's expedition in Syria during the beginning of Napoleon's first expedition in Egypt and five months before Napoleon proclaimed himself First Consul with a *coup d'état* on 9-10 November 1799.

Despite an imperial libretto, *Adrien* is still quoting the rhetoric of democratic 'collectivity' from the French Revolution:

Soldats, vous m'offrez un empire.
Et, soutenu par vos brillants exploits,
Puissé-je des Romains justifier le choix.
C'est la seule gloire à laquelle j'aspire.

---

[5]. Pertaining to the political controversy around Méhul's *Adrien*, see BARTLET 1992A.
[6]. From 2 March 1792, p. 277.
[7]. See BARTLET 1982, pp. 407-470 and pp. 1514-1553.

> Ce n'est point moi que vous servez;
> C'est Rome, Rome seule, à qui vous vous devez.
> Au trait des grandeurs je saurai reconnaître
> Que je suis votre chef et non pas votre maître.
> Respectons, vous le trône, et moi la Liberté.
> Empereur et sujets, ce saint nom nous rassemble.
> Réunis par l'honneur, nous servirons ensemble
> Pour la gloire de Rome et sa prosperité[8].

The libretto for *Adrien* visibly had its origins in 1792, during a time when the French were still working on a constitutional monarchy after the British model. Librettist François-Benoît Hoffman commented on this aspect of the libretto:

> Les seuls vers qui puissent s'appliquer aux circonstances sont, par un heureux hasard, aussi constitutionnels que s'ils eussent était faits à dessein. Mais en cela même je ne mérite aucun éloge, car ces vers sont presque littéralement traduits de Metastase[9].

A differentiation between *Adrien* and the propagandistic 'siege-opera' of the Revolution lies in the librettist's attempt to produce dramatic balance between the two parties, trying to illustrate not just the Romans', but also the Syrians' noble motives for doing battle. The grand-scale staging, the extreme realism of the physical details, and the flirting with the notion of exoticism were additional factors to set apart the Napoleonic 'expedition-opera' from the previous 'siege-opera' of the Revolution. The Finale I of *Adrien* showcases a battle in the tradition of the 'siege-opera' of the French Revolution, but with a pre-Revolutionary structure consisting of different Gluckian choruses that follow each other. Act II concentrates on the love triangle between the emperor, the Syrian princess Emirène, and the Roman lady Sabine but nevertheless ends by showcasing a long battle on the stage that follows the Revolutionary model of the 'siege-opera', but with an extremely complex staging that depicts chaotic battle action on the stage with the singers and the extras engaging in an almost athletic activity:

> On voit Cosroès et Pharnaspe qui repoussent Flaminius de l'autre côté du fleuve. Rutile sort avec sa troupe de droite, entre le fleuve et le temple. Adrien avec la sienne monte sur le pont et attaque le front des ennemis. Les prêtres ouvrent les portes du temple, les femmes et une partie du peuple s'y précipitent. Le reste avec les prêtres se posternent sur les marches et embrassent les statues des divinités. Le combat continue et s'anime. Cosroès et Pharnaspe repoussent la troupe d'Adrien et lui font repasser le pont. Mais Flaminius, qui revient par la rive qui est entre le fleuve

---

[8]. Acte I, scène 3.
[9]. In *Journal de Paris* from 3 March 1792.

et le palais, s'unit à l'empereur et l'aide à repousser les Parthes. Cosroès repasse le pont, et il est entraîné dans sa fuite par ses soldats. Mais au moment où il veut s'échapper par le côté droit de l'autre rive, Rutile arrive avec sa troupe et lui ferme le chemin. Le combat redouble avec fureur de l'autre côté du fleuve. Pharnaspe, investi sur le pont par Rutile, Adrien et Flaminius, s'y défend avec rage, mais enfin il est entraîné sur le devant, et, au moment où sa troupe résiste encore, le pont, sapé par les Romains, s'écroule avec fracas et renverse dans le fleuve tous les Parthes qui y restaient. Cosroès, qui voulait les secourir, voit s'écrouler le pont presque sous ses pieds, et il est entraîné dans la fuite par les siens. On entend des cris de victoire, et le peuple et les femmes sortent du temple, pour voir le vainqueur qui tient Pharnaspe prisonnier[10].

After this long battle scene there follows a collective oath-taking which directly imitates the Revolutionary model with 'que + subjonctif', including the idea of a 'traitor tyrant' as discussed above:

Percé de mille coups,
Que le tyran périsse,
Et que les fers des Romains égorgés
Soient l'instrument de son supplice.

In collective syllabic unison with *piano-forte*-effects, this oath is very similar to Méhul's at the time famous oath in his earlier Revolutionary opera *Horatius Coclés* (Paris, 1794), which inspired federalist Étienne de Jouy and Rossini in the second Act of *Guillaume Tell* (Paris, 1829)[11]. Act III of *Adrien* is just a *Divertissement* celebrating the emperor's *clemenza* as Adrien shows mercy for the Syrians who lost the war.

Librettist François-Benoît Hoffman critically discussed the spectacular staging for *Adrien*, which at the time was a novelty:

Adrien est attendu avec impatience pour la magnificence avec laquelle on sait qu'il doit être donné. Nous avons dans cet opéra tout ce qui peut piquer la grosse curiosité du vulgaire: des danses de tout genre, des combats, une marche triomphale qui passe sur un pont, un pont qui s'écroule dans un combat et qui renverse tous les combattants dans le fleuve, un char traîné par des chevaux réels, dont chacun coûte cent louis et les vaut[12], une montagne singulière, taillée à pic, de laquelle une armée descend d'une manière périlleuse et pittoresque, toutes les décorations neuves et riches, tous les habits neufs, costumes romains, parthes et syriens. Cent

---

[10]. Quoted from the printed score for the 1799 version, F-Po A 367, I-IV.
[11]. See BIRBILI 2014, pp. 55-72 and pp. 171-213, as well as BIRBILI 2013.
[12]. The French press misleadingly claimed that the horses engaged for the *Adrien* premiere from the notorious circus Franconi were supposedly financed by queen Marie-Antoinette.

vingt comparses, sans compter tous les chœurs et toute la danse de l'Opéra, enfin c'est une vraie lanterne magique, digne en tout du mauvais goût du siècle et de la décadence de la littérature. Aussi, mon frère, il est sûr que mon *Adrien* aura un très brillant et très honteux succès[13].

Another 'expedition opera' in honour of Napoleon, Jean-François Le Sueur's *Le Triomphe de Trajan*, was ordered by Napoleon himself in 1806, after his victory in Jena. Librettist Joseph-Alphonse Esménard and the *chef de la scène* of the Paris Opéra Loiseau Persuis were involved in the project. *Le Triomphe de Trajan* reached exorbitant costs as high as 72,000 francs, with 432 actors appearing on stage dressed as Roman soldiers and Daces, including 12 horses from the notorious circus Franconi. Cast with contemporary Parisian stars such as soprano Alexandrine-Caroline Branchu and star baritone Étienne Dérivis, the premiere of *Le Triomphe de Trajan* took place on 23 October 1807. As an imperial 'expedition-opera', *Le Triomphe de Trajan* depicts Trajan's expedition in the Middle East, transparently honouring Napoleon's victory in Jena. *Le Triomphe de Trajan* is musically less complex[14] than *Adrien* and *Fernand Cortez* but contains a collective oath-taking and a spectacular depiction of the Emperor's marching in the Middle East, with the use of a dozen real horses for the cavalry charge for the stage of the Opéra, rented from the reputable Circus Franconi, and with the participation of 432 extras as discussed above.

*Trajan* includes an oath-taking quartet in Act I for the two main soloists (Décéphale and Sigismond) together with two anonymous *coryphées* (*taille et basse*) as well as a collective oath for the chorus:

Que Rome à notre sang
Puisse mêler ses pleurs.

Nous avons tous
Les mêmes sentiments.
Les Daces à tes vœux
Unissent leur serment.

Another collective oath-taking for the chorus in Act II of *Le triomphe de Trajan* ('Heureux qui meurt pour la patrie') quotes a contemporaneously well-known oath chorus from Lemoyne's *Miltiade à Marathon*, a Revolutionary opera from the *Terreur* period that was kept in the Paris repertory until as late as in 1798.

---

13. Letter by the librettist François-Bénoît Hoffman to his brother, quoted in JACQUINET 1878, pp. 45-46.
14. For a critical discussion of *Le triomphe de Trajan*'s music and dramaturgy, see MONGRÈDIEN 1980. For additional, minor works honouring Napoleon, see MONGRÈDIEN 1986, pp. 53-61 and MONGRÈDIEN 1969.

The next Napoleonic 'expedition opera' of Le Sueur's was supposed to be an *Alexandre à Babylone* of 1815, a project which was abandoned after Napoleon's loss at Waterloo. While Le Sueur's *Le Triomphe de Trajan* showcases a staging that is much more interesting than the qualities of the music, and Méhul's *Adrien* appears rather too Gluckian in its musical idiom compared to Méhul's earlier operas, there is another contemporaneous Napoleonic opera that I would like to discuss, and this one is musically, dramaturgically, and politically most complex, fascinating, and significant for the future of French opera, since it appears to work as a link between Napoleonic 'expedition opera' and the later genre of *grand opéra*: I am referring, of course, to Étienne de Jouy's and Gasparre Spontini's *Fernand Cortez*.

Ordered by Napoleon as anti-Spanish propaganda during his expedition in Spain, luminary librettist Étienne de Jouy and Napoleon-friendly author Joseph Esménard worked on the libretto for a first version of *Fernand Cortez* that had its premiere on 28 November 1809.

*Fernand Cortez* is also one of the first operas in the 19th century that deals with the exotic, an elaborate demonstration of interculturality during the age of active colonialism, created at a particularly unstable historical moment, in the transitional period between the French Revolution and the restoration of monarchy in France. The challenges caused by the political agenda of this opera are reflected in the fact that it had to be rearranged five times into five more or less different versions, and therefore as a work it expresses an extremely unstable or at least ever-changing aesthetic and political statement, which is reflected in each of the five different versions[15]; these changed year after year, both in their structure and dramaturgy and in their location in two different cities, moving from 1809 in Paris to 1832 in Berlin. In this article I will concentrate on a discussion of the three Parisian versions of the opera, all of them directly or indirectly related to Napoleon.

*Fernand Cortez* embodies, musically as well as in its choice of subject and dramaturgy, the change of French opera from the politically charged works of the French Revolution to the historical opera of the 19th century, a genre known to musicology as *grand opéra*. Despite often being identified as merely a predecessor to the genre of *grand opéra*, *Fernand Cortez* and its historical, politicised dramaturgy did not occur in a vacuum, but in direct relation to its immediate past, after the occurrence of phenomena such as the revolutionary French 'siege-opera', the chorus gaining dramatic importance, and the collective oath-taking introduced by the French Revolution. Librettist Étienne de Jouy, who had witnessed the French Revolution

---

[15]. Not all five different versions of *Fernand Cortez* were set to music: After the first version of 1809 (which Napoleon disliked), a second version was prepared as a libretto in 1814-1815 (F-Po Livr. 19/189), but no sources or reports in the press have been found in Paris for this second version of the libretto having ever been set to music. The last French version of the opera from 1817 is the one usually performed today, while the 2 versions prepared by Spontini for Berlin (in 1824 and 1832) are not relevant for this discussion, especially since they celebrate Christianity.

and survived the *Terreur*, escaping to Switzerland and coming back after the fall of Robespierre, was careful to avoid the Revolutionaries' concept of 'neutralising the protagonist' in the libretto of *Fernand Cortez*, which was meant to celebrate imperial Napoleonic glory.

Another reminder of the opera of the Revolution to be found in *Fernand Cortez* is the collective oath. Reflecting ideas of the Revolution and an embellished version of its parliamentary procedures, the collective oath scene in the 'siege-opera' of the French Revolution invariably began with a recitative in active and equally engaged dialogue between a soloist and the homophonic chorus. Here is an example of an oath-taking from the 'siege-opera' *Fabius*, a Revolutionary battle transferred in the Roman antiquity, where the collective phrase «Oui, tous, nous le jurons» is repeated like a collective litany, a phenomenon that occurred in every single 'siege-opera' of the French Revolution:

| | |
|---|---|
| PAUL-ÉMILE: | Jurez de rétablir l'autorité des lois. |
| CHŒUR: | Oui, tous, nous le jurons. |
| PAUL-ÉMILE: | Jurez, au prix de votre vie de sauver la Patrie. |
| CHŒUR: | Oui, tous, nous le jurons. |
| PAUL-ÉMILE: | Jurez que les propriétés, que les hommes par vous seront respectés, et de la liberté pourront goûter les charmes. |
| CHŒUR: | Oui, tous, nous le jurons. |

*Fernand Cortez* contains a reminiscence of the Revolutionary oath scene in the scene in which Cortez subdues the insurrection of the Spanish fleet against his leadership:

| | |
|---|---|
| CORTEZ: | Vous me l'aviez promis. |
| MORALES: | Et je le jure encore. |
| CHŒUR (*noblement*): | Nous le jurons encore. |
| CORTEZ: | J'ai perdu mes soldats. |
| MORALES ET LE CHŒUR (*s'inclinant devant Cortez*): | Ils sont à tes genoux! |
| CORTEZ: | Je devrais les punir… |
| MORALES ET LE CHŒUR (*noblement, avec beaucoup de fierté*): | Nul d'entre eux/de nous ne t'implore Que pour suivre tes pas! |

The primarily physical, less politically charged business of battle and final liberation of the besieged town in the opera of the Revolution occurred with much visual realism on stage, in activity that was meant to be perceived as unruly. The siege theme was of such importance to the dramaturgy that the process of representing it visually completely dominated the staging. Since its very first appearance (with Nicolas Dezède's *Péronne sauvée* in 1783), 'siege-opera' established a formula and kept to it. After a march-like Ouverture (usually quoting *La Marseillaise*), a 'siege-opera' would open with a visually imposing, ominous view of the fortress of the besieged town. Between Act I and II the perspective would change to the other of the two rival camps. Act II of a 'siege-opera' took place at night, on a darkened stage, with effective, albeit technically simple, use of lighting effects and with continuous physical action, as a series of military troops, from the two sides, kept patrolling the darkened stage with torches, under the walls of the fortress. The activity on stage invariably culminated in a battle-scene, during which lighting effects would create a gradual sunrise. The autograph scores and manuscript copies of these operas at the Paris Bibliothèque de l'Opéra include lighting instructions in red pencil which produce the illusion of a gradual change from night in the woods to dawn and then sunrise («la nuit», «le contrejour», «le jour».) Act II of a 'siege-opera' would end inconclusively, in the middle of the battle-scene. After a short intermission, Act III began in the middle of the previous, supposedly ongoing battle, which went on and on, with complex physical manoeuvres, battle, fire, and pantomime on the stage. The final, predictable victory of the democratic side led to a *Divertissement* ending in a celebration of democracy and the ideals of the Revolution, with the performance of *La Marseillaise* and other Revolutionary songs.

These strong Revolutionary impressions lingered throughout the Napoleonic period, during which many of these 'siege-operas' were performed again, for example Lemoyne's *Miltiade à Marathon* and Méhul's *Horatius Coclès*. Méhul's *Le pont de Lodi*, first performed at the end of 1797 at the Théâtre Feydeau, presented an authentic siege from the Napoleonic wars, albeit without depicting Napoleon on stage.

*Fernand Cortez* stands out from the other Napoleonic œuvres de circonstance and 'expedition-operas' for its complex dramaturgy and the maturity of its musical idiom. Moreover, its politically ambiguous message not only makes it essentially the predecessor of *grand opéra* but also contributed to its failure with Napoleon. Napoleon had ordered prestigious librettist Étienne de Jouy and successful composer Gaspare Spontini to offer *Fernand Cortez* as a homage to the Napoleonic expedition in Spain. But during the premiere of the first version of the opera, on 28 November 1809, Napoleon was so disturbed by the ambiguous statements of the end-product that he left the theatre before the end of the performance. As a consequence, the first version of *Fernand Cortez* disappeared from the repertoire of the Opéra after only 24 performances (from 28 November 1809 to 24 January 1812).

There are some moments in *Fernand Cortez* that contribute to a very transparent glorification of Napoleon, particularly in the formal wedding ceremony between Cortez and the Aztec princess Amazily, which is a clear reference to Napoleon's plans to marry Marie Louise of Austria. Another direct reference to Napoleon's imperial glory and imperialistic intentions lies in the final *Divertissement* at the conclusion of the opera, as it alludes to a Spanish empire on which the 'sun never sets'.

Still, many aspects remain ambiguous. The violent fanaticism of the Aztec priests is a clear allusion to the Spanish Inquisition at the time of Napoleon's expedition in Spain. And Cortez/Napoleon is presented as a noble 'civilizer' just as much as a *conquistador*. But what about the corruption in the Spanish army? Does the fascination of the Spaniards with Aztec gold allude to contemporary 19$^{th}$ century Spain as an enemy of imperial France, or should we see a hidden allusion to the fact that France was getting tired of Napoleon's never-ending expeditions, especially after the disastrous effects of the Napoleonic campaign in Spain? Also surprising is the lack of an unambiguous propaganda against the Aztecs. There are no extremes of good and bad in the dramaturgy. The Aztecs are presented as at least as capable of heroism and noble patriotism as the Spaniards — perhaps even more, since they are mainly defending their native territory and are not shown to be greedy for gold. No wonder Napoleon left the *Fernand Cortez* performance early, disappointed.

The first version, performed in 1809, remains very close to the dramaturgy of the 'siege-opera' of the French Revolution. We have a first Act depicting the Spanish camp, with the Spaniards' view of the action and the problems that they experience with the organising of the *conquista* of the Aztec city of Tenochtitlàn. Soon after, we witness the insurrection of the Spanish soldiers which is presented, as in the Revolutionary 'siege-opera', by anonymous solo choristers («1$^{er}$ soldat», «2$^{ème}$ soldat») in recitative and in homophonic, short-chorus sections. The insurrection is cut short by Cortez' reckless act of burning down his own fleet so that his mutinous soldiers cannot desert Mexico by sea, and Act I ends with a collective oath-taking, reminiscent of the 'siege-opera' of the French Revolution. However, the concluding chorus of the *Fernand Cortez* oath features an Italian and not French Revolutionary musical structure, with a very early example of a 'Rossini crescendo' *avant la lettre*.

Act II of the first version of *Fernand Cortez* is staged under the fortress-like walls of Tenochtitlàn and contains ceaseless physical activity, very much like in the 'siege-opera' of the French Revolution, with the Spanish army executing various manoeuvres on stage, primarily building a bridge to the walls of Tenochtitlàn. Act II culminates with even more spectacular physical action, as the Aztec princess Amazily, on her own initiative and without Cortez' permission, jumps off a cliff into the Gulf of Mexico, swims to the other side, and reaches the Aztec city to negotiate an exchange of prisoners of war. This is depicted as a leap off-stage, with the female chorus of her Aztec servants commenting in recitative on the action as she swims to and finally reaches the opposite shore. Act III is shown at last from the Aztec perspective, from inside the besieged city of Tenochtitlàn, where the Aztec priests are preparing a ritualistic human sacrifice. Montezuma does not appear in this first version of *Fernand Cortez*, where Aztec leadership is reduced to either the violent, sanctimonious fanaticism of the Grand Prêtre (an allusion to the Spanish Inquisition?) or to the 'barbaric', frenetic martiality of the Aztec warrior

Télasco (baritone). Against these 'barbarians' there is the shining contrast of the Spaniards as not just *conquistadors*, but as 'civilisers' of an uneducated tribe of 'wild peoples', presented as being in complete ignorance of right and wrong and in desperate need of the civilising lights of the Napoleonic Code.

The next version of *Fernand Cortez*, created between 1814 and 1815 but only as a libretto[16] discovered by me in Paris, kept the same structure of Acts as in 1809, but the dramaturgy and political message were subtly changed. Instead of reminders of the 'siege-opera' of the French Revolution, we now have a purely imperial political statement, in the tradition of the libretti by Metastasio. If the 1809 version of *Fernand Cortez* depicted a decisive, martial, imperialistic conquest of the Aztec nation, in 1814 the conquest theme was changed into a humanistic imperial alliance between two different nations[17]. In this libretto version of *Fernand Cortez* from 1814 Montezuma appears on stage, albeit in a very brief role, in more symbolic than true dramatic fashion. Significantly his musical material is limited to archaic sounding baroque recitative. He is presented as an enlightened monarch who has no control over his governmental functions, trying in vain to regain power over the Grand Prêtre's barbaric religious fanaticism. At the end of the opera Montezuma seems relieved to hand over his kingdom and its many problems to Cortez, whom he recognises as better equipped to deal with them.

This libretto version from 1814-1815 contains some anti-Napoleonic, pacifist allusions. This appears not just in the celebration of peace between the nations, but, even more, in the unmistakably clear subtext of being worn out by constant war. Notice the allusion to the recognition of French Revolution roots in the Napoleonic empire, in the words of Aztec warrior Télasco:

> D'une vaine terreur qui fonda votre empire,
> N'espérez plus abuser à nos yeux.
>
> [Believe not that you can deceive us again:
> Your empire was founded upon the *Terreur*.]

In the next and last Paris version of *Fernand Cortez*, produced in 1817 and today established as the official version of the opera, the initial Acts I, II and III of the first two versions traded places with each other, creating an unprecedented dramaturgy. In this version of *Fernand Cortez* we are thrown, without any exposition, into the main action, which takes place inside the walls of ominous Aztec city Tenochtitlàn, and we are forced to witness the Aztec preparations for the ceremony of sacrificing a group of Spanish prisoners of war. The scene

---

[16]. F-Po Livr. 19/189.

[17]. On the various different compositions of eighteenth-century *Montezuma* libretti, including one by Friedrich the Great, see MAEHDER 1992.

derives from the opening of Act III of the previous versions of *Fernand Cortez*, but it has been musically developed. Even if there are still elements of propaganda in the dramatic structure of this opening scene, which contrasts 'barbaric' Aztecs with their bloodthirsty, primitive religion, against the noble, Deistic[18] stoicism of the Spanish prisoners, the original dramaturgy of *Fernand Cortez* has been completely altered in this third version of the opera. The dramatic conflict is no longer political, as in the previous two versions. It does not lie in physically depicting a heroic and action-packed war between two armies, as in 1809, nor in depicting a noble reconciliation between two emperors, as in 1814-1815. Instead, the main attraction in the 1817 version of *Fernand Cortez* lies in depicting the primarily exotic, sensorially overwhelming experience of the Aztec city of Tenochtitlàn. Instead of the political historicism of the French Revolution, we have now moved — for the first time in the history of opera — into historicism intended in an essentially anthropological sense. Napoleon's expeditions to Egypt and the Egyptomania which was soon to become popular in France are not unrelated to this phenomenon, where for the first time in the Western civilisation occurred an interest in systematically and accurately examining and depicting a foreign culture, an interest that continued to develop in the next genre of French *grand opéra* and its reception in Verdi's *Aida* (Cairo, 1871).

In both previous versions of *Fernand Cortez*, in 1809 and 1814, the dramatic action focuses on the siege of Mexico as a process, depicting the various actions taking place during this siege in a linear, chronologically accurate fashion. The siege of Tenochtitlàn was gradually and logically shown in stages, following the progress of the Spaniards' siege step by step on the operatic stage, and essentially creating a dramaturgy of suspense. Act I of the earlier versions only showed the Spaniards' camp and their growing problems with unruliness and insurrection, whereas Tenochtitlàn and the difficulties in attacking it were only mentioned verbally. Act II went on to show the ominous walls of the besieged Aztec city, under which the Spaniards were shown working like ants to build a bridge. The exotic factor found its physical concretisation for the very first time, as we see Aztec princess Amazily leaping off a cliff into the Gulf of Mexico, to swim to the other shore on the Aztec coast. And finally, Act III allowed the audience, with at least as much longing as the besieging Spaniards were experiencing, to take a first look into the mysterious, bizarre Aztec city of Tenochtitlàn and to witness directly the exotic local custom of human sacrifice, before seeing the city fall into the hands of the Spaniards.

The 1817 version of *Fernand Cortez* changed all that, creating a completely new, fragmented, short-cuts dramaturgy, which was soon to be assimilated into the future genre of

---

[18]. The text of the *a cappella* three-voice hymn sung by the Spanish prisoners, 'Créateur de ce nouveau monde', unmistakably evokes elements of freemasonry. We do not know for a fact, but musicologists such as Jacques Joly and Jouy's biographer, Paul Théodore Comeau suspect that librettist Étienne de Jouy was a member of a masonic lodge. At any rate the text is typical of the Napoleonic era, in which the ideas of the French Revolution were not completely erased, despite the emperor's later attempts to appear as imperial as possible, by having his coronation blessed by the Catholic Church. See COMEAU 1968.

*grand opéra* and is more characteristic of the medium of cinematography than the stage. After a fully unexpected, anthropologically charged first impression of Tenochtitlàn in full-blown human sacrifice fever, set up as an opening scene, we are anticlimactically moved back into the Spanish camp in Act II, to be informed in monotonous recitative of things we have already seen occurring on stage — and quite spectacularly so[19]. In Act II we are informed about the fate of Cortez' brother who is being held prisoner by the Aztecs, after we have just seen him on stage in Act I, chained up and ready to be slaughtered in honour of the gods of blood. The reason for these discrepancies is the fact that Acts I and III of the initial versions of *Fernand Cortez* traded places with each other. Act III of the 1817 version provides even less dramatic interest. Whereas in 1809 it contained the first glimpse inside Tenochtitlàn, in the 1817 version it is just a *pot-pourri* of various unrelated scenes, moving at a quick, even chaotic, pace. This dramaturgy might appear appropriate for the accelerating actions of war just before the final *conquista*, but the various scenes do not correspond with each other, having been randomly picked from the different Acts of the previous versions. Therefore we have the battle under the walls of Tenochtitlàn being held up for a brief recess, to allow for the wedding ceremony of Cortez and Princess Amazily to take place. Then the battle continues. On the other hand, one can say that the fragmented, highly incoherent conclusion of Act III of the 1817 version of *Fernand Cortez* intensifies the ambiguous, cynical political statement of the opera about the Spanish conquest of Mexico: something that Napoleon would definitely not accept.

Another aspect of exoticism in *Fernand Cortez* pertains to the — by this time obligatory in the Napoleonic era — cavalry charge, with the use of real horses on the opera stage. 17 horses from the Circus Franconi were hired for the first performance of *Fernand Cortez* in 1809, an addition of 5 more horses since *Le Triomphe de Trajan*. A clever dramatic twist in the first version of the opera allowed the use of the aforementioned horses to turn into an authentic anthropological commentary on the Aztec civilization, as the Aztecs were shown to be overwhelmed by their first experience of the dangerous looking and yet tame animals:

> Chœur:   Ô terreur! Ô prodige!
> Un effrayant prestige
> a-t-il troublé nos sens?
> Les enfants de la guerre
> font sortir de la terre
> des monstres bondissants,
> pour eux obéissants.
> Dans leur bouillante audace
> ils dévorent l'espace.
> Grâce, ô Dieux tout puissants!

---

[19]. One of the main characteristics of *grand opéra* is the interest in visually presenting action preferably in *tableaux* or pantomime, rather than depicting it verbally (per recitative) or musically (in a closed musical number).

*Fernand Cortez* exemplifies not just a fragmented dramaturgy, as discussed above, but also a mix of very unequal musical material: short, conservative solo pieces evocative of eighteenth-century opera, like Amazily's aria 'Dieu terrible, prêtre jaloux' and the aggressive, chromatically charged hate-chorus of the enraged Aztecs, 'Déchirons, frappons les victimes!' which is reinforced by an intense use of the cymbals. Such old-fashioned, Gluckian pieces are thrown together with longer, multi-sectional numbers *all'italiana*, exemplifying musical structures typical of the Italian, particularly Neapolitan, opera of the time, like the multi-sectional duet between Amazily and Télasco, which exemplifies an early use of Italian *solita forma*[20] duet form. Then there are the long, visually enriched, multi-mediatic scenes which, in their musical, visual, and scenic grand-scale complexity are an early predecessor of *grand opéra*, like the opening scene of Act I in the 1817 version, which contains different materials, first presented the one after the other, then superposed on each other so as to form a *tableau*. The scene begins with the pseudo-canon trio in g minor of the Spanish prisoners ('Champs de l'Ibérie'), followed by the solemn recitative of the Aztec Grand Prêtre, the ominous prayer of the Aztec chorus ('Que tout frémisse!'), and the exotic hate-chorus of the Aztec warriers ('Déchirons, frappons les victimes!'). Then follows another heroic trio of the Spanish prisoners preparing to die ('Voici notre dernier effort'), followed by their *a cappella* Deist hymn ('Créateur de ce nouveau monde'). What follows next is a superposition of parts from all these different materials, with the prayer of the Aztec chorus dominating the scene. Librettist Étienne de Jouy, a known federalist, had conceived this Aztec prayer as a solemn oath-taking, reminiscent, in its textual structure, of the French Revolution model. The composer Spontini, however, did not follow the Revolutionary model of an oath, but chose to follow the model of sacred music for this solemn, ominous chorus in g minor. 'Que tout frémisse!', with its syncopated motive in triplets, its old-fashioned suspensions, upward modulations over the diminished seventh chord, chromaticism in the woodwind instruments, and its ominous, repeated alliterations of '-isse' («frémisse..., gémisse..., s'appésantisse») contains transparent reminiscences of the *Lacrimosa* of the Mozart *Requiem*, which was previously very successfully performed in Paris in 1804 in the church of Saint Germain de l'Auxerrois, conducted by Parisian luminary composer Luigi Cherubini.

In its fragmented dramaturgy and mixture of very unequal musical material, *Fernand Cortez* stands out as a work suspended in several ways between two different worlds: between eighteenth- and nineteenth- century opera, between *opera seria* and *grand opéra*, between the early era of yet unquestioned colonialism and the more sophisticated, conflicted approach to colonial politics following the French Revolution. The subsequent German versions of the opera for Berlin (of 1824, in a modified arrangement of Acts II and III by the composer Spontini and in a German translation by Johann Cristoph May; and of 1832, in a new arrangement of

---

[20]. See POWERS 1987.

the third Act by Karl August von Lichtenstein) show an effort on Spontini's part to add more interest and spectacle to the third Act of the opera, in contrast to the weak third Act and hasty conclusion of the 1817 French version. Yet the spectacularly religious staging of the last, 1832 version for Berlin, showcasing a reconciliation of the entire population of Spaniards and Aztecs kneeling before a massive illuminated cross, remains as questionable and ambiguous a message as reflected in each of the three everchanging previous French versions of the opera. Thus Spontini's *Fernand Cortez*, due to its genesis at a particularly unstable historical time, in the transitional period between the French Revolution and the Restoration of monarchy in France, and a precursor of *grand opéra*, exemplifies interculturality and can be considered, thanks to the Napoleonic expeditions that brought about an interest in archeology and orientalism in France, as the first intent for an anthropological approach to colonialism that occurred on the opera stage. The challenges that such a political approach represented for its time are reflected in the fact that *Fernand Cortez* had to be rearranged five times[21] into different versions and therefore expresses an everchanging aesthetic and political statement, reflected in each and every one of these five different versions of the opera which shifted continuously from 1809 in Paris to 1832 in Berlin. Hence *Fernand Cortez* embodies, musically as well as in its choice of subject and in its dramaturgy, the shifting of French opera from the politically charged works of the French Revolution to the historical opera of the 19th century while at the same time depicting the involvement and the different political perceptions of Napoleon himself[22].

## Bibliography

Bartlet 1982
Bartlet, M. Elizabeth C. *Étienne-Nicolas Méhul and Opera during the French Revolution, Consulate and Empire: A Source, Archivial and Stylistic Study*, Ph.D. Diss., Chicago (IL), University of Chicago, 1982; Ann Arbor (MI), UMI Research Press, 1982.

Bartlet 1992a
Ead. 'On the Freedom of the Theatre and Censorship. The *Adrien* Controversy of 1792', in: *1789-1989: Musique, Histoire, Démocratie*, edited by Antoine Hennion, Paris, Éditions Maison des Sciences de l'Homme, 1992, pp. 13-30.

Bartlet 1992b
Ead. 'The New Repertory of the Opéra during the Reign of Terror: Revolutionary Rhetoric and Operatic Consequences', in: *Music and the French Revolution*, edited by Malcolm Boyd, Cambridge, Cambridge University Press, 1992, pp. 107-156.

---

[21]. As discussed above, the second French version (from 1814) exists only in libretto-form.
[22]. For a discussion of ossianic operas glorifying Napoleon such as Jean-François Le Sueur's *Ossian, ou Les Bardes* (1804) and Étienne-Nicolas Méhul's *Uthal* (1806), see Mongrédien 1969 and Mongrédien 1986.

BIRBILI 2013
BIRBILI, Maria. 'Conflict between State and Church in Verdi's Risorgimento Opera. French Influences in Models of Dramaturgy', in: *VIVA V.E.R.D.I.: Music from Risorgimento to the Unification of Italy*, edited by Roberto Illiano, Turnhout, Brepols, 2013 (Studies on Italian Music History, 8), pp. 255-276.

BIRBILI 2014
EAD. *Die Politisierung der Oper im 19. Jahrhundert*, Frankfurt, Peter Lang, 2014 (Perspektiven der Opernforschung, 21).

COMEAU 1968
COMEAU, Paul Théodore. *Étienne Jouy: His Life and his Paris Essays*, Ph.D. Diss., Princeton University (NJ), 1968; Ann Arbor (MI), UMI Research Press, 1968.

JACQUINET 1878
JACQUINET, Paul. *François Hoffman, sa vie et ses œuvres*, Paris, Aux Éditions du Livre, 1878.

JOLY 1985
JOLY, Jacques. 'Les ambiguïtés de la guerre napoléonienne dans *Fernand Cortez* de Spontini', in: *La bataille, l'armée, la gloire, 1745-1871. Actes du colloque Clermont-Ferrand 1983*, edited by Paul Vialleneix and Jean Ehrard, 2 vols., Clermont-Ferrand, Association des Publications de l'Université de Clermont-Ferrand 2, 1985, vol. I, pp. 239-255.

MAEHDER 1992
MAEHDER, Jürgen. 'Mentalitätskonflikt und Fürstenpflicht. Die Begegnung zwischen Conquistadór und mittelamerikanischem Herrscher auf der barocken Opernbühne', in: *Text und Musik. Neue Perspektiven der Theorie*, edited by Michael Walter, Munich, Fink, 1992, pp. 131-80.

MONGRÈDIEN 1969
MONGRÈDIEN, Jean. 'L'opéra au service de l'Empereur', in: *Europe*, no. 32 (April 1969), pp. 328-333.

MONGRÈDIEN 1980
ID. *Jean-François Le Sueur. Contribution à l'étude d'un démi-siècle de musique française*, Bern, Peter Lang, 1980.

MONGRÈDIEN 1986
ID. *La musique en France des Lumières au Romantisme, 1789-1830*, Paris, Flammarion, 1986.

POWERS 1987
POWERS, Harold Stone. '«La solita forma» and the Uses of Convention', in: *Acta Musicologica*, LIX/1 (1987), pp. 65-90 [also in: *Atti del convegno internazionale in occasione della prima del «Rigoletto» in edizione critica, Vienna 12/13 marzo 1983*, Parma-Milan, Istituto di studi verdiani-Ricordi, 1987, pp. 74-109].

# Dans l'ombre de Paris. Circulation et diffusion de la musique de scène sous l'Empire: l'exemple du théâtre de Versailles

*Martin Barré*
(Conservatoire National Supérieur
de Musique et de Danse de Paris)

Les histoires de la musique en France se sont longtemps focalisées sur la ville de Paris, ce qui était compréhensible au regard du foisonnement artistique de la capitale. Néanmoins, l'importance donnée à l'activité parisienne a eu pour conséquence d'éclipser le reste du pays. Exceptées quelques parutions marginales[1], l'intérêt pour la vie musicale en province est relativement récent[2]. De nombreux sujets ont été abordés depuis comme l'étude d'une ville spécifique[3], la mise en parallèle de plusieurs institutions[4], les publics[5] ou encore les rapports de pouvoir entre les provinces et l'État[6]. L'étude de la circulation des répertoires a souvent été menée à travers une échelle continentale mais plus rarement nationale, du moins concernant le XIXe siècle[7]. Le théâtre de Versailles représente, à ce sujet, un exemple inédit des rapports entre la capitale et le reste du pays[8]. Fondée en 1777 par Marguerite Brunet, plus connue sous le nom de la Montansier, l'institution a fait l'objet, comme beaucoup

---

[1]. Fuchs 1933; *La vie musicale* 1972-1993 qui regroupe des articles d'érudits locaux du XIXe et du XXe siècle; *Musique et société* 1982; Lesure 1999.

[2]. Élart – Simon 2018; Ellis 2022. Pour une bibliographie quasi exhaustive concernant les théâtres de province voir Carrère-Saucède 2020.

[3]. Naugrette – Taïeb 2009; Gosselin 1994.

[4]. Jardin 2006; Élart 2005.

[5]. Leterrier 2009; Corbin 2014.

[6]. Féret 2009; Triolaire 2012.

[7]. Charle 2013.

[8]. Nous entendons par théâtre de Versailles l'actuel théâtre Montansier qui prend le nom de sa fondatrice en 1936 et qui est une institution différente de l'Opéra royal.

d'établissements patrimoniaux, d'un ouvrage destiné à un large public, retraçant son histoire de manière chronologique et mettant en valeur ses archives[9]. Les publications de l'historien Romuald Féret, portant sur les rapports de pouvoir entre l'État et les théâtres à travers la mise en place du privilège, sont quasiment les seuls travaux universitaires dédiés aux théâtres de Seine-et-Marne et de Seine-et-Oise auxquels se rattache celui de Versailles[10]. Les musicologues, de leur côté, ne se sont intéressés à la ville qu'au moment de la période d'Ancien régime, délaissant par ailleurs l'activité locale post-révolutionnaire.

Le théâtre de Versailles présente pourtant un intérêt majeur par la qualité de conservation de ses archives qui sont quasiment intactes pour le XIX[e] siècle[11]. L'ensemble des recettes et des dépenses, les tableaux de troupes ainsi qu'une grande partie de la correspondance administrative sont conservés et il est presque possible de suivre quotidiennement l'activité du théâtre sur l'ensemble du siècle. Gardons tout de même à l'esprit que, bien que cette situation soit tout à fait exceptionnelle, elle ne permet en rien de saisir le fonctionnement de l'ensemble des théâtres du pays: elle reflète plutôt l'activité spécifique à l'établissement versaillais. Les études concernant les rapports entre Paris et la province ont montré comment cet « ailleurs » n'a longtemps existé que dans sa relation à la capitale qui portait souvent sur lui un regard dépréciatif. La vision « parisianiste »[12] qui considère tout ce qui se situe en dehors de la capitale comme un bloc monolithique et passif a d'ailleurs suscité tout un imaginaire jusqu'à la période de décentralisation[13]. Il convient donc de se défaire du regard parisianocentré pour considérer les villes en dehors de Paris dans leur pluralité et leur singularité. Le cas du théâtre de Versailles est unique par la position de la ville et sa situation politique. Nous continuerons tout de même à utiliser le terme réducteur de *province* au fil de l'article car il reflète la position qu'occupe l'ancien siège du pouvoir royal du point de vue de Paris[14].

---

[9]. VILLARD 1998.

[10]. FÉRET 2009. On mentionnera également le mémoire PICCIN 2000 ainsi que notre travail, BARRÉ 2021.

[11]. Celles-ci sont réparties entre les Archives communales de Versailles sous la série R2, les Archives départementales des Yvelines sous la série 4T1 et enfin dans le carton B XVIII du fonds Paul Fromageot conservé à la bibliothèque centrale de Versailles.

[12]. Néologisme inventé par Balzac dans 'La femme de province', in: *Les Français peints par eux-mêmes. 1*, Paris, Curmer, 1841, p. 5.

[13]. Nous entendons par période de décentralisation le lent mouvement qui débute à partir des années 1830 pour se défaire de la politique centralisatrice du Premier Empire et qui aboutira aux lois de 1982. Si le mot décentralisation apparaît dès les années 1830, il se réfère davantage à l'idée de déconcentration qui consiste à déléguer un pouvoir étatique à des administrations locales. Voir à ce sujet CORBIN 1992 et GEORGE 1998.

[14]. Bien que cela paraisse difficilement concevable aujourd'hui, Versailles est longtemps considérée comme une ville de province en raison de son accès laborieux depuis la capitale qui sera compensé par l'arrivé du chemin de fer en 1840. Le théâtre communal fait par exemple partie de la liste des 'Théâtres des grandes villes de province' qui figure dans SAINT-ROMAIN 1831, p. 72.

## Dans l'ombre de Paris

Notre étude s'appuie sur le dépouillement d'un fonds inédit de matériels d'orchestre utilisés au théâtre de Versailles et conservés à la bibliothèque centrale de la ville[15]. Il représente un ensemble de 589 pochettes contenant des matériels d'orchestre manuscrits qui servaient à l'accompagnement des pièces de théâtres, plus particulièrement des vaudevilles et des mélodrames, entre 1792 et 1832. Ces deux genres considérés comme populaires ont aujourd'hui disparu des scènes, emportant avec eux les pratiques dramatiques qui leur étaient spécifiques. À travers son statut d'ancienne capitale monarchique, Versailles occupe une position singulière par rapport à Paris, ce qui impacte directement l'activité du théâtre local. Afin de mettre au jour certaines pratiques spécifiques à un théâtre de province dont les moyens sont plus modestes que ceux de la capitale, nous nous concentrerons sur l'analyse du fonds inédit, qui présente la particularité d'appartenir autant à la sphère dramatique que musicale. Enfin, l'étude de la diffusion et de la circulation des musiques de scène est rendue possible grâce à la conservation d'un fonds parisien semblable à celui de Versailles, aussi terminerons-nous par la comparaison des matériels entre les deux villes.

L'objectif de cette étude, tout en participant à la remise au jour de pratiques tombées dans l'oubli, est aussi de réfuter l'idée d'une hégémonie culturelle parisienne qui s'exercerait sur l'ensemble du pays[16]. Certes, l'effervescence de la capitale suscite fantasmes et admiration mais les villes de province développent chacune leurs spécificités locales et ne sont pas seulement des réceptacles passifs de la production parisienne. À travers l'étude du fonds, nous verrons qu'une certaine autonomie locale se révèle dès lors qu'on se détache des textes littéraires des pièces de théâtre pour s'intéresser à la musique qui les accompagne.

## Le théâtre qui se croyait parisien

L'activité lyrique et dramatique connaît d'importants bouleversements sous l'Empire. La signature de trois décrets entre 1806 et 1807 vient assoir la nouvelle politique d'encadrement et de réforme des théâtres[17]. Le premier, publié le 8 juin 1806, rétablit le système de demande d'autorisation d'ouverture des théâtres et divise la France en vingt-cinq arrondissements théâtraux. Alors que quiconque était libre d'ouvrir un établissement depuis la loi du 13 janvier 1791 qui assurait la liberté des théâtres, un accord préalable du gouvernement est désormais nécessaire. Le deuxième décret du 25 avril 1807 concerne les genres dramatiques. Finies les salles à la programmation hybride où les œuvres sérieuses cohabitent avec les populaires, le

---

[15]. Pour le catalogue complet voir BARRÉ 2021. Nous remercions très chaleureusement le directeur de la bibliothèque, Vincent Haegele, de nous avoir indiqué l'existence de ce fonds.

[16]. Comme l'affirme par exemple LESURE 1999.

[17]. YON 2012; WILD 2012.

gouvernement impose désormais une stricte répartition des genres entre les salles. Comme de nombreuses lois, celle-ci peine à être appliquée et la porosité générique persiste au fil du siècle. Enfin, pour clore cette grande réforme de l'art dramatique, le troisième et dernier décret, le plus développé et publié le 29 juillet 1807, rétablit le privilège théâtral et fait passer le nombre des théâtres parisiens de vingt-cinq à huit[18]. Les établissements sont répartis en deux classes: d'une part les grands théâtres ou les établissements impériaux auxquels se rattachent l'Académie Impériale de Musique, l'Opéra-Comique, le théâtre de l'Impératrice ou le Théâtre-Français et d'autre part les théâtres secondaires (Vaudeville, Variétés, Gaîté et Ambigu-Comique).

À la suite de la réforme impériale du système dramatique, Versailles devient l'une des trois villes de la vaste Seine-et-Oise à disposer du privilège d'avoir une troupe sédentaire tout comme Étampes et Saint-Germain-en-Laye. La position de Versailles est assez singulière au sortir de la Révolution. Siège du gouvernement royal sous l'Ancien Régime, la ville se retrouve en quelques années réduite à l'état de cité morte[19]. Jusqu'aux événements révolutionnaires, la population versaillaise était presque intégralement constituée d'employés du château, centre de gravité de l'activité locale. Une fois le roi parti, en octobre 1789, c'est le fondement même de la ville qui se trouve ébranlé, tandis que le peuple versaillais, animé d'un sentiment prérévolutionnaire, se retrouve malgré lui spectateur des révoltes du pays. Versailles n'est plus alors qu'une «image figée»[20] où flotte le souvenir des splendeurs d'antan. Les classes populaires se retrouvent privées d'emploi, dépourvues de la machine commerciale qu'était le château lorsque la cour y résidait. La Révolution entraîne une baisse constante de la population qui passe de 50 000 habitants avant 1789 à 25 000 en 1796[21]. Versailles, «ville de toutes les tristesses et de tous les deuils»[22] selon Alexandre Dumas, traverse le XIXe siècle dans l'ombre de Paris.

Le théâtre local se retrouve donc dans une situation délicate, essayant de maintenir son activité dans une ville désertée — trop proche de Paris pour avoir sa propre autonomie culturelle, mais d'un accès laborieux depuis la capitale, ce qui lui vaut d'être considérée comme une ville de province. L'établissement connait pourtant jusqu'à la Révolution une période faste sous la direction de la Montansier, mais qui est brutalement interrompue par les évènements révolutionnaires. Délaissée par sa directrice, qui poursuit ses activités à Paris, la salle ferme ses portes après la parution du décret de 1806. Versailles, désormais considérée comme une ville secondaire, n'a plus le droit de posséder une troupe sédentaire et ne peut qu'accueillir des troupes ambulantes. La Montansier, parvient néanmoins, mais non sans difficultés, à obtenir le privilège exceptionnel de fixer une troupe à Versailles et en abandonne la direction, tout en

---

[18]. Le privilège est l'objet de l'étude citée plus haut: FÉRET 2009.
[19]. VERMANDER 2018, pp. 135-177.
[20]. *Ibidem*, p. 151.
[21]. *Ibidem*, p. 147.
[22]. DUMAS 1863, p. 242.

restant propriétaire, à une troupe parisienne dirigée par Jacques Robillon qui prend la tête de l'institution en 1807.

Issue du théâtre des Jeunes-Artistes, la troupe fait partie des victimes des décrets napoléoniens qui avaient entraîné la fermeture de nombreux établissements. À son arrivée à Versailles, elle est constituée de dix hommes, six femmes, vingt-trois danseuses et danseurs placés sous la direction du jeune frère du directeur, Claudius, et enfin d'un orchestre de douze musiciens dirigés par Antoine-François Heudier[23]. L'ère des frères Robillon, qui s'étale sur près de trente ans, est rythmée par les faillites et les tumultes. La qualité des représentations est particulièrement décriée à en croire le préfet de Seine-et-Oise:

> Tout ce que les dernières doublures des Funambules peuvent offrir de plus misérable, tout ce qu'il y a de plus sale sur les tréteaux des foires, ne peut être comparé à ce qu'on a osé offrir sur le théâtre d'une ville de douze mille âmes, la seconde d'un département qui ceint la capitale et possède une belle garnison[24].

Les troupes sont souvent incomplètes et beaucoup de témoignages déplorent le manque de talent des artistes qui ne connaissent pas leur texte ou souffrent de problèmes de diction.

Le public étant relativement statique et très demandeur, le théâtre se démarque par son impressionnante capacité de renouvellement de répertoire qui est alors essentiellement constitué de vaudevilles, de mélodrames et d'opéras-comiques. Romuald Féret, qui consacre une partie de son ouvrage au théâtre de Versailles, prend comme exemple l'année 1852 où 153 pièces différentes sont représentées et 13 des 14 représentations du mois d'octobre sont des créations[25]. Le théâtre possède donc un répertoire extrêmement varié par rapport aux institutions parisiennes qui voient leur public constamment renouvelé. Chaque représentation étant accompagnée de musique à cette époque, le théâtre de Versailles possède une importante bibliothèque de matériels d'orchestre qui vient seulement d'être redécouverte.

## Un riche fonds inédit

Afin de saisir les spécificités des pratiques versaillaises, il faut d'abord comprendre la place qu'occupe la musique de scène au sein du vaudeville et du mélodrame qui, à la suite de

---

[23]. Villard 1998, p. 62.

[24]. Lettre adressée au ministre du Commerce, le 25 octobre 1834, Archives Nationales, F21 1219, cité par Féret 2009, p. 140.

[25]. *Ibidem*, p. 200. À titre d'exemple, le théâtre du Vaudeville à Paris n'en donne que 48 la même année et celui du Gymnase, 69.

la Révolution, «reprennent les rôles de la comédie et de la tragédie en supprimant la barrière entre littérature d'élite et théâtre populaire»[26]. Appartenant à la sphère dite populaire, ces deux genres n'ont que très tardivement suscité l'intérêt des universitaires et il faut attendre les travaux pionniers de Jean-Marie Thomasseau sur le mélodrame pour voir réhabiliter un genre totalement tombé dans l'oubli[27]. Une seconde hiérarchie s'installe alors car, le vaudeville relevant du comique, il est d'abord occulté par le mélodrame considéré comme plus noble. Malgré ce regain d'intérêt scientifique, les pièces sont souvent restées à l'état d'objet d'étude et n'ont a priori pas encore connu de tentative de reconstitution. D'un autre côté, le vaudeville a été redécouvert à travers les travaux réalisés autour de l'un de ses auteurs les plus prolifiques, Eugène Scribe[28].

Circonscrits au champ des études théâtrales, le vaudeville et le mélodrame ont surtout été étudiés à travers un prisme littéraire. Si la musique est évoquée et fait même l'objet d'une édition dans le cadre de la publication intégrale des mélodrames de Pixerécourt[29], elle est plus rarement analysée et rares sont les musicologues à s'être emparés de la question[30]. Se rattachant à des traditions plus anciennes que le mélodrame, le vaudeville appartient en grande partie au domaine chansonnier et soulève donc des problématiques spécifiques qui ont notamment été abordées en musicologie à propos des XVII$^e$ et XVIII$^e$ siècles[31]. La première moitié du XIX$^e$ siècle, qui est pourtant une période cruciale dans le développement des deux genres, n'a donc quasiment pas été étudiée d'un point de vue musical et l'étude du fonds versaillais permet une première entrée en la matière.

Les matériels de la musique de scène sont curieusement absents du très complet catalogue des riches fonds musicaux de la bibliothèque de Versailles publié dans les années 1990 par le

---

[26]. THOMASSEAU 1995, pp. 127-128.

[27]. THOMASSEAU 1974; *Europe* 1987. Pour le vaudeville voir GIDEL 1986.

[28]. YON 2000; YON – BARA 2016.

[29]. PIXERÉCOURT 2013-2021. Bien que cette édition présente l'avantage exceptionnel de donner à lire la musique de certains mélodrames en la joignant au déroulé de l'action, il s'agit toujours de celle de la création, recopiée uniquement lorsque la source était complète. Sur les 29 mélodrames actuellement édités, seuls six sont donc accompagnés d'une partition.

[30]. Seule Nicole Wild semble s'être intéressée dans les années 1980 à la vaste collection de matériels d'orchestre des mélodrames parisiens durant la première moitié du XIX$^e$ siècle: WILD 1995. Si depuis quelques dizaines d'années le genre de la musique de scène suscite des travaux, ceux-ci concernent essentiellement d'autres périodes que celle qui nous occupe. Voir MENNERET 1973; STEINEGGER 2005; DOUCHE 2018. Un important colloque *La musique de scène dans le théâtre parlé de Diderot à Hugo* s'est également tenu en mai 2017 à Paris et donnera lieu prochainement à une publication aux Presses Universitaires de Rennes. Voir également l'important travail de thèse en cours de Fernando Morrison qui porte notamment sur la circulation des musiques de scène en province. Voir Morrison en cours.

[31]. Notamment par Herbert Schneider mais dont les travaux n'ont malheureusement pas été traduits. Voir aussi LE BLANC 2014.

musicologue Denis Herlin[32]. Cette carence peut s'expliquer par le statut hybride du genre de la musique de scène qui oscille entre le champ des études dramatiques et de la musicologie. La simplicité musicale, la pratique du timbre pour les vaudevilles et la désuétude des pièces, ajoutées à l'ampleur colossale du fonds peuvent justifier le peu d'intérêt qui lui a été porté jusqu'ici.

Les matériels de l'orchestre du théâtre semblent avoir été versés à la bibliothèque de Versailles vers la fin du XIX[e] siècle, moment où ils sont transformés en fonds patrimonial. Classés chronologiquement et cotés, ces matériels, contrairement à ceux d'opéra-comique, ne font pourtant pas l'objet d'un catalogage. Le fonds se divise en trois cotes, chacune correspondant à un genre dramatique de façon à ce que M.S.H. in-fol corresponde aux vaudevilles, M.S.I. in-fol aux mélodrames et M.S.J. in-fol aux ballets ainsi qu'à deux pochettes contenant des ouvertures et des œuvres du compositeur Antoine-François Heudier, chef de l'orchestre du théâtre[33].

Le fonds est exclusivement constitué de musique manuscrite. Les partitions de vaudevilles dépassent de loin en nombre celles des deux autres genres avec un total de 457 pochettes, soit 77, 59% du fonds, alors que ne sont conservés que 80 mélodrames et 52 ballets[34]. Cet écart important s'explique en partie par les dimensions beaucoup plus modestes, autant d'un point de vue de la durée que de l'effectif, du vaudeville, considéré comme un genre plus léger que le mélodrame. Les dates des pièces s'échelonnent entre 1792, date de création du théâtre du Vaudeville à Paris qui devient un réservoir pour la programmation des théâtres de province, et 1832, qui correspond à peu près à la première faillite de l'institution sous la direction de Claudius Robillon[35]. Le dépouillement systématique des matériels a permis de retracer une partie de l'historique du fonds.

Avant d'arriver au théâtre de Versailles, la troupe des frères Robillon occupait le théâtre des Jeunes-Artistes qui, malgré ses modestes dimensions et sa courte période d'activité de douze années[36], accueille de nombreuses créations parisiennes dont les matériels d'orchestre constituent une partie du fonds versaillais. Cela est confirmé par les multiples inscriptions manuscrites figurant sur les partitions. On peut lire, par exemple, sur la partie de flûte du matériel pour le ballet *Les Deux coffrets*[37]: «Desbais, Théâtre des Jeunes-Artistes», ou encore sur les parties de basses et de timbales du *Solitaire des Pyrénées*[38]: «Création au Théâtre des Jeunes-Artistes».

---

[32]. HERLIN 1995. Soulignons que les matériels des opéras-comiques y figurent mais ne semblent pas avoir encore fait l'objet d'une étude approfondie.

[33]. (1782-?). La date de sa mort reste inconnue mais il apparaît comme chef de l'orchestre du théâtre de la Porte Saint-Martin en 1828 dans l'*Almanach des spectacles* de la même année, p. 131.

[34]. Nous avons volontairement mis de côté les ballets car les genres chorégraphiques sortaient du cadre de ce travail et nécessiteraient une étude à part entière.

[35]. (c.1780-?). Nous n'avons pas trouvé de trace de Robillon à la suite de sa dernière démission en 1843.

[36]. WILD 2012, pp. 209-210.

[37]. Bibliothèque de Versailles (BV), M.S.J. 11.

[38]. BV, M.S.I. 80.

Malgré ses dimensions, le fonds de la bibliothèque de Versailles est en grande partie lacunaire et la part de matériels conservés est bien maigre face à la quantité de pièces programmées. En effet, les archives communales de Versailles possèdent la liste des recettes et dépenses du théâtre de 1812 à 1880, ce qui permet de connaître l'ensemble des représentations données au cours de cette période[39]. On s'aperçoit alors que le nombre de pièces représentées est bien supérieur à celui des matériels d'orchestre conservés. Le constat est d'ailleurs le même concernant le théâtre des Jeunes-Artistes dont la liste exhaustive du répertoire nous apprend que, non seulement la très grande majorité des pièces représentées n'a jamais été éditée, mais la musique qui les accompagnait a été perdue en très grande partie[40].

La perte des matériels peut s'expliquer par les multiples saisies puis rachats entraînés par les faillites que connaît le théâtre. Lors d'une énième vente des mobiliers de l'établissement en 1832, l'inventaire de la saisie révèle que le nombre de partitions est le même qu'aujourd'hui et ne semble pas avoir augmenté depuis[41]. En revanche, leur absence au-delà de la saisie de 1832 est plus mystérieuse alors que la programmation musicale et dramatique se poursuit notamment avec le succès croissant des œuvres d'Offenbach. Certains matériels sont encore en usage dans la seconde moitié du siècle comme l'indique la date du 7 janvier 1855 inscrite au crayon à côté d'un dessin, à l'intérieur de la partie de premier violon de *Trente ans ou La Vie d'un joueur*[42]. La disparition des matériels qui servaient à l'accompagnement des œuvres écrites au-delà de 1832 semble paradoxale face à la qualité de conservation de ceux du premier tiers du siècle et l'enquête mériterait d'être approfondie.

Les matériels, constitués des parties séparées, ont pour la plupart été mutilés lors de leur transformation en fonds. Pour les cordes, seules les parties de premier pupitre ont été conservées, celles qui contiennent le plus d'indication. Le reste semble avoir été recyclé en étiquettes au moment du classement du fonds. Les parties de vents en revanche sont intactes. Ficelés, classés et rangés, ces matériels d'orchestre abondamment utilisés sont devenus à la fin du XIXe siècle un fonds patrimonial figé et conservé en bibliothèque.

Malgré ces mutilations, le fonds se démarque par son exceptionnelle stabilité et les manques sont quasiment inexistants. La nomenclature étant détaillée de manière quasi systématique sur la couverture de la partie de second violon, y compris les pertes ou les doublons, il est possible d'avoir une idée précise de l'effectif orchestral du théâtre. Celui-ci varie selon les genres car, alors que l'écrasante majorité des vaudevilles est accompagnée par un orchestre à cordes à quatre parties, les mélodrames, de leur côté, requièrent des effectifs bien

---

[39]. Série 2R, «Recettes et dépenses».
[40]. *Note sur le théâtre des Jeunes artistes. 1779-1807*, manuscrit, Bibliothèque nationale, Département Arts du spectacle, 8-RT-3100.
[41]. Archives Départementales des Yvelines, Giroud-Mollier, Répertoire n° 169, 20 mars 1832, Vente, 3E43 524.
[42]. M.S.I. 49.

plus larges qui atteignent parfois les vingt-cinq parties[43]. Ce cas reste exceptionnel et l'effectif est le plus souvent constitué de deux parties de violons, une d'alto, une de basse, souvent une partie de contrebasse, deux flûtes, deux hautbois, deux clarinettes, deux bassons, deux cors et les timbales. Parfois des trompettes et des trombones se joignent à l'effectif mais cela reste occasionnel. En revanche, des instruments moins courants intègrent ponctuellement l'orchestre, notamment lorsqu'ils sont évoqués dans le livret. C'est le cas de l'ophicléide qui apparaît dans *Hernani*[44] ou du cor de chasse, présent dans *Harnali*[45], parodie du drame de Hugo. C'est encore le cas de la guitare[46], souvent présente dans les scènes de sérénade, ou du serpent encore assez courant sous l'Empire[47].

Chaque pochette contient une partie de répétiteur utilisée par le chef qui dirigeait alors du poste de premier violon. Nicole Wild, à propos des matériels d'orchestre conservés à la bibliothèque de l'Opéra, distingue les «conducteurs», réductions ne conservant que les parties principales de l'orchestre et utilisés par les chefs lors des répétitions, et les «répétiteurs» de ballets qui, jusqu'en 1870, ne sont constitués que de deux parties de violons avant de passer au piano[48]. À suivre cette distinction, le matériel de Versailles présenterait surtout des «conducteurs» bien qu'il soit toujours écrit «répétiteur» sur la couverture de cette partie. Dans le cas des vaudevilles, cette partie est nommée la plupart du temps «chant» ou «canto» et ne contient que la mélodie de l'air avec les paroles écrites sous la portée. Ces exemples fournissent par ailleurs de précieuses informations quant aux choix prosodiques des arrangeurs. Le texte est intégralement dit de manière syllabique avec très peu de répétitions. Les répétiteurs de mélodrames, où n'apparaissent que les parties les plus importantes regroupées sur deux ou trois portées, correspondent davantage à la définition qu'en donne Wild.

Les matériels ont été abondamment utilisés et les nombreuses indications manuscrites deviennent de précieux indices à propos des répétitions, des musiciens d'orchestre ou du répétiteur. Certaines partitions sont épinglées sur parfois plusieurs feuillets, des numéros sont rayés et il est souvent mentionné «bon», «bon pour ce soir» ou encore «passé» ce qui signifie que la musique était constamment arrangée selon les situations. L'orchestre s'adapte aux conditions de représentation et la musique n'est jamais figée. Mais les inscriptions ne sont pas seulement d'ordre musical. Des comptes, des dessins, des plaisanteries cohabitent dans les marges des numéros musicaux et sont peut-être les témoignages les plus directs des pratiques qui pouvaient régner au sein d'un orchestre de théâtre. Ces notes révèlent la manière dont les musiciens passaient le temps lors des répétitions, voire des représentations, étant donné que

---

[43]. *Jean de Calais*, M.S.I 8 in-fol.
[44]. M.S.I 58 in-fol.
[45]. M.S.I 59 in-fol.
[46]. *L'Égoïste par régime*, M.S.H 242 in-fol.
[47]. *Voltaire chez les capucins*, M.S.H 294 in-fol et *La Mort de Turenne*, M.S.I 76 in-fol.
[48]. Wild 1995, p. 284.

certains instruments ne jouaient que dans un ou deux numéros seulement. Certains dessins trahissent une attention aiguisée à ce qui se passait sur scène, comme l'illustrent les beaux portraits qui ornent la partie de flûte de la pièce *Le Proscrit et la fiancée*[49] (Ill. 1) ou la partie de premier violon du ballet *Psyché*[50] (Ill. 2). D'autres relèvent d'une franche grivoiserie quand ils ne sont pas obscènes comme les très nombreux dessins à caractère pornographique et scatologique qui couvrent la partie de premier violon du mélodrame *Trente ans ou La Vie d'un joueur*[51]. Quelle que soit leur valeur artistique, ces inscriptions permettent d'être au plus proche des sensibilités des musiciens d'orchestre, de comprendre leur rapport aux œuvres qu'ils accompagnaient et de reconstruire l'ambiance qui pouvait régner au théâtre de Versailles.

Ill. 1: partie de flûte, *Le Proscrit et la fiancée*, M.S.I 28 in-fol.

[49]. M.S.I 28 in-fol.

[50]. M.S.J 42 in-fol.

[51]. M.S.I 49 in-fol. Ces dessins sont loin d'être marginaux et s'inscrivent dans un contexte de libération des mœurs entraînée par la Révolution française. Voir à ce propos: BIARD – DUPUY 2010.

Ill. 2: partie de premier violon, *Psyché*, M.S.J 42 in-fol.

Enfin, le fonds permet la réhabilitation d'un compositeur tombé dans l'oubli: Antoine-François Heudier qui est alors chef d'orchestre du théâtre. Sa fonction est également celle d'arrangeur pour les vaudevilles et de compositeur pour les mélodrames. À la tête de l'orchestre du théâtre des Jeunes Artistes de 1804 à 1807 où il dirigeait une vingtaine de musiciens, Heudier suit, à la fermeture de ce dernier, la troupe de Robillon au théâtre de Versailles[52]. Peu d'informations nous sont parvenues le concernant. Choron, dans une courte notice de son *Dictionnaire*, mentionne des mélodrames, ballets d'action et quelques œuvres de musique de chambre de sa composition[53]. Il est admis au Conservatoire le 28 Messidor an VII [16 juillet 1799] et étudie en l'an VIII [1799-1800] dans la classe de violon de Frédéric Blasius[54]. Nous

---

[52]. Wild 2012, pp. 209-210.
[53]. Choron – Fayolle 1817, p. 331. La même notice est reprise ensuite par Fétis 1860-1881, p. 323
[54]. Granville 2014, p. 360.

ignorons à quelle date exactement il quitte le théâtre de Versailles, mais on le retrouve à la tête de l'orchestre du théâtre du Gymnase-Dramatique, alors appelé théâtre de Madame, de 1824 à 1830[55]. Il compose lors de ses années à Versailles la musique de nombreux mélodrames[56] et la cote M.S.J se referme sur deux pochettes contenant des œuvres de sa plume, dont le conducteur complet d'un mélodrame intitulé *Calas*[57].

Le fonds de la bibliothèque de Versailles représente donc un témoignage inestimable dès lors qu'on s'intéresse aux pratiques concernant les musiques de scène. Malgré sa programmation presque exclusivement parisienne, le théâtre de Versailles fait preuve d'une certaine autonomie musicale, notamment à travers la figure de Heudier, comme le montre la confrontation des matériels versaillais avec leurs équivalents parisiens.

## Reconstituer les pratiques versaillaises au regard des matériels parisiens

Si le fonds versaillais de musique de scène est tout à fait exceptionnel par son ampleur et la qualité de sa conservation[58], ceux des théâtres parisiens sont beaucoup plus lacunaires. C'est le cas du fonds redécouvert dans les années 1980 et inventorié par Pauline Girard[59]. Le catalogue, qui, faute de temps, ne contient que les drames et mélodrames, compte tout de même 382 notices et permet de se faire une idée de ce qu'était la pratique de la musique de scène à Paris sous l'Empire. Trois théâtres sont particulièrement représentés dans cet inventaire: la Gaîté, l'Ambigu-Comique et la Porte Saint-Martin, foyers du mélodrame où régnait le chef d'orchestre et compositeur Alexandre Piccinni[60]. Bien que les bibliothèques des théâtres du Vaudeville, des Variétés ou encore du Gymnase-Dramatique n'aient pas été conservées, le catalogue, désormais complet depuis sa mise en ligne, contient tout de même la musique des vaudevilles donnés dans les théâtres cités plus haut.

En comparant ce catalogue à celui que nous avons établi à Versailles, nous avons pu relever les pièces communes aux divers théâtres soit vingt-neuf vaudevilles et trente-trois mélodrames[61]. L'écrasante majorité de ces pièces provient des théâtres de la Gaîté et de la Porte Saint-Martin

---

[55]. Wild 2012, pp. 181-185.

[56]. *Le Bourgmestre de Saardam*, M.S.I 27 in-fol ou *Le Solitaire des Pyrénées*, M.S.I 80 in-fol.

[57]. M.S.J 51 in-fol. Cette musique accompagnait probablement la pièce du même nom de Victor Ducange.

[58]. D'autres fonds semblables sont également conservés notamment à Lille, Avignon, Montpellier et surtout Genève dont la Bibliothèque Musicale de la Ville conserve les matériels d'orchestre de 724 pièces.

[59]. Pour le récit de la redécouverte du fonds voir Wild 1995. Pour le catalogue voir Girard 1993.

[60]. Piccinni dirigeait simultanément les orchestres du théâtre de la Gaîté de 1818 à 1831 et celui de la Porte Saint-Martin de 1814 à 1837. 'Gaîté' et 'Porte Saint-Martin', in: Wild 2012, pp. 165-170 et pp. 367-372.

[61]. Pour la liste détaillée des pièces communes aux théâtres voir l'annexe n° 6 dans Barré 2021, p. 70.

et plusieurs des matériels des vaudevilles sont issus d'une reprise et non de la création. Alors que la musique des vaudevilles est bien souvent anonyme, celle des mélodrames est signée par des chefs d'orchestre locaux, notamment Alexandre Piccinni mais aussi Gérardin-Lacour, Hus-Desforges, Taix ou encore Lanusse.

Si les musiques de scènes parisiennes sont peu étudiées, leur mise en parallèle avec celles des villes de province semble inexistante. Après avoir sélectionné un échantillon de pièces communes aux deux théâtres, nous nous sommes livrés à la comparaison des matériels pour tenter de comprendre non seulement le processus de mise en musique d'une pièce mais également les différences de pratiques entre la capitale et une ville considérée comme la province. Le vaudeville et le mélodrame ayant leurs caractéristiques musicales propres, la méthode comparative ne pouvait être la même, c'est pourquoi nous avons décidé de leur dédier deux parties distinctes.

## « *Tout finit par des chansons* »[62]

La tradition du vaudeville est extrêmement ancienne et le terme désigne pendant plusieurs siècles un air connu, qu'on nomme *timbre*, dont le texte d'origine a été modifié. La fin du XVIII[e] siècle marque un déplacement sémantique car *vaudeville* se met à désigner non plus seulement une chanson mais bien un nouveau genre dramatique qui se caractérise par la présence de coupures lyriques qu'on nomme couplets et que les dramaturges indiquent par la mention « Sur l'air de… ». Chantés par les comédiens et les comédiennes et non de véritables artistes lyriques, les couplets interrompent régulièrement l'action, certaines pièces peuvent en compter jusqu'à 70, et la qualité de l'air choisie est remarquée et attendue comme le montre cette phrase issue du *Journal de Seine-et-Oise* à propos d'une pièce qui connaît un échec à Versailles: « Les auteurs auraient au moins dû appeler, au secours de leur intrigue, la puissante alliance de couplets bien tournés. Mais ceux qu'on chante dans leur pièce sont fades et affectés: ce sont de véritables madrigaux, des couplets à l'eau rose [*sic*] »[63]. La comparaison des vaudevilles s'est faite à travers quatre supports: les matériels parisiens et versaillais, le livret de la pièce et le recueil de timbre *La Clé du Caveau*[64]. Deux situations ressortent de cette confrontation.

Premièrement, lorsque l'air indiqué dans le livret figure dans le recueil de Pierre Capelle, les mélodies des deux matériels sont identiques au timbre d'origine. Si nous prenons par

---

[62]. BEAUMARCHAIS 1785, p. 233.
[63]. À propos de la pièce *Le Colonel*, 14 avril 1821.
[64]. À la suite de l'engouement pour ce nouveau genre dramatique, des recueils de mélodies sont édités et le plus célèbre d'entre eux, *La Clé du Caveau* de Pierre Capelle, ne compte pas moins de 2 350 timbres dans sa quatrième édition en 1848 (Capelle 1848). L'ouvrage, qui emprunte son nom à la plus célèbre des sociétés chansonnières, fait vite office de référence au sein des milieux chansonniers et dramatiques. Voir LEVEL 1988 et CHEYRONNAUD 2007.

exemple le premier couplet de la pièce *Femme à vendre*[65], il est indiqué « Air: Un rigaudon zig zag don don ». Cet air apparaît en tant qu' « Air de la ronde du Rival confident ou vaudeville du Chaudronnier de Saint-Flour » dans la *Clé du Caveau* et correspond au timbre n° 711. Il s'agit alors de la même mélodie entre les deux matériels et le recueil à quelques différences près sur lesquelles nous reviendrons. D'un autre côté, lorsque l'air indiqué dans le livret n'apparaît pas dans le recueil de Capelle alors les mélodies sont systématiquement différentes entre les deux matériels. Par exemple le deuxième air de la pièce *Le Chaudronnier de Saint-Flour*[66] intitulé 'Cet or que vous daignez m'offrir' ne figure pas, sous ce nom du moins, dans la *Clé du Caveau*. Les mélodies des deux matériels sont alors totalement différentes puisque ce numéro est à 2/4 à Versailles et à 6/8 à l'Odéon. Reste à savoir si ces mélodies sont originales, ce qui est peu probable étant donné la tradition du vaudeville et il y a fort à parier que les chefs d'orchestres prenaient eux-mêmes la liberté de choisir l'air de leur choix qui correspondait à la coupe du texte.

Toutefois, il arrive que, alors que le titre de l'air n'apparaît pas dans la *Clé du Caveau*, le même timbre soit utilisé dans les deux matériels. C'est le cas de l'air 'Belle meunière' dans *Le Marquis de Carabas*[67] dont le titre ne figure pas dans le recueil alors que les mélodies sont strictement les mêmes, à la note près dans les matériels ce qui pourrait laisser penser que ceux de Paris ont été copié pour la représentation versaillaise.

Lorsque le timbre est le même dans les trois sources, de subtiles différences subsistent entre elles. Reprenons l'exemple de l'air 'Un rigaudon zig zag don don' dans la pièce *Femme à vendre*[68] qui clôture également l'un des mélodrames les plus célèbres de Pixerécourt, *Cœlina*. Nous avons mis en parallèle les trois portées pour pouvoir comparer plus aisément (Ex. 1). On constate de nombreuses différences entre les deux théâtres par rapport à la mélodie d'origine. Deux hypothèses peuvent être formulées. Les différences rythmiques peuvent s'expliquer par des choix prosodiques de la part de l'arrangeur qui est obligé d'adapter le timbre d'origine au nouveau texte. La seconde hypothèse concerne la mémoire. Il est fort probable que les chefs d'orchestre dont le métier était, entre autres, d'arranger les airs, finissaient par ne plus avoir besoin des recueils pour se souvenir des timbres. Cela pourrait expliquer les légères différences entre les versions, situation qu'on retrouve dans le cas des entreprises de collectages de musiques traditionnelles qui, par leur tradition de transmission orale, existent à travers de multiples versions[69].

Partant de ce timbre imposé, le talent des arrangeurs va prendre forme dans l'instrumentation. De manière générale, l'effectif de l'orchestre du théâtre de Versailles reste

---

[65]. MAT TH-774 à Paris et M.S.H 77 in-fol à Versailles. GENTILHOMME – BELLE 1817.
[66]. MAT TH-585 à Paris et M.S.H 10 in-fol à Versailles. GOUFFÉ – HENRIQUEZ 1802.
[67]. Acte I, Scène 2.
[68]. Acte I, Scène 1.
[69]. BELLY 2014.

Ex. 1: Comparaison du timbre 'Un rigaudon zig zag don don' (Gentilhomme – Belle 1817).

plus modeste que celui des théâtres parisiens. Il comprend, en 1825, 22 musiciens[70] alors que l'orchestre de la Gaîté en compte 24 vers 1830, celui de la Porte-Saint-Martin 30 et celui de l'Ambigu-Comique de 17 à 28[71]. Alors que les vaudevilles à Versailles sont accompagnés la plupart du temps par un orchestre à cordes, des instruments à vent se joignent aux effectifs parisiens. Par exemple, la pièce *La Brouille et le raccommodement*[72] est accompagnée par un orchestre à cordes à Versailles (V1/V2/Alto/Basse) alors que des parties de flûte, hautbois, clarinette, basson et cor sont présentes dans le matériel de la Porte-Saint-Martin[73].

Quand bien même la mélodie est similaire entre les deux théâtres, les choix d'instrumentation peuvent être radicalement différents, comme on peut le voir dans un autre passage de la pièce *Femme à vendre*[74], l'air 'Contredanse de la Rosière' (Ex. 2). Exceptés quelques ornements rajoutés à la mélodie dans le matériel de Paris, l'air est, dans les deux cas, accompagné d'un orchestre à cordes. En revanche, les choix d'accompagnements différent selon les arrangeurs. Dans la première partie de l'air, un accompagnement en tenues est préféré à Paris alors qu'à Versailles, les autres instruments ponctuent la mélodie tous les temps. Dans la seconde partie, alors qu'à Versailles cette fois les longues tenues sont privilégiées, le second violon double le premier à la sixte à Paris. Ces différences, qui paraissent dérisoires, sont pourtant la preuve d'une certaine indépendance des théâtres en matière d'arrangement. Chaque chef d'orchestre organisait et arrangeait les airs à sa guise sans forcément reproduire les pratiques parisiennes comme on pourrait le penser. Le cas du mélodrame est à ce propos encore plus saillant.

---

70. Villard 1998, p. 98.
71. Wild 2012, pp. 165-170, 367-372 et 24-31.
72. M.S.H 78 in-fol. Dupetit-Méré 1817.
73. MAT TH-1168.
74. Acte I, Scène 4.

Ex. 2: Comparaison de l'orchestration de l'air 'de la contredanse de la Rosière' dans le vaudeville *Femme à vendre ou Le Marché écossais*.

## Dans l'ombre de Paris

### *Un opéra dénué de chant*

Si le vaudeville se caractérise par la chanson sur un air connu, le mélodrame se distingue par l'absence de chant. Cette caractéristique formelle constitue l'identité du genre comme l'affirme l'un de ses pionniers, René-Charles Guilbert de Pixerécourt, pour qui le mélodrame n'est «autre chose qu'un drame lyrique dont la musique est exécutée par l'orchestre au lieu d'être chantée»[75]. Lorsqu'un personnage se met à chanter, c'est que la chanson est intégrée à l'action et tient une fonction dramaturgique. Au-delà de la contrainte du timbre préexistant qui caractérise le vaudeville, le mélodrame présente des occurrences musicales beaucoup plus variées[76]. La musique mélodramatique est donc bien souvent originale. Malgré le fait qu'il n'échappe pas à l'étiquette populaire, le genre du mélodrame semble plus noble que celui du vaudeville, que ce soit par le sérieux des sujets qu'il traite, ses dimensions ou encore ses moyens techniques de mise en scène et cela se retrouve dans la musique. Les informations musicales contenues dans les livrets se limitent souvent au signe (M.) qui signifie que le dramaturge souhaite qu'il y ait de la musique à cet endroit suivi de quelques indications, ce qui laisse une grande liberté aux compositeurs. Les descriptions restent dans l'ensemble assez vagues comme cette note de Hapdé dans *Le Pont du diable* qui demande une «musique qui annonce l'arrivée précipitée d'une multitude»[77]. Cette liberté est tout de même soumise à certaines conventions établies au fil des tentatives de théorisations du genre[78].

Si les études théâtrales n'évoquaient la musique mélodramatique qu'à travers l'analyse des livrets, Nicole Wild est la première à l'étudier d'après les partitions. La musicologue distingue quatre fonctions de la musique mélodramatique: l'accompagnement des acteurs par l'orchestre, les airs sur timbre, l'ouverture et les ballets[79]. Les deux dernières de ces formes ne sont pas propres au mélodrame: une ouverture précède n'importe quelle représentation dramatique et le ballet est également omniprésent dans le paysage musical et dramatique parisien. L'utilisation d'airs sur timbre est une pratique qui se rattache davantage au vaudeville, mais alors que les airs surgissent de manière totalement arbitraire au sein de ce dernier, elle est justifiée par la dramaturgie du texte dans le mélodrame. Seuls les accompagnements des acteurs par l'orchestre sont caractéristiques du mélodrame. Nicole Wild insiste d'ailleurs sur l'importance de ce fond sonore qui annonce les entrées et sorties des acteurs et qui ménage des respirations dans les dialogues. La musique est mise au service de l'émotion qui la canalise et lui fournit les occasions de se déployer, elle renforce le pouvoir des mots en suggérant une sorte de méta-texte qui décuple les effets dramatiques.

---

[75]. Pixerécourt 1818, p. 4.

[76]. Voir notamment à propos des mélodrames dits musicaux l'important ouvrage de Waeber 2005 ainsi que les travaux de Sala 1998 et aussi son ouvrage malheureusement non traduit, Sala 1995.

[77]. Acte II, Scène 6.

[78]. Hugo – Ader – Malitourne 1817; Pixerécourt 1818; Pixerécourt 1841-1943.

[79]. Wild 1987.

L'analyse des matériels des mélodrames vient confirmer les deux fonctions de la musique comme accompagnement. La première, et la plus importante en termes d'occurrence, est la fonction transitoire de la musique[80]. Un court passage musical sert de liant entre les scènes et installe bien souvent le climat de l'action suivante. La musique commence fréquemment avant que les personnages aient terminé de parler comme l'indiquent les extraits de texte placés au-dessus des numéros musicaux.

La seconde sous-catégorie d'accompagnement des acteurs par l'orchestre se révèle dans les passages où la tension dramatique est la plus forte. La musique ne sert plus de transition mais intervient au sein même de la scène, accompagnant de courtes ponctuations et de tremolos la progression dramaturgique. On trouve un exemple de cette fonction dans la pièce *Le Couvent de Tonnington* de Victor Ducange et d'Auguste Anicet-Bourgeois[81] lorsque Lady Worcester retrouve sa fille[82]. Il s'agit tout d'abord d'une scène de reconnaissance, scène clé de l'esthétique mélodramatique[83], lorsque Lady, qui cueillait paisiblement des fleurs, reconnaît tout d'un coup sa fille, scène à laquelle s'enchaine toute une série d'aveux. La musique d'Alexandre Piccinni est présente tout au long des trois scènes. Lorsque Lady cueille des fleurs «d'un air distrait», une flûte soliste l'accompagne avec l'indication «mollement» puis trois mesures de traits rapides et *forte* aux violons soulignent la reconnaissance de sa fille. Dans la scène suivante, celle de l'aveu, les didascalies indiquent que Lady «réfléchit profondément à ce qu'elle va dire». Pour accompagner cette suspension temporelle, le cor joue des triolets *piano* puis s'en suit un solo de hautbois soutenu par l'orchestre. Nous avons là un parfait exemple d'une musique qui sert de «multiplicateur et amplificateur dramatique»[84].

La comparaison des matériels de Paris et Versailles permet une nouvelle fois de relever deux situations. Soit la musique est strictement la même entre les deux théâtres. C'est le cas des matériels du *Couvent de Tonnington* qui, à quelques ligatures et articulations près, contiennent la même musique. Les partitions de Versailles sont une copie de celles du théâtre de la Gaîté contenant la musique de Piccinni dont la renommée déborde les frontières de la capitale. Soit la musique est fondamentalement différente entre les deux théâtres. C'est le cas, parmi d'autres, de la pièce *Les Ruines de Babylone*[85] de Pixerécourt. Dès l'ouverture, les moyens techniques et musicaux sont radicalement différents (Tableau 1). Le matériel de la Gaîté, dont la musiques est écrite par Gérardin-Lacour, contient une vaste ouverture en trois parties contenant une marche introductive, une cadence de harpe et enfin la véritable ouverture pour un totale de 251

---

[80]. Les transitions peuvent être extrêmement courtes comme celle entre les scènes 3 et 4 du premier acte des *Ruines de Babylone* de Pixerécourt dans le matériel de Versailles qui ne fait que deux mesures.
[81]. Ducange – Anicet-Bourgeois 1838.
[82]. Acte I, Scène 14-16.
[83]. Thomasseau 1984, p. 28.
[84]. Thomasseau 1974, p. 434.
[85]. Pixerécourt 1810.

mesures. Celle de Versailles, d'une longueur de 68 mesures, n'est constituée que d'une partie dont l'écriture musicale est beaucoup moins ambitieuse et aucun instrument ne se voit confier de cadence ni même de solo. Une ouverture introduit d'ailleurs systématiquement les actes à la Gaîté, ce qui n'est pas le cas à Versailles.

Cette asymétrie entre les deux théâtres à propos du niveau technique des musiciens se retrouve aussi dans le n° 7 de l'Acte I des deux matériels correspondant à la scène 6 dans le livret. Dans cette scène, le personnage de Raymond est censé préluder sur son luth mais les deux matériels contiennent à ce moment un solo de flûte accompagné par les cordes jouant *pizzicato*. Ce solo, très bref dans les deux cas, est beaucoup plus véloce à la Gaîté. Le thème est ornementé, diminué alors que la flûte ne joue que des triolets à Versailles.

Pourtant, en dépit de cette différence de niveau technique, le théâtre de Versailles affirme son indépendance musicale. On constate, au fil de la comparaison, une grande liberté dans le choix des passages mis en musique. Le choix des transitions par exemple varie selon les théâtres comme c'est le cas de la fin de la scène 2 de l'Acte I qui n'en contient pas à la Gaîté contrairement à Versailles ou de la fin du troisième acte de la pièce *La Femme à deux maris*[86] où trois scènes (12, 14 et 15) contiennent de la musique à Versailles et non à Paris.

Les choix varient également à propos de la musique qui accompagne les acteurs. Les compositeurs, à la lecture du livret, ne distinguent pas forcément les mêmes apogées dramatiques. La scène 12 du premier acte des *Ruines de Babylone*, lorsque Haroun comprend la trahison de Giafar en observant le selam[87], est soutenue par une musique *pianissimo* dans le matériel de Versailles alors qu'elle se déroule sans accompagnement dans celui de la Gaîté. Gérardin-Lacour semble avoir favorisé la scène précédente où Issouf découvre le selam, scène accompagnée par une intervention de trois mesures ce qui n'est pas le cas à Versailles. Les choix d'insertions musicales varient donc considérablement entre les compositeurs.

Cette diversité de sensibilité s'illustre aussi lorsqu'un même passage est mis en musique dans les deux théâtres. La poétique mélodramatique peut sensiblement varier d'un théâtre à l'autre et donc susciter des effets totalement opposés. Le n° 6 des deux matériels, qui sert de transition entre les scènes 5 et 6 du premier acte, présente deux musiques relativement différentes. Alors qu'à Versailles la musique, en *do* majeur à deux temps, installe un caractère assez solennel par ses rythmes pointés et sa cadence parfaite, la musique de la Gaîté, en *si*♭ majeur, est beaucoup plus agitée et se termine sur un cinquième degré de *sol* mineur dont l'effet est beaucoup plus suspensif et installe une tension par rapport à la suite de la pièce.

Enfin, les figuralismes varient eux aussi selon les compositeurs. Alors qu'il est précisé à la fin de la scène 10 du troisième acte de *La Femme à deux maris* que le personnage, seul, entend quelqu'un arriver, cet évènement est figuré à la Gaîté par un *ostinato* de noires aux

---

[86]. Pixerécourt 1813.

[87]. Au Moyen-Orient, le selam est un bouquet de fleurs dont l'arrangement porte une symbolique.

basses *pianissimo* alors qu'à Versailles ce passage est accompagné d'une musique *forte*, en *do* majeur et à 6/8. Au milieu de la scène 12 de la même pièce, lorsque Walter surprend Fritz, l'attente de ce dernier est figurée à Versailles par des tremolos «sombres» puis des fusées *forte* accompagnent la surprise là où Gérardin-Lacour n'a pas jugé utile de mettre en musique ce passage.

La comparaison des matériels des mélodrames permet, encore plus que pour le vaudeville, de constater une réelle indépendance du théâtre de Versailles. Bien que certains matériels parisiens aient été copiés pour être rejoués à Versailles, de nombreuses œuvres se voient attribuer une nouvelle musique selon le lieu de leur représentation. Évidemment, un travail de comparaison exhaustif reste à faire entre les deux villes mais l'accès difficile aux matériels rend l'étude laborieuse. Au-delà même de Paris, la mise en parallèle des matériels de Versailles avec ceux présents dans les fonds des autres villes de France et de Suisse permettrait d'élargir les questions autour de la diffusion et de la circulation des musiques de scène. Une même pièce donnée dans différents théâtres du pays aurait-elle systématiquement une nouvelle musique? Dans ce cas, l'hégémonie parisienne se limiterait surtout au répertoire dramatique mais devrait être totalement reconsidérée d'un point de vue musical.

L'exemple du théâtre de Versailles vient nuancer l'idée d'un Paris hégémonique d'un point de vue dramatique et musical. Bien que la programmation des salles de la capitale serve de réservoir pour les théâtres du pays, la circulation des matériels d'orchestre semble plus complexe et moins univoque. S'il se peut que la musique des pièces données à Versailles soit la même que celle de la création parisienne, il arrive bien plus souvent qu'elle soit de la plume de compositeurs ou d'arrangeurs locaux comme Antoine-François Heudier. L'idée de circulation semble être fragilisée dès lors qu'on s'intéresse à la musique plus qu'aux textes littéraires.

Nous espérons que cette première approche du fonds versaillais contribuera à la reconsidération du genre de la musique de scène qui a longtemps souffert d'un défaut de légitimité alors qu'il est consubstantiel à toute activité dramatique au XIX[e] siècle. Néanmoins, un vaste chantier reste à entreprendre car la comparaison des matériels versaillais et parisiens pourrait être non seulement poursuivie mais élargie à ceux d'autres villes. Comme l'a montré Katharine Ellis dans son récent ouvrage, qui ouvre de nouvelles perspectives historiographiques sur l'étude de la vie musicale en province[88], il faut se défaire de l'idée d'un pays dont l'activité se concentrerait entièrement dans sa capitale: une prise de recul révèle des dynamiques locales spécifiques, que ce soit à l'échelle des provinces ou à celle des villes, comme le cas du théâtre de Versailles a permis de le montrer.

---

[88]. Ellis 2022.

# Dans l'ombre de Paris

## Tableau 1

Comparaison des matériels des *Ruines de Babylone* de Pixerécourt[89].

| Paris (Musique de Gérardin-Lacour) | Versailles |
|---|---|
| Dix-huit parties: vl princ-cond, V1 (2 ex.), V2 (2 ex.), alto, b/cb (3 ex.), fl, fag 1, cl 1, cl 2, trb, cor 1, cor 2, tb, (harpe seulement dans partie de conducteur). | Dix parties: répé, V1, V2, alto, b, fl, cl, fg, cor 1, cor 2. |
| Acte I: 22 numéros + un long ballet. | Acte I: 22 numéros, pas de ballet. |
| Acte II: 19 numéros. | Acte II: 21 numéros. |
| Acte III: introduction + long ballet + 20 numéros. | Acte III: 25 numéros. |

Comparaison des parties de répétiteur du premier acte

| Paris (Musique de Gérardin-Lacour) | Versailles (Musique d'Antoine-François Heudier) |
|---|---|
| Trois parties:<br>- «Ouverture/marche» à ¢ avec rythmes pointés, *smorzando* (54 mes.) puis seconde partie *Allegro à 2* (74 mes.).<br>- Cadence harpe<br>- «Commencement de l'ouverture» (91 mes.)<br>Total: 251 mes. | Ouverture plus modeste en une partie.<br>Musique différente.<br>68 mes. |
| N° 1: *ré* M, 6/8<br>Numéro concertant pour flûte. | N° 1: *do* M, 2/4<br>La flûte double les premiers violons dans le thème de la ritournelle. Pas d'écriture concertante. |
| N° 2 (un personnage chante une chanson en s'accompagnant d'un luth dans le livret): luth représenté par un «clavicorde» jouant une ritournelle introductive, la mélodie vocale et les paroles sont écrites, *la* M, ¢.<br>Dans le livret seul le premier couplet (4 vers) figure à la fois dans le livret et dans le matériel comme dans les matériels de Paris et Versailles.<br>Les autres couplets apparaissent dans les scènes suivantes.<br>La succession des vers est la suivante: ABCDDCDD (seule la fin de D est répétée la 2ème fois).<br>Dans le livret, il est écrit que «les muets dansent de manière grotesque» pendant le refrain. Dans la partition, le couplet est suivi d'une partie instrumentale plus martiale. | N° 2: même mélodie que dans le matériel de la Gaîté jusqu'à «moi je préfère un baiser qu'on me donne».<br>La mélodie de la Gaîté est plus chromatique alors que celle de Versailles est plus simple.<br>La succession des vers est la suivante: ABCDCD (pas de répétition de la fin de D).<br>Pas de musique après le couplet.<br>Dans les parties d'orchestre, ce numéro est barré et il est écrit «la feuille volante» mais la pochette n'en contenait pas. |
| N° 3: la suite de la chanson se trouve dans la seconde scène mais il s'agit de la même musique. | N° 3: ici le numéro correspond à la fin de la scène 2 de l'Acte I, moment qui n'a pas de musique dans le matériel de la Gaîté. Morceau court, *ré* M, ¢, répété deux fois. |
| N° 4 (fin de la scène 3 de l'Acte I): *ré* M, 6/8, morceau très court, 9 mes. | N° 4: même endroit que Gaîté, musique différente, seulement deux mesures, ¢, fusées ascendantes *ff*: ponctuation du discours. |
| N° 5 (fin de la scène 4): *Allegretto louré*, 6/8, *fa* M, 10 mes. | N° 5 (*ibidem*): *Allegro vivace*, *ré* M, 2/4, 8 mes. |
| N° 6 (fin scène 5): Allegro, 2/4, *si♭* M, dernier accord sur v de *sol* m. | N° 6 (*ibidem*): *Allegro*, *do* M, C, cadence parfait en *do*. |

---

[89]. Pixerécourt 1810.

| | |
|---|---|
| N° 7 (fin scène 6): Raymond prélude sur son luth (livret). Solo de flûte sous cordes en *pizzicato*, 6/8, *ré* M. | N° 7 (*ibidem*): il est réécrit sur le matériel que le prélude se fait sur un luth pourtant ici aussi on trouve un solo de flûte sous accompagnement de *pizzicato* mais il ne s'agit pas de la même musique: plus court et moins véloce qu'à la Gaîté, ¢. |
| N° 8 («nous nous reverrons bientôt», ne correspond pas exactement à la fin de la scène mais à la sortie de Giafar): *Agitato*, ¢, se termine sur un accord V de la m. | N° 8 («pour nous réunir», plus tôt dans la scène qu'à la Gaîté, moment où Giafar donne le selam à Zaïda): *do* m, C barré, rythmes pointés, syncopes, fin sur V. |
| N° 9 (fin scène 7). | N° 9 (*ibidem*). |
| N° 10 («le moment est favorable», milieu scène 8, quand Raymond entre dans le kiosque): 4 mes. | Il n'y pas de musique à ce moment dans les matériels de Versailles le numéro 10 correspondra donc au numéro 11 du matériel de la Gaîté. |
| N° 11 (fin de la scène 8): Raymond chante le troisième couplet de la chanson de la première scène. Même musique avec ritournelle de clavicorde, sur le matériel il est écrit les paroles du premier couplet. | N° 10 (*ibidem*): même musique que pour la première scène, les paroles ne sont pas écrites cette fois. |
| | N° 11 («les cadeaux de ces messieurs», milieu de la scène, moment de pantomime de Raymond): solo de basson, rayé sur la partie de répétiteur. |
| N° 12 (fin de la scène 9): la musique commence avant la dernière intervention, il est écrit «silence» avec un point d'orgue général pour ce dernier vers. | N° 12 (*ibidem*): musique différente, pas de point d'orgue silence pour le dernier vers. |
| N° 13 (fin de la scène 10 qui correspond à une scène de marche militaire): à 2, 5 mesures, rythme croche/deux doubles puis legato après autre réplique puis croches avec des points après autre réplique. | N° 13 (*ibidem*): à 2, rythmes pointés, solo de clarinette (militaire), répétée plusieurs fois entre les répliques de Raymond. |
| N° 14 (fin de la scène 10): Raymond sort en dansant, 6/8. | N° 14 (*ibidem*): 6/8 mais musique différente, solo de petite flûte. |
| N° 15 (milieu de la scène 11 quand Issouf découvre le selam): trois mesures. | |
| N° 16 (fin scène 11). | N° 15 (*ibidem*): musiques différentes mais de proportion semblable. |
| | N° 16 (milieu de la scène 12, quand Haroun examine le selam): brève intervention pour marquer un moment fort dramatiquement. |
| N° 17 (fin scène 12). | |
| N° 19 (le n° 18 est rayé) (fin scène 13): caractère de marche avec les vents. | N° 17 (*ibidem*): petite marche avec flûte. |
| N° 20 («coup d'œil», milieu scène 14): moment de contemplation d'un décor. | N° 18 (*ibidem*). |
| N° 21 (fin scène 14): transition avec final de l'acte, «musique bruyante et guerrière» dans le livret, «marche turque» dans les matériels. Long moment de musique. | N° 19 (*ibidem*): solo de timbale et petite flûte, aussi long moment. |
| N° 22 («que je rends à l'héroïsme», milieu final): Haroun pose une couronne d'or sur Giafar | N° 20 (*ibidem*): fanfare avec cors. |
| Le matériel de la Gaîté enchaîne sur un très long moment de ballet (une vingtaine de feuillets dans la partie de répétiteur) divisé en plusieurs numéros. | N° 21 («formée par les mains de Zaïda»): Allegro agitato, C, 8 mes. |
| | N° 22 (fin de l'acte): de nouveau la marche avec les timbales et la petite flûte. |

# Dans l'ombre de Paris

## Bibliographie

Barré 2021
Barré, Martin. *Dans l'ombre de Paris. La musique de scène au début du XIXe siècle au théâtre de Versailles*, mémoire d'histoire de la musique, Paris, CNSMDP, 2021.

Beaumarchais 1785
Beaumarchais, Pierre-Augustin de. *La folle Journée, ou Le mariage de Figaro*, Lyon, d'après la copie envoyée par l'auteur, 1785.

Belly 2014
Belly, Marlène. 'Trace écrite d'une mémoire collective: l'usage du timbre dans la chanson de tradition orale', in: Schneider, Herbert – Le Blanc, Judith. *Pratique du timbre et de la parodie d'opéra en Europe: XVIe-XIXe siècle*, Olms, Hildesheim, 2014, pp. 85-100.

Biard – Dupuy 2010
Biard, Michel – Dupuy, Pascal. 'Entre scatologie et fantasmes sexuels, le cul et son imaginaire', in: *Annales historiques de la Révolution française*, n° 361 (2010), pp. 3-11.

Capelle 1848
Capelle, Pierre. *La Clé du Caveau à l'usage des chansonniers français et étrangers des amateurs auteurs acteurs chefs d'orchestre*, (1811), Paris, Cotelle, ⁴1848.

Carrère-Saucède 2020
Carrère-Saucède, Christine. 'Recensement des salles de spectacle et bibliographie de la vie théâtrale en province au XIXe siècle', in: *Publications numériques du CÉRÉdI*, 2020, <http://publis-shs.univ-rouen.fr/ceredi/index.php?id=689>, visité en August 2023.

Charle 2013
Charle, Christophe. 'La circulation des opéras en Europe au XIXe siècle', in: *Relations internationales*, CLV/3 (2013), pp. 11-31.

Cheyronnaud 2007
Cheyronnaud, Jacques. *Des airs et des coupes. La Clé du Caveau, bréviaire des chansonniers. Introduction à une histoire de la chanson en France au XIXe siècle*, Paris, René Viénet, 2007.

Choron – Fayolle 1817
Choron, Alexandre – Fayolle, François. *Dictionnaire historique des musiciens, artistes et amateurs, morts ou vivans. 1*, Paris, Chimot, 1817.

Corbin 1992
Corbin, Alain. 'Paris-Province', in: *Les Lieux de Mémoire. 3/1: Les France*, Pierre Nora dir., Paris, Gallimard, 1992, pp. 777-823.

Corbin 2014
Id. 'L'agitation dans les théâtres de province sous la Restauration', in: *Le Temps, le désir et l'horreur*, Paris, Flammarion, ²2014, pp. 53-79.

Douche 2018
*Musiques de scène sous la III<sup>e</sup> République*, Sylvie Douche dir., Lyon, Microsillon éditions, 2018.

Ducange – Anicet-Bourgeois 1838
Ducange, Victor – Anicet-Bourgeois, Auguste. *Le Couvent de Tonnington ou La pensionnaire, drame en trois actes et en prose, représenté pour la première fois à Paris sur le théâtre de la Gaîté le 12 mai 1830*, Paris, Barba, 1838.

Dumas 1863
Dumas, Alexandre. *Mes mémoires. T. 5*, Paris, M. Lévy frères, 1863.

Dupetit-Méré 1817
Dupetit-Méré, Frédéric. *La Brouille et le raccommodement, comédie en 1 acte, mêlée de vaudevilles. Paris, Théâtre de la Porte Saint-Martin, 13 novembre 1817*, Paris, Barba, 1817.

Élart 2005
Élart, Joann. *Musiciens et répertoire de concert en France à la fin de l'Ancien Régime*, thèse de doctorat, Rouen, Université de Rouen, 2005.

Élart – Simon 2018
*Nouvelles perspectives sur les spectacles en province (XVIII<sup>e</sup>-XX<sup>e</sup> siècle)*, Joann Élart et Yannick Simon dir., Mont-Saint-Aignan, Presses universitaires de Rouen et du Havre, 2018.

Ellis 2022
Ellis, Katharine. *French Musical Life: Local Dynamics in the Century to World War II*, Oxford, Oxford University Press, 2022.

Europe 1987
'Le Mélodrame', in: *Europe*, n° 703-704 (novembre-décembre 1987).

Féret 2009
Féret, Romuald. *Théâtre et pouvoir au XIX<sup>e</sup> siècle*, Paris, L'Harmattan, 2009.

Fétis 1874
Fétis, François-Joseph. *Biographie universelle des musiciens et bibliographie générale de la musique, Deuxième édition, entièrement refondue et augmentée de plus de moitié. Tome Quatrième*, Paris, Librairie de Firmin Didot frères, fils et Cie, 1860-1881.

Fuchs 1933
Fuchs, Max. *La vie théâtrale en province au XVIII<sup>e</sup> siècle*, Paris, Droz, 1933.

Gentilhomme – Belle 1817
Gentilhomme, Paul – Belle, Gabriel-Alexandre. *Femme à vendre, ou le Marché écossais, folie en 1 acte, mêlée de vaudevilles. Paris, Théâtre de la Gaîté, 2 juillet 1817*, Paris, Barba, 1817.

George 1998
George, Jocelyne. *Paris Province. De la révolution à la mondialisation*, Paris, Fayard, 1998.

Gidel 1986
Gidel, Henri. *Le Vaudeville*, Paris, PUF, 1986.

Girard 1993
Girard, Pauline. *Musiques de scène des théâtres parisiens conservées à la bibliothèque-musée de l'Opéra, 1778-1878. Inventaire*, Paris, Bibliothèque nationale de France, 1993.

Gosselin 1994
Gosselin, Guy. *L'Age d'or de la vie musicale à Douai: 1800-1850*, Liège, Mardaga, 1994 (Musique-Musicologie).

Gouffé – Henriquez 1802
Gouffé, Armand – Henriquez, Louis-Martin. *Le Chaudronnier de Saint-Flour, comédie en un acte, mêlée de vaudevilles. Paris, Théâtre de Louvois, 20 mai 1798*, Paris, Barba, 1802.

Granville 2014
Grandville, Frédéric de la. *Dictionnaire biographique des élèves et aspirants du Conservatoire de musique de Paris (1795-1815)*, IreMus, 10 mars 2014 (version mise à jour en février 2017 avec une centaine de pages supplémentaires), <https://api.nakala.fr/data/10.34847/nkl.ed21p61a/2079fbb15e2a476bfe290f328f539761f9064711>, visité en November 2023.

Herlin 1995
Herlin, Denis. *Catalogue du fonds musical de la bibliothèque de Versailles*, Paris, Société française de musicologie-Klincksieck, 1995.

Hugo – Ader – Malitourne 1817
Hugo, Abel – Ader, Jean-Joseph – Malitourne, Pierre-Armand. *Traité du mélodrame*, Paris, Delaunay, Pélicier, Plancher, et les marchands de nouveautés, 1817.

Jardin 2006
Jardin, Étienne. *Le conservatoire et la ville. Les écoles de musique de Besançon, Caen, Rennes, Roubaix et Saint-Étienne au XIXe siècle*, thèse de doctorat, Paris, École des Hautes Études en Sciences Sociales, 2006.

*La vie musicale* 1972-1993
*La vie musicale dans les provinces françaises*, 8 vols., Genève, Minkoff Reprint, 1972-1993.

Le Blanc 2014
Le Blanc, Judith. *Avatars d'opéras, parodies et circulation des airs chantés sur les scènes parisiennes*, Paris, Classique Garnier, 2014.

Lesure 1999
Lesure, François. *Dictionnaire musical des villes de province*, Paris, Klincksieck, 1999.

Leterrier 2009
*Le public de province au XIX<sup>e</sup> siècle. Actes de la journée d'études organisée le 21 février 2007 à l'Université d'Artois*, Anne-Sophie Leterrier éd., Publications numériques du CÉRÉdI, 2009, <http://ceredi.labos.univ-rouen.fr/public/>, visité en August 2023.

Level 1988
Level, Brigitte. *A travers deux siècles, 1726-1939: le Caveau, société bachique et chantante*, Paris, Presses de l'Université de Paris-Sorbonne, 1988.

Menneret 1973
Menneret, Pierre. *La Musique de scène en France de Napoléon III à Poincaré (1852-1914)*, thèse du Conservatoire de Paris, 1973.

Morrison en cours
Morrison, Fernando. *La dramaturgie musicale du théâtre parlé des Lumières au Romantisme (1791-1852)*, thèse de doctorat, Montpellier, Université Paul Valéry-Montpellier 3, en cours.

*Musique et société* 1982
*Musique et société. La vie musicale en province aux XVIII<sup>e</sup>, XIX<sup>e</sup> et XX<sup>e</sup> siècles. Actes des Journées d'études de la Société française de musicologie, Rennes, les 8 et 9 septembre 1981*, Rennes, Université de Haute-Bretagne, 1982.

Naugrette – Taïeb 2009
*Un siècle de spectacles à Rouen (1776-1876). Actes du colloque organisé en novembre 2003 à l'Université de Rouen*, Publications numériques du *CÉRÉdI*, 2009, <http://ceredi.labos.univ-rouen.fr/public/?un-siecle-de-spectacles-a-rouen.html>, visité en August 2023.

Piccin 2000
Piccin, Linda. *Les difficultés d'un théâtre de province au XIX<sup>e</sup> siècle: le cas du théâtre de Montansier, 1807-1866*, mémoire de maitrise, Versailles, Université de Versailles Saint-Quentin-en-Yvelines, 2000.

Pixerécourt 1810
Pixerécourt, René-Charles Guilbert de. *Les Ruines de Babylone, ou Giafar et Zaïda, Mélodrame historique en 3 actes, en prose et à grand spectacle. Paris, Gaîté, 30 octobre 1810*, Paris, Barba, 1810.

Pixerécourt 1813
Id. *La Femme à deux maris. Mélodrame en 3 actes, en prose et à spectacle. Paris, Ambigu-Comique, 14 septembre 1802*, Paris, Barba, 1813.

PIXERÉCOURT 1818
ID. *Guerre au mélodrame!*, Paris, Delaunay, Barba, Mongie, 1818.

PIXERÉCOURT 1841-1843
ID. *Théâtre choisi. Précédé d'une introduction par Charles Nodier*, Paris, l'auteur, 1841-1843.

PIXERÉCOURT 2013-2021
ID. *Mélodrames*, 6 vol., Paris, Classique Garnier, 2013-2021 [édition critique intégrale en cours].

SAINT-ROMAIN 1831
SAINT-ROMAIN, A.-L. *Coup d'œil sur les théâtres du royaume*, Paris, Everat, 1831.

SALA 1995
SALA, Emilio. *L'Opera sanza canto: il mélo romantico e l'invenzione della colonna sonora*, Venise, Marsilio, 1995.

SALA 1998
ID. 'Définitions et métamorphoses d'un genre quasi-opératique', in: *Revue de Musicologie*, LXXXIV/2 (1998), pp. 235-246.

STEINEGGER 2005
STEINEGGER, Catherine. *La musique à la Comédie française de 1921 à 1964. Aspects de l'évolution d'un genre*, Sprimont, Mardaga, 2005.

THOMASSEAU 1974
THOMASSEAU, Jean-Marie. *Le Mélodrame sur les scènes parisiennes, de «Cœlina» (1800) à «L'Auberge des Adrets» (1823)*, Lille, Service de reproduction des thèses de l'université, 1974.

THOMASSEAU 1984
ID. *Le Mélodrame*, Paris, P.U.F, 1984.

THOMASSEAU 1995
ID. *Drame et tragédie*, Paris, Hachette Supérieur, 1995.

TRIOLAIRE 2012
TRIOLAIRE, Cyril. *Le théâtre en province pendant le Consulat et l'Empire*, Clermont-Ferrand, Presses Universitaires Blaise Pascal, 2012.

VERMANDER 2018
VERMANDER, Benoît. *Versailles, la République et la Nation*, Paris, Les Belles Lettres, 2018.

VILLARD 1998
VILLARD, Jacques. *Le Théâtre Montansier: de la Montansier à Francis Perrin*, Marly-le-Roi, Champflour, 1998.

WAEBER 2005
WAEBER, Jacqueline. *En musique dans le texte: le mélodrame de Rousseau à Schoenberg*, Paris, Van Dieren, 2005.

WILD 1987
WILD, Nicole. 'La musique dans le mélodrame des théâtres parisiens', in: *Musique à Paris dans les années 1830*, Peter Bloom dir., New York, Pendragon Press, 1987, pp. 589-610.

WILD 1995
EAD. 'Le théâtre lyrique français du xix$^e$ siècle dans les collections de la bibliothèque de l'Opéra', in: *Le théâtre lyrique en France au xix$^e$ siècle*, Paul Prévost dir., Metz, Serpenoise, 1995, pp. 279-295.

WILD 2012
EAD. *Dictionnaire des théâtres parisiens, 1807-1914*, Lyon, Symétrie, 2012.

YON 2000
YON, Jean-Claude. *Eugène Scribe: la fortune et la liberté*, Paris, Nizet, 2000.

YON 2012
ID. *Une histoire du théâtre à Paris, de la Révolution à la Grande guerre*, Aubier, Paris, 2012.

YON – BARA 2016
ID. – BARA, Olivier. *Eugène Scribe: un maître de la scène théâtrale et lyrique au XIX$^e$ siècle*, Rennes, Presses universitaires de Rennes, 2016.

# Caroline Branchu:
# A Model of Nineteenth-Century Womanhood?[*]

*Annelies Andries*
(Universiteit Utrecht)

> *Je puis donc aujourd'hui affirmer ici, en toute conscience, que rarement j'ai rencontré dans le monde une plus respectueuse fille, une plus vertueuse épouse, une plus tendre et soigneuse mère, que ne le fut et que ne l'est madame Branchu! Et que chez elle ses hautes qualités sont encore, s'il est possible, au-dessus du mérite de son beau et sublime talent.*
> Henri-Montan Berton, 12 juin 1829[1]

This glowing portrayal, written by the composer and music educator Henri-Montan Berton, is of Caroline Branchu[2]. Employed at the Opéra since 1798, she rose to fame around the turn of the century performing in *tragédies lyriques* of Christoph Willibald Gluck, Niccolò Piccinni and Antonio Sacchini. Her true triumph came when she originated the leading role of Julia in Gaspare Spontini's *La Vestale* (1807). During the next two decades she remained a prominent presence at the Opéra, premiering many new operas until her retirement in 1826. Notwithstanding her immensely successful operatic career, Berton suggested that she had equally excelled at the more standard roles expected of an early nineteenth-century woman, namely being a daughter, a wife, and a mother.

---

[*]. For their generous and insightful comments, the author thanks Julia Doe, Gundula Kreuzer, Emmanuela Wroth, and the editors of this volume. The archival research for this article was financially supported by the Institute for Cultural Inquiry at Utrecht University.

[1]. Hennequin 1829, p. 40.

[2]. Caroline Branchu is known under various names. Marie-Rose Chevalier is the name that appears on her birth certificate. In her first contract with the Opéra, she is named Thimoléon Caroline Beloved Chevalier Lavite. Because of her marriage to Isaac Branchu in 1800, she was mostly known as Caroline Branchu during her career. Therefore, I have chosen the latter as the principal name used in the chapter.

There is, of course, an agenda behind this overwhelmingly positive character sketch. It was written to serve as evidence in the Lefebvre court case: Branchu's daughter, Paméla, was seeking to separate from her abusive husband, the dancer Auguste Lefebvre[3]. Domestic abuse could be grounds for divorce under the post-revolutionary law of 20 September 1792 and the 1804 civil code, commonly known as the Code Napoléon[4]. Yet the Bourbon Restoration in 1815 resulted in the abolishment of divorce. The only option was to seek a separation of property alone or of property and person. The latter allowed spouses to live apart but did not annul the marriage — only the Catholic Church had the power to do so[5]. Paméla's case, that of spousal abuse, was one of the most common reasons for women to seek a separation[6]. Yet the experience was neither easy nor pleasant. It involved a court case with testimonies, character sketches, and pleas. Moreover, it quite frequently resulted in libellous gossip and attempts at character assassination from the opposing parties. Not only were the relationships and moral character of the spouses investigated, but those of their parents too, hence Berton's character sketch.

Branchu's celebrity status made this court case a more public matter than usual. Presumably for this reason, Berton thought it necessary to support the truthfulness of his character sketch by specifying that «Madame Branchu n'a jamais joué la comédie que sur la scène»[7]. His insistence on distinguishing between on- and off-stage worlds was warranted, as they were often mingled in the public imagination. Evidence of this is a report on the Lefebvre court case in the *Messager des chambres*: it is found amid the theatrical news[8]. Moreover, rather than report on the spousal disputes, the author's focus is on Branchu, and more specifically, on her motherly virtue. To this end he quoted a letter with advice she sent to her daughter. The advice in the letter perfectly fits within contemporary patriarchal notions, namely that a wife's life should revolve around that of her husband. Paméla is counselled to take care of her looks and the household, be good humoured and economical, and always ready to please her spouse. When things were not going smoothly, Branchu urged her to look at herself first, before pointing the finger at her husband. According to the journalist, the contents showed «une modèle de tendresse et de bons conseils»[9]. And he ends the article with the rhetorical question: «Jean-Jacques [Rousseau] écrirait-il encore qu'on ne trouve au théâtre que des mœurs corrompues?»[10].

---

[3]. HENNEQUIN 1829.
[4]. MCBRIDE 1992, pp. 749-750.
[5]. *Ibidem*, p. 751.
[6]. *Ibidem*, fn. 15.
[7]. HENNEQUIN 1829, p. 40.
[8]. *Messager des chambres*, 11 August 1828.
[9]. *Ibidem*.
[10]. *Ibidem*.

## Caroline Branchu: A Model of Nineteenth-Century Womanhood?

The changing legal status of actors had impacted perceptions about their morality and how they could serve as models. During the *ancien régime*, actors were barred from obtaining civil status by the French government and they were put in a perpetual state of excommunication by the Catholic Church, largely due to prejudices against their lifestyle[11]. Besides, Rousseau was concerned about the impact of them performing roles, which put them in danger of annihilating the self by continuously adopting other selves[12]. This situation changed following the French Revolution of 1789. Actors were now admitted to society as citizens, which granted them the option to partake in politics. The *Messager des chambres* claimed that they also sought domestic bliss: «depuis que nos artistes ne sont plus élevés sur les genoux de la haute aristocratie, ils sont pour ainsi dire réfugiés dans les vertus domestiques, dans les joies de l'économie, dans les vanités de cœur de la paternité»[13]. The Lefebvre court case, he continued, was «une preuve malheureuse mais convaincante des mœurs généralement rangées, modestes et vertueuses des grands et des petits talents de nos théâtres»[14].

Of course, actors and singers were not suddenly exclusively put forward as model citizens. Many of the prejudices continued. While nineteenth-century female star singers became objects of admiration — gaining a status as mythological creatures and immortal 'divas' — the press also revelled in criticising inappropriate on- and off-stage behaviour and gossiping about scandals and misfortunes[15]. As James Q. Davies has argued, these constructed images attest to a combination of both worship and fear toward female performers and their cultural impact[16]. Branchu caused little public scandal during her career; she seems to have stood out as an exceptional model of womanhood. The Lefebvre court case was not alone in presenting her as a paragon of womanly virtue; this image was repeatedly conjured up during and after her career. When she died in 1850, obituaries mentioned her charitable nature and emphasised her pious passing assisted by a priest. *L'Assemblée nationale* even mentioned that these characteristics gave her the epithet «la sainte de l'Opéra»[17].

In this chapter, I analyse Branchu's public persona, paying attention to three important dimensions of her identity: being a free person of colour[18], a woman, and a French singer

---

[11]. Friedland 2002, p. 167.
[12]. Marshall 2006, pp. 146-152.
[13]. *Messager des chambres*, 11 August 1828.
[14]. *Ibidem*.
[15]. See, for instance, Cowgill 2012 and Frigau Manning 2014.
[16]. Davies 2012.
[17]. See, for instance, *Messager des théâtres et des arts*, 23 October 1850; *L'Indicateur de Bordeaux*, 24 October 1850; *L'Assemblée nationale*, 29 October 1850; and *L'Indépendance belge*, 20 October 1850. The *Constitutionnel* even explicitly contrasted a past era when actors and singers were refused the last sacraments with the present situation in which they were all but canonized.
[18]. It is worth noting that in eighteenth- and nineteenth-century France the term 'gens de couleur' was used to indicate both free and enslaved people of non-white ethnic background. Duprat 2021, pp. 32-33.

educated at the Conservatoire. I understand this persona as constructed in the interplay between her various public appearances (as an individual, as a singer, as a performer of operatic roles) and how they were perceived by the public. Drawing on performance materials, articles in the press, and private correspondence, I examine how she came to exemplify imaginations of womanhood in early nineteenth-century France, when legal and cultural notions about women's rights and duties were continuously in flux. While scholars have shown that operatic characters generally reflected contemporaneous perspectives on gender roles[19], the Opéra's early nineteenth-century programming mixed older with new repertoire — approximately half of the performed works at the Opéra between 1789 and 1815 were created before the French Revolution[20]. Therefore, the chapter also points out how Branchu's performance career allowed for the creation of continuities between older and newer imaginations of womanhood.

## A Free Person of Colour

Caroline Branchu was born Marie-Rose Chevalier on 2 November 1778 in Paris[21]. She was then described as a «quarteronne»: a woman of African descent who had one Black grandparent and three white ones[22]. She was one of the thousands of people of African descent living in France at the end of the eighteenth century — a population largely brought to the metropole as a result of French involvement in the Atlantic slave trade[23]. The entrance of enslaved and free people of colour into *ancien régime* France was governed by a complicated bureaucratic system that sought to circumvent the law (Medieval in origin) that made mainland France «une terre libre de tout esclavage»[24]. Abuses of the system were frequent as more and more people of colour were forcibly transported into France by colonial planters and military officials. In an attempt to take back control, the government established the *Déclaration pour la police des noirs* in 1777[25]. In this and other legal texts the word 'Black', meaning generally 'person of colour', was used to avoid the term 'slave', which made a distinction between free and enslaved people

---

[19]. See WHITE 2018; FREITAS 2018; RAY 2020; LEGRAND 2021.

[20]. See ANDRIES 2018, pp. 14 and 21-22.

[21]. This is the date, place, and name that appear on a late nineteenth-century copy of the birth certificate found at the *Archives de Paris*. However, other dates of birth (between 1780 and 1782) and places of birth (Saint Domingue) are also found in legal documents of Branchu and are reproduced in multiple biographies.

[22]. This definition was most often used in legal texts in mainland France. Yet it was not always used in a very strict manner, and in different locales definitions could be used in varying manners. See DUPRAT 2021, p. 33.

[23]. *Ibidem*, pp. 27-28; NOËL 2011, p. xviii.

[24]. DUPRAT 2021, p. 21.

[25]. This police force did not just have Black people under its jurisdiction, but everyone considered 'of colour' including people of Middle-Eastern-, Asian-, and Native-American-descent. NOËL 2011, pp. xiv-xv.

## Caroline Branchu: A Model of Nineteenth-Century Womanhood?

purposefully obtuse. One mandate established that people of colour could only enter France for limited terms of religious education or apprenticeship in a trade[26]. In accordance with this legislation, Caroline's father, Jean-Joseph Chevalier, was brought into France in the 1770s as the «valet» of his white father with the reported goal of learning the bather's profession[27]. Chevalier was the son of a white French military colonel in Saint Domingue and a free Black woman named Martoune Valentin[28]. Before coming to Paris, he had built a career in the French Caribbean military. He would continue in this profession after his arrival in mainland France[29]. In 1777, he married the white woman Marie-Madeleine Brocard, even though miscegenation was officially forbidden[30]. A year later, in 1778, its illegality was put into the spotlight when marriages between European and Afro-descendant people were decreed to be punishable by deportation[31]. This did not, however, put an end to the practice, as forging familial ties with the white population was one means of seeking further integration into French society[32].

The Chevalier family dwelled in the elite circles of Paris — both of Caroline's godparents were French aristocrats — and she received an intellectual, artistic, and musical education[33]. In the 1790s, Caroline seems to have taught music to support her family after her father reportedly lost his fortune due to the revolutionary uprisings in Saint Domingue[34]. Yet the post-revolutionary decade also brought new possibilities for people of colour. Following the *Déclaration des droits de l'homme et du citoyen*, they sought access to citizenship in France; indeed, Caroline's father was one of the signees of a document on this topic submitted to the National Assembly in 1790[35]. Citizenship in mainland France was granted on 15 May 1791, first to those born of free mothers and fathers, and a few months later to those who had been enslaved[36]. It was only in 1794 that slavery was finally abolished in France and all its colonial territories.

During the following years, those marked by better conditions for people of colour, Caroline began to be recognised for her musical talent. In 1797, she was admitted to the

---

[26]. DUPRAT 2021, p. 25.
[27]. NOËL 2011, p. 153.
[28]. ROUANET DE VIGNE-LAVIT 1992, p. 45.
[29]. *Ibidem*, p. 46.
[30]. SANDERS 2022, pp. 195-198. Sanders refers to a study by Eric Saugera (SAUGERA 2002) who found only 12 examples of men of African ancestry marrying women of European ancestry and only three cases where it was the other way around. SANDERS 2022, p. 229.
[31]. *Ibidem*, p. 195.
[32]. DUPRAT 2021, pp. 166-167.
[33]. ROUANET DE VIGNE-LAVIT 1992, p. 47.
[34]. *Ibidem*. Branchu also discusses this in an autobiography she writes for the Lefebvre court case. BRANCHU 1828, p. [2].
[35]. *LETTRES DES CITOYENS DE COULEUR* 1790, p. 3.
[36]. DUPRAT 2021, p. 25.

Conservatoire in one of the first classes of students entering this new institute for music education established in 1795[37]. In the same year she received her first prize for singing and started performing in *opéras-comiques* at the Théâtre Favart. In the newspapers she was named «citoyenne Chevalier», a sign that actors and people of colour were now accepted as part of the citizenry[38]. This does not mean that her identity as a woman of colour was not remarked upon; in at least one instance, she was described in a document from the Conservatoire as «une jeune femme brune»[39]. Her racial identity seems, however, not to have significantly impeded her studies. She continued her singing education in the class of Pierre-Jean Garat, who was highly complimentary of her abilities. He mentioned that «cette enfant a un instinct étonnant de la scène. Elle dépassera Madame de Saint-Huberty[40]. C'est une âme de feu ayant à son service une voix dont le timbre réveillerait Gluck»[41]. His predictions were quite accurate. In May 1798, she signed her contract as a double with the Opéra, where she would quickly move on to performing principal parts and hold the stage for more than a quarter century[42].

During her years at the Opéra, the climate for people of colour in France became increasingly hostile. It is true that several regiments of Napoleon's *grande armée* and his overseas armies included soldiers and officers of African descent, and that the emperor had sought to build on the loyalty of these groups upon his brief return to power during the Hundred Days[43]. Yet it was on his initiative that in 1802 the decree abolishing slavery was overturned, and his armies started to gruesomely repress the enslaved and people of colour in the French colonies[44]. The situation in mainland France also largely returned to that of the discriminatory laws of the 1777 *Déclaration pour la police des noirs*[45]. The situation did not improve after Napoleon's fall in 1815 and the restoration of the Bourbon monarchy, not least because of the process of Haitian «reparation» that was initiated in this period[46]. In mainland France, some of Napoleon's 'Black' troops were persecuted as bandits, leading to many of them being sentenced to death or

---

[37]. *Ibidem*, p. [5].

[38]. See, for instance, *Le Courrier des spectacles*, 30 December 1798.

[39]. Cited in Noël 2011, p. 216.

[40]. Saint-Huberty was a star soprano at the Opéra in the 1780s, being celebrated for her performance of the principal parts in the *tragédies lyriques* of Gluck, Piccinni and Sacchini — repertoire in which Caroline Branchu would later also shine. Dratwicki 2020, p. 538.

[41]. Rouanet de Vigne-Lavit 1992, p. 48.

[42]. See 'Théâtre de la République et des Arts: Engagement' 1798, P-an AJ13/54/15.

[43]. Duprat 2021, p. 153.

[44]. For a discussion of the various reasons behind this gruesome treatment of people of colour in the French colonies and the historiography on this topic, see Dwyer 2008.

[45]. Duprat 2021, p. 152. On the treatment of people of colour in Metropolitan France under Napoleon, see Ngaire Heuer 2022.

[46]. On this process, see Dewhurst Lewis 2017.

deported[47]. In the colonies, horrid acts of violence and repression continued, though abolitionist movements were also on the rise and led to several moments of public outcry. A particularly notable event was the public vociferation concerning a large group of unduly deported people from Martinique in 1823 and 1824[48]. In the aftermath of these events, the government sought to identify possible incendiaries among people of colour in France. It is perhaps in this context that the prefect of the Gironde department asked for a recommendation from his colleague from the Hérault department to let Branchu perform in Bordeaux. The latter, however, reassured him of «tout l'intérêt qu'elle inspire par son caractère comme par son talent encore si remarquable et si beau»[49].

No documents suggest that Branchu was explicitly affected by these laws against people of colour; it is unclear whether the legal system was extended as far as a «quarteronne»[50]. Yet this does not mean that she was spared encounters with racism. Her main rival at the Opéra, Marie Thérèse Davoux Maillard, for instance, complained about the supposedly preferential treatment she received as a student of the Conservatoire at her debut: «Les voilà qui font jouer des sujets de leurs écoles et nous restons-là. En effet, le 8, il doit y en avoir une, la nommée Chevalier, une mulâtre qui chante assez bien, a-t-on dit»[51]. Defining her as «mulâtre» may have been an intentional mistake, as legally that was a different category than «quarteronne» and emphasised Branchu's identity as a woman of colour. It is noteworthy, though, that overtly racial terms were not often used to describe her while she was performing at the Opéra. In fact, they are more often found in biographical entrees written after the end of her career in 1826 and her death in 1850. Her obituary in *L'Assemblée nationale* mentioned that she was born in Saint Domingue (which contradicts her birth certificate) and that she «was a woman of colour»[52]. More explicitly racialised is the description in the *Dictionnaire de la conversation et de la nature* (1852): «De taille médiocre, d'un embonpoint assez marqué, de peau, de nez, de lèvres et de visage reflétant la race noire, quoiqu'au troisième degré, elle avait à la scène une apparence qui n'était dépourvue ni d'éclat, ni d'attrait»[53]. Such descriptions can be framed within contemporary ideologies of biological racism.

These ideologies had become increasingly virulent in the nineteenth century. A popular publication in this vein was Julien-Joseph Virey's *Histoire naturelle du genre humain*, first

---

47. DUPRAT 2021, p. 152.
48. See *AFFAIRE DES DÉPORTÉS* 1824. On the abolitionist movements see JENNINGS 2000.
49. Letter from de Creuzé de Lesser, préfet de l'Hérault, to baron d'Haussez, préfet de la Gironde, 12 September 1826. F-bmo NLAS-169. Julie Duprat has suggested that this letter should be read in the context of the *affaire des déportés* in a brief online biography of Branchu. DUPRAT 2019.
50. NOËL 2011, pp. xiv-xv.
51. Cited in ROUANET DE VIGNE-LAVIT 1992, p. 48.
52. *L'Assemblée nationale*, 29 October 1850.
53. DELAFOREST 1852, p. 644.

published in 1800-1801. While it may have taken some time for these ideas to take hold, their growing attraction to European consumers is suggested by reprints of this volume in the 1820s. Drawing on earlier eighteenth-century French, German, and British writings, Virey divided humanity into six different races, based on physical characteristics such as facial features, musculature, height and, importantly, skin tone[54]. He also explicitly linked physical beauty to the degree a race was «civilised». These assumptions were underlined with prejudiced descriptions and drawings showing the greater proximity of the darker coloured races to apes — drawings on which artists such as Géricault modelled the Black figures in their paintings[55]. Even if Branchu's racial identity was seldom mentioned explicitly, descriptions of her appearance in unflattering terms such as 'laid' or 'bossu', including by Napoleon's brother Lucien, drew upon and resonated with these harmful tropes then circulating in broader discourse[56].

## IMAGINATIONS OF WOMANHOOD C.1800

While Branchu's identity as a person of colour was not always foregrounded, her identity as a woman unmistakably was — as the epigraph to this article shows[57]. She grew up in a period when the rights and roles of women were considerably in flux. During the *ancien régime*, women had largely been subjected to the patriarchal framework of the monarchy and the Catholic Church. This situation was also reflected in operatic plots. According to musicologist Raphaëlle Legrand, eighteenth-century operas mostly featured two categories of women: the woman *au mouchoir* who passively suffers and eventually will marry her beloved, and the woman *à la baguette* who uses her (evil) powers to get her way, but ultimately fails[58]. Female characters that did not conform to the patriarchal system were usually the victim of character assassination or eventually reined in by marriage[59]. And yet, several scholars have argued that off stage, in the eighteenth-century salon, some women found a semi-public means to partake in politics[60].

---

[54]. VIREY 1800-1801, pp. 125, 129-138 (division of the races).

[55]. For its influence on the depiction of people of colour see DOY 1998, pp. 207-255 and CHILDS – LIBBY 2014.

[56]. Lucien described Branchu as «terriblement laide» in his memoirs. Cited in GAVOTY 1961, p. 126. In notes related to her 1803 request for promotion, she is described as «laide, rouge, bossue, et allemande». P-bmo, NLAS-171-171bis. On pseudo-scientific racism in the eighteenth century, see also GATES – CURRAN 2022.

[57]. Following the end of her career, Branchu also mentioned in a letter that her identity as a woman played a part in her desire no longer to be a celebrity figure. Letter cited by Emmanuela Wroth in an article that discusses Branchu's gender identity in relation to her agency and celebrity as a Black woman. WROTH forthcoming.

[58]. See LEGRAND 2021, pp. 1069-1072.

[59]. RAY 2020.

[60]. Scholarly opinions on women's importance to salons and their political culture differ. Some note that their influence did not reach far beyond the salon, others warn against focusing on the exceptionalism of certain figures

## Caroline Branchu: A Model of Nineteenth-Century Womanhood?

Moreover, in the form of «seigneurial and inheritance rights», aristocratic women could have some authority over their own properties and lives[61].

After the Revolution, the *Déclaration des droits de l'homme et du citoyen* also generated discourse on greater equality between the sexes, with Olympe de Gouges writing the counterpart «Déclaration des droits de la femme et du citoyenne» in 1791 to expose «les droits naturels, inaltérables et sacrés de la femme»[62]. In France, this briefly resulted in laws giving certain liberties to women regarding property and marital rights, such as the right to divorce[63]. Besides, women were important in the revolutionary imagination, frequently venerated as goddesses, warriors, and mothers[64]. In these roles, they could serve the nation in public by taking up arms, but also in private by raising their children as good citizens ready to die for the fatherland. While offering women certain rights and a broader conception of their societal roles, it is worth noting that these progressive efforts were mostly still imagined from a patriarchal perspective.

This period of better conditions for women was short-lived. Many of the progressive regulations enacted between 1791 and 1794 were undone by the 1804 Code Napoléon, which granted renewed supremacy to marital and paternal authority. The oft-quoted article 213 states that «Le mari doit protection à sa femme, la femme obéissance à son mari»[65]. Unmarried mothers and their children were not given any rights. It also made all women equal before the law, eradicating the aforementioned *ancien régime* differences based on social rank[66]. Now, women of aristocratic, bourgeois, or other backgrounds were given little security outside of the domestic framework of the family. Napoleon's own denigratory opinions on women are likewise infamous[67]. In a diatribe against the liberal-oriented salons of Mme de Staël, he supposedly remarked that: «On fait de la politique en parlant de littérature, de morale, de beaux arts, de tout au monde. Il faut que les femmes tricotent»[68]. The emperor's influence went beyond

---

or male constructed narratives. See, for instance, GOODMAN 1989, pp. 332-334; and KALE 2004, pp. 7-8. On women's impact on musical activities in the salons, see CYPESS 2022.

[61]. GERHARD – MEUNIER 2016, p. 254.

[62]. GOUGES 1791, p. 6.

[63]. GERHARD – MEUNIER 2016, pp. 256-257.

[64]. See GUTWIRTH 1992.

[65]. *CODE CIVIL DES FRANÇAIS* 1804, p. 53.

[66]. Florence Launay argues that the true impact of the domestication of women inscribed into the Code Napoléon only came into effect later in the nineteenth century, because early nineteenth-century women had in their youth and adolescence still experienced the more varied spectrum of womanhood of the late eighteenth century. LAUNAY 2006, pp. 87-88.

[67]. Many are cited in KALE 2004; BURTON 2007; and MAIERHOFER – ROESCH – BLAND 2007.

[68]. In *MÉMOIRES DE M. DE BOURRIENNE* 1829, p. 95. Domestic imagery is also found in an anecdote, written down by Hortense de Beauharnais, concerning Napoleon mocking women who meddled in politics. When she or her mother Joséphine requested a favour for one of their protégés, Napoleon reportedly responded: «Allons, nous allons tomber en quenouille, et moi je ferai de la tapisserie». BEAUHARNAIS 1930, p. 113.

mere rhetoric: he also closed the salons of those with the potential to critique his regime[69]. The Bourbon restoration continued on the path that the Code Napoléon had taken, and with the return of the authority of the Catholic Church, society's patriarchal framework was further strengthened. One clear example is the above-mentioned abolishment of divorce.

In the operatic realm, the potential impact of the law on a woman's life was conspicuously thematised, most famously in the work with which Branchu's name was inextricably linked: Spontini's *La Vestale* of 1807, with a libretto by Étienne de Jouy. The opera tells the story of a Roman woman named Julia who was forced to enter the college of vestals, priestesses that guard a flame symbolising Rome's safety. During a nightly visit from her beloved, the military hero Licinius, she fails to keep the sacred flame burning and subsequently is sentenced to being buried alive. Ultimately, she is saved by divine intervention and the lovers marry. *La Vestale* became one of the few truly popular operas from the Napoleonic era; it reached one hundred performances by Napoleon's fall in 1815[70]. While the historical introduction in the libretto states that the plot was based on an event included in Johann Joachim Winckelmann's *Monumenti antichi inediti* (1767)[71], a similar plot had already appeared in two earlier French theatrical works. In 1768, Joseph-Gaspard Dubois-Fontanelle wrote the spoken tragedy, *Ericie ou la Vestale*[72]. The censors forbade its performance on grounds of its critique of institutionalised religion[73]. Nonetheless, it was clandestinely published in London and performed in French provincial theatres, getting its Parisian premiere in 1789[74]. In addition, a pantomime under the title *Julia ou la Vestale* was performed at the Théâtre Variétés in 1786[75].

All three plots emphasise the patriarchal and legal context of the leading character's suffering: her father forced her to become a vestal virgin, and under the Roman laws governing the life of vestals, her love is understood as a crime. This legal framework is repeatedly invoked in de Jouy's and Spontini's *La Vestale*. In the opening scene, Licinius is asked by his friend, Cinna, why he is so sombre. He then introduces the story about his passionate love for Julia with the line «partage donc mon crime et ma fureur»[76]. Cinna later warns against this illicit love and its consequences with the words: «songe aux lois»[77]. In the next scene, the high priestess cautions the vestal virgins against «les vœux impurs, les désirs criminels»[78]. And when the visibly

---

[69]. KALE 2004, pp. 90-92.
[70]. Performance data has been collected from the *JOURNAL DE L'OPÉRA* [1671-1981].
[71]. JOUY 1807, p. vii.
[72]. DUBOIS-FONTENANELLE 1769.
[73]. On its censorship see MARTIN 2004.
[74]. Information taken from *LE THÉÂTRE FRANÇAIS* 2022.
[75]. PARISAU 1786.
[76]. JOUY 1807, p. 3.
[77]. *Ibidem*, p. 4.
[78]. *Ibidem*, p. 6.

unhappy Julia is addressed, she responds: «J'obéis à vos lois en pleurant sur mon sort»[79]. The words 'crime' and 'criminel' are also frequently repeated during the lovers' illicit encounter in Act II[80]. Licinius and to an even greater extent Julia are thus depicted as oppressed by the law. This is further underscored when Julia is condemned to death by the prelate and answers: «Le trépas m'affranchit de votre autorité et mon supplice au moins sera ma liberté»[81]. She then questions whether a law can overcome nature, thus implicitly critiquing the unnaturalness of Roman religious legislation.

This critique of (religious) law as unnatural is present in all three pieces but addressed in different ways. In Dubois-Fontanelle's tragedy, it is addressed by having the prelate be the father of the eponymous vestal, Ericie. The character struggles, in consequence, with the conflict between his public (but supposedly unnatural) duty to condemn his daughter to death and his private (and natural) fatherly love for his child. The pantomime, for its part, spotlights the legality of Julia's condemnation by tying it to the public reputation of Rome. When the flame dies out during the lovers' nightly encounter, Rome is literally in danger: the Gauls are besieging the city. Julia's beloved, who had earlier deserted the army to be with her, runs to fight them and eventually conquers the attackers. As a reward he wishes to marry Julia and claims that through their love «les Dieux l'auront sauvée»[82]. Julia's crime is then literally expunged as the prelate rips the page with her condemnation out of the book of sacrilegious vestals. The opera similarly focuses on supposed divine intervention to overturn the verdict. A lightning bolt sets flame to Julia's black veil — a symbol of her sacrilege — which is interpreted as a sign that the gods believe Julia innocent[83]. A more conspicuous critique on the legal system is present in the libretto's historical preface, where the Roman laws are defined as «inflexible» and «terrible»[84].

There are, however, different outcomes for the pieces. Dubois-Fontanelle's tragedy ends in the suicide of both lovers, suggesting in part that death might be woman's only escape from being oppressed by various laws. Such an interpretation is underlined by the tragedy's larger critique of the patriarchal system. One of Ericie's friends questions whether liberty is truly possible for a woman:

> Mais cette liberté, qui cause vos regrets,
> Jamais de notre sexe est-elle partage?
> Victime de la mode, esclave de l'usage,
> Il faut prendre un époux par devoir, non par choix,

---

[79]. *Ibidem*, p. 8.
[80]. *Ibidem*, pp. 21-22.
[81]. *Ibidem*, p. 28.
[82]. Parisau 1786, p. 29.
[83]. Jouy 1807, p. viii.
[84]. *Ibidem*.

> Ramper sous son pouvoir, obéir à ses lois,
> Supporter ses défauts, honorer ses caprices,
> Le chérir, respecter jusqu'à ses injustices[85].

The comment is waved away by Ericie, who remarks that her friend clearly does not know the all-consuming nature of passionate, natural love. It is this love that provides an escape in the pantomime as well as the opera. Both works end with the former vestal's marriage to her lover. It is a convenient solution within the patriarchal system: a switch from paternal to marital authority.

This solution had particular relevance with regard to Napoleonic society. As a vestal virgin, Julia was a representative of an ancient Roman tradition whose equivalent was no longer practiced in France: religious orders had been disbanded during the Revolution when successive governments sought to reduce the power of the Catholic Church as much as possible[86]. Even though Napoleon had restored France's bonds with Rome with the Concordat of 1801, religious orders were not reinstated until 1825[87]. *La Vestale* seems to have been read within this context: several reviewers contextualised the plot within broader discourses on religious practices and the nature of women. One critic, for example, suggested that the constancy and chastity required of vestals was unnatural, remarking that it was very difficult «d'exiger d'une femme qu'elle renonçât pendant trente ans aux affections de la nature»[88]. Another expressed a more general critique of female religious orders, wondering «pourquoi chez presque tous les peoples du monde on a toujours cru qu'une demoiselle soit plus agréable à Dieu qu'une dame»[89]. By eventually marrying, *La Vestale*'s heroine instead chooses that all-important, and supposedly more natural, female role as a spouse.

This role was not only enshrined in the Code Napoléon, but in multiple biological treatises on women too. Besides dividing humanity into races, the abovementioned Virey also wrote extensively on women's place in society in his *Histoire naturelle du genre humain*. One of his most succinct formulations is the following: «la femme semble n'exister que pour offrir un appui secourable au malheureux, ne vivre que pour calmer les peines de l'homme, ne respirer enfin que pour aimer; c'est là sa première et son unique destination; c'est la seule loi qui lui soit imposée»[90]. Note the reference to the law in the last sentence. Women's supposedly lesser control over their feelings justified the need for patriarchal control. A similar image of women as highly emotional and weak is found in a short biography of Branchu in the *Galérie théâtrale ou collections des portraits en pieds* (1834) attempting to explain *La Vestale*'s popularity:

---

[85]. DUBOIS-FONTENANELLE 1769, p. 7.
[86]. On the approach to religion during and after the French Revolution, see TALLETT 1991 and ASTON 2000.
[87]. FORD 2005, p. 38.
[88]. *Affiches, annonces et avis divers*, 17 December 1807.
[89]. *Courrier de l'Europe*, 15 December 1807.
[90]. VIREY 1800-1801, p. 307.

## Caroline Branchu: A Model of Nineteenth-Century Womanhood?

> La plupart des tragédies lyriques ne sont que d'un intérêt local ou de convention. L'intérêt de la *Vestale* est celui de l'humanité tout entière ; c'est au moins l'intérêt du sexe le plus faible et le plus doux, de celui dont on excuse plus volontiers les fautes, et on plaint plus facilement les infortunes[91].

The popularity of *La Vestale* and its titular character may well have derived from how well Julia fitted within cultural, legal, and biological imaginations of womanhood.

### Branchu as a Sacrificing Heroine

Branchu's personal life seems to have conformed to this ideal of the virtuous, caring — and critically — married woman. At 22 years old, she married the dancer Isaac Branchu[92]. In subsequent years, while both were building their careers, the couple welcomed two children: a son in 1802 and a daughter, Paméla, in 1808[93]. Many later biographers and scholars have suggested that Branchu briefly was the mistress of Napoleon (but the evidence is very thin)[94]. Even if this were true, no affirmation of this or any other extramarital affair seems to have circulated publicly during her career. The only verifiable liaison was with Claude-Charles Pierquin, a medical doctor employed at the Hôpital de la Charité in Paris in the 1820s. Branchu and Pierquin began an extensive and rather intimate correspondence in late 1826, a few months after the singer's retirement from the Opéra and two years after the death of her husband[95].

Branchu's caring, sacrificing nature was often highlighted by observers, especially in the documents related to the Lefebvre court case. For this case, she wrote a brief autobiography that thematised the love, but also the sacrifices and pain caused by her family life; in many respects, indeed, the biography reads as that of a stereotypical woman *au mouchoir*. Branchu describes how the celebration of her daughter's birth was clouded by the death of her beloved father[96]. Ten years later, in 1818, she tragically lost her son to an unexpected illness and was temporarily unable to perform[97]. Moreover, from 1817 onwards, she bore the financial responsibility of the household. Her husband had been let go from Opéra because he was increasingly suffering

---

[91]. Galérie théâtrale 1834, p. 2.
[92]. Rouanet de Vigne-Lavit 1992, p. 48.
[93]. Noël 2011, p. 217.
[94]. Gavoty cites a British diplomatic document unearthed by the historian Frédéric Barbey as the only source that provides concrete evidence of the affair. His quotation suggests that the affair must have been very brief. This is the only direct evidence. Other remarks, such as Branchu mentioning that Napoleon was her friend, cannot be seen as conclusive. Gavoty 1961, p. 132, fn.
[95]. Their correspondence is preserved at P-bmo Dossier d'artiste-BRANCHU.
[96]. Branchu 1828, p. [4].
[97]. *Ibidem*, pp. [6-7].

from a war injury (a dislodged bullet in his brain) dating back to his military service in the 1790s[98]. From the 1810s onward, it started causing physical and mental health problems which eventually debilitated him. The biography's emphasis on her duty to her family is to be expected; after all it served to establish her character and parenting qualities in the court case. And it is certainly possible to scrutinise this image. Branchu's career made it impossible for her to raise her children by herself. Instead, she had them raised in the countryside. Still, she mentioned that she had done so in their best interest — namely, to keep them away from the possible corrupting influence of the theatre[99]. And even though her husband spent his last years in a medical facility, she did visit him often[100]. The more public displays of her love, care, and dedication to her family are further corroborated in her private correspondence.

This correspondence also highlights that performer and operatic character were sometimes conflated in Branchu's persona. This is evidenced, for instance, in the case of the title role of Gluck's *Alceste* (1767, but reworked for Paris in 1776). Alceste is one of many characters she performed who are willing to sacrifice their own lives to save their husbands from death. Branchu first performed this role in March 1805, and it would remain in her repertoire for most of her career, with reviews highlighting both her musical and dramatic interpretation[101]. In an ode to Branchu[102], the author quoted the first lines of Alceste's most famous aria 'Divinité du Styx' suggesting that her touching interpretation of the character would secure her eternal fame:

> Ne crains rien pour ton nom, il ne mourra jamais;
> Et prête à déposer ta dépouille mortelle,
> Tu pourras dire avec transport:
> *Divinités du Styx, ministre de la mort,*
> *Je n'invoquerai point votre pitié cruelle.*

Branchu's performances reached such acclaim that she would at times be conflated with the character, as in this review from 1825:

> Alceste-Branchu (car l'artiste s'est réellement identifiée avec le personnage) s'est montrée de nouveau la digne interprète de cette sublime composition. [...] J'essaierais vainement de donner à ceux qui ne l'ont pas vue une idée de son jeu profond et pathétique, de sa pantomime si éloquente, de l'entraînante chaleur avec laquelle elle a chanté tout ce rôle[103].

---

98. *Ibidem*, p. [6].
99. *Ibidem*, p. [7].
100. *Ibidem*, p. [8].
101. See, for instance, *Le Courrier des spectacles*, 12 March 1805, and *Le Courrier des spectacles*, 23 March 1805.
102. Branchu received dozens of laudatory poems in manuscript or print form. The roles most often mentioned are Alceste and Didon. Many of these odes are preserved at F-Pbmo Dossier d'artiste BRANCHU.
103. *Journal de Paris*, 22 April 1825.

## Caroline Branchu: A Model of Nineteenth-Century Womanhood?

Branchu's personal experience may have helped her interpret the role with «pathos» and «depth». It had been just over six months since the death of her husband. In her autobiography for the Lefebvre court case, she underscored that she had taken marriage very seriously, writing that «mon mari et moi nous nous étions promis de nous soigner, de nous consoler mutuellement, de nous jamais abandonner, Dieu avoit reçu nos serments, ils ont été tenus»[104]. Moreover, in her private correspondences later in life, she mentioned not wanting to remarry — a choice that seems to have been partly motivated by her religious belief in the attachment to her spouse, even after death[105]. These letters provide further evidence of the conflation between Branchu and Alceste, as she is at times addressed as «Alceste» by friends. The poet Marceline Desbordes-Valmores does so, for instance, when discussing their unconditional friendship and the hardships they endured[106].

Thus, it was likely with due reason that Berton in his character sketch quoted at the beginning of this article warned against conflating Branchu's on- and off-stage performances. After all, a few years prior to the court case, she had ended her career with celebrated performances not of sacrificial spouses, but of mothers seeking to protect their children. In 1823, she premiered the role of Valérie in *Virginie ou les Décemvirs*, with a libretto by August-Félix Désaugiers and music by Berton. Valérie and her husband try to protect their daughter Virginie from being forcibly taken by Rome's leader Appius Claudius. Upon failing to do so, the father decides it is better to kill his daughter than to soil her virtue. Letters of admirers and members of the press lauded Branchu's touching and «sublime» portrayal of the mother figure, praising «la vive expression qu'elle a donné au sentiment d'amour maternelle»[107]. The piece was unexpectedly successful and performed regularly in the following years[108].

Branchu would take leave of the stage in 1826 with another maternal role: Statira, the widow of Alexander the Great and mother of the title character in Spontini's *Olimpie* (on a libretto by Armand-Michel Dieulafoy and Charles Brifaut). The opera premiered in 1819 and was revised for the 1826 revival. In the first version, Statira stabs herself because she cannot bear seeing her daughter marry the murderer of Alexander — an act that causes Olimpie to choose death over marriage as well[109]. In the second version, Olimpie's fiancée is ultimately

---

[104]. Branchu 1828, p. [5].

[105]. See, for instance, letter from Branchu to Charles Pierquin, 7 May 1827. F-Pbmo Dossier d'artiste BRANCHU.

[106]. Rivière 1896, p. 17 (letter of 4 March 1830) and p. 82 (letter of 7 June 1835).

[107]. *La Quotidienne*, 17 June 1823. Similar praise is found in *Le Drapeau blanc*, 15 June 1823; and *Gazette de France*, 22 November 1823. A highly lyrical description of her performance, including some detailed descriptions of excerpts of the performance, is found in a letter by an anonymous admirer dated 20 June 1823. F-Pbmo NLAS-150 (3).

[108]. It was performed 18 times in 1823 and another 14 times before being taken off the repertoire in 1827. Performance data collected from *Journal de l'Opéra* [1671-1981].

[109]. Dieulafoy – Brifaut 1819, pp. 52-53.

exculpated, causing Statira to welcome and celebrate the marriage[110]. While the two versions end differently, Statira's purpose remains largely the same: keeping her daughter safe from marrying a criminal. In most reviews, the intense relationship between mother and daughter was considered very moving. In an article on Branchu's final performance, the author especially highlighted extracts from Act II: «L'air de Mme Branchu, et son duo avec Olympie, où brille la tendresse maternelle, est tracé avec des couleurs si vives, qu'ils ont fait tressaillir le public»[111]. Notwithstanding Berton's warning, Branchu's successful onstage performances may well have reflected positively on the portrait she sought to present in the court case.

## A Woman with a Public Role

Yet the court case and its press rapportage also brought to the fore that Branchu, unlike many women, had a public career — she was not the model of a purely domestic woman. This combination of taking on traditional female roles, while simultaneously providing a public service, was one often found in the new characters that Branchu premiered. In *La Vestale*, Julia's role as priestess and later as a wife largely denote a secluded life away from the public eye. Still, these roles had important, if indirect, ramifications for public politics. By protecting the flame, vestal priestesses were (at least symbolically) safeguarding the nation. When Julia failed to protect the flame, she still saved the nation's reputation and risked her own death by not betraying her lover, Rome's most recent military hero. Thus, Julia had a role in public life that fitted within the patriarchal framework: sacrificing herself for *la patrie* and her (soon to be) husband; she fittingly marries him in the end, domestic bliss and the required happy ending restored[112]. Similar arguments can of course be made for many of the sacrificing women in earlier *tragédies lyriques*. Yet more than previous operas, *La Vestale* foregrounds the national context by including a large procession scene for Licinius' victory in Act II and by having the «peuple» present to witness the events. As such, the political ramifications of Julia's actions are more in focus.

The notion of heroic, public sacrifice is even more conspicuously present in several of the roles that Branchu subsequently premiered (especially those written by de Jouy, who also was the librettist of *La Vestale*). In Spontini's *Fernand Cortez*, she interpreted the role of Amazily, an Aztec princess who is the lover of Cortez. In the plot, she is willing to sacrifice her life to save Cortez's brother. In a poem addressed to Branchu, de Jouy mentioned that Amazily «à Cortez ouvrit le chemin de la gloire»[113]. He was not the only one to make such a remark. Press reviews

---

[110]. Dieulafoy – Brifaut 1826, pp. 47-52.
[111]. *Courrier des nouvelles de Paris*, 28 February 1826.
[112]. On the need for a happy ending, see Andries 2018, pp. 254-262.
[113]. Manuscript entitled «vers mis sur la partition de Fernand Cortez de Spontini» and signed «Jouï». F-Pbmo NLAS 151(3). They are identified as coming from de Jouy in a letter from Branchu to Pierquin, 27 April 1827.

suggest that her actions outshone those of a «passive» Cortez, making one reviewer wonder whether the opera's title should perhaps be changed[114].

Amazily was another character with whom Branchu sometimes self-identified in her correspondence with the abovementioned Pierquin. In a letter from 7 May 1827, she declared to be his Amazily and he her Cortez, to then quote from the opening of her Act II aria: «Arbitre de ma destinée pour les donner mes jours sont-ils à moi, Amazilie [*sic*] ne vit plus que pour toi»[115]. The operatic character's identity as a woman of colour and her relationship with the white Cortez may well have informed this identification[116]. After all, Branchu's and Pierquin's different ethnic backgrounds were prominently present in their correspondence. She at times explained «créole» expressions to him[117]. And, in a letter sent in 1829, she included a poem entitled «Réponse au petit blanc», which opens as follows:

> La négresse sans vie
> Ne sait plus que pleurer:
> Un méchant l'a trahie
> En disant l'adorer
> Il ajoute l'outrage
> Au cruel abandon
> Et rend son esclavage
> Digne du pardon[118]!

The text was not specifically framed as a reflection on their relationship; they often exchanged poetry[119]. Yet the characters in this poem do reflect their ethnic identities, and, like Cortez and Amazily, they are an example of miscegenation. As mentioned, miscegenation was not legally allowed in mainland France at the time. Nonetheless, most of Branchu's family was guilty of it: her father married a white woman and she and her sisters married white men[120]. While illicit, musicologist Scott Sanders has shown how eighteenth-century operas sometimes served as models for individuals in this situation or as spaces for more general societal reflections on the issue — it is likely that later ones such as *Fernand Cortez* did so too[121].

---

[114]. *Petites affiches de Paris*, 14 December 1809.

[115]. JOUY 1810, p. 36. Letter from Branchu to Pierquin, 7 May 1827.

[116]. For an extensive discussion of the imperial narratives that run through the relationship between the Aztecs and the European conquerors in *Fernand Cortez*, see ANDRIES 2022.

[117]. See, for instance, letter from Branchu to Pierquin, 13 February 1827.

[118]. Cited in ROUANET DE VIGNE-LAVIT 1992, p. 53. Letter from Branchu to Pierquin, 2 September 1827.

[119]. Branchu was the one most often sending poems, with Pierquin answering with corrections in his next letter. Still, Branchu figured among the four dedicatees of a poetry album that he wrote in 1828. PIERQUIN 1828.

[120]. ROUANET DE VIGNE-LAVIT 1992, p. 47.

[121]. Sanders has investigated how versions of the Beauty and the Beast plot, such as André Grétry's *Zémire et Azor* (1771), served this function in the late eighteenth century. SANDERS 2022.

Interestingly, no reviews of *Fernand Cortez* explicitly remarked on Branchu's identity as a woman of colour, nor did they when discussing another similar character that she performed a year later: Laméa, the principal role in *Les Bayadères* (1810) with music by Charles-Simon Catel and again a libretto by de Jouy. Laméa is an even more heroic character than her predecessors. She is a so-called 'bayadère', the nineteenth-century French translation for a *devadasi*, a woman in service of a deity or temple in India. After the rajah of the city Benares is captured, Laméa leads the campaign to free him[122]. Despite loving him, she refuses his marriage proposal because of her holy vows. As in *La Vestale*, she invokes the law: «Du devoir rigoureux | c'est la loi qu'il faut suivre | elle a brisé nos nœuds»[123]. Only when the rajah feigns a mortal wound and requires that his bride die with him on the funeral pyre is she persuaded to be released from her vows and they celebrate their wedding. The kinship between figures like Julia and Laméa is highlighted in the historical introduction of the libretto, which points out that «bayadères» and vestal virgins «ont le même emploi et jouissent les mêmes prérogatives»[124]. In doing so de Jouy actively created connections between the characters performed by Branchu and underlined the similarities between these embodiments of womanhood with public responsibilities from supposedly different cultures and times.

Branchu's role as a singer can also be interpreted as having an element of public responsibility: she served the artistic prestige of the nation. Despite never having performed in public theatres outside of France, many of her obituaries suggested she earned international acclaim and was a «nom européen»[125]. She was one of the most famous, long-lasting early nineteenth-century stars of the Opéra, which was often thought to be France's most prestigious theatre. Thus, she significantly contributed to France's cultural reputation. With her success in *La Vestale*[126], she had helped the institution overcome a period of decline or at least stagnation. Between 1789 and 1807, but a handful newly created works were (moderately) successful and none had done well on other European stages[127]. In the years prior to the premiere of *La Vestale*, the Opéra was also plagued by illnesses of singers, such as of her rival, Maillard. Maillard had started her career at the institution in 1782 and was thus Branchu's senior[128]. Because of the Opéra's strictly hierarchical organisation, this kept the junior singer from achieving the status

---

[122]. Jouy 1810.

[123]. *Ibidem*, p. 58.

[124]. *Ibidem*, p. 12.

[125]. See, for instance, *L'Hermine*, 18 October 1850; *Journal des villes et des campagnes*, 17 October 1850; *L'Événement*, 18 October 1850; *Messager des théâtres*, 23 October 1850.

[126]. When Branchu fell ill in late 1807, the official overseeing the Parisian theatres, Auguste de Rémusat, suggested replacing *La Vestale* with a different work. He feared that the opera's success could not be maintained without her. See correspondence between Rémusat and the administrators of December 1807. F-Pan AJ13/74/415-422.

[127]. I have written more extensively about this situation in Andries 2018, pp. 13-17.

[128]. Dratwicki 2020, p. 538.

of «première cantatrice» until the former's retirement in 1813[129]. Nonetheless, Branchu profited from her colleague's illness to start performing more principal parts — a «service extraordinaire»[130] that was lauded and financially rewarded by the Opéra's administrators. *La Vestale* cemented her standing as the Opéra's principal star in all but hierarchical position[131]. Even though in 1821, some performances were less favourably received[132], she generally continued to be popular. After a performance in 1822, a reviewer protested rumours about her retirement[133]. He claimed that she had sounded as strong as ten years ago and that «Mme Branchu peut encore être extrêmement utile comme actrice et comme modèle»[134]. Hector Berlioz, having seen her perform in those years, also considered her a model for younger singers against the growing taste for Italian embellishment[135].

Aside from the fame she had brought to the Opéra, she also served as a model product of the Conservatoire and its supposedly unique, method-based teaching practices[136]. This was already evident in the review of her début. After describing her as an «élève du Conservatoire», the author explicitly linked her qualities to the idea of method: «une prononciation très nette, une voix agréable, etc. Dans toutes les parties du chant; les indices d'une méthode sage et profonde lui ont procuré de fréquents applaudissements»[137]. Her long and successful career is often credited to how she combined Garat's education, based on Italian techniques[138], with a particular instinct for simplicity and depth in her singing and acting. While profiting from the achievements of the Italian singing schools, she is thought to have stayed true to the French emphasis on tragic acting and simplicity. Even better, by introducing this combination into her

---

[129]. Branchu was confronted with this hierarchy at several points in her career. In 1801 there is a conflict with the more senior singer Elise Henry, who claims Branchu gets too many performances. Correspondence from messidor an 9 [June 1801]. F-Pan, AJ13/51. In 1803, Branchu's request for promotion to «cantatrice première» is refused because of Maillard's seniority. Correspondence of December 1802, January 1803 and revisited in April 1805. F-Pbmo NLAS-150.

[130]. Letter from the *maîtres de chant* to the Opéra's director, Louis-Benoît Picard, 18 April 1805. F-Pbmo NLAS-150.

[131]. The surviving reports from the *maîtres de chant* in the years 1807 until 1811 are extremely laudatory. In 1811, the report just contains «Branchu!!!!!!!» suggesting that her success is too great to express in words. F-Pan AJ13/78.

[132]. See, for instance, a review of *Les Bayadères* in *Journal des débats politiques et littéraires*, 18 August 1821.

[133]. *Gazette de France*, 22 November 1822.

[134]. *Ibidem*.

[135]. See, for instance, a reader's letter Berlioz wrote to *Le Corsair* on 11 January 1824. Cited in KOLB – ROSENBERG 2015, pp. 27-29.

[136]. On the prestige that the Conservatoire attached to its methods-based teachings, see GEOFFROY-SCHWINDEN 2022, pp. 192-210.

[137]. *Le Courrier des spectacles*, 30 December 1798.

[138]. On the methods for teaching singing at the Conservatoire see HONDRÉ 1996.

performances and showing its impact on the audiences, the author of an article in the *Galerie théâtrale* argued in 1834 that she contributed to «une heureuse révolution» at the Opéra[139]. New composers, such as Spontini, were part of this revolution as they sought to build on the operatic traditions of the *tragédies lyriques* of the 1770s and 1780s, but added an intensified, highly emotional musical language as in *La Vestale*. Because of her technique and acting talents, Branchu thus became an ideal interpreter for this new repertoire while also keeping audiences emotionally moved by the older repertoire — thus she created continuities between a French operatic past and present while also forging bridges between older and newer imagination of womanhood.

*\*\*\**

Branchu's life and career took place in the highly turbulent decades straddling 1800, when notions about women's place and roles in society were continuously in flux. In my analysis of her public persona, I have shown how she and the characters that she interpreted gave embodied, lived form to biological, cultural, and legal notions about women's roles. Thus, the chapter analysed how singers interacted with — and at times may even have directed — contemporary imaginations of what it meant to be a person of colour, a woman and a singer in early nineteenth-century France. In doing so, singers, especially those with long careers, could offer more stable points of reference that connected older and newer roles in unstable legal and cultural environments.

## Bibliography

*Affaires des déportés* 1824
*Affaires des déportés de La Martinique 1823-1824. Mémoires, consultations, et pièces justificatives*, Paris, Constantin, 1824.

Andries 2018
Andries, Annelies. *Modernizing Spectacle in Napoleon's Paris, 1799-1815*, Ph.D. Diss., Ann Arbor (MI), UMI Research Press, 2018.

Andries 2022
Ead. 'Mobilizing Historicity and Local Color in *Fernand Cortez* (1809): Narratives of Empire at the Opéra', in: *French Historical Studies*, XLV/2 (2022), pp. 245-285.

Aston 2000
Aston, Nigel. *Religion and Revolution in France, 1780-1804*, London, Macmillan Press, 2000.

---

[139]. *Galerie théâtrale* 1834, pp. 1-2.

## Caroline Branchu: A Model of Nineteenth-Century Womanhood?

Beauharnais 1930
Beauharnais, Hortense de. *Mémoires de la Reine Hortense, publiés par le Prince Napoléon. Tome premier*, with notes by Jean Hanoteau, Paris, Plon, 1930.

Branchu 1828
Branchu, Caroline. [Autobiographie], [c.1828]. P-bmo LAS BRANCHU 59.

Burton 2007
Burton, June K. *Napoleon and the Woman Question: Discourses of the Other Sex in French Education, Medicine and Medical Law, 1799-1815*, Lubbock, Texas Tech University, 2007.

Childs – Libby 2014
*Blacks and Blackness in European Art of the Long Nineteenth Century*, edited by Adrienne L. Childs and Susan H. Libby, Farnham, Ashgate, 2014.

*Code civil des Français* 1804
*Code civil des Français*. Édition originale et seule officielle, Paris, Imprimérie de la République, 1804.

Cowgill 2012
Cowgill, Rachel. '«Attitudes with a Shawl»: Performance, Femininity, and Spectatorship at the Italian Opera in Early Nineteenth-Century London', in: *The Arts of the Prima Donna in the Long Nineteenth Century*, edited by Rachel Cowgill and Hilary Poriss, Oxford, Oxford University Press, 2012, pp. 217-251.

Cypess 2022
Cypess, Rebecca. *Women and Musical Salons in the Enlightenment*, Chicago, The University of Chicago Press, 2022.

Davies 2012
Davies, James Q. 'Gautier's «Diva»: The First French Uses of the Word', in: *The Arts of the Prima Donna in the Long Nineteenth Century, op. cit.*, pp. 123-146.

Delaforest 1852
Delaforest, A. 'Branchu', in: *Dictionnaire de la conversation et de la lecture. 3*, edited by M. William Duckett, Paris, Aux comptoirs de la direction, ²1852, p. 644.

Dewhurst Lewis 2017
Dewhurst Lewis, Mary. 'Legacies of French Slave-Ownership, or the Long Decolonization of Saint-Domingue', in: *History Workshop Journal*, LXXXIII/1 (2017), pp. 151-175.

Dieulafoy – Brifaut 1819
Dieulafoy, Armand-Michel – Brifaut, Charles. *Olympie*, Paris, Roullet, 1819.

DIEULAFOY – BRIFAUT 1826
ID – ID. *Olympie*, Paris, Roullet, 1826.

DOY 1998
DOY, Gen. *Women & Visual Culture in 19th-Century France, 1800-1852*, London, Leicester University Press, 1998.

DRATWICKI 2020
DRATWICKI, Benoit. 'Saint-Huberty', in: *Dictionnaire de l'Opéra de Paris sous l'Ancien Régime (1669-1791). 4*, Paris, Classique Garnier, 2020, pp. 537-540.

DUBOIS-FONTANELLE 1769
DUBOIS-FONTANELLE, Jean Gaspar. *Ericie ou la Vestale*, London, s.n., 1769.

DUPRAT 2019
DUPRAT, Julie. 'Caroline Branchu, une créole sur le devant de la scene', in: *Noire metropole*, 2019, <https://minorhist.hypotheses.org/1053>, accessed September 2023.

DUPRAT 2021
EAD. *Bordeaux Métisse: Esclaves et Affranchis du XVIIIᵉ à l'Empire*, Abbéville, Mollat, 2021.

DWYER 2008
DWYER, Philip. 'Remembering and Forgetting in Contemporary France: Napoleon, Slavery, and the French History Wars', in: *French Politics, Culture & Society*, XXVI/3 (2008), pp. 110-122.

FORD 2005
FORD, Caroline. *Divided Houses: Religion and Gender in Modern France*, Ithaca, Cornell University Press, 2005.

FREITAS 2018
FREITAS, Roger. 'Singing Herself: Adelina Patti and the Performance of Femininity', in: *Journal of the American Musicological Society*, LXXI/2 (2018), pp. 287-369.

FRIEDLAND 2002
FRIEDLAND, Paul. *Political Actors: Representative Bodies and Theatricality in the Age of the French Revolution*, Ithaca (NY), Cornell University Press, 2002.

FRIGAU MANNING 2014
FRIGAU MANNING, Céline. 'Playing with Excess: Maria Malibran as Clari at the Théâtre Italien', in: *Art, Theatre and Opera in Paris (1750-1850): Exchanges and Tensions*, edited by Sarah Hibberd and Richard Wrigley, Farnham, Ashgate, 2014, pp. 203-221.

*GALÉRIE THÉÂTRALE* 1834
*Galerie théâtrale ou collection des portrait en pieds. 1*, Paris, Chez Bance ainé, 1834.

## Caroline Branchu: A Model of Nineteenth-Century Womanhood?

Gates – Curran 2022
*Who's Black and Why? A Hidden Chapter from the Eighteenth-Century Invention of Race*, edited by Henry Louis Gates and Andrew S. Curran, Cambridge (MA), The Belknap Press of Harvard University, 2022.

Gavoty 1961
Gavoty, André. 'La cantatrice Branchu et le premier Consul', in: *Revue des deux mondes*, 1 January 1961, pp. 126-135.

Geoffroy-Schwinden 2022
Geoffroy-Schwinden, Rebecca Dowd. *From Servant to Savant: Musical Privilege, Property and the French Revolution*, Oxford, Oxford University Press, 2022.

Gerhard – Meunier 2016
Gerhard, Ute – Meunier, Valentine. 'Civil Law and Gender in Nineteenth-Century Europe', in: *Clio: Women, Gender, History*, no. 43 (2016), pp. 250-275.

Goodman 1989
Goodman, Dena. 'Enlightenment Salons: The Convergence of Female and Philosophic Ambitions', in: *Eighteenth-Century Studies*, XXII/3 (1989), pp. 329-350.

Gouges 1791
Gouges, Olympe de. *Les droits de la femme*, [Paris, s.n., 1791].

Gutwirth 1992
Gutwirth, Madelyn. *The Twilight of the Goddesses: Women and Representation in the French Revolutionary Era*, New Brunswick, Rutgers University Press, 1992.

Hennequin 1829
Hennequin, Antoine Louis Marie. *Mémoire pour la dame Lefebvre, contre le sieur Lefebvre*, Paris, Pillet aîné, [1829].

Hondré 1996
Hondré, M. Emmanuel. 'Le Conservatoire du Paris et le renouveau du « chant français »', in: *Romantisme*, no. 93 (1996), pp. 83-94.

Jennings 2000
Jennings, Lawrence C. *French Anti-Slavery: The Movement for the Abolition of Slavery in France, 1802-1848*, Cambridge, Cambridge University Press, 2000.

Journal de l'Opéra [1671-1981]
*Journal de l'Opéra*, [1671-1981], digitized on Gallica, <http://gallica.bnf.fr/ark:/12148/cb426079139/date.r=Journal+de+Paris>, accessed September 2023.

Jouy 1807
Jouy, Étienne de. *La Vestale*, Paris, Roullet, 1807.

Jouy 1810
Id. *Les Bayadères*, Paris, Roullet, 1810.

Kale 2004
Kale, Steven. *French Salons: High Society and Political Sociability from the Old Regime to the Revolution of 1848*, Baltimore, The Johns Hopkins University Press, 2004.

Kolb – Rosenberg 2015
*Berlioz on Music: Selected Criticism 1824-1837*, edited by Katherine Kolb and Samuel N. Rosenberg, Oxford, Oxford University Press, 2015.

Launay 2006
Launay, Florence. *Les Compositrices en France au xix$^e$ siècle*, Paris, Fayard, 2006.

Le Théâtre français 2022
*Le Théâtre français de la Révolution à l'Empire*, <http://theatre1789-1815.e-monsite.com/pages/pieces-gens-et-lieux/les-pieces/e/ericie-ou-la-vestale.html>, accessed September 2023.

Legrand 2021
Legrand, Raphaëlle. 'Héroïnes d'opéra à l'Académie royale de musique: La défaite des femmes?', in: *Histoire de l'opéra français: Du Roi-Soleil à la Révolution*, edited by Hervé Lacombe, Paris, Fayard, 2021, pp. 1068-1073.

Lettres des citoyens de couleur 1790
*Lettres des citoyens de couleur à M. le président de l'Assemblée Nationale*, Paris, Imprimerie du patriote françois, 1790.

Maierhofer – Roesch – Bland 2007
*Women Against Napoleon: Historical and Fictional Responses to his Rise and Legacy*, edited by Waltraud Maierhofer, Gertrud M. Roesch and Caroline Bland, Frankfurt, Campus Verlag, 2007.

Marshall 2006
Marshall, David. 'Rousseau and the State of Theatre', in: *Jean-Jacques Rousseau: Critical Assessments of Leading Political Philosophers. 4: Politics, Arts and Autobiography*, edited by John T. Scott, Abingdon-New York, Routledge, 2006, pp. 139-170.

Martin 2004
Martin, Isabelle. 'Colportage théâtral: *Ericie ou la Vestale* de Dubois-Fontanelle, les risques du métier: Les Interdits Religieux', in: *Revue d'histoire du théâtre*, LVI/1-2 (2004), pp. 111-120.

McBride 1992
McBride, Theresa. 'Public Authority and Private Lives: Divorce after the French Revolution', in: *French Historical Studies*, XVII/3 (1992), pp. 747-768.

## Caroline Branchu: A Model of Nineteenth-Century Womanhood?

*Mémoires de M. de Bourrienne* 1829
*Mémoires de M. de Bourrienne, Ministre de l'état sur Napoléon, le directoire, le consulat, l'empire et la restauration*, Brussels, H. Tallier et Auguste Wahlen, 1829.

Ngaire Heuer 2022
Ngaire Heuer, Jennifer. 'Race, Law, and Contested Heritage: Toussaint Louverture's Family in France', in: *The Journal of Modern History*, xcIV/4 (2022), pp. 790-821.

Noël 2011
*Dictionnaire des gens de couleur dans la France modern: Paris et son bassin*, edited by Érick Noël, Geneva, Droz, 2011.

Parisau 1786
[Parisau, Pierre-Germain]. *Julia ou la Vestale*, Paris, Lormet, 1786.

Pierquin 1828
Pierquin, Claude-Charles. *Poésies Nouvelles*, Bruxelles, Tarlier, 1828.

Ray 2020
Ray, Marcie. *Coquettes, Wives, and Widows: Gender Politics in French Baroque Opera and Theater*, Rochester (NY)-Woodbridge, University of Rochester Press-Boydell & Brewer, 2020 (Eastman Studies in Music, 72).

Rivière 1896
*Correspondence intime de Marceline Desbordes-Valmore*, edited by Benjamin Rivière, Paris, Alphonse Lemerre, 1896.

Rouanet de Vigne-Lavit 1992
Rouanet de Vigne-Lavit, André. 'Caroline Branchu: Diva de l'Opéra et amie de Napoléon', in: *Cahiers du Centre de généalogie et d'histoire des Iles d'Amerique*, no. 40 (1992), pp. 43-58.

Sanders 2022
Sanders, Scott M. 'Beastly Variations: Allegories on Race, Migration and Marriage', in: *Opera Quarterly*, xxxvi/3-4 (2022), pp. 190-220.

Saugera 2002
Saugera, Eric. *Bordeaux port neérier (XVII$^e$-XIX$^e$ siècles)*, Paris, Karthala, 2002.

Tallett 1991
Tallett, Frank. 'Dechristianizing France: The Year II and the Revolutionary Experience', in: *Religion, Society, and Politics in France since 1789*, edited by Frank Tallett and Nicholas Atkin, London, The Hambeldon Press, 1991, pp. 1-28.

VIREY 1800-1801
VIREY, Julien-Joseph. *Histoire naturelle du genre humain. 1*, Paris, L'imprimerie du F. Dufart, an IX [1800-1801].

WHITE 2018
WHITE, Kimberly. *Female Singers on the French Stage, 1830-1848*, Cambridge, Cambridge University Press, 2018.

WROTH forthcoming
WROTH, Emmanuela. 'From Branchu to Baker: Tracing Innovative Diasporic Performance Practices Through Time and Space in Nineteenth-Century Paris', in: *Women's Innovations in Theatre, Dance, and Performance. 1: Performers*, edited by Colleen Kim Daniher and Marlis Schweitzer, London, Bloomsbury, forthcoming.

# Moving towards Exclusion:
# A Case Study of the 'Female Viennese School'

*Claudia Chibici-Revneanu*
(Escuela Nacional de Estudios Superiores / UNAM, León, Mexico)

## Introduction

This chapter focuses on the insufficiently discussed notion that the rise of Romanticism and the Napoleonic era in some ways mark a 'regression' for female composers. It will be argued that this was due to complex socio-historical changes in the music world and beyond. During the French Revolution, claims for female rights started to be explicitly formulated and within the musical sphere women had gained considerable presence in some European regions. It seems that «among the ruins of the ancient regime», there was a brief «age of women»[1], a glimpse of hope for women in music. Yet, in some ways comparable to the backlash against women's rights powerfully represented by the «Napoleonic code»[2] (1804), the classical music world began to ideologically shut composing women out with new rigour, partly due to the rise of the male-centred genius ideology. Although the latter also affected so-called 'minor' male composers, the exclusion of female creators tended to be more extreme, with womanhood acting as a kind of genius antithesis. According to Helmig and Brand, «the creative competition of a woman» with figures such as Beethoven became «unthinkable»[3].

The analysis will centre around three Viennese women composers from the late 18th and early 19th century, Marianna Martinez, Maria Theresia von Paradis and Josepha Barbara Auernhammer, here referred to as the 'female Viennese School'. There were other women composers active in Vienna during that time, such as Josepha Müllner Gollenhofer (1768-

---

[1]. Bubenik-Bauer – Schalz-Laurenze 1995, p. 11, my translation.
[2]. E.g., Varela 2021.
[3]. Helmig – Brand 2001, p. 7, my translation.

1843), Magdalena von Kurzböck (1767-1845), Marianna von Auenbrugger (1759-1782), Karoline Bayer (1758-1803) as well as, somewhat later, Kozeluch's daughter Cibbini-Kozeluch (1785-1858) and Auernhammer's daughter Marianna Czega (1786-1849)[4]. But Martinez, Paradis and Auernhammer may be regarded as the most important musical women during the period in question, with Martinez sometimes seen as the most outstanding[5].

The allusion to the 'First Viennese School' (or Adler's «Viennese Classical School») of Haydn, Mozart and Beethoven might seem forced, yet has been deliberately chosen to highlight several factors. Firstly, it refers to the fact that the six composers were roughly contemporaries and musically connected in many ways. Secondly, it aims to give a sense of a 'female tradition', which has been difficult to maintain given the continuous 'disappearance' of women composers from musical history[6]. Thirdly, it provocatively hints at what Gates calls «The Woman Composer Question»[7] which — among other aspects related to women in music — hovers around the supposed absence of 'great' female composers.

There is a long tradition, particularly common during Romanticism, of ascribing this perceived 'absence' to women's inherent lack of compositional abilities[8]. From a political point of view, this can be seen as promoting a sense of men's creative superiority and serving as a justification for male dominance[9] and patriarchy, a hierarchical system which, in its «modern» version, «[e]levates some men over other men and all men over women»[10].

Over the past decades, scholars have not only demonstrated the presence of women composers since the origins of known musical history, but also shown that a 'female Mozart' or 'female Beethoven' could not have existed for socio-historical reasons[11], including ideological barriers such as the genius cult[12]. This chapter will argue that the rise of (male) 'musical genius' partly[13] influenced a certain ideological 'fall' of female composers through a cyclical process in which the creators to be discussed were directly involved.

Many of the concepts and historical developments underlying this chapter are complex and will be discussed in a generalised manner, relying on a map-like representation of aspects

---

[4]. See, for instance, NOPP 1995.
[5]. WYN JONES 2016.
[6]. See, for instance, CHIBICI-REVNEANU 2013.
[7]. GATES 2006.
[8]. See, for instance, HALSTEAD 2016, p. 3 and GATES 2006.
[9]. HALSTEAD 2016, p. 3.
[10]. GILLIGAN – SNIDER 2018, p. 6.
[11]. OSTLEITNER – DORFFNER 2006, p. 16.
[12]. Given the chapter's interest in social influences on musical evaluations and the loss of much of the female composers' oeuvre to be mentioned, it will side-step questions of 'intrinsic' musical quality.
[13]. Of course, not all gendered dynamics within the classical music world are related to the notion of genius. Still, it can be seen as an ideology which both 'sums up' and helps enforce restrictive tendencies which also powerfully influenced musical women composers during the 19th century (see CHIBICI-REVNEANU 2013).

considered most relevant. The gendered nature of genius and the lives of Martinez, Paradis and Auernhammer have already been well researched. However, questions such as their intersection with the rise of genius have not yet received sufficient attention. The chapter therefore aims to bring together previously disconnected discussions and provide a more detailed analysis of (gendered) patterns related to the 'female' and 'male Viennese School'.

It will begin with a brief outline of pertinent notions and historical developments, then turn towards the three composers and their interconnections with the 'male Viennese School'. Subsequently, it will examine the 'rise' of the latter as opposed to the 'fall' — primarily into oblivion — of Martinez, Paradis and Auernhammer.

## The Context

As is well known, the late 18th and early 19th century marked the onset of significant changes. Although regions central to this discussion such as Austria and France were largely opposing forces, the fall of the *ancien régime*, the French Revolution and the First French Empire reconfigured Europe in general. The rise of the modern nation-state, the shifting of social hierarchies and celebrations of (at least rhetorical) equality, as well as the implementation of new, meritocratic social ideals, are only some of the developments worth mentioning.

Related to these changes, and as is common knowledge, the musical field (in modern-day Austria and partly Southern Germany) witnessed the shift from Classicism towards Romanticism, musical patronage gradually gave way to the 'music market' and the concept of 'serious' music started to take hold. Romanticism marks a notable and related rise in the status of (some) creators of music and heroic artist figures began to attract more attention than their work. As Bruno observes, already hinting at the importance of genius regarding this matter: «this reorientation [...] lay[s] the groundwork for the Romantic movement, and it brings with it its own fascination with the artist. In fact, we must recognize the various musings on genius as part and parcel of this shift, for the study of genius is nothing if not the concentration on the relationship between the artist and the work»[14].

### The (Musical) Ideology of Genius

The word 'genius' has a complex history. It arose as a merging of the Latin 'ingenium' (ability) and 'genius', among other meanings a tutelary spirit and, in the Middle-Ages, an allegorical figure[15]. The period in question sees a gradual shift from genius as an inclination

---

[14]. BRUNO 2010, p. 24.
[15]. NITZSCHE 1975.

(something one *has*) to an embodied category (something one *is*). This change can be traced to the English literary sphere through writers such as Addison and Young. Theorists such as Kant, Herder and Diderot then expanded upon and promoted the idea[16].

According to Heinich, personified genius gained unprecedented power around the fall of the *ancien régime*, as it provided a new system of social distinction and justification of social inequality. The innate superiority associated with the aristocracy now became related to a few innate and godlike creators and, by extension, those capable of appreciating their work. The genius ideology thus helped retain a paradoxical sense of 'aristocratic' distinction while celebrating arising ideals such as 'equality' and meritocracy[17].

Within music, Rousseau already refers to musical genius in his *Dictionnaire de Musique* (1768) and E. T. A. Hoffmann is often credited with developing and popularising the notion. Moreover, DeNora suggests that musical genius became increasingly codified in and with reference to 18th-century and early 19th-century Vienna[18], where it indeed acted as a means of (re-)negotiating social status.

Importantly, genius is also a gendered notion from its very origins[19]. The Latin 'genius' was the tutelary spirit of men, often represented by phallic images, while women had their own spirit, Juno. The allegorical genius in the Middle Ages was male[20]. Rousseau believed that «Women, in general, do not like any art, know nothing about any, and have no genius»[21]. Citron further suggests that the associations between genius and divinity, imagined as singular and male in the Judeo-Christian tradition, emphasises its normative masculinity[22]. Even the rising belief that geniuses are innate, overcome all obstacles and achieve full appreciation from a discerning posterity, arguably has gender-exclusive effects. For these notions belittle the force of circumstantial restrictions many female composers had to face to varying degrees throughout musical history.

## Gender and Women Composers

Gender dynamics of the (late) 18th and early 19th century were contradictory and complex, both because of the ambiguous roles of women during the Enlightenment and the changes to follow. Despite multiple and powerful forms of gender oppression, Head argues that

---

[16]. Bruno 2010.
[17]. Heinich 2016. Of course, Napoleon himself was often regarded as a 'genius' figure.
[18]. DeNora 1997.
[19]. Citron 2000; Dunbar 2011; Battersby 1989; Shiner 2001.
[20]. Nitzsche 1975.
[21]. Quoted in Gates 2006, p. 2.
[22]. Citron 2000.

women's voices during the Enlightenment were present in many fields including the arts and they were rarely regarded as a cultural «other»[23]. Class distinctions were of crucial significance and women from the ruling classes, such as Empress Maria Theresia (1740-1780), were, despite some conflicts with traditional gender roles, considered entitled to rule[24]. In fact, it appears as if the modern patriarchal system which, as shown, tends to place men as a group over women, was not yet fully in place. In simplistic terms, it seems that aristocratic women at least partly hierarchically 'trumped' non-aristocratic males.

At the same time, revolutionary discourses of equality during the late 18th century also made matters of gender equality more thinkable. Some historians of feminism refer to this period as the first wave of feminism[25]. The Woman's March of Versailles in 1789, a significant event of the Revolution, was followed by women's petition that male privileges should be abolished alongside those of the aristocracy. Olympe de Gouge published 'The Declaration of the Rights of Woman and of the Female Citizen' in 1791, two years after 'The Declaration of the Rights of Man and of the Citizen'. In England, Mary Wollstonecraft released *A Vindication of the Rights of Woman* (1792). However, these developments were soon pushed back. Olympe de Gouge met her death by the guillotine in 1793. Women lost many of their new rights and were excluded from political meetings in 1795[26]. Once Napoleon rose to power, the 'Napoleonic code', as said, proved immensely restrictive for women. The 'rights of men' were for men only and women were «written out of the description of mankind»[27].

According to Dunbar, «women's documented musical activity in the Baroque (approximately 1600-1750) surpasses that of the Classical era (1750-1800)»[28]. Others, however, consider the latter a very positive age for women composers. Head mentions that «between 1756 and 1806 about fifty women in north German states [...] published music under their own names»[29]. Weissweiler stresses that women composers in Austria were particularly empowered and, unlike their German contemporaries, did not stick to «small forms»[30]. The idea of Vienna as a special place for female (evidently as well as male) composers is emphasised by Krones[31], who speaks of near gender equality in the musical sphere. Among other sources, he bases his argument on *The Yearbook of Music in Vienna and Prague* (1796). Indistinctly listing 'professionals' and 'amateurs', the latter mentions a total of 131 men and 77 women active in

---

[23]. HEAD 2013, p. 4.
[24]. BRAUN – KUSBER – SCHNETTGER 2002, p. 9.
[25]. E.g., VARELA 2021.
[26]. *Ibidem*, p. 41.
[27]. BUBENIK-BAUER – SCHALZ-LAURENZE 1995, p. 7.
[28]. DUNBAR 2011, p. 89.
[29]. HEAD 2013, p. 6.
[30]. WEISSWEILER 1999, p. 163.
[31]. KRONES 2006.

music[32]. Like Head, he also points to the frequent absence of 'othering' women (e.g. presenting them as exceptions to a male norm) in musical discourse during that time.

Evidently, a gender ratio of 131 men to 77 women does not imply equality and examples from the lives of Martinez, Paradis and Auernhammer will illustrate that musical women faced multiple gender restrictions. Joseph II, who succeeded Maria Theresia, for instance, implemented a reform of Church music which prohibited the participation of women, except those of particularly high social standing[33]. Gendered factors which severely affected Anna Maria Mozart's musical career have also already been extensively analysed[34].

Nonetheless, one does note a cultural space for women in music. Apart from a common absence of discursive 'othering', there is even a, presumably unselfconscious, use of what may be called gender inclusive language. One finds writings with a specific deployment of male and female forms (in German), such as an article on male and female pianists to be mentioned or a piece on Paradis which refers to her using the female version of «master» («Meisterin»)[35]. Even the deployment of genius, although arguably never free of historically male associations, tends to be gender neutral. The *Yearbook*, for example, moves freely between genius as a feature and a person and applies both to women and men[36].

## The Composers

### Marianna Martinez (1744-1812)

Marianna Martinez, also often named Marianne and/or Martines, was born in Vienna, although she belonged to an aristocratic family of Spanish-Italian origins. Like Joseph Haydn and Metastasio, a close friend of her family, she lived in the 'Michaela House' on the Michaela Platz in central Vienna. Metastasio noticed her musical abilities from an early age onwards and oversaw her education which included lessons from Haydn, Porpora, Hasse and Bonno. She was renowned as a pianist as well as a singer.

Martinez apparently first performed one of her compositions before a large audience in 1761[37]. Many presentations of her work took place in more private settings, such as the frequent musical soirées in her house where Mozart and Haydn were allegedly often invited, and Martinez and Mozart played together. In fact, Martinez's compositions influenced some of

---

[32]. *Ibidem*, p. 179.
[33]. Nopp 1985, p. 36.
[34]. See, for instance, Neumayr 2019. Mozart's sister lived outside the Viennese context here discussed.
[35]. *AmZ* 1799a, pp. 523-526; *AmZ* 1817, p. 322.
[36]. Schönfeld 1796 describes «Mademoiselle» Müller as «a strange genius», p. 45, my translation.
[37]. Unseld 2018. It is not entirely certain if this was the first public presentation of her work.

Mozart's work. As Godt observes: «More than twenty years after the publication of Marianna's sonata, Mozart used a plainer version of her first two phrases... at the beginning of his Sonata in C, K. 545»[38]. Her 'Christe eleison' also acted as a model for Mozart's 'Christe eleison' in the *Waisenhausmesse* (K. 139)[39]. In 1782, her oratorio *Isacco, figura del Redentore* was performed by the Viennese Tonkunst Sozietät. Metastasio died soon after and left her a considerable inheritance. After his death, Martinez lived at different locations in Vienna and, between 1780 and 1790, led a singing school, sometimes regarded as a precursor of the Viennese conservatoire.

Her musical abilities and compositions received much recognition during her lifetime. She was often invited to perform at Maria Theresia's court, where Joseph II turned the pages for her. She was praised by many important musical figures such as Charles Burney. The latter recounts how he had heard of Martinez as possessing «the greatest genius for music, in all its branches of playing, singing, and composing, of any one living»[40]. After meeting her in Vienna, he speaks highly of her performance and two of her «very well written»[41] pieces, adding that she «has composed a Miserere [...] and is a most excellent contrapuntist»[42]. In 1773, she became the first woman to be accepted by the Accademia Filarmonica di Bologna, a great honour also awarded to Mozart in 1770.

Her oeuvre comprises 4(-5) masses, 9 litanies and other liturgical works, 6 motets, 2 oratorios, 11 cantatas, her Symphony in C major (1770), 4 concerts for cembalo, 3 cembalo sonatas and one collection named *Saggio di composizioni della Sig.ª Anna Maria Martines: Kyrie und Et vitam venturi*[43]. Much of her work is extant. However, and although Korntner emphasises that she does not have further information on this matter, Martinez allegedly composed a lot more — an apparent total of 156 arias, as well as another oratorio and symphony[44]. Given her attraction to sacred works, Martinez was negatively impacted by Joseph II's previously mentioned Church reforms. She remained single and died in 1812, a few days after her sister.

*Maria Theresia von Paradis (1759-1824)*

The Vienna-born Maria Theresia was blind from an early age onward and became a patient of Franz Anton Mesmer. Her family was connected to the court, and she was often assumed to

---

[38]. GODT 2010, p. 30.
[39]. *Ibidem*, p. 37.
[40]. BURNEY 1773, p. 246.
[41]. *Ibidem*, p. 308.
[42]. *Ibidem*, pp. 309-310.
[43]. UNSELD 2018.
[44]. KORNTNER 2018, p. 42.

be aristocratic, yet this is probably not true[45]. Her musical teachers included Kozeluch, Righini, Salieri, as well as Frieberth and Vogler who instructed her in composition[46]. As a renowned pianist, Paradis undertook a European tour between 1783 and 1786, including stops in London, Paris, Berlin and Prague. She was accompanied by her mother and met her friend and later partner Johann Riedinger. In Paris, Paradis had met and collaborated with Valentin Haüy who had opened the first school for the blind. Back in Vienna, Paradis gradually withdrew from public performances and focused mainly on composing and teaching. She founded a music school for girls in 1808, another forerunner of the conservatoire. Mozart and Paradis knew of each other, although it is not certain if they met in person[47].

Paradis' compositions include the stage works *Der Schulkandidat* (*The School Candidate*, written 1791/1792, performed six times), *Ariadne und Bacchus* (first performed in 1791), *Rinaldo und Alcina* (first performed in 1797, in Prague), and the *Große militärische Oper* (*Great Military Opera*, 1805). With the exception of part of *Der Schulkandidat*, the music to all of these works is lost. She also wrote three cantatas (one lost), two ballads (one lost), several songs (some lost), including a song-collection published by Breitkopf in 1786, two piano concertos (lost), a piano trio (lost) and two fantasies for piano, among other piano works[48]. Although an unresolved matter, Matsushita argues that her most famous composition, the *Sicilienne*, is probably not by her[49].

Due to the loss of many of her compositions[50], it is impossible to evaluate her complete oeuvre. It is, however, known that during her lifetime, her work was generally very well received. Among many examples, Frankl alludes to the fact that Joseph II desired to meet her and exclaimed during their encounter: «I'm very glad to have met you in person, as I've known you as a composer for a long time»[51]. An article published by the *Wiener allgemeine musikalische Zeitung* states that her *Ariadne und Bacchus* showed an «inexhaustible wealth of ideas», and — indeed implying a meeting between them — that «Mozart liked it so much that he was present at every performance and always sat next to her at the piano»[52]. Paradis died on the 1st of February 1824. Despite her musical importance, her death protocol only mentions her as the daughter of a governing council[53].

---

[45]. Fürst 2005, p. 22.
[46]. Korntner 2018, p. 44, p. 51.
[47]. See, for instance, *ibidem*, pp. 48-49.
[48]. *Ibidem*, pp. 82-83.
[49]. Matsushita 2006, p. 35.
[50]. However, several pieces are available at the Gesellschaft der Musikfreunde in Vienna, for example.
[51]. Frankl 1876, p. 18, my translation.
[52]. *WamZ* 1813, p. 496, my translation.
[53]. Nopp 1995, p. 118.

# Moving towards Exclusion: A Case Study of the 'Female Viennese School'

## *Josepha Barbara Auernhammer (1758-1820)*

Josepha Barbara Auernhammer (Aurnhammer, Bösenhönig and Bessenig)[54], was also born in Vienna and received excellent musical training. She studied piano with Richter, Kozeluch and Mozart, who dedicated several pieces to her (K. 296 and K. 448, among others). She, in turn, was in charge of several editions of his work[55].

Auernhammer was born a year earlier than Paradis, yet this section mentions her last, due to some difference with regard to the other two composers. She was the only one who married, had (two) children and aspired to work as a professional musician. Also, she published extensively and had a strong public presence, partly through her yearly musical Academies where she often performed her own compositions and sometimes played with Mozart. Her professional aspirations and greater public presence may be partly connected to the fact that she was not from an aristocratic background, nor apparently close to the court.

Although better known as a pianist, her compositions started to appear around 1790. According to an article to be mentioned, she produced at least 63 works, yet Korntner lists only 15 as known[56]. These are chiefly piano variations such as her *Six Variations on the Aria 'Der Vogelfänger bin ich ja'* from Mozart's *Die Zauberflöte* and her *Six variations on a Hungarian theme*. But the list also includes her Sonata in C major for piano and violin, six songs and two sonatas for piano. All compositions mentioned are extant. Yet if she indeed composed 63 works, the great majority of her oeuvre is lost.

In a previously alluded to article on the most famous 'female' and 'male' pianists in Vienna, Auernhammer is named alongside Kurzböck, Beethoven and Wölfl. The (unnamed) author assumes that readers are familiar with her «outstanding compositions»[57] and recounts that, during a performance, the audience «particularly liked her variations on the Duet: *La stessa, la stessissima* — from Salieri's opera Falstaff which she composed»[58]. The piece also criticises (as well as praises) her piano playing, while incidentally considering Wölfl a better pianist than Beethoven. In fact, Auernhammer herself was increasingly questioned as a pianist, which may be why she eventually withdrew[59].

Her 'case' already forces one to address gender ambiguities. Firstly, her professional ambitions are known because Mozart mentioned them in a letter to his father, explaining that she considered herself too unattractive to find a husband who would financially provide for

---

[54]. *Ibidem*, pp. 66-67.
[55]. Unseld 2006, p. 47.
[56]. *AmZ* 1799b, pp. 90-91; Kortner 2018, p. 77.
[57]. *AmZ* 1799a, p. 523, my translation.
[58]. *Ibidem*, my translation.
[59]. Nopp 1995, p. 97.

her[60]. This shows both an 'opening' and a persistent 'closure' for women during the period in question. While Mozart supported this plan and a professional career in music had become thinkable, it also proves the persistent role of marriage as a basic financial survival strategy, with looks acting as a key social currency for many women. As said, Auernhammer did eventually marry — a Mr. Bessenig — in 1786 and retained a strong musical presence under her maiden name. Again, this may be linked to her social status and perhaps illustrates that her desire to become 'professional' was not just a financial concern.

Secondly, Auernhammer's reception became increasingly marked by signs of female 'othering'. In 1791, a review of one of her variations starts by commenting on how rare it is for women to write with «male understanding and taste»[61], a 'feat' which Auernhammer is considered to have achieved. In 1792, her variations on Mozart's 'Vogelfänger' are praised as deserving «to be placed alongside some male works of this kind»[62]. Although meant as compliments, these comments clearly illustrate the assumed superiority of male musical creativity. The gendered nature of her reception became even more evident in an article previously alluded to which states on the publication of her 63rd composition: «The 63rd work? – ay, ay, that's a little much for the outer work of a lady»[63].

## Ascent and Decline

### Becoming Geniuses

As indicated, Haydn, Mozart and Beethoven's now largely «undisputed primacy [...] did not match outlooks in Vienna around 1800»[64]. This is not to question their musical achievements, but their growing hagiographic veneration which stands in sharp contrast to the gradual 'diminishment' and (near) disappearance of Martinez, Paradis, Auernhammer, as well as, albeit to a lesser extent, that of many so-called 'minor' composers[65].

Now, celebratory writings on Mozart, Haydn and Beethoven are so abundant and well-known, they will not be presently explored in detail. Rather, this section aims to show that they were not simply judged as qualifying for the accolade of musical genius, but that the idea of embodied musical genius was built to a considerable extent with their work and personae

---

[60]. Unseld 2006.
[61]. *MK* 1791, p. 361.
[62]. *MK* 1792, p. 195.
[63]. *AmZ* 1799b, pp. 90-91, my translation.
[64]. Wyn Jones 2016, p. 15.
[65]. In fact, this is consistent with the previous definition of modern patriarchy as elevating «some men over other men and all men over women», Gilligan – Snider 2018, p. 6.

in mind. This leads to a cyclicality which may be illustrated through an article that praises «St. Mozart's» work as typical of «this genius» and «so beautiful that if it didn't display Mozart's name already, one would be tempted to put it there»[66].

The involvement of Haydn, Mozart and Beethoven in the configuration of embodied musical genius may also be depicted through some writings by E. T. A. Hoffmann. In one of his most influential texts on musical Romanticism, he muses that «Romantic taste is rare; even rarer is romantic talent», attributing this distinctive accolade to Haydn, Mozart (who «draws upon the superhuman») and, above all, Beethoven[67]. He seems to be rhetorically designing what may be called a 'Romantic genius suit' specifically tailored to the 'male Viennese School'.

In fact, several scholars have analysed the configuration of musical genius with reference to these three composers (and a few others). Baumann discusses Haydn's (self) construction as an «original» composer in his later years[68]. Kivy not only writes about Händel and Beethoven, but also highlights the genius myth-formation surrounding Mozart, which was, for instance, taken up in Schopenhauer's genius philosophy[69]. DeNora outlines «the links between Beethoven's eminence and the articulation of the notion of master composers in Vienna during the early part of the nineteenth century»[70]. As said, she traces the rise of the musical genius cult to specific musical developments in Vienna, where, among other aspects, figures such as the powerful Gottfried van Swieten — at some stage the patron of Haydn, Mozart and Beethoven and under the spell of pre-Romantic ideals from Germany — had a decisive impact on the interest in (historical) musical 'masters' and the configuration of the musical genius ideology. In a complex manner partly explored by DeNora, van Swieten also influenced some compositions by the 'male Viennese School', thus arguably even contributing to the 'inscription' of some of his values into their music.

## Almost Vanishing

In sharp contrast to aspects outlined in the previous section, Martinez, Paradis and Auernhammer seemed to have experienced a notable 'fall' in public opinion. This is traceable through several sources to be mentioned, yet also partly 'immeasurable' as they were above all assigned to invisibility and silence. The absence of much of their work — or the «complete loss» falsely assumed by Hanslick to be explored — not only contributed to this invisibility

---

[66]. *AmZ* 1799B, pp. 88-89, my translation.
[67]. Hoffman cited in Cassedy 2010, p. 6.
[68]. Baumann 2004.
[69]. Kivy 2001, p. 69. Schopenhauer's genius notions explicitly excluded women (see Gates 2006).
[70]. DeNora 1997, p. xii.

but also removed them from 'music-based' discourse. What little information circulated about them tended to be based on subjective opinions — and, as will be shown, particular credence was given to negative ones.

Reception processes are complicated and cannot be attributed to a single cause. It has been stated, for instance, that Martinez's compositional style fell out of fashion[71]. Moreover, and although many grey areas surround this claim, Martinez, Paradis and Auernhammer were not 'professional' musicians like Haydn, Mozart and Beethoven. In the patronage system, «playing for pay was a low status employment»[72]. But the rise of the music market and meritocratic ideals largely altered this, possibly affecting posterior evaluations of their musical legitimacy. Also, as said, the three composers were not left unscathed by gendered rules and prohibitions.

Most importantly, not all writing on them promoted a negative view. Martinez and Paradis in particular received posterity's occasional mention as important musicians and composers, in publications such as Frankl's work on Paradis (1876), Schmid's article on Martinez in the *Allgemeine Wiener Musikzeitung* (1846)[73] or Le Beau's 'Women Composers of the Previous Century'[74]. Still, there is a notable consensus among scholars that 'negative' sources to be mentioned significantly influenced the way they were posthumously perceived[75].

In the case of Auernhammer, part of her role in Mozart's life became a source of her historical 'decline'. In another letter to his father, Mozart comments that: «If a painter wanted to paint the devil accurately, it would be her face he'd have to choose. She's as fat as a farm wench, sweats so much that it makes you sick and goes about so scantily clad...»[76]. Here, Mozart appears as somewhat threatened by her 'uncontained' femininity. Most strikingly, however, this statement largely ended up eclipsing her many achievements and «she remains known to posterity due to her ugly appearance rather than her artistic activity»[77].

The 'fall' of Martinez and Paradis is usually traced to Caroline Pichler — a somewhat younger writer and salonnière — and her posthumously published memoire, where she twice mentions their alleged musical mediocrity. She claims she knew «several compositions of Miss Paradis herself; and yet I thought that neither her compositions nor the compositions by Miss Martinez (the only works by women composers which I got to know) were of great importance»[78]. Later, she observes that women have displayed notable abilities in other art forms, whereas «there is not even one [woman composer] who has managed anything with

---

[71]. E.g. GODT 1995, p. 538.
[72]. SHINER 2001, p. 108.
[73]. SCHMID 1846.
[74]. See UNSELD 2001.
[75]. See, for instance, GODT 2010; KORTNER 2018; GARVEY JACKSON 2001, NOPP 1995.
[76]. Mozart quoted in TOMES 2021, p. 43.
[77]. KORNTNER 2018, p. 31, my translation.
[78]. PICHLER 1844, vol. I, pp. 217-218, my translation.

notable success. I only met two during my long life [...] a Miss Martinez [...] and my friend, the blind Miss von Paradis. Both achieved charming things, but they barely reached above — indeed not quite a middle level»[79]. Pichler disregards their many musical distinctions and seems unaware of the existence of other women composers in Vienna and beyond.

Yet her rather uninformed writing and its negative evaluation of Martinez and Paradis was passed down as musical history. This may be exemplified by looking at *Geschichte des Concertwesens in Wien* (*History of Concert Life in Vienna*, 1869) by the previously mentioned music critic Eduard Hanslick. When documenting the city's musical life during the second half of the 18th century, he does mention both Auernhammer and Paradis as Kozeluch's students and notable pianists. As to the former, however, he also explicitly draws on Mozart's letter(s) when he describes the «fat Miss Auernhammer» as «a proper monster»[80]. Regarding Paradis, he comments that she was less publicly active and adds in a mere footnote: «At this time, Vienna was in the happy and rare possession of two female composers: Therese von Paradis and Marianne v. Martinez [...] The compositions of both ladies are lost. Caroline Pichler, a friend of both in her youth and who had frequently heard them play, says [...] that both Miss Paradis and Miss von Martinez did not appear to have reached "above, indeed not quite a middle level" — a judgment, which strikes us as quite believable»[81]. Auernhammer's compositions go unmentioned. And if Hanslick had tried to look for pieces by Paradis and Martinez, he could have quite easily located some of them[82] and evaluated them himself. Yet strangely, Pichler's opinion — as a writer, not a musician — was sufficiently 'believable' for this eminent critic and his musical history.

## The Threat of Women's (Musical) Eminence?

At the beginning of this chapter, it was suggested that the fall of the *ancien régime* allowed some women to voice their demands for gender equality which were then pushed back by a strengthened system of male dominance. In fact, it appears as if the revolutionary notion of all men being equal paradoxically tended to push all women (who, like men, were of course also lastingly affected by other hierarchical structures such as class or 'race') into lower positions which relied on the justification of their presumed inferiority. This needed to be codified, and, as previously implied, the category of genius, at least to an extent, increasingly fulfilled this

---

[79]. *Ibidem*, vol. II, p. 96, my translation.
[80]. Hanslick 1869, p. 125, my translation.
[81]. *Ibidem*, p. 124, my translation.
[82]. As implied with reference to Paradis, sheet music and bibliographical information on both would have, for instance, been available at the Gesellschaft der Musikfreunde in Vienna.

sociocultural function. Albeit theoretically open to all, embodied genius became normatively represented by (white) men.

If this system is partly based on assumptions of female (creative) 'inferiority', however, then highly creative women plausibly represent(ed) a menace to its underlying logic. As Citron states, women «as professional composers may be considered subversive — a threat to the cultural order. Behaviors beyond prescribed boundaries may appear as excess or display»[83]. During the final section of this chapter, it will be argued that highly achieving women in music such as Paradis, Auernhammer and Martinez may have indeed begun to pose an ideological threat which needed to be discursively minimised. In fact, it seems that Paradis was increasingly aware of the subversive nature of being a (blind) woman composer. In 1810, she replied when asked why she had not published her recent compositions: «Would my male artistic companions forgive me if I, as a woman — and especially a blind one — dared to measure myself against them?»[84].

Women's potential claim to outstanding musical creativity or 'genius' had to be oppressed, both internally and externally, with regard to their social reception. As to the former, one may allude to a statement by Heydenreich on women's education, published in c.1800, which stresses «an educator's duty to supress a girl's emergent genius and to prevent through all available means that she becomes aware of the size of her abilities»[85]. With regard to the latter, discourses on women's (musically) creative inferiority (which promptly appeared as an apparent backlash against a growing awareness of claims for gender equality made during the French Revolution in the German-speaking world[86]) and the minimisation of their achievements arguably acted as useful ideological tools. As Garvey Jackson notes with reference to Martinez, but may also be applied to Auernhammer and Paradis, their «creative contributions were downgraded (usually by persons who had neither seen nor heard them) in the fashionable debates about whether women possessed creativity»[87].

Turning again towards Auernhammer, the outcry against her «63rd work» in the *Allgemeine musikalische Zeitung* (1799) may be regarded as a way of highlighting her «excess» as a married woman and mother with a public presence and rhetorically re-establishing appropriate boundaries for musically creative women. In fact, the same newspaper page also contains the «cyclical» statement about Mozart cited earlier[88], illustrating the involvement of both 'Viennese Schools' in a discursive re-negotiation of (musical) gender roles.

---

[83]. CITRON 2000, p. 87.
[84]. Cited in FÜRST 2007, p. 1, my translation.
[85]. Heydenreich cited in NOPP 1995, p. 6, my translation.
[86]. HECKMANN 2016, p. 9.
[87]. GARVEY JACKSON 2001, p. 134.
[88]. *AmZ* 1799B, pp. 89-90.

# Moving towards Exclusion: A Case Study of the 'Female Viennese School'

As to Paradis and Martinez, it is worth returning to Pichler's memoire. For the latter did not simply make negative statements about them as individuals, but as representatives of (inferior) women composers. The previously quoted section taken up by Hanslick begins with the observation that «there is not even one [woman composer] who has managed anything with notable success»[89]. Paradis and Martinez are mentioned as *examples*. Furthermore, the 1914 edition (based on Pichler's hand-written manuscript and containing many elements absent from the 1844 version Hanslick relied on), not only refers to their works' lack of importance. It also affirms women's ability to reach certain heights in other arts, whereas «no woman has yet managed to distinguish herself as a creating musician»[90]. Pichler thus partly seems to *use* the two composers to make an affirmation of limited female compositional capacities, especially when compared to other arts.

Yet why would Pichler do this? While her intentions may not be pinned down with certainty (even less so because the later edition includes aspects which she may not have wished to publish[91]), it appears as if she were attempting to carve out a place for herself as a female writer. She seems to ward off potentially negative reactions like the ones Paradis anticipated by simultaneously endorsing and gently challenging the status quo[92]. Paradis and Martinez can thus be seen as collateral casualties of Pichler's own threat reaction and attempt at careful self-elevation. This argument can be further strengthened by the fact that she writes about the two women composers in the context of her own creative process (described in highly Romantic terms) and her personal knowledge of Haydn, Mozart and Schubert.

Incidentally, her celebration of these 'geniuses' is by no means unambiguous. Pichler also highlights their lack of mental abilities («no other outstanding mental powers [...] unwitty jokes»[93]) which she allegedly detected during their personal encounters. Hanslick, however, whose *Concertwesen* describes Haydn, Mozart, Schubert and Beethoven as the greatest composers of the context analysed, is not influenced by Pichler's 'eye-witness account' of their supposed mental limitations. It is her negative comments about women composers which he considered «believable», against available evidence and in an otherwise well-researched work. Given that Hanslick displays a belief that women composers are «rare» others, a partial dismissal of female musical creativity probably confirmed his own bias.

---

[89]. Pichler 1844, vol. II, p. 96 my translation.
[90]. Pichler 1914, p. 191, my translation.
[91]. This double rhetoric is considered a frequent feature of Pichler's writing. See, for instance, Lauková 2011.
[92]. Blümml 1914, pp. liv-lv.
[93]. Pichler 1914, pp. 293-294, my translation.

CLAUDIA CHIBICI-REVNEANU

CONCLUSION

This chapter discussed the paradox that the rise of 'equality' the French Revolution and fall of the *ancien régime* are often associated with, in some ways marks a regression for women. In musical terms, it depicted a partial 'opening' for female composers in 'Classical' Vienna before an ideological backlash occurred, partly through the ideology of genius. Focusing specifically on the 'female Viennese School' of Martinez, Paradis and Auernhammer and members of the 'male Viennese School', it has been shown that they were all active and often interconnected figures within the same musical context. Martinez and Mozart, for instance, received similar distinctions such as their acceptance by the Accademia Filarmonica di Bologna and both Auernhammer and Beethoven were considered among the best Viennese pianists. Still, Haydn, Mozart and Beethoven rose to godlike genius status, whereas Martinez, Paradis and Auernhammer were virtually forgotten.

Moreover, it has been argued that the 'male' and 'female Viennese Schools' were not only affected, but directly involved, albeit to varying degrees, in the configuration of the (male) genius ideology and its subtle female antithesis in the music world and beyond. The highly exclusive genius ideology affected male and female composers. Many men also had to be put 'down' for a few to become extremely distinguished. But male composers did not become representatives of a collective entity often regarded as incapable of musical creativity.

The matters presented have many nuances which need to be explored in more detail in future research. Most importantly, perhaps, it has to be stressed that the 'regression' mentioned is only partial, for 19th century women in music naturally also had several 'advantages' such as greater access to musical education[94]. Still, this chapter has been chiefly concerned with raising questions regarding a certain 'ideological' downfall of female creators of music. 19th century women composers such as Clara Schumann, Fanny Mendelssohn, Louise Adolpha Le Beau or Leopoldine Blahetka apparently had to face the full force of by now often explicit declarations of women's lack of compositional ability and misguiding beliefs in their absence from musical history. The critic Ludwig Rellstab, for instance, advised the Austrian Blahetka in 1825: «not to play too many of her own compositions, but rather concentrate on the presentation of the greatest piano masters. For what do compositions by women ultimately consist of? [...] production disgusts the sex»[95]. Clara Schumann could believe that «a woman must not wish to compose — there never was one able to do it»[96]. And by the end of the 19th century, Le Beau

---

[94]. See, for instance, REICH 2001A for a more detailed discussion.
[95]. RELLSTAB 1825, p. 153, my translation.
[96]. Clara Schumann cited in REICH 2001B, p. 344.

becomes hailed as the «first woman» to write a symphony[97] — although Martinez had figured prominently in her own article on women composers.

Finally, and despite the supposed 'demise' of the genius ideology during the 20th century, many of the emergent ideological structures here explored seem to lastingly impact the musical sphere. Also, apart from some notable initiatives, Martinez, Paradis and Auernhammer remain largely absent from Vienna's active 'composer-cult'.

## Bibliography

AmZ 1799a
'Die berühmtesten Klavierspielerinnen und Klavierspieler Wiens', in: *Allgemeine musikalische Zeitung*, xxx (15 May 1799), pp. 523-526.

AmZ 1799b
'Recensionen', in: *Allgemeine musikalische Zeitung*, v (30 October 1799), pp. 87-95.

AmZ 1817
'Die vorzüglichsten gesichtslosen Musik-Virtuosen neuerer Zeit: Ein Ehrendenkmahl', in: *Allgemeine musikalische Zeitung, mit besonderer Rücksicht auf den österreichischen Kaiserstaat*, 1817, pp. 249-251; pp. 265-267; pp. 288-290; pp. 314-317; pp. 321-324.

Battersby 1989
Battersby, Christine. *Gender and Genius: Towards a Feminist Aesthetics*, London, Women's Press, 1989.

Baumann 2004
Baumann, Thomas. 'Becoming Original: Haydn and the Cult of Genius', in: *The Musical Quarterly*, lxxxvii/2 (2004), pp. 333-357.

Blümml 1914
Blümml, Emil K. 'Einleitung', in: Pichler, Caroline. *Denkwürdigkeiten aus meinem Leben*, 2 vols., Munich, Georg Müller, 1914, pp. vii-lxxxvii.

Braun – Kusber – Schnettger 2020
*Weibliche Herrschaft im 18. Jahrhundert: Maria Theresia und Katharina die Große*, edited by Bettina Braun, Jan Kusber and Matthias Schnettger, Bielefeld, transcript, 2020.

Bruno 2010
Bruno, Paul W. *Kant's Concept of Genius: Its Origin and Function in the Third Critique*, New York-London, Continuum, 2010.

---

[97]. Unseld 2001, p. 33.

BUBENIK-BAUER – SCHALZ-LAURENZE 1995
BUBENIK-BAUER, Iris – SCHALZ-LAURENZE, Ute. 'Vorwort', in: *Frauen in der Aufklärung: ihr werten Frauenzimmer, auf!*, edited by Iris Bubenik Bauer and Ute Schalz-Laurenze, Frankfurt, Ulrike Helmer Verlag, 1995, pp. 7-13.

BURNEY 1773
BURNEY, Charles. *The Present State of Music in Germany, the Netherlands, and United Provinces. 1*, London, T. Becket and Co., 1773.

CASSEDY 2010
CASSEDY, Steven. 'Beethoven the Romantic: How E. T. A. Hoffmann Got It Right', in: *Journal of the History of Ideas*, LXXI/1 (2010), pp. 1-37.

CHIBICI-REVNEANU 2013
CHIBICI-REVNEANU, Claudia. 'Composing Disappearances: The Mythical Power behind the Woman Composer Question', in: *Entreciencias: diálogos en la Sociedad del Conocimiento*, 1/2 (2013), pp. 189-206.

CITRON 2000
CITRON, Marcia. *Gender and the Musical Canon*, Urbana-Chicago, University of Illinois Press, 2000.

DENORA 1997
DENORA, Tia. *Beethoven and the Construction of Genius: Musical Politics in Vienna, 1792-1803*, Berkeley-Los Angeles, London, University of California Press, 1997.

DUNBAR 2011
DUNBAR, Julie C. *Women, Music, Culture: An Introduction*, Abingdon-New York, Routledge, 2011.

FRANKL 1876
FRANKL, Ludwig August. *Maria Theresia von Paradis' Biographie*, Linz, Verlag des oberösterreichischen Privat-Blinden-Institutes, 1876.

FÜRST 2005
FÜRST, Marion. *Maria Theresia Paradis: Mozarts berühmte Zeitgenossin*, Vienna, Böhlau, 2005.

FÜRST 2007
EAD. 'Maria Theresia (von) Paradis', in: *MUGI: Musik und Gender im Internet*, 2007, <https://mugi.hfmt-hamburg.de/receive/mugi_person_00000615>, accessed September 2022.

GARVEY JACKSON 2001
GARVEY JACKSON, Barbara. 'Musical Women of the Seventeenth and Eighteenth Centuries', in: *Women & Music: A History*, edited by Karin Pendle, Bloomington-Indianapolis, Indiana University Press, [2]2001, pp. 97-146.

GATES 2006
GATES, Eugene. 'The Woman Composer Question: Philosophical and Historical Perspectives', in: *The Kapralova Society Journal: A Journal of Women in Music*, IV/2 (2006), pp. 1-11.

GILLIGAN – SNIDER 2018
GILLIGAN, Carol – SNIDER, Noemi. *Why Does Patriarchy Persist*, Cambridge, Medford, Polity Press, 2018.

GODT 1995
GODT, Irving. 'Marianna in Italy: The International Reputation of Marianna Martines (1744-1812)', in: *The Journal of Musicology*, XIII/4 (1995), pp. 538-561.

GODT 2010
ID. *Marianna Martines: A Woman Composer in the Vienna of Mozart and Haydn*, Rochester-Woodbridge, University of Rochester Press-Boydell & Brewer, 2010 (Eastman Studies in Music, 77).

HALSTEAD 2016
HALSTEAD, Jill. *The Woman Composer: Creativity and the Gendered Politics of Musical Composition*, Abingdon-New York, Routledge, ²2016.

HANSLICK 1869
HANSLICK, Eduard. *Geschichte des Konzertwesens in Wien*, Vienna, Wilhelm Braumüller, 1869.

HEAD 2013
HEAD, Matthew. *Sovereign Feminine: Music and Gender in Eighteenth-Century Germany*, Berkeley-London, University of California Press, 2013.

HECKMANN 2016
HECKMANN, Ruth. *Tonsetzerinnen: Zur Rezeption von Komponistinnen in Deutschland um 1800*, Wiesbaden, Springer VS, 2016.

HEINICH 2016
HEINICH, Nathalie. 'Genius versus Democracy: Excellence and Singularity in Postrevolutionary France', in: *Genealogies of Genius*, edited by Joyce E. Chaplin and Darrin M. McMahon, New York, Palgrave Macmillan, 2016, pp. 29-41.

HELMIG – BRAND 2001
HELMIG, Martina – BRAND, Bettina. 'Vorwort', in: *Maßstab Beethoven?: Komponistinnen im Schatten des des Geniekults*, edited by Bettina Brand and Martina Helmig, Munich, Edition text + kritik, 2001, pp. 7-8.

KIVY 2001
KIVY, Peter. *The Possessor and the Possessed: Handel, Mozart, Beethoven, and the Idea of Musical Genius*, New Haven (CT), Yale University Press, 2001.

KORNTNER 2018
KORNTNER, Beate. *Frauen als Komponistinnen im Umfeld Mozarts mit einem besonderen Augenmerk auf Maria Theresia Paradis*, Munich, AVM Press, 2018.

KRONES 2006
KRONES, Harmut. 'Zum Stellenwert der Komponistinnen in Wien um 1800: Archivbestände, Publikationen, Verlagssituation', in: «*Ein unerschöpflicher Reichtum an Ideen...» Komponistinnen zur Zeit Mozarts*, edited by Elena Ostleitner and Gabriele Dorffner, Vienna, Vier-Viertel-Verlag, 2006 (Frauentöne, 6), pp. 177-190.

LAUKOVÁ 2011
LAUKOVÁ, Lucia. 'Die emanzipierte Emanzipationsgegnerin: Caroline Pichlers theoretische Schriften', in: *New German Review*, XXIV/1 (2011), pp. 94-111.

MATSUSHITA 2006
MATSUSHITA, Hidemi. 'The Blind Composer Maria Theresia Paradis. Facts, Fictions, and Speculations', in: «*Ein unerschöpflicher Reichtum an Ideen...» Komponistinnen zur Zeit Mozarts, op. cit.*, pp. 29-39.

*MK* 1792
'Rezensionen', in: *Musikalische Korrespondenz*, XXV (20 June 1792), pp. 193-196.

NEUMAYR 2019
*Maria Anna Mozart: Facetten einer Künstlerin*, edited by Eva Neumayr, Vienna, Hollitzer Verlag, 2019 (Schriftenreihe des Archivs der Erzdiözese Salzburg, 20).

NITZSCHE 1975
NITZSCHE, Jane Chance. *The Genius Figure in Antiquity and the Middle Ages*, London-New York, Columbia University Press, 1975.

NOPP 1995
NOPP, Regina. *Frau und Musik: Komponistinnen zur Zeit der Wiener Klassik*, Linz, Universitätsverlag R. Trauner, 1995.

OSTLEITNER – DORFFNER 2006
OSTLEITNER, Elena – DORFFNER, Gabriele. 'Einleitung', in: «*Ein unerschöpflicher Reichtum an Ideen...» Komponistinnen zur Zeit Mozarts, op. cit.*, pp. 13-16.

PICHLER 1844
PICHLER, Caroline. *Denkwürdigkeiten aus meinem Leben – 1769-1798*, 2 vols., Vienna, Verlag von A. Pichler's sel. Witwe, 1844.

PICHLER 1914
EAD. *Denkwürdigkeiten aus meinem Leben*, edited by Emil Karl Blümml, 2 vols., Munich, Georg Müller, 1914.

REICH 2001A
REICH, Nancy. 'European Composers and Musicians, ca. 1800-1890', in: *Women & Music: A History*, edited by Karin Pendle, Bloomington, Indiana University Press, 2001, pp. 147-174.

Reich 2001b
Ead. *Clara Schumann: The Artist and the Woman*, Ithaca-London, Cornell University Press, ²2001.

Rellstab 1825
Rellstab, Ludwig. 'Reiseberichte von Rellstab No. 4 (Schluß)', in: *Berliner Allgemeine musikalische Zeitung*, xix (11 May 1825), pp. 153-154.

Schmid 1846
Schmid, Anton. 'Zwei musikalische Berühmtheiten Wiens aus dem Schönen Geschlecht in der zweiten Hälfte des verflossenen Jahrhunderts', in: *Allgemeine Wiener Musikzeitung*, 6 October 1846, pp. 509-510, 513-514, 517-518.

Schönfeld 1796
Schönfeld, Johann Ferdinand Ritter von. *Jahrbuch der Tonkunst von Wien und Prag*, Vienna, Schönfeldischer Verlag, 1796.

Shiner 2001
Shiner, Larry. *The Invention of Art: A Cultural History*, Chicago-London, University of Chicago Press, 2001.

Tomes 2021
Tomes, Susan. *The Piano – A History in 100 Pieces*, New Haven (CT), Yale University Press, 2021.

Unseld 2001
Unseld, Melanie. 'Eine weibliche Sinfonietradition jenseits von Beethoven? Louise Adolpha Le Beau und ihre Sinfonie Op. 41', in: *Maßstab Beethoven?: Komponistinnen im Schatten des des Geniekults*, op. cit., pp. 24-44.

Unseld 2006
Ead. '«Studiren [...] und Metier davon zu machen»: Mozarts Schülerinnen Josepha Auernhammer und Babette Ployer', in: *«Ein unerschöpflicher Reichtum an Ideen...» Komponistinnen zur Zeit Mozarts*, op. cit., pp. 41-52.

Unseld 2018
Ead. 'Marianne Martines', in: *MUGI: Musik und Gender im Internet*, 2018, <https://mugi.hfmt-hamburg.de/receive/mugi_person_00000528>, accessed September 2022.

Varela 2021
Varela, Nuria. *Feminismo para principiantes*, Mexico City, Penguin, ²2021.

Weissweiler 1999
Weissweiler, Eva. *Komponistinnen vom Mittelalter bis zur Gegenwart: Eine Kultur-und Wirkungsgeschichte in Biographien und Werkbeispielen*, Munich, Deutscher Taschenbuch Verlag, 1999.

*WAMZ* 1813
'Fräulein Marie Therese Paradis', in: *Wiener allgemeine musikalische Zeitung*, 1813, pp. 483-498.

WYN JONES 2016
WYN JONES, David. *Music in Vienna 1700, 1800, 1900*, Woodbridge, Boydell & Brewer, 2016.

# Music Publishing and Teaching

# Les relations entre Jean-Jérôme Imbault et ses compositeurs d'après des lettres de Jean-Louis Duport et Ferdinando Paër[*]

*Henri Vanhulst*
(Université libre de Bruxelles / Académie royale de Belgique)

Jean-Jérôme Imbault (1753-1832) débute comme violoniste avant de se lancer dans l'édition musicale. Associé d'abord à Jean-Georges Sieber[1], il s'établit à son compte en 1784, peu de temps après son mariage avec Henriette Gudin. Sa firme acquiert une telle importance qu'Imbault se voit attribuer vers 1811 le titre de « marchand de musique de Leurs Majestés Impériales et Royales et musicien de leur Chapelle ». En juillet 1812, il vend son affaire à Pierre Honoré Janet et Alexandre Cotelle pour 300 000 francs. L'acte notarié contient l'inventaire des 38 555 planches gravées qu'il leur cède et ce nombre impressionnant démontre combien l'entreprise s'est développée en près de trois décennies. Si Imbault est l'éditeur d'une centaine de chants révolutionnaires, sa production est axée sur la musique instrumentale, tant pour orchestre — symphonies et concertos — que pour des ensembles réduits — du duo au septuor — ou encore le piano, voire la harpe. Dans le domaine lyrique, il publie peu de partitions complètes, préférant les ouvertures et des extraits vocaux dont il propose aussi divers arrangements à effectifs réduits. On lui doit également des centaines de romances et autres mélodies avec accompagnement de piano ou harpe. Imbault est le seul éditeur parisien de l'époque à publier vers 1791-1792 le *Catalogue thématique* de son fonds[2]. Il laisse en outre le plus grand nombre de catalogues séparés, qui paraissent entre 1792 et juillet 1801 et font de huit à quatorze pages[3]. Tout comme les autres éditeurs parisiens, il

---

[*]. Nous tenons à remercier Marie Cornaz, Catherine Massip et Olivia Wahnon de Oliveira pour leur aide.
[1]. Benton 1976 reste la meilleure synthèse de la biographie d'Imbault. Voir Devriès – Lesure 1979, vol. I, pp. 85-86, pour le résumé de ses activités d'éditeur.
[2]. Benton 1972.
[3]. Johansson 1955, facs. 39-40 (exemplaire incomplet), facs. app. 1-12, 13-20; B-Br, Fétis 5.193 C 19 Mus.; coll. H. Vanhulst.

insère évidemment aussi des listes — de une à quatre pages — de ses publications dans de nombreux exemplaires de ses éditions.

Les relations entre Imbault et ses compositeurs sont très mal connues à cause de l'absence de sources. En décembre 1786, il signe à Strasbourg avec Ignace Pleyel (1757-1831), qui est au service de la cathédrale de la ville, un contrat à propos de l'édition de ses *XII Nouveaux quatuors dédiés... au Roi de Prusse* et de onze symphonies périodiques[4]. À ce document d'un grand intérêt s'ajoutent maintenant trois lettres de deux compositeurs. Elles révèlent des pratiques parfois surprenantes tant pour ce qui est de l'élaboration, la production et la diffusion d'une méthode instrumentale que pour l'aspect financier des relations entre les deux parties, ou encore la stratégie éditoriale d'Imbault. Ce ne sont guère plus que des bribes et il convient dès lors de n'en tirer aucune conclusion générale, d'autant que les réponses de l'éditeur manquent.

## Deux lettres autographes de Jean-Louis Duport à propos de son *Essai sur le doigté du violoncelle*[5]

Le violoncelliste Jean-Louis Duport (1749-1819) entame en 1768 à Paris une carrière d'interprète qui se révèlera brillante. Entre 1794 et 1788, il publie chez Imbault trois concertos[6], dont chaque page de titre est ornée d'un cadre surmonté d'un ovale, signé Sophie Beaublé, contenant le monogramme du compositeur — une exception dans la production d'Imbault de ces années-là. À la Révolution. Duport quitte la France et rejoint son frère aîné Jean-Pierre, lui aussi violoncelliste, à Berlin. Il y poursuit sa carrière tant à la cour de Potsdam qu'au sein de l'orchestre de l'Opéra. Le 6 mars 1804, il écrit de Potsdam une lettre[7], dont le début manque, à son « cher ami » Imbault. Bien qu'il envoie même « mille choses aimables » à l'épouse de l'éditeur, ce ton familier ne prouve nullement que les deux hommes aient eu des contacts dans un passé récent. L'adresse figurant sur la lettre — « entre la rue de l'arbre sec... » — n'est d'ailleurs plus utilisée par Imbault depuis 1800[8]. Le post-scriptum confirme pourtant les liens cordiaux entre le violoncelliste et l'éditeur: le compositeur et pianiste Friedrich Heinrich Himmel, qui est lui aussi actif à Potsdam, a raconté à Duport sa rencontre avec Imbault à Paris, où ils ont à plusieurs reprises trinqué à la santé du violoncelliste[9]. Ce dernier ne manque pas d'ajouter qu'il s'est « vengé » à Berlin.

---

[4]. Benton 1977, pp. 26-28.
[5]. F-Pn, LA-DUPORT JEAN LOUIS-6 et LA-DUPORT JEAN LOUIS-3.
[6]. Devriès-Lesure 2005, p. 172.
[7]. F-Pn, LA-DUPORT JEAN LOUIS-6 et LA-DUPORT JEAN LOUIS-3.
[8]. Devriès – Lesure 1979, vol. i, p. 85. La seconde lettre a une adresse différente mais tout aussi dépassée.
[9]. Imbault a édité les *Trois sonates pour le piano forte avec accompagnement de violon & violoncelle*, Op. 16 de Himmel (*RISM* H 5553).

# Les relations entre Jean-Jérôme Imbault et ses compositeurs

Se vantant d'avoir acquis «un peu de réputation», Duport s'étend dans sa lettre sur son *Traité sur le doigter du violoncelle* dont l'idée lui est venue à plusieurs reprises et qu'il a rédigé lentement et relu plusieurs fois, avant de le soumettre à d'autres violoncellistes. Il estime maintenant que l'ouvrage est terminé et cherche à le publier. S'il pense évidemment à Imbault, sans le dire en toutes lettres, il évoque d'autres possibilités qui lui ont été suggérées par des amis. Il pense ainsi à une version bilingue, son texte étant accompagné d'une traduction allemande. Il envisage apparemment une édition à compte d'auteur, puisqu'il estime nécessaire de réunir deux cents souscripteurs, et semble persuadé d'en trouver beaucoup dans la seule ville de Berlin. Ce procédé lui paraît un moyen particulièrement adéquat tant pour décourager les contrefacteurs que pour tirer quelque profit financier de l'ouvrage. Si Duport demande l'avis d'Imbault, il veut sans doute l'informer en même temps au sujet de ses projets. Avant d'accepter de publier le *Traité*, Imbault doit savoir qu'il ne sera pas le seul à le faire, puisqu'il y aura aussi une version bilingue. Cette édition lithographiée paraîtra chez Johann André à Offenbach vers 1809-1810[10]. Elle part de la version française éditée par Imbault et il serait intéressant de connaître les modalités de l'arrangement qui a dû intervenir entre les deux éditeurs.

Comme Duport n'ajoute pas le manuscrit de son ouvrage à sa lettre, il en détaille le contenu. Il cite l'intitulé des seize «articles» et précise la longueur de certains d'entre eux. Il se déclare déjà d'accord de supprimer le quinzième, intitulé «de la coalition des vibrations», car il reconnaît que ce sujet est sa «manie» ou «folie». Il sait aussi que son ouvrage sera soumis à deux «censeurs» qu'il ne semble pas connaître et dont on ignore toujours les noms, et les remercie déjà de leurs avis, tout comme il demande celui d'Imbault sur le contenu de sa méthode.

Duport termine sa lettre par une pique contre Jean-Baptiste Bréval (1753-1823), l'auteur du *Traité de violoncelle* qui vient de paraître chez Imbault, et il n'est pas le seul à se montrer critique[11]. Dans une phrase absconse, Duport reproche à Bréval, qui est à ce moment membre de l'orchestre du Concert spirituel et a dans un passé récent publié plusieurs compositions à compte d'auteur, un manque total de clairvoyance à propos des doigtés. Comme ce dernier affirme: «Le doigté du violoncel n'est en quelque sorte que le produit des habitudes des différens maîtres»[12], Duport en tire la conclusion que Bréval n'hésite pas à ériger ces «mauvaises habitudes» en «principes», alors qu'il est convaincu qu'un «peu de réflexion» suffit pour s'en défaire. Il faut, au contraire, procéder de manière rationnelle, comme lui-même déclare l'avoir fait. S'il en avait été incapable, il aurait renoncé à rédiger sa méthode!

Bien que la réponse d'Imbault ne soit pas été conservée, il ne fait aucun doute qu'il décide de publier l'ouvrage. La mention «propriété de l'éditeur» sur la page de titre prouve même

---

[10]. Voir Twyman 1996, pp. 156, 207 et 299.

[11]. Voir la recension dans la *Correspondance des professeurs et amateurs de musique*, II/50 (20 juin 1804), col. 395-400, et II/51 (23 juin 1804), col. 403-405.

[12]. Bréval 1804, p. 4.

que l'affaire lui semble rentable puisqu'il a racheté les droits à Duport. Il faut plus d'un an à Imbault pour préparer la publication car ce n'est que le 11 juin 1805 qu'il envoie à l'auteur la version remaniée de l'ouvrage, intitulé dorénavant *Essai* au lieu de *Traité* — pour éviter toute confusion avec la méthode de Bréval? — avant d'en entamer l'impression. Comme le document — les épreuves? — est perdu, c'est la réponse du violoncelliste, écrite à Potsdam le 29 juin, qui fournit quelques éclaircissements. Duport n'a manifestement pas été tenu au courant des modifications qui ont été apportées à son manuscrit. Il remercie Imbault d'avoir corrigé son texte et Pierre-François Levasseur, un membre de l'orchestre de l'Opéra, qui a vérifié les doigtés ajoutés aux exemples. Duport revient aussi sur la partie consacrée à l'archet. Il parle à ce propos, sans s'en expliquer, de «métaphysique» de l'instrument, et rappelle qu'il s'agit de «simples réflexions jetées à la hâte», tandis que les pages relatives aux doigtés sont le résultat d'un quart de siècle d'étude sans cesse approfondie et de trois ans de travail de rédaction. Il regrette manifestement le libellé de la page de titre qui met les deux sujets sur le même pied — *Essai sur le doigté du violoncelle et sur la conduite de l'archet* — et affirme qu'il ne voit toujours aucun inconvénient à la suppression de tout ce qu'il a écrit sur l'archet[13]. Comme il se rend compte qu'Imbault ne le fera pas, il insiste pour l'insertion d'une note précisant l'origine de cette partie de sa méthode. Accédant à sa demande, l'éditeur ajoute au début du «titre XVIII» la phrase: «L'intention de M. Duport n'étoit pas de parler de l'archet. Ce n'est qu'à la sollicitation de ses amis et depuis que la gravure de l'ouvrage est commencée, qu'il s'est décidé à jeter rapidement sur le papier, les réflexions qui forment ce présent titre»[14]. Duport tient aussi à ce que la page de titre cite son titre à la cour de Frédéric II et la mention «Premier violoncelle de la chapelle de S. M. le roi de Prusse» y sera jointe à nom.

La comparaison de l'espèce de table des matières insérée dans la lettre de 1804 et la version imprimée de l'*Essai* révèle des modifications tantôt superficielles et tantôt fondamentales, qui ont sans doute été introduites par Imbault. Dans l'édition, le mot «titre» remplace «article» et les intitulés de ces chapitres sont reformulés. Le texte même a dû subir lui aussi de substantiels changements, à en juger d'après les deux lettres de Duport qui sont truffées de fautes d'orthographe et mal écrites[15]. En outre, la version imprimée insère une section supplémentaire, «De la différence du doigté de la quarte superflue et de la fausse quinte», dans le «titre X». Elle ajoute aussi un nouveau «titre XV», qui est consacré à la manière d'accorder le violoncelle. La lettre ignore évidemment le «titre XVIII», puisque ce long développement sur l'archet a été rédigé ultérieurement, car jugé indispensable par les «amis» de l'auteur — et aussi, voire surtout, par Imbault lui-même, qui en tant que violoniste a probablement aussi son opinion sur

---

[13]. DUPORT 1806, pp. 156-175.
[14]. *Ibidem*, p. 156.
[15]. Voir MILLIOT 1985, pp. 660-663, qui cite quelques passages de la lettre du 6 mars 1804 en respectant l'orthographe de Duport.

le sujet. Comme la première lettre de Duport ne fait pas mention des vingt et un exercices qui constituent le «titre» final et un seul est attribué Martin Berteau, que l'on considère comme le fondateur de l'école française de violoncelle, et deux autres Jean-Pierre Duport, il s'agit peut-être aussi d'un ajout au projet initial, mais Imbault les avait déjà reçus puisque Levasseur en avait revu les doigtés[16].

D'après la note marginale dans la lettre de 1805, Imbault interroge Duport sur l'opportunité de diffuser l'*Essai* à l'étranger avant Paris. Comme le Conservatoire publie la même année la *Méthode de violoncelle et de basse d'accompagnement* signée par P.-M. Baillot, J.-H. Levasseur, C.-S. Catel et C.-N. Baudiot, l'éditeur craint sinon une réaction défavorable de la part de ces derniers, du moins la concurrence. Résidant à Berlin, le violoncelliste ne semble guère partager cette inquiétude car il n'a aucun lien avec le Conservatoire et envisage une diffusion internationale de son ouvrage qu'il dédie intentionnellement à l'ensemble des professeurs de violoncelle. Il ne sait évidemment pas encore que les événements politiques l'amèneront en 1807 à retourner en France. Entré au service de Charles IV, roi d'Espagne qui vit en exil à Marseille, il intégrera en 1812 à Paris la chapelle musicale de l'Empereur et sera nommé l'année suivante professeur de violoncelle au Conservatoire à côté de Baudiot et Levasseur.

Puisqu'une lettre met environ une quinzaine jours pour arriver de Paris à Berlin, Imbault n'a pu recevoir la réponse de Duport que vers le milieu du mois de juillet 1805, à condition que le courrier circule à la même vitesse dans les deux sens. Vu le nombre très réduit d'ajouts souhaités par le violoncelliste, l'impression de l'*Essai* a pu débuter peu après. L'ouvrage est déjà sorti de presse au tout début de 1806, puisqu'en février Johann Friedrich Reichardt en rend déjà compte en termes élogieux dans l'hebdomadaire berlinois dont il est l'éditeur[17]. Notons à propos de l'année de parution que l'exemplaire de la Bibliothèque nationale de France[18] commence par un catalogue de quatre pages qu'Imbault incorpore déjà dans des éditions de 1803[19]. Voilà la preuve irréfutable qu'une telle insertion ne permet nullement de dater l'édition ni même l'exemplaire auquel elle est jointe! Quant au prix de vente, fixé à 36 livres pour 269 pages, il est proportionnellement le même que pour le *Traité* de Bréval qui fait 206 pages et coûte 24 livres[20]. Rappelons qu'en 1814 Imbault demande 20 francs pour l'autographe de *l'Essai*, en deux volumes, dans le catalogue manuscrit des musiques qu'il met en vente «après

---

[16]. *Ibidem* et WALDEN 1998 situent l'*Essai* dans l'évolution des méthodes de violoncelle publiées depuis le XVIIIe siècle.

[17]. R[EICHARDT], J. F. 'Recensionen', in: *Berlinische Musikalische Zeitung*, n° 8 ([février] 1806), pp. 29-30. C'est, en revanche, seulement en septembre 1807 que l'*Intelligenz-Blatt zur Allgemeine musikalische Zeitung*, n° 11 (septembre 1807), col. 46, signale l'ouvrage parmi les nouveautés disponibles chez Breitkopf & Härtel à Leipzig.

[18]. F-Pn, VM8 E-20. L'exemplaire est disponible sur le site <Gallica.bnf.fr>.

[19]. DEVRIÈS - LESURE 1979, vol. I, planches 111-114.

[20]. F-Pn, VM8 E-9 à 11. Puisque l'adresse bibliographique de l'exemplaire disponible sur le site Gallica, est celle de Janet et Cotelle, les successeurs d'Imbault, il s'agit d'un tirage postérieur à 1812, comme le confirme le prix de 30 francs.

cessation de commerce»²¹. C'est l'un des lots chers de la liste, mais il est impossible d'en tirer des conclusions car l'éditeur ne se sépare d'aucun autre autographe.

Comme Imbault l'interroge dans sa lettre de 1805 sur le nombre d'exemplaires qu'il souhaite recevoir en sa qualité d'auteur, Duport en demande quatre. Il les destine respectivement aux deux élèves, restés inconnus, qui l'ont aidé à copier son *Essai*, à son frère Jean-Pierre — en guise de remerciement pour les exercices insérés dans l'ouvrage? — et à lui-même. Il en demande par ailleurs quarante qu'il compte vendre. Il espère que ce premier lot ne suffira pas car c'est visiblement par cette voie qu'il compte tirer un avantage financier supplémentaire de son *Essai*, puisqu'il l'a cédé à Imbault. Le nombre d'exemplaires semble pourtant dérisoire quand on se souvient que le violoncelliste se vantait dans sa première lettre de trouver facilement deux cents souscripteurs.

D'après Duport, Imbault lui a déjà plusieurs fois demandé de lui trouver un agent à Berlin, mais le violoncelliste ne lui a jamais fait de proposition, faute de candidat fiable. Il prétend maintenant en avoir trouvé un en la personne d'un certain Deroudville et il se porte garant de son honnêteté. Ce dernier veut cependant en savoir plus au sujet des conditions financières avant d'entreprendre les démarches nécessaires l'autorisant à lancer «un petit commerce de musique». Si Duport sert d'intermédiaire, il avoue qu'il a l'intention de s'associer à Deroudville et tient à assurer Imbault et de leur engagement commun à respecter scrupuleusement ses conditions et notamment son refus de donner ses éditions en location. Duport sait déjà qu'un agent bénéficie d'une remise de cinquante pourcent du prix de vente, mais il ignore si Imbault veut être payé à la livraison des partitions ou après leur vente. Il est clair que le projet ne lui semble intéressant que dans le cas où Imbault accepte d'attendre que les exemplaires aient trouvé acquéreurs avant de recevoir son dû. Duport termine en lui demandant de trouver un arrangement avec Deroudville et un accord est certainement intervenu. D'après la recension déjà citée de Reichardt, l'*Essai* s'achète à Berlin chez Deroudville, qui habite «Wilhelmstrasse 71». Nous ignorons si la collaboration s'est maintenue longtemps, mais la liste des débiteurs qui est dressée en 1812, au moment où Imbault vend son affaire à Janet et Cotelle, ne mentionne en tout cas qu'un seul marchand de musique à Berlin, Adolphe Schlesinger²².

## LA LETTRE AUTOGRAPHE DE FERNANDO PAËR À PROPOS DE L'ARRANGEMENT DE *CAMILLA* POUR DEUX FLÛTES ET ALTO

Le compositeur italien Fernando Paër (1771-1839) a été actif à Vienne et dans quelques villes allemandes quand Napoléon, qui est charmé par ses œuvres lyriques, le nomme en 1807

---

[21]. VANHULST 2012, pp. 432 et 445.
[22]. VANHULST 2016, pp. 249 et 253.

# Les relations entre Jean-Jérôme Imbault et ses compositeurs

à sa cour avant de lui attribuer la direction de l'Opéra-Comique, où Imbault dispose depuis 1799 d'un point de vente. Paër devient «directeur des concerts et des théâtres de S. M. l'Empereur et Roi», comme le clame la page de titre de sa romance *Marie-Louise au berceau de son fils*, composée à la naissance du «prince impérial» en 1811 et publiée par Imbault. Ce dernier a déjà édité d'autres œuvres de Paër. *Camilla, dramma serio-giocoso* créé à Vienne en 1799, a retenu son attention dès le lendemain de sa première représentation au Théâtre Italien le 5 novembre 1804. Imbault en publie très rapidement l'ouverture dans une version pour clavier[23]. On lui doit aussi un ensemble de dix airs arrangés pour chant et clavier dont les paroles sont accompagnées d'une adaptation française et dont les titres citent les chanteurs tels que Teresa Strinasacchi qui ont interprété l'œuvre sur la scène parisienne[24]. Ces deux éditions sont signalées dans le *Catalogue de musique de fond et d'assortiment* que l'éditeur et marchand de musique bruxellois Weissenbruch insère de décembre 1804 à mai 1805 en cinq livraisons dans son mensuel *L'Esprit des journaux*[25]. Bien qu'Imbault édite aussi «l'ouverture à grand orchestre»[26], son intérêt pour l'œuvre semble de courte durée car cette dernière publication figure déjà dans le catalogue de Weissenbruch daté de juillet 1809[27]. En même temps, on ne peut oublier qu'Imbault est depuis le mois de février 1811 le dépositaire de Nicolas Simrock, éditeur établi à Bonn, qui a publié *Camilla* dans une version bilingue italien/allemand avec accompagnement de piano. D'après son catalogue manuscrit de 1814 déjà cité, Imbault en possède deux exemplaires «reliés en parchemin vert»[28].

Paër aurait-il pensé que la collaboration avec Simrock inciterait Imbault à s'intéresser à nouveau à *Camilla*? Adoptant un ton nettement plus neutre que Duport et n'hésitant même pas à conclure par une formule obséquieuse, Paër lui écrit en tout cas le 12 juillet 1811 qu'il a fait adapter *Camilla* pour deux flûtes et alto par un musicien dont il dit seulement qu'il réside à Parme[29]. Il se déclare satisfait du travail et joint les trois parties à sa lettre. Il ajoute que l'auteur de l'arrangement ne s'attend pas à un cachet et «se contente» de cinquante exemplaires. Paër s'occupera de les lui faire parvenir à ses frais car il a toujours des contacts à Parme, où son opéra *Agnese* a été créé à l'automne de 1809. Il termine sa lettre en se félicitant d'avoir «bien négocié [l']intérêt» d'Imbault et feint d'oublier non seulement qu'une édition implique d'autres frais et mais aussi que cinquante exemplaires représentent une part importante du tirage. Pacini soupçonne clairement l'éditeur d'être réticent à investir dans de nouvelles

---

[23]. F-Pn, VM4-103.
[24]. F-Pn, VM4-103 (2)
[25]. *L'Esprit des journaux*, janvier 1805, p. 65 (l'ouverture); février 1805, p. 120 (les airs). Voir aussi le numéro de mai 1805, p. 152, qui recense la partition manuscrite de *Camilla*.
[26]. F-Pn, VM26-459.
[27]. *Catalogue de musique vocale et instrumentale de fond et d'assortiment*, Bruxelles, Weissenbruch, 1809, p. 8.
[28]. Vanhulst 2012, p. 444.
[29]. B-Bc, P 00268/087.

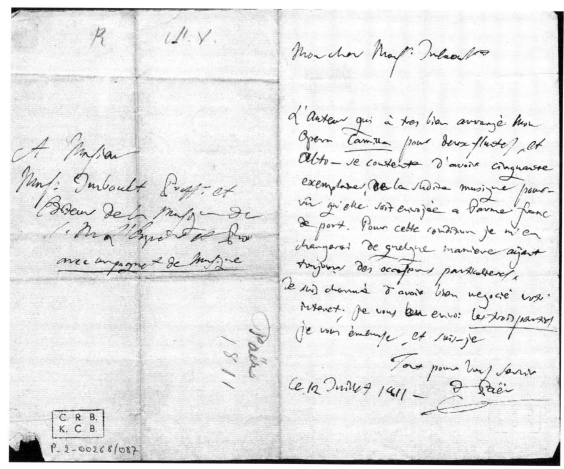

Ill. 1: Lettre du 12 juillet 1811 de Ferdinando Paër à Jean-Jérôme Imbault (B-Bc, P 00268/087).

versions instrumentales de *Camilla* et croit que l'argument financier sera décisif. Qu'Imbault y soit insensible ou qu'il soit irrité par le reproche implicite, il ne semble pas avoir donné suite à la proposition, à moins qu'il ne subsiste plus aucun exemplaire de l'édition. Les extraits de *Camilla* qu'il a déjà mis sur le marché lui ont sans doute appris que l'œuvre ne suscite plus grand intérêt. En outre l'effectif choisi ne correspond pas aux ensembles habituels. Les œuvres pour un trio composé de deux flûtes et un alto sont très rares dans les catalogues d'Imbault[30]. On y trouve de nombreux extraits d'opéra qui sont le plus souvent destinés à un duo, que ce soit chant et clavier/harpe ou deux instruments sinon identiques du moins de la même famille.

L'initiative de Paër est-elle conforme aux usages ou croit-il que sa position à la cour l'investit de quelque prérogative? Si un compositeur décide du type d'arrangement de son œuvre et de la personne qu'il chargera du travail, sans consulter l'éditeur au préalable, il risque

---

[30]. Voir Devriès – Lesure 1979, vol. i, planche 112.

# Les relations entre Jean-Jérôme Imbault et ses compositeurs

d'essuyer un refus. Il aurait certes été éclairant de connaître la réponse qu'Imbault a envoyée au compositeur. Ce dernier a dû être surpris par le refus, voire vexé, mais cette déconvenue ne mettra pas fin aux relations entre les deux parties, comme nous le savons déjà.

\*\*\*

Les trois lettres mettent en évidence la position de force d'un éditeur face à ses compositeurs. Imbault oblige Duport à ajouter à son *Essai* une partie substantielle sur l'archet, alors que le violoncelliste avait décidé d'ignorer cet aspect. La page de titre ne manque même pas — contre l'avis de l'auteur — d'attirer l'attention sur le sujet. D'autre part, Imbault a dû corriger le texte du violoncelliste, voire le reformuler, mais en même temps ce dernier lui a trouvé un agent à Berlin. Pour ce qui de la lettre de Paër, la réaction négative d'Imbault prouve que ce dernier ne se laisse pas imposer la publication d'un arrangement d'une œuvre faisant pourtant partie de son catalogue. Son attitude tient peut-être au fait qu'il n'a pu intervenir ni dans le choix de l'effectif ni dans celui de l'arrangeur. Ce n'est pas parce que ce dernier se contente d'une rémunération présentée comme modeste par Paër, qu'Imbault se laisse convaincre car il est uniquement guidé par des considérations d'ordre commercial et sait que l'arrangement ne se vendra guère. Son intransigeance explique certainement pourquoi son affaire est si florissante quand il la vend en 1812, soit un an après la lettre de Paër.

## Annexe

Afin de faciliter la lecture, nous avons corrigé les erreurs d'orthographe, particulièrement nombreuses dans les lettres de Duport, et adapté la ponctuation.

1

Lettre de Jean-Louis Duport à Jean-Jérôme Imbault (Potsdam, le 6 mars 1804)
2 feuillets

**f. 1 recto**

La chose change de face, je suis violoncelle ayant acquis un peu de réputation. Si je fais un pauvre ouvrage, je la perds et suis déshonoré. Voilà pourquoi j'y ai pensé plus d'une fois, et pourquoi j'ai travaillé lentement. Enfin après l'avoir relu plusieurs fois, j'ai cru pouvoir y mettre mon nom, si surtout mes anciens amis et confrères l'approuvent. On me conseille ici de ne faire paroître cet ouvrage qu'après avoir fait une souscription. Il est certain que j'aurai beaucoup de souscripteurs pour la seule ville de Berlin parce que quelques professeurs à qui je l'ai communiqué l'ont beaucoup prôné. On veut aussi me persuader de le faire traduire en allemand afin qu'il puisse paroître dans les deux langues. Je vous serois bien obligé de me dire votre façon de penser là-dessus. Quant à moi je ne voudrois pas qu'il paroisse avant que d'avoir au moins deux cents souscriptions, ce que je crois qu'il sera facile d'avoir, vu que par ce moyen on dégoûte les contrefacteurs et que l'auteur, qui s'est donné de la peine, peut espérer un dédommagement de ses soins.

Le titre de cet ouvrage est *Traité sur le doigter du violoncelle* et en voici à peu près le plan:

Article 1ᵉʳ de la position de l'instrument

 2 de son accord

 3 de la position de la main; cet article est assez étendu

 4 des gammes dans le bas du manche dans tous les tons majeurs et mineurs

 5 des gammes sur la même corde et supplément aux mêmes gammes

 6 des positions dans le manche

 7 des gammes par trois et sans à-vide

 8 la gamme chromatique qui s'adapte à tous les tons

 9 des sons harmoniques

 10 de la double corde. Cet article est divisé de la manière suivante

| | |
|---|---|
| 1ᵉʳ de la tierce, suite de tierces | 9 de la sixte et suite |
| 2 tierce et seconde, et suite | 10 sixte et quinte suite |
| 3 tierce, sixte et seconde | 11 sixte et septième |
| 4 tierce et sixte | 12 septième diminuée |
| 5 de la quarte | 13 récapitulation de ces différents accords |
| 6 de la quinte | |
| 7 de la fausse quinte | |
| 8 de la quarte superflue | |

**f. 1 verso**

 11 quelques coups d'archet et principalement sur le doigter de l'arpeggio et des différentes extensions qu'on y rencontre

 12 une assez grande quantité de passages propres à s'exercer et à développer le doigter de l'instrument et surtout à prouver qu'il n'existe pas de contrariété dans le doigter. La manière de monter et descendre sur les mêmes cordes dans différents tons et toujours régulièrement. La preuve de la nécessité de ne pas lever les doigts inutilement. Les inconvénients qui en résultent, ainsi que de ne pas changer de position sans raison… et une infinité d'autres choses que j'ai tâché de présenter de mon mieux

 13 mon opinion sur la manière de battre la cadence

 14 sur la nécessité de la révision des unissons et des octaves avec les à-vides, ainsi que mon opinion sur la manière d'accorder l'instrument

 15 de la coalition des vibrations. Cet article est ma manie ou ma folie. S'il n'est pas approuvé, il n'y aura rien de si aisé que de le supprimer

16ᵐᵉ et dernier article explication de la distance que les doigts doivent avoir entre eux dans les 4 premières positions du manche et la preuve de l'unité de ces 4 premières positions du manche en comparant la 2ᵐᵉ, la 3ᵐᵉ, la 4ᵐᵉ avec la 1ʳᵉ. sous tous ces rapports

Si Bréval avoit fait ce travail, il se seroit convaincu qu'il n'existe pas de contrariété dans le doigter du violoncelle, mais que ce sont nos mauvaises habitudes qui en sont, et que ceci dépend beaucoup des premières leçons qu'on a reçues et du peu de réflexion qu'on a faite ensuite en travaillant pour les déraciner. Mais il me semble qu'un homme qui fait un ouvrage doit bien se garder de les passer en principes, et c'est ce qu'on pourra peut-être lui reprocher. Je vous avouerai que si j'en avois trouvé d'insurmontables, j'aurois abandonné la besogne. Adieu, mon cher ami, je vous embrasse de tout mon cœur et vous demande pardon de vous en avoir écrit si long, mais vous m'avez attaqué sur ma manie du moment. Je vous prie de vouloir bien embrasser madame Imbault pour moi et de lui dire mil choses aimables de ma part. Mil compliments à tous mes amis et particulièrement à mes deux censeurs. Croyez-moi toujours pour la vie avec toute l'amitié

**f. 2 recto**
possible tout à vous.

Duport cadet

Potzdam ce 6 mars 1804

Himmel me prie de vous faire bien des compliments. Il n'a pas manqué de me dire que vous m'aimiez de tout votre cœur, que vous avez bu à ma santé toutes les fois que vous vous êtes trouvés ensemble. Vous pouvez croire que je me suis vengé de cela à Berlin avec bien du plaisir, attendu que je ne suis pas un ingrat...
Donnez-moi, je vous prie, votre avis sur la traduction ainsi que sur la souscription. Vous pourriez sur le dernier article me donner des avis salutaires.

**f. 2 verso**

[cachet:] PRUSSE PAR MAASEYCK

À Monsieur
Monsieur Imbault, marchand de musique Rue S$^t$ Honoré au mont d'or – entre la rue de l'arbre sec et celle des poulies.
À Paris

2
Lettre de Jean-Louis Duport à Jean-Jérôme Imbault (Potsdam, le 29 juin 1805)
2 feuillets

**f. 1 recto**

Potsdam ce 29 Juin 1805

Mon cher ami,
Je n'ai reçu votre lettre du 11 juin que le 25 et cela parce que vous me l'avez adressée à Berlin au lieu de Potsdam où je suis toujours, excepté le temps du Carnaval où je suis à Berlin pour les opéras. Vous êtes le plus aimable garçon du monde et vous arrangez les choses pour le mieux. Je vous remercie bien des corrections d'orthographe que vous m'avez faites. Je remercie aussi M$^r$ Le Vasseur l'aîné des chiffres qu'il a bien voulu remettre en ordre dans le doigter. Je m'étois bien douté que malgré toute l'attention possible, il me seroit échappé quelques fautes. Je ne puis pas vous dissimuler que j'aurois été charmé que vous ayez laissé quelque mots qui disent que j'ai entrepris absolument cet ouvrage pour traiter du doigter, et que ce que je dis sur l'archet n'est que de simples réflexions car, soit dit entre nous, je regarde l'archet comme la métaphysique des instruments à cordes, et voilà pourquoi je n'en voulois pas dire un mot. Le fait est que je n'aurois pas entrepris l'article du doigté si je ne l'avois pas cru absolument utile, et que je ne l'aurois pas mis au jour si je n'avois pas eu l'espoir de ramener les professeurs eux-mêmes à la vraie unité de principe qui n'étoit pas encore bien établie. Ceci est le fruit de 25 ans de réflexions et d'observations, et le

travail de trois années, au lieu que ce que je dis sur l'archet n'est que de simples réflexions jetées à la hâte dessus le papier parce que vous l'avez voulu car je n'avois jamais pensé de ma vie à écrire sur l'archet.

**f. 1 verso**

Vu que je n'y vois aucune utilité, vous sentez que je ne fais pas de comparaison de l'un à l'autre, j'abandonne mes idées sur l'archet et je les verrois retranchées du livre avec la plus grande indifférence, au lieu que je crois qu'il n'y a pas une page du doigté qui ne soit utile au tout. Voilà pourquoi j'aurois désiré que ce que je dis sur l'archet fût annoncé avec beaucoup de modestie, et comme un article qui n'entroit pas dans mes projets.

À présent parlons d'autres choses! J'ai un ami à Berlin qui désireroit faire un petit commerce de musique. L'idée lui est venue sur ce que je lui ai dit que vous aviez désiré plusieurs fois de trouver quelqu'un qui voulut se charger de vendre ici de la musique de votre firme et que vous lui feriez des avantages, mais que je n'avois jamais pu vous recommander des gens sûrs. À la vérité, j'en ai rencontré plusieurs qui m'avoient chargé de vous écrire pour cela, mais je ne l'ai jamais fait parce que je vous aurois fait faire de mauvaises connaissances. Ici ce n'est pas le cas, la personne dont il est question est très honnête, et je puis vous en répondre comme de moi-même. Il seroit question de savoir vos arrangements, vous me parlez de 50 pour cent, mais est-ce quand on achète ou bien en commission car pour acheter à son compte, il pourroit y avoir des risques à courir car malgré le gros bénéfice que présente 50 pour cent, si on ne vendoit que la moitié de la musique que l'on feroit venir, il y auroit encore de

**f. 2 recto**

la perte à cause des frais de port etc. Je vous serois donc bien obligé de me dire comment vous traitez avec les débitants étrangers et sur votre réponse nous vous ferons une commande. N[o]ta Bene. Je vous donne ma parole d'honneur que vous n'avez pas à craindre qu'on donne votre musique en loyer.

À présent parlons de mon ouvrage! Vous me demandez combien vous devez m'en donner comme auteur. Je réponds à cela le moins possible. Je vous en demanderai 4, un pour moi, un pour mon frère et d[eux pour[31]] deux écoliers qui m'ont infiniment aidé pour la copie. [De] plus je vous en demanderai 40 exemplaires pour vendre [et je] souhaite être dans le cas de vous en demander davant[age] mais cela me paroît suffisant pour commencer.

La personne dont je viens de vous parler n'a pas encore fait de démarche pour la permission de ce commerce, mais elle la fera et j'espère que d'après votre réponse nous pourrons vous faire une demande, qui sera soumise à votre jugement à cause des nouveautés, et vous pourriez joindre mon envoi à celui-là.

Adieu, cher ami, je vous embrasse de tout mon cœur et suis pour la vie avec toute l'amitié possible tout à vous

Duport cadet

Dans le cas où vous vous arrangeriez avec M$^r$ Deroudville qui est le nom de la personne dont je vous parle plus haut, je ferois annoncer mon ouvrage dans les gazettes à son adresse avec la note des ouvrages que vous me marquez dans votre lettre.

Potzdam, ce 29 juin 1805

Mil compliments respectueux à Madame Imbault

[Note marginale, f. 1v] Je ne suis pas assez instruit pour vous dire si vous ferez bien ou mal de faire paroître dans l'étranger ou à Paris en premier, mais je crains peu le travail du Conservatoire. Comme je n'ai pas l'honneur d'être membre de cette corporation, donnez-moi mon titre de Premier violoncelle de la chapelle du roi de Prusse.

---

[31]. Une petite partie de la page a été déchirée et les mots entre crochets sont manquants.

# Les relations entre Jean-Jérôme Imbault et ses compositeurs

**f. 2 verso**

[cachet:] PRUSSE PAR MAASEYCK

    À Monsieur
    Monsieur Imbault, marchand de musique Rue S<sup>t</sup> Honoré au mont d'or, près de l'ancien hôtel d'Aligre
    À Paris

3

Lettre de Ferdinando Paër à Jean-Jérôme Imbault (sans lieu, le 12 juillet 1811)
1 feuillet

**recto**

    À Monsieur
    Mons[ieu]r Imbault Prof[esseu]r et Éditeur de la Musique de S[a] M[ajesté] l'Emp[ereu]r et Roi *avec un paquet de Musique*

**verso**

    Mon cher Mons[ieu]r Imbault
    L'Auteur qui a tres bien arrangé mon opéra *Camilla* pour deux flûtes et alto se contente d'avoir cinquante exemplaires de la susdite musique pourvu qu'elle soit envoyée à Parme franc de port. Pour cette condition je m'en chargerai de quelque manière, ayant toujours des occasions particulières.
    Je suis charmé d'avoir bien négocié votre intérêt; je vous en envoie *les trois parties*.
    Je vous embrasse et suis-je
    Tout pour vous servir
    F. Paër
    Le 12 juillet 1811

## Bibliographie

**Benton 1972**
*Catalogue thématique des ouvrages de musique, mis au jour par Imbault*, Paris, Imbault, s.d., fac-similé avec un index des compositeurs cités, Rita Benton éd., Genève, Minkoff, 1972 (Archives de l'édition musicale française, 7).

**Benton 1976**
Benton, Rita. 'J.-J. Imbault (1753-1832), violoniste et éditeur de musique à Paris', in: *Revue de Musicologie*, LXII/1 (1976), pp. 86-103.

**Benton 1977**
Ead. *Ignace Pleyel: A Thematic Catalogue of His Compositions*, New York, Pendragon Press, 1977 (Thematic Catalogues, 2).

**Bréval 1804**
Bréval, J[ean]-B[aptiste]. *Traité du violoncel*, Op. 42, Paris, Imbault, [1804].

Devriès-Lesure 2005
Devriès-Lesure, Anik. *L'édition musicale dans la presse parisienne au XVIIIe siècle. Catalogue des annonces*, Paris, C.N.R.S., 2005 (Sciences de la musique, série Références).

Devriès – Lesure 1979
Ead. – Lesure, François. *Dictionnaire des éditeurs de musique français*, 2 vol., Genève, Minkoff, 1979 (Archives de l'édition musicale française, 4).

Duport 1806
Duport, J[ean]-L[ouis]. *Essai sur le doigté du violoncelle et sur la conduite de l'archet*, Paris, Imbault, [1806].

Johansson, 1955
Johansson, Cari. *French Music Publishers' Catalogues of the Second Half of the Eigtheenth Century*, 2 vol., Stockholm, Royal Swedish Academi of Music, 1955 (Publications of the Library of the Royal Swedish Academy of Music, 2).

Milliot 1985
Milliot, Sylvette. *Le violoncelle en France au XVIIIe siècle*, Paris-Genève, Champion-Slatkine, 1985.

Twytman 1996
Twytman, Michael. *Early Lithographed Music: A Study Based on the H. Baron Collection*, London, Farrand Press, 1996.

Vanhulst 2012
Vanhulst, Henri. 'Un catalogue manuscrit de Jean-Jérôme Imbault postérieur à 1812', in: *Noter, annoter, éditer la musique. Mélanges offerts à Catherine Massip*, Cécile Reynaud et Herbert Schneider dir., Paris, École pratique des Hautes Études-Bibliothèque nationale de France, 2012, pp. 429-446.

Vanhulst 2016
Id. 'Les relations commerciales de J.-J. Imbault d'après l'acte de vente du 14 juillet 1812', in: *Music and War from French Revolution to WWI*, Étienne Jardin dir., Turnhout, Brepols, 2016 (Music, Criticism & Politics, 2), pp. 233-254.

Walden 1998
Walden, Valerie. *One Hundred Years of Violoncello: A History of Technique and Performance Practice, 1740-1840*, Cambridge, Cambridge University Press, 1998.

# Music Publishing and Markets c.1750-1830

*David Rowland*
(The Open University)

The late eighteenth and early nineteenth centuries were turbulent yet formative times for the modern music publishing industry. The context is familiar. These were times of war and social unrest during which the *ancien régime* was under threat throughout Europe and it was a period during which modern societies and modern economies emerged. Underpinning many of these developments was the Enlightenment, with its emphasis on human endeavour. This chapter will argue that although music publishing was affected by all of these factors it was predominantly changing economic fortunes and social structures around Europe that gave rise to the emergence of the markets which shaped the industry. By comparison, war — of which there was plenty — could be seen as little more than an inconvenience which did not fundamentally affect the development of music publishing. A similar observation was made by Hans Lenneberg about the effects of the Thirty Years' War in the first half of the seventeenth century who writes «it is true [...] that during the Thirty Years' War music publishing actually flourished in Germany; on the whole, the war seems not to have had a devastating influence on the book trade»[1].

In order to understand music publishing businesses in our period we need to know the basis on which they operated. Perhaps it goes without saying that music publishers needed to cover their costs and to make profits. This was achieved according to two essentially different models. The first model was characterised by the production of relatively small quantities of high-value, multi-page volumes which were sold for the sort of money that only the very richest in society could afford. This model tended to be used for the production of substantial scores such as oratorios which in the eighteenth century were often published by subscription.

---

[1]. Lenneberg 2003, p. 60.

Compiling a subscribers' list, as Charles Burney did for the British sales of Haydn's *Creation*[2], had the benefit of reassuring publishers of sufficient income. But when the required number of subscribers could not be found, a publication could be aborted before any production costs were incurred[3].

The second model required publishers to speculate and to publish music that they hoped would sell over the counter without any guarantees that the market would like what was published. By the eighteenth century there had already been a long tradition of publishing short, inexpensive pieces in this way that were cheap to produce and designed to appeal to a wide market; sixteenth- and seventeenth-century broadside publications were produced and sold according to this model. But as the market expanded, especially in the eighteenth century, publishers took risks with more substantial publications of several, or even dozens, of pages. The increasing market for music and therefore the profitability of this second model caused the virtual demise of the subscription model in the early nineteenth century.

The success of the second model depended not only on an expanding market, but on the development of a more efficient and therefore cheaper means of production, particularly with the introduction of engraving and lithography. The benefit of these technologies over the use of moveable type, which had been the usual means of production in earlier times, was that engraved or lithographed publishing plates could easily be stored and re-used for a series of later print runs. Initial print runs could therefore be kept relatively small, a definite advantage because paper was a significantly costly part of the publishing process. Only later would further print runs be made if a work showed signs of selling well. In contrast, the use of moveable type matrices, which tended to be used for a single print run and then dissembled because publishers needed the expensive pieces of type for another publication, could be wasteful and expensive. Engraving and lithography were therefore ideal methods of publishing for markets in which demand was uncertain and this was the model that was increasingly used in the rapidly expanding market for music in our period[4].

What sort of people provided the market that caused the second model of music publishing to flourish? They were the same people who fuelled the growth in concert-going and instrument purchasing. At the beginning of the period under discussion that market was by no means as large as it was to become in the nineteenth century. Writing about England, which almost certainly had a bigger market than any other in the second half of the eighteenth

---

[2]. Charles Burney was responsible for compiling the subscribers' list and Clementi & Co. managed the publication's distribution. See ROWLAND 2010, p. 46.

[3]. An example of an aborted publication is Johann Bernhard Logier's *A Treatise on Practical Composition and Harmony*. Notice of its publication was given in Dublin's *Freeman's Journal and Daily Commercial Advertiser* on 28 June 1813 with an endorsement by Clementi, but there is no evidence in newspaper or other advertisements, or in physical copies, that it was ever published.

[4]. The merits of various nineteenth-century music publishing processes are discussed in ROWLAND 2019.

century, Robert Hume comments that the sort of music regularly published and heard in concert performances «was consumed by the top 1 per cent or 0.5 per cent of the English population»[5]. But the growth of the market in England was inexorable, as judged by the increase in instrument manufacture, the expansion of the concert world and the sheer amount of music put into the public domain by music publishers[6]. And it was the gradual emergence of the middle classes during our period who were largely responsible for the expansion of this market, not just in England, but elsewhere in Europe. This sector of society had increasing amounts of disposable income to spend on cultural commodities such as music. Writing of the end of the period under discussion William Weber comments on the situation in London, Paris and Vienna:

> [...] after the end of the Napoleonic wars a new era began in the history of the concert world, one in which the middle class began taking on dramatic new roles. The most fundamental fact underlying the growth of concerts was the good health and stability of the capitals' economies. After the period of rapid economic expansion and rising prices in the second half of the eighteenth century and the wild price fluctuations during the wars, prices levelled off and economic growth resumed at an even pace [...] The middle class thereby gained a rising standard of living and, thanks to the continuing peace, had little worry over general economic crisis.
>
> These conditions affected musical life initially by stimulating a boom in the sale of instruments and publications. Musical activities in the home, although common previously, were rapidly becoming almost standard within substantial middle-class households. Publishing and instrument manufacture had grown steadily since the middle of the eighteenth century, but as home musical activities increased, their production and sales picked up speed rapidly[7].

However dramatic these developments may have been, they did not occur uniformly across Europe. It was only where there was a suitably strong economic environment that music publishing began to thrive, first in the north and then, several decades later, in the south and east, although in some countries where music in the public domain had thrived in earlier centuries, publishing activity actually reduced before increasing once again as the nineteenth century progressed[8]. In Italy, for example, high-quality music publishing famously reached an early peak of sophistication in the sixteenth century as epitomised in the publishing activities of the Venetian Ottaviano Petrucci, but its significance there was to diminish. By 1600 the economic

---

[5]. HUME 2014, p. 415.
[6]. ROWLAND 2020, especially pp. 87-89.
[7]. WEBER 2004, pp. 6-7.
[8]. BEREND 2013 provides a very useful summary for the underpinning economic observations made in this chapter.

might of centres such as Venice and Genoa had waned and music publishing fell into decline, just as it did in seventeenth century Germany[9].

It was in The Netherlands, Britain and France that the strongest markets for music publishing emerged in the seventeenth and eighteenth centuries. The Netherlands, with its modern economy and growing population, its overseas trade, its abandonment of archaic systems of government and its modern political and economic institutions, flourished as the most prominent centre of music publishing in the seventeenth century. The merchant classes who were so important to the economy had disposable income to spend, and they spent some of it on published music.

Britain followed a similar pattern, although music publishing flourished somewhat later than it did in the Netherlands. As prosperity gradually declined in the Netherlands, Britain emerged as a highly successful economy in which social and economic freedoms and structures, along with the absence of an environment tightly controlled by monarchy, provided ideal conditions for music publishing.

It is not difficult to understand the success of music publishing in The Netherlands and Britain, with their emphasis on free trade and a relatively modern market economy with fewer controls than elsewhere. But the success of the French music publishing industry in the eighteenth century is perhaps a little more perplexing. How could a music publishing industry thrive in a country with a tightly controlling, absolutist monarchy where the social and political freedoms enjoyed by the Dutch and British did not exist? I can think of two reasons. The first is that the monarchy had invested significantly in musical culture over many years, just as it valued and promoted the intellectual endeavour that was such a hallmark of French culture in the eighteenth century. The second reason is the size of the French population, which had been the largest in Europe for hundreds of years and which by 1820 exceeded 31 million; the population of France was more than 30% bigger than the area which is modern Germany and 50% bigger than Britain[10]. Although the vast majority of the French were unable to purchase music, there was nevertheless a sizeable number of people at the top end of society who provided a market for it[11].

The early success of music publishing in The Netherlands, Britain and France during the eighteenth century contrasted sharply with the poor state of music publishing further south and there are many examples of music composed and played in poorer, less open southern countries which was published in the comparatively affluent north, rather than in the country in which it was produced. For example, many of Vivaldi's sonatas and concertos were first published in

---

[9]. See LENNEBERG 2003, Chapter 3 for an overview.
[10]. MADDISON 2001, Appendix B.
[11]. This group of people provided significant impetus to the development of new music: see, for example, BROOK 1994, especially pp. 144ff.

Amsterdam from 1711 to 1729, rather than in Italy, and Scarlatti's *Essercizi*, a collection of his sonatas, were published in London in 1739. Many more examples exist of composers in countries such as Italy, Spain and Portugal, as well as in poorer countries to the east, turning to the north-western countries of Europe for the publication of their works.

As mentioned above, music publishing in German-speaking lands declined in the seventeenth century. By the early eighteenth century these societies had still not thrown off their feudal structures. Their economies failed to flourish and whatever wealth there was did not often flow to more than a handful of people who wanted to buy printed music. Consequently, the market for music was very small in some places. Even as late as 1783, Carl Friedrich Cramer wrote that there were «not more than four or six persons in Kiel and the neighbourhood who buy music»[12]. The situation was not quite so bad elsewhere, but in many places there was simply an insufficient critical mass of people who could afford music to justify a mass printing industry. Instead, a great deal of music circulated in manuscript. This was the case in Vienna, for example, where there were thriving music-copyist business throughout the eighteenth century. Even after the prominent firm Artaria was established as a music printer in the 1770s, manuscript copies continued to be produced in significant numbers. This was a feature, too, of other countries where a music publishing industry was slow to develop; music circulated in manuscript rather than in printed copies or, in some cases, musicians depended on imported rather than locally produced scores.

But in spite of the relative lack of music publishing in German-speaking lands society began to benefit from the 'enlightened absolutism' that characterised the reigns of Frederick the Great of Prussia and Maria Theresa of the Hapsburg Dominions from the middle of the eighteenth century onwards. These rulers effected the social reforms and economic development that allowed music publishing to develop rapidly in the late eighteenth and early nineteenth centuries. By the end of the eighteenth century there were some thriving music publishers who were able to compete in the international arena, notably in Leipzig, where Breitkopk & Härtel were based, and in Vienna where a number of well-known music publishers had thriving businesses.

Among the slowest countries in Europe to develop a music-publishing industry were Spain and Portugal. Spain's economy was much slower to mature than economies in countries further north: the country boasted nothing like a market economy or free trade in the period under discussion. And most aspects of society were tightly controlled by the monarchy, including music publishing. So, when the Portuguese publisher Marchal left Portugal in 1796 and moved to Spain, where he was nominated musician of the Royal Camera of King Carlos IV, his request to start a music printing business was refused by the Spanish crown, which did not permit

---

[12]. Quoted and translated in BEER 2005, p. 173.

music publishing[13]. Even in the first quarter of the nineteenth century there was no significant music publishing industry in Spain. Discussing music publishing in the second decade of the nineteenth century Gloria Araceli Rodríguez-Lorenzo comments that «a specialized music press did not exist in Spain at this time, although music had a growing presence in different types of newspapers and magazines»[14].

More enlightened policies operated under the Portuguese monarchy. Music publishing was actively encouraged by the crown and from the end of the 1780s music publishers began to open shops[15]. But Portugal remained a poor country with one of the smallest populations in Europe[16]. And its capital transferred to Brazil from 1808 to 1821. Under these conditions Portugal's music publishing industry did not thrive to any great extent until well into the nineteenth century.

To discuss music publishing in countries to the east in Europe would be to duplicate many of the themes already mentioned in connection with Austria, Germany, Portugal and Spain. Suffice it to say that the antiquated societies and economies of countries such as Hungary and Poland provided little stimulus for music publishing, which developed at a much slower pace there than in the north-western economies of Europe.

***

In comparison with the impact of economic and societal change around Europe, what was the effect on European music publishing of the French Revolution and Napoleonic wars? Broadly speaking, publishing industries in Britain, France and in German-speaking lands continued, or began to thrive and to expand even during those times, which is all the more remarkable in the case of Britain since Napoleon tried to restrict British trade and to bring the country to its economic knees. Meanwhile, developments in Italy, on the Iberian Peninsula and in many of the countries to the east continued at a slower pace, though not uniformly so. Italy, for example, was able to support publishers such as the well-known firm founded by Giovanni Ricordi in 1808, while there remained few music publishers in other countries for some years.

Following the cessation of hostilities, the situation from 1815 onwards was complex. The developments of that year saw a return to entrenched monarchical government in many countries, but at the same time some of the societal and governmental innovations brought about by Napoleon continued to modernise economies, as many of the social and institutional changes brought about by Napoleon remained, even in conservative countries. These changes

---

[13]. ALBUQUERQUE 2020, p. 243.
[14]. RODRÍGUEZ-LORENZO 2020, p. 279.
[15]. ALBUQUERQUE 2020, pp. 239-241.
[16]. MADDISON 2001, Appendix B.

fostered the emergence of the middle classes and consequently a market for music that stimulated the development of music publishing.

Aside from this general picture, at a more local level the volatile times of the French Revolution and Napoleonic wars provided an unstable environment for music publishers. There was a high rate of business failure, but at the same time there were many opportunities and successes. So, in Britain, for example, one of the country's highest-profile companies, Corri, Dussek & Co., became bankrupt in 1800[17]. Yet at around the same time, from the remains of Longman & Broderip's bankruptcy in 1798, Clementi & Co. emerged to become an extremely successful business while war was raging; a spreadsheet of partners' business stakes from 1811, calculated on the occasion of the withdrawal of Frederick Augustus Hyde from the business, shows that Clementi and other partners had made profits of around 1300% in the decade to 1810[18]. In Paris, according to Gribenski, there were nineteen music publishers just before the Revolution[19]. Between then and the end of the eighteenth century, seven of those businesses failed (over one-third), yet eight new ones were founded. The overwhelming impression of all these comings and goings among music businesses is that if sound management was in place companies could not only survive, but thrive, whereas poor management easily led to failure in such a volatile environment. In turn, good management often depended on relevant business skills being available within partnerships. The success of Clementi & Co., for example, was in no small measure the result of its well-balanced partnership which consisted of an internationally renowned musician (Clementi), someone with experience of running previous music businesses (Hyde), instrument makers (Collard and Davis) and a partner with financial expertise (Banger). Some of these men had also been assignees of Longman & Broderip's bankruptcy and must therefore have learned salutary lessons in business failure.

International cooperation was a growing feature of Europe's music industries throughout the period and during the French Revolution there are several examples of business relationships being forged and developed across the English Channel. This environment lasted well beyond the beginning of the French Revolution and continued until after the signing of the Treaty of Amiens in March 1802. But once hostilities resumed a year later, and Napoleon came to power, France's attention moved from internal affairs to war with other countries, a consequence of which was that international cooperation became more difficult, especially between England and the continent. The business relationship between Pleyel and the music industry in London illustrates the point. Pleyel was in the English capital in the early 1790s before establishing his publishing company in Paris in 1795. Once established as a businessman he began to work very closely with Corri, Dussek & Co. in London. The two companies published a number of works

---

[17]. ROWLAND 2012, pp. 99-103.
[18]. ROWLAND 2010, pp. 423-425.
[19]. GRIBENSKI 1991.

more or less simultaneously in their respective cities and in 1797 they collaborated on a musical journal of vocal, harp and piano music, which was published in more or less identical form in both Paris and London[20]. The cooperation slowed and finally ended with the London firm's bankruptcy in 1800. The decline of Pleyel's business relationship with Corri, Dussek & Co. coincided with the establishment of strong business relations between Pleyel's and Clementi's music businesses. Collaboration between the two men began at least by 1799, when Clementi and Pleyel began to exchange music for publication in their respective companies. Clementi then arranged to visit Pleyel in Paris in 1802 at the beginning of his extended tour of Europe (1802-1810), staying with him and proposing a joint venture to manufacture pianos in France. But as far as it is possible to tell (not least because many letters between the two men are either lost or currently inaccessible), correspondence between the two businessmen ceased after Clementi left Paris in the autumn of 1802 and their joint ventures came to a halt. Instead, Pleyel looked towards other parts of continental Europe for collaborators. In 1804 he opened a branch of his business in Regensburg and in 1805 he attempted, but failed, to open a music shop in Vienna[21]. At the same time, Clementi seems to have abandoned his efforts to expand his business in France and began to concentrate on selling pianos and acquiring publishing contracts further east and south in Europe, in Austria, Germany, Italy, Russia, and Switzerland.

The suspension of cooperation between British and continental publishers was temporary and collaboration gained impetus once again after 1815. Signs of increasing international collaboration can be seen in Clementi's correspondence. Towards the end of 1816 August Alexander Klengel wrote to Clementi, sending him a catalogue of music sold by the Parisian music publisher Erard. On 3 February 1817 Gottfried Christoph Härtel wrote to Clementi wishing to set up closer business relations and on 7 May in the same year Frederick William Collard wrote to Artaria & Co. asking for some of the firm's musical publications[22]. Further signs of growing international cooperation around this time are found in the publishing arrangements for a number of works whose title pages include the names of publishers in more than one country. The trend grew from 1815 and a particular concentration of examples can be seen in publications by the London firm Cocks & Co. In the 1820s the firm registered a number of works at Stationers' Hall noting in the records their joint publication relationships with various French publishers such as Pleyel (20 March, 26 May 1824; 1 and 15 November and 1 December 1825; 10 April, 13 and 31 October 1826, 14 June 1828, 13 January 1829), Leduc (24 January 1829) and Troupenas (28 February 1829).

One of the main difficulties during the Napoleonic wars was the absence of a free flow of goods between Britain and France because of the latter's policy of restricting trade between the

---

[20]. ROWLAND 2012, pp. 96-98.
[21]. BENTON 1979, pp. 134-135.
[22]. See ROWLAND 2010, pp. 237, 244 and 246 for transcriptions and translations of the letters.

continent and Britain, especially after the formation of Napoleon's so-called 'Continental System' in 1806. The system aimed to starve Britain of its European trade in order to bring its economy to its knees. But the policy failed for a variety of reasons, not least Napoleon's underestimation of the success of Britain's trade outside Europe. Although Britain's exports to Europe declined, its naval superiority enabled it to trade freely elsewhere.

From 1806 British music publishers found trade with Europe difficult, but they nevertheless benefitted from trade with the country's colonies and former colonies. Trade with India in music and musical instruments had been gathering pace towards the end of the eighteenth century with individuals selling items that were advertised in the local newspapers. In the 1780s and 1790s John Bland advertised his music for export to merchants, ships' captains and other dealers. Around the same time a man called Stone opened a musical warehouse in Calcutta[23] and Longman & Broderip established a music shop in the same city[24]. Their successor firm Clementi & Co. continued to trade with the Indian sub-continent via the East India Company selling, among other things, sets of brass instruments[25]. British companies also traded with America and several workers in the music industry spent time across the Atlantic. Broadwood's agent in New York, Daniel Stewart, wrote to James Shudi Broadwood, 'Clementi & Co have sold a good many instruments to people in this country'[26], a fact confirmed by other correspondence and advertisements in the American press[27]. However, it seems that several American makers were copying British instruments with greater or lesser success and since British publications were liberally pirated by American firms[28], the North American market may not have been as lucrative as the Indian sub-continent. At the same time as British musical goods were being sent to far-flung places, and in spite of French restrictions, some trade continued with Europe. Although British goods were liable to be seized at France's borders and at other checkpoints, the borders could never be sealed entirely, and goods were still able to be moved between the two countries. And as Clementi's letters make clear, it was still possible for trade to flow to Europe through the Baltic ports[29].

One affect of the blockade of Britain by France seems to have been a reduction in the exchange of repertoire between Britain and the continent. A much fuller investigation of this topic needs to be undertaken, but there were certainly gaps in British publishers' catalogues during the period of the French Revolution and Napoleonic wars. While some extracts from

---

[23]. WOODFIELD 2000B, pp. 3 and 9.
[24]. WOODFIELD 2000A, pp. 68-69.
[25]. ROWLAND 2011, pp. 139 and 155.
[26]. WAINWRIGHT 1982, p. 108.
[27]. KASSLER 2020.
[28]. GRAY 2020, especially pp. 74-79.
[29]. See, for example, Clementi's activities in St. Petersburg and Riga as described in his letters of 17 August 1803, 14 September [1805] and 22 June/4 July 1806 in ROWLAND 2010, pp. 104-110, 158-159 and 166-168.

operas performed in Paris found their way to London, other repertoires fared badly. For example, almost no piano music by the likes of Louis Adam, François-Adrien Boieldieu and Hyacinthe Jadin published in Paris during the period found its way into the hands of London publishers. Whether this was a direct effect of the blockade, or because the British shunned French piano music for partisan reasons, is unclear.

A further, practical effect of the period's wars, especially Napoleon's, was the increasing unreliability of the international postal network, which seriously affected the publication of continental music in Britain. The saga of Beethoven's contract with Clementi amply illustrates the problem[30]. In 1807 the two men signed a contract for the publication in London of some of Beethoven's works. Scores were to be sent to London in two packages, but one of those packages failed to reach its destination. The other one arrived, but some two years after it had been sent from Vienna. This was not only irritating for Clementi, but potentially injurious to his business, since because of the lack of any international copyright protection it was important to arrange for works to be published more or less simultaneously in different countries in order to avoid piracy.

Further evidence of communication problems is found in the breakdown of publishing negotiations between Clementi, Beethoven and the Leipzig firm Breitkopf & Härtel. On 22 April 1807 Clementi wrote to Gottfried Christoph Härtel, saying

> Beethoven and I have become good friends in the end. We have reached an agreement whereby he grants me the rights in the British Dominions for 3 quartets, a symphony, an overture, a violin concerto and a pianoforte concerto. I made this agreement with him following on from your letter dated 20 January, in which you told me you were unable to accept his proposals because of the war[31].

Exactly why, beyond the general reason of the war, Beethoven's proposals could not be accepted is unknown, but the problem of war was also a theme in another of Clementi's letters, this time with his London business partner, Frederick William Collard. Clementi was in St Petersburg in 1806, anxious to return home to London, but aware that travel was difficult. His access to the French ports was impeded by war, and he had no stomach for a long sea voyage around the Baltic and across the North Sea. As he said in his letter of 9 June 1806, «Oh this damned war! – or that I could bear a long sea voyage!»[32].

There can be no doubt that the French Revolution and Napoleonic wars were major inconveniences for the music industry in Europe. They hindered business between countries and affected the way in which printed music and musical instruments were disseminated.

---

[30]. COOPER 2002.
[31]. ROWLAND 2010, p. 181.
[32]. *Ibidem*, p. 165.

# Music Publishing and Markets c.1750-1830

But ultimately these events did little to slow the pace of the industry's development. Those companies that found ways around the difficulties, and which were sufficiently disciplined not to over-stretch themselves during challenging times, were able to grow and to prosper. During the period discussed here, many in the music trade became wealthy and in general terms the foundations were laid for further expansion in the decades that followed.

## Bibliography

ALBUQUERQUE 2020
ALBUQUERQUE, Maria João. 'Music Printing and Publishing in Portugal (1750-1850)', in: *Music Publishing and Composers (1750-1850)*, edited by Massimiliano Sala, Turnhout, Brepols, 2020 (Speculum Musicae, 37), pp. 239-255.

BEER 2005
BEER, Axel. 'Composers and Publishers: Germany 1700-1830', in: *Music Publishing in Europe 1600-1900: Concepts and Issues, Bibliography*, edited by Rudolf Rasch, Berlin, Berliner Wissenschafts-Verlag, 2005 (The Circulation of Music, 1), pp. 159-181.

BENTON 1979
BENTON, Rita. 'Pleyel as Music Publisher', in: *Journal of the American Musicological Society*, XXXII/1, (1979), pp. 125-140.

BEREND 2013
BEREND, Ivan T. *An Economic History of Nineteenth-Century Europe*, Cambridge, Cambridge University Press, 2013.

BROOK 1994
BROOK, Barry. 'The Symphonie Concertante: Its Musical and Sociological Bases', in: *International Review of the Aesthetics and Sociology of Music*, XXV/1-2 (June-December 1994), pp. 131-148.

COOPER 2002
COOPER, Barry. 'The Clementi-Beethoven Contract of 1807: A Reinvestigation', in: *Muzio Clementi: Studies and Prospects*, edited by Roberto Illiano, Luca Lévi Sala and Massimiliano Sala, Bologna, Ut Orpheus Edizioni, 2002 (MC, 61), pp. 337-353.

GRAY 2020
GRAY, Myron. 'What is an Author of Early American Music?', in: *Music Publishing and Composers (1750-1850)*, op. cit., pp. 67-81.

GRIBENSKI 1991
GRIBENSKI, Jean. 'Un Métier Difficile: Editeur de Musique à Paris sous la Révolution', in: *Le Tambour et la Harpe: Œuvres, Pratiques et Manifestations sous la Révolution 1788-1800*, edited by Jean-Rémy Julien and Jean Mongrédien, Paris, Editions Du May, 1991, pp. 21-36.

HUME 2014
HUME, Robert D. 'The Value of Music in Eighteenth-Century England: Incomes, Prices, Buying Power – and Some Problems in Cultural Economics', in: *The Huntingdon Library Quarterly*, LXXVII/4 (2014), pp. 373-416.

KASSLER 2020
KASSLER, Michael. 'Dominick Mazzinghi, Seller of Clementi & Co. Instruments in New York City', in: *Galpin Society Journal*, LXXIII (2020), pp. 223-225.

LENNEBERG 2003
LENNEBERG, Hans. *On the Publishing and Dissemination of Music, 1500-1850*, Hillside (NY), Pendragon Press, 2003.

MADDISON 2001
MADDISON, Angus. *The World Economy: A Millennial Perspective*, Paris, OECD, 2001.

RODRÍGUEZ-LORENZO 2020
RODRÍGUEZ-LORENZO, Gloria Araceli. 'La Iberia Musical y Literaria (1842-1846): Connecting the Public and Private Sphere', in: *Music Publishing and Composers (1750-1850), op. cit.*, pp. 279-297.

ROWLAND 2010
*The Correspondence of Muzio Clementi / La corrispondenza di Muzio Clementi*, critical edition by David Rowland, Bologna, Ut Orpheus Edizioni, 2010 (Muzio Clementi Opera Omnia, vol. XIV, CCE, 1).

ROWLAND 2011
ID. 'Clementi's Music Business', in: *The Music Trade in Georgian England*, edited by Michael Kassler, Farnham-Burlington (VT), Ashgate, 2011, pp. 125-157.

ROWLAND 2012
ID. 'Dussek in London's Commercial World', in: *Jan Ladislav Dussek (1760-1812): A Bohemian Composer «en voyage» through Europe*, edited by Roberto Illiano and Rohan H. Stewart-MacDonald, Bologna, Ut Orpheus Edizioni, 2012 (Quaderni Clementiani, 4), pp. 87-111.

ROWLAND 2019
ID. 'Music Publishing in Britain ca. 1840-1900', in: *Music and the Second Industrial Revolution*, edited by Massimiliano Sala, Turnhout, Brepols, 2019 (Music, Science & Technology, 2), pp. 223-244.

ROWLAND 2020
ID. 'Composers, Publishers and the Market in late Georgian Britain', in: *Music Publishing and Composers (1750-1850), op. cit.*, pp. 85-112.

WAINWRIGHT 1982
WAINWRIGHT, David. *Broadwood by Appointment*, London, Quiller, 1982.

WEBER 2004
WEBER, William. *Music and the Middle Classes: The Social Structure of Concert Life in London, Paris and Vienna between 1830 and 1848*, Aldershot-Burlington (VT), Ashgate, ²2004 (Music in Nineteenth-Century Britain).

WOODFIELD 2000A
WOODFIELD, Ian. *Music of the Raj: A Social and Economic History of Music in Late Eighenth-Century Anglo-Indian Society*, Oxford-New York, Oxford University Press, 2000.

WOODFIELD 2000B
ID. 'The Calcutta Piano Trade in the Late Eighteenth Century', in: *Music and British Culture, 1785-1914*, edited by Christina Bashford and Leanne Langley, Oxford, Oxford University Press, 2000, pp. 1-21.

# Soundscapes and Aesthetics

# The Empire's Mechanical Musics: From Soundscape to Reception

*Emmanuel Reibel*
(École normale supérieure de Lyon /
Conservatoire National Supérieur de Musique de Paris)

Mechanical instruments have suffered a bad reputation. In the collective imaginary, they remain tethered to the popular universe of barrel organs, fairgrounds, or to the childish world of musical boxes. They have been the subject of several engrossing studies over the years[1]; but the privileged approach has always been organological — as though the only way to take these instruments seriously was to demonstrate their operational complexity, their brilliant construction, or the ingenuity of their inventors, as if the emphasis placed on the technology of these instruments served to justify the interest one might have for them.

As an alternative to this approach, I propose to examine mechanical musics from the dual perspective of aesthetics and culture. Such a task is facilitated by musicology's efforts, for some time now, to disassemble the musical canon, to contest the hierarchisation of learned and popular cultures, and to reconsider the elements that constitute musical knowledge. More recently, the field of sound studies has shifted the centre of attention away from works in themselves and toward the question of sound. What would the nineteenth century be, after all, without the sound of these mechanical instruments, which filled the streets with a varied repertoire of fashionable songs, military anthems, and opera arias?

To evoke the sound of the Empire requires us, therefore, to take an interest in these mechanical instruments and in these sounds that music history literature has so often silenced. Take, by way of example, the marriage of Napoleon to Marie-Louise I, in early April 1810. Musicologists will typically evoke, first and foremost, Gluck's *Iphigénie en Aulide*, performed at

---

[1]. SIMON 1960; BOWERS 1967-1968; ORD-HUME 1973; HASPELS 1987.

the court theatre at Saint-Cloud on 1 April, and the concert the following night at the Louvre featuring the cantata composed for the occasion by Méhul, the *Ode à l'hymen* written specially by Cherubini, and Gluck's choruses. But the official music was not all that resonated that day: the historic press reveals that, on 2 April, over fifty singers were invited to sing popular songs on the Champs-Élysées, alongside «street orchestras, musettes, barrel organs, viols, jesters, and tightrope dancers»[2].

Mechanical instruments thus played their part in the soundscape of the Empire, and it is worth listening out for them through the evidence provided by the press from that era[3]. I will show how these instruments were not merely components of the soundscape: they also conditioned the ear, thereby contributing to the creation of what I would call more broadly a 'sound culture'. Yet the impact of this sound culture was crucial — for one, because it was a process of circulation, and moreover, because it contributed to conditioning perception and to structuring judgments of taste.

To demonstrate this, I shall begin by evoking, with the support of certain texts, the mechanical soundscape of the Empire; I shall then pause to examine at greater length Maelzel's instruments, displayed in Paris during this period; and finally, I will show how familiarity with these instruments constructed a system of positively and negatively defined values, by which performers and opera singers subsequently come to be judged.

## The Mechanical Soundscape of the Empire

Upon opening newspapers from the Empire, it is not uncommon to land on descriptions of the streets of Paris, such as in this article evoking the Boulevard des Italiens in 1808: «groups of onlookers, stock still, gathered around a mime who is singing the most lively vaudevilles & making abominable faces; a small travelling musician who is trying to produce with residential doorbells the effect of the Dunkerque carillon; and an organ grinder accompanied by two young violinists who are not without talent»[4]. Barrel organs were as much a part of the soundscape of the Parisian street as the sound of horses and carriages over cobblestones, or the various 'cris de Paris', the calls of street vendors. In those days, it should be noted, these organs did not

---

[2]. *Moniteur* 1810: «[…] des orchestres ambulants, de musettes, d'orgues de Barbarie et de vielles, des bouffons, des danseurs de cordes».

[3]. This article is based on a vast historical press corpus of fifteen newspapers from the Empire, and on a digital analysis of the articles on the Théâtre-Italien collected by Jean Mongrédien (Mongrédien 2008).

[4]. *Journal de Paris* 1808a: «[…] badauds groupés, & immobiles comme des poutres, autour d'un mime qui chante des vaudevilles très-gaillards, & fait des grimaces abominables; d'un petit musicien ambulant, qui essaye sur des sonnettes d'appartements l'effet du carillon de Dunkerque, d'un joueur d'orgue de barbarie, qu'accompagnent deux jeunes violons qui ne sont pas sans talent».

play from perforated rolls, which were only invented in the 1840s; it was only in the second half of the century that this borrowed technology, first developed by Joseph Marie Jacquard of the Lyon textile industry, would play its role in the rise of mechanical music right through its Golden Age in the Belle Époque[5]. Before then, these organs played inscribed cylinders, defined by Momigny in the *Encyclopédie méthodique* (1818) like so: «The cylinder organ is the kind that operates by means of a cylinder on which a certain number of pieces have been notated with pins. These pins move the keys of a keyboard which has been fitted to them. Then, by means of a crank handle which one turns, the cylinder moves & places the pins, in succession or several at a time, in contact with the keys that correspond to the pipes. What we call an *orgue de Barbarie* is nothing other than a portable cylinder organ»[6].

If the article quoted above offers no indication of the instrument's repertoire, other texts prove more precise in this regard. The *Mercure de France*, for example, depicts an animated image of the boulevards of Paris in 1811, mentioning — among the peddlers and a thousand other attractions — a barrel organ «playing the Romance from *Le Jardinier Fleuriste*» (referring to the opera by Luigi Giuseppe Balocchi, which had been the recent subject of popular variations)[7]. Another article refers to a passerby stopped in his tracks «by groups of bourgeois pedestrians, awestruck — some by a child doing "Saint Bernard's wheel" between two candles; others around a merchant selling cologne at thirteen sous a roll; some more next to a barrel organ playing Cendrillon's aria out of tune; others around a fortune teller who, for two sous, promises love, happiness, or wealth to all who approach; and others still, next to a young girl, her head humbly wrapped in a dirty veil, and who is singing *Bocage que l'aurore*, etc., or *Mon cœur soupire*, accompanied by a clanking guitar»[8]. Beneath the narrator's obvious disdain for the Parisian populace lies a fascinating soundscape: the aria from *Cendrillon* emanating from the cylinder

---

[5]. That era would see the triumph of Carpentier's Mélotrope, Thibouville-Lamy's Organina, Gavioli's organs, and every model of mechanical piano — before the phonographic age would render all these reproducing instruments obsolete.

[6]. Momigny 1818 (the name of the Panharmonicon appears under the entry 'Métromètre'). «[L']Orgue à cylindre est celui qui va par le moyen d'un cylindre sur lequel on a noté un certain nombre de morceaux avec des pointes. Ces pointes font mouvoir les touches d'un clavier qui leur est approprié. C'est au moyen d'une manivelle que l'on tourne, que le cylindre se meut & présente successivement, ou plusieurs à la fois, ses pointes aux touches qui répondent aux tuyaux. Ce qu'on nomme *orgue de Barbarie* n'est pas autre chose qu'un orgue portatif & à cylindre».

[7]. Mercure de France 1811. The aria from the *Jardinier Fleuriste* is in vogue thanks to the variations published by Xavier Désargus, announced in the *Gazette de France*, 1 February 1811.

[8]. Mercure de France 1810: «[...] par des groupes de bourgeois ébahis, les uns, devant un enfant qui fait la roue de saint Bernard entre deux bouts de chandelle; ceux-ci autour d'un marchand d'eau de Cologne à treize sous le rouleau; ceux-là près d'un orgue de Barbarie qui joue faux l'air de Cendrillon; d'autres autour d'une tireuse de cartes qui, pour deux sous, promet à tout venant de l'amour, du bonheur et des richesses; d'autres enfin auprès d'une jeune fille, dont la tête est modestement enveloppée d'un voile sale, et qui chante en s'accompagnant d'une aigre guitare: *Bocage que l'aurore*, etc. ou *mon cœur soupire*».

organ is an excerpt from Isouard's *opéra-comique*, which had premiered six months prior at the Salle Feydeau; *Bocage que l'aurore* is the title of a Romance by Plantade, while *Mon cœur soupire* is none other than the French translation of 'Voi che sapete', from Mozart's *Marriage of Figaro*. As may be seen, diverse musical horizons commingled freely in the Parisian soundscape.

But mechanical instruments' close association with Parisian street life is only part of a broader picture. Part of what makes cylinder organs so fascinating is their transcendence of spatial boundaries: they could be found as often in Paris as in the provinces, in urban settings as in the countryside, outdoors as well as indoors. Accordingly, mechanical instruments occupied a wide range of functions. Some were used to create dance music, as shown in this engraving drawn from Engramelle's work[9] on musical cylinders; others served as church organs (as, for example, the instrument in the church at Villars-sur-Var, made by Antoine Nicolas Lété in 1816, still preserved and listed as a historical monument). Even if few of them have survived, such instruments were nothing special in those days: several communes had procured them since the eighteenth century in order to compensate for the absence of an instrumentalist. The press occasionally bears a trace of these church-bound mechanical organs — as in this brief in *L'Écho du midi* evoking a cylinder on which are inscribed «the royal mass, hymns, prose pieces, canticles, two beautiful symphonic overtures, etc.»[10]. Elsewhere, far afield from dance or from prayer, were other instruments intended to train captive birds — serinettes, perroquettes, merlines, and other turlutaines — very popular between 1750 and 1850, as demonstrated by Chardin's *La Serinette ou dame variant ses amusements* (1751). These instruments with their high-pitched whistles could perform a wide range of tunes, as was the case of the 'Ferry' serinette, now conserved at the Musée de la Musique in Paris: among its eight offerings are the folksong, 'Malgrough s'en va t'en guerre', and the romance, 'Je suis Lindor', from Nicolas Dezède's incidental music for Beaumarchais's *Barbier de Séville*.

Mechanical instruments also transcended social boundaries. Cylinder organs were not only the province of ambulant musicians; they could also be inlaid with marquetry and figure among the most sought-after aristocratic furnishings. In the 1804 record of a property sale of a count who had been a French ambassador, one finds — in addition to precious items of furniture and a table service for a hundred — several musical instruments, including an organ with five cylinders «in a modern taste, made of solid mahogany»[11]. Beyond cylinder organs, several mechanical instruments became collectors' objects under the Empire, just as they were under the *ancien régime*, when they figured in cabinets of curiosities and in aristocratic salons. These included cylinder clocks and pendulums, which played a different refrain each hour; usually manufactured in Switzerland, these spread various tunes across all of Europe — even

---

[9]. See also instruments à valser, engraving, from ENGRAMELLE 1775.
[10]. ÉCHO 1823: «[...] la messe royale, des hymnes, proses, cantiques, deux belles ouvertures en symphonie, etc.».
[11]. JOURNAL DE PARIS 1804: «[...] d'un goût moderne en acajou massif».

Revolutionary songs, like *La Carmagnole*. These also included collectable snuffboxes containing musical boxes, of the sort that Napoleon would sometimes offer to his most deserving officers[12].

A news article from 1805 describes one such luxury snuffbox containing a musical automaton: «Messieurs Maillardet possess a fifth article about which I will speak separately, because it has the advantage over the others of forming a precious jewel, above any reproach for those of good taste: it's a snuffbox in enamelled gold, further enriched with pearls. The contents of this snuffbox, of ordinary size, are twofold: first, a clock mechanism that makes appear, out from underneath one of the medallions, a bird the size of the smallest hummingbird — which very distinctly sings a serinette tune by swiveling its beak and its wings of gold and azure; after which, it returns all by itself into the box, which closes behind it to leave only an ordinary snuffbox, for the use of whosoever might be rich enough to pay for it»[13].

The tradition of musical automata in France reaches back to Vaucanson's flutist and tambourine player. The first of these concealed beneath its human form an assemblage of pipes, cylinders, pullies, gears, valves, levers, pivots, screws, and cords: these set into motion the artificial lips and fingers of the automaton which made the instrument sound. The second also consisted of thousands of levers and springs, and held in one hand a flageolet into which it blew, and in the other hand a stick beating a drum: he would 'play' some twenty songs, minuets, rigaudons, and contradances. These jewels of science and ingenuity were admired far beyond French borders: the technical apparatuses drawn up by Vaucanson were swiftly translated into English, and Diderot and d'Alembert's *Encyclopédie* accorded them pride of place in the articles titled 'Androïde' and 'Automate'[14]. Such automata would continue to stimulate many mechanicians. In 1801, it was announced that one of them had perfected Vaucauson's flute player: «he has created a young shepherd who plays sixteen songs on the galoubet with clarity and precision». The only drawback: «its sounds are a bit weak»[15]. There was also the trumpeter-automaton of Étienne-Gaspard Robertson, another mechanician who gained an international reputation exhibiting his inventions that mixed science and mystification.

---

[12]. The website of one Toulouse manufacturer (<http://www.leludion.com/event/tabatieres.htm>, accessed September 2023) displays certain models, such as a snuffbox from the 1810s made of ronce de thuya, with tortoiseshell interior, a golden pushbutton, and a musical mechanism with twenty-five pitched lamellae.

[13]. JOURNAL DE L'EMPIRE 1805: «MM. Maillardet possèdent une cinquième pièce dont je parle à part, parce qu'elle a sur les autres l'avantage de former un bijou précieux, et contre lequel le bon goût n'a pas du moins à réclamer; c'est une tabatière en or émaillé, et enrichie de perles: cette tabatière, de grandeur ordinaire, renferme dans un double fond un mouvement d'horlogerie, qui fait sortir de dessous l'un des médaillons un oiseau de la grosseur du plus petit des colibris, et qui chante très distinctement un air de serinette, en agitant son bec et ses ailes d'or et d'azur; après quoi, il rentre de lui-même dans la boîte, qui se referme pour ne plus laisser apercevoir qu'une tabatière ordinaire, et à l'usage de quiconque serait assez riche pour y mettre le prix».

[14]. See REIBEL 2023, Chapter 2.

[15]. MONITEUR 1801: «[...] il a fait un jeune berger qui joue sur le galoubet seize airs de suite, avec beaucoup de netteté et de précision»; «les sons en sont un peu faibles».

Often associated with rare and expensive horological experiments, these mechanical instruments generally displayed an artistic craft worthy of the highest of high society. In the eighteenth century, composers including Handel, Haydn, and Mozart (both father and son) took no exception to writing tunes for these princely toys[16]. It was in this context that Cherubini wrote a piece for cylinder organ in 1805, destined for Peter von Braun's Temple of Night in his domain at Schönau, Austria[17]. The manuscript of this *Andantino* in F Major, written for four voices, is held at the Bibliothèque nationale de France.

This brief panorama of mechanical music that resonated under the Empire is striking in its diversity, extending from Parisian streets to rural churches by way of wealthy aristocratic interiors. Beyond their technological interest, these mechanical instruments participated in what Judith Le Blanc, speaking of operatic parodies, has called a «circular culture», facilitating the circulation of certain music outside of their original milieu: just as they introduced folk or military songs into spaces of higher society, so did they bring selections of learned repertoire to popular spaces. And yet this culture did not only circulate across social boundaries, but also national ones — as we shall see next, with reference to Maelzel's mechanical instruments, presented in Paris during the Empire.

## Maelzel's Automata in the Paris of the Empire

If the story is little known, the name Johann Nepomuk Maelzel (1772-1838) is already familiar to us: the Bavarian, and «first mechanician of H. M. the Emperor of Austria»[18], is primarily remembered by posterity as the inventor of the metronome. But in his day, he earned an extraordinary reputation for his automata, which he presented with the flair of a showman in highly popular spectacles: a mechanical doll, a gymnast android, automated dancers and horsemen, not to mention the famous mechanical Turk — an automated chess player which, it turned out, was a hoax, since it relied on a man to operate the mechanism in hiding. Being also a musician and composer, Maelzel took an interest in mechanical music, and was one of the first to construct automated orchestras. His Panharmonicon, an ancestor of the orchestrion, is known for having captured the attention of Beethoven, who wrote for it his *Wellington's Victory* before falling out with the inventor. What is less well-known is that the Panharmonicon known to Beethoven in the 1810s was the second Panharmonicon; this had been preceded by a first instrument, constructed in 1805[19].

---

[16]. See ORD-HUME 1982.

[17]. See RICE 2006.

[18]. *JOURNAL DU COMMERCE* 1807: «[...] premier mécanicien de S. M. l'empereur d'Autriche».

[19]. See STERL 1981; CHARBON s.d.; WOLF 2012. The information given by Fétis in his *Biographie universelle des musiciens* is partly erroneous. The information contained in the 'Maelzel' article in the *Grove Music Online*

# The Empire's Mechanical Musics

Measuring 4.22 m high, 1.62 m wide, and 97 cm in depth, this first Panharmonicon resembled a small theatre in military decoration; it contained not only organ pipes but actual wind instruments activated mechanically — flutes, piccolos, clarinets, bassoons, oboes, serpents, trumpets, hunting horns, and, to top it all off, a percussion section comprising bass drum (occupying the central throne), timpani, cymbals, and a triangle. He staged demonstrations of his orchestra-machine, attracting large crowds and arousing the interests of impresarios: after two years in Vienna, Maelzel decided in 1807 to cast a wider net by exhibiting it in Paris, first in the open-air setting of the Champ de Mars, then in concerts with paid admission.

The *Journal de l'Empire* was the first to announce Maelzel's arrival, on 28 February 1807: as it explained, Cherubini, Méhul, Pleyel, and Rigel had already offered the mechanician pieces of music written for the instrument. Beginning on 4 March, two daily concerts were organised at the Hôtel Montmorency on the Rue du Montblanc at the corner of the Chaussée d'Antin (not far from the Salle Favart), a private mansion rented by Maelzel for 1000 francs per month. We know, thanks to the memoirs of Count Ludwig von Bentheim-Steinfurt who was living in Paris at the time, that the instrument was placed in a rotunda with a high, domed ceiling, opening onto a superb and richly decorated oval salon that could seat 60 to 70 listeners[20]. The cost of a ticket was high (6 francs), with Maelzel wishing to attract a refined audience.

The concert program, over two hours long, appears in the *Affiches, annonces et avis divers* of 8 March: the first half offered Haydn's Symphony No. 100 ('Military'), Cherubini's *L'Écho* (composed specially), the overture to *Médée* (also by Cherubini), and the Finale of another unspecified Haydn symphony. On the second half: six fanfares by Maelzel himself, four French marches, the overture to Mozart's *Clemenza di Tito*, and a suite of German dances also by Maelzel[21]. The mix of genres is utterly characteristic of the repertoire for mechanical

---

*Dictionary* (see Thayer 2021) is partly inexact: Maelzel's first mechanical orchestra was already known as the 'Panharmonicon', and he only arrived in Paris in 1807.

[20]. See Monheim 1997. Count von Bentheim-Steinfurt contains, in somewhat shaky French, an interesting description (15 April 1807, p. 269): «[Le panharmonicon] est placé dans une très belle rotonde avec un plafond en dome très élevé, et puis un superbe salon oval pour l'auditoire avec six portes forment aussi fenetres, et postiches en glaces les banaux [bandeaux] entre deux sont ornées de belles sculptures richement dorés sur un fond soupe au lait, du luxe qui brilloit chez les grands avant la revolution, dans le genre de l'hotel de Biron (qu'habite Caprara) mais la dorure a l'hotel de Montmorenci est bien placée et fraiche encore, enfin il seroit impossible a trouver un emplacement mieux choisir et plus analogue pour placer le Panharmonicon, c'est come s'il auroit eté fait exprès pour cela».

[21]. Further details are offered in Count Ludwig von Bentheim-Steinfurt's journal. Regarding the four French marches: «[...] la première est de M. Nadermann. On les entend d'abord dans le lointain; elles se rapprochent peu à peu, et parviennent par un crescendo, jusqu'au plus grand *forte*». Regarding Haydn's 'Military' Symphony: «Ce morceau fait connaître la perfection du Panharmonicon, par les différents solos qu'il contient pour la flûte, le hautbois et la trompette, et par plusieurs passages de musique turque». On Maelzel's fanfares: «Elles sont exécutées par quatre trompettes et par les timbales». On his German dances: «Elles réunissent des solos de tous les instruments. Il est à remarquer que ces danses, au nombre de douze, sont chacune dans un ton différent, et se

instruments; but the presence of Mozart and Haydn is noteworthy, at a time when their music was just starting to be heard in Paris: the Panharmonicon thus contributed to the circulation and diffusion of Viennese repertoire in Paris.

This mechanical orchestra's sojourn in Paris turned out to be anything but incidental. For one, it caught the attention of the imperial family: the *Gazette de France* reveals that the Empress appeared in person at the Hotel Montmorency on 5 March to discover the instrument. Furthermore, it won over the press: on 9 March, the *Journal de l'Empire* devoted a three-page *feuilleton* to the Panharmonicon, no less coverage than given to premieres at the Opéra. But above all, it provoked a major success among the broader public, to such an extent that the daily concerts continued over several weeks. Announcements of these sessions are publicised in several newspapers — the *Journal de l'Empire*, the *Journal du commerce*, the *Journal de Paris*, the *Gazette de France*, the *Gazette national ou moniteur universel*, the *Journal des arts* — and one even finds mention of them in provincial papers, such as the *Journal du département de la Haute-Vienne*. Maelzel's two daily concerts figured on the calendar of spectacles alongside theatrical or lyrical performances (as shown here, for example, in the *Gazette de France* of 21 April), and newspapers occasionally published the reactions of enthusiastic attendees. The success was such that during the summer Maelzel opened the room adjoining the salon in which the Panharmonicon was kept: these less well-placed auditors paid half-price admission (3 francs rather than 6 francs, which was not nothing, even so). The ingenious mechanician knew how to prolong his success by rekindling the curiosity of his Parisian public over time: he later engraved a cylinder with a new piece composed by Steibelt to show off the sonorities of the instrument. This was a descriptive piece, evoking a day in the countryside, representing successively the sounds of «the calm of the night, sunrise, the cockcrow, the shepherd and the labourer heading to the fields, the hunter with hounds, etc., etc.»[22].

After a brief interruption in November 1807 — during which the Panharmonicon was moved to the Rue du Lycée, near the Palais-Royal — the daily séances resumed from 12 December, even once Maelzel left Paris. The longevity of these concerts beggars belief: they continued each day until July 1808, at which point the pace was reduced to four weekly concerts for the summer. On 12 August, the *Journal de l'Empire* announced the Viennese mechanician's return to Paris to present a new invention, albeit a more modest one: the trumpet-automaton. A description may be found in the *Journal de Paris* shortly thereafter:

---

succèdent sans interruption: ce qui développe la faculté unique du Panharmonicon». Journal entry of 15 April 1807, p. 270, cited in MONHEIM 1997, p. 141.

[22]. MONITEUR 1807: «[...] le calme de la nuit, le lever du soleil, le chant du coq, le berger et le laboureur allant aux champs, le chasseur avec sa meute, etc. etc.».

## The Empire's Mechanical Musics

> The inventor of the Panharmonicon, M. Maelhel [sic], of Vienna, has just arrived in Paris with an automaton representing a life-sized trumpeter. He is not placed upon a stand like those of the famed Vaucanson; rather, the entire mechanism is placed within *the body itself*. He is kept under a tent, from which it emerges, dressed in the uniform of the cuirassiers of the regiment of Archduke Albert de Saxe Teschen, and he executes all the Austrian manoeuvres and marches. Following which he returns inside his tent, changes costume, and re-emerges a moment later, having transformed into a trumpeter of the guard of H. M. the Emperor of the French. As such, he executes all the manoeuvres and marches of the imperial guard. This automaton is currently placed in the hall of the old Palais du Tribunat, and has only been seen by certain people of the imperial court, of the art world, and some amateurs; but we hope that it will be brought elsewhere without delay, such that the public may also see it[23].

Maelzel's automaton constitutes something of a burlesque echo of the broader history taking place in the European theatre. Recall that after the French victory at Austerlitz on 2 December 1805, the Austrians were obliged to sign the Peace of Pressburg; in 1808, Austria had not yet renewed the hostilities that would lead to its defeat at Wagram on 6 July 1809. It was during this window that Maelzel, who kept company with the entire Viennese aristocracy, could be received by Napoleon and present to him this automaton that could perform all the French and Austrian military marches. Maelzel's mechanical instruments thus did not merely bring music from one side of the border to the other; they were rather singular agents of a transcultural dialogue.

One can continue tracking Maelzel's subsequent adventures in France through the press, which contains a nearly continuous record of the daily Panharmonicon concerts, now centred around the trumpeter-automaton, up until 3 July 1809 — thus spanning over two years in total. In the autumn, it was announced in the press that Maelzel was working on a second Panharmonicon in Austria: «the French government has granted him rooms in the imperial castle of Vienna, where he is working for the Prince Viceroy of Italy on what is perhaps an even more perfect Panharmonicon». The Viceroy of Italy was none other than Eugène

---

[23]. *Journal de Paris* 1808b: «L'auteur du panharmonicon, M. Maelhel [sic], de Vienne, vient d'arriver à Paris avec un automate, représentant un trompette de grandeur naturelle. Il n'est placé sur aucun piedestal, comme sont ceux du célèbre Vaucanson; mais le mécanisme entier est placé *dans le corps même*. Il est logé sous une tente, d'où il sort vêtu de l'uniforme des cuirassiers du régiment de l'Archiduc Albert de Saxe Teschen, et exécute toutes les manœuvres et marches autrichiennes. D'après cela il rentre dans la tente, change de costume, et en sort un moment après transformé en trompette de la garde de S. M. L'Empereur des Français. Il exécute comme tel toutes les manœuvres, et marches de la garde impériale. Cet automate est placé dans ce moment dans la salle de l'ancien palais du Tribunat, et n'a été vu que par quelques personnes de la cour impériale, et par les gens de l'art et amateurs; mais on espère qu'il sera incessamment transporté ailleurs, où le public pourra aussi le voir».

de Beauharnais, Napoleon's stepson. It may be inferred from this that Napoleon placed an order with Maelzel for a new mechanical orchestra[24]. One finds traces of the Panharmonicon being heard at the Cour des Fontaines from the summer of 1810 until November of that year. But the *Mercure de France* announced on 11 August 1810 the sale of this mechanical orchestra for the colossal sum of 100,000 francs. It is possible that Napoleon ended up purchasing this instrument directly for Eugène de Beauharnais; further sources would be required in order to confirm this. And certain other points also remain unclear: what instrument was being referred to when, in April 1814, the press announced séances with a 'Panharmonicon-métallico' on Rue Saint-Honoré? And when Maelzel was back in Paris in the autumn of 1815 to showcase his Panharmonicon at the Salle Louvois, was this the second instrument that had since been constructed in Vienna, and for which Beethoven composed *Wellington's Victory*?

For the time being, two main observations will have to suffice. First: the concerts organised by Maelzel became so ritualised as to enter the Panharmonicon into the soundscape of the Empire. Even if his name is mangled by the press in a thousand different ways, the Viennese mechanician became well known to Parisians of the time. It may be said that the Panharmonicon contributed to Maelzel's growing reputation in Paris, and that his fame was critical to the subsequent battle he would wage there: the presentation of the metronome to the French musical and scientific milieu, in order to patent it in 1815[25]. It was this new machine — adapted from Winckel's chronometer, which differed from the pendulum then in use by sounding out the beats — that characterised the soundscape of the Empire at its close. In 1815, Maelzel received the unanimous support of the Conservatoire and of the Institut; and it is reasonable to hypothesise that the relationships Maelzel had established during his precious stay in Paris, with his Panharmonicon seances, proved decisive in this respect. Second: the story of the Panharmonicon showcases the homogenous and dynamic nature of the soundscape of the Empire — homogenous insofar as mechanical music enabled a sort of sonic continuum between the military marches that resounded over battlegrounds and the musics that filled private salons; and dynamic insofar as this mechanical music served as a means of transcultural circulation between France and Austria. The story would continue beyond Maelzel and into the years of the Bourbon Restoration: for example, the Dresden mechanician Friedrich Kaufmann — himself an inventor of an automatic orchestra in 1805 (the belloneon, deploying 24 trumpets and two drums), and of a trumpeter-automaton in 1812 — would also come to Paris and exhibit a variety of mechanical instruments, including the harmonichord and the cordaulodion, in his shop located at 21 Rue de la Paix.

---

[24]. Ebeling – Leben 2016; Ebeling 2017.
[25]. Reibel 2023.

# The Empire's Mechanical Musics

## Music Criticism and the Anti-Mechanical Ideal

Yet the impact of these mechanical musics goes beyond the creation of this homogeneous and dynamic soundscape: mechanical musics established new parameters by which to structure a value system. Indeed, the rise of mechanical music in this era was a factor in reshaping how music in general was heard and judged, from the perspective of both performance and composition[26].

### *From the Point of View of Performance*

At the time of the Empire, people did not fear, as they would in the mid nineteenth century, that machines would entirely replace musicians. Even so, however, improvements in mechanical organology led some to observe a narrowing gap between man and machine: cylinder organs and mechanical orchestras, no longer mere toys, appeared as potential rivals to interpreters. That, in particular, is what struck those who heard Maelzel's Panharmonicon. The testimony is virtually unanimous: although it was occasionally judged too loud during *tutti* effects (perhaps due to the acoustic of the salon in the Hotel Montmorency)[27], the instrument's precision and versatility were admired. As may be read in the press, «Never before had mechanical movement come so near to the inimitable perfection of human movement»[28]. Just as mechanical music was approaching human performance ever more closely — just as the murmurings increasingly ventured, sometimes jokingly, that machines have become more steady, more precise, more reliable, and less expensive than musicians — performers urgently needed to distinguish themselves from the machines. Good interpretation at the dawn of the nineteenth century, therefore, came to be often considered that which did not content itself with technical precision, but which cultivated those elements that the machine did not possess: soul, fire, warmth, life. As early as 1804, in his preface to the *Méthode de piano du Conservatoire*, Méhul excoriated «those pianists condemned to be nothing but brilliant machines», who «would one day regret the time they had devoted exclusively to purely mechanical labour»[29].

Mechanical instruments thus became something of a foil undergirding contemporaneous critical discourse. This could even extend to the voice — such as in this appreciative review of Mademoiselle Laurenzetti at the Théâtre-Italien: «Her performance, her singing, sparkle with ardour [...]; this is nothing like a singing-machine, like Vaucanson's flute-player or M.

---

[26]. This section draws directly from Chapter 2 of *ibidem*.

[27]. See the diary of Count Ludwig von Bentheim-Steinfurt, entry of 15 April 1807 (cited above): «Ces fanfares font un tres bon effet mais crient un peu trop».

[28]. *Journal de l'Empire* 1807: «Jamais le mouvement mécanique ne s'était autant rapproché de l'inimitable perfection des mouvements de l'homme».

[29]. Adam 1804, p. ii: «[...] regretteront un jour le temps qu'ils auront exclusivement employé à un travail purement mécanique». The quotation is drawn from a speech delivered by Méhul and presented as an epigraph.

Olivier's automata, this is a young actress with a most promising intellect»[30]. In contrast, in 1810, singers without expression were castigated for privileging their throats over their hearts: «these trilling machines, like serinettes, never tire out; they remain just as cool as their cold, embellished tapestry»[31].

The reference to the serinette — very popular between 1750 and 1850, as discussed above — is especially interesting. This instrument, operated with a crank handle, allowed one to make birds in an aviary sing. But with growing awareness over time, the use of the serinette came increasingly under debate[32]. For in fact, this mechanical instrument was provoking a purely artificial effect: it was distorting the song of the serin itself, in favour of a learned melody. The serinette thus came to represent a type of superficial learning, as demonstrated by the appearance, in 1808, under the Empire of the French verb '*seriner*' ('to play the serinette', but also figuratively, 'to repeat' or 'to bang on about'): whether the object of *seriner* was a melody or a lesson, the word absorbed a pejorative connotation, reflecting an idea of servile, and sterile, repetition.

Such vocabulary already began to pepper music criticism at the beginning of the century. Regarding the singer François Laÿs, for example: «All of those chirping or warbling Italians would be mistaken for serinettes compared to this French singer»[33]. The image of the serinette became a means of reducing Italian singers to the rung of machines, suitable for training serins and parakeets — thereby enhancing the value of French artists. One might perceive a conflict between Italian and French aesthetics starting to surface from beneath this cutthroat critique — the disdain for 'warbling' (*ramage*) refers to a melody learned mechanically, by force, in contrast to the natural motion of singing. Recourse to this metaphor would only intensify during the Restoration. How was the singer Carolina Naldi, for example? She sang «like a serinette» and played «like an automaton»[34]. And the tenor Marco Bordogni? An «agreeable serinette»[35]. What about Laure Cinti-Damoreau? Another «agreeable serinette, but rather weak»[36]. As for Maria García, on the other hand: «All the singing serinettes pale in comparison to such a live and manifest talent»[37].

---

[30]. COURRIER 1807: «Son jeu, son chant étincellent d'ardeur [...]; ce n'est point une machine chantante comme le joueur de flûte de Vaucanson et les automates de M. Olivier, c'est une jeune actrice dont l'intelligence promet beaucoup».

[31]. JOURNAL DE L'EMPIRE 1810: «[...] ces machines à roulades ne se fatiguent pas plus que des serinettes; elles restent aussi froides que les froids canevas qu'elles brodent».

[32]. DEPLANCK 1860.

[33]. DÉBATS 1802B: «Il n'y a point d'italien à gazouillement et à ramage qu'on ne prenne pour une serinette auprès de ce chanteur français».

[34]. MIROIR 1822.

[35]. JOURNAL DES THÉÂTRES 1826.

[36]. FIGARO 1826: «[...] serinette agréable, mais bien faible».

[37]. PANDORE 1826: «Toutes les serinettes chantantes semblent bien pâles à côté d'un talent si vif et si franc».

# The Empire's Mechanical Musics

## *From the Point of View of Composition*

If mechanical music was beginning to constitute a negative image against which to contrast ideals of musical performance, it was also coming to structure compositional values. To reduce a work to 'mechanical music' was tantamount to excluding it from the field of art, or to demean it as simple artisanry. It was not rare for a critic to reduce a work to 'mechanical procedures'; and to do so was always to discredit the work, assimilating it to a manufactured product. As it happened, the real or supposed 'mechanisation' of music became above all a choice weapon in the aesthetic debates between national schools. Already in 1802, torchbearers for Italian music panned French opera, arguing that «clever combinations of chords and brilliant orchestral effects are nothing but overcomplicated trifles and mechanical procedures so long as they are stripped of melody, as melody alone gives life and soul to musical productions»[38]. This point of view relied upon an old and intransigent critical trope, according to which the French possessed the greatest science of harmony and of orchestration, whereas the Italians surpassed them in the art of melody. Partisans of the Italian school clearly set the realm of melody (music's soul and spiritual dimension) in opposition against that of harmony (music's mechanical and material dimension). In the quarrels over Rossinism some years later, similar reproaches would be made toward French music, «that deluge of notes, that instrumental racket so prevalent in the modern school, which threatens to reduce art to purely mechanical schemes, in accordance with the methods of the Conservatoire and the Institut»[39].

In a twist of historical irony, the other camp — partisans of the French school — used the same image to deprecate Italian opera. Since the start of the century, they condemned composers south of the Alps who sought to «turn the art music into a mechanical game», this time on the grounds that they neglected the poetic text, reducing opera to a simple vocal demonstration dissociated from any dramatic intelligence[40]. Music that was pleasing in itself, lacking any link to sentiment or dramatic context, could risk being labelled 'mechanical'. Partisans of the French school never missed an opportunity to point out the Italians' lack of

---

[38]. *Débats* 1802A (in an article on *Gli zingari in fiera* by Paisiello): «[...] de savantes combinaisons d'accords, de brillants effets d'orchestre ne sont que des bagatelles difficiles et des procédés mécaniques, s'ils sont absolument dépouillés de cette mélodie qui, seule, donne la vie et l'âme aux productions musicales».

[39]. *Quotidienne* 1824: «[...] ce déluge de notes, ce fracas d'instruments qui prévaut dans l'école moderne et qui menace de réduire l'art à des combinaisons purement mécaniques, selon la méthode du Conservatoire et de l'Institut».

[40]. *Journal du commerce* 1804A: «Plusieurs de nos artistes, soit compositeurs, soit exécutants, s'efforcent de faire de l'art musical un jeu mécanique; ils voudraient le détacher entièrement de l'esprit et de l'âme pour le réduire à des combinaisons de manœuvres; mais notre goût pour la poésie dramatique lutte encore contre cette dégradation et conserve encore à la musique quelques rapports avec le sentiment et l'intelligence, tandis qu'en Italie, la rupture est depuis longtemps déclarée».

dramatic sensibility, which they likened to the stiffness and repetitiveness of an automaton. As one critic put it, writing about Ferdinando Paer in 1812: «Vaucanson's flute-player, even though it may charm our ears, has never rendered feeling»[41]. Attention was drawn as early as 1804 to «those mechanical refinements that have been introduced [...] into Italian music, which may well have produced a keen effect when first used, but which have since been deadened by abuse at every opportunity»[42].

The 'mechanistic' quality of musical composition thus appears as a critical weapon at the heart of aesthetic debates, used by the anti-French camp to point out failings in melodic invention, brandished by the anti-Italian camp to denounce the reduction of art to formulas, to something like a mere manufactured product. If such quarrels were already bubbling beneath the surface since the start of the century, they erupted with Rossini's arrival to Paris. His adversaries would find their spokesman in the form of composer Henri-Montan Berton, professor at the Conservatoire and member of the Institut. Berton authored an anti-Rossinist tract titled *De la musique mécanique et de la musique philosophique*. In the conclusion of the pamphlet, he staged a dialogue designed to «prove» the mechanicity of Rossini's music. Having discovered some days prior the chess-playing automaton designed by Maelzel, the famed inventor of the metronome and the Panharmonicon, Berton reportedly asked the following question: «Because you have calculated all of the potentialities on the chessboard and found them to be far more numerous than the harmonic potentialities of our musical system, would you also be able to invent a machine capable of composing music?». To which Maelzel is said to have responded: «Yes, I could make one capable of composing music like to that of MM.\*\*\*, but it would not be able to produce anything like the works of the Mozarts, the Cimarosas, the Sacchinis, etc., etc.; I have not been granted such power. "My art has no entitlement, only to Divinity does such a claim belong"»[43].

This no doubt fictitious dialogue suggests that the work of MM\*\*\* [Rossini] is akin to that of a simple musical box, infinitely reproducible. But only a few years earlier, it was Rossini's

---

[41]. *Journal de Paris* 1812 (writing about Paer's *Camilla*): «[...] le flûteur de Vaucanson, tout en charmant nos oreilles, n'a jamais peint un sentiment».

[42]. *Journal du commerce* 1804B: «[...] ces raffinements mécaniques qui se sont introduits [...] dans la musique italienne, dont l'effet a pu être piquant la première fois qu'on les a employés, mais qui s'est émoussé par l'abus qu'on en a fait à tout propos». See also Fétis 1829, on Rossini's *Mathilde di Shabran*: «On ne peut disconvenir qu'il y ait dans *Matilda* beaucoup de *crescendo*, de mouvements de valse et tous les moyens mécaniques d'effet imaginés par Rossini, et prodigués par lui dans les ouvrages de sa seconde manière, c'est-à-dire, dans ceux qu'il écrivit depuis 1816 jusqu'en 1824».

[43]. Berton 1826, p 42. The idea of an instrument able to compose music recalls the story of the Componium, an «improvising mechanical orchestra», exhibited in Paris in 1824, which caused the members of the Académie des Beaux-Arts, including Berton, to refute the epithet of «improviser» (see *Le Moniteur universel*, 4 and 6 February 1824). But Berton's text is issued from articles in *L'Abeille* written as early as 1821, and thus before the Componium. I thank Étienne Jardin for drawing my attention to this detail.

imitators who had been decried as mechanical, mere reflections of the living model. What conclusion might one draw from this? Perhaps that in the early days of the industrial revolution, the worst possible accusation consisted in knocking the music of the rival camp down to the status of a manufactured product — without soul, therefore without art. The new benchmarks of value were, in composition as in performance, that which a machine did not possess — in other words, taste would thenceforth be structured in opposition to mechanical music.

## Conclusion

Under the Empire, mechanical music never ceased to develop, continuing along the flourishing path that had begun in the previous century. It is of particular interest insofar as it crossed social, geographic, and institutional boundaries: from Paris to the provinces; from collectors' items preserved by wealthy aristocrats to cylinder organs animating the street and countryside alike, from churches and popular fairgrounds to private concerts. Mechanical music was thus omnipresent, sometimes one simple element of a soundscape, sometimes a spectacular object on display.

Maelzel's instruments, discussed here at particular length, contributed in particular to the circulation of melodies in such a way as to blur the boundaries between the learned and the popular. They facilitated transcultural dynamics insofar as they disseminated Austrian music in France, boldly placing the two cultures in close contact at a moment when the nations faced each other on the battlefield. Moreover, they facilitated transgenerational dynamics, because, prior to recorded music, these mechanical instruments were a medium that could travel not only from one country to another, but from one generation to the next.

In those days, listeners and critics grew so familiar with mechanical music that it came to structure their perception and judgments of taste. And yet, while the machine may appear to have represented certain ideals (regularity, precision, efficiency, speed), in critical discourse, the 'mechanisation' of performers was most often perceived negatively. The machine thus became an anti-ideal, connoting boredom and the absence of expression or of life. From then on, it was expected that pianists should be more than mere musical machines, that singers should no longer content themselves with being agreeable serinettes, and even that composers should guard against mechanical facility. Should one conclude from this that the aesthetic of Romanticism was nourished by a rejection of mechanical musics? The question is rather complex, given that when Berton demolished Rossini by reducing his music to a potential Maelzel invention, it was the Romantics themselves — Rossini and his school — who were being denounced as mechanical. On the other hand, the ideal of non-mechanicity would soon become widely held, transcending the various quarrels and national rivalries, eventually becoming a strong marker of Romantic sensibility. One might thus interpret Romanticism as the shadow or the flipside of technical modernity: as Michael Löwy and Robert Sayre have shown, it was a reaction against a science that would rationalise the world; it was a revolt against the desecration of nature brought about by machines; it opposed scientific evidence with metaphysical doubt; and, up against the mechanisation of industrial rationality, it brandished the spiritualism of artistic experience[44]. The mechanical soundscape of the Empire is, therefore, of far more than anecdotal interest: one may affirm that it contributed to shaping nineteenth-century taste.

*Translation: Peter Asimov*

## Bibliography

Adam 1804
Adam, Louis. *Méthode de piano du Conservatoire*, Paris, Imprimerie du Conservatoire de musique, 1804.

Berton 1826
Berton, Henri-Montan. *De la musique mécanique et de la musique philosophique*, Paris, A. Eymery, 1826.

Bowers 1967-1968
Bowers, Q. David. *A Guidebook of Automatic Musical Instruments*, New York, Vestal, 1967-1968.

Charbon s.d.
Charbon, Paul. 'La carrière aventureuse de Johann Nepomuck Maelzel et son rôle dans la création du métronome', <https://www.leducation-musicale.com/nepomuck_maelzel.pdf>, accessed September 2023.

*Courrier* 1807
*Le Courrier des spectacles ou journal des théâtres*, 27 April 1807.

*Débats* 1802a
*Journal des débats*, 15 May 1802.

*Débats* 1802b
*Journal des débats*, 8 September 1802.

Deplanck 1860
Deplanck, Alexandre. 'Le merle et la serinette', in: Id. *Petit Recueil poétique dédié au jeune âge*, Lille, Horemans, 1860.

---

[44]. Löwy – Sayre 1992.

EBELING 2017
EBELING, Jörg. '«Objets d'une affection particulière»': le collezioni di Eugenio di Beauharnais a Milano', in: *Il palazzo reale di Milano in età napoleonica (1796-1814)*, edited by Giovanna D'Amia, Viterbo, BetaGamma, 2017, pp. 95-11.

EBELING – LEBEN 2016
ID. – LEBEN, Ernst Ulrich. 'La Salle à manger', in: *Le style Empire: l'hôtel de Beauharnais à Paris. La résidence de l'ambassadeur d'Allemagne*, edited by Jörg Ebeling and Ernst Ulrich Leben, Paris, Flammarion, 2016, pp. 211-215.

ÉCHO 1823
*L'Écho du midi*, 8 August 1823, p. 4.

ENGRAMELLE 1775
ENGRAMELLE, Marie-Dominique-Joseph. *La Tonotechnie ou l'art de noter les cylindres*, Paris, P.-M. Delaguette, 1775.

FÉTIS 1829
FÉTIS, François-Joseph. *Revue musicale*, VI (1829), pp. 304-309.

FIGARO 1826
*Le Figaro*, 18 August 1826.

HASPELS 1987
HASPELS, Jan Jaap L. *Automatic Musical Instruments: Their Mechanics and Their Music, 1580-1820*, Utrecht, Kluwer, 1987.

JOURNAL DE L'EMPIRE 1805
'Arts mécaniques. Pièces automates de Maillardet, père et fils', in: *Journal de l'Empire*, 10 November 1805, p. 1.

JOURNAL DE L'EMPIRE 1807
*Journal de l'Empire*, 9 March 1807.

JOURNAL DE L'EMPIRE 1810
'Académie impériale de musique', in: *Journal de l'Empire*, 24 March 1810, p. 1.

JOURNAL DE PARIS 1804
*Journal de Paris*, 21 June 1804, p. 10.

JOURNAL DE PARIS 1808A
G****. 'Des pipes, des grosses pierres et des badauds', in: *Journal de Paris*, 11 August 1808, p. 5.

*Journal de Paris* 1808b
*Journal de Paris*, 20 September 1808, p. 4.

*Journal de Paris* 1812
*Journal de Paris*, 26 May 1812.

*Journal des théâtres* 1826
*Journal des théâtres, de la literature et des arts*, 21 December 1826.

*Journal du commerce* 1804a
*Journal du commerce, de politique et de littérature*, 8 April 1804.

*Journal du commerce* 1804b
*Journal du commerce, de politique et de littérature*, 19 July 1804.

*Journal du commerce* 1807
*Journal du commerce*, 8 March 1807, p. 267.

Löwy – Sayre 1992
Löwy, Michael – Sayre, Robert. *Révolte et mélancolie. Le romantisme à contre-courant de la modernité*, Paris, Payot, 1992.

*Mercure de France* 1810
'Variétés. Chronique de Paris', in: *Mercure de France*, 8 September 1810, p. 46.

*Mercure de France* 1811
'Variétés. Chronique de Paris', in: *Le Mercure de France*, 25 May 1811, p. 362.

*Miroir* 1822
*Le Miroir des spectacles*, 13 December 1822.

Momigny 1818
Momigny, Jérôme Joseph. 'Orgue à Cylindre', in: *Encyclopédie méthodique. 2: Musique*, Paris, Panckoucke, 1818, p. 243.

Mongrédien 2008
Mongrédien, Jean. *Le Théâtre-Italien de Paris, 1801-1831: chronologie et documents*, 8 vols., Lyon-Venice, Symétrie-Palazzetto Bru Zane, 2008.

Monheim 1997
Monheim, Annette. *Ein Westfale in Paris. Die Tagebücher des Ludwig Grafen von Bentheim-Steinfurt aus den Jahren 1806-1807*, Münster, Lit Verlag, 1997.

## The Empire's Mechanical Musics

Moniteur 1801
*Gazette nationale ou le moniteur universel*, 18 September 1801, p. 1.

Moniteur 1810
'Intérieur. Paris, le 9 avril', in: *Gazette nationale ou le moniteur universel*, 10 April 1810, p. 3.

Ord-Hume 1973
Ord-Hume, Arthur Wolfgang Julius Gerald. *Clockwork Music: An Illustrated Musical History of Mechanical Musical Instruments*, London, G. Allen and Unwin, 1973.

Ord-Hume 1982
Id. *Joseph Haydn and the Mechanical Organ*, Cardiff, University College Cardiff Press, 1982.

Pandore 1826
*La Pandore*, 30 June 1826.

Quotidienne 1824
*La Quotidienne*, 12 January 1824.

Reibel 2023
Reibel, Emmanuel. *Du métronome au gramophone. Musique et révolution industrielle*, Paris, Fayard, 2023.

Rice 2006
Rice, John A. *The Temple of Night at Schönau: Architecture, Music, and Theater in a Late Eighteenth-Century Viennese Garden*, Philadelphia, American Philosophical Society, 2006.

Simon 1960
Simon, Ernst. *Mechanische Musikinstrumente füherer Zeiten und ihre Musik*, Wiesbaden, Breitkopf & Härtel, 1960.

Sterl 1981
Sterl, Raimund W.
'Johann Nepomuk Maelzel und seine Erfindungen', in: *Musik in Bayern*, XXII (1981), pp. 139-150.

Thayer 2021
Thayer, Alexander Wheelock. 'Johann Nepomuk Maelzel' (revised by Dixie Harvey), in: *New Grove Online*, 2021, <www.oxfordmusiconline.com/grovemusic/>, accessed November 2023.

Wolf 2012
Wolf, Rebecca. *Die Musikmaschinen von Kaufmann, Mälzel und Robertson: eine Quellenedition*, Munich, Deutsches Museum, 2012.

# Imaginary Soundscapes: The Sounds of Portuguese Music as Captured by German Travellers at the End of the *Ancien Régime*

*Inês Thomas Almeida*
(IELT – FCSH, Universidade Nova de Lisboa)[1]

THE SIGNIFICANT INCREASE, in the second half of the 18th century, of travels to Portugal from northern and central Europe led to an exponential growth of travel accounts that portrayed, in different ways, the Portuguese reality through foreign eyes. Even if it is true that the information they contain is precious for the characterisation of the musical practices of the time, great caution is required in using this type of source. Not only the description, but also what they describe and how they do it, varies according to the geographical origin of the travellers, their religious orientation, their political, cultural, and socio-economic positioning, their personal biography, and the target audience for whom the account is intended. These, among other parameters, are indispensable elements in the methodological analysis of travel literature, aiming, as far as possible, at separating objective elements (e.g., the day and place of a particular musical event, type and number of instruments, or the kind of repertoire performed) from the subjective ones (e.g., opinions, positive or negative appreciation of a particular practice, description of a certain object in detriment of another, etc.[2]).

Among these accounts, we find several written by German visitors, which are the object of the present study[3]. In this article, I will attempt to present in broad strokes some of the

---

[1]. The author is a Postdoctoral Research Fellow funded by the FCT – Fundação para a Ciência e Tecnologia, Reference UIDB/00657/2020.

[2]. On the methodology of analysis of travel reports in musicological studies, see ALMEIDA 2022.

[3]. I am deeply grateful to Rui Vieira Nery, who over the course of several years compiled and identified more than three hundred accounts of foreign travellers in Portugal between 1750 and 1834 with music descriptions, in a study that is expected to be published soon, and without which my research could not have taken place.

observations made by German visitors regarding sound involvement in Portugal and suggest possible approaches to contextualise these observations. The list of examples, far from being exhaustive, should be taken as an illustration of the dynamics between the real and the projected. The original German version of each quotation is placed in a footnote. All translations and transcriptions, unless otherwise indicated, have been made by the author.

## Expected Soundscapes: Hearing the Streets

German travellers of this period tended to seek the manifestation of a national character, mirroring the pre-Romantic sensitivity of their homeland, and to react negatively when they did not find in Portugal the same elements they had in their own country[4]. Portuguese musical practice, embedded with Iberian, Italian and Counter-Reformist influences, was viewed with perplexity, rejection, and vivid critique by these visitors, who searched for the imagined elements of what they thought to be the true Portuguese nation. These elements would be found — so they believed — in the common people, expressing a primordial naturalness that had not yet been corrupted. Thus, one of the practices travellers positively described were traditional dances, the sensuality of the women's natural voices, the streets filled with the strange polyphony of the church bells and cannon roars, the chants of the shepherds, the cries of water carriers and the sad songs of the blind, a soundscape focused on what the traveller, according to their conception of reality, expected to find.

In January 1797, a Dutch-German businessman allegedly traveled through Portugal. His travelogue, which has no indication of authorship except the abbreviation 'H\*\*', was published in 1799 in German translation. The text mainly focuses on the description of a bullfight in Lisbon and Portuguese life in the province of Alentejo, a predominantly rural region in the interior of the country. The arrival of a Portuguese prince and future King John VI in Évora, on 12 January 1797, was described as follows:

> Just as we were returning from the convent, the Prince and Princess of Brazil arrived with their entourage. [...] The Prince was seated on a chaise coupée pulled by two mules, beside him his nephew, the Infant. A detachment of cavalry escorted the car: [...] Many chaises and carriages finished the procession. All the bells of the countless churches were ringing and making such a noise as to make you lose your eyesight and your hearing[5].

---

[4]. The detailed study of the German view on musical practice in Portugal in the second half of the 18th century was the subject of my doctoral thesis, *The German Gaze: Musical Practice in Portugal at the End of the Ancien Régime According to German Sources*. See ALMEIDA 2021.

[5]. «Gerade als wir aus dem Kloster zurück gingen, kam der Prinz und die Prinzessin von Brasilien mit ihrem ganzen Gefolge an. Dieser Zug war nicht ausnehmend glänzend. Der Prinz saß in einer *Chaise coupée*, die durch zwei

## Imaginary Soundscapes

The critique of the traveller is directed towards the fact that the bells were part of the royal performance, overlapping the profane and sacred spheres: in their incessant ringing, they reinforced and underlined the connection of the Church to the royal family and gave the sacred guarantee to the secular codes of distinction. This is the kind of Portugal a Dutch or German traveller (as was the writer, and his audience) would expect to see and hear: a country bound by atavistic customs, where religion was present in all spheres of public and private life and which would be the main cause of Portuguese backwardness, in opposition to the civilisational advance of the enlightened German-speaking nations.

One of the most interesting descriptions of Portuguese musical practice as seen by foreigners is that of Wilhelm Gottlieb Tilesius von Tilenau (1769-1857), a German scientist who visited Portugal from 1795 to 1796. As a promising young scholar with a bachelor's degree in medicine and natural sciences from the University of Leipzig, and an enormous talent for drawing, which made him a renowned scientific illustrator, Tilesius was hired by Count Johann Centurius von Hoffmannsegg (1766-1849) in an expedition whose aim was to study and catalogue the Portuguese flora. The venture went badly — partly because of bad weather that made botanical observation impossible or difficult, partly because of bureaucratic issues, and partly because of personal disagreements between Tilesius and the Count — and the journey that had begun in the autumn of 1795 and was to last two years eventually ended in March 1796. Back in Germany, Tilesius returned to the University of Leipzig, where in the following year he became a Doctor of Philosophy and in 1801 a Doctor of Medicine and Surgery. The fame of his illustrations and research on marine species on the Portuguese coast earned him an invitation from the University of Moscow to take part in the first Russian circumnavigation voyage, which left in the summer of 1803 on the ship *Nadejda* under the command of the captain, Baron Adam Johann von Krusenstern (1770-1846) and only returned three years later. After the trip, acclaimed for his scientific achievements, Tilesius was elevated to noble status by Tsar Alexander I and was decorated Knight of the Order of Vladimir and the French Legion. He became a member of the Academies of Sciences of numerous cities such as Erfurt, Berlin, Göttingen, Munich, and St. Petersburg, published several essays on the taxonomy of marine species, and distinguished himself in medicine by describing neurofibromatosis and many other skin diseases. He returned to his hometown of Mühlhausen in 1814 and died there in 1857, in financial difficulties, isolated, and in total oblivion.

---

Maulesel gezogen wurde, neben ihm sein Neffe, der Infant. Ein Detachement Kavallerie escortirte den Wagen: nun folgte eine 4 sitzige Kutsche mit 6 Mauleseln bespannt. Die Prinzessin und drei Damen saßen darin. Sie wurde wie die vorige durch ein Detachement Kavallerie begleitet. Viele Chaisen und Wagen mit dem Gefolge endigten den Zug. Alle Glocken der zahllosen Kirchen lauteten, und machten einen solchen Lärm, daß einem Jeden Hören und Sehen verging. Der Prinz logirte dise Nacht in dem Pallast des Bischofs. Den Abend wurde die Stadt illuminirt». *Tagebuch* 1799, pp. 43-44.

In 1799 Tilesius published a German translation of *Tableau de Lisbonne en 1796*, the account of the French physician Joseph-Barthélemy-François Carrère (1740-1803). To his translation, Tilesius added a supplement of five hundred pages, called *Nachtrag zur Berichtung einselner Ansichten in dem Gemälde von Lissabon*, in which he proposed to make all the necessary amendments to Carrère's text, making use of his status (much appreciated in these years of pre-romantic sensitivity or *Empfindsamkeit*) as an eyewitness. His description of Portugal is based on the travel notes he took in his handwritten diary[6], never published, which is now in the Müllhausen municipal archive[7].

Tilesius was a great connoisseur of music. He played the violin, the viola, the harp, the piano, and the organ, he often ordered scores from musicians of his time, such as Mozart, Beethoven, and Haydn, for his personal use[8], and he even made a musicological analysis of traditional songs and dances that he collected in the Kamchatka Peninsula, in the easternmost region of Russia, and the Marquesas Islands, in French Polynesia, during his circumnavigation trip[9]. Throughout his account in Portugal — both in the *Nachtrag* and in the handwritten diary — there are numerous detailed musical descriptions, revealing a degree of theoretical and practical knowledge that equals that of a professional musician.

As for the depiction of Portuguese musical practice, Tilesius made a vivid description of Lisbon streets which also included the bells and their connection to the bad influence of the Catholic monks:

> Throughout the day and at all hours of the night, the bells ring, in their own way, in the countless monasteries and towers of the city, in such a way that during the day you cannot think without being disturbed and at night you cannot sleep well. The monks who receive the order beat with hammers on two or three different bells, in a strange rhythm or beat, so that from the various towers a peculiar mixture of sounds descends. My stay in Hamburg, where you can often hear the ringing of bells in the towers, prepared me in a way for this music, however, the endless ringing, the unusual form of hammer strokes, and the compass which (as in military service) is observed here caught my attention. In some of the monasteries that were completely or partially destroyed by the earthquake of 1755, 3 to 4 bells were placed on the ground among the ruins, which can be rung, which is seen by the monks as an activity that pleases God. However, the sounds of the bells serve as sensory impressions only to help the priests deceive the poor people[10].

---

[6]. See Tilesius 1795.

[7]. This diary, written in German *Kurrentschrift*, was transcribed, translated, and analysed in my doctoral dissertation. See Almeida 2021.

[8]. See Tilesius 1818.

[9]. See Tilesius 1805.

[10]. «Den ganzen Tag lang und zu allen Stunden in der Nacht wird auf eine ganz eigene Art von den unzähligen Klöstern und Thürmen der Stadt mit den Klocken gebümmelt, so daß man weder am Tage ungestört denken

# Imaginary Soundscapes

Expectations aside, the description of the hammer blows is interesting, testifying to the adaptation to the vicissitudes caused by the Lisbon Earthquake, preventing the normal ringing of bells and leading to the adoption of new practices. On festive days, the sound of roaring cannons was added to all this hubbub:

> The 17th of December [1795] was the birthday of Queen Maria I. There was a strong roaring of cannons on the river, coming from the boats, that were decorated with coloured flags and silk ribbons, which provided an excellent show.
> The 18th of December was the Queen's name day, and there was again a strong volley of cannons in the river and coming from the forts.
> On 28 December, as on the 2nd day of Christmas [...], there was again a strong roaring in the Tagus and the forts[11].

Continuing his portrayals of the streets, Tilesius von Tilenau adds a magnificent piece of 18th-century soundscape description in his diary, on 18 December 1795:

> There's such a roar in the streets all day long that you can't hear a conversation in your own room. Now a coloured old man shouts with his head half covered like a charlatan or a Moor, dressed in surplices and a short sleeveless cassock, holding a tin bowl by a stick, and asking for spiritual alms, which are more or less here obligatory, with the words: *Que dei mol' à os almas, almas centi beniti*. Then comes a blind man who is guided through the streets by a little boy and in two deep and reverberating bass tones he repeats uninterruptedly a short prayer: *uu-/-uu/uu-/---/uu/-uuuuu Christum possessim en povesi mossâve ube mille movve bum, um min moll...* There is a blind woman, who lets herself be guided through the streets by a dog held by the hand on a leash, who cries out her prayer in a clear, shrill voice; there's a guy with a donkey, loaded with vegetables and that makes *Quirri quirri, quirri*! There, there comes the goats or a group of shepherds, descending the Estrela sidewalk and

---

noch des Nachts ungestört schlafen kann. Die Mönche, welche hierzu beordert sind, schlagen mit Hämmern mit sonderbaren Rythmuß oder Tackt an 2 oder 3 verschiedenen Klocken wodurch von den vielen Thürmen herab ein sonderbares Gemisch von Tönen hervorgebracht wird. Der Aufenthalt in Hamburg wo man häufiges Glockenspiel von den Thürmen hört, hatte mich zwar etwas zu dieser Musik vorbereitet, indeß fiel mir doch das Unaufhörliche und die eigener Art des Aufschlags mit den Hämmern und der Tackt den man, (wie das Militär) darin beobachtet auf. An einigen halb oder ganz durch das Erdbeben von 55 zerrütteten Klöstern hat man doch 3 – bis 4 Glocken auf der Erde in den Ruinen angebracht um anzuschlagen, welches die Mönche schon an sich für eine Gott wohlgefällige Handlung ansehen müßen. Eigentlich aber sollen wohl die Klockentöne als sinnliche Eindrükke der Pfaffenbetrügereien zur Täuschung des armen Volkes mit hinwürken». TILESIUS 1795, p. 320.

[11]. «Am 17t Decembr war der Geburtstag der Königin Maria I. wurde auf den Tagus von den Schiffen die mit bunten Flaggen und seidnen Bändern geschmückt waren, stark *canonirt*, welches ein vortreffliches Schauspiel gab. / d. 18 Dec. war der Nahmenstag der Königin, wurde wieder stark auf den *Tagus* und aus den *Forts canonirt*. / d. 28 Dec, als der 2te Weyhnachts Feyertag gingen die äthiopischen Prinzen aus unserem Gasthofe nach Ajuda {u *Quelus*} nach Hofe, wurde wiederum stark auf dem Tagus und aus den Forts *canonirt*». Ibidem, p. 322.

shouting *milk, milk, who wants milk, good milk, fresh milk*. The goats bring the milk in their womb for sale in Lisbon and the group consists of a peasant woman, who is dressed in boots and a black peaked cap under a shawl, mounted on a donkey loaded on both sides with baskets or saddlebags, [...] and by a man or even children who carry with them the cup to measure the milk. In front and behind the donkey is a herd of goats with clappers, which make a constant peal. If someone asks for milk, the whole group stops in front of this house, and a goat is chosen and milked as much as requested. Afterwards, the procession continues its way, with new screams and tinkles. There is a similar peasant woman who comes with vegetables, mounted on her overloaded donkey, and touts her cauliflowers and artichokes, etc: *Artichokes! Garlic, leeks, cauliflower, cucumber! who wants?* Afterwards come the young men from the convents with their little boxes, where the Mother of God and the baby Jesus are stuffed and the people in the streets fall on the excrement and the Moor or the saint who carries the box opens the glass door and leaves the beggars to kiss the figures in exchange for a penny. There are oxen hitched to carts, the guide skewers the oxen in the horseshoe with a spike and thus guides them, according to the old custom, and lets them lick the wound... the wheels are out of gear and quite deformed, the cart too, and the whole makes a creaking and horrible screeching noise in the streets. And it's like that in front of my window all day. The Galicians or water carriers, waterboys, walk around with their red canteens and shout *water*, *água*, or rather *auga*. Children with ribbons, beads, or wineskins scream *wine*! In addition, two people arrive with a container and shout *fish*, and the street is never empty of beggars and miserable people, who partly lie there, partly wander[12].

The description is so vivid that we can almost hear the soundscape resounding on the pages of the diary. This passage, which was written by Tilesius after his return to Germany, clearly shows the strong impact that this amalgam of sounds caused on the Thuringian scientist, possibly even more than the opera, sacred music, or the concerts he attended, and which even outside Portugal occupied his memory, oscillating between repulsion and fascination for the exotic.

## Seeking the *Natural*

Another expected trait of the Portuguese was their naturality, their supposed primal characteristics, which had not yet been damaged by superstition or religion. This idea is very much present in the travelogue of the writer, essayist, and translator Esther Bernard (c.1767-after 1833). Born into a Jewish family in Breslau, Prussia, as Esther Gad, she changed her name after marrying the merchant Samuel Bernard, from whom she divorced; later she married the

---

[12]. *Ibidem*, pp. 320-321.

physician Wilhelm Domeier, adopted the Christian faith, and changed her name to Lucie Domeier[13]. She was what we now would call a true activist and was involved in public discussions on women's rights to civic participation, education, visibility, and financial independence. Around 1796 she moved to Berlin, where she quickly became a regular presence at literary salons, notably that of Henriette Herz, with whom she became friends. In this context, she connected with several important personalities of the German culture of her time, such as Friedrich and August Wilhelm Schlegel, the poet Jean-Paul Richter, the writer Madame de Genlis and the salonnière Rahel Varnhagen. Bernard could speak and write fluently in German, French, English, and Italian; she was a regular presence at the Berlin opera and published a theatre review of Friedrich Schiller's *Die Piccolomini*. With a keen sense of public relations (and the use of numerous subterfuges, such as the use of initials in the name to hide female authorship, the targeted choice of subjects and magazines according to the intended audience, or the dedication of the book to an important figure in certain social circles, such as the poet Jean-Paul Richter, to increase the probability of its being read in those same circles), Esther Bernard managed to position herself in a publishing market that was frankly dominated by men, even being quite explicit and outspoken about the striking differences in the treatment of male and female writers[14].

Her second husband was the doctor of the Duke of Sussex, the youngest son of the King of England, who had to settle business in Portugal and, being asthmatic, did not dispense with the doctor's presence. Esther Bernard spent a year in Lisbon, from 1801 to 1802, and wrote a travelogue of her experiences in the form of letters to a friend. This account, published in two volumes between 1802 and 1803, was listed in the press of the time and presented for two consecutive years at the Frankfurt and Leipzig book fairs. Some chapters were also published separately as articles in various magazines, and even had a reprint in 1808.

In her Lisbon inn at Rua de Buenos Aires, Bernard depicts the voices of the Portuguese women under the light of their natural, primordial characteristics:

> The chit-chat of women does not sound the least pleasant, and anyone who
> dared to compare the Portuguese language in terms of harmony with the Italian

---

[13]. For more biographical information about Esther Bernard, see SCHEITLER 1999, MEIER 2010, and ALMEIDA 2021.

[14]. In 1814, already living in London, Esther Bernard became vocal about the strategies she used to succeed as a female writer. In the introduction to the German translation of her essay on a book by Madame de Staël, which Bernard had dedicated to Jean-Paul Richter, she explicitly says that she did it as a decoy and that it is her «wish to provoke, through your name on the cover, a favourable opinion to this little work of mine». She also writes that she managed to hide her name and gender from the original English version because the reader's judgment would thus be less biased and more impartial if they don't know both. She ends this introduction by assertively signing it as «a German woman». See BERNARD 1814.

language has incurred the latter an enormous injustice. However, with so little melody in the language of these women, so much more exists in their singing. Most of them have beautiful voices, penetrating and with something very touching, as is not even found in Italian voices. But Portuguese women sing like birds in the forest; they lack education and art. However, graceful singing, even without art, is already art, just as beauty without ornaments is also beauty[15].

Nature, well emphasised by the association with birds in the forest, is an element valued by Bernard's pre-Romantic sensitivity, who compared the beauty of pure Portuguese voices, even lacking education and artistry, as being even more touching than the Italian ones. This comment is reinforced by her description of Lisbon's Opera House, where she attended Gluck's *Orfeo ed Euridice*, to whose music she spared no praise[16]. Her greatest admiration was for the ballerina Monroi, whose delicate body reminded her of a sylphid, or spirit of the air, delicate and sensitive, as opposed to the soloists of the Italian school, whom she considered heavy and tasteless. Curiously, in a theatre where most of the repertoire was Italian, the only performance description made by Bernard during the whole year she spent in Lisbon related also to Gluck, the reformer of opera who proposed more importance to choruses and recitatives, the introduction of French dances and the placing of text and personal drama in the foreground. We distinctly see Esther Bernard's adherence to an aesthetic of what she considers to be authentic: the search for naturalism and a primordial emotion, to the detriment of the Italian models, which she considered artificial.

## Desired Soundscapes: Feminisation and Masculinisation

Sometimes German accounts adopted a frankly more sensual and sexualising posture, for example in the report of Karl August Engelhardt (1768-1834), a Dresden-born archivist, writer, and pedagogue. He studied theology at the University of Wittenberg and started a career in public administration, which he later interrupted to devote himself exclusively to literature. Ten years later, in 1804, he was appointed archivist at the Dresden Public Library and remained there until his death. He published twelve volumes of stories for children and many pedagogical

---

[15]. «In völlig portugiesischen Familien (denn viele Familien sind mit Engländern, Italienern oder Franzosen verbunden, und haben mehr fremde Sitten angenommen) sitzen die Frauenzimmer äusserst selten auf Stühlen, sondern gewöhnlich in einem Kreise umher auf der Erde. [...] Aber so wenig Melodie in der Sprach der hiesigen Frauenzimmer liegt, so viel liegt in ihrem Gesang. Die mehrsten haben liebliche, eindringende Stimmen, und so viel rührendes, was selbst die italienischen Stimmen nicht haben. Aber die Portugiesinnen singen wie die Vögel im Walde; es fehlt ihnen an Schule und Kunst. Doch ein lieblicher Gesang ist ohne alle Kunst schon Kunst, so wie die Schönheit ohne alle Putz Schön heit ist». BERNARD 1802, pp. 280-281.

[16]. See *ibidem*, pp. 261-263.

works, books on the history of Saxony, and travel accounts in Germany, Spain, and Portugal, based on his privileged access to little-known sources. Engelhardt is a particularly interesting case because although he most likely never came to Portugal, having only read accounts in the archive of the library where he worked, his particular choice of texts to describe the Portuguese reality says a lot about what he expected to find in this country. In 1797 he published in Bautzen a two-volume account of Portugal and Spain, with many descriptions of what he thought to be the Iberian reality. In the second volume we find a description, possibly taken from another source he found in the Dresden library, of a popular dance in Vila Viçosa, in the countryside, near the Spanish borderline:

> While I was in Vila Viçosa and having just taken off my coat, the muleteer immediately started playing his guitar, and a fellow who seemed to be made of rags accompanied him with a very sweet little song. About twenty pairs of friendly and very dirty people quickly got together, who writhed on the floor with the most admirable frolics and sometimes approached each other gently, sometimes walked away quickly, always tapping their heels and tiptoes, at the same time as they snapped the fingers of their hands. All this time, the man stared into his woman's face, and the woman stared at the ground, seeming to be modesty itself. This was then the famous Portuguese dance of Fofa, which is almost the same as the Spanish Fandango, but has to be seen with your own eyes, it cannot be described, if you want to have a precise idea[17].

The man was looking directly at the woman, who, in an example of chastity and expected modesty, was looking at the floor. The resulting sexual tension was absorbed by the visitor himself, the voyeur who completed the triangle, and attributed to the Portuguese as a whole the erotic charge that would be an inherent characteristic, documented for centuries, as seen in his following passage:

> Already in Roman times, the inhabitants of this land, as well as those from Andalusia and Granada, were known for their agility in dance. The most beautiful

---

[17]. «Kaum hatte ich in Villa vicosa meinen Ueberrock ein wenig auf die Seite gelegt, so fieng ein Mauleseltreiber auf seiner Guitarre an zu spielen und ein Kerl, der aus Lumpen zusammengelegt zu seyn schien, akkompagnirte mit einem sehr zärtlichen Liedchen. Bald fanden sich über 20 nette und ekelhafte Pärchen ein, die sich mit den wunderlichsten Kapriolen auf dem Boden herumdrehten, sich bald einander zärtlich näherten, bald wieder geschwind entfernten, mit den Fersen und Zehen dabei saftmäßig stampften und eben so mit den Fingern schnippten. Der Chapeau laß seiner Dame dabei beständig starr ins Gesicht und diese sah denn eben so starr zur Erde und schien die Bescheidenheit selbst zu seyn. Dies war denn der so berühmte Foffatanz der Portugiesen, der dem spanischen Fandango beinahe ganz gleicht, aber selbst gesehen, nicht beschrieben werden mus, wenn man sich einen genauen Begriff davon machen will; denn er besteht nicht in abgemessene Schritten, sondern vielmehr in Bewegungen und Wendungen, wie jeder Tänzer mit einer, nur ihme, gefälligen Grazie bald mehr, bald weniger künstlich macht». ENGELHARDT 1797, pp. 74-75.

dancers travelled from here to Rome and throughout the Roman provinces and made many wise people lose their minds. We know well, at present, what dancers are capable of[18].

Voyeurism, the sexualisation of reality, and the enactment of masculinity itself are visible in the descriptions of German scientist Heinrich Friedrich Link (1767-1851), a renowned botanist who had come to Portugal with the Count of Hoffmannsegg[19], in the Count's second attempt to write a compendium on Portuguese flora (after the failure of his previous journey with Tilesius). About the region of Peso da Régua, he writes:

> Here we had the opportunity to observe the effects of such intense heat on society. At noon everything was dead and silent; at four o'clock the working class could be seen at last; after the sun went down, the nobles came out of their houses. The night was a constant tumult. The women, lightly dressed, were sitting on the balconies in front of the windows, to cool themselves, and their beauty lost nothing with the night twilight. They seemed, if a traveller is allowed to make general judgments of this kind, to have more generous forms than the rest of the Portuguese women, and they had, like the flowers in their valley, a more Spanish nature. But perhaps it was a coincidence that the author of these lines witnessed things that the upper-class women in Portugal would never allow themselves, not so soon or in such a way. But can one blame them there[20]?

The «lightly dressed» and «generously shaped» women would have offered the traveller during the «long night» a behaviour that «upper-class women in Portugal would never allow themselves», a behaviour that the traveller visibly enjoyed and was far from criticising.

---

[18]. «Schon in den Römerzeiten waren die hiesigen Einwohner, so wie die von Andalusien und Granada, ihrer Tanzfertigkeit wegen berühmt. Die schönsten Tänzerinnen reiseten von da nach Rom und in den römischen Provinzen herum und machten so manche Weisen zum Narren. Man weis ia wohl, was Tänzerinnen in den neuern Zeiten vermocht haben und noch vermögen». *Ibidem*, p. 75.

[19]. Heinrich Friedrich Link is a much-studied figure in German and Portuguese academic works. For more biographical information, see CLARA 2005, OLIVEIRA 2015, MARTIUS 1851, WUNSCHMANN 1883, BUTZIN 1985, and POMMER 2008.

[20]. «Wir hatten hier Gelegenheit, die Wirkungen einer so starken Hitze auf die menschliche Gesellschaft zu beobachten. Um Mittage war alles todt und still; um vier Uhr sah man erst die beschäftigte Volksklasse; nach Untergang der Sonne kamen die Vornehmen aus den Häusern. Die Nacht war ein beständiges Getümmel, die Frauenzimmer saßen leicht gekleidet auf den Balkons vor den Fenstern, um sich zu lüften, und ihre Schönheit verlor durch die nächtliche Dämmerung nicht. Sie schienen, wenn ein Reisender allgemeine Urtheile von dieser Art wagen darf, üppiger zu seyn, als sonst das portugiesische Frauenzimmer zu seyn pflegt, und hatten hierin, wie die Blüthen ihres Thals, mehr spanische Natur. Doch vielleicht war es Zufall, daß der Verfasser Zeuge von Schritten seyn mußte, welche sich sonst Frauenzimmer vom Stande in Portugal nie so bald und nie so breit erlauben. Aber kann man es ihnen verdenken?». LINK 1801, pp. 108-109.

# Imaginary Soundscapes

Sometimes, feminine attributes stopped being confined to a woman to apply to an entire region, in a kind of 'gendered geography', describing Portuguese reality with the same words and the same attributes they would use to describe women — docility, beauty, softness, while the more masculine attributes of braveness, courage, intellect are used exclusively for the traveller themselves, in a kind of conquest and appropriation of an entire region, through its description by gender stereotypes. This is exactly what Link does when he states that songs in Portugal were marked by the «suffering of love», chastity, modesty, and tenderness, all associated with the female world, as opposed to the German style, which had «beautiful opera arias» and «masterpieces by the greatest poets of the nation», referring to an ideal of intellectuality, culture, and sophistication associated with the male world[21].

## The Desire Killer: Beards and Colours

A desire killer was the use of male singers for female roles in the opera. For about 15 years, female singers in Portugal were banned from opera theatres, all roles being replaced by castrati. This was a break with the previous tradition since there had been many Portuguese female singers singing in the opera for decades, some of them well known, like Luisa Todi (1753-1833), who made an international career in France, Russia, and Berlin and was one of the best singers of her time. But Germans travelling to Portugal during these prohibition years could not hide their discomfort with what they called some heavily bearded men playing the role of fragile mistresses, as stated in Heinrich Friedrich Link's performance description at the Salitre Theatre:

> Here, too, no women are allowed to enter the theatre; their roles are played by men who can barely conceal their beards. The actors, moreover, are partly craftsmen; a cobbler who worked at his trade during the day played, among others, comic old men, and was not the worst actor. Mostly there are translations from Italian; rarely imitations of plays from other languages, and even more rarely originals. [...] All tragedies and serious plays are bad, or badly acted; there is nothing more detestable than the gallant or naïve leading ladies of this Theatre[22].

---

[21]. See *ibidem*, pp. 109-111.

[22]. «Auch hier darf kein Frauenzimmer das Theater betreten; ihre Rollen werden von Männern gemacht, welche kaum den Bart verbergen können. Die Schauspieler sind überdies zum Theil Handwerker; ein Schuster, der am Tage sein Handwerk trieb, spielte unter andern komische Alte, und war nicht der schlechteste Schauspieler. Meistens gieb man Uebersetzungen aus dem Italiänischen; seltener Nachahmungen von Stücken aus andern Sprachen, und noch seltener Originale. [...] Alle Trauerspiele und ernsthafte Schauspiele sind schlecht, oder werden schlecht gegeben; nichts ist abscheulicher, als die ersten Liebhaber und Liebhaberinnen dieses Theaters». Link 1804, p. 232.

In 1799 the ban was lifted and women returned to the stage of theatres, prompting Link to breathe a sigh of relief:

> The theatres in Lisbon have, moreover, undergone a great improvement in the fact that women have been allowed to step on stage. Now the naïve maidens no longer have to be played by bearded characters, whose black beard shows through the white make-up, and who speak in falsetto when they want to say something delicate[23].

Carl Israel Ruders (1761-1837), a Swedish Protestant pastor who was in Portugal from 1798 to 1802 as chaplain to the Swedish delegation in Lisbon, suggested, in a passage dating back to 1800, this make-up method to whiten the skin colour of the Brazilian-born opera singer Joaquina Maria da Conceição Lapa (before 1786-after 1811). Known as Lapinha, the talented singer had a brown skin colour, a result of her multiethnic Afro-Brazilian-Portuguese background, and was considered an attraction. For Ruders, Lapinha being the «daughter of a mulatto woman», and although possessing a «good voice and very dramatic feeling», had a «very dark skin colour», an «inconvenience» which could be «remedied with cosmetics»[24].

## Imagined Soundscapes: The *Modinha*

Paradoxically, most German travellers believed they had found the pureness of Portuguese music in the *Modinha*, a very popular urban song accompanied by the guitar, unaware that this type of composition, far from being an expression of a national archetype, was the result of a seething mix of European, Brazilian, and African influences. Link thus described the songs he heard on the streets at night:

> The guitar and the popular song of the Portuguese, elegiac and monotonous, continued throughout the night until the sun rose again. [...] Imagine a guitar so bad you can only hear the fingers tapping on the wood and you'll get an idea of the tender songs that lovers sing at night to their beauties. [...] The popular Portuguese song is always complaining: it almost always talks about the sufferings of love, it is very rarely obscene and even less humorous[25].

---

[23]. «Uebrigens haben die Theater in Lissabon dadurch eine grobe Verbesserung erhalten, daß man dem Frauenzimmer wiederum erlaubt hat, sie zu betreten. Nun werden die naiven Mädchen nicht mehr durch bärtige Personen vorgestellt, denen der schwarze Bart durch die weibe Schminke hervorscheint, und die durch die Fistel reden, wenn sie etwas Zierliches sagen wollen». *Ibidem*, pp. 191-193.

[24]. Ruders 2002, pp. 93-94.

[25]. «Die Guitarre und der elegische einförmige Volksgesang der Portugiesen dauerte die ganze Nacht, bis die Sonne wieder aufging. [...] Man denke sich dazu eine so schlechte Guitarre, dab man nur das Klappern auf

# Imaginary Soundscapes

These songs, played and sung in an urban environment, strophic, sentimental, accompanied by the guitar and with percussive rhythmic parts made by the tapping of fingers, as Link rightly observed, were *Modinhas*, a kind of repertoire strongly influenced both by European models, conveyed in good part by the existence of foreign communities that brought their musical practices and made them popular, and by the significant presence of Africans and Afro-Brazilians, both in the metropolis and in Brazil, who had brought their musical practices as well. The circulation and reciprocal exchange of models between Portugal and Brazil was the fertile ground where *Modinha* took shape, which quickly spread to the upper classes, being a case par excellence of geographical, cultural, and social transversality.

The travellers' assumption that these were popular Portuguese songs, failing to see the tangled web of musical influences they carried, reflects primarily their propensity and willingness to find a national song model that was the equivalent of the German *Lied*, believing, in the good pre-Romantic spirit, that they had found a pure form, springing from the people, which would mirror the intrinsic essence of the Portuguese nation.

## Elaborated Soundscapes: A Flight and a Royal Marriage

In 1807, Napoleonic troops invaded Lisbon and demanded the Portuguese surrender. In a gesture as risky as it was unusual, the royal family chose not to do so but to flee instead to Brazil, at the time a Portuguese colony, maintaining that the kingdom was still independent (and protected by its British allies), with only the capital changing from Lisbon to Rio de Janeiro. This measure did indeed preserve sovereignty in the face of Napoleon, but a huge effort was needed to build the infrastructure in Brazil, from courts to schools, factories, palaces, and theatres, which would transform the whole land and above all the new city, from an administrative point of view and in European eyes, into the capital of a kingdom.

To ensure that its importance was maintained in the delicate balance of power in Europe, the Portuguese crown tried to convey the image of a prosperous and wealthy country to its partners in the Old World. The high point of this policy came in 1816, with the marriage of the crown prince Dom Pedro (1798-1834), later Pedro IV of Portugal and Pedro I of Brazil, to princess Maria Leopoldina of Austria (1797-1826), daughter of the Holy Roman Emperor Francis II (1768-1835), which occurred in 1817 by proxy. On the pretext of the wedding festivities, the Portuguese crown invited numerous personalities and paid for expeditions

---

dem Holze hört, und man hat einen Begriff von den zärtlichen Liedchen, welche die Liebhaber ihren Schönen die Nächte vorsingen. [...] Das portugiesische Volkslied ist beständig klagend; es redet fast immer von den Leiden der Liebe, es ist äuberst selten unzüchtig, noch seltener witzig». Link 1801, pp. 108-111.

by European scientists and artists to the new capital, Rio de Janeiro, aiming to reinforce Portugal's role in European politics, even if the court was temporarily overseas. From 1816 to 1832, scientists and artists such as Auguste Saint-Hilaire (1779-1853), Prince Maximilian zu Wied-Neuwied (1782-1867), Carl Martius (1794-1868), Johann Baptist von Spix (1781-1826), Johann Moritz Rugendas (1802-1858) and even Charles Darwin (1809-1882) went to Brazil to study and describe the new European state out of Europe. This caused a proliferation of Portuguese-related publications, no longer the result of independent travel experiences but instead part of a continued political effort. In 1816, the *Allgemeine musikalische Zeitung* published for the first time an extensive article on Portuguese music, systematising its various aspects and shifting to a more cosmopolitan view of concert life, opera, and church music, under a new general light[26]. The Portuguese royal family returned to Lisbon in 1821, which only added more interest to the country.

It is important to stress that concerts, opera, and church music had existed there long before the *Allgemeine musikalische Zeitung* first took notice of it. Its history could be traced back many decades in the case of opera and concerts, and many centuries in the case of church music. Indeed, as we have seen, German travellers had described the Portuguese operatic life in the public theatres, showing their approval and often surprise at the quality of the Portuguese orchestras, as stated by Tilesius von Tilenau in his 'Nachtrag': «The orchestra is made up of Italians who belong to the Royal Chapel, but I also met some Germans there. The music is as perfect and pleasant as that of the Capelle in Dresden»[27]. Many reports praise the quality of the Lisbon orchestra, a description of which would exceed the aim of this text. But with the wedding of the prince of Brazil and, before that, the departure of the royal family to Rio de Janeiro, a more insistent and systematic look at the Portuguese reality was brought about. In an extensive article on Portuguese music, the *Allgemeine musikalische Zeitung* of 1808 talked about the popularity of Haydn's symphonies and Mozart's songs among the Lisbon public, moving away from the picturesque version and presenting a more cosmopolitan view of musical practices in Lisbon[28].

---

[26]. This eleven-page essay in the most important German music magazine of the time, published by the renowned Breitkopf & Härtel, covered public concerts, orchestras, operas, famous singers and instrumentalists, repertoire, composers, music life in Lisbon and Porto, and of course the *Modinha*, which was depicted as «the national music of the Portuguese». See ROCHLITZ 1816.

[27]. «Das Orchester besteht aus Italienern, welche die königliche Capelle formiren, auch habe ich einige Deutsche darunter gefunden. Die Musik ist eben so gleichförmig und gefällig, als die von der Dresdner Capelle, die Herren Musiker sind im Stande die Compositionen eines *Dalairac, Alessandri, Gretri*, u.s.w. nach vielmahligen vorhergegangenen Uebungen sehr gut darzustellen; von Mozart habe ich nichts hier gehört, man sagte: seine Compositionen seyen für dieses Orchester zu schwer — und doch ist die Besoldung dieser Tonkünstler verhältnißmäßig um die Hälfte ansehnlicher in Portugal als in Sachsen». TILESIUS 1797, pp. 402-403.

[28]. See ROCHLITZ 1808.

# Imaginary Soundscapes

Until the beginning of the 19th century, the news in German newspapers referring to Portuguese music was usually very short and mainly reported issues related to Luísa Todi (in the 1780s and 1790s), or the sporadic visit of a German musician to Portugal, or to the superficial mention of a Portuguese opera that had been performed abroad. The main source of information was the travel report. Thanks to the work of Rui Vieira Nery, who collected over three hundred accounts of foreign travellers to Portugal and Brazil between 1750 and 1834 with musical references, we can get an approximate idea of the number of existing travelogues. Between 1750 and 1807 (the date of the royal family's departure for Brazil), we have ten travel reports by German authors about Portugal, with a growing interest in the country after the death of the Marquis of Pombal in 1782. From 1807 until the end of the Portuguese civil war in 1834, which determined a new political course and the end of the *ancien régime*, we find not only in-depth articles in German newspapers, very far from the previous fait divers but also eleven travelogues by German travellers, i.e. there were more travelogues in these 27 years than in the previous 57 years. Many still had several of the prejudices that had proliferated in previous reports, such as the idea that orchestral music would not be appreciated, or would not exist at all, in Portugal, or the tendency, still and always, towards an association between the Portuguese and a candid *naïveté* that would make them a prime example of Rousseau's myth of the 'noble savage', for whom a little enlightened civilisation could only do good. However, the interest in Portugal after the Napoleonic invasion and the flight of the royal family to Brazil led to a closer look, a search for information, and a desire to see Portugal and its musical practices as part of a European mosaic, which would soon ensure the entry of Portugal as a subject of academic studies and would lead to the creation of Lusitanistics[29].

# Conclusion

The Portuguese music soundscape as captured by German travellers at the end of the *ancien régime* was a mixture of *in-loco* observations and imagined projections that portray the country of origin and the wider context not only of the writers but also of the contemporary scene and their readers. It showed, to the traveller's eyes, the rich sound of the streets, with all kinds of beggars, vendors, animals, and criers; the female voices, pure and free because they were not moulded or tarnished by education or art; the constant mixture of sacred and profane, altar and stage, church and street, where bells rang and cannons resounded; also a docile and melancholic music, seductive and feminine, ready to be dominated by the powerful and virile northern traveller; the prominence of Italian opera, which was seen by German travellers as

---

[29]. For the history of Lusitanistics see BRIESEMEISTER 2014 and BRIESEMEISTER – SCHÖNBERGER s.d.

almost incomprehensible, preferring models related to the *Empfindsamkeit*; and a type of tune resulting from various transatlantic mixtures between peoples and influences, which to the ears of travellers sounded like the true national song. Gradually, after Napoleon, this type of description would be complemented by another in which the connection to cosmopolitan practices was sought. It went from a markedly Pre-Romantic individual projection, which valued the natural, the primordial, the national characteristics, and the connection to nature, to a more sophisticated vision that prized Portugal's place in Europe, curiously at a time when the country's capital was in an extra-European territory. As the end of the *ancien régime* approached, the depiction, by German travellers, of Portuguese music and culture moved from a series of punctual reports to an attempt at detailed study, even though maintaining antiquated narratives: the image of a backward Portugal was now added to the image of a backward Portugal *with* opera and concerts. It was an image that only now, with the musicological study of the last decades, has finally been updated.

## Bibliography

Almeida 2021
Almeida, Inês Thomas. *O olhar alemão: A prática musical em Portugal em finais do antigo regime segundo fontes alemãs*, Ph.D. Diss., Lisbon, Faculdade de Ciências Sociais e Humanas da Universidade Nova de Lisboa, 2021.

Almeida 2022
Ead. 'Bias or Factuality? Music in Majestic Representation and Public State Ceremonies in Late 18th-Century Portugal, as Seen by German Travellers', in: *Advances in Design, Music and Arts II*, edited by Daniel Raposo, João Neves, Ricardo Silva, Luísa Correia Castilho, and Rui Dias, New York, Springer International Publishing, 2021, pp. 587-602.

Bernard 1802
Bernard, Esther. *Briefe während meines Aufenthalts in England und Portugal an einen Freund*, Hamburg, August Campe, 1802.

Bernard 1814
Ead. *Kritische Auseinandersetzung mehrerer Stellen in dem Buche der Frau von Stael über Deutschland*, Hannover, Hahn, 1814.

Briesemeister 2014
Briesemeister, Dietrich. 'Zur Geschichte des Fachs – Deutscher Lusitanistenverband', in: *Deutscher Lusitanistenverband e.V.*, 2014, <http://lusitanistenverband.de/was-ist-lusitanistik/zur-geschichte-des-fachs/>, accessed September 2023.

## Imaginary Soundscapes

BRIESEMEISTER – SCHÖNBERGER 2022 s.d.
BRIESEMEISTER, Dietrich – SCHÖNBERGER, Axel. 'Geschichte der Lusitanistik in Deutschland', s.d., <http://www.lusitanistik.de/Geschichte/geschichte.htm>, accessed September 2023.

BUTZIN 1985
BUTZIN, Friedhelm. 'Link, Heinrich Friedrich', in: *Neue Deutsche Biographie. 14*, edited by Historischen Kommission bei der Bayerischen Akademie der Wissenschaften, Berlin, Duncker & Humblot, 1985, p. 629.

CLARA 2005
CLARA, Fernando. 'Luzes e sombras', in: LINK, Heinrich Friedrich. *Notas de uma viagem a Portugal e através de Espanha e França*, Lisbon, Biblioteca Nacional, 2005, pp. ix-xxviii.

ENGELHARDT 1797
ENGELHARDT, Karl August. *Portugall und Spanien: geographisch durchreiset. 2*, Bautzen, Arnold, 1797.

LINK 1801
LINK, Heinrich Friedrich. *Bemerkungen auf einer Reise durch Frankreich, Spanien, und vorzüglich Portugal. 2*, Kiel, Neue akademische Buchhandlung, 1801.

LINK 1804
ID. *Bemerkungen auf einer Reise durch Frankreich, Spanien, und vorzüglich Portugal. 3*, Kiel, Neue akademische Buchhandlung, 1804.

MARTIUS 1851
MARTIUS, Carl Friedrich Philipp von. 'Denkrede auf Heinrich Friedrich Link: Gehalten in der öffentlichen Sitzung der Königlich Bayerischen Akademie der Wissenschaften am 28. März 1851', in: *Münchener Gelehrte Anzeigen*, nos. 59-69 (1851), pp. 473-555.

MEIER 2010
MEIER, Monika. 'Lucie Domeier Geb. Esther Gad (1770 (?) - Nach 1835)', in: *Brüche und Umbrüche: Frauen, Literatur und soziale Bewegungen*, edited by Margrid Bircken, Marianne Lüdeke and Helmut Peitsch, Potsdam, Universitätsverlag Potsdam, 2010, pp. 43-63.

OLIVEIRA 2015
OLIVEIRA, Nuno Gomes. *A flore Portugaise e as viagens em Portugal de Hoffmannsegg e Link (1795 a 1801)*, Lisbon, Chiado Editora, 2015.

POMMER 2008
POMMER, Christine-Kai. *Heinrich Friedrich Link. Die Reise eines Naturforschers und Mediziners nach Frankreich, Spanien und Portugal. Protokoll eines aussergewöhnlichen Lebens*, Ph.D. Diss., Lübeck, Institut für Medizin- und Wissenschaftsgeschichte der Universität zu Lübeck, 2008.

ROCHLITZ 1808
[ROCHLITZ, Friedrich]. 'Musik in Portugall', in: *Allgemeine musikalische Zeitung*, x/40 (1808), pp. 635-640.

ROCHLITZ 1816
[ID.] 'Musik in Portugal', in: *Allgemeine musikalische Zeitung*, XVIII/26 (1816), pp. 429-440.

RUDERS 2002
RUDERS, Carl Israel. *Viagem em Portugal 1798-1802. 1*, (1809), Portuguese translation by António Feijó, Lisbon, Biblioteca Nacional, 2002.

SCHEITLER 1999
SCHEITLER, Irmgard. *Gattung und Geschlecht: Reisebeschreibungen deutscher Frauen 1780-1850*, Tübingen, Max Niemeyer Verlag, 1999.

TAGEBUCH 1799
*Tagebuch einer Reise durch die portugiesische Provinz Alentejo im Januar 1797. Mit einer Beschreibung der Stiergefechte in Portugal*, Hildesheim, Gerstenberg, 1799.

TILESIUS 1795
TILESIUS, Wilhelm Gottlieb. *Tagebuch auf meiner Reise von Hamburg nach Lissabon etc. von 1795 bis 1797*, unpublished diary, Mühlhausen, Tilesius-Bibliothek, Stadtarchiv Mühlhausen, 1795.

TILESIUS 1797
ID. 'Nachtrag zur Berichtigung einzelner Ansichten in dem Gemälde von Lissabon', in: CARRÈRE, Joseph-Barthélemy-François. *Neuste Gemälde von Lissabon*, Leipzig, Karl Wilhelm Küchler, 1797, pp. 321-504.

TILESIUS 1805
ID. 'Bachia, oder Kamtschadalischer Bärentanz, Nationalmusik und Tanz, und Das Menschenfresser-Lied der Marquezas-Insulaner Auf Nukahiwah, ein Nationalgesang', in: *Allgemeine musikalische Zeitung*, XVII (January 1805), pp. 261-171.

TILESIUS 1818
ID. *Wilhelm Gottlieb Tilesius von Tilenau to Johann Martin Peters-Steffenhagen*, unpublished letter, Berlin, Handschriftenabteilung, Staatsbibliothek Berlin, 1818.

WUNSCHMANN 1883
WUNSCHMANN, Ernst. 'Link, Heinrich Friedrich', in: *Allgemeine Deutsche Biographie*, XVIII (1883), pp. 714-720.

# Le Napoléon d'Hector Berlioz,
## proposition de lecture

*Alban Ramaut*
(Université Jean Monnet, Saint-Étienne)

Jean-François Le Sueur écrit au docteur Louis Berlioz le 25 août 1830[1] au sujet de son fils Hector qui quatre jours auparavant vient de «remporter à l'unanimité»[2] le premier grand prix de Rome. Cette lettre de deux pages, très unique en son genre, développe tout d'abord des arguments assez matérialistes sur les revenus qu'Hector peut espérer bientôt obtenir; puis elle se termine de façon amphigourique sur un parallèle établi entre Hector et Napoléon!

Évoquant les qualités d'attention dont fait preuve le jeune musicien envers les artistes et plus particulièrement les interprètes, Le Sueur remarque tout d'abord: «Cette manière de faire le bien dans sa sphère particulière, sera une image de celle de Napoléon dans sa sphère immense»[3]. Puis, en qualité de compositeur, l'épistolier file la métaphore qu'il mène à son apothéose: «Qui sait? il sera peut-être, un jour, le Napoléon de la science musicale, par les pas de géants qu'il lui fera faire [...]»[4]. L'affirmation a donc glissé de la relation d'Hector aux interprètes jusqu'à l'originalité de son style. Elle pose en sa qualité prédictive diverses questions que les lendemains immédiats de la Révolution de juillet rendent particulièrement vives.

Le régime politique juste-milieu qui s'ouvre, si discuté soit-il et que chacun peut encore rêver, cherchera de fait à concilier Napoléon avec une monarchie de plus en plus bourgeoise. Aussi en quoi l'avenir promis à Berlioz s'y retrouve-t-il? Des éléments antérieurs ou parallèles à

---

[1]. Le Hir 2020A. L'original de cette lettre ainsi que la réponse du Docteur Berlioz sont entrés depuis 2021 dans les collections du Musée Hector Berlioz de la Côte-Saint-André, suite à un don de l'Association Nationale Hector Berlioz (ANHB) qui les avait acquises. Sur l'analyse du contenu de la lettre de Le Sueur, voir Le Hir 2021.

[2]. Le jury après un premier tour (19 août) qui n'avait retenu que Berlioz proposa le 21 de lui adjoindre un second lauréat. Voilà pourquoi Berlioz parle d'«unanimité».

[3]. Le Hir 2020B.

[4]. Le Hir 2020C.

l'enseignement de Le Sueur font-ils par ailleurs écho à l'audace de sa métaphore napoléonienne? Deux questions qui s'intéressent à l'empreinte, sensible jusque dans la musique, du «plus puissant souffle de vie qui jamais anima l'argile humaine»[5].

\*\*\*

Or si ces interrogations mêlent la réalité politique de la France à l'originalité créatrice de Berlioz, elles s'inscrivent également dans la montée en puissance du courant romantique, à l'égard duquel Le Sueur exprime, comme on le verra, les plus vives réticences. Aussi s'agit-il ici de cerner au plus juste ce qu'exprime Le Sueur de Napoléon et de saisir au plus près ce qu'il nomme, au travers d'une formule qu'il reprend entre autres aux encyclopédistes, la «science musicale».

## Science musicale

Comme auteur lui-même d'un traité — *Exposé d'une Musique une, imitative, et particulière à chaque solennité* — qu'il publie en 1787 chez la veuve Hérissant à vingt-sept ans, Le Sueur semble bien placé en effet vis-à-vis de l'idée de «science musicale». Le sous-titre de son ouvrage mérite d'être intégralement donné tant il trace avec bonne volonté des perspectives esthétiques: «[Exposé…] Où l'auteur, […] donne à ceux de ses Élèves qui se destinent à composer la Musique de nos Temples, les Préceptes qu'il leur a cru nécessaires pour mettre le plus de Poésie, de Peinture & d'Expression possible dans leurs Ouvrages». Vingt-sept ans est l'âge auquel Berlioz atteint le 11 décembre 1830. Tout converge ainsi vers des similitudes et peut-être plus encore vers la notion d'une transmission non dépourvue de mimétisme mais qui repose cependant sur un écart de plus de quarante années. La *Messe solennelle* de 1825 porte à l'évidence les signes d'une filiation esthétique alors largement consentie. Le Sueur y reconnut du reste un esprit cultivé, réfléchi, doublé d'un goût sûr pour l'énergie de la musique, tous éléments de jugement et de culture qui à ses yeux participaient à la complexion d'un compositeur. Aussi est-ce en toute logique que sa lettre, pour étayer son parallèle napoléonien, revient sur l'une de ses plus profondes convictions: «Il sera peut-être le Napoléon de la science musicale […] vu ses autres connaissances acquises et adjointes aux beaux-arts, et particulièrement à cette musique si puissante sur le cœur et l'imagination des hommes, quand elle est composée de génie»[6]. Comme l'a montré Sabine Le Hir[7] d'autres textes de Le Sueur confirment l'idéologie classicisante, digne des idéologues, du musicien. Notamment sa *Lettre en réponse à Guillard*, véritable ouvrage de préceptes pédagogiques et de réflexions esthétiques qu'il publie en novembre 1801[8].

---

[5]. Chateaubriand 1951, livre vingt-quatrième, chapitre II, p. 1022.
[6]. Le Hir 2020[D].
[7]. Le Hir 2021.
[8]. Le Sueur 1801.

# Le Napoléon d'Hector Berlioz

Si l'avènement politique nouveau de 1830 et la consécration d'un tempérament artistique inspirent à Le Sueur parvenu au seuil de sa carrière, une forme de reconnaissance, c'est aussi une espérance qui est prononcée d'un style nouveau. Car comment traduire par les sons la puissance des conceptions de l'Empereur dont la fulgurance visionnaire arpenta l'Europe en quelque sorte «à pas de géants» et que ses successeurs commencent à faire entrer dans la légende et l'épopée?

## Préalables à une lettre de compositeur

On peut saisir la formule prudemment hypothétique — «il sera peut-être un jour» — en la comprenant comme exclusivement destinée au docteur Berlioz, que Le Sueur veut convaincre. Certes le musicien désire ne pas heurter l'opinion ni blesser la sensibilité d'un homme dont il aurait selon le chapitre x des *Mémoires* déjà éprouvé la «roideur» des principes[9]. Après l'envoi de ce 25 août 1830 Le Sueur n'aura de fait plus de raison d'écrire au docteur Berlioz puisque son intention d'accompagner Berlioz au seuil de sa carrière vient d'être couronnée. Et du reste la réponse un peu distante que lui adressa début septembre le Docteur, comme on y reviendra, met assez clairement fin à un échange douloureux pour Louis Berlioz.

Les arguments avancés par le vieux compositeur sont donc à la fois choisis à partir de ce qu'il a appris de la bouche même d'Hector sur ce milieu provincial et plus particulièrement sur son chef de famille tels que l'évoque les *Mémoires* et de ce qu'il porte lui-même dans son cœur, comme proche musicien de l'Empereur. Mais Le Sueur trouve-t-il pour autant les arguments aptes à émouvoir la personnalité du Docteur Berlioz, ou au contraire à l'exaspérer? N'y avait-il pas un risque à brandir l'image de Napoléon auprès d'un propriétaire terrien que tout rattachait, par une filiation bourgeoise déjà bien établie à la sensibilité critique des encyclopédistes? Un «incrédule» que l'occupation de la Côte-Saint-André par les Autrichiens en 1814 avait dit-on fortement marqué. Son épouse Joséphine nourrissait plus encore un culte intransigeant pour les principes catholiques liés à l'ancien régime.

Pourtant par-delà la sincérité dramatisée qui anime la métaphore de Le Sueur, et qui n'est peut-être qu'un effet de théâtre, voire de rhétorique d'à-propos, c'est bien l'intuition que Le Sueur a de l'exceptionnelle personnalité créatrice de son élève qui s'exprime. C'est même l'unique réalité qu'il veut affirmer. En cela il ne fait que répéter avec une comparaison

---

[9]. Par un échange épistolaire antérieur hélas perdu de nos jours. Berlioz évoque en effet une lettre de 1826 suite à son élimination au concours de Rome: «Mon père le sut et cette fois, sans hésiter, m'avertit de ne plus compter sur lui […] Mon bon maître lui écrivit aussitôt une lettre pressante, pour l'engager à revenir sur cette décision […] Il mêlait à ses arguments […] certaines idées religieuses dont le poids lui paraissait considérable […] Aussi la réponse brusque, roide et presque impolie de mon père ne manqua pas de froisser violemment la susceptibilité et les croyances intimes de Le Sueur. Elle commençait ainsi: "Je suis un incrédule, monsieur!" On juge du reste». Berlioz 2019[A].

nouvelle impensable sous la Restauration et que l'actualité politique rend possible, un propos déjà affirmé avec assurance depuis 1825[10] et repris le 20 août 1828[11]. À travers les mots et les figures qu'il convoque, Le Sueur martèle un seul message, celui du caractère indiscutable de la vocation d'Hector.

Comme souvent dans une lettre destinée à apaiser des tensions d'opinion, le scripteur pour convaincre son lecteur en appelle à des figures majeures. Pour qu'un échange entre Le Sueur et Louis Berlioz ait une réelle densité, Le Sueur prend soin d'évoquer au préalable dans sa lettre nombre de figures de musiciens jusqu'à en venir à Napoléon. Cependant Napoléon et Hector demeurent pour le docteur comme on peut sans peine l'imaginer des figures qui souffrent mal le rapprochement. Ce qui suggère à Le Sueur de recourir à cette l'image ne peut d'autant pas impressionner Louis Berlioz qu'il a de bonnes raisons de croire bien connaître la nature de son fils. Et de fait, nous devons le constater, ni Le Sueur ni le Docteur ne se trompent sur l'avenir d'Hector, car si Berlioz est bien devenu la grande figure française du romantisme musical, il n'a jamais, à l'instar des Haendel, Gluck ou Rossini, cités en exemple dans les premières lignes de la lettre de Le Sueur, su en tirer fortune!

## Les forces en présence

Ces distinctions de tempérament et de vécu posées entre le père et le maître augurent-elles d'un impossible dialogue? La réponse que Louis Berlioz adresse à Le Sueur révèle jusque dans le maniéré de son style, son désir de mettre fin à un échange qui le tourmente. «Si mon fils atteint à quelque célébrité, si déjà il se trouve sur le seuil du temple de la gloire et de la fortune; c'est à vos conseils affectueux, c'est à vos savantes leçons, c'est à vous, son maître, et son ami, qu'il le doit»[12], écrit-il, avant de tirer sa révérence: «Ses mœurs sont demeurées pures au milieu de la corruption et sous votre égide. […] Le cœur d'un père ressent cette obligation par-dessus toute autre; et il vous assure des droits à l'éternelle reconnaissance»[13].

Il est vrai que le rapprochement des deux figures — Napoléon et Hector — peut créer un malaise dans le cœur d'un père. Car celle de Napoléon est omniprésente et célèbre, non pas indiscutable mais incontournable. Elle revêt particulièrement en août 1830 l'autorité de celui qui a su seul conjurer les violences révolutionnaires et en tirer une «sphère immense» d'action et d'entreprise. Napoléon mort devient plus que jamais dans la conscience politique française

---

[10]. Berlioz 1972^A. «Venez que je vous embrasse; morbleu vous ne serez ni médecin, ni apothicaire, mais un grand compositeur; vous avez du génie, je vous le dis parce que c'est vrai».

[11]. Berlioz 1972^B.

[12]. Le Hir 2020^E.

[13]. Le Hir 2020^F.

et européenne celui qui a définitivement refondé la société. Il est l'œil de l'esprit qui dans une fulgurance visionnaire a pressenti le monde nouveau, il est la main dont le geste créateur a réalisé des prodiges.

Hector, ardent musicien, s'il gravite dans l'orbe idéal de l'aigle impérial, au risque de paraître insensé dans ses engagements, reste encore en revanche en quête de victoire. La *Symphonie fantastique* bien que déjà composée ne l'imposera au public romantique que dans quelques mois. Dans sa famille sa vocation musicale est toujours à cette époque taxée de «folie». Joséphine, lorsqu'elle évoque la lettre d'Hector[14] qui dit son succès, écrit ce même 25 août (!) à Nanci[15]: «Il me serait trop long de détailler toutes les folies qui courent sous sa plume, et sa lettre est trop barbouillée pour te l'envoyer». Cela fait écho à la lettre sans doute du 27 août 1827 où Joséphine rend compte de l'échec d'Hector (dans une lettre désormais perdue) au concours de Rome, il s'agit de *La Mort d'Orphée*, «[…] Néanmoins […] trois pages de sa lettre ne le sortent pas de ses folies musicales et puis son budget vient après. […] Il est fou, voilà tout ce que je puis dire pour sa justification…»[16]. L'oncle de Berlioz, frère de Madame Berlioz, Félix Marmion, même s'il sera par la suite le plus proche de la carrière d'Hector s'était déterminé en 1823 à combattre la vocation de son neveu qu'il taxait aussi de «folie»[17].

Loin de rassembler et de réjouir, le courrier de Le Sueur a semble-t-il confirmé les réticences de la famille envers le monde artiste. Tel est tout au moins ce que permet de penser l'usage que fit le docteur de ce papier[18]. S'il n'a probablement pas été communiqué à Hector, il a en revanche circulé entre plusieurs mains sans quitter la maison. Joséphine informe Nanci de son existence et se promet de le lui montrer. «Ton père a seulement répondu hier à ton frère de même qu'à M. Lesueur qui lui écrit une lettre de félicitations qui t'amusera quand tu la verras»[19]. Franchise de ton par laquelle on vérifie comment l'assimilation proposée au docteur des dons de son fils à ceux de l'Empereur a manqué son effet au sein du microcosme familial.

## La lettre «interdite»

Le Sueur se doutait-il du huis-clos qui entourerait sa lettre? Cela est difficile à trancher. Il pouvait sans doute l'imaginer. Mais, par ce geste qui l'honore, cet habitué des textes bibliques prononçait ici son *Nunc dimittis* face à la consécration de son élève. Aussi peut-on se demander si en écrivant au père il n'espérait pas secrètement dans sa bienveillance admirative s'adresser

---

[14]. Berlioz 1972[C].
[15]. Berlioz 2016[A].
[16]. Berlioz 2016[B].
[17]. Berlioz 2016[C].
[18]. Cairns 2002; Lesure 1972.
[19]. Beyls 2019.

au fils avec lequel il avait l'habitude de s'entretenir de musique et de Napoléon[20]? De là le ton possiblement allusif «Qui sait?», et aussi cette emphase qui voudrait prendre l'univers entier à témoin. Car si Le Sueur parle au docteur Berlioz comme à un homme de sa génération — un ainé s'adressant à un plus jeune frère (seize ans les séparent) —, il fait d'Hector quasiment le fils qu'il a peut-être rêvé d'avoir[21], ou à défaut le gendre qu'il aurait pu espérer[22]. Quoi qu'on en pense, il l'introduit dans la sphère immense des génies.

Quelles que soient ces hypothèses, on sait que Le Sueur a écrit cette lettre à l'insu de Berlioz. Berlioz pense-t-on aujourd'hui n'accéda que plus tard, si cela se fit, à ce courrier qui nous est parvenu, relié dans un des exemplaires de la livraison des *Mémoires* publiés à compte d'auteur en 1865. Par qui et à quelle date cette lettre a-t-elle été associée à cet exemplaire? Par Hector ou par ses héritiers? L'avenir débrouillera peut-être cette question.

Au mieux, actuellement on peut penser qu'Hector a eu connaissance de cette lettre qu'il ne mentionne nulle part, à la fin de l'été 1848[23], dans le contexte doublement particulier pour lui des lendemains de la mort de son père (28 juillet) et du naufrage de la Monarchie de juillet. Mais en 1848 ce témoignage n'avait plus la même intensité que celle dont l'actualité quasi solennelle et inaugurale du mois d'août 1830 la revêtait.

Faut-il conclure que l'initiative en quelque sorte déjouée de le Sueur achève symboliquement d'émanciper Berlioz de toute tutelle? Elle le livre à une liberté souveraine, une indépendance de pensée, qui est sans doute ce que le jeune prix de Rome prisait le plus dans les gestes inspirés de la vie de Napoléon. C'est peut-être «qui sait» en ce cas Le Sueur qui donne à Berlioz la liberté de devenir le «Napoléon de la science musicale».

Cependant une autre source napoléonienne à la fois plus romanesque et plus matérialiste doit être évoquée.

## Autre source

Si les termes de la lettre donnent à comprendre par les jeux d'une circulation de pensée et d'admiration comment Hector Berlioz a pu, par son maître, concevoir Napoléon en idéal artistique, voire en imagination sonore, un autre témoignage napoléonien antérieur à cette formation doit être avancé. Il porte en réalité sur la première imprégnation que reçut Hector

---

20. Berlioz 2019<sup>B</sup>.
21. Berlioz 1972<sup>D</sup>: «Mais je [Hector] me suis dit [...] et si jamais la patience excessive et les bontés d'un maître, la reconnaissance et (j'ose le dire) l'amour filial de ses élèves lui ont acquis sur eux le titre de Père, je suis du nombre de ses enfants».
22. Boschot 1906 et Boschot 1927. Pourtalès 1939.
23. Hector séjourna à la Côte-Saint-André du 28 août à la mi-septembre pour régler avec ses sœurs l'héritage de leur père.

sans même sans doute y prendre garde dans le contexte de sa propre famille, et dans l'ignorance entière de sa vocation musicale.

Cette initiation napoléonienne a permis à l'idéalisme romanesque de Berlioz, alors au seuil de son adolescence, de se fixer sur une représentation quasi de terrain de l'Empereur à travers l'horizon tout à la fois affectif et fantastique qu'animaient les récits de son oncle Félix Marmion (1787-1872). La présence dans l'entourage familial d'une figure masculine de militaire si différente de celle de son père a en outre contribué à la construction d'une image quasi réaliste et sensitive de Napoléon. Car même si en son appropriation elle est devenue poétique, elle reste inspirée d'actes héroïques violents, de gestes à l'éloquence sans limite et du fracas inouï des batailles.

> Mon oncle [...] venait quelque fois nous y joindre [à Meylan] tout chaud encore de l'haleine du canons, orné tantôt d'un simple coup de lance, tantôt d'un coup de mitraille dans le pied ou d'un magnifique coup de sabre en travers de la figure[24].

Frère de Joséphine Berlioz, Félix Marmion, sous-lieutenant au I[er] Dragons en 1806 a accompagné l'Empereur sur presque tous les fronts jusqu'à Waterloo. Étonnamment proche de la famille Berlioz il fut un témoin de l'Empereur. Il a semé très tôt dans l'affection imaginative et admirative d'Hector l'idée de la grandeur de ses entreprises comme il a inscrit l'image du dévouement et de la foi qu'imposait cette autorité proprement impériale à ses soldats. La figure tutélaire à travers la carrière de cet oncle qu'Hector aimait et qui est l'un, on l'a dit, des rares membres de la famille à avoir assisté à certains de ses concerts, pouvait trouver de quoi alimenter la fantaisie et la fièvre naissante du lecteur du roman d'aventures du très royaliste Montjoye, *Manuscrit trouvé au mont Pausilippe*[25]. Or Félix Marmion joignait pour Hector au prestige des descriptions des batailles et à la vénération pour les traces des blessures qu'il portait sur son visage, un goût d'amateur de musique qu'il semble avoir été le seul dans la famille à avoir réellement possédé[26]:

> Il n'était encore qu'adjudant-major de lanciers; jeune épris de la gloire, prêt à donner sa vie pour un de ses regards, croyant le trône de Napoléon inébranlable comme le Mont Blanc; et joyeux et galant, grand amateur de violon [il faut comprendre, sachant bien jouer du violon] et chantant fort bien l'opéra-comique[27].

---

[24]. BERLIOZ 2019[C].
[25]. MONTJOYE 1802 et BERLIOZ 2019[D].
[26]. Même si les sœurs de Berlioz, plus particulièrement Adèle, faisaient un peu de musique.
[27]. BERLIOZ 2019[E].

Tel apparaît ce premier paysage napoléonien fait de récits. Une légende sans doute assez répandue dans les esprits français de la jeunesse romantique. Il s'agit à l'évidence d'un paysage préparatoire à celui que lui a ouvert Le Sueur dès 1823, le lui présentant à son tour comme une perspective sublime à l'inspiration artistique. Ces récits sont enfin là peut-être comme les prémices à ces visions grandioses et désolées, ces espaces illimités, les proportions inédites ces «pas» suggérés par Le Sueur.

Alors qu'il est lui-même trahi par Camille Moke, Hector au printemps 1831 traverse revenant sur ses pas depuis Rome vers Paris, certains des sites des victoires de la campagne d'Italie. Au pont de Lodi, il songe au génie inspiré de Napoléon qui le conduisit à renverser les mondes, haïr la médiocrité, et avancer à la tête de son armée:

> Ô Napoléon, Napoléon, génie, puissance, force, volonté!... Que n'as-tu dans ta main de fer écrasé une poignée de plus de cette vermine humaine!... Colosse aux pieds d'airain, comme tu renverserais du moindre de tes mouvements tous leurs beaux édifices patriotiques, philanthropiques, philosophiques! Absurde racaille[28]!

La fureur amoureuse de Berlioz se transforme ensuite, comme on sait, en ferveur artistique. Le déplacement du culte amoureux pour une femme à celui pour la muse peut avoir trouvé dans la figure de la ténacité napoléonienne, mais aussi de sa fatale solitude, son vrai champ d'horizon, ce qu'il avait déjà nommé ailleurs la «sphère sublime rêvée par les poètes»[29]. Ainsi, force, poésie, création se conjuguent jusqu'à rencontrer en la figure de Napoléon devenue elle-même ossianique une possible incarnation dans la musique.

## Napoléon et le romantisme

Les jeux de rôles établis par la métaphore de Le Sueur et que les récits de Félix Marmion avaient déjà préparés montrent comment dans un mouvement général dont Berlioz n'est pas excepté, Napoléon devient l'indiscutable référence de ceux qui ne l'ont pas connu. Ce mouvement déjà perceptible dans les milieux plutôt légitimistes, ignorants des arts, mais attentifs au relèvement de la France, s'accentue et s'accélère encore lorsque la Monarchie de juillet se met en place. Napoléon devient par l'universalité de son action, certes un possible modèle d'idéologie politique mais plus encore une force transposable au domaine des arts, comme aussi un enjeu manipulable bien qu'à risques, comme l'histoire l'a prouvé, pour la politique de Louis-Philippe. Ainsi, à mesure que Napoléon devient immortel le *sui generis* de sa gloire s'étend à tous les domaines[30].

---

[28]. BERLIOZ 1972[E].
[29]. BERLIOZ 1996.
[30]. LENZ – LAGRANGE 2021.

# Le Napoléon d'Hector Berlioz

Si l'évolution de la figure de Napoléon est d'autant plus sensible à la suite des événements de 1830, c'est la date du 5 mai 1821 jour de la mort de l'Empereur, qui décide du basculement de l'opinion. Or Berlioz arrive à Paris à l'automne de cette même année. La jeunesse romantique en effet souvent alors ultraroyaliste s'empare à partir de la mort de l'Empereur de la figure de l'aigle terrassé comme d'un thème essentiel à sa propre recherche du sublime et de la souveraineté. Auparavant, Napoléon s'apparente, explique Emmanuel Fureix[31] sous la forme du néo-classicisme davidien à l'éthique classique elle-même conjuguée au modèle louis-quatorzien. Sa mort en exil l'introduit dans le panthéon plus pathétique des romantiques.

La parution du *Mémorial de Sainte-Hélène* publié par le comte de Las Cases ravive pour sa part dès 1823 le culte du génie de Napoléon. Ce livre certes politique qui conforte le bonapartisme contribue aussi à la construction de la légende poétique qu'adoptent les artistes. Las Cases sait avec adresse relier dès les premières pages de son ouvrage l'activisme visionnaire des années du directoire et du consulat auxquelles rien ne résista, aux propos recueillis à Sainte-Hélène de l'Empereur «vaincu». Ultimes paroles dont le mémorialiste met en évidence la tonalité intemporelle pour mieux construire la légende: «Ces conversations du dernier abandon, et qui se passaient comme étant déjà de l'autre monde»[32]. Dans le 'Préambule' où il justifie son ralliement à une forme d'autorité contraire aux intérêts de sa caste, Las Cases a des phrases enthousiastes que tout romantique pouvait aussitôt prendre pour siennes.

> Cependant [dans l'immédiat après 1789] des événements sans exemple se succédaient autour de nous; ils étaient d'une telle nature et portaient un tel caractère, qu'il devenait impossible à quiconque avait dans le cœur l'amour du grand, du noble et du beau, d'y demeurer insensible[33].

La «nature» et le «caractère» posent avec des traits sûrs l'autorité et expliquent l'indiscutable sidération qu'exerce le génie. Quelques autres lignes prises à la 'Préface' traduisent encore la puissance de fascination qu'exerçait la prestance du grand homme sur son entourage immédiat au point d'en faire un legs imprescriptible:

> Les circonstances les plus extraordinaires m'ont tenu longtemps auprès de l'homme le plus extraordinaire que présentent les siècles.
>
> L'admiration me le fit suivre sans le connaître; l'amour m'eut fixé pour jamais près de lui dès que je l'eus connu.
>
> L'univers est plein de sa gloire, de ses actes, de ses monumens; mais personne ne connaît les nuances véritables de son caractère, ses qualités privées, les dispositions

---

[31]. Fureix 2012.
[32]. Las Cases 1823[A].
[33]. Las Cases 1823[B].

naturelles de son âme. Or, c'est ce grand vide que j'entreprends de remplir ici, et cela avec un avantage peut être unique dans l'histoire[34].

Or c'est bien à l'appel provoqué par la béance d'un destin brisé — *remplir le grand vide* — qui se pose comme une imprescriptible force intérieure, que les dernières années de la Restauration, durant lesquelles Berlioz est devenu compositeur, doivent une part de leur vocation. Si ces années sont surtout redevables du choix accompli dans une forme inédite d'empressement lyrique pour la voie romantique, elles choisissent de placer l'autorité de Napoléon au cœur de leur conviction. Ce devenir de Napoléon n'est cependant pas sans poser quelques problèmes.

## Devenir d'une dette

Les générations éloignées auxquelles appartiennent Le Sueur (1760-1837) et son élève Berlioz (1803-1869) entretiennent une inévitable différence de point de vue. L'écart des âges se trouve encore conforté, comme on va désormais l'étudier, par celui qu'implique aussi la complexe relation d'autorité maître/disciple. Berlioz en effet acquiert peu à peu la certitude de devoir s'émanciper du conformisme formel auquel son maître identifie l'art suprême.

La musique de Le Sueur, aussi attachée qu'elle soit à une esthétique compassée, représente tout d'abord pour Berlioz une vraie dette d'initiation. Le partage des situations et des expériences vécues a certes motivé l'admiration à cet égard non expérimentée de Berlioz, mais ce processus de transmission a aussi rapidement séparé les deux artistes. Ainsi autant le culte de Napoléon les rassemble, autant la manière de le célébrer les désunit. Le jeune Berlioz devient attentif, en quelque sorte, à la réparation à faire à la mémoire de Napoléon. Il est alors essentiellement sensible au destin héroïque de l'Empereur destitué, celui du maître du monde détenu sur un rocher. C'est ce destin qui fait écrire à Victor Hugo le 9 octobre 1830 dans son poème 'À la colonne' réuni en 1835 aux recueil *Les chants du crépuscule*: «Dors, nous t'irons chercher! ce jour viendra peut-être! / Car nous t'avons pour dieu sans t'avoir eu pour maître!»[35]. La distance qui transforme pour la génération romantique le «maître» en «dieu» explique la position privilégiée qu'occupe Berlioz par rapport à Le Sueur pour façonner en son esthétique un analogue inédit de Napoléon et non plus proposer avec les moyens usuels à la pompe des rois, l'illustration d'un homme à honorer.

---

[34]. Las Cases 1823[C].

[35]. Cette apostrophe correspond à une réaction d'humeur de Hugo face à la tiédeur de la chambre qui le 7 octobre 1830, ne retint pas la proposition de pétitionnaires qui réclamaient une démarche afin que les cendres de Napoléon soient rapportées sous la colonne Vendôme.

# Le Napoléon d'Hector Berlioz

Le jeu de transfert auquel il se prête tend alors moins dans le domaine des arts à faire passer l'ostentation de la puissance politique que le génie de ses enjeux. La recherche compositionnelle vise moins à approcher l'éblouissement des conquêtes que l'intuition du génie militaire et la puissance sidérante des actions sur les champs de bataille. Comme Napoléon a conçu des stratégies militaires uniques et a modifié les règles de l'équilibre européen, il est question de reconsidérer en musique une tradition contrainte et de la libérer avec audace en se fiant à la force des moyens et des circonstances.

À cet égard on doit comprendre que le conformisme de Le Sueur, plus particulièrement son attachement à une logique imitative laborieuse, posèrent vite problème à Berlioz. Il est intéressant d'observer qu'un double article de Berlioz consacré à «l'imitation», apparaît quelques mois avant la mort de Le Sueur (6 octobre 1837) dans la *Revue et gazette musicale de Paris* (1er et 8 janvier[36]). Berlioz n'y mentionne pas les idées de son maître qu'il connaît assurément. Sur le même sujet il s'élance au-delà des principes de l'*Exposé* déjà cité et aussi de la *Lettre en réponse à Guillard*. On peut voir en ces articles un remaniement des idées de Le Sueur, une reprise très transformée de certains éléments.

Si donc Le Sueur dans la bienveillance incontestable de son courrier tente le rôle compliqué de médiateur entre Hector et sa famille, dans quelle mesure ses intuitions justes coïncident-elles avec des intentions esthétiques qu'il ne saurait au fond admettre?

## Le même est un autre

Berlioz écrit à Nanci le 5 septembre 1830: «Cette révolution est faite exprès pour la liberté des arts»[37], tandis que Le Sueur s'émeut des risques que court l'époque de perdre toute morale esthétique. Ce doute, à vrai dire, s'empare de Le Sueur dès les dernières années de la Restauration, à l'orée du printemps 1828 lorsque les premiers concerts de la Société du Conservatoire révèlent aux Parisiens les symphonies de Beethoven, ce Viennois sourd, juste plus jeune que lui de dix années et qui vient de disparaître.

Berlioz rapporte dans ses *Mémoires* le jugement de son maître après une audition de la *Cinquième symphonie* de Beethoven que l'on peut situer entre le 4 mai 1828 et le 30 mai 1830[38]. Le Sueur, au comble d'une émotion, aurait cependant déclaré: «C'est égal, il ne faut pas faire de la musique comme celle-ci»[39]. Aveu flagrant d'une forme d'impréparation à l'essor du romantisme que Beethoven inaugure dès les années 1803-1805, durant lesquelles Le Sueur crée *Ossian ou les Bardes*, l'opéra préféré de l'Empereur!

---

[36]. Berlioz 2001.
[37]. Berlioz 1972F.
[38]. Berlioz 2019F.
[39]. Berlioz 2019G.

Ainsi l'évocation de la figure de Napoléon propose selon qu'on se range du côté de ce que Le Sueur écrit ou de celui de Berlioz à cause duquel ces paroles sont écrites, deux appréhensions de Napoléon. Ce qu'il a été d'une part comme empereur à servir et ce que d'autre part son ascendant d'empereur en disgrâce est en train de désigner comme modèle aux jeunes artistes. Si ces lectures s'entremêlent et peuvent parfois se rejoindre, elles risquent surtout de différer du tout au tout.

La lecture de Le Sueur s'enracine sur une part de son vécu néo-classique qu'on peut qualifier hâtivement de davidien et que l'on peut aussi plus sûrement rapprocher de l'art du baron Guérin[40].

La lecture napoléonienne de Berlioz existe en revanche à travers un imaginaire fantasmé, romantique, né du rocher prométhéen de Sainte-Hélène, et dans le sillage de la manière de Géricault sinon de Delacroix.

Ce que Le Sueur ne percevait peut-être pas totalement de l'Empereur — mais le pouvait-il? trop plongé qu'il se trouvait lui-même dans l'accélération d'un quotidien étonnant, et de la refondation d'un prestige qui pouvait renouer par certains aspects avec les fastes de la cour —, c'est à Berlioz qu'il appartient de l'inventer.

La préférence que Berlioz découvre dès 1828 pour la musique révélée de Beethoven accuse la divergence de perception de la flamme que l'Empereur a fait briller sur l'Europe entière et dont Beethoven a cru pour un temps, comme on sait, pouvoir associer l'éclat à sa propre recherche créatrice. Si Berlioz saisit très vite la supériorité musicale de Beethoven, sa désillusion vis-à-vis de l'art de Le Sueur le déstabilise aussi:

> J'ai éprouvé une contrariété assez vive dernièrement à l'occasion de M. Le Sueur; il faut que je vous dise que cet excellent homme est du siècle de Louis XIV en musique. Il a néanmoins voulu faire exécuter deux de ses compositions dans un des superbes concerts du Conservatoire; j'étais bien sûr d'avance de ce qui est arrivé; ses deux morceaux placés à côté de Beethoven et de Weber ont éprouvé le plus complet échec; et il était loin de s'y attendre [...] Mon rôle se borne à lui déguiser le mieux que je puis ce qu'on dit dans le monde[41].

En quoi par conséquent la musique de Berlioz, si elle souscrit à la prophétie de Le Sueur, peut-elle prétendre à être dite «napoléonienne», sinon par l'invention qu'il faut bien admettre «posthume», d'une couleur musicale qu'on préférerait dire «empire» — non pas «philipparde» — mais qui est plus simplement déclarée «romantique»? Napoléon, se

---

[40]. Il faut penser à son *Andromaque et Pyrrhus* (1813) conservé au Louvre. Notons que Berlioz se recommandera bien plus tard pour le sextuor des *Troyens* du tableau de Guérin, Énée racontant à Didon les malheurs de Troie également au musée du Louvre.

[41]. BERLIOZ 1972[G].

campe pour Berlioz comme une figure saisissable, insaisissable, qui conserve quelque chose d'*inaccessible*[42], voire d'intouchable mais de galvanisant et de terrifiant.

## Napoléon présent ou caché

Si des déclarations napoléoniennes sont fréquentes et constantes dans les propos de Berlioz, le modèle de Napoléon ne donne pourtant pas lieu à de nombreuses œuvres musicales où l'Empereur apparaît nommément. Une forme de procrastination semble tout d'abord avoir retenu Hector jusqu'à la réalisation d'une entité sonore napoléonienne plus implicite que déclarée. Une résistance existe chez Berlioz à réussir à incarner le génie dans l'homme public que fut aussi Napoléon. Comment en effet maintenir la hauteur des implications symboliques de cette figure dans sa représentation littérale, sinon en la répandant dans toute musique sans la dévoiler?

Il est par conséquent nécessaire de constater aussi et surtout comment Napoléon présent, en réalité, presque en permanence dans l'esprit de Berlioz, en est néanmoins presque le plus souvent absent dans son œuvre musical. C'est peut-être par l'ajournement de Napoléon comme homme incarné au profit de sa sanctuarisation comme énergie que se construit le napoléonisme esthétique de Berlioz. Ce processus n'est au demeurant pas réservé à l'Empereur. Gluck, Beethoven, Goethe, Shakespeare, Virgile connaissent aussi la même ferveur et le même travail de réinvention, de réappropriation dans la durée. Mais la différence reste qu'il existe bien une revendication de filiation artistique assez immédiate chez ces auteurs qui ne peut pas être affichée avec autant de lucidité et de détermination à l'égard de Napoléon. Seules des comparaisons, des métaphores permettent d'établir des ponts réels. Parmi les plus directes il faut penser aux comptes rendus de voyages de Berlioz dans toutes les grandes villes d'Europe et jusqu'à Moscou, qu'il nomme ses «Bulletins de la grande armée». Expression logique puisqu'il compare ses tournées à des «campagnes»[43]. Mais aussi des passerelles moins déclarées comme l'idée de l'orchestre pensé à l'image de la grande armée, autant dans ses parades que dans ses manœuvres sur le champ de bataille et bien sûr avec ses mitrailles comme l'a indiqué la caricature bien

---

[42]. Adjectif utilisé par Napoléon pour qualifier le second acte des *Bardes* de Le Sueur. Voir la vingtième soirée des *Soirées de l'orchestre*, où Berlioz relate cet épisode, soulignant lui-même le mot «inaccessible».

[43]. BERLIOZ 1989[A]. Il s'agit de la dédicace à George Kastner du manuscrit autographe de la partition de *Roméo et Juliette*. Le manuscrit réalisé en 1838 a beaucoup accompagné les voyages de Berlioz, le compositeur en explique l'état endommagé par ces mots: «Vous me pardonnerez, mon cher Kastner, de vous donner un manuscrit pareil, ce sont les campagnes d'allemagne [sic] et de Russie qui l'ont ainsi couvert de blessures. Il est comme ces drapeaux *qui reviennent des guerre plus beaux* (dit Hugo) *quand ils sont déchirés*». [Victor Hugo, *Odes et ballades*, livre 4ème, n° 17 (décembre 1827)] Berlioz modifie le texte: «[Ami] Viens; cette gloire, en butte, à tant de traits vulgaires, / Ressemble à ces drapeaux qu'on rapporte des guerres, / Plus beaux quand ils sont déchirés!».

connue de Grandville. Puis et surtout c'est au gigantisme architectural des conceptions sonores des partitions qu'il faut penser comme à des analogues des vues audacieuses que la politique de Napoléon donna à l'Europe jusqu'à remodeler ses frontières et modifier l'urbanisme de ses villes. Est-ce de même un mimétisme historique inconscient qui dans le *Grand Traité d'instrumentation et d'orchestration modernes* met en outre en présence l'orchestre et l'orgue comme l'Empereur et le Pape?

L'Histoire étant le plus souvent comme on sait ironique, elle ne s'est pas privée de brouiller les cartes face cependant à autant d'évidence. Berlioz qui n'a pu connaître Napoléon I[er] que d'après les témoins de son entourage a été en revanche le contemporain de Napoléon III, autre récurrence bien particulière propice à certaines confusions et à certains désenchantements pour ne pas dire certaines désillusions mais aussi certaine affection de filiation. Le compositeur ne tint jamais, et même tout au contraire, l'attitude de Victor Hugo, il chercha à être reçu par Napoléon III comme il imagina dans une version non retenue du final des *Troyens*, à placer en apothéose impériale la conquête de l'Algérie. À cet égard, le phénomène de répétition place presque Berlioz face à Napoléon III qu'il ne saurait vraiment suivre et qui resta plutôt indifférent, comme Le Sueur le fut face à Napoléon I[er].

C'est donc à travers Napoléon I[er] et qui sait par la fabrication d'une survie de son image, quelque chose d'analogue à l'élan du *Anch'io sono pittore*[44] si souvent évoqué par les romantiques et dont Berlioz lui-même n'a pas été avare[45], qui se joue. Ce sont par conséquent toutes les accommodations et toute l'indépendance que cela suppose qu'il convient de mettre en valeur au gré d'un relevé qui suit les fluctuations d'une ligne en quelque sorte en pointillée tant elle procède de quelques indispensables opérations de transmissions/transferts. Ainsi le travail de la mémoire, celui des rêves de l'enfance, des émotions populaires et patriciennes, se traduisent et inventent, réinventent ses modèles. Mais les conditions ne sont pas toujours aussi complices et limpides. Voyons l'exemple du silence de Berlioz lors du retour des cendres le 15 décembre 1840.

## Le retour des cendres et la cantate du *Cinq mai*, épisodes de la vie d'un artiste

C'est a priori le même mouvement de lucidité ou de probité artistique qui inspire officiellement à Hector de refuser pour cet événement de composer «au pied levé» une marche

---

[44]. «Moi aussi je suis peintre», profession de foi prêtée au Corrège lorsqu'il se trouva face à *l'Extase de Sainte Cécile* de Raphaël, toile actuellement conservée à la Pinacothèque nationale de Bologne.

[45]. Berlioz reprend cette formule en français au moins deux fois, Berlioz 2019[H] et Berlioz 2001[B]. Tout d'abord lorsqu'il explique les motivations de son premier concert du 28 mai 1828, ensuite lors de l'article nécrologique qu'il consacre à Le Sueur pour le *Journal des débats*.

pour accompagner le cortège du Retour des Cendres. Pourtant Berlioz confie à son père au sujet de sa *Symphonie funèbre et triomphale*: «Je suis vraiment fâché d'avoir écrit cette marche triomphale pour nos petits Héros de Juillet, elle eût presque convenu pour le grand Héros»[46]. Mais face à ces considérations idéales, d'autres enjeux moins avouables expliquent autrement son retrait de cette manifestation musicale. Hector donne à sa sœur Adèle les motivations secrètes que dissimulent ses arguments officiels, là où l'homme dans son quotidien l'emporte sur le héros.

> Tu sais qu'on m'a demandé une marche triomphale pour l'empereur [*sic*], quinze jours avant la cérémonie [du Retour des Cendres] et que j'ai refusé *sous prétexte* qu'il ne s'agissait pas là d'un couplet de mariage qu'on peut improviser un soir en se couchant. Au fond je voulais me donner le plaisir de voir Auber, Halévy et Adam se casser les reins sur mon apothéose de Juillet; et j'ai réussi à tel point que j'en ai eu le cœur saignant[47].

Or Adolphe Adam de son côté avait assez attendu que la *Symphonie funèbre et triomphale* dont il aurait aimé avoir la commande, soit un fiasco…[48]

Au concert qu'il dirige le 13 décembre Hector programme néanmoins sa cantate *le Cinq mai* officiellement dédicacée à Horace Vernet mais initialement destinée à Louis-Philippe[49] et qui en réalité est aussi sous-titrée *Chant sur la mort de l'Empereur Napoléon*, mais que Berlioz peut nommer *Napoléon*[50]. Horace Vernet après une audition de l'œuvre également déjà donnée en juillet, adresse un court billet à Berlioz pour le remercier de la dédicace. Certaines phrases donnent en quelque sorte un aperçu de la difficulté que le «cycle napoléonien» de Berlioz rencontre à exister:

> Mon cher Berlioz […] Je ne voulais le faire [vous remercier pour la dédicace] qu'en joignant à l'expression de toute ma gratitude pour votre bon souvenir, celle de mon admiration pour cette dernière production de votre vigoureux génie, dont le sujet, il faut le dire aussi, est si digne de lui[51].

Ainsi, dix ans après Le Sueur, l'hommage d'Horace Vernet au «vigoureux génie» de Berlioz «si digne» de celui de Napoléon vérifie la justesse de la prophétie du maître. Certes le

---

[46]. BERLIOZ 1975[A].
[47]. BERLIOZ 1975[B].
[48]. BERLIOZ 1975[C].
[49]. BERLIOZ 1975[D]. «La *cérémonie sublime qui se prépare* et que vous devra la France donne à la publication de cet ouvrage, l'avantage de l'à-propos, et le succès en sera assuré si le Roi daignait en accepter la dédicace».
[50]. BERLIOZ 1975[E].
[51]. BERLIOZ 2003.

moment du retour des Cendres facilite le parallèle dans les esprits français qui reconnaissent ouvertement et unanimement la grandeur de l'Empereur. Mais la cantate de Berlioz a été mise en chantier en 1831, lorsque Berlioz séjournait à la Villa Médicis alors dirigée par Horace Vernet, elle ne fut cependant réellement complétée et créée que le 22 novembre 1835, dans un temps moins déterminant au culte de l'Empereur et dans une phase créatrice d'attente. Cette partition illustre ainsi un exemple de ce que « l'épiphanie »[52] napoléonienne lui suggère lorsqu'il choisit de mettre en musique ce qu'il nomme lui-même « les mauvais vers de Béranger », dont l'élan lui avait néanmoins « paru musical »[53]. Si Vernet, en flatteur, perçoit de façon un peu facile une identité d'échelle entre Napoléon et Berlioz, nous y voyons relativement à d'autres partitions une entreprise certes aboutie mais secondaire, et qui sait laborieuse dans son achèvement peut-être en raison même des interférences entre les intérêts politiques du bonapartisme et le culte idéaliste voué à l'esprit de l'Empereur. Pourtant rien de l'esprit patriote de Béranger ne correspond à l'admiration aristocratique de Berlioz, il ne s'agit pas du même napoléonisme.

Il n'est donc pas aisé pour Berlioz d'aborder Napoléon en musique dans un discours en somme littéral et une mise en scène explicite[54]. À ces sujets, le compositeur préfère d'autres mises en situations, d'autres analogies. C'est bien donc principalement en dehors de Napoléon qu'il faut trouver la présence du Napoléon de Berlioz.

## Solitude

Les grandes admirations de Berlioz pour le génie de l'homme, passent ainsi par des figures qu'il s'est appropriées, mais qu'il ne représente pas nécessairement de façon directe. Espace poétique dans lequel il déploie ce style unique d'un discours à la fois littéral et fantaisiste. Pour être omniprésentes ces entités de l'humain, tel le panthéon qu'il apostrophe dans la lettre souvent citée adressée à Humbert Ferrand qui mêle, il faut le remarquer, des personnages de fiction à leurs créateurs, demeurent le plus souvent secondaires. « Arrivez au plus tôt, je vous en prie [...] Nous lirons Hamlet et Faust, Shakespeare et Goethe ! les muets confidents de mes tourments, les explicateurs de ma vie. Venez, oh ! venez ! personne ici [dans sa famille] ne comprend cette rage de génie. Le soleil les aveugle »[55]. Certes il s'agit ici d'une lettre enflammée d'un jeune-homme de vingt-cinq ans dont l'énergie s'épuise en fébrilité, mais on retrouve plus de trente ans plus tard la même conviction notamment dans la si précieuse correspondance

---

[52]. Van Rij 2015.
[53]. Berlioz 1975F.
[54]. On peut remarquer que le récit de Goguelat du *Médecin de campagne* de Balzac reste également un moment compliqué dans l'énergie littéraire du roman.
[55]. Berlioz 1972H.

échangée avec Carolyne Sayn-Wittgenstein lors de la composition des *Troyens*. Le 20 juin 1859, par exemple, Berlioz écrit: «Quant à l'objet principal de l'œuvre, à l'expression de la passion et des sentiments, à la reproduction musicale des caractères, ce fut dès l'origine la partie la plus facile de ma tâche. J'ai passé ma vie avec ce peuple de demi dieux; je me figure qu'ils m'ont connu, tant je les connais»[56]. Une autre fois il évoque et appelle Napoléon avec une forme d'enthousiasme fanatique et agglutinant qui le lui fait assimiler aussi à Alexandre le Grand:

> Je suis pour la musique appelée par vous-même *libre*. Oui, libre et fière et souveraine et conquérante, je veux qu'elle prenne tout, qu'elle s'assimile tout, qu'il n'y ait plus pour elle ni Alpes ni Pyrénées; mais pour ses conquêtes il faut qu'elle combatte en personne et non par ses lieutenants, je veux bien qu'elle ait, s'il se peut, de bons vers rangés en bataille, mais il faut qu'elle aille elle-même au feu comme Napoléon, qu'elle marche au premier rang de la phalange comme Alexandre[57].

Par cette analogie dont son maître avait été l'instigateur, Berlioz dans le sillage de sa génération a sans cesse développé une singulière forme de métonymie musicale dont le génie de Napoléon est l'un des objets à la manière d'un levier permanent. Mais comme tout levier, il n'est jamais une fin en soi, seulement l'instrument d'une mécanique qui doit aussi s'oublier.

Dans le cas de l'impression que Napoléon exerce sur le compositeur, la particularité tient à la transformation d'une puissance non artistique en sa traduction esthétique. Il s'agit a priori de transposer au domaine de l'imaginaire musical, la réalité d'une énergie qui était la manifestation de l'immanence du génie. À cet égard la scène de la fonte du Persée au dernier acte de *Benvenuto Cellini* a quelque chose d'exemplaire, un affrontement qui fait basculer le cours de l'intrigue, suspend dans l'action de la naissance du chef-d'œuvre le cours du temps et dévore toutes les sculptures de l'atelier. Par ce processus, ce sont les idées de grandeur, d'audace, de clairvoyance ou de perspicacité inspirée qui semblent avoir intéressé l'idéalisme et l'esprit d'invention de Berlioz. Napoléon en ce cas est-il un modèle que l'on peut reconnaître ou est-il une présence diffuse, une figure tutélaire comme Berlioz aime à en invoquer selon des associations qui confondent sous un même élan les personnages réels et les êtres de fictions jusqu'à tenter de fondre la réalité en une mythologie? De là l'errance maladive du compositeur dans l'existence qu'il désigne par ailleurs comme une mystification dont le but est «de connaître ce qui est beau, c'est d'aimer»[58]. De là, par incompréhension, la fatale et exceptionnelle solitude du génie. Aussi la fin de Napoléon demeure-t-elle sans doute pour Berlioz le point vers lequel il se sent comme artiste le plus appelé, le plus aimanté.

---

[56]. Berlioz 1989[B].

[57]. Berlioz 1989[C].

[58]. Berlioz 1989[D]. «Je me suis bien souvent demandé quel pouvait être le but de cette mystification qu'on nomme la vie…».

# Alban Ramaut

## Bibliographie

**Berlioz 1972**
Berlioz, Hector. *Correspondance générale. 1*, Pierre Citron éd., Paris, Flammarion, 1972.

[A] Lettre de recommandation, datée du 20 août 1828, jointe à une lettre de Berlioz au récent Ministre de l'Intérieur Jean-Baptiste de Martignac (4 janvier 1828), p. 205.

[B] Lettre adressée à Albert du Boys, le 20 juillet 1825, qui rend compte de la déclaration de Le Sueur après l'audition de la *Messe solennelle*, p. 97.

[C] Lettre adressée à Joséphine Berlioz, le 23 août 1830, p. 349.

[D] Lettre adressée à Jean-François Le Sueur, [mois de juillet 1824?], pp. 59-60.

[E] Lettre adressée à Humbert Ferrand, le 12 avril 1831, pp. 424-425.

[F] Lettre adressée à Nanci, le 5 septembre 1830, p. 35.

[G] Lettre adressée à sa mère, le 10 Mai 1829, p. 252.

[H] Lettre adressée à Humbert Ferrand, le 16 septembre 1828, p. 208.

**Berlioz 1975**
Id. *Correspondance générale. 2*, Pierre Citron éd., Paris, Flammarion, 1975.

[A] Lettre adressée à son père, le 30 juillet 1840, pp. 649-650.

[B] Lettre adressée à sa sœur Adèle, le 17-20 décembre 1840, p. 670.

[C] Lettre d'Edmond Cavé à Hector Berlioz, le 29 juillet 1840, p. 647, note 1.

[D] Lettre adressée au Roi Louis-Philippe I[er], le 14 mai 1840, p. 642.

[E] Lettre adressée à Adolphe Catelin, le 9 novembre 1840, p. 664.

[F] Lettre adressée à Humbert Ferrand, le 23 janvier 1836, p. 279.

**Berlioz 1989**
Id. *Correspondance générale. 5*, Pierre Citron éd., Paris, Flammarion, 1989.

[A] Lettre adressée à Jean-Georges Kastner, le 17 septembre 1858, p. 592.

[B] Lettre adressée à la princesse Carolyne Sayn-Wittgenstein, le 20 juin 1859, pp. 693-694.

[C] Lettre adressée à la princesse Carolyne Sayn-Wittgenstein, 12 août 1856, p. 352.

[D] Lettre adressée à la princesse Carolyne Sayn-Wittgenstein, le 20 juin 1859, p. 694.

**Berlioz 1996**
Id. 'Aperçu sur la musique classique et la musique romantique', in: *Le Correspondant*, 22 octobre 1830, in: Berlioz, Hector. *Critique musicale. 1*, Yves Gérard, Anne Bongrain et Marie-Hélène Coudroy-Saghaï éds., Paris, Buchet-Chastel, 1996, pp. 63-68.

**Berlioz 2001**
Id. *Critique musicale. 3*, Yves Gérard, Anne Bongrain et Marie-Hélène Coudroy-Saghaï éds., Paris, Buchet-Chastel, 2001.

[A] 'Imitation', in: *Revue et gazette musicale*, 1[er] et 8 janvier 1837, pp. 1-14.

[B] 'Le Sueur', in : *Journal des débats*, 15 octobre 1837, p. 296.

# Le Napoléon d'Hector Berlioz

BERLIOZ 2003
ID. Lettre d'Horace Vernet adressée à Hector Berlioz, le 28 août 1840, in: *Correspondance générale. 8*, Pierre Citron éd., Paris, Flammarion, 2003, p. 186.

BERLIOZ 2016
ID. *Nouvelles lettres de Berlioz, de sa famille, de ses contemporains*, [*Correspondance générale*, vol. IX], Peter Bloom, Joël-Marie Fauquet *et al.* éds., Arles-Venice, Actes Sud-Palazzetto Bru Zane, 2016.
  [A] Lettre de Joséphine Berlioz à Nanci Berlioz, le 25 août 1830, p. 89.
  [B] Lettre de Joséphine Berlioz à Nanci Berlioz, probablement du 27 août 1827, p. 57.
  [C] Lettre de Félix Marmion à sa nièce Nanci Berlioz, le 25 mars [1823], p. 41.

BERLIOZ 2019
ID. *Mémoires d'Hector Berlioz de 1803 à 1865 et ses voyages en Italie, en Allemagne, en Russie et en Angleterre écrits par lui-même*, Peter Bloom éd., Paris, Vrin, (MusicologieS), 2019.
  [A] Ch. X, p. 179.
  [B] Ch. VI, pp. 162-163.
  [C] Ch. III, p. 136.
  [D] Ch. XL, p. 370.
  [E] Ch. III, p. 136.
  [F] Ch. XX, p 239, note 8.
  [G] Ch. XX, p 240.
  [H] Ch. XVIII, p. 230.

BEYLS 2019
Lettre de Joséphine Berlioz adressée à Nanci Berlioz, le 4 septembre 1830, in: *Correspondance de la famille de Berlioz. 1*, Pascal Beyls éd, Grenoble, Pascal Beyls, 2019, p. 473.

BOSCHOT 1906
BOSCHOT, Adolphe. 'Un fils de famille', in: *Hector Berlioz. 1: La jeunesse d'un romantique 1803-1831*, Paris, Plon, 1906, p. 125.

BOSCHOT 1927
ID. *Hector Berlioz. Une vie romantique*, Paris, Librairie de France, 1927, p. 14.

CAIRNS 2002
CAIRNS, David. *Hector Berlioz. 1*, trad. française par Denis Collins, Paris, Fayard, 2002, pp. 456-459.

CHATEAUBRIAND 1951
CHATEAUBRIAND, François René de. *Mémoires d'Outre-Tombe. 1*, Maurice Levaillant et Georges Moulinier éds., Paris, Gallimard, 1951 (Bibliothèque de la Pléiade).

FUREIX 2012
FUREIX, Emmanuel. 'Napoléon Bonaparte', in: *Dictionnaire du romantisme*, Alain Vaillant dir., CNRS Éditions, Paris, 2012, pp. 494-496.

LAS CASES 1823
LAS CASES, Emmanuel (comte de). *Mémorial de Sainte-Hélène*, 8 vol., Paris, l'Auteur, 1823.
[A] 'Préface' [15 août 1822], tome I, p. 1.
[B] 'Préambule', tome I, p. 13.
[C] 'Préface', tome I, p. 1.

LE HIR 2020
LE HIR, Sabine. *Lélio*, n° 43 (novembre 2020).
[A] 'lettre de Le Sueur et du Dr Berlioz', transcrites par Sabine Le Hir avec les facsimilés des lettres, pp. 4-9; sur l'historique des diverses publications de la lettre de Le Sueur: 'Lettres voyageuses', pp. 12-14.
[B] Lettre de Jean-François Le Sueur au Docteur Berlioz, le 25 août 1825, p. 7 (Sabine Le Hir corrige ici une coquille qui rendait le sens incertain, maintenue dans les éditions précédentes).
[C] Lettre de Jean-François Le Sueur au Docteur Berlioz, le 25 août 1825, p. 7.
[D] Lettre de Jean-François Le Sueur au Docteur Berlioz, le 25 août 1825, p. 7.
[E] Lettre de Louis Berlioz à Jean-François Le Sueur, le 2 septembre 1830, p. 9.
[F] Lettre de Louis Berlioz à Jean-François Le Sueur, le 2 septembre 1830, p. 9.

LE HIR 2021
EAD. 'Un don au musée Berlioz', in: *Bulletin de liaison - Association Nationale Hector Berlioz*, n° 55 (2021), pp. 59-80.

LENZ – LAGRANGE 2021
*Le plus puissant souffle de vie: la mort de Napoléon (1821-2021)*, Thierry Lenz et François Lagrange (dir.), Paris, CNRS éditions, 2021.

LE SUEUR 1801
LE SUEUR, Jean-François. *Lettre en réponse à Guillard*, Paris, Baudouin, brumaire an X (novembre 1801), pp. 60-96 et note p. 94.

LESURE 1972
LESURE François. 'Recension *Correspondance générale d'Hector Berlioz, 1803-1832, tome I*', in: *Revue de Musicologie*, LVIII/2 (1972), pp. 274-276.

MONTJOYE 1802
MONTJOYE, Christophe Félix Louis, [Christophe Félix Louis Ventre de la Toulourbe, dit Galart de Montjoye]. *Histoire d'un manuscrit trouvé sur le mont Pausilype*, 4 vol., Paris, Le Normant, 1802.

POURTALÈS 1939
POURTALÈS, Guy de. *Berlioz et l'Europe romantique*, Paris, Gallimard, p. 24.

VAN RIJ 2015
VAN RIJ, Inge. *The Other Worlds of Berlioz: Travels with the Orchestra*, Cambridge, Cambridge University Press, 2015.

# Abstracts and Biographies

Galliano Ciliberti, *Francesco Morlacchi, Napoleone I e il sound imperiale tra Italia e Germania*

When the composer Francesco Morlacchi arrived in Dresden as director of the royal chapel on 5 July 1810, the king of Saxony Frederick Augustus I, allied with France and Napoleon, reigned in the European political arena. And this was the reason why Bonaparte convened the Congress of Dresden in the Saxon capital in May 1812 in which the Emperor of Austria and the kings of Prussia and Saxony swore to him before the Russian campaign. Morlacchi took an active part in the event, having taken care of the entire musical content with the royal chapel, both at court and at the theatre. The most important result of this event was the composition of two cantatas ([1.4.1812] Cantata in praise of Napoleon *Quella che qui s'aggira*; [12.5.1812] Cantata in the presence of Napoleon I and the royal participants in the Congress *No non menton gli dei*) and the offertory *Domine salvum fac imperatorem nostrum Napoleonem* (22.5.1812). The Congress had been 'prepared' not only politically but also from a musical point of view during the previous year. Morlacchi, in fact, had composed the gigantic pro-French opera *Raoul di Créquy* (Royal Theatre, February 1811) — where in one passage the «hammers and pickaxes» are used among the instruments — and the Cantata for the birth of the King of Rome *Anche sì frettoloso* (18.4.1811). Through an examination of the music, the liturgical ceremonial, the poetic texts of the cantatas, and other documents, the sound world of the Congress of Dresden is reconstructed, and in particular the imperial sonorities in Morlacchi's melodramas (such as the use of winds, the band on stage, choirs), as well as his activity as a Bach interpreter.

Galliano Ciliberti is Professor of Music History at the 'Nino Rota' Conservatory of Monopoli. Having graduated in Literature from the University of Perugia, he obtained a Doctorate in Musicology from the University of Liège and a post-doctoral degree from the École Pratique des Hautes Études in Paris. He has received several research contracts from the C.N.R. and was a research fellow at the Department of Musicological and Philological Paleographic Sciences of the University of Pavia, Cremona branch. The author of many essays and numerous books, he has participated in various conferences in Italy and abroad. Winner of the Bertini Calosso Award (1998-2000 edition), he deals with the musical relations between Rome and Paris in the seventeenth century and with Roman sacred music in the seventeenth century.

*\*\*\**

Magdalena Oliferko-Storck, *Napoleonic Warsaw: The Emperor's Sojourns and the French Culture in the Soundscape of the Capital of Poland before Chopin*

The common musical history of France and Poland deepened especially in the Napoleonic era. It was a period not only of enhanced military cooperation, but also in the cultural field, which prepared the foundations for the 'Great Polish Emigration' to France after 1831. The capital of Poland, deprived of its identity, was

# Abstracts and Biographies

incorporated into Prussia after the last partition in 1795. It was liberated for a short time in 1806 by Napoleon Bonaparte, who established the Duchy of Warsaw, a state with its own constitution, government and army, actually dependent on the French Empire and subordinated to the French Emperor. It was perceived as 'new Poland', a substitute for statehood. In 1812, during the attack on Russia, Napoleon was accompanied by over 100,000 Poles who naively believed that their country would be rebuilt after a possible triumphant victory. The defeat of Napoleon ended the reign of France in Warsaw, opening the period of Russian rule, in which the cultural efforts of the capital were constantly suppressed. Although the Napoleonic period in Warsaw was short-lived in the sense of time (1806-1814), it had a more spectacular influence on Polish culture than the devastating, over 100-year-old invasion of the Russian oppressor. A true francophilia and a cult of Napoleon, perceived as the saviour of the nation, the resurrector of lost Poland, in whom there were hopes for the revival of pre-partition Poland, prevailed in the Duchy of Warsaw. It was documented also in works of fine art and music of that time, including in the opera *Andromeda* by Elsner, created in honour of Napoleon. The Napoleonic era significantly contributed to the future cultural exchange between both nations. In post-Napoleonic Warsaw, French language and culture were widespread, deepening the cosmopolitan aspirations of the Polish capital. After the fall of the November Uprising, France opened up to Polish culture in a gesture of gratitude, giving shelter to its nearly 6,000 emigrants. They contributed to the assimilation of Polish-French themes, establishing a number of cultural and educational Polish institutions in France, producing art in private salons and publishing Polish national compositions. Chopin became the iconic symbol of the merger of Polish-French culture in the post-restoration era. The present paper presents the musical landscape of Napoleonic Warsaw: the socio-political situation, cultural institutions, public space, music publishing and repertoire. A large part is also devoted to Napoleon's extended stay in Warsaw in 1807, which had a spectacular impact on the musical life of the capital.

MAGDALENA OLIFERKO-STORCK is a musicologist and concert organist. She graduated in musicology from the University of Warsaw (2005), awarded for her MA thesis on Organ Concertos by J. S. Bach. There followed organ studies at the Hochschule für Musik und Theater in Hamburg (2010) as well as a Specialized MA at the Department of Historical Keyboard Instruments at the Hochschule für Alte Musik in Basel (2011). She was awarded a Ph.D. in Musicology *summa cum laude* from the Université de Genève and the University of Warsaw for her monograph on the life and work of Julian Fontana (2019). She is the author of over 50 academic publications (books, articles). Since 2007, she has been cooperating with the Fryderyk Chopin Institute in Warsaw. She is a Research Associate at the Universität Bern.

***

ERIC BOARO, «*Non essendovi più capelle in veruna chiesa...*». *Finanziamento e impiego musicale nella Modena giacobina e la stagione al Teatro Rangone tra il 1798 e il 1799*

This article examines various unpublished archival papers relating to certain events that took place in Modena between 1798 and 1799. Preserved at the State Archive in Milan, they illustrate how the city's musical job market had been affected negatively by the anti-aristocratic sentiment and laicism of the new Napoleonic state, the Repubblica Cisalpina. Due to the fact that the local aristocracy and clergy lost their of power and wealth suddenly, all of the city's operatic and musical activities, including those that took place within religious institutions, ceased, leaving many musicians without any source of income. Therefore, some among them presented several petitions to representatives of the Modenese government. They accepted them, and persuaded the Minister of the Interior to reopen the local theatre, the Teatro Rangone. The plan was to use funds originally allocated for the theatrical activities organised by a local boarding school for aristocrats, the Civico Collegio. Yet these activities ceased with the advent of the Repubblica Cisalpina. The petitions of the musicians bear dramatic witness to the consequences of the renewed socio-political order on the daily lives of musicians during the early Napoleonic age in Italy. Also, the lengthy correspondence between the various levels of government — local and central — provide evidence of the strategy that the Repubblica Cisalpina adopted to aid the poverty-stricken musicians of Modena. In a more general sense, this article shows how the sudden change of government negatively affected the musical labour market in Italy, due to the loss of power and wealth of two key players in the history of music in pre-Revolutionary Italy: the clergy and the aristocracy.

Eric Boaro studied Musicology at the State University in Milan, where he earned a degree in 2015 (Highest Honours). He also graduated in Piano at the Conservatory 'G. Puccini' in Gallarate (Honours). In 2021 he earned a Ph.D. in Musicology at the University of Nottingham. His main research interest is the Neapolitan music of the early eighteenth century. He has published in journals such as *Eighteenth-Century Music*, *Ad Parnassum*, *Current Musicology*, *Early Music*, and *Acta Musicologica*. He teaches music history in various Italian conservatories.

***

Federico Gon, *'Feast, Flour, and Gallows': Haydn's «Creation» in Naples (1821) and the Politics of Restoration*

During Lent of 1821 (specifically the evenings of 10 and 12 April) Joseph Haydn's *The Creation* was performed at the Teatro San Carlo in Naples under direction of Gioachino Rossini, with a cast of great renown: there were, among others, Andrea Nozzari, Giovanni Battista Rubini, Filippo Galli, Michele Benedetti and Adelaide Comelli. This Neapolitan staging assumed a certain importance because it was part of a particular and very delicate political-social context: the year before (June-July 1820) Naples had been the scene of violent clashes and insurrections which culminated with the king's flight to Palermo and the concession of the Constitution, a libertarian act frowned upon by the great European powers, Austria first and foremost. After the Troppau Congress (27 October), Metternich summoned King Ferdinand I to Ljubljana to clarify his intentions: he decided on armed intervention, and the Habsburg troops entered Naples in March 1821 bringing back to the throne Ferdinand I, who suspended the Constitution and began a harsh repression of the insurgents and collaborators. In the very days in which *The Creation* was prepared, the Marquis of Circello, Prime Minister of the King, promulgated two edicts (9 and 12 April) through which punitive measures and capital punishments were arranged for those guilty of 'revolution', which led from there to 13 life sentences and 30 death sentences. Hence the particularly symbolic choice of performing this *oratorio* (through precise lexical and musical choices made by Rossini, an expert connoisseur both of the Haydn repertoire and of Bourbon politics) can be read as a clear desire to musically underline the restoration of the *status quo* by the Habsburgs, through a work that could not only represent a peak of the Viennese musical school, but could also establish a clear link both to the people and to the Neapolitan nobility and bourgeoisie thanks to the exercise of the creative power of divine majesty and the rediscovered political stability, embodied by the majesty of Ferdinand I.

Federico Gon is a musicologist and composer. He studied musicology (Masters Degree and Ph.D.) at the University of Padua, and has to his credit numerous participations in conferences as well as the publication of books and essays in academic journals specialising in opera and instrumental music of the xviii-xix centuries. He is a winner of the 'Tesi Rossiniane' award (Fondazione Rossini, Pesaro, 2013). He is member of

# Abstracts and Biographies

the Committee of the Italian National Edition of the Comedies for Music by Domenico Cimarosa and has been a post-doctoral researcher at the University of Vienna (2016-2019). He currently teaches at the Conservatorio 'G. Tartini' in Trieste.

\*\*\*

Matthieu Cailliez, *Étude des transferts musicaux franco-allemands à l'époque napoléonienne à travers le prisme de l'«Allgemeine musikalische Zeitung»*

On 3 October 1798, the weekly publication of the *Allgemeine musikalische Zeitung*, the most important German music periodical of the first half of the 19th century, founded by the Breitkopf & Härtel publishing house, began in Leipzig. One year later, the *coup d'état* of 9 November 1799 and the establishment of the Consulate symbolically marked the end of the French Revolution, the assumption of power by Napoleon Bonaparte and the beginning of the Napoleonic era in Europe. This examination of the *Allgemeine musikalische Zeitung* between 1798 and 1815 offers a wealth of additional information on the extent and intensity of Franco-German musical transfers in action during the Consulate and the Empire. The central role of music publishing was favoured by the establishment of numerous German professionals in this sector in the French capital. The circulation of scores in both directions between Paris and Leipzig was thus greatly facilitated. Whether in the original language or in translation, Breitkopf & Härtel offered the German public privileged access to an extensive repertoire of French works, instrumental methods from the Paris Conservatory, and essays on music, as well as the latest in Parisian instrument making, such as pedal harps and bows. While Parisian musical news was followed with the greatest attention, the incredible diffusion of French opera in the German-speaking world was attested to by hundreds of performance reports and by numerous reviews of opera scores and related products. The readership was also informed in detail about the performances of German works given in Paris. Whereas the editorial staff of the periodical rarely expressed a political position in the 1800s and seemed to adopt a form of neutrality towards the Napoleonic regime, this changed in the early 1810s with the editorial emphasis on German patriotic songs at the time of the *Befreiungskriege* or wars of liberation.

Matthieu Cailliez is a Lecturer (*Maître de conférences*) of History and analysis of music in the Department of Musicology at the Jean Monnet University in Saint-Étienne and is also a permanent member of the Institut d'Histoire des Représentations et des Idées dans les Modernités (IHRIM: UMR 5317). He holds a doctorate from the Universities of Bonn, Florence and Paris-Sorbonne in the framework of the «Trinational Doctoral Programme in Europe's Founding Myths of Europe in Literature, Art and Music». He is the author of some thirty articles mainly devoted to lyrical theatre in Europe in the nineteenth century.

\*\*\*

Maria Bribili, *The Sound of Empire: Politicised Dramaturgy in French Opera from the French Revolution to Napoleon*

My article discusses the profound changes in the aesthetics, the politicised dramaturgy, and the music brought upon French opera during the French Revolution and the Napoleonic wars. Phenomena will be explored such as the diminishing of the protagonist vs. the chorus as a dramatis persona, the collective revolutionary oath-taking, and the realistically staged depiction of a siege and battle on stage, all introduced by the French Revolution but still dominant during the Napoleonic era. As discussed in my first book, the specific 'siege-opera' and 'expedition-opera' sub-genres not only reflect the organised propaganda of the Revolutionary regime and of

# Abstracts and Biographies

Napoleon's regime (both as a consul and as an emperor), but they constitute a direct acculturisation process, with the representation of a number of contemporary historic events on the opera stage, often just months after their occurrence. The 'siege-opera' sub-genre depicts various authentic sieges and battles from the Revolutionary wars against the European coalition, often transposed into Greek or Roman antiquity. With the intention of depicting the political ideas of democracy in 'siege-opera', specific new models in dramaturgy, staging, and music were created. These strong Revolutionary impressions lingered throughout the Napoleonic period, during which many of these 'siege-operas' were frequently performed. The evolution of the genre from the Revolution into the Napoleonic era can be identified in Méhul's *Le pont de Lodi* and *Adrien* and Spontini's/Jouy's *Fernand Cortez*. The latter two 'expedition-operas' were ordered so as to celebrate Napoleon's glory just before the first Napoleonic expeditions in Egypt and in Spain. *Fernand Cortez*, which Napoleon hated (he left the premiere before the ending of the opera), is the most complex of these works, remaining politically ambiguous in its sophisticated dramaturgy and conflicted approach to colonialism, while, in its complex historicism, it paves the road to the later genre of *grand opéra*.

Maria Birbili studied piano, voice and French literature at the Sorbonne Université, and musicology and theatre studies at the Freie Universität Berlin. After her Ph.D. (*Die Politisierung der Oper im 19. Jahrhundert*, Peter Lang, 2014), she has been a Fellow of the Gerda Henkel Stiftung in Italy, a *chercheur associé* at the Maison des Sciences de l'Homme in Paris, a Visiting Scholar at the University of Chicago, and a collaborator in the critical edition projects for Rossini, Verdi (University of Chicago), and Meyerbeer (Schloß Thurnau). She is currently completing her habilitation and teaching in different Universities in Germany, with a second book on Rossini to appear soon.

\*\*\*

Martin Barré, *Dans l'ombre de Paris. Circulation et diffusion de la musique de scène sous l'Empire: l'exemple du théâtre de Versailles*

The municipal theatre of Versailles, which was founded in 1777 by Marguerite Brunet, and which adopted the name 'la Montansier' in 1936 in hommage to its founder, experienced difficulties throughout the 19th century, in particular because of its proximity to Paris. Like most theatres of the time, the Versailles establishment had its own orchestra which, in 1813, was comprised of twelve musicians under the direction of Antoine-François Heudier. The repertoire mostly consisted of *opéras-comiques*, ballets as well as popular drama, notably vaudevilles and melodramas. Even though French incidental music composed during and after the second half of the 19th century has recently been the subject of several publications, earlier works in this genre are still not well known. Only one article by Nicole Wild has offered a first approach to the music that accompanied the melodramas in the first half of the century, but vaudeville music from this period has not given rise to any systematic work so far. We will analyse here the dramatic repertoire and the musical practices of the theatre of Versailles from a rich collection of orchestral material (not yet inventoried) that was used in the city theatre and kept in the municipal library of Versailles. This includes in particular the separate parts of the incidental music that accompanied the *vaudevilles*, melodramas and ballets. Through an examination of this unpublished collection of 589 manuscripts, our study therefore analyses the musical practices of a provincial town too close to Paris to have developed an artistic identity of its own. The Versailles case will thus make it possible to examine the diffusion and circulation of incidental music between the capital and its suburbs, as well as their reception. The objective of this study, in addition to participating in the resurgence of forgotten practices, is also to refute the idea of a Parisian cultural hegemony that would spread throughout the country.

# Abstracts and Biographies

As much a musicologist as a cellist, MARTIN BARRÉ has been trying for several years to establish a dialogue between the two disciplines. That is why, alongside his training as an instrumentalist, he completed a master's degree in musicology at the Paris Conservatoire in the aesthetics and history of music classes, graduating in 2023. He then began a music history thesis under contract to the École des Hautes Études en Sciences Sociales on the history of stage fright, under the supervision of Rémy Campos and Céline Frigau Manning. His work in musicology was rewarded in 2020 by the Monique Rollin Prize awarded by the Fondation de France, and he was one of the winners of the SYLFF 2022-2023 grant awarded by the Tokyo Foundation for Policy Research for the project *Stage Fright through History: When the Past Serves the Present*. After obtaining a bachelor's degree in modern cello at the Pôle Supérieur de Paris-Boulogne, he began a new bachelor's degree in baroque cello at the CNSM in Lyon in 2023.

\*\*\*

ANNELIES ANDRIES, *Caroline Branchu: A Model of Nineteenth-Century Womanhood?*

This chapter analyses the public persona of Caroline Branchu, a star singer at the Paris Opéra during the first quarter of the nineteenth century. After making her name in revivals of *tragédies lyriques* by Gluck, Piccinni and Sacchini, she triumphed premiering the leading role in Gaspare Spontini's *La Vestale* (1807). Branchu's career took place against the highly turbulent background of early nineteenth-century France, when legal and cultural notions about the societal roles of women and of people of colour were continuously in flux. More progressive regulations concerning their rights dating from the 1790s were short-lived as the revolutionary decade made way for the Napoleonic era, and rights were even further curbed at the return of the Bourbon Monarchy. Drawing on performance materials, press articles, and private correspondence, this chapter examines Branchu's public images (as an individual, as a singer, as a performer of operatic roles) and their entwinement with changing legal and cultural imaginations. It analyses how a singer interacted with — and may even have directed — contemporary imaginations of what it meant to be a person of colour, a woman, and a singer in early nineteenth-century France. In doing so, it shows that these artists gave living, embodied form to pseudo-scientific, cultural, and legal notions about individuals with these identities. Ultimately, I argue that singers, especially those with long careers like Branchu, could offer points of reference that connected older and newer roles for women, people of colour, and other artists that found themselves in unstable legal and cultural environments.

ANNELIES ANDRIES is Assistant Professor at Utrecht University. Her research investigates how European musical culture developed in the wake of long-nineteenth-century military conflicts from the perspectives of gender and trauma in connection to identity. She is writing a book on elite identity formation through opera in Napoleonic France. Her work has been published in *Cambridge Opera Journal*, *Journal of Culture and War Studies*, *French Historical Studies* and others. She is also active as a performance-researcher examining nineteenth-century musico-theatrical and salon genres, and writes programme notes for opera houses.

\*\*\*

CLAUDIA CHIBICI-REVNEANU, *Moving towards Exclusion: A Case Study of the 'Female Viennese School'*

The chapter focuses on the notion that the rise of Romanticism and the Napoleonic era in some ways mark a 'regression' for female composers. It is argued that this was due to complex socio-historical changes in the music world and beyond. During the French Revolution, claims for female rights started to be explicitly formulated and, within the music world, women had gained considerable presence in some European regions. It seems that during

## Abstracts and Biographies

the fall of the *ancien régime*, there was a glimpse of hope for musical women. Yet, somewhat like the backlash against women's rights represented by the 'Napoleonic code' (1804), the classical music world began to shut composing women out with new rigour, partly through the increasing adoption of an embodied (male) 'genius' ideology which may, at least hypothetically, be seen as a threat-response to (gender) developments, again within and beyond the musical sphere. The discussion centres on the Viennese composers Marianna Martinez, Maria Theresia von Paradis and Josepha Auernhammer, provocatively referred to as the 'female Viennese School'. It explores their lives, works and musical connections to the (first) 'male Viennese School' of their contemporaries Haydn, Mozart and Beethoven. Whereas all six composers, albeit to different degrees and within individual contexts, reached remarkable musical success, Haydn, Mozart and Beethoven were elevated to godlike genius status, whereas Martinez, Paradis and Auernhammer were forgotten or chiefly remembered as grotesque or musically mediocre figures. It will be argued that they were not only affected by the rise of personified genius during Romanticism, but — like the male Viennese School — partly involved in the configuration of this ideology which normatively celebrates male composers and helps to ideologically push female creators back and out. The gendered nature of genius, as well as the lives of Martinez, Paradis and Auernhammer have already been well researched. This chapter is original in its concern with the intersection of the rise of genius and a historical 'regression' for women composers and a detailed analysis of (gendered) patterns related to the 'female' and 'male' Viennese School which have not yet been sufficiently explored.

CLAUDIA CHIBICI-REVNEANU is Lecturer of Gender and Intercultural Development at the National Autonomous University of Mexico (UNAM) in León. She holds a Ph.D. in Cultural Policy Studies from the University of Warwick (UK) and is a member of the Mexican research program SNI. She has published two novels and numerous book chapters and academic articles in international books and journals, mainly focused on women composers, whose work she also promotes through concert-conferences. In 2017 she received the UNAM's prestigious Sor Juana Inés de Cruz award for women in academia.

\*\*\*

HENRI VANHULST, *Les relations entre Jean-Jérôme Imbault et ses compositeurs d'après des lettres de Jean-Louis Duport et Ferdinando Paër*

In his letter to Jean-Jérôme Imbault written in Potsdam on 6 March 1804, Jean-Louis Duport presented the content of his *Essai sur le doigté du violoncelle* which he wanted to publish. A second letter, written by Duport in Potsdam on 29 June 1805, proves that Imbault had accepted it. He had, however, asked for some additions and had revised Duport's writing. Imbault had also sent the revised and corrected version of the manuscript and asked for the author's agreement. In addition, Duport informed his publisher that a certain Derondville was planning to open a bookshop in Berlin and wanted to know the financial conditions for the distribution of Imbault's prints. Ferdinando Paer's letter to Imbault of 12 July 1811 reveals that the composer had decided himself to order an arrangement for two flutes and alto of his opera *Camilla*. A musician in Parma, whose name is not mentioned, wrote it and asked for fifty copies as payment. Apparently Imbault did not publish the arrangement.

HENRI VANHULST is Emeritus Professor of Musicology at the Université Libre de Bruxelles. He is a member of the Académie royale de Belgique and director of the series 'Études de musicologie' (Brussels, Peter Lang). He is also the president of the Belgian Musicological Society and the editor of the *Revue belge de Musicologie*. His research focuses mainly on vocal and instrumental Renaissance music, the history of music publishing in the

# Abstracts and Biographies

Low Countries and in France, studies on printed or manuscript sources, the circulation of music in Europe in the 16th-19th centuries, the history of the Brussels Conservatory and the Brussels concert life.

\*\*\*

DAVID ROWLAND, *Music Publishing and Markets c.1750-1830*

The period 1750-1830 saw the growth of music industries across Europe and further afield, especially in those countries where the economic and social conditions supported their development. Where the environment allowed it, as it did throughout the period in parts of northern Europe, music publishing and instrument making flourished. Elsewhere, such as in German-speaking lands, the industry took a little while to develop into a major force, but was firmly established by the beginning of the nineteenth century. In other countries to the south and east, progress was very slow and even at the end of the period music industries were still in their infancies in some places. This was a period of growing internationalism, when music publishers took steps to cooperate with each other across borders insofar as they were able at a time when copyright provision was inadequate. But the major upheavals that occurred with the French Revolution and the Napoleonic wars had a major impact on the ways in which these businesses were able to trade with each other. Britain was especially, though not uniquely, affected. However, in spite of prolonged attempts by the French to weaken British trade with Europe and the upheavals caused by war, the internationalisation of the music business continued even through uncertain times during which the free movement of goods and intellectual property were hampered. Part of the continuing success of Britain's music businesses lay in the development of trade with current and former colonies. This chapter outlines the varied fortunes of music businesses during this critical period, demonstrating how the dissemination of music was affected. It shows how some of the major figures of the period, including Beethoven, Clementi and Pleyel, fared as composers and as leaders of the music industry.

DAVID ROWLAND is Professor of Music and former Dean of Arts at The Open University. He is the author of three books and numerous chapters and articles on the performance history of the piano and early keyboard instruments. He has edited the first scholarly edition of Clementi's correspondence, which provided the impetus for a much broader investigation of the London music trade during the French Revolution and Napoleonic wars, on which he has published extensively. His research has also focused on listening history, with the assistance of two large Arts and Humanities Research Council grants. David also performs on early keyboard instruments and has been Director of Music at Christ's College, Cambridge since 1984.

\*\*\*

EMMANUEL REIBEL, *The Empire's Mechanical Musics: From Soundscape to Reception*

Under the Empire, mechanical musics never ceased to develop, continuing along the flourishing path begun in the previous century. It is of particular interest insofar as it crossed social, geographic, and institutional frontiers: from Paris to the provinces; from collectors' items preserved by wealthy aristocrats to cylinder organs animating the street and countryside alike, from churches and popular fairgrounds to private concerts. Mechanical music was thus omnipresent, sometimes one simple element of a soundscape, sometimes a spectacular object on display. In this chapter, special attention is paid to Maelzel's instruments, the history of which is less well known. In reconstructing the Parisian trajectory of the first Panharmonicon and the trumpet player automaton in light of contemporaneous primary sources, it will be shown that these instruments contributed to the circulation of melodies — transcending the boundary between the learned and the popular — and that they also served a

## Abstracts and Biographies

transcultural dynamic, disseminating Austrian music in France and boldly placing the two cultures in close contact at a moment when the nations faced each other on the battlefield. In those days, listeners and critics became so familiar with mechanical music that it came to structure their perception and judgments of taste. And yet, while the machine may appear to represent certain ideals (regularity, precision, efficiency, speed), in critical discourse, the 'mechanisation' of performers is most often perceived as negative. The machine thus becomes an anti-ideal, connoting boredom and the absence of expression or of life. Thenceforth, it is expected that pianists should be more than mere musical machines, that singers should no longer content themselves with being agreeable serinettes, and even that composers should guard against mechanical facility. The ideal of non-mechanicity would soon become widely held, transcending the various quarrels and national rivalries, eventually becoming a strong marker of Romantic sensibility.

Emmanuel Reibel is Professor of Musicology at the École Normale Supérieure de Lyon and Professor of Aesthetics at the Conservatoire de Paris. His work focuses in particular on music discourses and the history of romanticism. He is the author of a number of renowned works (including *Comment la musique est devenue romantique. De Rousseau à Berlioz*, Paris, Fayard, 2013) and director of the Dictéco (*Dictionnaire d'écrits de compositeurs*) program, which he cofounded with Valérie Dufour and Michel Duchesneau (<dicteco.huma-num.fr>). His latest book has just been published: *Du métronome au gramophone: musique et révolution industrielle* (Paris, Fayard, 2023).

\*\*\*

Inês Thomas Almeida, *Imaginary Soundscapes: The Sounds of Portuguese Music as Captured by German Travellers at the End of the «Ancien Régime»*

In the second half of the 18th century, Portugal, which until then had been a destination of little importance for European travellers, mainly due to its peripheral geographical location and its political action turned toward the Atlantic, became increasingly visited by foreigners, partly because of the sudden interest caused by the Lisbon Earthquake, partly because of the growth of the phenomenon of scientific expeditions and leisure travel, and partly by the arrival in Portugal of army officers during the Peninsular Wars. Their descriptions, especially those concerning musical manifestations, help us to recreate the soundscape of the Portuguese streets, the music, and sounds echoing in the public sphere, from merchants to royal festivities and sacred processions. Nevertheless, the way that soundscape is perceived varies according to the regional, religious, socio-economic, and cultural background of the traveller, as well as the public they were addressing. The historical and political context, not only of the traveller but of the moment itself, also played a very important role, and this is how we find a change, in the first quarter of the 19th century, in the type of description given, accompanying the royal family's flight to Brazil after the Napoleonic invasions and the crown's continued efforts to show that Portugal was a solid and promising kingdom, even if, for the moment, with an extra-European capital in Rio de Janeiro. The traveller's depiction, more than a kind of snapshot of the cultural practice it intends to portray, is a starting point that often reflects, first and foremost, their projections and expectations. Based on the analysis of several German sources between 1762 and 1816, this article presents an overview of the perceived Portuguese soundscapes before and after Napoleon, pointing out filters and stressing the delicate balance between the observed and the imagined.

Inês Thomas Almeida is a musicologist, Ph.D. in Music Historical Sciences from Universidade Nova de Lisboa and a Postdoctoral Research Fellow at IELT/FCSH. Her dissertation *The German Gaze: Musical Practices in Portugal at the End of the Ancien Régime According to German Sources*, supervised by Rui Vieira Nery and funded

# Abstracts and Biographies

by FCT, was unanimously awarded the highest classification. Her research focuses on Iberian music and literature of the 15th to 17th centuries, Portuguese and German music in the 18th century, travelogues, women and music, and transnational cultural networks. She is a lecturer at the Faculty for Social and Human Sciences at the Universidade Nova de Lisboa and regularly publishes peer-reviewed articles in scientific journals in her research field.

*∗∗∗*

Alban Ramaut, *Le Napoléon d'Hector Berlioz, proposition de lecture*

On 25 August 1830, Jean-François Le Sueur wrote to Dr Louis Berlioz about his son Hector, who had been awarded First Prize of the Prix de Rome on the 21st: «He might one day become the Napoleon of musical Science, because of how greatly he will impact it». What intuition gave birth to his opinion? The composer of *Les Bardes* and successor of Paisiello as *maître de chapelle* at the Tuileries knew that the Emperor's ascendency must have inspired the arts. What ardent images did Berlioz himself draw from the aesthetic upheaval that the great man's actions engendered in the music of Berlioz's master, but also in that of Spontini, and Beethoven later? What did the tales of his uncle Félix Marmion, a cavalry officer who took part in the *Grande Armée*'s campaigns all the way to the battlefield of Waterloo, suggest to him? Why does Napoleon, whom Berlioz seemed to admire so much, appear so little in the composer's public and private writings? Of the specifically Napoleonian musical projects, few works came to fruition, apart from the *Cinq Mai* cantata (which Berlioz dubbed *Napoléon* on 9 November 1840). However, fragments of these musical pieces he imagined and drafted have migrated to other works including his most remarkable — the *Grande messe des morts*, the *Symphonie funèbre et triomphale*, and the *Te Deum*, which ironically premiered under Napoleon III. Thus, traces of Napoleonic influence have subtly seeped through Berlioz's work.

A former student at the CNSMD of Paris, Alban Ramaut is Emeritus Professor at the Jean Monnet University of Saint-Étienne, France. He works at the IHRIM research laboratory. His research focuses on Berlioz and the genealogies of French musical Romanticism. He also studies the vocabulary of music, from the *Encyclopédie* to Castil-Blaze's *Dictionnaire de musique moderne*. He published *Hector Berlioz 1869-2019, 150 ans de passions* with Emmanuel Reibel (Aedam Musicae, 2019).

# Index of Names

## A

ADAM, Adolphe 327
ADAM, (Jean-)Louis [Johann Ludwig] 115, 268
ADDISON, Joseph 224
ALEMBERT, Jean le Rond d' 279
ALEXANDER I, Emperor of Russia 297
ALEXANDER III, the Great, King of Macedonia 329
ALMEIDA, Inês Thomas xiii, 295
AMBROGI [Ambrosi], Antonio 101
ANDRÉ, Johann 247
ANDRIES, Annelies xii, 195
ANICET-BOURGEOIS, Auguste 184
ASIMOV, Peter 290
AUBER, Daniel-François-Esprit 24, 327
AUBERT, Olivier 114
AUENBRUGGER, Marianna von 222
AUERNHAMMER [Aurnhammer], Josepha Barbara xii, 221-223, 226, 229-234, 236-237

## B

BACCIARELLI, Marcello 43
BACH, Carl Philipp Emanuel 118
BACH, Johann Sebastian 6, 25-29, 118
BAILLOT, Pierre(-Marie-François de Sales) 249
BALDESCHI, Lodovico 26
BALOCCHI, Luigi Giuseppe 277
BALZAC, Honoré de 168, 328
BANGER, Josiah 265
BARBEY, Frédéric 207
BARRÉ, Martin xii, 167
BAUDIOT, Charles-Nicolas 249

BAUMANN, Thomas 231
BAYER, Karoline 222
BEAUBLÉ, Sophie 246
BEAUHARNAIS, Eugène de 283-284
BEAUHARNAIS, Hortense de 203
BEAUMARCHAIS, Pierre-Augustin Caron de 278
BEAUVARLET-CHARPENTIER, Jacques-Marie 130
BEETHOVEN, Ludwig van ix-xiii, 6, 13, 25, 29, 48, 110, 126, 132, 221-222, 229-232, 235-236, 268, 280, 284, 298, 323-325
BELLINI, Vincenzo 4, 98, 100
BELLOTTO, Bernardo 42
BENEDETTI, Michele 95, 101
BENINCASA, Gioacchino 14
BENTHEIM-STEINFURT, Ludwig von 281, 285
BERLIOZ, Hector xiv, 124, 213, 313-329
BERLIOZ, Joséphine 317, 319
BERLIOZ, Louis 313, 315-316
BERNARD, Esther 300-302
BERNARD, Samuel 300
BERTEAU, Martin 249
BERTON, Henri-Montan 67, 114, 120, 195, 196, 209-210, 288
BIRBILI, Maria xi, 151
BLAHETKA, Leopoldine 236
BLAND, John 267
BLASIUS, Frédéric 112, 114, 177
BOARO, Eric xi, 77
BOCCHERINI, Luigi 110
BOGUSŁAWSKI, Wojciech 45-46, 48, 56, 60, 62-63

# Index of Names

Boieldieu, François-Adrien 6, 47, 52, 114, 119-120, 132, 268
Bonaparte, Girolamo [Jérôme, Hieronymus], King of Westphalia 10
Bonaparte, Luciano [Lucien], Prince of Canino and Musignano 202
Bonno, Giuseppe 226
Bordesi, Giovanni Battista 22
Bordogni, Marco 286
Borghese, Camillo Filippo Ludovico 56
Bottioni, Luigi 22
Bourgoing, Jean-François de 9
Branchu, (Alexandrine-)Caroline xii, 156, 195-202, 206-214
Branchu, Isaac 207
Branchu, Paméla 196
Brand, Bettina 221
Braun, Peter von 280
Bréval, Jean-Baptiste 247-249, 254
Brifaut, Charles 209
Brizzi, Antonio 56
Broadwood, James Shudi 267
Brocard, Marie-Madeleine 199
Brühl, Alojzy Fryderyk 66
Brunet, Marguerite 167
Bruni, Antonio Bartolomeo 120
Bruno, Paul W. 223
Brzezina, Jan 49
Burney, Charles 227, 260

### C

Cailliez, Matthieu xi, 109
Cambini, Giuseppe Maria 112, 114
Capece Minutolo, Antonio, Prince of Canosa 98-99, 101, 103, 105
Capelle, Pierre 179
Carbonel, Joseph-François-Narcisse 114
Carlos III, King of Spain 98
Carpani, Giuseppe 101, 103-105
Carpentier, Jules 277
Carrascosa, Michele 97
Carrère, Joseph-Barthélemy-François 298
Caruso, Luigi 6
Castelli, Ignaz Franz xi, 109, 123

Catalani, Angelica 49
Catel, Charles-Simon xii, 120, 212, 249
Chardin, Jean-Baptiste Simeon 278
Chassé de Chinais, Charles-Louis-Dominique 121
Chédeville, Étienne Morel de 113, 123
Cherubini, Luigi ix-x, 4, 17, 25, 48, 66, 113-115, 118-120, 164, 276, 280-281
Chevalier, Jean-Joseph 199
Chevalier, Marie-Rose see Branchu, (Aléxandrine-) Caroline
Chibici-Revneanu, Claudia xii, 221
Chladni, Ernst Florens Friedrich 118
Chopin, Fryderyk x, 42, 46-47, 51, 54, 70
Chopin, Mikołaj 54
Choron, Alexandre 116
Cibbini-Kozeluch, Catherine 222
Ciccimarra, Giuseppe 101
Ciliberti, Galliano x, 3
Cimarosa, Domenico 4, 13, 121
Cinti-Damoreau, Laure 286
Citron, Marcia Judith 234
Clementi, Muzio xiii, 110-112, 260, 265-266, 268
Collard, Frederick William 265-266, 268
Colletta, Pietro 97
Comeau, Paul Théodore 162
Comelli, Adelaide 95, 101
Contri, Valentino 80-83
Cornaz, Marie 245
Corneille, Pierre 128
Cortese, Diotebo 83, 87
Cotelle, Alexandre 245, 249-250
Cramer, Carl Friedrich 125, 263
Creuzé de Lesser, Auguste 201
Cybulski, Izydor Józef 49
Czega, Marianna 222

### D

Dąbrowski, Jan Henryk 51, 54
Dahlhaus, Carl xiv
Dalayrac, Nicolas-Marie 23, 52, 114-115, 120, 128
D'Almivare, Martin Pierre 110-111
D'Ambrosio, Angelo 98
Darwin, Charles 308

# Index of Names

DAUTRIVE, Richard 114
DAVIES, James Q. 197
DAVIS, David 265
DELACROIX, Eugène 324
DELLA MARIA, Domenico 113
DENORA, Tia 224, 231
DEPUIS, J. J. 114
DÉRIVIS, Étienne 156
DEROUDVILLE, Mr 250, 256
DE SANTIS, Luigi 56
DÉSARGUS, Xavier 277
DÉSAUGIERS, August-Félix 209
DESBORDES-VALMORES, Marceline 209
DESRIAUX, Philippe 102
DEVIENNE, François 114, 120
DEZÈDE, Nicolas 152, 159, 278
DICKENS, Charles vii
DIDEROT, Denis 116, 224, 279
DIEULAFOY, Armand-Michel 209
DI SOMMA, Tommaso Maria, Marquis of Circello 99, 101
DITTERSDORF, Karl Ditters von 125-126
DMUSZEWSKA, Zofia 62
DMUSZEWSKI, Ludwik 52, 67
DOE, Julia 195
DOISY, Charles 114
DOMEIER, Lucie 301
DOMEIER, Wilhelm 301
DONIZETTI, Gaetano 4
DOURLEN, Victor 114
DROZDOWSKA, Karolina 67
DUBOIS-FONTANELLE, Joseph-Gaspard 204-205
DUCANGE, Victor 178, 184
DUMAS, Alexandre 105, 170
DUNBAR, Julie C. 225
DUPORT, Jean-Louis xii, 121, 246-251, 253, 255-256
DUPORT, Jean-Pierre 246, 249-250
DUPRAT, Julie 201
DUQUÉNOY, François 118
DÜRR, Alfred 26
DU TAILLIS, Adrien Jean-Baptiste-Amable du Bosc, Count 67
DUVAL, Jérôme 114
DUVERNOY, Frédéric 114-115

## E

ELER, André-Frédéric 114
ELLIS, Katharine 186
ELSNER, Józef 46-50, 52, 54, 56-57, 59, 62-63, 66-68
ELSNER, Karolina 67
ENGEL, Jan 49
ENGELHARDT, Karl August 302
ENGRAMELLE, Marie-Dominique-Joseph 278
ESMÉNARD, Joseph-Alphonse 156-157
ESTE, Ercole III, Duke of Modena and Reggio 78
ESTERHÁZY, Nikolaus I, Prince 96

## F

FANAN, Giorgio 89
FASCH, Carl Friedrich Christian 118
FAYOLLE, François 116
FERDINANDO I, Borbone, King of Two Sicilies [Ferdinand IV, King of Naples] 96-98, 101, 103, 105
FERDINANDO III, Grand Duke of Tuscany 10
FERDINANDO CARLO GIUSEPPE, Archduke of Austria-Este 45
FÉRET, Romuald 168, 171
FERRAND, Humbert 328
FERRARI, Giacomo Gotifredo 110-111
FERRETTI, Jacopo 22
FÉTIS, François-Joseph 280
FINK, Gottfried Wilhelm 21, 24
FISCHER, Michael Gotthard 117
FONSECA SIMÃO, Marcos António da 89
FONTANA, Julian 51
FORCE, David xv
FORESTIER, A. H. 114
FORKEL, Johann Nikolaus 118
FRANCESCO I, Borbone, King of Two Sicilies 96
FRANKL, Ludwig August 228, 232
FRANZ II, Holy Roman Emperor [Franz I, Emperor of Austria] 10, 307
FRIBERTH [Frieberth, Friebert, Friedberg], Carl [Karl] 228
FRIEDRICH II, the Great, King of Prussia 161, 263
FRIEDRICH AUGUST I, King of Saxony x, 8-10, 15, 44
FRIEDRICH WILHELM III, King of Prussia 10

# Index of Names

Fuchs, Georg Friedrich 114
Fureix, Emmanuel 321

## G

Galli, Filippo 95, 101
Gandini, Alessandro 86, 88-90
Garat, Pierre-Jean 113-114, 200
Garnier, Joseph-François 114
Gaveaux, Pierre 120
Gavioli, Lodovico 277
Gavoty, André 207
Gérard, François-Pascal-Simon 55
Gérardin-Lacour 179, 184-187
Géricault, Théodore 324
Gianella, Luigi 114
Girard, Pauline 178
Gluck, Christoph Willibald 48, 66, 118, 120-121, 128, 131, 195, 200, 208, 275-276, 302, 316, 325
Gobbi, Giuseppe 81
Goethe, Johann Wolfgang von ix, 115-116, 325, 328
Goguelat, François 328
Gollenhofer, Josepha Müllner 221
Gon, Federico xi, xv, 95
Gossec, François-Joseph 115
Gouge, Olympe de 225
Gouges, Olympe de 203
Graun, Carl Heinrich 25
Greco, Ottavio 81
Grétry, André-Ernest-Modeste 6, 114-116, 119-211
Gribenski, Jean 265
Gudin, Henriette 245
Guérin, Pierre-Narcisse 324
Guicciardi, Diego 79, 87, 89

## H

Hadrava, Norbert 95
Haegele, Vincent 169
Haibel, Jakob 126
Halévy, Jacques-François-Fromental-Élie 327
Handel, George Frideric 6, 25, 118, 231, 280, 316
Hanslick, Eduard 231, 233, 235
Härtel, Gottfried Christoph 266, 268
Hasse, Johann Adolf [Adolph] 118, 226
Haüy, Valentin 228
Haydn, Franz Joseph xi-xii, 6, 16, 25, 95, 100-103, 105-106, 109-110, 118, 127, 222, 226, 230-232, 235-236, 260, 280-282, 298, 308
Heibel, Jakob 125
Heinich, Nathalie 224
Helmig, Martina 221
Hennig, Johann Christian 110
Henri IV, King of France 98
Henry, Elise 213
Hensel [née Mendelssohn], Fanny 236
Herder, Johann Gottfried 224
Herlin, Denis 173
Hérold, François-Joseph 110
Hérold, (Louis-Joseph-)Ferdinand 6, 101, 124
Herz, Henriette 301
Heudier, Antoine-François 171, 173, 177-178, 186-187
Heydenreich, Karl Heinrich 234
Hiller, Ferdinand 102
Hiller, Johann Adam 118
Himmel, Friedrich Heinrich 246, 255
Hoffman, François-Bénoît 16, 154-156
Hoffmann, Ernst Theodor Amadeus 48, 66, 115, 132, 224, 231
Hoffmann, Heinrich Anton 131
Hoffmannsegg, Johann Centurius von 297
Hoffmeister, Franz Anton 110, 112
Hugo, Victor ix, 175, 322, 326
Hugot, Antoine 115
Hume, Robert 261
Hummel, Johann Nepomuk 49, 110
Hus-Desforges, Pierre-Louis 179
Hyde, Frederick Augustus 265

## I

Illiano, Roberto xv
Imbault, Jean-Jérôme 245-253, 255, 257
Isouard, Nicolas 114, 119-120, 278

## J

Jackson, Garvey 234
Jacquard, Joseph Marie 277

# Index of Names

Jadin, Hyacinthe 120, 128, 268
Jadin, Louis 152
Janet, Pierre Honoré 245, 249-250
Jardin, Étienne 288
João VI, King of Portugal and Brazil 296
Joly, Jacques 162
Joseph II, Holy Roman Emperor 226-228
Jouy, Étienne de [Victor-Joseph Étienne] 204, 210, 212, 152-153, 155, 157, 159, 162, 164

## K

Kalkbrenner, Christian 16
Kandler, Franz Sales 25
Kant, Immanuel 224
Kastner, George 325
Katharina Sophie Dorothea, Princess of Württemberg 10
Kaufmann, Friedrich 284
Kirnberger, Johann Philipp 118
Klengel, August Alexander 266
Klukowski, Franciszek 49
Korntner, Beate 229
Kotzebue, August von xi, 109, 123
Kozeluch [Koželuh], Leopold [Jan Antonín] 222, 228-229, 233
Koźmian, Kajetan 63, 65
Kraus, Joseph Martin 110
Kreutzer, Rodolphe 16, 114, 120
Kreuzer, Gundula 195
Krones, Harmut 225
Krusenstern, Adam Johann von 297
Kurpiński, Karol Kazimierz 46-47, 51, 68-70
Kurzböck [Kurzbeck], Magdalena von 222, 229

## L

Lachnith, Ludwig Wenzel 113, 123-124
Lacroix, Antoine 114
Lanusse, J. 179
Lapa, Joaquina Maria da Conceição 306
Launay, Florence 203
Laÿs, François 286
Le Beau, Louise Adolpha 232, 236
Le Blanc, Judith 280
Le Breton, Joachim 116, 127

Ledóchowska, Józefa 60
Lefebvre, Auguste 196
Lefèvre [Lefèbvre], Jean-Xavier 114
Le Froid de Méraux, Nicolas 152
Legrand, Raphaëlle 202
Le Gros, Joseph 114
Le Hir, Sabine 314
Lelewel, Prot 45, 65
Le Mercher de Longpré d'Haussez, Charles Étienne de, Baron 201
Lemoyne, Jean-Baptiste 152, 156
Lenneberg, Hans 259
Leopold II, Holy Roman Emperor 153
Le Sueur [Lesueur], Jean-François 114-115, 130, 156-157, 313-318, 320, 322-327
Lété, Antoine Nicolas 278
Le Vasseur, Pierre-François 248-249, 255
Lichtenstein, Karl August von 165
Ligber, Jan 60-61
Link, Heinrich Friedrich 304-307
Logier, Johann Bernhard 260
Louis XVI, King of France 152
Löwy, Michael 290
Lully, Jean-Baptiste 121

## M

Maelzel, Johann Nepomuk xiii, 276, 280-285, 288-289
Maillard, Marie Thérèse Davoux 201-212
Malibran [née García], Maria 286
Manzoni, Alessandro xiv
Marchesi, Tommaso 7
Marcolini, Camillo 8
Maria I, Queen of Portugal 299
Maria Karolina, of Austria, Queen of Naples and Sicily 96
Maria Leopoldina, of Austria, Princess 307
Maria Theresia, Holy Roman Empress 225-227, 263
Marie-Antoinette, Queen of France 153, 155
Marie Louise, of Austria, Empress consort 159, 275
Marmion, Félix 317, 319-320
Martinez [Martines], Marianna [Marianne] xii, 221, 223, 226-227, 230-237

# Index of Names

Martini, Johann Paul Aegidius [Jean-Paul-Gilles] 113-114
Martius, Carl 308
Marx, Adolf Bernhard 29
Massip, Catherine 245
Matsushita, Hidemi 228
Mattei, Stanislao, father 7-8
Maupin, Mademoiselle de 121
May, Johann Cristoph 164
Mayr, Johann Simon 9
Mazzoni, G. Federico 81
Méhul, Étienne-Nicolas ix, 6. 48, 52, 114-115, 119-120, 130, 152-153, 155, 157, 159, 276, 281, 285
Mendelssohn Bartholdy, Felix 111
Merelli, Bartolomeo 22
Mesmer, Franz Anton 227
Metastasio, Pietro 15-16, 153-154, 161, 226-227
Methfessel, Albert 130
Metternich, Klemens von 97, 105
Meyerbeer, Giacomo 6
Mezzanotte, Antonio 6, 15
Michel, J. 114
Michotte, Edmond 102
Mila, Massimo x
Milton, John 103
Moke, Camille 320
Momigny, Jérôme-Joseph de 116, 277
Mongrédien, Jean 276
Monti, Vincenzo 6
Monvel [Jacques-Marie Boutet] 23
Morabito, Fulvia xv
Morelli, Michele 96, 100
Moritz, Carl Theodor 131
Morlacchi, Alessandro 10-11
Morlacchi, Francesco x, 3-4, 6-11, 13-31, 34
Morrison, Fernando 172
Mozart, Anna Maria 226-227
Mozart, Wolfgang Amadeus xii, 4, 6, 13, 25, 47-48, 67, 109, 112-113, 118, 123-126, 164, 222, 226-227, 229-236, 278, 280-282, 298, 308
Müller, August Eberhard 129
Müller, Wenzel 125-127
Murat, Joachim 44, 53, 56

N

Naldi, Carolina 286
Napoleon I, Bonaparte, Emperor ix-x, 6, 8-10, 12-14, 16, 41-42, 44-46, 48, 51, 53-55, 57, 59-60, 62-63, 65, 67-69, 71, 78-79, 109, 121, 129-130, 151-153, 156-157, 159-160, 162, 165, 200, 202-204, 207, 224-225, 250, 264, 267-268, 275, 279, 283-284, 313, 315-316, 318-319, 321-326, 328-329
Napoleon II, Bonaparte, Emperor and King of Rome 9
Napoleon III, Bonaparte, Emperor 326
Navi, Vincenzo 84-85, 90
Nery, Rui Vieira 295, 309
Niemcewicz, Julian Ursyn 45, 67
Nompère de Champagny, Jean-Baptiste de 151
Nozzari, Andrea 95, 101

O

Offenbach, Jacques 112, 174, 247
Ogiński, Michał Kleofas 68
Oliferko-Storck, Magdalena x, 41
Orlandi, Ferdinando 12
Osiński, Ludwik 57, 62-67
Ozi, Étienne 114-115

P

Pacini, Giovanni 251
Paer, Ferdinando xii, 10, 48, 52, 56, 63, 250-253, 257, 288
Paganini, Nicolò 49
Paisiello, Giovanni x, 3-4, 23, 89, 121, 287
Palestrina, Giovanni Pierluigi da 118
Paltrinieri, Antonio 81
Paradis [Paradies], Maria Theresia von xii, 221, 223, 226, 228-237
Pedro IV, King of Portugal [Pedro I, Emperor of Brasil] 307
Pepe, Florestano 97
Pepe, Guglielmo 96-97
Pergolesi, Giovanni Battista 25
Perotti, Giannagostino 20
Perotti, Niccolò 22-23
Persuis, Louis-Luc Loiseau de 114, 156

## Index of Names

Peszka, Józef 53
Petrucci, Ottaviano 261
Picard, Louis-Benoît 213
Picchioretti, Ignazio 84-85, 90
Piccinni, Louis Alexandre [Luigi Alessandro] 178-179, 184
Piccinni, Niccolò x, 121, 195, 200
Pichler, Caroline 232-233, 235
Pierquin, Claude-Charles 207, 209, 211
Pixerécourt, René-Charles Guilbert de 172, 180, 183-184, 187
Płachecki, Antoni 49
Plantade, Charles-Henri 278
Plersch, Jan Bogumił 59, 60-62, 66-67
Pleyel, Ignace Joseph [Ignaz Josef] xiii, 102, 104-105, 110-112, 114, 246, 265-266, 281
Porpora, Nicola 226
Puccini, Giacomo 66

### R

Racine, Jean 128
Ramaut, Alban xiv, 313
Rameau, Jean-Philippe 118
Rangone, Ghirardo 82
Raphael [Raffaello Sanzio] 326
Rastrelli, Vincenzo 8
Rault, Félix 114
Reibel, Emmanuel xiii, xv, 275
Reicha [Rejcha], Anton [Antonín] 114
Reichardt, Johann Friedrich xi, 109, 115, 118, 123-124, 126, 249-250
Reissiger, Carl Gottlieb 27
Rellstab, Ludwig 236
Révéroni Saint-Cyr, Jacques-Antoine de 116
Riccardi, Francesca 56
Richter, Georg Friedrich 229
Richter, Jean-Paul 301
Ricordi, Giovanni 6, 264
Riedinger, Johann 228
Rigel, Henri-Jean 281
Righini, Vincenzo (Maria) 228
Robertson, Étienne-Gaspard 279
Robespierre, Maximilien de 158
Robillon, Claudius 171, 173

Robillon, Jacques 171
Rochefort, Antoine 152
Rochlitz, Johann Friedrich 125
Rode, Pierre 114
Rodolphe, Jean-Joseph 114
Rodríguez-Lorenzo, Gloria Araceli 264
Romanelli, Luigi 22
Romani, Felice 22
Romberg, Bernhard Heinrich 126
Rosen, Alexander von 15
Rossetti, Gabriele 99
Rossi, Gaetano 22
Rossini, Gioachino x, 3-4, 6-7, 47, 95, 97, 100-103, 105, 152, 155, 288-289, 316
Rossi-Scotti, Giovanni Battista 7
Rousseau, Jean-Jacques 114, 116, 121, 196-197, 224, 309
Rowland, David xiii, 259
Roze, Nicolas 114, 130
Rubini, Giovanni Battista 95, 101
Ruders, Carl Israel 306
Rugendas, Johann Moritz 308

### S

Sacchini, Antonio 195, 200
Saint-Hilaire, Auguste 308
Saint-Huberty, Antoinette 200
Sala, Massimiliano xv
Salieri, Antonio 16, 228-229
Salin, F. de 114
Salingre, F. H. 110
Sanders, Scott 199, 211
Sanvitale, Stefano 8
Sapieha, Aleksander Antoni, Prince 60, 62
Sassaroli, Germano 14
Saugera, Eric 199
Saxe-Teschen, Albert Kasimir, Duke of 283
Sayn-Wittgenstein, Carolyne 329
Sayre, Robert 290
Scarlatti, Domenico 263
Scatizzi, Stefano 22
Schaum, Johann Otto Heinrich 132
Schikaneder, Emanuel 123
Schiller, Friedrich 301

## Index of Names

Schlegel, August Wilhelm 301
Schlegel, Friedrich 301
Schlesinger, Adolphe 250
Schmid, Anton 232
Schmidt, Johann Philipp Samuel 131
Schneider, Friedrich 25
Schneider, Herbert 112, 172
Schopenhauer, Arthur 231
Schubert, Franz 235
Schulze, Johann Abraham Peter 118
Schumann [née Wieck], Clara 236
Schuster, Joseph 8
Scribe, Eugène 172
Shakespeare, William 325, 328
Sieber, Jean-Georges 245
Silvati, Giuseppe 96, 100
Simrock, Nicolas 251
Sografi, Antonio 22
Solignani, Lorenzo 84, 86, 89-90
Spazier, Karl 115
Spix, Johann Baptist von 308
Spohr, Louis xi, 109, 123-124, 132
Spontini, Gaspare x, xii, 4, 13, 17, 29, 47, 114, 120, 153, 157, 159, 164-165, 195, 204, 209-210, 214
Staël-Holstein, Anne-Louise Germaine Necker de 203, 301
Stanisław II August, King of Poland 42, 48
Stefani, Jan 52, 54
Steibelt, Daniel 117, 124, 126, 129, 282
Stendhal [Marie-Henri Beyle] xiv
Stewart, Daniel 267
Strinasacchi, Teresa 251
Süssmayer, Franz Xaver 125-126
Swieten, Gottfried van 103, 231

### T

Tadini, Antonio 79, 84
Taix, conductor 179
Talleyrand-Périgord, Charles-Maurice de 55
Thibouville-Lamy, Jérôme 277
Thomasseau, Jean-Marie 172

Tilesius von Tilenau, Wilhelm Gottlieb 297-299, 308
Todi, Luisa 305, 309
Trial, Antoine 111
Trial, Armand-Emmanuel 110-111, 152

### V

Vaccai, Nicola 3
Vaccari, Luigi 87-88
Valentin, Martoune 199
Valois, Henri de 41
Vanderhagen, Armand 112, 114
Vanhulst, Henri xii, 245
Varnhagen, Rahel 301
Vaucanson, Jacques de 279, 283, 285, 288
Verdi, Giuseppe 162
Vernet, Horace 327-328
Veronese, Paolo 58
Viguerie, Bernard 114
Villeblanche, Armand de 117
Viotti, Giovanni Battista 110, 114
Virey, Julien-Joseph 201
Virgil [Publius Vergilius Maro] 53, 325
Vivaldi, Antonio 262
Vogel von Vogelstein, Carl Christian 5
Vogler, Georg Joseph [Abbé Vogler] 228
Vranický, Pavel 70

### W

Wagner, Richard 24
Wahnon de Oliveira, Olivia 245
Walewska, Maria 53-55
Weber, Aloysia 125
Weber, Bernhard Anselm 131
Weber, Carl Maria von 6, 25, 116, 132, 324
Weber, William 261
Weigl, Joseph 126
Weissenbruch, Johan Hendrik 251
Weissweiler, Eva 225
Wied-Neuwied, Maximilian zu, Prince 308
Wild, Nicole 172, 175, 183
Winckel, Dietrich Nikolaus 284

## Index of Names

Winckelmann, Johann Joachim 204
Wojniakowski, Kazimierz 60-61
Woldemar, Michel 115
Wölfl [Wölffl, Woelfl], Joseph 126, 229
Wollstonecraft, Mary 225
Wroth, Emmanuele 195, 202
Wunderlich, Fritz 115

### Y
Young, Edward 224

### Z
Zurla, Odoardo 8